THE ALL-TIME GREATS

of

BRITISH and IRISH SPORT

Peter Matthews

Ian Buchanan

GUINNESS PUBLISHING

First published 1995
Reprint 10 9 8 7 6 5 4 3 2 1

Published in Great Britain by Guinness Publishing Ltd,
33 London Road, Enfield, Middlesex

Typeset in Times and Gill Sans
Printed and bound in Great Britain by The Bath Press, Bath, Avon

A catalogue record for this book is available friom the British Library

ISBN 0-85112-678-2

PETER MATTHEWS

Peter Matthews is Editor of *The New Guinness Book of Records*, having previously been its sports editor for ten years. He commentates on his speciality, athletics, for ITV and Channel 4. Guinness published the fourth edition of his *Encyclopedia of International Sports Records and Results* in 1995. He has been a member of the Association of Track & Field Statisticians since 1970 and has edited their *International Athletics Annual* since 1984. His other works include *Who's Who in British Athletics* (1990).

IAN BUCHANAN

Ian Buchanan is a leading athletics and Olympic historian whose previous books include *British Olympians*, published by Guinness in 1991, the *Encyclopedia of British Athletics Records*, and *The US National Championships in Track & Field* with Bill Mallon. He is President of the International Society of Olympic Historians (ISOH), a member of the British Society of Sports Historians, the Association of Track & Field Statisticians, and the British Olympic Association.

Peter Matthews and **Ian Buchanan** wrote, with Bill Mallon MD, the *Guinness International Who's Who of Sport*, which was published in 1993.

Introduction

This book contains biographies of the top names in the history of British and Irish sport from the days of prize fighting and racing at Newmarket, through the development of modern sport in the final decades of the 19th century to the big business of today,

The leading sports are massively represented, with nearly 200 footballers and over 150 cricketers and rugby players, but the minor sports are not forgotten, so that the most successful sportsmen and women from the likes of bobsleigh, bowls, croquet, darts, gliding, polo, real tennis and triathlon are also included.

Our subjects come from the whole of the British Isles, so that many Irish sports men and sports women are included as well as those from England, Scotland, Wales and the Channel Islands. Such sports as boxing and rugby feature strongly in the Irish representation, but there are also the leading exponents of gaelic football and hurling.

The profiles vary in length, but we have endeavoured to give full details of names, dates and places of birth and death, with leading honours won and career highlights and records. Families feature strongly, and when a sportsman or woman has relatives who have also achieved prominence at sport, brief details are given of them. We have not stuck to rigid structures for the biographies, the length of which vary considerably. Career statistics are usually up to the end of the last completed season, although the text may include more topical details.

At the back of this book there is an index by sport, and also a check on individuals who were close to having their own entry, but for whom details are included with a relative.

As with our previous book, the *Guinness International Who's Who of Sport*, Ian Buchanan and I have had to face the invidious task of deciding just who and who not to include. We sincerely hope that we have not missed anybody that sports experts might regard as being amongst the true élite, but when it comes to a full list of over 1500 names, then there must be areas of disagreement. As authors we had a go at all-time Top 10 lists for men and women; as can be seen on page 6, we were only in agreement on half the names!

This can be regarded as a complementary publication to my *Guinness Encyclopedia of Sports Records and Results*, the 4th edition of which is published virtually simultaneously. Like that volume, which is published biennially, I hope that this book may appear in subsequent editions. Every year new stars emerge and their biographies can be added in future. We will, of course, also be happy to consider adding any names from the past that readers may feel should belong in such a work.

This is the first comprehensive all-time who's who of British sport to be published, so we trust that it fills a gap in bookshelves and libraries.

We have endeavoured to include as much information as possible up to the very last stage of the production process at the beginning of July 1995.

Peter Matthews

July 1995

Acknowledgements

To repeat what we said in the introduction to our *International Who's Who of Sport*, in the course of compiling these books we have consulted many reference sources and many experts. We have also, of course, tapped into our accumulated data over lifetimes of sports 'nuttery', and many others have helped us with our various projects over the years. It is very difficult, therefore, for this list to be comprehensive, so if we have missed anybody then please accept our apologies and thanks.

We would, then, like to mention the following, some of whom have helped with just one or two queries and some whose assistance has been profound.

Patricia Arthur

Stan Greenberg

Andrew Huxtable

Howard Bass, winter sports

Rex Bellamy, squash

Dennis Bird, ice skating

Paul Campion, The Croquet Association

Clive Carpenter, geography

Marion Collin, women's cricket

Terry Dooris, orienteering

Phil Drackett, ice hockey

Sylvia Eastley, All England Netball Association

Malcolm Fare, fencing

Cris Freddi, football

Robert Gate, rugby league

David Guiney, Ireland

Maryanne Henchy, Badminton Association of England

Elisabeth Hussey, skiing

John Jenkins

Maurice Jones, speedway

Fred Lake, archery

Alan Little, tennis

Peter Lovesey, athletics

Bob Mason, hockey

Brian Mellowship, football

T Morris, women's hockey

Graham Morrison, fencing

A J Oldham

Guy Oliver, football

Paul Owen, British Canoe Union

Sue Peard, badminton

John Randall, horse racing

Chris Rhys, rugby union

Barry Rolfe, British Gliding Association

Chloe Ronaldson, roller skating

R H Sinclair, English Table Tennis Association

Hugh Soar

Major John Watson, polo

Ian Wright, squash

Editor's Notes

Certain conventions have been used for displaying statistical material for various sports.

Seasons that cross over years are shown in the format e.g. 1994/5. A span of successive years is shown in the format e.g. 1961-7, for each year from 1961 to 1967. Thus 1994-5 indicates both of the calendar years 1994 and 1995, rather than the 1994/5 season.

Measurements are generally given in metric units, and Imperial units, if used, follow in italics. Exceptions to ths rule include some measurements made originally in Imperial units.

Note that career figures are generally given to the end of the last completed season before press date, although references may be made in the biographies of current players to milestones achieved since that cut-off date.

Name details

Where known, full names are given on the third line of each entry, followed by date and place of birth, and, if relevant, date and place of death. Changes of name are shown, né for males with different names at birth, née for women's maiden names. In general women are shown under the name, married or single, by which they are best known. Later married names are shown at the end of this line.

In certain instances it has not been possible to trace the exact location of births and deaths and information is limited to the appropriate registration district.

Counties are shown for many place names, but not for major cities or towns, such as Bristol, Sheffield, Edinburgh or Belfast, nor for county towns such as Oxford or Hertford. County names and boundaries have changed over the years, and in general current county or district names have been used, even though the name may not have been in use when a sportsman or woman was born. So, for instance, Powys has been used rather than Breconshire, and Highland rather than Inverness-shire or Caithness. We have also incorporated the new Scottish and Welsh boundary changes, being introduced soon after the publication of this book.

Athletics

Event distances are shown in metres (m), yards (y), kilometres (km) or miles (M). Distances recorded for field events are generally shown in metres, although some Imperial measurements are shown where they are of historical significance.

Times are in seconds or minutes and seconds (e.g. 27:39.4 is 27 minutes, 39.4 seconds) or for very long distances hours, minutes and seconds (e.g. 2:06:50 is 2 hours, 6 minutes, 50 seconds).

The letter w after a time indicates wind-assistance in excess of the limit permitted for record purposes of 2 metres per second *4.47 mph.*

The letter i indicates an indoor performance. A personal best performance may be indicated by the letters pb.

Boxing

Career records list number of wins (W) followed, where known, by wins inside the full distance in parentheses, losses (L), and draws (D). Biographies may detail wins by knockout (KO) and technical knockout (TKO).

Canoeing

Races are designated with K for kayak

canoes and C for Canadian canoes, followed by the number of canoeists, e.g. C2 is Canadian pairs.

Cricket

Career figures are shown for the following three categories: a) Test matches, b) One-day internationals, c) First-class matches.

The number of Tests or one-day internationals is shown, with the career span for each. Then batting figures: number of runs, and average runs per completed innings, number of centuries (100s) and highest score (HS). Then bowling figures: wickets and average runs per wicket, best bowling in an innings (BB). Then total catches and stumpings.

* indicates an unfinished (not out) innings.

Cycling

Times are in seconds or minutes and seconds (e.g. 3:40.62 is 3 minutes, 40.62 seconds).

Speed skating

Times are in seconds or minutes and seconds (e.g. 3:40.62 is 3 minutes, 40.62 seconds).

Swimming

Times are in seconds or minutes and seconds (e.g. 3:40.62 is 3 minutes, 40.62 seconds). IM is individual medley.

Tennis

For Davis Cup and Wightman Cup players' records show number of wins and matches played (e.g. 5/12 is five wins in 12 matches).

Triathlon

Times are shown in hours: minutes: seconds for the total times for swimming, cycling and running.

Weightlifting

Weights lifted and weight-categories are shown in kilograms.

Abbreviations

General

av.	average
cc	cubic capacity
d	days
hr	hours
kg	kilograms
km	kilometres
km/h	kilometres per hour
m	metres
M	miles
min	minutes
mph	miles per hour
m/s	metres per second
sec	seconds
y	yards
yr	years

In dates, months are usually abbreviated to their first three letters.

Greater Manchester has been abbreviated to Gt. Manchester.

Countries

Alg	Algeria
Arg	Argentina
Aus	Australia
Bel	Belgium
Bra	Brazil
Bul	Bulgaria
Can	Canada
Chn	China
Cs	Czechoslovakia
Cze	Czech Republic
Den	Denmark
Egy	Egypt
Eng	England
Fin	Finland
Fra	France
FRG	Federal Republic of Germany
GDR	German Democratic Republic
Ger	Germany
Gre	Greece
Hol	Holland/Netherlands
Hun	Hungary
Ind	India
Ire	Ireland
Ita	Italy
Jam	Jamaica
Ken	Kenya
NI	Northern Ireland
Nor	Norway
NZ	New Zealand
Pak	Pakistan
Phi	Philippines
Pol	Poland
Por	Portugal
PR	Puerto Rico
Rom	Romania
SAf	South Africa
Sco	Scotland
SL	Sri Lanka
Spa	Spain
Swe	Sweden
Swi	Switzerland
Tun	Tunisia
USA	United States
USSR	Soviet Union
Wal	Wales
WI	West Indies
Yug	Yugoslavia

Governing Bodies, Sports Organisations, Awards etc

AAA   Amateur Athletic Association (UK)
AAU   Amateur Athletic Union (USA)
ABA   Amateur Boxing Association
AC   Athletics Club
ACS   Association of Cricket Statisticians
A-CU   Auto-Cycle Union
AFA   Amateur Fencing Association
ARA   Amateur Rowing Association
ASA   Amateur Swimming Association
ATP   Association of Tennis Professionals
BSJA   British Show Jumping Association
CC   Cricket Club
CG   Commonwealth Games
EBA   English Bowling Association
EIBA   English Indoor Bowling
       Association
FA   Football Association
FEI   International Equestrian Federation
FIBA   International Basketball Federation
FIDE   International Chess Federation
FIE   International Fencing Federation
FIFA   International Association Football
       Federation
FIG   International Gymnastic Federation
FIH   International Hockey Federation
FIM   International Motorcycling
       Federation
FINA   International Amateur Swimming
       Federation
FIS   International Ski Federation
FITA   International Archery Federation
GAA   Gaelic Athletic Association
GP   Grand Prix

IAAF   International Amateur Athletic
       Federation
IBF   International Boxing Federation
IOC   Interntional Olympic Committee
ISU   International Skating Union
ITF   International Tennis Federation
LPGA   Ladies Professional Golfers
       Association
LTA   Lawn Tennis Association
MCC   Marylebone Cricket Club
NCAA   National Collegiate Athletic
       Association (USA)
NH   National Hunt (horse racing)
NL   National League (NL)
OG   Olympic Games
PFA   Professional Footballers
       Association
PGA   Professional Golfers Association
RAC   Royal Automobile Club
SRA   Squash Rackets Association
TT   Tourist Trophy
UCI   International Cycling Union
UEFA   Union of European Football
       Associations
UIT   International Shooting Union
WAAA   Women's Amateur Athletic
       Association
WBA   World Boxing Association
WBC   World Boxing Council
WBO   World Boxing Organisation

See also Editor's Notes for specific abbreviations for particular sports.

Carl AARVOLD

Rugby Union
(Sir) Carl Douglas Aarvold. b. 7 Jun 1907
West Hartlepool, Durham. d. 17 Mar
1991.

Aarvold, a long-striding, classic centre, also won international honours as a winger. From Durham School he went to Cambridge, winning his Blue 1925-8 before playing club rugby for West Hartlepool, Headingley and Blackheath. He scored four tries in 16 internationals 1928-33 and captained England six times. He was president of the Lawn Tennis Association from 1962 to 1981 and also chairman of the RAC 1978-81.

Called to the bar in 1932, he became a circuit judge, described in his obituary as London's most colourful and well-liked judge, and he was knighted in 1968. Following a distnguished war record he was awarded the OBE in 1945.

Bobby ABEL

Cricket
Robert Abel. b. 30 Nov 1857 Rotherhithe, London. d. 10 Dec 1936 Stockwell, London.

'The Guv'nor' was one of the smallest top-class batsmen (1.62m *5 ft 4 in*) but was a patient and masterly opener. He played for Surrey and was 31 when he made his Test debut. He exceeded 2000 runs in eight successive seasons 1895-1902, including a record 12 centuries in 1900 and then a record 3309 runs (at 55.15) in a season in England in 1901. He scored eight double centuries with a best of 357* when he carried his bat through Surrey's 811 v Somerset at The Oval in 1899. He was also a right-arm slow round-arm bowler and a fine slip fielder.

13 Tests 1888-1902: 744 runs at 37.20, 2 100s HS 132*; 13 catches.

First-class 1881-1904: 33, 124 runs at 35.46, 74 100s HS 357*; 263 wickets at 24.00, BB 6-15; 586 catches.

Lord ABERDARE – see Hon. Clarence BRUCE

Harold ABRAHAMS

Athletics
Harold Maurice Abrahams. b. 15 Dec 1899 Bedford. d. 14 Jan 1978 Enfield, London.

The Olympic 100m victory by Abrahams in 1924 was later immortalised in the film *Chariots of Fire* (1981). He set British 100m records at 10.6 in heat, semi-final and final and also won a silver medal in the sprint relay.

In his first Olympics in 1920 he was eliminated in the quarter-finals of the 100m and 200m and helped Britain to 6th in the 4x100m. He set four British records at the long jump from 7.19m in 1923 to 7.38m in 1924, which remained the record for 30 years. He might have become the first English 25-footer (7.52m) but for breaking his leg in May 1925, an injury that terminated his career. He set a record with eight individual event wins for Cambridge University in the annual match against Oxford: 100y 1920-3, 440y 1923, and long jump 1920, 1922-3. AAA champion at 100y 1924 and long jump 1923-4, he was coached by Sam Mussabini. Other bests: 100y 9.6w downhill and 9.9 (1924), 220y straight track 21.6 (1923), 200m 22.0 (1924).

Following his retirement he devoted a lifetime of service to the sport, as team manager, broadcaster, journalist, statistician and official, serving on the AAA's General Committee from 1926, becoming secretary in 1931 and president in 1976. He was Hon. Treasurer of the BAAB 1946-69 and its chairman 1969-75. He was awarded the CBE in 1957 as secretary of the National Parks Commission, which he joined after 13 years as a barrister.

Harold's elder brothers Adolph and Sidney were both knighted, the former for services to medicine and the latter for legal work. **Sidney** Solomon (b. 11 Feb 1885. d. 14 May 1957) was also a fine long jumper, AAA champion in 1913, and placed 5th in 1906 and 11th in 1912 at the Olympic Games. His best was 7.03m for 3rd in the 1911 AAAs.

Paul ACKFORD

Rugby Union
Paul John Ackford. b. 26 Feb 1958
Hannover, Germany.

Having played for England B in 1979, Ackford did not win his first full cap until nine years later when he was 30. He went on, however, to play in the second row for England 22 times, partnering Wade Dooley (qv) in most of these matches. He won representative honours at many levels culminating with the 1989 British Lions tour of Australia where he played in three Tests. He played for the Harlequins and was variously a schoolteacher, post-graduate student at Cambridge University (Blue 1979) and police inspector before resigning to become the rugby correspondent of the *Sunday Telegraph*.

Janet ACKLAND

Bowls
Dorothy Janet Ackland. b. 19 Dec 1938
Ystrad Mynach, Caerphilly.

Representing Wales, after winning bronze medals in the pairs and fours at the 1977 World Championships, Ackland won the singles 11 years later to become the second UK player to win this title. She was Welsh champion in singles, triples and fours and won her first international cap in 1973. In 1980 she gave up her job as an art teacher to become a full-time bowler.

Eleanor ADAMS

Athletics
Eleanor Adams. b. 20 Nov 1947
Middlesbrough. née Puckrin. Later Mrs Robinson.

In the 1980s Adams compiled a hugely impressive collection of ultra long-distance running records. Having taken up jogging following the birth of her third child in 1979, she ran her first ultra marathon in 1982, and in that race set a world best for 50 miles of 6:41:02. Her records range in distance from 30 miles to becoming the first woman to cover 500 miles in a six-day race in 1984, a record 143:11:23 for 500 miles (1986) and 1000 miles on the road in

16 days 22:51:00 in 1987. Other major records include track times of 19:28:48 and 500km 77:53:46 in 1989 and 200km and 24 hours indoors at 19:00:31 and 237.861 km in 1990. She has won the world's longest race of the current era, the Sydney-Melbourne, three times, and other major wins have included the Spartathlon 1983, London-Brighton 1987 and the World 100km title in 1990. She is a PE teacher.

Neil ADAMS

Judo
Adrian Neil Adams. b. 27 Sep 1958 Rugby, Warwickshire.

A great stylist, Adams has the most successful international record of any British judo player, winning espoir (1974), junior (1977) and five senior (1979-80 and 1983-5) European titles, four World Championship medals and two Olympic silver medals. At the Olympics in 1980 he needed less than four minutes to defeat his first three opponents but lost a unanimous decision in the 71 kg final to Ezio Gamba (Ita). He was the clear favourite in 1984, but lost in the final of the 78 kg category to Frank Wieneke (FRG), the only time in his entire career in which he lost a match by ippon. At the World Championships he became Britain's first ever champion, at 78 kg in 1981, but had to settle for silver in 1983 when he lost on a disputed split decision to Nobutoshi Hitage (Japan); he won bronze medals at 71 kg in 1979 and at 78 kg 1985. He also won eight senior British Open titles: two at 71 kg, 1977 and 1979, and six at 78 kg: 1980-4 and 1988. He won British junior titles each year 1969-73.
He retired from competition after the 1988 Olympics and became a highly successful coach at his club in Coventry. He was awarded the MBE in 1982.

Tony ADAMS

Football
Tony Alexander Adams. b. 10 Oct 1966
Romford, London.

Adams has played all his senior club football with Arsenal, becoming their youngest ever captain, and a determined central defender. He was voted PFA Young Footballer of the Year in 1987. He played for England Youth, B and under-21 teams and in 34 internationals for England 1987-95. He was touted as a future captain of England, and indeed that came to pass but first he had to overcome a three-month ban for a professional foul followed by a four-month prison sentence for drunken driving in 1990.

Tim AHEARNE (Ireland)

Athletics, Triple Jump
Timothy Ahearne. b. 18 Aug 1885 Dirreen, Athea, Co. Limerick. d. Nov 1968 USA.

At the 1908 Olympics Ahearne won gold and set a new world record of 14.92m *48 ft 11 ¹⁄₄in* in the triple jump. He jumped an Olympic record 14.73 in the 2nd round, was passed by Garfield MacDonald (Can) 14.76 and then won with the final jump of the competition. His record was improved by his brother Dan Ahearn (he dropped the final "e'), who in May 1911 in New York jumped 15.52m, the first record officially accepted by the IAAF.

Ahearne was also 8th in the 1908 Olympic long jump, and at that event his best was 7.61m with 7.63m on a downhill runway, both in 1901. He was AAA champion at long jump in 1909, no triple jump being contested at these championships until 1914.

His brother **Daniel F Ahearn** (b. 2 Apr 1888) emigrated to the USA with Tim in 1909 and was AAU champion at the triple jump eight times, 1910-11, 1913-18. Tim was runner-up four times, in 1911, 1913-4 and 1916. Dan, who was not eligible for the US team at the 1912 Olympics, would have been clear favourite in1916 when the Games were cancelled due to World War I, but did compete in 1920, placing 6th when past his best.

Kriss AKABUSI

Athletics, Hurdling
Kriss Kezie Uche Chukwu Duru-Akabusi. b. 28 Nov 1958 Paddington, London.

Akabusi gave marvellous service to British athletics for a decade from his international debut in 1983, although that, at the age of 24, was quite a late start after several years at 48-second 400m standard in Army athletics. He became an invaluable member of 4 x 400m relay teams, with silver at the 1984 Olympics, and gold medals at the Europeans of 1986 and 1990, Commonwealth 1986 and the 1991 Worlds, when he anchored the British team to an epic victory over the Americans. At the end of that year he was voted the British Sports Writers' male sportsman of the year. He also won a relay bronze at the 1987 Worlds and ran on three successive British European Cup winning relay teams 1987-91.

Not quite making the very highest level at 400m, with a best time of 44.93 in 1988, and a 4th place at the 1986 Commonwealth Games, he turned to 400m hurdling in 1987, and reached world class very rapidly. He was 7th at the 1987 Worlds and 6th at the 1988 Olympics before, in 1990, after winning the Commonwealth title, he finally smashed David Hemery's 22-year-old UK and ex-world record of 48.12 when he ran 47.92 to win the European title.

Akabusi improved twice more in the 1991 World Championships, with 47.91 in his semi-final and 47.86 for 3rd in the final, and to 47.82 for the Olympic bronze in 1992. He also won the 400m hurdles at the 1989 and 1991 European Cup, was UK champion at 400m 1984 and 400m hurdles 1987 (tie) and 1990; and won the AAA 400m 1988 and 400m hurdles 1992. He was awarded the MBE in 1991, he retired in 1993 and is making a career as a television personality.

Other bests: 100m 10.7 (1983), 200m 21.22 (1991) and 21.1 (1990), 300m 32.59 (1991), 600m 1:17.1 (1991), 800m 1:48.2 (1985), 110m hurdles 14.6 (1989).

Charles ALCOCK

Football & Administration
Charles William Alcock. b. 2 Dec 1842 Sunderland. d. 26 Feb 1907 Brighton.

Alcock played a remarkable part in the organisation of British sport. He was secretary of the Football Association 1870-96 and of Surrey County Cricket Club from 1872 to his death in 1907. During this time he founded the FA Cup and organised the first Test match to be played in England, although it was not so named until 1895.

An Old Harrovian and a forward with the Wanderers club, he took the concept of the school inter-house competition and inaugurated the nationwide knockout competition for the FA Cup, which he proposed to the FA in July 1871. The competition started later that year and he captained Wanderers in the first FA Cup Final in 1872

In 1875 he became the only current FA secretary to play for England when he captained the side that drew 2-2 with Scotland, scoring one of the goals. In 1880 he persuaded Lord Harris and W G Grace (qqv) to raise a representative England cricket side and this played against Australia at The Oval in 1880. He edited *James Lillywhite's Cricket Annual* throughout its life 1872-1900 and also founded the weekly magazine *Cricket* in 1882.

John ALDRIDGE

Football
John William Aldridge. b. 18 Sep 1958 Liverpool.

A high-scoring forward with Newport County and Oxford, Aldridge joined Liverpool in 1987 where he took over from Ian Rush (qv), who had moved to Italy. He played a major part in Liverpool's League (1988) and FA Cup (1989) successes before going to Real Sociedad. After two seasons in Spain he returned home, signing for Tranmere Rovers in 1991. He had scored 276 goals in Football League matches to April 1995, and 17 goals in his 64 internationals for the Republic of Ireland from 1986 to June 1995.

Alister ALLAN

Shooting
Alister Miller Allan. b. 28 Jan 1944 Freuchie, Fife.

Allan won double gold at the 1981 European Championships, setting an unbeatable world record with 600 out of 600 for 3-positions small-bore rifle. At the Olympics Games, having first competed in 1976, at small-bore rifle he was 3rd in 1984 and 2nd in 1988 at three positions, and 4th and 5th respectively at prone position. At the World Championships he set a world record score of 599 when he won the small-bore rifle, prone in 1978. His Commonwealth Games medal haul 1978-86 was four gold, four silver and three bronze. He was awarded the MBE in 1990.

Ivor ALLCHURCH

Football
Ivor John Allchurch. b. 16 Dec 1929 Swansea.

A talented inside-forward with Swansea, Newcastle United and Cardiff, Allchurch's 68 Welsh caps, 1950-66, stood as a record until beaten by Joey Jones (qv) in 1986. After completing his National Service, he made his first team debut with Swansea Town in 1949 and despite many attractive offers from wealthier clubs remained loyal to his Welsh roots for ten years. He eventually moved to Newcastle in 1958, shortly after he had done much to take Wales into the quarter-finals in the World Cup, but returned to Wales, joining Cardiff, when Newcastle were relegated in 1961. After three seasons he went back to Swansea but they dropped to Division Four in 1967 and Allchurch spent his final season in League football in undistinguished company.

With his precision passing, fierce shooting and deceptive dribbling he was one of the most talented players of his time but only 103 of his 692 League games were in Division One. He scored 251 goals in league matches and his 23 goals for Wales equalled the record set by Trevor Ford (qv). He was awarded the MBE in 1966. In eight of his international matches he played with his younger brother **Len** (b. 12 Sep 1933), who in all earned 11 caps for Wales.

Tony ALLCOCK

Bowls
Anthony Allcock. b. 11 Jun 1955 Thurmaston, Leicestershire.

A specialist at the indoor game, Allcock won two World Indoor singles titles, 1986-

7, and six pairs titles, 1986-7 and 1989-92 partnering David Bryant (qv). He also won the English Indoor singles twice.

He made his England debut indoors in 1976 and outdoors in 1978 and outdoors he became the youngest ever world champion when he joined with Jim Hobday and David Bryant to win the triples in 1980 at the age of 24. He won further gold medals at fours in 1984 and team in 1980 and 1988, with silvers at pairs 1984 and 1988 and bronze at fours 1988. In August 1987 he gave up his job as principal of a day centre for mentally handicapped adults in Stroud to devote more time to the game. He did not win his first English outdoor singles title until 1990 but he was again the champion in 1991; he also won the triples in 1990. In 1992 he had a great year, winning the British Isles singles and then the World title. In 1994 he won the singles silver medal at the Commonwealth Games. He was awarded the MBE in 1989.

Suzanne ALLDAY

Athletics, Shot
Suzanne Allday. b. 26 Nov 1934 Shoreham, West Sussex. née Farmer.

With eight improvements Allday took the British record for the shot from 13.33m in 1956 to 15.18 in 1964 and made ten improvements to the discus record from 40.37 in 1952 to 47.70 in 1958. She set a record (since surpassed by Judy Oakes (qv)) with 14 WAAA titles, seven each at shot (1954, 1956, 1958-62) and discus (1952-3, 1956, 1958-61) with a further two indoors, 1962-3. Her 35 international appearances for Britain 1951-64 was at the time a record. After 13 years in retirement she returned to reach 12th ranking in Britain in both events in 1977.

At the Commonwealth Games she was 6th and 2nd in 1954, 2nd and 1st in 1958 and 3rd and 4th in 1962 at shot and discus respectively. Her best European placing was 5th in the 1958 shot, and she competed at the Olympic Games of 1956 and 1960. Accompanying her at the former was her husband **Peter Allday** (b. 27 Jun 1927), who set a British hammer record at 59.61 in 1956.

Gubby ALLEN

Cricket
(Sir) George Oswald Browning Allen. b. 31 Jul 1902 Sydney, Australia. d. 29 Nov 1989 London.

While he was a fine, hostile fast bowler and a fearless, hard-hitting batsman, Allen's cricket was limited by his business career, and he made an even bigger impact as an administrator. He became a member of the Middlesex committee in 1931 and of the MCC in 1935. He was treasurer of the MCC 1964-76 and its president 1963-4, and chairman of the Test selectors 1955-61. After Eton and Cambridge University (Blue 1922-3) he played infrequently for Middlesex, but had many successes in major games. He took 21 wickets in the 'bodyline' series in 1932/3, although not bowling that style himself, and he did much to restore his nation's reputation in Australia when he led the England team to tour there in 1936/7. When not really fit enough, at the age of 45, he was persuaded to take the England team to the West Indies in 1947/8. Awarded the CBE in 1962, he was knighted in 1986 for services to cricket.

25 Tests 1930-48: 750 runs at 24.19, 1 100 HS 122; 81 wickets at 29.37, BB 7-80; 20 catches.

First-class 1921-50: 9232 runs at 28.67, 11 100s HS 180; 788 wickets at 22.23, BB 10-40; 131 catches.

His uncle Reginald Allen (1858-1952) played once for Australia against England in 1887.

Terry ALLEN

Boxing
né Edward Albert Govier. b. 18 Aug 1925 Islington, London. d. 8 Apr 1987 London.

As an amateur Allen lost only five of his 107 contests before turning professional shortly after leaving school in 1942. He changed his name from Teddy Govier to Terry Allen in memory of a shipmate killed in the war, and soon established a reputation as a tough two-fisted fighter. It was not, however, until after the war, when the sport returned to normalcy and Allen returned from military service in Egypt that he was able to mount a serious challenge for top honours. In 1949 he fought a 15-round draw with the world flyweight champion, Rinty Monaghan (qv), and after the Irishman had relinquished his title, Allen became the world champion the following year by outpointing Honoré Pratesi (Fra). He lost his world title to Dado Marino (USA) after only 98 days and his two attempts to recover his world crown were unsuccessful, losing a return match with Marino (1951) and to Yoshio Shirai of Japan (1953).

At home, apart from a six-month period in 1952, Allen held the British flyweight title 1951-4 before he retired as the undefeated champion.

Career record 1942-54: 77 contests. Won 62 (18 KO), Drew 1, Lost 14.

Derek ALLHUSEN

Equestrian events
Derek Swithin Allhusen. b. 9 Jan 1914 Chelsea, London.

Major Derek Allhusen won an Olympic gold medal in Mexico City in 1968 at the age of 54 as a member of the British team in the three-day event. Ending with a clear round in the show jumping he also took the individual silver medal. These triumphs came 20 years after his Olympic debut, but that, in 1948, had been at the Winter Games when he placed 6th in the pentathlon, a special demonstration event comprising cross-country skiing, pistol shooting, fencing and riding.

Allhusen was a member of the winning British three-day event team at the European Championships in 1957 and again, riding his famous mare *Lochinvar* in 1967 and 1969, placing 3rd in the individual at the former. After retiring from the Army he bred and trained horses in Norfolk. He was awarded the CVO in 1984.

Percy ALLISS

Golf
Percy Alliss b. 8 Jan 1897 Sheffield. d. 31 Mar 1975 Ferndown, Dorset.

The father of Peter Alliss (qv) finished in the top five of The Open five times between 1928 and 1939. They were the first father and son to play in the Ryder Cup, in which Percy's record was three wins, two losses and a half in four ties for which he was selected 1929-37.

Like his son, his fine striking of the ball was let down by inconsistent putting. He had 16 European wins, including the *News of the World* Match Play Championship in 1933 and 1937, the German Open five times between 1926 and 1932 while he was the pro at the Wannsee Club in Berlin, and the Italian Open twice, in 1927 and in 1935, when he set a European low aggregate record of 262. Another son, Percy, was also a professional golfer.

Peter ALLISS

Golf
Peter Alliss b. 28 Feb 1931 Berlin, Germany.

One of the most prominent British golfers of the 1950s and 1960s, Alliss has become the voice of the game as a TV commentator for the BBC and in the USA. A gifted player, his suspect putting was perhaps the major reason that he did not win a major, but he played in eight Ryder Cups for Britain and Ireland, from his debut as the youngest ever player at 22 in 1953 to 1969. His playing record was 10 wins, 15 losses and 5 halves in 30 matches. He also played for England in ten World Cups between 1954 and 1967.

Encouraged by his father Percy (qv), he turned pro in 1946 after being a boy international. He had 20 European wins in his career, including the Dunlop Masters in 1955 and 1959, and in 1958 three Opens in successive weeks: the Spanish, Italian and Portuguese. He won the Vardon Trophy for the lowest stroke average on the tour in 1964 and 1966, but his greatest disappointment was that his best place in the Open was just 8th (in 1969 and three times jointly).

Fred ALSOP

Athletics, Triple Jump
Frederick John Alsop. b. 20 Oct 1938 Plaistow, London.

Alsop was AAA junior champion for triple jump in 1957 and burst into prominence with an English Native record 14.94m in 1959 to win the Essex county title, more than 70 cm more than he had jumped before. He broke the British record of Ken Wilmshurst (born in India) with 15.65 in the qualifying round of the 1960 Olympics, before placing 12th in the final, and made seven more improvements to the 16.46 with which he was 4th at the 1964 Olympics.

He won Commonwealth bronze medals in 1962, when he exceeded 16m for the first time, and again in 1966. In 1965 he produced his best ever jump, a wind-assisted 16.65 and retired in 1969 a year after competing at his third Olympics.

He was AAA champion outdoors at long jump in 1960, 1963 and 1965 and at triple jump in 1960-1, 1964-5 and 1967 and indoors at long jump 1962 and 1965 and at triple jump 1965 and 1967-8. His long jump best was 7.74 in 1964. He was an engineer by profession.

Jeannette ALTWEGG

Figure Skating
Jeannette Eleanor Altwegg. b. 8 Sep 1930 India. Later Mrs Wirz.

The only British woman to win both a world and an Olympic figure skating title since Madge Syers (qv) in 1908, Altwegg made her debut at the World Championships in 1947 when she placed 5th and later that year was runner-up in the junior lawn tennis championships at Wimbledon. She then decided to concentrate on skating and showed consistent improvement each year. She finished 4th at the 1948 World Championships, 3rd in 1949, 2nd in 1950 and finally took the title in 1951. She won a bronze medal at the 1948 Olympics before winning a gold medal at the 1952 Games, after which she retired.

She was also British champion four times, 1947-50, and twice European champion, 1951-2. She declined all offers to turn professional and took up a teaching post at the Pestalozzi children's orphanage in Switzerland. Awarded the CBE in 1953, she married a Swiss, Marc Wirz, but they were divorced in 1973. One of their daughters, Cristina, won a world championship gold medal at curling in 1983.

Leslie AMES

Cricket
Leslie Ethlebert George Ames. b. 3 Dec 1905 Elham, Kent. d. 26 Feb 1990 Canterbury, Kent.

A high-class wicket-keeper/batsman, Ames three times achieved the wicket-keeper's double of 1000 runs and 100 dismissals; only John Murray (qv), in 1957, has also done this. His 128 dismissals (79 ct, 49 st) in 1929 and 122 (70, 52) in 1928 remain unassailable as the two highest totals of dismissals in a first-class season. In 1932 he scored 2482 runs as well as taking 104 dismissals, which included 64 stumpings, again an all-time record, as is his 418 career stumpings, many off the Kent leg-spinner 'Tich' Freeman (qv).

A free-scoring batsman, particularly accomplished as a cutter and hooker and easily good enough to play for England in that role alone, he scored over 1000 runs in a season 17 times, with a peak of 3058 at 58.80 in 1933. He was England's first-choice 'keeper almost throughout the 1930s, but back problems caused him to concentrate virtually exclusively on his batting from 1939.

He was manager and secretary of Kent 1960-74, playing a major part in that county's outstanding success after his own playing days were over. In 1950 he was the first professional ever to be appointed an England selector, serving for eight seasons, and he also managed MCC touring teams. He played League football for Clapton Orient and Gillingham and was a squadron leader in the RAF during the war. He was awarded the CBE in 1973.

47 Tests 1929-39: 2434 runs at 40.56, 8 100s HS 149; 74 catches, 23 stumpings.
First-class 1926-51: 37,248 runs at 43.51, 102 100s HS 295; 24 wickets at 33.37, BB 3-23; 703 catches, 418 stumpings.

Dennis AMISS

Cricket
Dennis Leslie Amiss. b. 7 Apr 1943
Harborne, Birmingham.

Although he made his debut in Test cricket in 1966, Amiss did not establish himself for several years until he became Warwickshire's opening batsman in 1972 and he opened for the first time in his tenthTest in the 1972/3 series against India. Also in 1972 he scored the first ever century in one-day internationals for England v Australia at Old Trafford. From then he was England's most prolific scorer, until in common with many others he struggled against the pace of Dennis Lillee and Jeff Thomson in 1974/5. Against the West Indies in 1973/4 he made 663 runs at 82.87 in five Tests, with a great match-saving 262* at Kingston. In eight of his 11 Test centuries he passed 150.

His Test career ended in 1977 when he went to play in World Series Cricket in Australia and he also toured South Africa with the England 'rebels' in 1982, but he continued to score massively for his county. He exceeded 1000 runs for 23 successive seasons in England 1965-87, with bests of 2239 at 55.97 in 1984 and 2110 at 65.93 in 1976. He was awarded the MBE 1988. He became Warwickshire CC's chief executive in 1994, when the county won a unique treble of Championship, Sunday League and Benson & Hedges Cup.

50 Tests 1966-77: 3612 runs at 46.30, 11 100s HS 262*; 24 catches.
18 One-day Ints 1972-7: 859 runs at 47.72, 4 100s HS 137; 2 catches.
First-class 1960-87: 43,423 runs at 42.86, 102 100s HS 262*; 18 wickets at 39.88, BB 3-21; 418 catches.

Bob ANDERSON

Darts
Robert Charles Anderson. b. 7 Nov 1947
Winchester, Hampshire.

A civil servant from Swindon, Anderson began playing darts at five but did not represent England until he was 33. He steadily reached the top, winning his first major title in 1986. That year he partnered John Lowe (qv) to win the first World Pairs title, and won the first of three successive World Masters titles. In 1987 he won the British Open and World Matchplay and in 1988 he became the World Professional champion. He was also British Matchplay champion in 1988-9, won the Canadian Open 1990 and 1992 and the North American Open 1993.

Jamie ANDERSON

Golf
James Anderson. b. 1842 St Andrews, Fife.
d. 1912 Perth.

Having been runner-up in 1873, Anderson won the Open Championship three years in succession 1877-9. He was again runner-up in 1881 and joint 3rd in 1882.

The son of David Anderson, 'Old Daw', a caddie at St Andrews, Jamie started to play golf at the age of ten. A very steady player, noted for his accuracy, he was a professional at Ardeer Club and then at St Andrews.

Rob ANDREW

Rugby Union
Christopher Robert Andrew. b. 18 Feb 1963 Richmond, Yorkshire.

England's most capped fly-half, playing 69 times in that position and once at full back from 1985 to 1995, Andrew captained England once and holds English records of 396 points and 21 dropped goals. He added a further 11 points, including two dropped goals in his five Tests for the British Isles, two in 1989 against Australia and three in 1993 against New Zealand. Andrew had lost his England place to Stuart Barnes in 1993, but was then preferred to Barnes on the Lions' tour and regained his England place, playing a major part in the great win over the All-Blacks in November 1993. In 1986 he set a then England record with 21 points (six penalties and dropped goal) against Wales, and, having remodelled his kicking technique with the help of David Alred, he regained his England kicking job and scored 27 points against South Africa in June and 30 points against Canada in

December 1994, when he succeeded with all six penalties and all six conversion attempts. He added all 24 points against Scotland in March 1995 to seal England's Grand Slam triumph that season. He maintained his brilliant form into the World Cup, and it was his thrilling 40-yard dropped goal that took England to victory over Australia in a pulsating quarter-final. Days later his award of the MBE was announced.

His first club was Middlesbrough and he later played for Nottingham and Wasps, whom he captained when they won the 1989/90 Courage Championship. He also played for a brief spells with Gordon, Sydney, in Australia and for Toulouse when he worked in France in 1991-2.

A Cambridge Blue 1982-4, he also captained the University at cricket, with a century against Nottinghamshire in 1984. He is a chartered surveyor.

Dennis ANDRIES

Boxing
Dennis Andries. b. 5 Nov 1953
Georgetown, Guyana.

Andries began his professional career in 1973 and, after unsuccessfully challenging for the British light-heavyweight crown in 1980 and 1982, finally won the title by outpointing Tom Collins in 1984. Two years later he won the WBC World light-heavyweight championship but lost the title to Thomas Hearns (USA) in Detroit in 1987. In America in 1989 he regained the title by defeating Tony Willis (USA) in February but then lost to Jeff Harding (USA) in June. In July 1990 Andries became the only British boxer ever to recapture a world title twice when he beat Harding in a return bout and after two successful title defences he met Harding for a third time in September 1991. This time it was the American's turn to regain the title and the reign of Andries as world champion was finally ended. He continued, however, to box, but lost his British cruiserweight title in May 1995. He was awarded the MBE 1991.

Career record 1978-May 1995: 62 contests. Won 48, Drew 2, Lost 12.

Howard ANGUS

Rackets and Real Tennis
Howard Rea Angus. b. 25 Jun 1944
Watford, Hertfordshire.

Angus matched Peter Latham and Jim Dear's (qqv) achievement of winning world titles at both rackets and real tennis, and was the first amateur to do so.

He excelled at all racket games at Winchester and Cambridge. At real tennis he was the British Amateur champion 16 times between 1966 and 1982, when he failed to win the title only in 1981. He also won the doubles eight times. After an unsuccessful challenge for the World title in 1974, he beat Gene Scott (USA) two years later and remained the champion until 1981.

His record as a rackets player was equally impressive, winning the British Amateur singles and doubles title four times each. Between 1972 and 1977 he played Willie Surtees (GB/USA) four times in challenge matches for the world title and was successful in his second challenge in 1973. He was particularly disappointed to lose the fourth challenge in 1977 as he was, at the time, the world real tennis champion and he had hoped to match Latham's record of holding both titles simultaneously.

Princess ANNE

Equestrianism, Three-day Event
HRH The Princess Royal, Princess Anne
Elizabeth Alice Louise. b. 15 Aug 1950
London.

Princess Anne was the winner of the European three-day event title on *Doublet* in 1971, when she was voted BBC Sports Personality of the Year, and second on *Goodwill* in 1975, when she also won a team silver. She also competed for Britain at the 1976 Olympics. She was president of the British Olympic Association from 1983, succeeded her father, Prince Philip, as president of the International Equestrian Federation (FEI) in 1986, and has been a determined, independent-minded member of the International Olympic Committee from 1988. She was married to Mark Phillips (qv) 1973-92.

William APPLEGARTH

Athletics
William Reuben Applegarth. b. 11 May 1890 Guisborough, North Yorkshire. d. 5 Dec 1958 Schenectady, New York, USA.

In 1914 Applegarth ran 220 yards in 21¹/₅, secs a time that matched the ratified world record for an event that, at the time, was also run on straight tracks. It remained unbeaten around a turn for 18 years and was his fourth British record for 220y, his first 21¹/₅ in 1913. He also equalled the British records of 10⁴/₅ for 100m four times in 1912 and 9⁴/₅ for 100y in 1913 and 1914, with another record for 150y of 14³/₅ in 1913, and ran on two British sprint relay teams that set world records. At the 1912 Olympics he won a gold medal in the 4x100m relay and was third at 200m after being eliminated in the semi-finals of the 100m.

The Post Office worker first made his name in 1910, when he was 3rd in the AAA 100y, and he won the AAA 220y in 1912 and both 100y and 220y in 1913 and 1914. He then turned professional and beat the Australian Jack Donaldson, then the top professional sprinter, in November 1914 at 100y and in April 1915 at 220y. In 1922 he emigrated to the USA where he coached soccer and track and field athletics for three years before working as a welder.

Bob APPLEYARD

Cricket
Robert Appleyard. b. 27 Jun 1924 Wibsey, Bradford, West Yorkshire.

Appleyard first played for Yorkshire at the age of 26 in 1950, taking 11 first-class wickets at 16.09. He then caused a sensation by taking 200 wickets at 14.14 in 1951 with his medium-paced inswingers and slower off-breaks. His unerring accuracy from his high, easy action made him a formidable proposition, but he was struck down by illness and after just one match in 1952 did not reappear until 1954.

On his return he was again highly successful with 154 wickets at 14.42 and made his way into the England team, taking seven wickets in his first Test against Pakistan and heading the Test averages with 11 wickets at 20.36 against Australia in 1954/5. His Test career, however, lasted only two years and his last year with Yorkshire was 1958.

9 Tests 1954-6: 51 runs at 17.00, HS 19*; 31 wickets at 17.87, BB 5-51; 4 catches.
First-class 1950-8: 776 runs at 8.52, HS 63; 708 wickets at 15.48, BB 8-76; 80 catches.

Fred ARCHER

Horse Racing
Frederick James Archer. b. 11 Jan 1857 Cheltenham. d. 8 Nov 1886 Newmarket.

The greatest jockey of the 19th century, Fred Archer was champion in England for 13 successive years, 1874-86, up to his suicide at the age of 29.

He had ridden 2748 winners from 8084 mounts since 1870. His annual tally of winners rose each year from 1870 to 1878: 2, 3, 27, 107, 147, 172, 207, 218, 229; the last four were new annual records. After again totalling over 200 in 1881-2, he set further new records from 1883 to 1885: 232, 241, 246. He rode five Derby winners, and in all won 21 classics, 12 of them for Lord Falmouth. At 1.78m *5 ft 10 in* tall, Archer was forced to adopt savage dieting in order to ride at some 3 stone below his natural weight of 11 stone. This wasting drastically affected his health and while seriously ill with typhoid fever, and also affected by the death of his wife Nellie two years earlier, he shot himself.

The son of **William**, who rode the winner of the 1858 Grand National, Fred was apprenticed to Mathew Dawson (qv) at the age of 11 and was stable jockey for that great trainer from 1874. Allied to his masterly natural horsemanship he possessed enormous drive and determination to succeed, making him very hard on his horses, but a great friend to backers of them.

His younger brother **Charles** Edward (1858-1922) rode on the flat for a short while, and after excess weight forced him to give up, took to training.

Jimmy ARMFIELD

Football
James Christopher Armfield. b. 21 Sep 1935 Denton, Manchester.

Armfield was the winner of 43 caps for England at right-back 1959-66, including a run of 37 consecutive appearances, 15 as captain. Although he represented Lancashire Schools at rugby, he decided on a football career and signed for Blackpool as an amateur in 1951. He turned professional in September 1954 and made his League debut three months later, going on to make 566 League appearances for Blackpool before he retired in 1971. He also played nine times for England in Under-23 internationals and made 12 appearances for the Football League. The outstanding feature of his game was the strength of his tackle and he was at his peak in the 1962 World Cup.

Two months after retiring in May 1971 he was appointed manager of Bolton Wanderers and after moving to Leeds United in 1974/5 guided them to the European Cup final that season. On leaving Leeds in July 1978, he became a regular broadcaster on BBC radio.

Gary ARMSTRONG

Rugby Union
Gary Armstrong. b. 30 Sep 1966 Edinburgh.

A scrum-half from Jed-Forest, Armstrong played for Scotland at Under-18, Youth, Under-21 and 'B' levels before making his full international debut against Australia in 1988. His partnership with fly-half Craig Chalmers (qv) was particularly effective and was a key factor in Scotland's 1990 Grand Slam. He toured Australia with the British Lions in 1989 but did not play in the Tests.

He was troubled by injury throughout his career. A torn knee ligament kept him out of the 1992 international season and then a groin injury almost certainly cost him his place on the 1993 Lions' tour. He then announced his intention of retiring from the international game but was persuaded to continue for the 1993/94 season during which he won his 30th cap, although a hand injury playing against Ireland resulted in his missing the matches against Wales and France.

Gerry ARMSTRONG

Football
Gerard Joseph Armstrong. b. 23 May 1954 Belfast.

Signed by Tottenham from the Northern Irish club Bangor, he spent five seasons (1976-80) with Spurs before moving to Watford. A spell in Spain with Real Mallorca followed and on his return to the English League he played for West Bromwich, Chesterfield, Brighton and Millwall. A strong, unselfish target man he won 63 caps for Northern Ireland and, with 12 goals, he is their second highest goalscorer.

Bill ARNULL

Horse Racing
William Arnull. b. 1785. d. 29 Apr 1835.

Between 1804 and 1832 Arnull rode nine Classic winners: three each of the 2000 Guineas, 1000 Guineas and Derby. This followed the success of his father and uncle.

His father **John** (1753-1815) rode five Derby winners and one Oaks winner between 1784 and 1807, and his uncle **Samuel** (c.1760- Feb 1800) rode the first Derby winner, Sir Charles Bunbury's *Diomed* in 1780 with three more Derby winners and one of the Oaks to 1798. Of the first 35 Derbys, the Arnull family rode the winner 12 times.

Eric ASHTON

Rugby League
Eric Ashton. b. 24 Jan 1935 St Helens.

An outstanding leader, Ashton captained Wigan in a record six Challenge Cup finals, taking the trophy in 1958-9 and 1965. He won 26 caps for Great Britain, 15 as captain, scoring 14 tries, and led them to victory in the 1960 World Cup and the Ashes on the 1960 tour of Australia.

After being turned down by his home-town club, St Helens, he was signed by Wigan who had noted his talents while he was playing rugby union as a national ser-viceman. He scored 319 tries in his senior career and also kicked 481 goals 1955-68, including 231 tries with 448 goals for Wigan, but his major contribution was as a playmaker for his winger, Billy Boston (qv). On the 1958 and 1962 Great Britain tours of Australia he scored a total of 51 tries but again created many openings for his wing men. He was player-coach at Wigan 1963-9 and after retirement remained as coach until 1973 when he moved to St Helens. A natural leader and master tactician who coached Great Britain and England, he was awarded the MBE in 1966 and was the first rugby league player to be honoured in this manner. He is now chairman of St Helens.

Nigel ASPINALL

Croquet
George Nigel Aspinall. b. 29 July 1946 Reading, Berkshire.

Winner of the President's Cup a record 11 times between 1969 and 1985, Aspinall also won the Open Championship eight times and his total of ten wins (with three different partners) in the men's doubles equalled the record set by John Solomon and Edmund Cotter (qqv). Other successes included victories in the men's champi-onship (1973, 1983) and the mixed doubles (1973, 1982, 1987). An accom-plished all-round player from the Bristol club, he favoured a straightforward style of play, eschewing unnecessary embellish-ments and his particular strength was his shooting. A graduate of Bristol University and a freelance computer programmer, he was recognised as the world's best player from 1969, when he won all his matches in the Test series against Australia.

Andrew ASTBURY

Swimming
Andrew Astbury. b. 29 Nov 1960 Leeds.

Astbury reached his peak with Common-wealth titles in 1982 in British records at 200m 1:51.52, and 400m 3:53.29, his third record at this distance from 1979, adding a silver medal at 4 x 200m. He had won the Commonwealth bronze at 1500m in 1978, placing 5th at 400m and won an Olympic bronze medal at 4 x 200m in 1984.

He was ASA freestyle champion: long course: 200m 1981, 400m 1980-2, 1500m 1979-83; short course: 400m 1978-9, 200m and 1500m 1979, and he also set a British long course record with 8:13.86 from 800m in 1980.

Mike ATHERTON

Cricket
Michael Andrew Atherton. b. 23 Mar 1968 Failsworth, Manchester.

Tough, resolute and a highly skilful open-ing batsman, Atherton was the ideal choice as England cricket captain when he was appointed to succeed Graham Gooch (qv) in 1993. The job these days, like that of the England football manager, is made well-nigh untenable by the attentions of the media unless success is continuous. Atherton's team's record has been far from that, but his own form has been marvel-lously well sustained.

He made 553 runs at an average of 46.08 against Australia in 1993, when he took over as captain for the last two Tests, and followed that with 510 at 56.66 against the West Indies and 273 at 68.25 against New Zealand in 1994. That year his record was marred by the ball tampering incident at Lord's against South Africa, for which he was twice fined. However, he put that behind him, and maintained his form on the tour to Australia. He started the summer of 1995 as man of the series in the Texaco Trophy matches against the West Indies, with an exceptionally brilliant 127 in the third match, his first one-day international century.

Educated at Manchester Grammar School and Cambridge University, whom he cap-tained in 1988-9, he captained Young England in 1987 and in 1988 at the World Youth Cup before making his Test debut in 1989. In 1990, his first full season with Lancashire, he had his best season to date in English first-class cricket, scoring 1924

his leg breaks. A back injury the following year brought a temporary lull in his Test career and the end of his bowling, but he was soon back in the England team.

45 Tests 1989-95: 3324 runs at 40.04, 7 100s HS 151; 1 wicket at 282.00, BB 1-60; 34 catches.

25 One-day Ints 1990-5: runs at 46.43, 1 100 HS 127; 8 catches.

First-class 1987-95: 12,399 runs at 44.12, 34 100s HS 199; 107 wickets at 43.83, BB 6-78; 153 catches.

Geoffrey ATKINS

Rackets
Geoffrey Willoughby Thomas Atkins.
b. 20 Jan 1927.

By successfully challenging Jim Dear (qv) in 1954, Atkins became only the third amateur to win the world rackets title since the championship was instituted in 1820. He successfully defended the title against challenges from James Leonard (1963 and 1968) and Charles Swallow (1964 and 1970). When he resigned the title in 1971, at the age of 44, he had been champion for 17 years which beat Peter Latham's record for the longest tenure.

Between 1952 and 1963 he won the British Amateur title five times and the doubles three times. After winning the world rackets title in 1954, he lived in Chicago for the next 20 years winning the US Open in 1958 and 1968 and the US Amateur eight times between 1954 and 1970. A classic stylist with effortless footwork, his outstanding career could hardly have been predicted as, while at Rugby School, he was only second string in the school pair for one year.

John ATKINS

Cyclo Cross
John Atkins. b. 7 Apr 1942.

Britain's most successful cyclo-cross rider, Atkins won five national titles as an amateur, 1961-2 and 1966-8, and a further seven in succession as a professional 1969-75, adding the Open title in 1977. His 5th place in the World Championships in 1968 was the best ever by a British rider.

John ATKINSON

Rugby League
John Atkinson. b. 30 Oct 1946 Leeds.

With 26 caps 1968-80, Atkinson became one of Great Britain's most capped players. A winger, he scored 12 international tries and was top scorer in the League three times. 1970, 1972-3. He was a vital member of the Leeds team which won every major honour, including the League title five times (1967-70, 1972) and the Challenge Cup three times (1968, 1977-8). Atkinson scored a try in each of these Challenge Cup finals and was also a member of the losing team at Wembley in 1971-2.

He toured with Great Britain in 1970 and 1974 and was on the winning team at the 1972 World Cup. In February 1983 he became player-coach at Carlisle but the appointment came too late to save the club from relegation and in his first and only season in the Second Division (1983/4) he suffered a serious injury. This prompted his decision and concentrate on coaching and he remained with Carlisle in that capacity until 1986. He scored 401 tries in his career 1966-83, 340 for Leeds.

Bunny AUSTIN

Tennis
Henry Wilfred Austin. b. 26 Aug 1906 Croydon, London. D 26/8/2000

Austin was a stalwart of the British team which held the Davis Cup from 1933 to 1936. After winning the Public Schools' title while at Repton, he went on to captain Cambridge and the year after leaving University he made his Davis Cup debut. Between 1929 and 1937 he played in 48 Davis Cup rubbers (all of them singles) and won 36. A singles semi-finalist at Wimbledon five times, and quarter-finalist ten times, he lost in the final to Ellworth Vines (USA) in 1932 and Donald Budge (USA) in 1938. He was also runner-up to Henner Henkel (Ger) at the 1937 French Championships.

His only significant singles success outdoors was at the 1937 British Hard Court Championships, but he won the British

His only significant singles success outdoors was at the 1937 British Hard Court Championships, but he won the British Indoor title in 1934 and 1937.

As a doubles player, he again narrowly missed top honours; in the mixed doubles he was the losing finalist at the US Championships 1929, the French 1931 and Wimbledon 1934. At men's doubles he reached the semi-finals at Wimbledon 1926-7 and the French 1931. Seeded No. 1 in the Wimbledon singles in 1939, he went out in the quarter-finals and retired at the end of the season. He later devoted himself to the cause of Moral Rearmament.

'Bunny' Austin lacked the physique to play a power game but his superlative armoury of ground strokes made him one of the most respected players of his era.

Steve BACKLEY

Athletics
Steven James Backley. b. 12 Feb 1969 Sidcup, London.

Backley was the world's top javelin thrower in his first two years as a senior in 1989, when he won at the European Cup and World Cup and took the World Student Games gold medal, and in 1990, when he won Commonwealth and European titles and became the first British male thrower ever to set a world record.

After retaining his World Student title, he was held back in 1991 by an adductor muscle injury, and met his first failure at a major event when he did not qualify for the final of the World Championships. He rebounded with a UK record three weeks later, and in New Zealand in January 1992 he achieved the first 90m throw (91.46) with the revised javelin specification, but with further injury problems was restricted to the bronze medal at the Olympics. A shoulder injury then kept him out of action until July 1993, a month before he took 4th place in the World Championships. Although not quite back to his best in 1994, he retained both European and Commonwealth titles and also won the World Cup javelin.

He had won the European Juniors in 1987 and in 1988 set a world junior record and placed 2nd at the World Juniors. His first world records in 1990 were 89.58 in Stockholm with a Sandvik javelin, and 90.98 at Crystal Palace on just his second throw with a Németh model. When this was banned at the end of 1991, his 89.58 was reinstated as the record. UK champion 1988-92, AAA 1989 and 1992. He competes for Cambridge Harriers and was awarded the MBE in 1995.

Steve BADDELEY

Badminton
Stephen John Baddeley. b. 28 Mar 1961 Hove, East Sussex.

A left-hander, Baddeley won a record 143 England caps 1979-90. After winning the English National under-18 doubles with D Burden in 1978-9 he went on to take the senior singles in 1982, 1985 and 1987, and the doubles in 1985 and 1987 and 1989. He also won the singles at the 1986 Commonwealth Games, with team gold at the three Games 1982-90, and took the European men's singles title in 1990 before retiring at the end of the year. A biology and psychology graduate, he was the manager of the British team when badminton was introduced into the Olympics in 1992 and now coaches in Switzerland.

Wilfred and Herbert BADDELEY

Tennis
Herbert Baddeley. b. 11 Jan 1872 Bromley, London. d. 20 Jul 1931 Cannes, France.

Wilfred Baddeley. b. 11 Jan 1872 Bromley, London. d. 24 Jan 1929 Menton, France

The early days of tennis (then lawn tennis) in Britain were notable for the number of brothers who dominated the game. Firstly came the Renshaw twins (qv) and then the Baddeley twins who were followed by the Doherty brothers (qv). The Baddeleys won the Wimbledon doubles four times (1891, 1894-6) and the Irish Championships twice (1896-7). Wilfred was undoubtedly the stronger player, the first of his three victories in the Wimbledon singles (1891-2, 1895) coming when he was only 19 years old and he held the record as the youngest-

performance as a singles player was to reach the semi-finals at Wimbledon for three consecutive years 1894-6. Sons of a London solicitor, both twins died in the south of France.

Edgar BAERLEIN

Rackets and Real Tennis
Edgar Maximilian Baerlein. b. 13 Dec 1879 Manchester. d 3 Jun 1971 Midhurst, West Sussex.

Baerlein was winner of the British Amateur rackets singles a record 9 times and the British Amateur real tennis singles 13 times. The promise he had shown as a player of court games at Eton and Cambridge was quickly fulfilled in the senior ranks. His run of championship successes at rackets was only interrupted when he fractured his skull in a motorcycle accident. He also won the Amateur rackets doubles six times between 1902 and 1920. Although Baerlein did not concentrate on real tennis until after World War I, he won the British Amateur singles 13 times between 1912 and 1930 and this remained the record until Howard Angus (qv) won for a 14th time in 1979. He also won the doubles 11 times between 1920 and 1937. In 1931 he won the first British Open Championship at the age of 51 and at the time of his final Championship victory in the 1937 doubles he was, incredibly, aged 57. Despite this host of Championship successes, his finest victory came in the Bathurst Cup in 1923 when he became the only man to beat the great American, Jay Gould, at real tennis in a 20-year period extending from 1907 to 1926.

His son **Richard** Edgar Baerlein (1910-95) was a distinguished horse racing journalist.

Bill BAILEY

Cycling
William James Bailey. b. 6 Apr 1888. d. 12 Feb 1971 Chiswick, London.

World amateur sprint champion four times, 1909-11 and 1913, and British Empire sprint champion each year 1909-11, Bailey was the leading attraction as a track racer in the years prior to World War I. His run as world champion was interrupted in 1912, when the National Cyclists' Union could not afford to send him to the USA. His matinée idol good looks and marvellous physique brought him widespread adulation as he contested match races against local champions around the world. His appearances were often heralded by the popular song 'Won't You Come Home, Bill Bailey?' He was also national champion at 1 mile 1909, 1912-13; 5 miles 1909 and quarter-mile 1910 and 1913 and won the Grand Prix de Paris each year 1910-13 before turning professional on the outbreak of war in 1914, only to lose years of potential profit through World War I. He was 3rd in the world professional sprint in 1920. He was also a talented footballer, at that sport playing for Middlesex.

McDonald BAILEY

Athletics
Emmanuel McDonald Bailey. b. 8 Dec 1920 Williamsville, Trinidad

A beautiful stylist, Bailey dominated British sprinting in the late 1940s and early 1950s, collecting a record 14 AAA titles by winning the 100y and 220y each year 1946-53, except for 1948. That was Olympic year, but Bailey has well below form, running only 3rd in the AAA 100y, before, suffering from a throat infection, he was 6th in the 100m final. Four years later he took the Olympic 100m bronze in a blanket finish with 4th place at 200m. Although resident in Britain he was not permitted to compete at the European Championships.

Bailey had first run at the AAAs in 1939 before war service in the RAF and he was also champion of Trinidad during the war. From 1946 to 1952 he set British records at 100y (14 at 9.7 and 9.6), 100m (5 from 10.4 to a world record 10.2 in 1951), 200m (7 from 21.2 to 20.9) and had a wind assisted bests for 100y of 9.4 and 220y of 20.5 on a straight track. In 1953 he became a professional rugby league player, but only played one friendly match for Leigh.

He returned to his native Trinidad, where he became a leading administrator.

He returned to his native Trinidad, where he became a leading administrator.

Trevor BAILEY

Cricket
Trevor Edward Bailey. b. 3 Dec 1923 Westcliff-on-Sea, Essex.

'Barnacle' Bailey's epic partnership with Willie Watson (qv) to save England from defeat by Australia at Lord's in 1953 made him a national hero. By then however he was mid-way through a Test career which lasted for just under ten years and which many experts felt ended prematurely. A most astute tactician, he could well have made a successful captain at Test level, as he was for Essex 1961-6.
He won his Blue at Cambridge University 1947-8 and played for Essex 1946-67. He was a true all-rounder as he proved his worth in Tests as a fast-medium bowler and a generally obdurate batsman, who once went 79 minutes without adding to his score in a Test match (v South Africa 1955), and as a very fine close-in fielder. He achieved the double of 1000 runs and 100 wickets in eight seasons, and in 1959 became the only player since 1937 to have scored 2000 runs and taken 100 wickets in a season. For many years he has provided expert analysis for the BBC Radio team on cricket. At soccer he won his blue at Cambridge and an FA Amateur Cup winners' medal in 1952 with Walthamstow. He was awarded the CBE in 1994.
61 Tests 1949-59: 2290 runs at 29.74, 1 100 HS 134*; 132 wickets at 29.21, BB 7-34; 32 catches.
First-class 1945-67: 28,642 runs at 33.42, 28 100s HS 205; 2082 wickets at 23.13, BB 10-90; 428 catches.

Chris BAILLIEU

Rowing
Christopher Latham Baillieu. b. 12 Dec 1949 Marylebone, London.

Baillieu was educated at Radley College and Jesus College, Cambridge, where he distinguished himself by becoming only the second Cantab to row in four winning Boat Race crews 1970-3. He then had a remarkable record at double sculls with Michael Hart, winning a gold medal at the World Championships in 1977, as well as silver in 1978 and bronze in 1974 and 1975, and Olympic silver in 1976 as well as wins at Henley 1973, 1975 and 1977-8. He went on to place 4th with Tim Clark at the 1980 Olympics and to have two more Henley double sculls victories, 1979 and 1983. As a single sculler he was a three-time winner of the Diamonds, 1981-2 and 1984, won the Scullers Head 9 times in 11 years to 1984, and had a world championships best placing of 4th in 1981. He was awarded the MBE and was later appointed a Steward of the Henley Royal Regatta.

Ben Howard BAKER

Athletics, High Jump
Benjamin Howard Baker. b. 15 Feb 1892 Aigburth, Liverpool. d. 10 Sep 1987 Warminster, Wiltshire.

A fine all-round sportsman, Baker won a record six AAA high jump titles either side of World War I, 1910, 1912-3, 1919-21 After British records of 1.91 and 1.92 in 1920, he set the inaugural English native record of 1.95m in 1921, and this lasted as a British record for 25 years.
He competed at the Olympic Games of 1912 and 1920, when he was 6th at high jump, 8th at triple jump (in a pb 13.67m) and also threw the discus. Soon afterwards he beat the Olympic champion Dick Landon (USA) at high jump in the British Empire v USA match. As a goalkeeper at soccer he won eight amateur caps and made full international appearances in 1921 while with Everton and 1926 while with Chelsea, not conceding a goal. He was also an international class water polo player. At tennis he played in the Wimbledon doubles and won the Welsh covered court doubles title in 1929 and 1932.

Percy BAKER

Bowls
Edwin Percy Baker. b. 18 Jul 1895 Weston-super-Mare, Somerset. d. 3 Jan 1990 Poole, Dorset.

Winning four singles titles over a 23-year period, 1932, 1946, 1952 and 1955, Baker was the most successful bowler at the English Championships until the arrival of David Bryant (qv). He also won the pairs in 1950 and 1962 and the triples in 1960, and won a silver in the singles at the 1958 Commonwealth Games.

A professional photographer, he settled in Dorset after serving in France and the Balkans in World War I and took up bowls at Poole Park in 1921. A tall, elegant player, he represented Dorset 1927-69, winning 11 county singles titles over a 37-year period. He first played for England in 1933 and last in 1959, but was not a regular member of the team until 1949, becoming captain in 1950. His distinguished career ended in 1971 when, at the age of 76, he won the Bournemouth Open pairs. In his last years he was totally blind.

Philip Noel BAKER

Athletics
Philip John Baker, later Noel-Baker, then Lord Noel-Baker. b. 1 Nov 1883 Hendon, London. d. 9 Oct 1982 Westminster, London,

The Nobel Peace Prize winner of 1959 gave a lifetime's service to peace causes. He entered Parliament as Labour MP for Coventry 1929-31 before representing Derby from 1936 until 1970. During and after World War II he held several ministerial posts and was created a life peer in 1977. He served on the secretariat of the peace conference 1919 and of the League of Nations 1919-22 and was Cassel professor of international relations at London 1924-9 and a lecturer at Yale in 1934.

He was an Olympic finalist at 1500m in 1912 and 1920, helping his team-mates Arnold Jackson and Albert Hill (qqv) to victory, placing 6th in 1912 and 2nd in 1920. He had started running while at school in the USA and then won his Blue at Cambridge, winning the 880y each year 1910-12 and the mile in 1909 and 1911 against Oxford. He was the first honorary secretary of the Achilles Club, formed in 1920.

Best times (all 1912): 880y 1:56.8, 1500m 3:59.6, mile 4:24.8.

Enid BAKEWELL

Cricket
Enid Bakewell. b. 18 Dec 1940 Newstead, Notts. née Turton.

England's finest all-round woman cricketer, Bakewell was a right-hand opening bat and left-arm orthodox spinner. She made 113 v Australia on her Test debut in 1968, and was the first woman player to do a double of 1000 runs and 100 wickets on tour, with 1031 runs at 39.65 and 118 wickets at 9.77 in Australia and New Zealand in 1968/9. With 68 and 112 not out and match figures of 10-75 (3-14 and 7-61) for England v West Indies at Edgbaston in 1979, she achieved a match double never before achieved by a man or woman in a Test match for England. This was also one of three occasions in which she took five wickets in an innings and scored a century in the same Test. First selected for Nottinghamshire at the age of 14, she has been a county player for 40 years, continuing to play for East Midlands and in 1993-5 for Surrey as well as for Redoubtables. She holds the National Cricket Association advanced coaching award and is an England selector.

12 Tests 1968-79: 1078 runs at 59.88, 4 100s HS 124; 50 wickets at 16.62, BB 7-61; 9 catches.

23 One-day Ints 1973-82: 500 runs at 35.71, 2 100s HS 118; 25 wickets at 21.12, BB 3-13; 7 catches.

Gerald BALDING

Polo
(Capt.) Gerald Matthews Balding. b. 24 Aug 1903 Market Harborough, Leics. d. 16 Sep 1957 Marylebone. London.

British leading polo player of the 1930s, Balding was the sixth and (to-date last) British player to be given a 10-goal handicap. He played for Britain in the Westchester Cup in 1930, 1936 (a narrow defeat) and 1939 (captain), and on the team that in 1953 lost to Argentina in the final of a 6-nation tournament. Thereafter he became one of the leading teachers of the game. He played regularly in America as a member of the Greentree team which twice won the US

National Open Championship 1935-6, and he represented the USA against Argentina in the Cup de las Americas in 1936. Still in America on the outbreak of war, he caught the first boat home and was commissioned into the Royal Horse Guards.

His sons Toby and Ian followed him as racehorse trainers. Gerald Barnard 'Toby' **Balding** (b. 23 Sep 1936) has trained two winners of the Grand National *Highland Wedding* in 1969 and *Little Polveir* in 1989, with 59 National Hunt winners in his best season of 1988/9.

Ian Antony **Balding** (b. 7 Nov 1938) was a top amateur jockey, with over 70 National Hunt winners, and gained his training licence in 1964 when he took over from his father-in-law Peter Hastings-Bass. He was champion trainer on the flat in 1971, when his most famous horse, *Mill Reef*, won five major races, including the Derby, King George VI and Queen Elizabeth Stakes and the Prix de l'Arc de Triomphe.

Alan BALL

Football
Alan James Ball. b. 12 May 1945
Farnworth, Gt. Manchester.

A resolute and constructive midfield player, Ball was the youngest member of England's World Cup winning team in 1966.

Encouraged by his father, James (1924-82), a former professional and manager of Halifax Town and Preston North End, he signed amateur forms for Blackpool in 1961, turning professional the following year. He was transferred for British record fees to Everton in August 1966 for £110,000 and then in December 1971 when he went to Arsenal for £220,000.

He moved in 1976 to Southampton, where he became the first player to play over 100 league games for four different First Division clubs, before returning to Blackpool as player-manager in 1980; he then returned to Southampton in 1981 and he closed his playing career with Bristol Rovers in 1983. During this period he also played in the USA, Canada and Hong Kong. After only a few months at Bristol he moved to Portsmouth, serving first as youth coach and then as manager before reverting to a coaching position. He has subsequently been manager of Stoke City 1989-91, Exeter City 1991-4, Southampton 1994-5 and Manchester City from July 1995.

During his outstanding career he won a host of honours: 72 England caps 1965-75; six appearances for the Football League and eight England Under-23 caps. He played in two FA Cup finals, for Everton 1968 and Arsenal 1972, and one League Cup final for Southampton 1979, but was on the losing side on each occasion. He was, however, a member of the Everton team which took the Football League title in 1970.

John BALL

Golf
John Ball Jr. b. 24 Dec 1861 Hoylake, Merseyside. d. 2 Dec 1940 Halkyn, Flintshire.

The greatest amateur golfer of his time, Ball won the British Amateur a record eight times, 1888, 1890, 1892, 1894, 1899, 1907, 1910 and 1912, the last at age 50, and he played in the tournament from the first time it was staged in 1885 until 1921, when he reached the sixth round at the age of 60. He would surely have won even more titles, but the Amateur was not founded until 1885, when he beat his father in the third round. Ball was joint 4th in the Open at the age of 16 in 1878 and in 1890 became the first amateur and the first Englishman to win the Open, achieving another first by completing a double with the Amateur that year. All this despite not playing for three years at his peak when he served with the Cheshire Yeomanry in the Boer War from 1899. He captained England against Scotland each year 1902-11.

Ball revolutionised swing theories with his technique. He was the first to use an open stance and an upright swing, enabling him to hit highly lofted shots landing near the target, rather than always playing a run-up game. He became a farmer in north Wales. His father, also John Ball, owned the Royal Hotel, which overlooked the links at Hoylake, and was a semi-finalist in the Amateur Championship in 1886 and 1887.

Joe BAMBRICK

Football
James Bambrick. b. 3 Nov 1905 Belfast. d. 1983.

A powerfully built centre-forward, he scored six goals for Northern Ireland v Wales in 1930 which still stands as a record for a Home International. This feat, coupled with his 94 goals in that season for the Irish club, Linfield, attracted the attention of English scouts and he signed for Chelsea in 1934. Although finding stiffer competition in the English League, he scored 37 goals in 66 appearances for the London club before moving to Walsall in 1939. He won seven caps for Northern Ireland with Linfield and a further four with Chelsea, scoring 12 goals in all.

Charles BAMBRIDGE

Football
Edward Charles Bambridge. b. 30 Jul 1858 Windsor, Berkshire. d. 8 Nov 1935 Wimbledon, London.

Bambridge was one of five footballing brothers three of whom were, uniquely, all capped by England. Winning 18 caps 1879-87 at outside-left he was the most successful of the talented trio and is rated as one of the outstanding players in the game's formative years. After leaving Malvern College, he played for a variety of clubs including Upton Park, Clapham Rovers, Swifts and Corinthians of whom he was a founder member and later served as Hon. Secretary 1923-32. While still a player, he served on the FA Committee 1883-6.
His brother, **Arthur** Leopold (1861-1923), won three caps for England 1881-4, and the eldest brother, **Ernest** Henry (1848-1917), was capped once in 1876.

Billy BANCROFT

Rugby Union
William John Bancroft. b. 2 Mar 1871 Swansea. d. 3 Mar 1959 Swansea.

An unorthodox full-back for Swansea, Bancroft played for Wales in 33 consecutive matches, 11 of them as captain. His international career lasted from 1890 to 1901 and he also played cricket for Glamorgan from 1897 to 1914. In 1893 he scored the decisive penalty from a drop kick which gave Wales their first home win over England. He is said to have invented the screw kick.
He was a cobbler by trade. His younger brother, **Jack** (1879-1942), won 18 caps as full back (1909-14) scoring 88 points which stood as a Welsh record for many years, including a record eight conversions against France in 1910.

Gordon BANKS

Football
Gordon Banks. b. 30 Dec 1937 Sheffield.

Universally recognised as the greatest goalkeeper in the world during his peak years, Banks was discovered while playing for a Sheffield works club. He played only one season for Third Division Chesterfield before moving to Leicester City in 1959 and to Stoke City in 1967. He set a (then) record for an England goalkeeper by winning 73 caps 1963-72. The highlight of his career was as a member of the England team which won the 1966 World Cup, although many other honours came his way. He won Football League Cup winners' medals with Leicester in 1964 and Stoke 1972 and his outstanding performance in the latter final did much to earn him the award as the Footballer of the Year. Perhaps the one outstanding save of his career was that against Pelé in the 1970 World Cup.
An eye injury sustained in a road accident in August 1972 virtually ended his career although he recovered sufficiently to play briefly in the USA. He later held coaching or managerial posts with Port Vale, Telford United and Stoke City. His game was built on brilliant positional play and superb anticipation and reflexes. He was awarded the MBE in 1970.

Johnny BANNERMAN

Rugby Union
(Lord) John Macdonald Bannerman. b. 1 Sep 1901 Glasgow. d. 10 Apr 1969 Tidworth, Hampshire.

Educated at Shawlands Academy, Glasgow High School and Glasgow University, he had already won 28 caps in the Scottish pack when he went up to Balliol College, Oxford to take a course in agricultural economics. He won his Blue in 1927 and 1928 and went on to win a total of 37 international caps 1921-9; this remained a Scottish record until 1962.

He was Factor to the Montrose Estates 1930-52 and held many civic and political posts. Notably, he served as President of the Scottish RU in 1954-5, as the Lord Rector of Aberdeen University and as Chairman and President of the Scottish Liberal Party. He was awarded the OBE in 1952 for his services to the Festival of Britain and created a Life Peer in 1967.

Roger BANNISTER

Athletics
(Sir) Roger Gilbert Bannister. b. 23 Mar 1929 Harrow, London.

On 6 May 1954 Bannister achieved one of the most celebrated deeds in the history of sport, with the first sub four-minute mile, running 3:59.4 at Iffley Road, Oxford. Six weeks later John Landy (Aus) improved the mile record to 3:57.9, but Bannister in this, his last season before concentrating on his medical career, beat Landy in a race dubbed 'The Mile of the Century' to win the Empire Games title at 1 mile in Vancouver. Bannister ran 3:58.8 and Landy 3:59.6, the first time two men had beaten four minutes in one race. Bannister then added the European title at 1500m. He set four British records at 1500m to 3:42.2 in 1954 and four at 1 mile, his first being 4:03.6 in 1953. He had been 3rd in the European 800m in 1950 and a disappointed 4th at 1500m in the 1952 Olympics. AAA champion at 880y 1952, 1 mile 1951, 1953-4. Best time for 880y 1:50.7 (1953).

He was awarded the CBE in 1955 and became a distinguished neurologist. He was knighted in 1975 for his services to medicine, was Chairman of the Sports Council 1971-4, and was Master of Pembroke College, Oxford 1985-93.

Paul BARBER

Hockey
Paul Jason Barber. b. 21 May 1955 Peterborough.

A penalty corner expert, Barber scored the majority of his 73 international goals (49 England, 24 GB) from the set piece. Playing 99 times for England 1977-88, he failed by the narrowest of margins to become only the third player to win 100 caps and he also won 67 caps for GB 1978-88. He was a medallist at all the major tournaments winning gold (1988) and bronze (1984) at the Olympics, silver (1986) at the World Cup and silver (1987) and bronze (1978) in the European Cup. On leaving King's School, Peterborough he joined the local town club but later played for Slough. He is a quantity surveyor by profession.

Capt. Robert BARCLAY

Walking
Robert Barclay Allardice. b. Aug 1779. d. 8 May 1854.

Allardice, a Scotsman known as Captain Barclay, achieved one of the earliest and most celebrated feats of pedestrianism when, from 1 June to 12 July 1809 on Newmarket Heath, watched by thousands of spectators in the closing stages, he walked 1 mile every hour for 1000 hours. Barclay must have been tough to achieve this, even if no speed was required; he must have been even tougher to have survived his training regimen, which included purging by the drastic use of medicines, sweating by walking under a weight of clothes and by lying between feather beds. His diet was lean meet, beef or mutton, no vegetables or milk, but butter and cheese were allowed, and, to drink, strong ale.

As a teenager he had won a wager of 100 guineas to walk six miles in the hour "fair heel and toe" and undertook a series of wagers in ensuing years, such as 300 miles in five days in hot weather in June 1801, but it was for the 1000 in 1000 that he is remembered. A few days after this feat he rejoined his regiment and his position as ADC to Lt Gen. the Marquis of Huntly. As well as his long distance efforts he also ran at distances as low as 440y, although usually at the mile.

Sandy BARCLAY

Horse Racing
Andrew Barclay. b. 13 Jun 1948 Ayr.

Barclay had a very rapid rise to the top as a jockey, Apprenticed to Harry Whiteman in Ayr, he had his first ride in public in April 1965 and rode his first winner the next month. From ten winners that first year his total rose to 71 in 1966 to make him champion apprentice and at the end of that season, when Lester Piggott (qv) turned freelance Barclay joined the stable of Noel Murless (qv) as deputy to the Australian George Moore. After 55 winners in 1967, and when Moore then returned to Australia, Barclay took over the top jockey's post in Britain, after just three years of racing. Faith in him was soon justified as he rode 116 winners in 1968, including his first Classic, the 1000 Guineas on *Caegwrle*, and four major races including the King George VI and Queen Elizabeth Stakes on *Royal Palace*, for Murless. After that brilliant start, however, he was to ride only one more Classic winner, *Lupe* in the 1970 Oaks and his association with Murless ended when he went to ride for François Boutin in France after that season. He returned to England in 1973 but could not recapture his old form. Although he did have some success later in India, his time at the top was brief.

Sue BARKER

Tennis
Susan Barker. b. 19 Apr 1956 Paignton, Devon. Now Mrs Lampard.

After a brilliant career as a junior she won the French and German singles in 1976 and was a singles quarter-finalist at Wimbledon that year, improving to reach the semi-final in 1977, when she reached her highest world ranking of sixth. Her powerful forehand was her key strength. After declining an invitation to join the Wightman Cup team in 1973, she became a regular member of the squad the follow-

ing year and also joined the Federation Cup team in 1974. In the Wightman Cup she played in ten ties, 1974-83 (5/18 singles, 4/9 doubles) and in the Federation Cup she played in 27 ties, 1974-82 (16/24 singles, 16/21 doubles). She was named Sports Presenter of the Year in 1994 for her work first on BSkyB and then for the BBC.

Woolf BARNATO

Motor Racing
Joel Woolf Barnato. b. 27 Sep 1895 Westminster, London. d. 27 Jul 1948 Marylebone, London

'Babe' Barnato, whose family had made a fortune in South African diamond mining, was one of the leading 'Bentley Boys' of the late 1920s. He won the Le Mans 24-hour race each year 1928-30 in Bentleys. His co-drivers were successively Bernard Rubin, Sir Henry Birkin (qv) and Glen Kidston. The son of the diamond merchant, Barney Barnato, he played six first-class cricket matches for Surrey as a wicket-keeper/batsman in 1928-30.

Brian BARNES

Golf
Brian W Barnes. b. 3 Jun 1945 Addington, London.

A very powerful player and popular man, Barnes was among the top British golfers of the 1970s, but achieved less than he promised to, although he was in the top ten in the Order of Merit in 1968 and each year 1971-80. Perhaps he enjoyed life and a drink or two a little too much!
A fine all-round sportsman at Millfield School he won the British Youths Championship in 1964 just before turning pro. His first European Tour wins came in 1969, when he made the first of six Ryder Cup appearances, His overall Ryder Cup record 1969-79 was 10 wins, 14 losses and 1 half, achieving particular success in partnership with Bernard Gallacher (qv), and then in 1975 when he twice beat Jack Nicklaus (USA) in one day. He also played for Scotland in the World Cup each year 1974-7. His major wins on the European

Tour included the Dutch Open 1974, French Open 1975, Spanish Open 1978, Italian and Portuguese Opens 1979. In Britain his best win was the PGA Match Play in 1976. He withdrew from the European Tour in 1983, but returned in 1991.

John BARNES

Football
John Charles Bryan Barnes. b. 7 Nov 1963 Kingston, Jamaica.

One of the most gifted players of recent years, Barnes has not always been able to reproduce his brilliant club form at international level. With speed, strength, superb ball control and devastating shooting power, particularly from free kicks, his play on the left flank or as a roamer brought a new dimension to British football. He started his League career at Watford in 1981 and became instrumental to the club's rise to prominence in the mid-1980s. Under the management of Graham Taylor, Barnes formed a lethal attacking partnership with Luther Blissett which led the club to finish runners-up in the first division in 1983, and to reach the final of the FA Cup the following year.

In 1987 Barnes moved to Liverpool for a surprisingly low figure of £900,000. Immediately, the club reaped the benefits as Liverpool romped to the title in 1987/8, losing only twice, and then again in 1989/90. Barnes helped them to win the FA Cup in 1989 and the Coca-Cola Cup in 1995. He was the Football Writers' Player of the Year in 1988 and 1990, also winning the PFA award in 1988. He has won 78 England caps, scoring 11 goals, from 1983 to June 1995. After being out of the side for a while he made a successful return to international football in 1994. At the age of 21 he scored what was described as the 'goal of a lifetime' for England against Brazil at the Maracana Stadium.

Sidney BARNES

Cricket
Sidney Francis Barnes. b 19 Apr 1873 Smethwick, West Midlands. d. 26 Dec 1967 Chadsmoor, Staffordshire.

Barnes was regarded by many as the greatest of bowlers. A tall man at 1.86m *6 ft 1 in* and broad-shouldered, he operated at varying paces from fast to slow-medium, employing a beautifully balanced action to impart both swing and spin, with immense accuracy and control of length.

He played only a limited amount of county cricket for Warwickshire 1894-6 and Lancashire 1899-1903, as for the rest of his career he played for minor counties and in the leagues. That, and perhaps his aloof attitude, meant that he played in only ten Tests in England. Yet his Test record is magnificent. In just four matches for England in South Africa 1913/4 he set an unchallenged record for a Test series with 49 wickets at an average of 10.93. That included a match analysis of 17-159 (8-56 and 9-103), a Test record until surpassed by Jim Laker (qv) in 1956. His 189 Test wickets remained the record until passed by Clarrie Grimmett (Aus) in 1936, and his last 100 wickets came in just 11 Tests.

In all matches in his career he took 6229 wickets at an average of 8.33, including 1432 wickets at 8.15 for Staffordshire in the Minor Counties Championship and 4069 wickets over 38 years in league and club cricket at the staggering average of just 6.03.

27 Tests 1901-14: 242 runs at 8.06, HS 38*; 189 wickets at 16.43, BB 9-103; 12 catches.
First-class 1895-1930: 1573 runs at 12.78, HS 93; 719 wickets at 17.09, BB 9-103; 72 catches.

Stuart BARNES

Rugby Union
Stuart Barnes. b. 22 Nov 1962 Grays, Essex.

As a boy Barnes moved from Essex to Wales and he captained the Welsh senior schools team before going up to Oxford University where he won his Blue, 1981-3. After declining an invitation to join the Welsh senior squad in 1981, he made his England debut in 1984 and won eight caps up to 1988. After a long interval, he was recalled to the England side in 1993 and won two further caps.

An attacking fly-half, with exceptional speed off the mark, he would almost certainly have won more caps had he not been a contemporary of Rob Andrew (qv) although his adventurous play was not well suited to the pedestrian style of play adopted by England at the time.

After a spell with Newport he was in Bristol's John Player Cup winning team in 1983 and was again in the winning side in 1986 after he had moved to Bath. He captained Bath for a number of seasons, playing at full-back or fly-half, and scored a memorable drop goal in extra time to defeat Harlequins in the 1992 Pilkington Cup final.

Long an outspoken and articulate critic of various aspects of the game ad its admiistration, on giving up playing he became rugby correspondent of the *Daily Telegraph*.

Walley BARNES

Football
Walley Barnes. b. 16 Jan 1920 Brecon. d. 4 Sep 1975 Hammersmith, London.

A Londoner by heritage, he was born in Wales where his father was serving in the Army. After playing as an amateur for Portsmouth and Southampton he signed with Arsenal in 1943 and stayed with the club until his retirement. Although the start of his career was delayed by the war, he soon established a reputation as one of the best full-backs in Britain. With his strong tackle, excellent positional sense and prudent ball distribution his reputation was fully justified. With Arsenal he won the League Championship in 1948 and an FA Cup winners medal in 1950 but he was out of the game for a year after being carried off with a severe injury in his second FA Cup final in 1952.

After making two appearances for Wales in wartime internationals, he won 22 full caps and captained his country in many of these matches. After his retirement, he joined the BBC as a commentator and, apart from a spell in South Africa as manager of Highland Park FC, he remained in the job until his sudden death.

Charles BARNETT

Cricket
Charles John Barnett. b. 3 Jul 1910 Fairview, Cheltenham. d. 28 May 1993 Stroud, Gloucestershire.

A dashing, hard-hitting batsman for England on either side of World War II, Barnett started in the middle order but after five years with Gloucestershire switched to opening. He reached 1000 runs in a season 12 times, and went over 2000 four times with a peak of 2489 at 40.14 in 1947. Highlights of his Test career, which had started in 1933 just three months after his first century for Gloucestershire, came with centuries against Australia in 1937, 129 at Adelaide, and in 1938, when he made 98 of 169 runs in partnership with Len Hutton (qv) before lunch at Trent Bridge. He reached his 100 off the first ball after lunch. He lost six years of his prime during World War II, but played four Tests for England as a middle-order batsman in 1947-8. He left county cricket in 1948 to play League cricket for Rochdale. He was also an effective medium-fast in-swing bowler and a fine outfielder.

His father, also Charles, played for Gloucestershire 1904-26, as did two uncles, all as amateurs.

20 Tests 1933-48: 1098 runs at 35.41, 2 100s HS 129; 14 catches.

First-class 1927-54: 25,389 runs at 32.71, 48 100s HS 259; 394 wickets at 30.98, BB 6-17; 319 catches.

Edward BARRETT (Ireland)

Wrestling
Edward (a.k.a. Edmund) Barrett. b. 3 Nov 1880 Ballyduff, Co. Kerry. d.?

Barrett achieved a unique double for an Irishman with medals at tug-of-war and wrestling at the 1908 Olympics. His gold medal was with the City of London Police tug-of-war team, but wrestling was his forte, and he also won Olympic bronze in the heavyweight freestyle event, at which he was British champion in 1908 and 1911. He was beaten by fellow-Irishman Con O'Kelly. Barrett also won an all-

Ireland hurling championship medal as a member of the 1901 London Irish team that beat Cork in the all-Ireland final.

His twin brother **John** was a shot putter who won the Irish title in 1903, 1906-08 and 1910-11, AAA in 1911 and 1923 and also competed at the 1908 Olympics.

Roper BARRETT

Tennis
Herbert Roper Barrett. b. 24 Nov 1873 Upton, London d. 27 Jul 1943 Horsham, WestSussex.

A member of Britain's first Davis Cup team in 1900, he played in eight ties until his retirement in 1919 (0/2 singles, 4/8 doubles) after which he became non-playing captain from 1926-39, guiding the team to four Challenge Round successes 1933-6. He was a notable doubles player and partnering Arthur Gore (qv) he won Wimbledon in 1909, reached the all-comers' final on three other occasions, and took the 1908 Olympic Indoor and 1909 British Indoor titles. He added two further Wimbledon titles 1912-3 with Charles Dixon (qv) as his partner. He reached the final of the all-comers' singles at Wimbledon four times, going through to the Challenge Round in 1911 when he was forced to retire against Tony Wilding (NZ) with the score level at two sets all. At the British Covered Court Championships he won the doubles in 1909 and the mixed doubles in 1910.

A prolific tournament player, he won many events on the Continent and at home he achieved a unique dominance at the Suffolk Championships winning the singles 17 times between 1898 and 1921. A London solicitor, he served as Chairman of the LTA in 1924.

Jonah BARRINGTON

Squash
Jonah Paul Barrington. b. 29 Apr 1941 Stratton, Cornwall.

The greatest British squash player, Barrington won many major tournaments, including the British Open every year from 1967 to 1973 except for 1969 when he lost to Cam Nancarrow (Aus) in the semi-finals, and the British Amateur three times, 1967-9. His greatest year was 1968 when he also won the Egyptian Open, the Australian Amateur and the South African Amateur.

His greatest rival was the Australian, Geoff Hunt, and although Barrington won many of their matches Hunt beat him in the final of the 1967 World Amateur and frustrated Barrington's plans to turn professional as the reigning world champion. He finally turned professional in February 1969 and through his match winnings, endorsements, coaching clinics and exhibitions he became the first man to be handsomely remunerated by the game. In 1994 he became president of the Squash Rackets Association.

A left-hander, his game was built on supreme physical fitness, tenacity and endurance. He was educated at Cheltenham College and Trinity College, Dublin, where he studied law for two years. In July 1973 he married Madeline (née Wooller), an international middle-distance runner and the former wife of Derek Ibbotson (qv).

Ken BARRINGTON

Cricket
Kenneth Frank Barrington. b. 24 Nov 1930 Reading, Berkshire. d. 14 Mar 1981 Needham's Point, Bridgetown, Barbados.

The news of Barrington's death from a heart attack during the Third Test of the England tour of the West Indies in 1981 deeply saddened cricket lovers all over the world. This much loved and respected man was assistant manager of the England team on what was a most troubled tour. His playing career had been cut short by a mild heart attack at the age of 38.

Initially joining Surrey as a bowler, his promise as a batsman was soon evident, although his leg-breaks later seemed under-utilised. He made his Test debut at the age of 24 with two matches in 1955, but had to wait four years for another chance. By then he had tightened up his defence and became a highly productive and sound batsman, ever determined to sell his wicket dearly. This led at times to

accusations of slow play, and he was omitted from the Test team for a match against New Zealand in 1967 after taking over seven hours to make 137, but otherwise England were very glad of his determination and consistency virtually throughout the 1960s. He averaged 101.60 for 508 runs in 1964/5 against South Africa, but his most vital contribution was probably his 582 runs at 72.75 against Australia in 1962/3, far ahead of the rest of the team (and 1763 at 80.13 in all first-class games). He scored over 2000 runs in a season three times: 2499 at 54.32 in 1959, 2070 at 59.14 in 1961 and 2059 at 68.63 in 1967.
82 Tests 1955-68: 6806 runs at 58.67, 20 100s HS 256; 29 wickets at 44.82, BB 3-4; 58 catches.
First-class 1953-68: 31,714 runs at 45.63, 76 100s HS 256; 273 wickets at 32.62, BB 7-40; 513 catches.

Ernest BARRY

Rowing
Ernest Barry. b. 12 Feb 1882 London. d. 21 Jul 1968 Twickenham, London.

Barry had a very long career as an oarsman, winning his first major title in 1900 with the Putney Coat and Badge, and he added Doggett's Coat and Badge in 1903. He lost to Frank Arnst (Aus) when he first challenged for the world professional title in 1910, but reversed that setback to claim the title in 1912, and defended it three times before World War I interrupted sporting matters. In 1919 Alf Felton (Aus) defeated him over the Putney to Mortlake course, but Barry reclaimed the title by defeating Felton a year later and retired shortly thereafter.

Ron BARRY (Ireland)

Horse Racing
Ron Barry b. 28 Feb 1943 Limerick.

Barry was champion National Hunt jockey in 1972/3 with 125 winners, including the Cheltenham Gold Cup on *The Dikler*. His total broke the 20-year-old record for a season, and he was champion again the following year, with 94 winners. He was apprenticed to Tommy Shaw in Ireland for five years, and came to Britain to ride initially for Wilf Craword in Scotland in 1964, riding his first winner that year at Ayr. At his retirement in 1983 he had ridden 823 winners under NH rules.

Pam BARTON

Golf
Pamela Barton. b. 4 Mar 1917 London. d. Nov 1943 Manston, Kent.

Killed on take-off in an off-duty flight in 1943 at the age of 26 when she was an officer in the WAAF, Barton had already achieved much in golf. After being runner-up in 1934 and 1935, she won the Ladies' British Open Amateur Championship in 1936 and in 1939. In 1936 she also became only the second player to also win the American title in the same year. She had won the French Ladies Championship in 1934 as a 17 year-old, played for England in each Home International 1935-9 and for Britain in the Curtis Cup of 1934 and 1936, losing three and halving one of her four matches.
Her sister **Mervyn** (later Mrs Sutherland Pilch) was also an international golfer, both playing at the Royal Mid-Surrey Club.

Billy BASSETT

Football
William Isaiah Bassett. b. 27 Jan 1869 West Bromwich. d. 8 Apr 1937 West Bromwich.

The greatest right-winger of the 19th century, Bassett won 16 England caps 1888-96 at a time when opportunities for international selection were restricted to matches between the Home Countries. He played for West Bromwich Albion throughout his senior career, winning FA Cup medals in 1888 and 1892 and playing in his third FA Cup final in 1895 when WBA lost to Aston Villa. Small and speedy, his accurate centres were a feature of his game during an era when wingers never strayed far from the touchline.
He was appointed a West Bromwich Albion director in 1905 and served as Chairman of the club from 1908 until his

death. From 1930 to 1937 he was a member of the FA Council and the Football League Management Committee.

Cliff BASTIN

Football
Clifford Sydney Bastin. b. 14 Mar 1912 Exeter, Devon. d. 3 Dec 1991 Exeter.

A brilliant outside-left Bastin, by the age of 19, had won the highest honours. He played in the League for Exeter City when aged only 15 and moved to Arsenal in 1929 soon after turning professional. He was a major contributor to the successes of their great team which won the League five times (1931, 1933-5, 1938) and the FA Cup twice (1930, 1936). He also played in the 1932 Cup Final, when Arsenal lost to Newcastle United. In 1930 he set a record, which was to last for 34 years, of being the youngest-ever Wembley Cup finalist. In the 1932/3 season he scored 33 League goals which was a record for a First Division winger.

He won 21 England caps 1931-8, scoring 12 goals, and made his last League appearance in 1946, having scored 150 goals in 350 appearances for Arsenal.

With his devastating shot and ice-cool temperament, Bastin was the most accomplished winger of his generation, although he also played at inside-left and occasionally at wing-half with notable success. Throughout his career he was troubled by deafness and the problem became more acute in his later years when he was a publican in Devon.

Jeremy BATES

Tennis
Michael Jeremy Bates. b. 19 Jun 1962 Solihull, West Midlands.

Consistently ranked as Britain's No. 1 from 1988, Bates reached the last 16 of the Wimbledon singles in 1992 and was a member of Britain's Olympic team that year. He made his Davis Cup debut in 1985 and played in 20 consecutive ties and 22 in all (18/38 singles, 9/15 doubles) until he announced his retirement from Cup tennis at the end of 1994. He won the

mixed doubles at Wimbledon in 1987 and at the Australian Championships in 1991 and his outstanding singles performance was to win the Korean Open in 1994. A serve and volleyer, best on grass, he reached his highest world ranking with 54th in April 1995, from a previous best of 63rd in March 1988. Having won the Under-12 title in 1974 and Under-18 in 1979-80, he was British national singles champion in 1985, 1988, 1990 and 1992-4, and doubles champion 1986-7, 1989-91 and 1993.

Billy BATTEN

Rugby League
William Batten. b. 26 May 1889 Kinsley, nr. Fitzwilliam, West Yorkshire. d. 27 Jan 1959 Wakefield, West Yorkshire.

One of the great pioneers of the game, Batten began as a winger with Hunslet but soon moved to centre and played in all three Tests in the first ever series against Australia in 1908/9, scoring two tries in the first Test. As an incisive runner in the centre and a devastating tackler, he was a great favourite with the crowd who particularly appreciated his ability to jump over would-be tacklers. When he moved to Hull in 1913 his transfer fee of £600 doubled the previous record and in 1920 he received the first benefit to exceed £1000. He won nine Great Britain caps with Hunslet from 1908 and his tenth and final cap in 1921 with Hull. After 11 years with Hull he played briefly for Wakefield Trinity and Castleford.

His son **Eric** was a winger who played in four internationals for Britain 1946-7, 14 internationals for England, and in a then record eight Challenge Cup finals, for Leeds in 1941 and 1943, five in six years for Bradford Northern 1944-9 and for Featherstone Rovers 1952. He was on the winning side in 1941, 1944, 1947 and 1949.

Jim BAXTER

Football
James Curran Baxter. b. 29 Sep 1939 Hill of Beath, Fife.   14/4/2001

Baxter was one of the finest attacking midfield players in the world in the 1960s. He began his career with Raith Rovers in 1957 and won a Scottish Under-23 cap in 1959, but his superlative talents were not fully appreciated until he moved to Rangers later that year. While he was at Ibrox he won the majority of his 34 Scottish caps (1960-7) and Rangers won the Scottish League and Scottish Cup three times each and the Scottish League Cup four times. They were also finalists in the European Cup Winners' Cup in 1961. He also played for the Rest of the World against England in 1963. A broken leg in December 1964 seemed to have ended his career but he still commanded a substantial fee when he was transferred to Sunderland 1965 and then Nottingham Forest 1967. After two undistinguished years at Nottingham he was given a free transfer in 1969 when he returned briefly to Rangers before becoming a publican in Glasgow.

With his superb distribution of the ball from the left-half position and his seemingly effortless control of his territory, he is remembered with respect by all who saw him play when he was at his best. Unfortunately, this memory is rather flawed by the lethargy and aloofness which marked his final seasons.

George BEAMISH

Rugby Union
(Sir) George Robert Beamish. b. 29 Apr 1905 Coleraine, Co. Londonderry. d. 13 Nov 1967 Castlerock, Co. Derry.

A forward of imposing physique and immense strength he won his first cap as Ireland's No. 8 as a 19-year-old in 1925. A broken leg then kept him out of the Irish team until 1928 after which he went on to win 25 caps before announcing his retirement in 1933. He played in all five Tests during the 1930 Lions' tour of New Zealand and Australia and the following season, while playing with Leicester, he led the East Midlands to a memorable victory over the touring South Africans, their only defeat of the tour.

He had a distinguished career with the RAF, rising to the rank of Air Marshal and after being awarded the CBE in 1942 he was knighted in 1955. His brother **Charles** (1908-1984) won 12 caps in the Irish front row 1933-38.

Peter BEARDSLEY

Football
Peter Andrew Beardsley. b. 18 Jan 1961 Newcastle.

An inspirational and creative striker and ballplayer Beardsley was surprisingly omitted from England's team for three years after playing 49 times from his international debut in 1986. At his best, he was the perfect foil for Gary Lineker (qv), but his lack of international goals led to his demotion from the England team. He was recalled in 1994 by Terry Venables (qv), after a resurgence of form under Kevin Keegan (qv) at Newcastle United and has so far scored a total of 9 goals in his 56 internationals for England to June 1995.

Having started his career at Carlisle United, he played in North America for Vancouver Whitecaps. While there he was brought back to Britain by Manchester United, but did not play for them. In 1983 he was signed by Arthur Cox for Newcastle United and moved to his hometown to form a partnership with Kevin Keegan. In his first season he helped Newcastle win promotion to the First Division by scoring 20 goals. In 1987, he was the subject of a then British record transfer fee of £1.9 million when he moved to Liverpool, who won the FA Cup 1989 and the League 1988 and 1990 while he was with them. After a less successful spell with Everton 1991-3, he was then transferred back to a resurgent Newcastle for £1.5 million in 1993. There he has linked up with Andy Cole, scorer of a club record 41 goals in season 1993/4 thanks to Beardsley's creative promptings. He was awarded the MBE in 1995.

Bill BEAUMONT

Rugby Union
William Blackledge Beaumont. b. 9 Mar 1952 Preston, Lancashire.

Although both totals have now been bettered, Beaumont held the record as

England's most capped lock (34) and for captaining England a record number of times (21). He was an inspirational captain and in 1980 led England to their first Grand Slam in 23 years. Later in the year he captained the British Lions in South Africa before his distinguished career was ended by injury in 1982. That year he was awarded the OBE.

After leaving Ellesmere College, he joined Fylde and represented England Under-23s, Lancashire, North Western Counties and the North of England who he led to a memorable victory over the 1979 All Blacks. He developed a successful career as a TV commentator and personality and is managing director of the family textile business.

Dewi BEBB

Rugby Union
Dewi Iorwerth Ellis Bebb. b. 7 Aug 1938 Bangor, Caernarfonshire and Merionethshire.

Scoring the winning try against England on his international debut assured his place as a favourite of the Welsh crowd. A winger of exceptional pace (9.6 100y) he scored 11 tries for Wales in 34 internationals 1959-67 and toured South Africa with the British Lions in 1962 and Australia and New Zealand in 1966. On the first tour he played in two Tests but in 1966 he was the first choice winger and was the only three-quarter to play in all five Tests. He also toured South Africa with Wales in 1964 and played a vital role in the team which won the Triple Crown in 1965.

He played for a variety of College and Service teams before joining Swansea. Formerly a teacher, he has now developed his career as a television producer and presenter.

Margaret BECK

Badminton
Margaret Beck. b. 9 Jan 1952 Cumbria. Later Mrs Lockwood.

First capped in 1969 while still a junior, she went on to play 46 times for England 1969-78. She won the All-England singles

in 1973 and partnered her great rival Gillian Gilks (qv) to take the doubles the following year. At the English National Championships she won the singles five times, 1972-5 and 1977, and the women's doubles in 1977. At the European Championships she won the singles in 1972 and the doubles in 1974, and at the Commonwealth Games she won the singles in 1970, when as an 18-year-old she beat Gilks (then Perrin) in a superb final, and the doubles in 1974. After reaching two semi-finals at the first-ever World Championships in 1977, she was forced to retire as a result of serious knee injuries, after which she devoted her time to golf, soon representing her county. She married England selector Ron Lockwood.

'Darkie' BEDELL-SIVRIGHT

Rugby Union
David Revell Bedell-Sivright. b. 8 Dec 1880 North Queensferry, Fife. d. 5 Sep 1915 Gallipoli, Turkey.

A tough, uncompromising forward, he was first capped by Scotland while playing for Cambridge University (Blue 1899-1902). He won 22 Scottish caps between 1900 and 1908 and led the British team which toured Australia and New Zealand in 1904 although he only played in the first Test. A man of many parts, he was the Scottish heavyweight boxing champion, spent a year in Australia as a stock rearer after the 1904 tour and on his return qualified as doctor at Edinburgh University. He died of blood poisoning while serving as a naval surgeon in World War I.

His brother, **John** (1881-1920), with whom he was not on speaking terms, also played once for Scotland in 1902.

David BEDFORD

Athletics
David Colin Bedford. b. 30 Dec 1949 London.

A hugely popular and flamboyant distance runner, Bedford played a major part in re-establishing the popularity of athletics in Britain in the early 1970s. His extrovert appearance, sometimes including red socks, delighted the crowds. An early example of his uninhibited approach was when he won the Southern junior and senior cross-country titles within an hour. He won the International cross-country titles as a junior in 1969 and senior in 1971, but disappointed in major track races, where his lack of a finishing kick let him down, so that he was 6th in the 1971 European 10,000m, 12th at 5000m and 6th at 10,000m in the 1972 Olympics, and 11th at 5000m and 4th at 10,000m at the 1974 Commonwealth Games.

He was National cross-country champion in 1971 and 1973, and won five successive AAA titles at 10,000m from 1970 to 1974, including the world record of 27:30.8 in 1973, adding the 5000m title in 1972. In addition to four at 10,000m from 28:24.4 at the age of 19, his British records included the following bests: 2000m 5:03.16 (1972), 3000m 7:46.4 (1972), 5000m 13:17.21 (1972), 3000m steeple-chase 8:28.6 (1971).

Persistent leg injuries brought his running career to a premature close, but he remained very actively involved with his club, Shaftesbury Barnet Harriers, and with the International Athletes Club in the promotion of athletics. He was secretary of the AAA of England 1993-4 and is now race director of the London Marathon.

Alec BEDSER

Cricket
Alec Victor Bedser. b. 4 Jul 1918 Reading, Berkshire.

World War II held back Alec Bedser's introduction to Test cricket, but he was an immediate success against India in 1946, when he took 24 wickets at 12.41 in three matches, including 7-49 and 4-96 on his debut.

For the next eight years his accurate in-swing bowling, with a most effective leg-cutter, was the mainstay of the England attack, and at times he seemed to carry the attack almost single-handed. He made his highest Test score of 79 when sent in as a night-watchman at No. 4 against Australia at Leeds in 1948.

He took 30 wickets at 16.06 against Australia in 1950/1 and reached his peak effectiveness against Australia in the Ashes-winning series of 1953, when he started with 7-55 and 7-44 at Trent Bridge and took 39 wickets at 17.48 in the five Tests, passing Grimmett's record number of wickets in a Test career. Amazingly within two years that was over, as the new young fast bowlers Frank Tyson, Brian Statham and Fred Trueman (qqv) took charge.

He was an England Test selector from 1961 and chairman for a record 13 seasons 1969-81; he also managed several England touring teams. He was awarded the OBE in 1964 and the CBE in 1982.

Alec's identical twin brother **Eric** was an off-spinning all-rounder (14,716 runs at 24.10, 833 wickets at 24.95), but did not progress beyond a Test trial (1950), although he accompanied Alec on many overseas tours. Both joined the Surrey staff in 1938 and gave stalwart service, playing major roles as the county won seven consecutive championships 1952-8.

51 Tests 1946-55: 714 runs at 12.75, HS 79; 236 wickets at 24.89, BB 7-44; 26 catches.
First-class 1939-60: 5735 runs at 14.52, 1 100 HS 126; 2082 wickets at 23.13, BB 10-90; 428 catches.

Colin BELL

Football
Colin Bell. b. 26 Feb 1946 Hesleden, Co. Durham.

A talented midfield player whose career was ended by injury, Bell was signed by Manchester City from Bury in 1966 and was one of the stars of the team which won the Football League in 1968, the FA Cup in 1969 and the European Cup Winners' Cup and Football League Cup in 1970 and 1976.

Between 1968 and 1975 he was capped 48 times by England, until injuries to a thigh and both knees in 1976 kept him out of the game for two years. Although he recovered sufficiently to resume playing he never completely regained his previous form and retired in 1979.

Derek BELL

Motor Racing
Derek Reginald Bell b. 31 Oct 1941
Pinner, London.

In a long career in motor sport Bell has achieved his greatest success as a sports car driver, headed by five wins in the Le Mans 24-Hours. The first of these was with Jacky Ickx (Belgium) in 1975 in a Gulf Mirage-Ford. Driving for Porsche, he won again with Ickx in 1981 and 1982, and with Hans Stück (FRG) and Al Holbert (USA) in 1986 and 1987. He won 23 World Championship races, and with Stück shared the title in 1985 and 1986, although in the latter year he was declared the champion, having finished higher in the one race in which they did not compete together, Bell was also 3rd in the first Drivers' Championship in 1982. He has also competed with distinction in a wide variety of motor sports.
Bell started racing with a Lotus Seven in 1964, soon moving up to Formula 3 with Lotus and in 1968 to Formula 2. He was offered a drive by Ferrari in Formula One in 1968, but there had surprisingly little success, starting just nine races from then to 1974 for a variety of teams, and gaining just one point with his 6th in the 1970 US Grand Prix for Surtees. In 1970 he was 2nd to Clay Regazzoni in the Formula 2 Championship.
In 1995 Derek drove at Le Mans with his son **Justin** and Andy Wallace; they placed third in their McLaren after leading for eight hours.

Diane BELL

Judo
Diane Bell. b. 11 Oct 1963 Cambridge.

At the 61 kg category Bell was world champion in 1986 and 1987, and when women's judo was held as a demonstration sport at the 1988 Olympics, she won again. She took world silver in 1991 and bronze in 1993, having won her first world bronze at 56 kg in 1982. She was European champion in 1984, 1986 and 1988, with silver 1994-5 and bronze 1985, 1987 and 1993.
She was British champion at 61 kg in 1985 and each year 1988-94 and also won the 61 kg title in 1990 on the only occasion that judo was included on the Commonwealth Games programme.

Nigel BENN

Boxing
Nigel Gregory Benn. b. 22 Jan 1964 Ilford, London.

Benn made his professional debut a year after winning the 1986 ABA middleweight title. A devastating puncher, he won his first 16 fights by a KO with nine of his opponents failing to survive the first round. He then met Abdul Amora Sanda in April 1988 for the vacant Commonwealth middleweight title and disposed of the Ghanaian in two rounds. After three successful defences he lost the title to Michael Watson (GB) in May 1989.
He went to Miami, USA where he remodelled his style and came back so well that in Atlantic City in April 1990 he took the WBO World middleweight title from Doug de Witt (USA) when the referee stopped the contest in the eighth round. In his first title defence he stopped Iran Barkley (USA) in the first round but in November 1990, Benn suffered the first defeat of his professional career when Chris Eubank (qv) took over as world title holder with a ninth round victory. Benn then successfully challenged Mauro Galvano (Italy) for the World (WBC) super-middleweight crown in October 1992 and has made seven successful defences of the title to his sensational win over Gerald McClellan in February 1995.
Career record 1987-95: 52 contests. Won 49, Lost 2, Drawn 1.

Alec BENNETT

Motorcycling
Alexander Bennett. b. 1898 near Belfast.

After war service as a fighter pilot, Bennett won the Senior TT on the Isle of Man three times, in 1922 on a Sunbeam, and in 1924 and 1927 on Nortons, and in Junior TT twice, 1926 and 1928 on Velocettes. He raced remarkably little for such success, with 18 races on the island and fewer than 30 in his career, yet he also won the French Grand Prix four times and the Belgian Grand Prix twice. His last race was in 1932 when he was 8th in the Junior TT. He was also a member of the winning British team in the international six-day trial.

Jack BENNETT

Hockey
John Hadfield Bennett. b. 11 Aug 1885 Chorlton, Gt. Manchester. d. 27 May 1973 Budleigh Salterton, Devon.

He made his international debut in 1911 and, although wounded in the war, went on to play full-back for England 34 times. On his retirement in 1924, only Stanley Shoveller (qv) with 35 caps had played more times for England. From Harrow, Bennett went up to Oxford, where he won his blue in 1907-08 as a full-back. He captained the winning England team at the 1920 Olympic Games and again from 1922-4. A lawyer by profession, he played for Hampstead.

Phil BENNETT

Rugby Union
Philip Bennett. b. 24 Oct 1948 Felinfoel, Carmarthenshire.

After progressing through the Welsh Secondary Schools and Youth teams Bennett went on to play for Llanelli, the Barbarians, Wales and the British Lions. His greatest asset was his ability to beat opponents with a jink, dummy or side-step and these talents led to 29 caps (8 as captain) for Wales and 8 Test appearances for the Lions. Bennett usually played at fly-half and in 25 of his matches for Wales and in all four Tests for the 1974 Lions he partnered scrum-half Gareth Edwards (qv). During his international career 1969-78 he set numerous scoring records including a then world record 210 points in international matches (166 for Wales, 44 Lions) and a record equalling 38 points in the 1976 Championship season. After touring with the Lions to South Africa in 1974 he captained the team in New Zealand in 1977 and is only the second Welsh player

to have captained the Lions. He played in every Test on each tour.
Awarded the OBE in 1978 after retiring from international rugby, he continued to play for Llanelli for a number of seasons. He is still involved in the game as a TV commentator.

Billy BENYON

Rugby League
William Benyon. b. 7 Mar 1945 St. Helens, Merseyside.

After signing for St. Helens on his 16th birthday Benyon went on to win virtually every major honour with the club playing in 16 major finals for them. With Benyon at centre or stand off, St Helens won three Challenge Cup finals (1966, 1972, 1976), two Premierships (1976-7) and the Division I title three times (1966, 1970-1).
He won five GB caps (plus one as a replacement) in 1971 and 1972 but was never chosen to tour. In 1977 he left St Helens for Warrington and in his first season won a John Player Trophy winners' medal and then, on taking over as coach, he guided the club to two more John Player finals before being sacked in 1982. After winning his case against Warrington at an Industrial Tribunal, he returned to St Helens as coach and remained there until 1985 when he handed over to the legendary Alex Murphy (qv). Benyon then moved to Leigh and remained their coach until 1990.
A talented soccer player, he turned down an offer to sign for West Bromwich Albion.

Jack BERESFORD

Rowing
Jack Beresford Jr. b. 1 Jan 1899 Chiswick, London. d. 3 Dec 1977 Shiplake-on-Thames, Oxfordshire.

Beresford was one of the most titled rowers ever and also had an amazingly long career. He won five Olympics medals: at single sculls silver 1920 and gold 1924, eights silver 1928, coxless fours gold 1932, and double sculls gold 1936. He was preparing to compete in 1940 when the war intervened. At Henley, he won the Diamond Sculls four times, 1920 and 1924-6; the Nickalls Challenge Cup at coxless pairs with Gordon Killick 1928-9, and the Double Sculls Challenge Cup with Dick Southwood 1939. Beresford also won the Wingfield Sculls for seven consecutive years from 1920. He rowed for the Thames, Leander and Kingston clubs, coached and managed the British Olympic rowing team in 1952 and was awarded the CBE in 1960.

His father **Julius** (né Wisniewski, b. 29 Jun 1868. d. 29 Sep 1959) was also a notable oarsman, winning the Silver Goblets in 1911 and a silver in the coxed fours at the 1912 Olympics.

Jackie 'Kid' BERG

Boxing
né Judah Bergman. b. 28 Jun 1909 Whitechapel, London. d. 22 Apr 1991 London.

A precocious young fighter from London's East End, at the age of 16, Berg outpointed British featherweight champion Johnny Curley over 15 rounds in a non-title bout. He continued fighting in England until 1928, losing only three times, after which most of his fights over the next five years were in America where he was held in far higher regard than most British boxers.

He returned to London in February 1930 and stopped Mushy Callahan (USA) with a tenth round KO to take the world junior welterweight title (NBA version) and made three successful defences of his title before losing on a third round KO to Tony Canzoneri (USA) in 1931. Later in the year he challenged Canzoneri for the world lightweight title and this time lost on points over 15 rounds. These defeats by Canzoneri marked the beginning of a gradual decline, but in 1934 he was still good enough to beat Harry Mizler to win the British lightweight crown. Strangely, this was the first British title for the 'Whitechapel Whirlwind' and he remained champion for two years before losing to Jimmy Walsh in 1936.

He served in the RAF during the war and continued fighting until 1945, after which he became a movie stuntman and opened a restaurant in Soho. Unfortunately, the venture was not a success and faced with financial hardship, he was forced to sell his Lonsdale belt.

Career record 1924-45: 197 contests. Won 162 (59 KO), Drew 9, Lost 26.

Verona BERNARD – see ELDER

Jack BESFORD

Swimming
John Charles Preston Besford. b. 30 Jan 1911. d. Mar 1993 Chorlton, Gt. Manchester.

Besford was the surprise winner of the European 100m backstroke title in 1:11.7 in 1934, receiving a trophy donated by Adolf Hitler for an event for which a German winner was confidently predicted. He was seven times ASA backstroke champion, at 150y 1927-8, 1930-2, 1935-6, and at the Empire Games he was 3rd in 1930 and 2nd in 1934 at 100y backstroke.

His wife **Pat Besford** became the leading British swimming journalist, *Daily Telegraph* correspondent for many years, president of the AIPS swimming commission and a leading officer of the Sports Writers' Association of Great Britain.

George BEST

Football
George Best. b. 22 May 1946 Belfast.

One of the most talented players in the history of the game, Best's sadly unacceptable off-field behaviour hastened his retirement and tarnished his image. Before being beset by alcohol-related problems, his skills as a striker or winger were universally admired. He made his Football League debut for Manchester United and won the first of his 31 international caps for Northern Ireland before he had reached his 18th birthday.

He was English and European Footballer of the Year in 1968 and played a vital part in Manchester United's defeat of Benfica in the European Cup that year. Between 1963 and 1973 he made 349 League appearances for Manchester United, scoring 134 goals but towards the end of this period signs of his excesses were already apparent. He began to miss club and international training sessions with worrying regularity and he was dropped from the Manchester United and Northern Ireland teams. After a while, the managers were prepared to overlook his lapses and he regained his place in both sides. The recovery was short-lived, the physical and mental decline continued and, although he made a brief comeback with Los Angeles Aztecs and Fulham (and won his final cap in 1977), his brilliant but tragic career in football was all but over, although he played briefly for league teams in the USA, Scotland and England, ending with five games for Bournemouth in 1983.

Denis BETTS

Rugby League
Denis Betts. b. 14 Sep 1969 Salford, Gt. Manchester.

Signed by Wigan from the amateur club Leigh Rangers in 1986, Betts has remained with the club ever since. From his international debut in 1990 to 1994 he won 24 GB caps (plus one as a replacement) and toured Australasia in 1990 and 1992 with the British Lions. A second-row forward of exceptional speed (11.1 for 100m) he played a vital role in the Wigan team which won the Challenge Cup 1989-95 (Betts taking the Lance Todd Trophy in 1991), the Regal Trophy in 1989, 1990, 1993 and 1995, and the Premiership 1992 and 1994-5. Four years after winning the young player award he was voted Man of Steel as rugby league's player of the year in 1995, having scored 21 tries in the season, before going to New Zealand to play for Auckland Warriors.

Dave BICKERS

Moto Cross
David Bickers. b. 17 Jan 1938 Gipping, Suffolk.

Britain's most successful scrambler of the 1960s, he was European 250cc champion in 1960 and 1961, before the event achieved World Championship status in 1962. Thereafter his best placing was 3rd

at 250cc in 1965 and at 500cc in 1967. He also rode on the winning British teams in the Moto Cross des Nations in 1966 and 1967. He started racing in Europe in 1959 and recorded his first Grand Prix win in Switzerland in 1960. He won six British Championships: A-CU Stars - 250cc 1960, 1962-5 and 500cc 1966. He ran a motorcycle business in his home of Codrenham, Suffolk.

Terry BIDDLECOMBE

Horse Racing
Terence Walter Biddlecombe. b. 2 Feb 1941 Hartbury Court, Gloucestershire.

Champion National Hunt jockey three times in the 1960s, Biddlecombe started his career in 1957/8, had his first winner at Wincanton in 1958 and turned professional in 1960. His first championship in 1964/5 was with 114 winners, when he was first jockey to Fred Rimell (qv), and he then placed successively 1st, 2nd, 3rd, 1st equal, and 3rd in the NH jockeys' championship, with one more century, 102 in 1965/6. In all he rode 909 winners under NH rules 1958-74. His biggest victory came with the Cheltenham Gold Cup on *Woodland Venture* in 1967.
The extrovert son of a Gloucestershire farmer, he was very tall for a jockey. He was a strong rider with fast reactions, renowned for his courage and horsemanship, as well as his cheerfulness.

Mary BIGNAL - see RAND

Billy BINGHAM

Football
William Laurie Bingham. b. 5 Aug 1931 Belfast.

One of Northern Ireland's greatest wingers, Bingham was later an outstanding manager for his country. After a brilliant display for the Irish League against the Football League in 1950 he was signed from Glentoran by Sunderland, for whom he played 206 games, scoring 45 goals, before moving to Luton Town in 1958. In his first season they reached the 1959 FA Cup Final before, after 27 goals in 87 games, he moved on the following year to Everton, whom he helped to win the League title in 1963. His Everton record was 26 goals in 98 games and he went to Port Vale for a couple of years 1964-5. Between 1951 and 1963 he won a then record 56 caps for Northern Ireland, having been a schoolboy international 1943-4, with nine youth caps 1946-8.

His managerial career took him to Southport, Plymouth Argyle, Linfield, Greece, where he was in charge of the national side, Everton, PAOK Salonika (Greece), Mansfield Town and Al Nasir (Saudi Arabia). He was not particularly successful during his first spell as manager of Northern Ireland (1968-70) but when he took over for a second time in 1980 he guided his team into the finals of the World Cup in 1982 and 1986. After more than 40 years active involvement with the game he finally retired in 1993 after 116 matches as manager. He was awarded the MBE in 1982.

Blanche BINGLEY

Tennis
Blanche Bingley. b. 3 Nov 1863 Greenford, London. d. 6 Aug 1946 Pulborough, West Sussex. Later Mrs Hillyard.

A player whose career was noted not only for its many successes but also for its longevity, Bingley first played at Wimbledon in 1884 and, at the age of 49, made her 27th and final appearance in 1913. During the intervening years she won the singles six times (1886, 1889, 1894, 1897, 1899, 1900) with a 14-year interval between her first and last title. She was unfortunate to be a contemporary of the incomparable Lottie Dod (qv) who beat her four times in the Challenge Round and once in the all-comers' final. She was also the singles champion of Germany (1897, 1900), Ireland (1888, 1894, 1897) and Wales (1888) and won the All England doubles in 1897, 1901 and 1906 before the event was given full Championship status. She generally played from the baseline, relying on her forehand power and speed about the court.

The majority of her titles were won after her marriage in July 1887 to Commander George Hillyard RN, secretary of the All England Club from 1907 to 1924.

Joe BINKS

Athletics
Joseph Benjamin Warden Binks. b. 14 Jul 1874 London. d. 28 Jan 1966 Salisbury, Wiltshire.

Binks won the 1902 AAA 1 mile title in 4:16 $^4/_5$ and this remained the British record until Albert Hill first equalled it in 1919 and then broke it in 1921. Binks was 2nd to Alf Shrubb in the AAA mile 1903. but claimed to be above all to be a master 'pot hunter', winning more open handicaps from scratch than any other runner at distances from 100y to 10 miles cross-country. He was athletics correspondent for the *News of the World* for over 50 years to 1957, and was the organiser and inspiration behind the popular British Games series, which became established as major events at the White City Stadium.

Dicky BIRD

Cricket
Harold Denis Bird. b. 19 Apr 1933 Barnsley, South Yorkshire.

Bird has umpired a record 62 Test matches from 1973 to June 1995 as well as the World Cup finals of 1979, 1979, 1983 and the women's World Cup 1982. With the introduction of an international panel of umpires, he has been one of the first umpires to officiate all over the world. His consistency and understanding of the game has made him hugely respected by the players, while his idiosyncrasies and enthusiasm have made him popular with the wide cricket audience. He was awarded the MBE in 1986.

He played for Yorkshire from 1956 to 1959 but could not break into the first team on a regular basis and then played for Leicestershire 1960-4, with a best season in 1960 when he scored 1028 runs.

First-class career 1956-64: 3314 runs at 20.71, 2 100s HS 181*; 28 catches.

Tim BIRKIN

Motor Racing
Sir Henry Ralph Stanley Birkin Bt. b. 26 Jul
1896 Basford, Nottinghamshire. d. 22 Jul
1933 London.

The dashing Captain 'Tim' Birkin, who
had been a Royal Flying Corps pilot in
World War I, won the Le Mans 24-hour
race twice, with Woolf Barnato (qv) in a
Bentley in 1929 and with Earl Howe in an
Alfa-Romeo in 1931. Also in Bentleys he
was 2nd in the 1930 French Grand Prix,
and set the Brooklands outer circuit lap
record at 135.34 mph in 1930 and again at
137.96 mph in 1932. It was in a Maserati,
however, that he won the 1931 Brooklands
Mountain Championship. He died of blood
poisoning three weeks after suffering an
arm burn from the exhaust pipe at the
Tripoli Grand Prix when racing a new 3-
litre Maserati for the first time. His first
race had been at Brooklands in 1921 and
he joined the Bentley team in 1927.

Tommy BISHOP

Rugby League
Thomas Bishop. b. 15 Oct 1940 St. Helens,
Merseyside.

A scrum-half, Bishop won 15 GB caps
1966-9, and helped St Helens to victory in
the Championship and Challenge Cup in
1966. After he gave up playing, he
coached in Australia for 12 years but
returned to take over as coach at
Workington in 1980. He left Workington in
1982 and after a year's interval was
appointed coach at Leigh. This appointment lasted one year after which he closed
his coaching career by spending three
months at Barrow.

Ian BLACK

Swimming
Ian Macintosh Black. b. 27 Jun 1941
Aberdeen.

Black was Britain's Sportsman of the Year
(both BBC and *Daily Express*) in 1958
after winning three gold medals at the
European Championships: 400m and
1500m freestyle and 200m butterfly, all
easily; along with the 220y butterfly gold
and silvers at 440y freestyle and 4 x 220y
relay at the British Empire Games.

His one world record was the inaugural
mark, 5:08.8 at the 440y individual
medley. He took 4th places at the Olympic
Games, at 400m in 4:21.8 (his fifth
European record at this event) and on
Britain's 4 x 200m relay team. He actually
dead-heated with John Konrads (Aus) for
bronze at 400m, but was relegated to 4th
on a technicality.

He then retired, although he returned
briefly in 1962, when he set a European
record of 2:02.6 at 200m freestyle. He also
set European records for 800m freestyle at
9:25.5 and twice at 1500m (best 18:05.8)
in 1958, at 200m butterfly, 2:18.7 in 1960,
and 400m IM, 5:08.8 in 1959. He was
ASA champion at each of 110y, 220y and
440y freestyle and 220y butterfly in 1958
and 1959. In 1958-9 he set British records
at all freestyle distances from 100y to 1
mile, as well as three of the four at butterfly and at 400m/440y IM.

Roger BLACK

Athletics
Roger Anthony Black. b. 31 Mar 1966
Portsmouth.

A powerfully built runner, Black made a
brilliant start to his international career
with six gold medals, both 400m and 4 x
400m relay, in three international championships: European Juniors 1985 and both
European Championships and Commonwealth Games in 1986. His first notable
performance had been 3rd in the 1983
English Schools 200m. In 1987, after placing a close 2nd to Thomas Schönlebe
(GDR) in the European Cup, he had to
miss the individual 400m at the World
Championships, but won a silver medal in
the relay.

He abandoned his medical studies to concentrate on athletics, but his career has
been blighted by foot injuries. He has,
however, proved highly resilient. After two
years out of competition he returned to
earn a place on England's 1990 Commonwealth Games team, but he was denied the
chance of a relay medal by officious dis-

qualification. That summer he again won gold medals at the European 400m and 4 x 400m and in 1991 he won the silver medal at 400m and helped the British team to a brilliant win over the USA in the relay at the World Championships. A serious foot injury and a virus illness further affected his career but he came back again in 1994 to add another European relay gold after being thwarted by Du'aine Ladejo in his bid to win a third successive 400m title; his five European gold medals equal's the men's record of Harald Schmid (Ger). He also won the European Cup 400m in 1991 and 1994, UK titles at 200m 1987 and 400m 1990, and the AAA 400m 1994. He was awarded the MBE in 1992.

Best times: 100m 10.49 (1995), 200m 20.60 (1990), 300m 32.08 (1986), 400m 44.59 (1986 and 1995), 600m 1:16.2 (1991), 800m 1:52.1 (1990).

Danny BLANCHFLOWER

Football
Robert Dennis Blanchflower. b. 10 Feb 1926 Belfast. d. 9 Dec 1993 London.

One of the most thoughtful players and inspirational captains of the post-war era, Blanchflower's skills at right-half provided countless opportunities for his forwards. After joining Barnsley from Glentoran of the Irish League in 1948, he was transferred to Aston Villa for £15,000 in 1951, but only after joining Tottenham in December 1954 were his talents fully appreciated. He captained Spurs to the Cup and League double 1961, the FA Cup 1962 and the European Cup Winners' Cup 1963. He was voted Footballer of the Year in 1958 and 1961.

After winning a record 56 caps for Northern Ireland, 1949-62, and having played 383 games for Spurs, a leg injury caused his retirement at the end of the 1963/4 season. Apart from a brief spell as manager of Chelsea, he concentrated on journalism, writing first for *The Observer* and then for 25 years for the *Sunday Express*. Unusually for a top-name sportsman, he wrote his own copy but his career as a television commentator never flourished. He undoubtedly had all the necessary qualities but he refused to compromise his views in order to conform with the authorities. He managed the Northern Ireland team 1976-9 and had a brief, but unsuccessful, spell as manager of Chelsea 1978-9.

His younger brother **Jackie** (b. 7 Mar 1933), who played for Manchester United and won 12 caps for Northern Ireland 1954-8, was injured in the Munich air crash of 1958.

Ernie BLENKINSOP

Football
Ernest Blenkinsop b. 20 Apr 1902 Cudworth, South Yorkshire. d. 24 Apr 1969 Sheffield.

For five years, 1928-33, Blenkinsop was ever present in the England team, winning all his 26 caps as a speedy and intelligent left back in consecutive matches. He was captain in his last match, against Scotland in 1933. He joined Hull City from Cudworth United Methodists in October 1921 for £100 and 80 pints of beer. He then moved to Sheffield Wednesday in 1922 and played for them until 1934, starring in their Football League title successes of 1928/9 and 1929/30. He then reformed his England back partnership with right-back Tom Cooper at Liverpool, before his top-class career ended with one season at Cardiff City 1937/8. He became a licensee in Sheffield.

Steve BLOOMER

Football
Stephen Bloomer. b. 20 Jan 1874 Cradley Heath, West Midlands. d. 16 Apr 1938 Derby.

A prolific scorer from the inside-right position, Bloomer's 28 goals for England in 23 appearances 1895-1907 remained a record for 50 years. His five goals against Wales in 1896 remains unsurpassed for England. After playing in local minor leagues he joined Derby County in 1892 and twice was in their losing FA Cup final team (1898-9) but because of injury he missed the 1903 final when Derby again lost. Shortly after he left for Middlesbrough in 1906, Derby County were relegated but after four years with Middlesbrough he returned to Derby for a final three seasons and led them to the Second Division championship in 1912 at the age of 38.

Despite his frail physique, he possessed an incredibly powerful shot and in 674 league and cup games he scored a total of 394 goals. The main criticism of his game was that he was more concerned with adding to his personal goal tally than with providing scoring chances for his team-mates. After playing his last game for Derby in 1914, he went to Berlin as a coach and was interned in Germany during World War I. After the war, he served Derby in various capacities until the time of his death, although his duties at the Baseball Ground were interrupted at various times by coaching appointments in Canada, Spain and Holland. His daughter married the Derby County footballer Alfred Quantrill (1897-1968), who won four England caps 1920-1.

Shirley BLOOMER-BRASHER

Tennis
Shirley Juliet Bloomer. b. 13 Jun 1934 Grimsby, Lincolnshire. Later Mrs Brasher.

A steady, consistent player with a style best suited to hard courts, Bloomer enjoyed her best year in 1957 when her victories in the singles at the French, Italian and British Hard Court Championships resulted in her being ranked No. 3 in the world. She won the British Hard Court singles for a second time in 1958. At Wimbledon, she was a singles quarter-finalist in 1956 and 1958 and won the Plate in 1959.

She also had a fine record as a doubles player, reaching the Wimbledon final in 1955 with Pat Ward (qv) and winning the French and British Hard Court titles in 1957 (both with Darlene Hard (USA)) and the Italian title in 1958 (with Christine Truman (qv)) when she also won the mixed doubles at the Italian and British Hard Court Championships. She played in six Wightman Cup matches, 1955-60, but only won three rubbers (1/7 singles: 2/6 doubles). In 1959 she married Chris

Brasher (qv), the 1956 Olympic steeplechase champion. Their daughter **Kate** won the British Junior title 1978-9. Another daughter, Amanda, was also a successful tournament player. Following the birth of her two daughters Mrs Brasher took a long break from top-class tennis but she returned in 1968 and in 1972 she became, at the age of 36, the oldest woman ever to be ranked in the top ten in Britain. In 1986-7 she won the Over-50 singles and the doubles with Lorna Cawthorne at the ITF Veteran Championships.

Colin BLYTHE

Cricket
Colin Blythe. b. 30 May 1879 Deptford, London. d. 8 Nov 1917 Passchendaele, Belgium.

A classical slow left-arm bowler, Blythe was killed in the Great War. He took 100 wickets or more in 14 of his 16 seasons with Kent, with a peak of 215 at 14.54 in 1909, despite suffering from epilepsy. He was a master of flight, and particularly formidable on 'sticky' wickets. In 1907 he had his most successful Test series, with 26 wickets at 10.38 against South Africa, and for Kent v Northants he took 17 wickets in a day (10-30 and 7-18).

19 Tests 1901-10: 183 runs at 9.63, HS 27; 100 wickets at 18.63, BB 8-59; 6 catches.
First-class 1899-1914: 4443 runs at 9.87, HS 82*; 2506 wickets at 16.81, BB 10-30; 206 catches.

Lillian BOARD

Athletics
Lillian Barbara Board. b. 13 Dec 1948 Durban, South Africa. d. 26 Dec 1970 Munich, Germany.

Lillian and her twin sister, Irene, were born in South Africa and returned with their parents to England in 1950. Her first important title came with the English Schools junior long jump in 1963 and she emerged into top class in 1966, when she was 5th in the Commonwealth Games 440y. In 1967 she won the WAAA 440y and took more than a second off her best for 400m with a brilliant win for the

Commonwealth v the USA.

Still a teenager, she went into the 1968 Olympics as the favourite for the 400m title, but in an epic race was pipped on the line by Colette Besson (Fra) in a British record time of 52.12. A year later she stepped up to 800m and won the European title in brilliant style by 10 metres, adding a second gold at 4x400m relay, when she anchored the British team to a great win over France, both teams sharing the world record time of 3:30.8. Board also ran on three other world record-setting relay teams, at 4 x 100y, 4 x 400m and 4 x 800m. She was awarded the MBE in the 1970 New Year Honours. After back problems during the winter she was affected by stomach problems in 1970, and having set a mile best of 4:44.6 these got progressively worse; cancer was diagnosed. Her tragically early death soon after her 22nd birthday was a terrible shock for her many friends and the British public who had regarded her as the new 'golden girl' of the sport.

Other best times: 100y 10.9 (1968), 10.6w (1966); 100m 11.9 & 11.8w (1968), 200m 23.42 (1968), 800m 2:01.50 (1969).

Chris BOARDMAN

Cycling
Christopher Miles Boardman. b. 26 Aug 1968 Clatterbridge, Merseyside.

When Chris Boardman won the Olympic pursuit title in 1992, much attention was focused on his revolutionary Lotus bicycle. That perhaps distracted attention from some of the greatest riding ever seen at an Olympics. From a pre-Games best of 4:31.4, he set Olympic records in the preliminary rounds with times of 4:27.357 and 4:24.496, and the latter was later recognised as the world record for the distance, when the lists were rationalised in 1993. Boardman went even faster in the Olympic final and completed 4000m in about 4:22, but by then he had eased up and the race was over, because he achieved the unprecedented feat of catching his opponent, Jens Lehmann (Ger), who started half a lap ahead, at 4:11 to end the race.

Boardman won Commonwealth bronze medals at team pursuit in 1986 and 1990 and at team trial in 1990 and also competed at the 1988 Olympics. He won the national amateur pursuit title in 1989 and 1991-2. Six days before his attempt on the classic world record for the 1 hour in 1993 the Scot Graeme Obree smashed the record set by Francesco Moser (Italy) at 51.151km in 1984, with 51.596km. Boardman was undaunted, however, and powered to a distance of 52.270km at Bordeaux on 23 Jul 1993. On the same day he was invited to join Miguel Induráin (Spain) on the rostrum of the Tour de France which swept into Bordeaux that day, and immediately began to receive offers to join the professional road racers.

He turned professional in September 1993 and had a highly successful first season in 1994. He won the prologue time trial of the Tour de France, and proudly wore the yellow jersey as race leader for the first three days, later retiring from the race to concentrate on preparation for the World Championships. There he won both the pursuit title (at which he had been 3rd in 1993) and the inaugural individual time trial on the roads. In 1995 he prepared well for the Tour de France, where he would need to add climbing ability to his time-trialing brilliance, but crashed in appalling conditions in the opening time trial.

He was awarded the MBE in 1993.

His father **Keith** was close to selection for the 1964 Olympic cycling team.

Angela BONALLACK

Golf
Angela Bonallack. b. 7 Apr 1937 Birchington, Kent. née Ward.

The wife of Michael Bonallack (qv), she won the championships of Sweden and Germany in 1955, Scandinavia 1956 and Portugal 1957 before her two wins in the English Ladies', 1958 and 1963, a tournament in which she was runner-up three times, 1960, 1962 and 1972. She was also runner-up in the Ladies' British Open Amateur Championship in 1962 and 1974. She began playing at the age of 13, was Kent junior champion 1952-4 and British Girls' champion 1955. She played in the

six Curtis Cup ties 1956-66 and was an England international for two decades.
Her sister **Shirley Ward** was the English Girls' champion of 1964.

Michael BONALLACK

Golf
Michael Francis Bonallack. b. 31 Dec 1934 Chigwell, Essex.

A master of the short game, Bonallack was the greatest British amateur player of the modern era. He is the only man to have won the British Amateur three consecutive times, 1968-70, following his earlier victories in 1961 and 1965. He was British Boys' champion in 1952 and set a record by winning the English Amateur title five times, 1962-3, 1965, and 1967-8, and in the final in 1968 went round Ganton in 61 strokes. He was also four times English Amateur Stroke Play champion, 1964, 1968-9 and 1971. He played on eight consecutive Walker Cup teams, 1959-73, with his record: won 8, lost 14, halved 3; he was also a member of the 1957 team but did not play. He played seven times in the World Amateur Team Championship, 1960-72, winning with the GB & Ireland team in 1964. He was awarded the OBE in 1971 and succeeded Keith McKenzie as chairman of the Royal & Ancient in 1983.
His sister **Sally** (b. 9 Apr 1938 Chigwell), later Mrs Barber, played for Britain in the Curtis Cup in 1962 and was English Ladies' champion in 1968, a year in which Michael was also English champion. His wife **Angela** (qv) was twice English Ladies' champion.

Billy BONDS

Football
William Arthur Bonds. b. 17 Sep 1946 Woolwich, London.

Bonds is one of the finest uncapped players in the history of the game. Moving to West Ham in 1967 after three seasons with Charlton Athletic, he spent the rest of his career at Upton Park making a record 782 appearances for West Ham between 1967 and 1989 to pass Bobby Moore's previous club record. He took over from Moore (qv)

as club captain in 1974 and led West Ham to victory in two FA Cup finals, 1975 and 1980, and played a key role in taking them back to the First Division in 1981 and to the League Cup final that year.
An inspired central defender, he was capped by England at Under-23 level and was selected once for a full international but had to withdraw through injury. After a playing career notable for its longevity and for his unwavering loyalty to West Ham, he continued to serve the club in various capacities before taking over as manager in 1990 after Lou Macari resigned. He remained as manager until August 1994 when he left Upton Park after 27 years unbroken service. He was awarded the MBE in 1988.

Pat BONNER (Ireland)

Football
Patrick Bonner, b. 25 May 1960 Co. Donegal.

In 1994 Bonner passed Liam Brady's (qv) record of 72 appearances for the Republic of Ireland and in October that year, against Liechtenstein, he was honoured with the captaincy of his country and his 78th cap. By then he was Celtic's reserve goalkeeper, having played for the Scottish club since he was signed from Keadie Rovers in 1978, but he was back in the first team for his fifth Scottish Cup winner's medal in May 1995 to add to four Championships and one League Cup.

Nigel BOOCOCK

Speedway
Nigel Boocock. b. 17 Sep 1937 Wakefield, West Yorkshire.

Having started his speedway career with Bradford in 1955, Boocock continued at top level until his retirement in 1979. He remains the leading scorer in league racing with 6471 points. Captain of England at home and in Australia, he rode in 151 Test matches for England, British Lions and Great Britain. From his ten World finals he scored 47 points. He was British champion and Midland Riders' champion and also won the South Australian title in 1968. He now lives in Sydney, Australia.

'Boy' BOON

Boxing
Eric Boon. b. 3 Jan 1919 Chatteris,
Cambridge.

The son of a blacksmith, Boon won the
British lightweight title in December 1938,
when 19 days short of his 19th birthday, by
knocking out Dave Crowley. He was
already a star attraction and his popularity
reached a peak with his first defence
against Arthur Danahar in February 1939.
The venue, Harringay Arena, was a sell-
out and the fight was the first to be
televised 'live' to a nearby cinema. After a
thrilling contest he stopped Danahar in the
14th round. He retained the title later that
year by knocking out Crowley, but lost it
in 1944 when knocked out by Ronnie
James after he had difficulty making the
weight. At his peak, 1937-9, he won 32
successive fights, 26 inside the distance,
and would probably have fought for a
world title but for war service in the RAF.
He was the first prominent boxer to be
managed by Jack Solomons, who became
the dominating force in boxing promotions
after the war. Boon made a comeback as a
welterweight in 1946, but after several
successes lost a British title fight to Ernie
Roderick in 1948 and retired in 1949.
Career record 1934-49: 117 contests. Won
93, Drew 5, Lost 18, No Contest 1.

Willie BOONE

Rackets
William Robin Boone. b. 12 July 1950
Norwich.

After winning the 1968 Public Schools
Championship for Eton, Boone developed
into the most consistent of players. He was
World champion from 1984 to 1986,
British Open champion in 1979, 1984,
1986 and again in 1995, and winner of the
British Amateur title eight times between
1976 and 1994. Remarkably, he was a
finalist every year in this period. He also
won the Amateur doubles 12 times
between 1975 and 1994. He also won the
British Open doubles in 1981-5 with
Randall Crawley and in 1994-5 with Tim
Cockroft.

A hard-hitting left-hander with a devastat-
ing service, he first challenged for the
world title in 1979 when he failed to take a
game off William Surtees. In 1984 he beat
John Prenn (qv) in Montreal and then at
Queen's to take the World Championship
but two years later the title again passed to
Prenn. He won many titles in North
America and was the US and Canadian
Open singles champion in 1994.

Dora BOOTHBY

Tennis
Penelope Dora Harvey Boothby. b. 2 Aug
1881 Finchley, London. d. 22 Feb 1970
Hammersmith, London. Later Mrs A C
Geen.

Boothby is renowned for her unique 6-0,
6-0 defeat by Dorothea Lambert Chambers
(qv) in the 1911 Wimbledon singles final
when she established the record of being
the only Wimbledon finalist who failed to
win a single game. The score was, however, apparently a true indication of the
difference in their abilities as Miss
Boothby had lost to Lambert Chambers by
an identical score at Beckenham earlier in
the season. Despite this shattering defeat,
she continued to compete at Wimbledon
after her marriage in 1914 and was a semi-
finalist in the doubles in 1922.
She had won the Wimbledon singles in
1909 after taking the third set 8-6 in a
close match with Agnes Morton. She also
won the first Wimbledon womens' doubles
to be given official Championship status
with Winifred McNair in 1913 after Sterry
and Chambers were forced to retire when
holding a commanding lead. She also won
a silver medal in the singles at the 1908
Olympic Games and was the British
Covered Court singles champion and the
All England mixed doubles badminton
champion in 1909.

Norman BORRETT

Hockey and Squash
Norman Francis Borrett. b. 1 Oct 1917
Wanstead, London.

Olympic hockey medallist, champion
squash player and first class cricketer,

Borrett was one of the finest all-rounders of his generation. As an inside-forward, he won 30 England caps at hockey 1939-53 and captained the GB team (7 caps) which won the silver medals at the 1948 Olympic Games. At squash he won the British Amateur Championship five times (1946-50) and made 12 appearances for England, and he played county cricket for Essex. He won a blue at Cambridge before the war for hockey and squash but surprisingly not for cricket, although he made the first of his three first class appearances for Essex while still at university. He also played cricket for Devon 1949-59 and served as president of the Squash Rackets Association. Educated at Framlingham College, he later taught at his old school.

Bernard BOSANQUET

Cricket
Bernard James Tindal Bosanquet. b. 13 Oct 1877 Enfield, London. d. 12 Oct 1936 Ewhurst, Surrey.

Perfecting the googly, Bosanquet gave his name to the Australian term for this off-break delivered with a leg-break action – the Bosie. In his third Test, against Australia in 1904, he bowled England to victory with a second innings 6-51 and that summer had his most successful season with the ball in England, taking 132 wickets at 21.62. His bowling declined from 1905, after which he played no more Tests but his batting flourished for Middlesex although he played infrequently after a splendid year in 1908, when he headed the first-class averages with 1081 runs at 54.05, including 214 in 195 minutes for the Rest of England against the champion county, Surrey. His 104 and 100*, 3-75 and 8-53 for Middlesex v Sussex in 1905 is one of only three instances of hundreds in each innings and ten wickets in a first-class match.

He was an Oxford cricket Blue 1898-1900 and also represented the university at throwing the hammer and at billiards; he was also a fine ice-hockey player. His son Reginald Bosanquet was the well-known television newsreader.

7 Tests 1903-05: 147 runs at 13.36, HS 27;

25 wickets at 24.16, BB 8-107; 9 catches. First-class 1898-1919: 11,696 runs at 33.41, 21 100s HS 214; 629 wickets at 23.80, BB 9-31; 191 catches.

Billy BOSTON

Rugby League
William John Boston. b. 6 Aug 1934 Cardiff.

A high-scoring winger, Boston attracted the attention of League scouts while playing the Union code as a national serviceman. He had been a Welsh youth international and played for Cardiff prior to signing for Wigan in 1953. The following year he became the first coloured British rugby league player to tour Australia. He won the first of his 31 Great Britain caps (24 tries) in the second Test against Australia and his four tries in the second Test against New Zealand equalled the individual try-scoring record for a Test match. His total of 36 tries was also a new record for a tour of Australia.

Boston again toured Australia in 1962 when he scored a further 22 tries and he played in the World Cup tournaments in 1957 and 1960. He scored a career total of 571 tries in 564 appearances 1953-70, of which 482 were for Wigan, achieving his first 100 tries in only 68 games 1953-5. His speed and powerful hand-off made him one of the most spectacular players of his era. He played for Wigan in six Challenge Cup finals and later played occasionally for Blackpool Borough before becoming the landlord of a hotel next to Wigan's Central Park ground.

Ian BOTHAM

Cricket
Ian Terence Botham. b. 24 Nov 1955 Heswall, Merseyside.

The charismatic all-rounder became a folk hero in England after his exploits in the 1981 Test series against Australia. He had quickly made his mark in Test cricket from his debut in 1977, taking his 100th wicket just two years and nine days later with hostile swing bowling. He achieved the double of 1000 runs and 100 wickets in a

Ian Botham in Test Cricket									
Year	v	Tests	Runs	Ave.	HS	Wkts	Ave.	BB	Catches
1977	Aus	2	25	12.50	25	10	20.20	5-21	1
1978	NZ	3	212	53.00	103	17	18.29	5-73	5
1978	Pak	3	212	70.67	108	13	16.08	8-34	4
1978	NZ	3	51	17.00	22	24	14.04	6-34	2
1978-9	Aus	6	291	29.10	74	23	24.65	4-42	9
1979	Ind	4	244	48.80	137	20	23.60	5-35	10
1979-80	Aus	3	187	37.40	119*	19	19.53	6-78	3
1980	Ind	1	114	114.00	114	13	8-15	7-48	0
1980	WI	5	169	18.77	57	13	29.61	3-50	2
1980-1	WI	4	73	10.42	26	15	32.80	4-77	5
1981	Aus	6	399	36.27	149*	34	20.59	6-95	12
1981-2	Ind	6	440	55.00	142	17	38.82	5-61	3
1982	SL	1	13	13.00	13	3	21.67	3-28	0
1982	Ind	3	403	134.33	208	9	35.55	5-46	1
1986-7	Aus	4	189	31.50	138	9	32.88	5-41	10
1987	Pak	5	232	33.14	51*	7	61.85	3-217	3
1989	Aus	3	62	15.50	46	3	80.33	2-53	3
1991	WI	1	35	35.00	31	3	22.33	2-40	3
1991	SL	1	22	22.00	22	1	41.00	1-26	2
1991-2	NZ	1	16	8.00	15	3	25.33	2-23	1
1992	Pak	2	8	4.00	6	0	-	-	2

record 21 Tests, and went on to further records, with 2000 runs and 200 wickets in 42 Tests and 3000 runs and 300 wickets in 71. He reached a record number of wickets in Tests with his 356th in 1986, and although he added to that figure afterwards, at a much slower pace, he has been overtaken by others.

For England against Pakistan at Lord's in 1978 he became the only player to score a century (108) and take eight wickets in an innings (8-34) in the same Test, and against India in the Bombay Jubilee Test of 1980 achieved a unique feat of a century (114) and 13 wickets (6-58 and 7-48) in a Test match.

He captained England for 12 Tests 1980-1, but that included two tough series against the West Indies, and he was unsuccessful. His form was affected and he stood down after two matches against Australia in 1981. He bounced back, however, with his greatest triumphs in the next four Tests. In the 3rd Test at Headingley came a match-winning 149 not out, scoring 100 off only 87 balls; in the 4th a spell of five wickets for 1 run in 28 balls, in the 5th an even better century, which came off 86 balls; and in the 6th ten wickets in the match. In 1982 against India

at Lord's he made 208, his 200 coming off 220 balls, the fastest Test double century ever, and in 1986 he scored England's fastest Test 50, off 32 balls v New Zealand at The Oval.

In his later years his experience was of value to England in one-day cricket, and on his day his majestic batting could turn any game, but after his triumphs of 1981, when he was voted BBC Sports Personality of the Year, his bowling was generally far less effective than in his first four years of Test cricket when he took 202 wickets at 21.20 in 41 Tests. In 1985 he hit a record 80 sixes during a first-class season. He played for Somerset 1974-86 (captain 1984-5), leaving acrimoniously after the county had dispensed with the services of the West Indians Vivian Richards and Joel Garner; Worcestershire 1987-91 and Durham 1992-3. He also played League football for Scunthorpe United as a striker 1980-5. He was awarded the OBE in 1992.

102 Tests 1977-92: 5200 runs at 33.54, 14 100s HS 208; 383 wickets at 28.40, BB 8-34; 120 catches.

116 One-day Ints 1977-92: 2113 runs at 23.21, HS 79; 145 wickets at 28.54, BB 4-31; 36 catches.

First-class 1974-93: 19,399 runs at 33.97, 38 100s HS 228; 1172 wickets at 27.22, BB 8-34; 354 catches.

Teddy BOURNE

Fencing
Edward Owen Bourne. b. 30 Sep 1948 Romford, London.

While still a pupil at Brentwood School, Bourne finished 2nd in the épée at the AFA Championships in 1965 and the following year won the first of his record six titles (1966, 1972, 1974, 1976-8). Although subsequently equalled by Ralph Johnson (qv), his total of six épée Championship victories has never been surpassed. Additionally, he placed 2nd four times (1965, 1967, 1971 and 1973) and was also a useful foilist, finishing 2nd in the AFA Championships in 1974. He competed in three Olympic Games 1968-76 and is a London solicitor.

Bill BOWES

Cricket
William Eric Bowes. b. 25 Jul 1908 Elland, West Yorkshire. d. 5 Sep 1987 Menston, Leeds.

A most intelligent fast bowler for Yorkshire and England, Bowes helped Yorkshire to win the championship eight times between 1931 and 1946. Tall (1.93m *6 ft 4 in*) and fair-haired, he generally bowled at a controlled fast-medium pace but was capable of a genuinely fast ball. Off a short run he was extremely accurate, swung the ball either way and had a sharp break-back. He took over 100 wickets in a season nine times, 1930-6 and 1938-9, with a best of 193 at 15.44 in 1935 and 190 at 15.14 in 1932 and averaged under 20 runs per wicket in every one of his 13 seasons of play in England.

His England appearances, and the fact that he only made one overseas tour, to Australia in 1932/3, were restricted by the fact that he was no batsman and also a poor fielder. Indeed he was one of those rare cricketers who took more wickets in his first-class career than he scored runs. He became a leading cricket writer, notably for the *Yorkshire Evening Post.*.

15 Tests 1932-46: 28 runs at 4.66, HS 10*; 68 wickets at 22.33, BB 6-33; 2 catches. First-class 1928-47: 1530 runs at 8.59, HS 43*; 1639 wickets at 16.76, BB 9-121; 138 catches.

George BOWMAN

Equestrianism, Carriage Driving
George Bowman. b. 14 Oct 1934 Penrith, Cumbria.

Bowman has been Britain's most successful four-in-hand trials driver, winning the horse teams title 17 times to 1994. At the World Championships he was 3rd in 1974 and 2nd in 1980, taking team gold on both occasions.

He worked for several years as a cowboy and rodeo rider in Canada and ran a demolition and scrap metal business. He took up carriage riding following a serious injury when the doors of an aircraft hangar fell on him. He is a member of the driving committee of the International Equestrian Federation.

Chris BOXER - see CAHILL

Geoffrey BOYCOTT

Cricket
Geoffrey Boycott. b. 21 Oct 1940 Fitzwilliam, West Yorkshire.

The most dedicated of batsmen, Boycott achieved a record number of runs for England, and in his penultimate Test at Delhi on 23 Dec 1981 passed the world record total of Gary Sobers (West Indies). He made his Yorkshire debut in 1962 and two years later first played for England. He was an obvious first-choice opener for the next two decades, except for the period 1974-7 when he made himself unavailable for Test cricket. That was in the middle of a generally unsuccessful eight years as captain of Yorkshire. He returned to Tests against Australia in 1977, and on his home ground at Headingley became the first player to score his 100th first-class 100 in a Test match. He captained England four times as deputy for Mike Brearley (qv) in 1977-8. In 1982 he played with the England 'rebels' in South Africa.

He averaged over 50 in 19 seasons in England, including a record 11 consecutive years 1970-80, and is the only batsman to average more than 100 in two English seasons: with his best aggregate of 2503 runs at 100.12 in 1971, and again with 1538 runs at 102.53 in 1979. He was awarded the OBE in 1980.

Seen by many as an obsessively selfish player, and a man who was in the midst of many turmoils at Yorkshire County Cricket Club, both as a player and as a committee member (elected 1984), his great batting was backed by profound knowledge of the game and he has become a most authoritative TV commentator.

108 Tests 1964-82: 8114 runs at 47.72, 33 100s HS 246*; 7 wickets, BB 3-47; 33 catches.

36 One-day Ints 1971-81: 1082 runs at 36.06, 1 100 HS 105; 5 wickets at 21.00, BB 2-14; 5 catches.

First-class 1960-87: 43,423 runs at 42.86, 102 100s HS 262*; 45 wickets at 32.02, BB 4-14; 264 catches.

Cecil BOYD-ROCHFORT

Horse Racing
(Sir) Cecil Boyd-Rochfort. b. 16 Apr 1887 Middleton Park, Co. Meath, Ireland. d. 17 Mar 1983 Kelnahard Castle, Co. Cavan.

The first trainer to win over £1 million in career prize money in Britain, he was leading trainer in 1937-8, 1954-5 and 1958. He joined Atty Persse in 1906 and became assistant trainer to Captain R H Dewhurst in 1908. In 1912 he was appointed racing manager to Sir Ernest Cassel. He started training at Newmarket in 1921, based at Freemason Lodge from 1923, and in his 47 years as a trainer, 25 of them for the Royal Family, he won 13 Classics. He won the St Leger six times and was especially noted for his stayers. His greatest horses included *Alcide* and *Meld*, and he had just one Derby winner, *Parthia* in 1959.

A tall and elegant Old Etonian, he was awarded the Croix de Gu:rre in World War I while serving in the Scots Guards with his elder brother Arthur, who won the VC and was later to breed many famous horses at the Tally-Ho Stud in Ireland. Boyd-

Rochfort was created KCVO in the 1968 New Year Honours List. On his retirement at the end of that year he handed over to his stepson Henry Cecil.

Aubrey BRABAZON (Ireland) .

Horse Racing
Aubrey Brabazon. b. 7 Jan 1920.

A stylish horseman, he was champion jockey on the flat in Ireland in 1945 and won the Irish 2000 Guineas and Oaks, but he was best known for his National Hunt wins for Vincent O'Brien at Cheltenham. He rode *Cottage Rake* to three successive wins in the Cheltenham Gold Cup 1948-50 and *Hatton's Grace* to win the Champion Hurdle in 1949 and 1950. He succeeded his father Cecil as a trainer at Rangers Lodge, the Curragh.

Caroline BRADLEY

Equestrianism, Show Jumping
Caroline Frances Bradley. b. 14 Apr 1946. d. 1 Jun 1983 Oxford.

As a member of the gold medal British team in 1978, Bradley was the first woman to win a gold medal when the World Championships were opened to men and women competing together. She had been 2nd in the 1973 European Ladies' and 4th in the World Ladies' Championship in 1974, and also won a European team gold in 1979, as well as winning the British Championship in 1977.

She produced a series of great horses, such as *Marius* and *Tigre* on whom she won the Queen Elizabeth II Cup in 1978 and 1980 respectively, and *Milton*, ridden for many years to enormous success by John Whitaker (qv), following Caroline's early death after a sudden heart attack at the Suffolk County Show in 1983. She was awarded the MBE.

Harry BRADSHAW (Ireland)

Golf
Harry Bradshaw. b. 9 Oct 1913 Delgany, Co. Wicklow. d. Dec 1990.

Harry Bradshaw was beaten by Bobby

Locke (SAf) in a play-off for the Open title at Sandwich in 1949. An incident at the 5th hole in the second round may have cost him the title for his ball came to rest from a drive in a broken beer bottle. He had to play the ball and the bottle, but the ball moved only about 30 yards; this led to a change in the Rules of Golf. His round was a 77 and his other three were 68, 69 and 70.

With Christy O'Connor (qv), Bradshaw won the Canada Cup (now World Cup) for Ireland in 1958 at the high altitude of Mexico City, when his 286 made him the joint individual leader, although he lost the play-off to Angel Miguel of Spain.

Bradshaw won the Irish Open in 1947 and 1949 and was Irish Professional champion ten times, 1941-4, 1947, 1950-1, 1953-4 and 1958. It was not until the age of 40, in 1953, that he won his first major British event, the Dunlop Masters and in that year he made his Ryder Cup debut, the first southern Irishman to be selected. In his three Cup appearances, 1953, 1955 and 1957, he won two, lost two and halved one of his five matches.

He had an unorthodox grip, with three fingers of his right hand overlapping his left, but he had a most consistent short game. He was professional at the Portmarnock Club, County Dublin.

Liam BRADY (Ireland)

Football
William Brady. b. 13 Feb 1956 Dublin.

Brady was one of the most gifted footballers ever to play for Ireland, for whom he made a record 72 international appearances between 1974 and 1990. Sadly he never had the opportunity to play in a World Cup competition or indeed the finals of any international competition. He was a highly skilful playmaker, particularly strong with his left foot. He came to England to make his Football League debut at the age of 17 with Arsenal, for whom he played in midfield in three successive FA Cup finals 1978-80, but was only on the winning team in 1979. He was also a member of the team which lost the 1980 European Cup Winners' Cup to Valencia on penalties.

In 1980 he went to Italy, where he played for seven years, successively with Juventus (guiding them to two League championships), Sampdoria, Internazionale and Ascoli, before returning to England to play for West Ham. He was elected Football Writers' Player of the Year in Britain in 1979. He was manager of Celtic for just over two years until resigning in October 1993; and in December 1993 was appointed manager of Brighton. His elder brothers Ray and Pat played for Millwall.

James BRAID

Golf
James Braid. b. 6 Feb 1870 Earlsferry, Fife. d. 27 Nov 1950 London.

The first man to win the British Open five times – 1901, 1905-06, 1908 and 1910 – Braid was also 2nd in 1897, 1902 (=), 1904 (=), 1909, and 3rd in 1900 and 1912. He was a tall, quiet man who drove the ball great distances, said by Horace Hutchinson to 'drive with divine fury'. At the turn of the century he was, with J H Taylor and Harry Vardon (qqv), one of the 'Great Triumvirate'.

Braid was a founding member of the Professional Golfers' Association, whose Matchplay Championship (the *News of the World*) he won four times, 1903 (the first year it was first held), 1905, 1907 and 1911.

He was a joiner by trade before going to London as a club-maker in 1893 and turning professional in 1896. He served as the professional at Romford for eight years and at Walton Heath for 45 years, helping make it one of England's finest courses, and was famed as a golf course architect, perhaps most notably of Gleneagles.

Bob BRAITHWAITE

Shooting
John Robert Braithwaite. b. 28 Sep 1925 Scarborough.

In 1968 Braithwaite became the first Briton to win an Olympic gold medal for shooting for 44 years. A veterinary surgeon, he had placed 7th in the clay pigeon shooting in 1964 and in Mexico City scored 198 out of a possible 200, hitting 187 consecutive clays after missing the 6th and the 13th.

His daughter **Norine** (b. 29 Jan 1951) was a British athletics international, placing 5th in the 1970 Commonwealth Games 1500m and winning the WAAA indoor title at 800m in 1973 and 1500m in 1974.

Chris BRASHER

Athletics
Christopher William Brasher. b. 21 Aug 1928 Georgetown, Guyana. *28/02/03*

Entering the 1956 Olympic Games only as the British third string to John Disley (qv) and Eric Shirley, Brasher emerged as steeplechase champion, winning in a British record time of 8:41.2 (8:41.35) on auto timing, 6 seconds better than his previous best. His pace-making of Bannister's first four-minute-mile had already made him well known, but perhaps his greatest achievement has been the founding of the London Marathon in 1981 and his subsequent hard work in establishing the race. He had been inspired to bring such a race to Britain's capital when he had run in the New York marathon. His varied career has included spells as Sports Editor of *The Observer* and Head of General Features, BBC Television. He married the tennis player Shirley Bloomer (qv).

A mountaineering enthusiast throughout his life and graduate of Cambridge University, Brasher won the 1951 World Student Games title at 5000m and was second at 1500m. He turned to the steeplechase and was 11th in the 1952 Olympics, but never won an AAA title. He also became a leading developer of the sport of orienteering in Britain.

Best times on the flat: 1500m 3:53.6 (1954), 1M 4:06.8 (1955), 3000m 8:15.4 (1955), 2M 8:45.6 (1956).

Len BRAUND

Cricket
Leonard Charles Braund. b. 18 Oct 1875 Clewer, Berkshire. d. 23 Dec 1955 Putney, London.

A most useful all-rounder, middle-order batsman, leg-break bowler and outstanding slip fielder, he played in all five Tests for the outstanding England team of 1902. His great years were 1901-03, when he did the double each year; he made over 1000 runs in a season six times and took over 100 wickets four times with a peak of 172 at 19.80 in 1902. He played for Surrey 1896-8, and London County 1900-04, but most of his career was with Somerset, who he joined in 1899, only to have to wait until 1901 before qualifying to play for them. After his retirement from county cricket he was a first-class umpire for 15 years.

23 Tests 1901-08: 987 runs at 25.97, 1 100 HS 104; 47 wickets at 38.51, BB 8-81; 39 catches.
First-class 1896-1920: 17,801 runs at 25.61, 25 100s HS 257*; 1114 wickets at 27.27, BB 9-41; 545 catches, 1 stumping.

Mike BREARLEY

Cricket
John Michael Brearley. b. 28 Apr 1942 Harrow, London.

Although he was a good-class county batsman, Brearley did not fulfil his early batting promise in Tests. He gained his place for his batting and also as a very fine slip fielder, but once he had taken over the England captaincy from Tony Greig (qv) in 1977, he played mainly because he was a genius as a captain; an inspiration to his team and a great communicator. He won 18 and lost 4 of his 31 matches as captain. He may have been fortunate that many of those wins were against Australian teams weakened by defections to World Series cricket, but his return in 1981 to take over from Ian Botham (qv) was the stuff of legend as he helped to revitalise Botham and the team, winning three of the four Tests. He scored a record 4310 runs in his four years at Cambridge where he also kept wicket and took a 1st in Classics. In 1964 he scored 2178 runs at 44.44 and was voted Best Young Cricketer of the Year. He captained the England Under-23 team to Pakistan in 1966/7, where he made his highest ever score of 312*. Remarkably that tour was in the middle of a period when he did not play first-class cricket but trained as a psychologist and taught philosophy at the University of California and Newcastle University. He returned to full-time cricket when asked to take on the Middlesex captaincy in 1971, and had considerable success in his 12 years in charge, during which time the county won three Championships and shared another, and two Gillette Cups. He was awarded the OBE in 1978.

39 Tests 1976-81: 1442 runs at 22.88, HS 91; 52 catches.

25 One-day Ints 1977-80: 510 runs at 24.28, HS 78; 12 catches.

First-class 1961-82: 25,185 runs at 37.81, 45 100s HS 312*; 3 wickets; 418 catches, 12 stumpings.

Billy BREMNER

Football
William John Bremner. b. 9 Dec 1942 Stirling.

Bremner was a player of fiery temperament which he had difficulty in controlling both on the field and in off-field clashes with authority. Initially a right-winger, he later took the field as a half-back but with his constantly roving style his nominal position in the line-up was academic. Only 1.65m *5 ft 5 in* tall, he was renowned for his fitness and energy.

He made his debut for Leeds United in 1960 as Don Revie's right-wing partner and with Revie (qv) as manager and Bremner as captain they later took Leeds into the most successful period in the club's history, winning the FA Cup (1972), the League Championship (1969, 1974), the League Cup (1968) and the European Fairs Cup (1968 and 1971). He was voted the Football Writers' Footballer of the Year in 1970. Between 1965 and 1975 he won 54 caps for Scotland (3 goals) and scored 115 goals in 771 games for Leeds before moving to Hull City in 1976. He then went to Doncaster Rovers in 1978 as player-manager but in 1985 he returned as manager to Leeds, where he remained for three years before being dismissed. His second spell as manager at Doncaster (1989-92) followed and he led them out of the Fourth Division for the second time.

Johnny BRIGGS

Cricket
John Briggs. b. 3 Oct 1862 Sutton-in-Ashfield, Nottinghamshire. d. 11 Jan 1902 Cheadle, Gt. Manchester.

Boy' Briggs, just 1.65m *5 ft 5 in* tall, was an outstanding all-rounder who made six tours to Australia in the 1880s and 1890s. He suffered, however, from epilepsy and was eventually confined to Cheadle Asylum, where he died at the age of 39. A left-handed batsman and slow left-arm bowler who exerted sharp spin on the ball, he first gained his place in the Lancashire team for his fielding and was mainly a batsman until 1885, the season after his Test debut, when he made his one Test century against Australia at Melbourne. Each year from 1887 to 1897 and again in his last season of 1900 he took over 100 wickets, with a peak of 166 in 1893. His batting declined, but he achieved some great bowling figures, headed by his 7-17 and 8-11 against South Africa at Cape Town on 26 Mar 1889, an unparalleled 15 wickets (14 bowled, 1 lbw) in a single day's Test cricket, and six wickets in each innings against Australia at Adelaide in 1892, after a hat trick in the previous Test.

33 Tests 1884-9: 815 runs at 18.11, 1 100 HS 121; 118 wickets at 17.74, BB 8-11; 12 catches.

First-class 1879-1900: 14,092 runs at 18.27, 10 100s HS 186; 2221 wickets at 15.95, BB 10-55; 259 catches.

Karen BRIGGS

Judo
Karen Valerie Briggs. b. 11 Apr 1963 Hull. Later Mrs Inman.

Britain's most successful judo player at world championships with four titles: under-48kg in 1982, 1984, 1986 and 1989, with the silver in 1991. She was also European champion in 1981-4 and 1986-7, with silver medals 1989-91 and bronze 1985. She won the Japanese Open title 1983-6 and 1988 and the British Open 1981-2, 1986-7, 1989-90 and 1992. When judo was included at the Commonwealth Games for the first (and so far only) time in 1990, she won the gold medal.

She started judo at the age of ten and won her first national junior title at under-30 kg in 1975. At her first British Open in 1980 she was beaten by Jane Bridge in the semi-finals, but she won a year later and in that year made her international debut. She also represented her county in the English Schools cross-country. She was awarded the MBE in 1990 and in 1994 she married Peter Inman, son of Ron Inman, the manager of the British judo team.

Robbie BRIGHTWELL

Athletics
Robbie Ian Brightwell. b. 27 Oct 1939 Rawalpindi, India (now Pakistan).

Having been a successful junior sprinter, but lacking the blazing speed to become world class, Brightwell moved up to 400m with immediate success in 1960. He set British records at 46.2 (46.31 automatic timing) and 46.1 (46.25), but the latter was for 4th in the semi-final and he just missed the final. He lost his record to his great rival Adrian Metcalfe in 1961, but set further British records with 45.9 for 440y (also a European record) in 1962 and when running 45.79 and 45.75 for 400m at the 1964 Olympics. There he had been the favourite, and he was bitterly disappointed by his 4th place behind the American Mike Larrabee. However that was almost compensated by the marvellous win at 800m of his fiancée Ann Packer (qv) and his own brilliant relay leg of 44.7 in gaining two places in the last 50 metres and securing for Britain the silver medal behind the Americans.

He was European champion at 400m in 1962, with a relay silver medal, having been 5th at 200m in 1958. At the Commonwealth Games he was a 220y semi-finalist in 1958 and in 1962 won silver medals at 440y and 4 x 440y relay. He was AAA 440y champion 1962 and 1964 and awarded the MBE in 1965. Other best times: 100y 9.7 (1958), 9.5w (1964); 100m 10.6 (1959), 200m 20.9 (1962).

His son **Gary** (b. 6 Oct 1965) ran 47.90 for 400m in 1984, and Gary's two younger brothers **Ian** (b. 9 Apr 1968) and **David** (b. 7 Jan 1971) became professional foot-ballers with Manchester City, Ian playing for England Schools, Youths and Under-21s.

Brian BRINKLEY

Swimming
Brian Brinkley. b. 28 Dec 1953 Bedford.

A most versatile swimmer, he won the 200m butterfly at the 1974 Commonwealth Games, when he was also 2nd at 200m and 400m individual medley and won a silver and two bronze medals in the relays. Later that year he won silver medals at 200m butterfly and medley relay at the Europeans. In 1975 he took bronze medals at 200m freestyle and butterfly and two relay bronze medals at the World Championships, having been 4th at 200m butterfly in 1973. At the Olympics he placed 5th at 400m freestyle in 1972 and 6th at 200m butterfly with a bronze at the 4 x 200m relay in 1976. He was awarded the MBE.

Tall and powerful, he won 43 national titles: 24 long-course - freestyle: 100m 1974-5, 200m and 400m 1971-5, 1500m 1972-3; butterfly: 100m 1974-5, 200m 1972-5; IM 200m 1971, 1973, 1975; 400m 1973; and 19 short-course - freestyle 100m 1974-5, 200m and 400m 1971-5, 1500m 1973; butterfly: 100m 1975, 200m 1973-5, IM 200m 1974, 400m 1973. At long course he set the following British records 1971-6: freestyle 100m 52.30 (1975), 200m eight to 1:53.07 (1976), 400m five to 4:01.37 (1976), 800m two to 8:42.60 (1972), 1500m two to 16:39.60 (1972); butterfly: 100m three to 56.68 (1975), 200m six to 2:01.49 (1976); 400m IM 4:36.29 (1973).

Eric BRISTOW

Darts
Eric John Bristow. b. 25 Apr 1957 Stoke Newington, London.

'The Crafty Cockney' became the leading player when darts reached its peak popularity as a television sport in the early 1980s. He was a precocious talent, making his England debut at 18 and taking over from John Lowe (qv) as World No. 1 in January 1980. In that year a film of his lifestyle *Arrows* was released.

Bristow has most wins in the World Masters (1977, 1979, 1981, 1983-4), the World Professional Championships (1980-1, 1984-6), World Matchplay (1985 and 1988), British Open (1978, 1981, 1983, 1985-6) and the World Cup singles (1983, 1985, 1987, 1989) and has played on seven winning England teams in the latter tournament. He also won the *News of the World* Championship in 1983-4, the British Matchplay in 1982-3 and 1986, and with Peter Locke the World Pairs in 1987. In addition to his five wins he has also been beaten in five World Championship finals. He was awarded the MBE in 1989.

Janette BRITTIN

Cricket
Janette Ann Brittin. b. 4 Jul 1959 Kingston-upon-Thames, London.

A fluent opening bat and brilliant fielder, Brittin scored her first Test century, 144*, in the 1st Test against New Zealand at Headingley in 1984. In the subsequent two Tests of that series her scores were 96, 63 and 35, for an overall average of 112.67, the highest for a woman in a three-match Test series. She also proved to be a useful occasional spinner and took 3-27 in the 2nd Test against Australia in 1984/5. Her 138* against the International XI at Hamilton in January 1982 is the highest ever in the World Cup by an England player.

She is now the second highest run-scorer in women's Test cricket and the highest ever in one-day internationals. In helping England to win the World Cup in 1993 she was the top run-scorer in the tournament with 410 at 51.25 and became the first player to score 1000 World Cup runs in her career. She also overtook Rachel Heyhoe-Flint's (qv) record of 2457 runs in all internationals, taking her total to 2789. She has played for Surrey since 1976 and played a major part in her club, Redoubtables, becoming League champions in 1994. She also played for England three times in indoor hockey internationals in 1988, and is a sales administrator for British Airways.

19 Tests 1979-92: 1193 runs at 45.88, 3 100s HS 144*; 9 wickets at 46.11, BB 2-15; 10 catches.
45 One-day Ints 1979-93: 1596 runs at 43.13, 4 100s HS 138*; 8 wickets at 23.75, BB 3-16; 22 catches.

John BROCKWAY

Swimming
William John Brockway. b. 8 Oct 1928 Bristol.

In 1954 he became the first Welshman to win an Empire Games swimming title, when he won the 110y backstroke, having taken the silver medal in 1950. He also won the European bronze medal at 100m backstroke in 1954. He was ASA backstroke champion a record-equalling seven times in eight years, at 100y 1948-51 and 110y 1953-5, and won eight Welsh titles between 1946 and 1956.

Stanley BROGDEN

Rugby League
Stanley Brogden. b. 15 Mar 1910 Bradford, West Yorkshire.

After winning county honours for soccer as a schoolboy, Brogden switched to rugby league and played his first game as professional for Bradford Northern v Huddersfield at the age of 16 years 7 months. In 1929 he moved to Huddersfield, where he won his first GB cap as a 19-year-old, and then to Leeds in 1933 for a world record fee of £1200. One of the outstanding three-quarters of the 1930s, he won 16 GB caps 1929-37 and toured Australia in 1932 and 1936 playing every Test on each tour. Sheer speed was his greatest asset and he scored many tries by simply outpacing his opponents. He scored 276 tries in his first-class career 1927-48.

Percy BROMFIELD

Table Tennis
Percival Bromfield. b. 1886. d. 1947.

Table tennis, or 'Ping Pong' as it was then known was hugely popular at the turn of the century, but collapsed in popularity a

couple of years after the Ping Pong Assoc-iation was formed in 1902. Bromfield won their championship in 1904, and he won again when the sport revived and he took the English Open title in 1924. He was a pioneer of the use of rubber-surfaced bats. Wooden bats had been used previously; the sound of the bat hitting ball giving rise to the name *ping pong*. Bromfield's uses of the rubber surface to produce swerve and spin helped to enable the game to flourish again. He captained the England team in the first Swaythling Cup match in 1926, and won the English Open mixed doubles in 1927.
His daughter **Valerie** (b. 1912) won English Open titles at women's singles and mixed doubles in 1931.

Eric BROOK

Football
Eric Fred Brook. b. 27 Nov 1907 Mexborough, South Yorkshire. d. 29 Mar 1965 Manchester.

An outside-left with a devastatingly pow-erful shot, Brook spent two seasons with Barnsley before moving to Manchester City in 1928 and remained with the club for the rest of his playing career. After being losing finalists in the 1933 FA Cup final, Manchester City won the trophy the follow-ing year and were league champions in 1937. Eric Brook contributed to all these successes and scored 158 goals in 453 League games for Manchester City before his retirement during World War II.
He won 18 caps for England 1929-37, scor-ing 10 international goals, including two in six minutes against Italy in the notorious 'Battle of Highbury' in 1934. There was no shortage of talented challengers for Brook's England place at outside-left but he played in 11 consecutive games after the selectors showed the foresight to play the great Cliff Bastin at inside-left.

Trevor BROOKING

Football
Trevor David Brooking. b. 2 Oct 1948 Barking, London.

After joining West Ham as an apprentice in 1965 he signed professional forms the

following year and remained with the club throughout his playing career. A poised and gifted midfield player, he never appeared to be hurried – always the hallmark of a class player. He made his League debut for West Ham in 1967 playing in 635 matches (102 goals) before his retirement in 1984. He won an FA Cup winners' medal in 1975 and again in 1980 when he scored the only goal of the match. He also won runners-up medals in the European Cup Winners' Cup 1976 and the League Cup 1981, and was a member of the team which took West Ham back into the First Division in 1981. He was capped 47 times (scoring 5 goals) by England between 1974 and 1982. He was awarded the MBE in 1981, he is today a popular and knowledgeable commentator on TV and radio.

Marshall BROOKS

Athletics, High Jump
Marshall Jones Brooks. b. 30 May 1855. d. 5 Jan 1944 Tarporley, Cheshire.

On 17 Mar 1876, after a snowstorm, Marshall Brooks produced the first ever 6 foot high jump, clearing a bar at Oxford set an eighth of an inch above this height. He improved the world record to 1.89m *6 ft 2 1/2in* three weeks later at the inter-Varsity sports from a grass take-off at Lillie Bridge, London before 15,000 spec-tators, the largest crowd to watch an athletics meeting to that date. This mark remained a British record for 44 years. He had earlier set bests of 5 ft 10 in and 5 ft 11 in in 1874 and was AAC champion in 1874 and 1876.
The second son of the 1st Baron Crawshaw, he played for England against Scotland at rugby football in 1874 and won his Blue at Oxford for rugby 1883 (playing with his elder brother William) and athletics 1884-6.

Tony BROOKS

Motor Racing
Charles Anthony Standish Brooks. b. 25 Feb 1932 Dukinfield, Gt. Manchester.

Brooks leapt to fame in 1955 when, still a dental student, he won the Syracuse Grand Prix in a Connaught. This was only his second race outside Britain and first in a Formula One car, and it was the first win on the continent by a British car and driver since Henry Segrave (qv) in 1925. Having started his first Formula One Grand Prix race in 1956, the stylish and determined driver was signed by Vanwall and was 2nd in his first race at Monaco. Next, he shared a great win at Aintree in the British Grand Prix with Stirling Moss (qv) and he ended the year 5th in the drivers' world championship. He improved to 3rd in 1958, when he won three Grands Prix: Belgian, German and Italian, and, with Moss and Stuart Lewis-Evans, ensured that Vanwall won the constructors' championship.

Vanwall owner Tony Vandervell withdrew from motor racing in 1959 and Brooks joined Ferrari, winning the French and German Grand Prix and finishing 2nd in the championship just four points behind Jack Brabham (Aus). He contested a limited Formula One programme in 1960 in a Cooper and he raced for BRM in 1961, but his best position in those seasons was his 3rd in the US GP, his last race before he retired to develop his garage business in Weybridge, Surrey. His Formula One record was 6 wins and 75 points from 38 starts 1956-61. Equally proficient at sports car racing driving Aston Martins, he won the Nürburgring 1000 km in 1957 and the Tourist Trophy (with Stirling Moss) in 1958.

Tim BROOKSHAW

Horse Racing
Stanley James Brookshaw. b. 25 Mar 1929 Shawbury, Shropshire. d. 8 Nov 1981 Oswestry, Shropshire.

Champion National Hunt jockey in 1958/9 with 83 winners, he increased his total to 90 in 1960/1, but then was some way behind Stan Mellor's winning figure of 118. From a farming family in Shropshire, Brookshaw's career was ended with a bad fall in 1964 as a result of which he was paralysed from the waist down. He overcame this disability so that he runs his farm and trains horses. The Injured Jockeys' Fund was set up following the injuries that he and Paddy Farrell suffered in 1964.

David BROOME

Equestrianism, Show Jumping
David McPherson Broome. b. 1 Mar 1940 Cardiff.

Broome has a record six wins in the King George V Gold Cup, on six different horses, between 1960 on *Sunsalve* and 1991 on *Lannegan*. He was three times European champion - on *Sunsalve* in 1961, and then riding *Mister Softee*, his greatest horse in 1967 and 1968; and was world champion on *Beethoven* in 1970 before helping Britain to win the team championship in 1978. He also won the world individual bronze medal in 1960 and team bronzes in 1982 and 1990 and won six national championships, 1961-2, 1967, 1973, 1979 and 1986. His sister Liz (see Liz Edgar) was also a national champion.

He won two individual show-jumping bronze medals at the Olympics in 1960 and 1968, but having turned professional in 1973 he could not compete at the Games, until the rules changed and he was selected again in 1988 and 1992. He would have achieved a record for any sport by a British competitor with a 32-year-span, but a last-minute injury meant that he was unable to compete in 1992.

A farmer in south Wales, he has competed at the highest level for 35 years, competing in a record 106 Nations Cup events for Britain 1959-94. He was voted BBC Sports Personality of the Year in 1960, awarded the OBE in 1970 and the CBE in 1995.

Jim BROUGH

Rugby League
James Wasdale Brough. b. 5 Nov 1903 Silloth, Cumbria. d. 16 Sep 1986 Workington, Cumbria.

Once on the books of Liverpool FC as an understudy to international goalkeeper Elisha Scott (qv), he turned to rugby union and was capped twice by England as a full-back while playing for the unfashionable Cumberland club, Silloth, where he was a local fisherman. In June 1925, he switched to rugby league, signing for Leeds for the then substantial fee of £600. The move proved a great success and

Brough won the highest honours. He toured Australia twice, 1928 and 1936, and was captain on the second occasion although he only played in one Test. His international appearances were limited to five, but had he not been a contemporary of the great Jim Sullivan he would undoubtedly have won many more caps. Because of Sullivan's firm hold on the full-back position, Brough made his international debut as a centre.

He was a member of the Leeds team which won the 1932 Challenge Cup, captaining them to a second victory in 1936. He retired in 1938 to take up a business appointment in South Africa but returned on the outbreak of war and played a few more games, including the wartime Challenge Cup final in 1942 when, as a 38 year-old, he was on the winning team for the third time. In all he played in 442 games for Leeds in 1925-44 before taking over the coaching duties. Then, after a brief spell at Whitehaven, he became manager of Workington Town in 1958 and that year was appointed as the first-ever coach to a GB touring team.

Eric BROWN

Golf
Eric Chalmers Brown. b. 15 Feb 1925 Edinburgh.

The top Scottish golfer of the 1950s and 1960s, he won the Scottish professional title eight times: 1956-8, 1960, 1962, 1965, 1966 (tied) and 1968, having first come to the fore when as a railway fireman he won the Scottish Amateur Championship in 1946.

He won the Dunlop Masters 1957, PGA Match Play 1960 and 1962 and his best placing in the Open was 3rd in 1957 and 1958. A tough match player with the ability and temperament to rise to the occasion, in four Ryder Cup appearances 1953-9 he won all four singles although he lost his four foursomes. He was then Ryder Cup captain in 1969, when the British team tied with the Americans, and in 1971. He also played 13 times for Scotland in the World Cup between 1954 and 1968.

Freddie BROWN

Cricket
Frederick Richard Brown. b. 16 Dec 1910 Lima, Peru. d. 24 Jul 1991 Ramsbury, Wiltshire.

Brown's all-round talent was recognised early. He was highly successful as a powerfully built schoolboy at The Leys and topped both batting and bowling averages in his two years at Cambridge University, where he also gained a hockey blue. He took 107 wickets with his leg breaks in 1931, when he made his Test debut against New Zealand, and in 1932, his first full season with Surrey, he did the double with 1135 runs and 120 wickets. He was then selected for the 1932/3 tour of Australia. After five Test appearances in 1931-3 he played only one more, in 1937, as he played irregularly as an amateur, before the War. An Army officer, he spent three years in a POW camp in Italy and on return took up a business appointment in Northampton. Not having played regular first-class cricket for ten years, he became Northamptonshire captain in 1949 and revitalised this struggling team with his ebullient personality. He was also immediately successful as a player, achieving his second double in 1949 and returning to the England team as captain. After scoring 122 out of 131 in 110 minutes for the Gentlemen against the Players at Lord's he took the England team to Australia in 1950/1, losing the series but inflicting on Australia their first post-war defeat in the final Test. Chairman of the Test selectors in his last year as Northants captain, 1953, he was persuaded to play in the Lord's Test and contributed well with scores of 22 and 28 and 4-82 in the second innings. He managed MCC touring teams in 1956/7 and 1958/9, was president of the MCC in 1971-2 and chairman of the Cricket Council 1974-9. He was awarded the MBE and then the CBE in 1980.

22 Tests 1931-53 (captain 15): 734 runs at 25.31, HS 79; 45 wickets at 31.06, BB 5-49; 22 catches.

First-class 1930-53: 13,335 runs at 27.36, 22 100s HS 212; 1221 wickets at 26.21, BB 8-34; 212 catches.

George BROWN

Motorcycling
George Brown. b. 1912. d. 1979.

Britain's supreme motorcycle sprinter of the 1950s, Brown set numerous world and national records. His racing career started in 1934 when he joined Vincent, later becoming that company's chief tester before leaving in 1951. In 1953 he retired from road racing to concentrate on sprints and hill climbs. His first world records came in 1961 and even when past the FIM age limit of 55 for world records he continued to set national speed records. He achieved particular success with the special machine that he built called Nero and later with his 1147cc Super Nero.

Godfrey BROWN

Athletics
Arthur Godfrey Kilner Brown. b. 21 Feb 1915 Bankura, India. d. 4 Feb 1995 Coneyhurst, West Sussex.

A highly talented runner at distances from 100y to the half mile, Brown set European records twice in the 1936 Olympic 400m. First he ran 47.3 (47.31 on automatic timing) in his semi and then ran a brilliant 46.68 in the final for the silver medal just 0.02 behind Archie Williams (USA), whom he just failed to catch after making up three metres over the last 100m. The next day his sister **Audrey** (b. 24 May 1913, later Lady Court) won a sprint relay silver medal and two days later Brown anchored the British team to victory in the 4 x 400m relay, the time a European record 3:09.0. In 1937 he won the World Student Games 400m, adding gold medals at both relays, and in 1938 he won the European 400m, with silver in the 4 x 400m relay and bronze at 4 x 100m. He had been Public Schools 880y champion each year 1932-4, won the 440y for Cambridge against Oxford each year 1935-7, adding the 100y in 1937, and AAA champion at 440y in 1936 and 1938 and at 880y in 1939. He was headmaster of Worcester Royal Grammar School 1950-78.
Other best times: 100y 9.9 and downhill 9.7 (1936), 880y 1:52.2 (1937).

His brother **Ralph** (b. 28 Aug 1909, later Sir Ralph Kilner Brown OBE) was 3rd in the 1934 Empire Games 440y hurdles, won the AAA title that year and ran his best time for 400m hurdles, 54.8, when second in the 1933 World Student Games.

Gordon BROWN

Rugby Union
Gordon Lamont Brown. b. 1 Nov 1947 Troon, South Ayrshire. *19/3/2001*

The son of a Scottish international goalkeeper and younger brother of Scotland's rugby captain Brown's sterling performances in the second row for Scotland and the British Lions were fully in keeping with the family tradition of sporting excellence. Capped 30 times 1969-76 by Scotland from the West of Scotland club, he went on three British Lions tours, New Zealand 1971 and 1977 and South Africa 1974, playing in a total of eight Tests. Always a major force in the line-out, he also had excellent ball-handling skills and, unusually for a lock, he scored two Test tries on the South African tour and made a significant contribution to the Lions winning the series.
Although gifted with a superb physique and awesome strength, his career was beset by injuries which prevented him from winning more international honours. He was also suspended for a season after being sent off in a District Championship match in 1976. His elder brother **Peter** (b. 16 Dec 1941 Troon) won 27 caps for Scotland (1964-73) and when he was injured in the match against Wales in 1970 it was brother Gordon who came on as a replacement.

Jackie BROWN

Boxing
John Brown. b. 29 Nov 1909 Ancoats, Manchester. d. 15 March 1971 Smethwick, West Midlands.

Brown was one of the best of an outstanding group of British flyweights in the 1930s. He took the vacant British title with a third round KO over Bert Kirby in 1929 and in a re-match the following year the fight again ended with a KO in the third round but this time Kirby was the winner. In a third match in February 1931, Brown regained the title by outpointing Kirby and then in May he beat Lucien Popescu (Rom) to take the European crown. Brown's finest moment came in his home town of Manchester in October 1932 when he challenged Young Perez (Tun) for the world flyweight title. After 13 gruelling rounds the Tunisian threw in the towel and Brown was the world champion.

In 1933 he successfully defended his title three times: twice against Valentin Angelmann (Fra), and once against Ginger Foran from Liverpool. A third meeting with Angelmann in 1934 resulted in a draw and then in September 1935 he lost his British, European and World titles to Benny Lynch (qv) when the referee stopped the contest in the second round. He lost even more decisively in a re-match when he was knocked down five times in the first round and six in the second before the referee stopped the fight. He then fought with some success as a bantamweight until 1939.

Career record 1926-39: 135 contests. Won 103, Drew 8, Lost 24.

Karen BROWN

Hockey
Karen Brown. b. 9 Jan 1963 Redhill, Surrey.

Brown is the most capped English woman hockey player. In 1991 she won a gold medal for England in the European Cup, having won silver in 1987, and she played for GB in the 1988 Olympic Games (4th) and again in 1992 when she won a bronze medal. After two and half years out of international action she returned to the England team as its midfield general in January 1995 and scored the winning goal against Russia. From 1982 to June 1995 she has played in 244 international matches: 105 GB (with 22 goals), 103 England (42 goals), 36 England Indoor. A bank official, she played for Orpington 1977-87 and since then for Slough and was voted UK player of the year in 1984 and 1994.

Her father **Leslie** (b. 27 Nov 1936) played soccer for Britain at the 1960 Olympic Games.

Hon. Clarence BRUCE

Rackets
Clarence Napier Bruce, Lord Aberdare. b. 2 Aug 1885 Pimlico, London. d. 4 Oct 1957 Moring near Kotor, Montenegro (Yugoslavia).

An outstanding all-round sportsman, Bruce won a Blue at Oxford for cricket, golf and rackets. While at Winchester, he won the Public Schools rackets championship in 1904 and went on to win the British Amateur singles in 1922 and 1931 and was runner-up on five other occasions. He also won the British Open singles in 1932 and the Canadian Amateur singles in 1928 and 1930. His record in the British Amateur doubles was even more notable: with eight victories (1921, 1924-8, 1930, 1934) he equalled the record of H K Foster (qv). He also won the US Amateur doubles in 1928 and 1930 and the Canadian Amateur doubles 1930. His later titles were won as Lord Aberdare after he succeeded to the title on the death of his father in 1929.

After Oxford, he gave up playing first-class cricket on a regular basis but up until 1929 he was still called on occasionally by Middlesex. He served as a member of the International Olympic Committee from 1929 until his death in 1957 and he played a major part in the organisation of the 1948 Olympic Games. He was drowned when his car went over a precipice into a river only a metre deep in Yugoslavia.

First class cricket 1905-29: 4326 runs at 29.03, 6 100s, HS 149.

Norman BRUCE

Rugby Union
Norman Scott Bruce. b. 24 Aug 1932 Edinburgh. d. 28 Mar 1992 Oswestry, Shropshire.

Although born and educated in Scotland he played most of his senior rugby in England for Blackheath, London Scottish, the Army and Combined Services. Twenty-nine of his 31 caps 1958-64 as

Scotland's hooker came in consecutive matches. With Hugh McLeod and David Rollo (qqv) he formed a formidable front row and they played together in 14 internationals. He toured South Africa with the Barbarians in 1958 and with Scotland in 1960. On retiring from the Army he taught at a prep school in Shropshire.

Martin BRUNDLE

Motor Racing
Martin John Brundle. b. 1 Jun 1959 King's Lynn, Norfolk.

Brundle has yet to win a race in eleven seasons of Formula One, but he has gained a solid reputation. He had started with Tyrrell 1984-6, and his overall record is 83 points from 131 starts to the end of 1994, with a best year in 1992 when he was 6th in the drivers' championship for Benetton, taking a 2nd (at Monza) and four 3rd places. He switched to Ligier in 1993, to McLaren in 1994, when he gained another 2nd, at Monaco, and back to Ligier in 1995. Brundle had a great contest against Ayrton Senna in F3 racing in 1983, as after Senna had won nine times, Brundle won six for 2nd overall.

Greatest success has come his way in sports car racing, in which he made his world championships debut in 1985. He became world champion in 1988, won the Daytona 24-hours in 1988 and Le Mans 24-hours in 1990, all in Jaguars.

Frank BRUNO

Boxing
Franklyn Roy Bruno. b. 16 Nov 1961 Hammersmith, London.

After winning the ABA heavyweight title in 1980, Bruno turned professional in 1982. He had a series of eye operations, but then, carefully managed by Terry Lawless, won his first 21 fights before being knocked out by James 'Bonecrusher' Smith (USA) in 1984. The following year a fourth round KO of Anders Eklund (Sweden) gave him the European heavyweight title after which he challenged twice for the world crown. In 1986 he lost to Tim Witherspoon (USA) in 11 rounds when he challenged for the WBA version of the title and he lasted only five rounds against Mike Tyson (USA) in 1989 when the WBC title was at stake.

Bruno dominated the domestic scene for a number of years but has surprisingly never won the British title and he has been found wanting when he faced truly world class opposition. An immensely popular man, with a superb physique, he starred in pantomime and TV panel games as his fighting career seemed to be drawing to a close. In 1995, however, he was being lined up for another crack at a world title. He was awarded the MBE in 1990.

Career record 1982-May 95: Contests 43. Won 39 (38 KO), Lost 4.

David BRYANT

Bowls
David John Bryant. b. 27 Oct 1931 Clevedon, Somerset.

The most successful bowler in the history of the game, Bryant has the greatest number of wins at all the major championships. He has a total of six victories at the World Outdoor Championships, winning the singles in 1966, 1980 and 1988, the triples 1980 and the Leonard Trophy (team) 1984 and 1988. At the World Indoors he won the singles the first three years the Championships were held, 1979-81, and the pairs, with Tony Allcock (qv), six times, 1986-7, 1989-92.

His record at the English Outdoor Championships is no less remarkable, winning (or sharing) 16 titles between 1957 and 1985. He won the singles six times, 1960, 1966, 1971-3, 1975; the pairs three times, 1965, 1969, 1974; the triples three times, 1966, 1977, 1985; and the fours with the Clevedon team four times, 1957 (his father Reg also playing in this team), 1968-9, 1971. He also won the English Indoor singles a record nine times between 1964 and 1983. Other notable successes, from his first club competition win in 1948, include seven British Isles titles (four singles, one pairs, one triples and one fours) from 1957 to 1987 and five gold medals at the Commonwealth Games, four singles between 1962 and 1978 and the fours 1962.

With his skill, showmanship and impeccable manners, he has done more than any man to promote and popularise the game and he was awarded the MBE in 1969 and CBE 1980 for his services to the sport.

Charles BUCHAN

Football

Charles Murray Buchan. b. 22 Sep 1891 Plumstead, London. d. 25 Jun 1960 Monte Carlo, Monaco.

Buchan was a brilliant attacking player in any of the three inside-forward positions, although his subtleties frequently confused his colleagues and limited his international appearances for England to only six matches, 1913-24.

After signing for Southern League club Leyton in 1910 he moved to Sunderland a year later. In the 1912/3 season he helped them to the First Division championship and the FA Cup final where they lost to Aston Villa. His career was interrupted by the War in which he won a Military Medal serving with the Grenadier Guards and was later commissioned in the Sherwood Foresters.

At the age of 33 in 1925, he was one of the first signings of the legendary Herbert Chapman (qv) at Highbury. Arsenal paid Sunderland a basic £2,000 plus a further £100 for each goal Buchan scored in his first season. He scored 21 and the original down-payment was more than doubled. His most important contribution at Highbury was the development of the 'third-back' game which he devised with Chapman to counter the new offside rule. He captained Arsenal to their first FA Cup final in 1927 and, as with Sunderland 15 years earlier, he was on the losing side.

He also played cricket for Durham in 1920. On his retirement in 1928, he became a journalist and was the football and golf correspondent for the *Daily News* and the *News Chronicle* following the amalgamation of the two papers. He was also a commentator for BBC Radio and in 1951 founded the popular magazine, *Football Monthly*. He died while on holiday with his wife.

Ken BUCHANAN

Boxing

Kenneth Buchanan. b. 28 Jun 1945 Edinburgh.

After winning the ABA featherweight title in 1965 he turned professional and took the British lightweight title from Maurice Cullen in 1968 with an 11th round KO after he had floored the champion five times. After one defence, he then relinquished the title in 1970 but regained it in 1973 beating Jim Watt (qv) before again relinquishing his crown. In September 1970 a points win over Ismael Laguna (Panama) gave Buchanan the British version of the world lightweight title and after two successful defences he challenged Roberto Duran (Panama) for the WBA title in 1972. Duran, renowned as a dirty fighter, crippled Buchanan with a blow to the groin at the end of the 13th round and when the Scotsman failed to come out for the next round the fight was awarded to Duran. The Panamanian carefully avoided any further meetings with Buchanan and was stripped of his title in 1973 for failing to honour a contract for a re-match. Eventually, Buchanan took on Guts Ishimatsu (Japan) in 1975 for the WBC championship but the Japanese fighter retained his title after 15 hard-fought rounds.

Career record 1965-81: 69 Contests. Won 61 (28 KO), Lost 8.

Frank BUCKLE

Horse Racing

Francis Buckle. b. 1766 Newmarket, Suffolk. d. 5 Feb 1832 Peterborough.

From his success on *John Bull* in the 1792 Derby to 1827 he rode 27 English Classic winners: nine Oaks, six 1000 Guineas, five each 2000 Guineas and Derby, two St Leger. This record was eventually passed by Lester Piggott (qv) in 1984. He started riding in 1783 at a weight of just 3st 13lb *25kg* and rode until the age of 65 in 1831. He was for many years first jockey to Robert Robson (qv). Renowned for his integrity, as well as being a great jockey, specialising in well-timed finishes, he was also a successful farmer near Peterborough.

Walter BUCKMASTER

Polo
Walter Selby Buckmaster. b. 16 Oct 1872 London. d. 30 Oct 1942 Warwick.

Buckmaster was one of the first polo players to receive the maximum ten-handicap. He played for the winning England team in the Westchester Cup against the USA in 1902 and captained first the Old Cantabs and then the Freebooters. He won Olympic silver medals in 1900 and 1908.

Jack BUCKNER

Athletics
Jack Richard Buckner. b. 22 Sep 1961 Wells, Somerset.

Buckner, who graduated in geography from Loughborough University, reached 5th ranking among UK 1500m runners before turning to the 5000m, at which he achieved his goal in 1986 with the European gold medal (in the second fastest ever time by a British athlete of 13:10.15), following the Commonwealth silver. He added a World bronze in 1987 and was ranked 3rd in the world in 1986 and 2nd in 1987, when he won in Zürich. In 1988 he was 6th at the Olympics and in 1989 he was 2nd in the European Cup and 4th in the World Cup and was appointed that year to the IAAF Athlete's Commission.

He missed the 1990 season through a stress fracture of the left foot, but although he came back to run in the 1992 Olympics he did not quite recapture his previous form. He had won the AAA junior 1500m in 1980 and the AAA road 10km in 1985. Other best times: 800m 1:49.8 (1981), 1000m 2:18.88 (1982), 1500m 3:35.28 (1986), 1M 3:51.57 (1984), 2000m 4:53.06 (1987), 3000m 7:40.43 (1986), 10,000m 28:13.36 (1991).

When his brother **Tom** (b. 16 Apr 1963) competed in the steeplechase in 1992 they were the first brothers to compete for Britain at one Olympic Games in athletics since the Whitlocks in 1952.

Joe BUGNER

Boxing
Joseph Bugner. b. 16 Mar 1950 Hungary. Now an Australian citizen.

Bugner had a superb physique and indeed a fine technique, yet perhaps the reason he never quite made it to the top as a boxer was his lack of a mean streak. He won the English Schools junior boys discus title in 1964 and was 2nd in the intermediate boys in 1965. He turned pro in 1967 after only a handful of amateur fights. After a careful initiation in the sport against nonentities, he beat several leading fighters and was thought ready to take on Henry Cooper (qv) for the British, Commonwealth and European heavyweight titles a few days after his 21st birthday. His controversial victory caused a sensation and his defeat of such a favourite did not endear him to the public.

Six months later he gave a poor show in losing his titles to Jack Bodell, but he regained the European title in 1972 and four times defended this before retiring in 1976. Meanwhile he beat the former WBA world champion Jimmy Ellis (USA) and went 12 rounds in losing in 1973 to both Mohammed Ali (USA) and Joe Frazier (USA), with a great display against the latter, including a ferocious fight back after being downed in thetenth round. Much less satisfactory was his continual backtracking in a title fight against Ali in 1975. He returned to beat Richard Dunn in one round in his first comeback in 1976 to regain his three titles, before another retirement in 1977. Finally, in 1987, he suffered a comprehensive defeat at the hands of Frank Bruno (qv).

Career record: 74 contests. Won 61, Drew 1, Lost 12.

Mike BULL

Athletics, Pole Vault
(Dr) Michael Anthony Bull. b. 11 Sep 1946 Belfast.

The first British pole vaulter to clear 16ft, 5 metres or 17 ft, as he set 11 British outdoor records from 4.72m *15 ft 6 in* in 1966, when he won the Commonwealth silver medal, to 5.25m *17' 2 ³/₄"* in 1973. After that first Commonwealth medal he went on to win gold for the pole vault in 1970, and in 1974 gold for decathlon and silver for pole vault, but at his final Games in 1978 he was out of contention at both events. At the pole vault he was AAA champion outdoors five times, 1966-7, 1969, 1971-2, and indoors eight times 1967-72, 1974 and 1977. He also competed at four European Championships outdoors and the Olympic Games of 1968 and 1972. Including the European Indoor Games, before they were given full international status, he made a men's record 69 international appearances for Britain 1965-77.

A Northern Ireland schools' swimming international, he started in athletics at shot put, and was a fine all-rounder winning the N.Ireland Schools shot, pole vault and discus on the same day that he won the senior decathlon. A graduate of Queen's University, Belfast, winning his doctorate in moral philosophy, he became a university lecturer.

Other bests: decathlon 7363 points (current tables) (1974), long jump 7.31m (1967), 100y 9.8 (1967), shot 14.17m (1972).

Jane BULLEN

Equestrian events, Three-day Event
Jane Mary Elizabeth Bullen. b. 7 Jan 1948 Bridport, Dorset. Later Mrs Holderness-Roddam.

In 1968 Jane Bullen took leave of her nursing duties at the Middlesex Hospital to compete at the Olympic Games in Mexico City, the first woman to compete for Britain at the three-day event. She placed 18th individually and although she failed to score was a member of the gold-medal winning British team, thus becoming the first woman event rider to step onto an Olympic podium. Earlier that year she had ridden her *Our Nobby* to victory at Badminton. After her marriage she rode *Warrior* to victory at Burghley in 1976 and Badminton in 1978. She became a leading administrator of the sport.

Her brother **Michael** (b. 20 May 1937) competed at three-day event at the 1960 and 1964 Olympics, and her sister **Jenny**

Loriston-Clarke (b. 22 Jan 1943 Charmouth, Dorset) competed at four Olympic Games 1972-88 at dressage. She became the only British competitor ever to win a dressage World Championships medal with the individual bronze in 1978.

Ron BURGESS

Football
William Arthur Ronald Burgess. b. 9 Apr 1917 Cwm, Ebbw Vale, Blaenau Gwent.

As an attacking left-half, he was the best of his time and was rated alongside the great players of the past. Although winning 32 caps for Wales 1946-54 he will be best remembered for the part he played in Tottenham's successful 'push-and-run' era when they won the League Division Two championship in 1950 and took the First Division title the following year. Although he had been dropped from the Spurs first team in 1954, he won his final Welsh cap that year at the age of 36. He also played for Great Britain v Rest of Europe in 1948. From Tottenham he went to Swansea as player-coach and then to Watford and later Hendon as manager.

David BURGHLEY

Athletics
David George Brownlow Cecil, Lord Burghley. b. 9 Feb 1905 Burghley House, Cambridgeshire. d. 22 Oct 1981 Burghley House. Later Marquess of Exeter KCMG.

The Olympic champion at 400m hurdles in 1928, he had also competed at 110m hurdles in 1924 and went on to win a relay silver medal and place 4th at 400m hurdles in 1932 (in his best ever time of 52.01). At the first Empire Games, in 1930, he won gold medals at both 440y hurdles and 4 x 440y relay, and he won five AAA titles at 440y hurdles, 1926-8, 1930 and 1932 and three at 120y hurdles, 1929-31. He held British records at all hurdles events, with bests of 14.5 for 120y and 24.3 for 220y.

Just a year after his last Olympic appearance he became a member of the International Olympic Committee (at the age of 28) and in 1936 he was elected president of the AAA and chairman of the British Olympic

Association. In 1946 he became president of the IAAF and was Chairman of the organising committee of the 1948 Olympic Games. A graduate of Cambridge University, he was MP for Peterborough from 1931 to 1943, when he was appointed the Governor of Bermuda. He succeeded his father to become the 6th Marquess of Exeter in 1956.

Richard BURNELL

Rowing
Richard Desborough Burnell. b. 26 Jul 1917 Henley-on-Thames, Oxon. d. 29 Jan 1995 Wallingford, Oxon.

Burnell, with his father 'Don' (Charles Desborough Burnell OBE) (1876-1969), who rowed four times for Oxford 1895-8 and was a member of the legendary Leander 'Old Man's' eight that won the gold medal at the 1908 Olympics, became the only father and son to have won Olympic gold medals for rowing.
Richard, who had won his Blue at Oxford in 1939, returned to rowing after war service to win the Wingfield Sculls in 1946. In 1948 he teamed up with Bert Bushnell to win the double sculls at Henley and Olympic gold. He also won the Grand in the Leander eight in 1946 and 1950 and at his final appearance at Henley won the double sculls with Pat Bradley in 1951. He also took a bronze medal at eights in the 1950 Empire Games. He had been rowing correspondent for *The Times* from 1946 and after a few years in the Channel Islands was rowing correspondent of the *Sunday Times* until his retirement in 1990. He became president of Leander and from 1965 a Steward at Henley.
Richard married Rosalind Garton, whose father Stanley (1889-1960) rowed in the winning 1912 Olympic eight. Their eldest son, **Peter**, maintained the family tradition by winning his Blue at Oxford in 1962.

Beryl BURTON

Cycling
Beryl Burton. b. 12 May 1937 Leeds. née Charnock.

The greatest distaff rider ever produced in

Britain, Burton was chiefly renowned as a time trialist, though in the early 1960s few women could beat her at any discipline. In 1967 she covered 446.19 km in a 12-hour time trial, which was then 9.25 km beyond the British men's record, and in 1968 she rode 100 miles in 3hrs 55:05, only 12 years after the first British man had broken four hours for that distance.
At the world championships her medal collection was as follows: individual pursuit - 5 gold (1959-60, 1962-3, 1966), 3 silver, 3 bronze; road race - 2 gold (1960, 1967), 1 silver. She was the first woman to be allowed to compete at the highest level against men when she rode in the Grand Prix des Nations. World outdoor records ratified: 3km 4:16.6 and 4:14.9 in 1964, 20km 28:58.4 in 1960.
She collected an unprecedented number of British titles, 25 times all-round time trial champion 1959-83 and winner of 72 individual road TT titles, 14 track pursuit titles and 12 road race titles to 1986. She was awarded the MBE 1964 and the OBE 1968.
She married Charles Burton in 1955. Her daughter **Denise** (b. Jan 1956) competed with her at the 1972 World Championships, and was 3rd in the 1975 world pursuit.

Matt BUSBY

Football
(Sir) Matthew Busby. b. 26 May 1909 Orbiston, North Lanarkshire. d. 20 Jan 1994 Cheadle, Manchester.

One Scottish international cap in 1933 (plus seven wartime internationals 1942-5) and an FA Cup winners' medal for Manchester City in 1934 were the highlights of a relatively modest playing career but as a manager he was one of the world's greatest. He joined Manchester City from Deeny Hibernians in 1928 and his career blossomed when he switched from inside forward to right half. At this position he was noted for his attacking play. In 1936 he was transferred to Liverpool for £8000 and played for them until 1939 and during the war.
He served as manager of Manchester United 1945-69 and guided them to

unprecedented heights as he formed four great teams. They won the European Cup in 1968, the FA Cup in 1948 and 1963, and the Football League Championship five times, 1952, 1956-7, 1965, 1967. Many of these successes were achieved after eight team members had tragically lost their lives in the Munich air disaster in 1958. Busby himself felt that that team, known as 'The Busby Babes', could have dominated the sport for a decade.

Busby was close to death after the air crash but he survived to rebuild his team and after a Football League record 24 years as a manager he continued to serve the game for many years. Appointed to the Manchester United board in 1971 he became club president in 1982 and held high office in the Football League Management Committee. He was awarded the CBE in 1958 and knighted in 1968.

Don BUTCHER

Squash
Donald George Butcher. b. 1905
Kingston-upon-Thames, London.

Playing in an era when the major Championships were decided on a challenge basis he beat Charles Read for the British professional title in 1930 and after successful defences in 1930 and 1931 he lost to James Dear (qv) in 1935 and failed to recapture the title when he met Dear again the following year. He won the British Open title in 1930 and defended his crown successfully in 1931 but the Egyptian amateur, Amr Bey, defeated Butcher for the Open title in 1932 and resisted his spirited challenge to recapture the title in 1934.

Butcher, who was noted for his elegant stroke play, was the professional at the Conservative Club and he emigrated to Melbourne in 1957.

Terry BUTCHER

Football
Terry Ian Butcher. b. 28 Dec 1958
Singapore.

Butcher was a central defender noted for using his imposing physique to dominate

his territory. Signing for Ipswich in 1976, he spent ten seasons with the East Anglian club, winning a UEFA Cup winners' medal in 1981, before moving to Rangers in 1986. He proved an inspirational captain of Rangers, taking them to wins in the Scottish League Cup 1987-9 and League 1987 and 1989-90. His successful years in Scotland were followed by brief spells as player-manager at Coventry City 1990-2 and Sunderland 1992-3. He won 77 caps for England 1980-90.

Frank BUTLER

Horse Racing
Francis Butler. b. 1818. d. 1 Feb 1856
Newmarket.

The son of a Newmarket trainer and grandson of Samuel Chifney Snr (qv), Butler rode the winners of 14 Classics in England, mostly for John Scott (qv), for whom he was the stable jockey. He won the Oaks six times and the 2000 Guineas, 1000 Guineas, Derby and St Leger twice each from 1843 to the first ever Triple Crown on *West Australia* in 1853. That was his last year of riding due to increasing weight. He was a heavy drinker and died after a long illness three years later. He had been apprenticed to his uncle William Chifney and learned much from Samuel Chifney Jnr. His forté was always that of producing a late finishing effort.

Guy BUTLER

Athletics
Guy Montagu Butler. b. 25 Aug 1899
Harrow, London. d. 22 Feb 1981 St Neots,
Huntingdonshire.

With four Olympic medals Butler shares the British record for athletics with Sebastian Coe (qv). He won gold for 4 x 400m and silver for 400m in 1920 and bronze for each in 1924 (after a British record 48.0m in his 400m semi) and also competed in 1928. He won the AAA 440y title aged 19 in 1919 and his blue at Cambridge each year 1920-2, winning the 440y against Oxford in the last two years after tying in 1920 with the South African Bevil Rudd, who went on to beat him at the Olympics. Surprisingly Butler's further AAA success was restricted to the 220y in his best time of 21.9 a week after setting a world record of 30.6 for 300y in 1926. He was a schoolmaster and then an athletics journalist and was a pioneer of filming athletes in action.

Jeff BUTTERFIELD
Rugby Union
Jeffrey Butterfield. b. 9 Aug 1929 Heckmondwike, West Yorkshire.

Winning 28 caps in consecutive matches 1953-9, Butterfield was England's most capped centre until David Duckham (qv) surpassed his record. After leaving Cleckheaton GS he played for the local club, the Army and Loughborough Colleges before becoming a regular in the Northampton and Yorkshire teams. Although Butterfield only played alongside Phil Davies in the centre nine times for England, they formed an outstanding partnership on the Lions' tour of South Africa in 1955 and were rated as one of the greatest pairs of centres in history. He went on a second Lions tour to Australia and New Zealand in 1959 but a thigh injury, which ended his representative career, kept him out of the Test team.
As the proprietor of the Rugby Club in London he maintains close contact with the sport and has served as an England selector.

Frank BUTTERS
Horse Racing
Joseph Arthur Frank Butters. b. 1878 near Vienna, Austria. d. 1 Jan 1958 Northampton.

From 1926 to 1949 he trained 1019 winners in Britain and was leading trainer eight times, 1927-8, 1932, 1934-5, 1944, 1946 and 1949. His 15 Classics winners included *Bahram*, winner of the Triple Crown in 1935, and *Mahmoud*, the 1936 Derby winner.
His father Joseph went to Austria in 1873 to ride for Emperor Franz Josef and later trained in Austria and in Newmarket from 1903 to 1926. Frank also trained in Austria prior to internment in World War I. He

then ran a stable in Italy before coming to Britain in 1926 to train for Lord Derby at Stanley House, Newmarket. His contract with Lord Derby expired in 1930, when he took a lease on the Fitzroy House stables. He was forced to retire in 1949, after he suffered brain damage when he was knocked off his bicycle by a lorry.

Angela BUXTON
Tennis
Angela Buxton. b. 16 Aug 1934 Liverpool. Later Mrs D Silk.

After reaching the semi-finals of the doubles at the French and US Championships in 1955 she established herself as a world-class player the following year. A 1956 Wimbledon singles finalist and the doubles champion, with Althea Gibson (USA), at the French Championships and Wimbledon, she also won the British Covered Court singles and Hard Court doubles (with Darlene Hard (USA)). Shortly after her Wimbledon success, when ranked 6th in the world, a highly promising career was cut short when, at the age of 22, she was forced to give up the game due to weak wrists.
She played in three Wightman Cup matches 1954-6, but lost all seven rubbers (4 singles, 3 doubles). Although not a naturally gifted player, she was a fine tactician and played with great determination.

Chris CAHILL
Athletics
Christina Tracy Cahill. b. 25 Mar 1957 Northolt, London. née Boxer.

From winning the National junior cross-country title in 1971 (second in 1970), to the AAA Indoor 1500m in 1992, Chris Boxer (later Cahill) had a long and distinguished career. At the Commonwealth Games she won the 1500m title in 1982 and the silver medal in 1990, with 11th place in 1978 and 4th in 1986. In 1979 she became the first British woman to run 800m in under 2 minutes, with 1:59.05 and she first made the world top ten at 1500m in 1985. She also set UK and Commonwealth records at 1500m (4:00.57) and 1 mile

(4:22.64) in 1984, and an English 1000m record of 2:34.92 in 1985. In 1988 she was a magnificent 4th at 1500m at the Olympics, having placed 6th in 1984, when the Eastern European nations had boycotted the Games. She won the UK 800m 1979-80, 1984 and 1988, and 1500m 1986; also the WAAA 800m 1977-8, 1985, and 1500m 1982, 1988, 1990. Other best times: 400m 55.14 (1979), 2000m 5:33.85 (1984), 3000m 8:49.89 (1985).

In 1986 she married **Sean Cahill** (b. 4 Mar 1958), who was the AAA junior 1500m champion in 1977 and had a mile best of 3:56.95 in 1979.

Harry CAHILL

Hockey
Harry Alexander Cahill. b. 9 Jun 1930.

Cahill won 72 caps for Ireland over 20 years from his international debut in 1953. He was also capped 33 times for Great Britain, including the Olympic Games of 1960, 1964 and 1968. He played for Belfast YMCA, Coventry & North Warwick and Tamworth.

Phil CAIRA

Weightlifting
Philip Mario Caira. b. 24 Feb 1933 Dunfermline, Fife.

The winner of seven British light-heavyweight titles, 1952, 1954-9, Caira was the Commonwealth champion, representing Scotland, in 1958 and 1962. A newsagent, he competed at the Olympic Games in 1956 and 1960.

Jim and Finlay CALDER

Rugby Union
James Hamilton Calder and Finlay Calder. Twins b. 20 Aug 1957 Haddington.

From 1981-90 one of the Calder twins from Stewart Melville's FP, Edinburgh took the field for Scotland in 55 of their 59 international matches. Jim was the first into the international side, winning 27 caps (1981-5) a total which Finlay with 34 caps (1986-91) subsequently bettered.

Both played as flankers and both toured with the British Lions, the only twins ever to do so. Jim played in one Test in New Zealand in 1983 while Finlay proved an inspiring leader of the Lions in Australia in 1989 when the tourists came back to win the series after losing the first Test. He was awarded the OBE in 1990.

Both contributed to a Scottish Grand Slam: Jim (1984) and Finlay (1990) and when they toured Australia together with Scotland in 1982, a third brother, John, was also in the party and was equal top try scorer on the tour. In all four brothers were Scottish Schools internationals.

Johnny CALDWELL

Boxing
John Caldwell. b. 7 May 1938 Belfast.

After winning a bronze medal representing Ireland as a flyweight at the 1956 Olympic Games he turned professional in 1958 and won the British title in 1960 with a third round KO over Frankie Jones. This was his last fight as a flyweight and he later relinquished his title after moving up to the bantamweight division. In May 1961 he won the EBU version of the world bantamweight title by outpointing Alphonse Halimi and in October he again beat Halimi on points when the Algerian made a bid to regain his title. In an attempt to achieve recognition as the undisputed world champion Caldwell was stopped in ten rounds by Eder Jofre (Bra) in January 1962. Later in the year he lost to fellow-Irishman, Freddie Gilroy, in a challenge for the British and Commonwealth bantamweight title but in 1962 the southpaw, Caldwell, claimed both titles by defeating George Bowes before losing them to Alan Rudkin a year later. He retired in 1965 and three of his five defeats as a professional were as a result of cuts.

Career record 1958-65: 35 contests. Won 29 (1 KO), Drew 1, Lost 5.

Donald CAMPBELL

Motor Racing
Donald Malcolm Campbell. b. 23 Mar 1921 Horley, Surrey. d. 4 Jan 1967 Coniston Water, Cumbria.

An engineer by training, and also with quite a reputation as a playboy, he emulated his father Malcolm (qv) by breaking both land and water speed records; they were two of only three men to hold both records simultaneously. Donald set the land speed record with 403.14 mph *648.77 km/h* on Lake Eyre salt flats, Australia in 1964, and broke the water speed record seven times from 202.32 mph *325.60 km/h* on Ullswater Lake in a jet-propelled hydroplane on 23 Jul 1955 to 276.279 mph *444.615 km/h* on Lake Dumbleyung, Australia on 31 Dec 1964.

In his last, and fatal water speed record attempt in his turbo-jet engined *Bluebird* he achieved an unofficial speed of 328 mph *528 km/h* on Coniston Water in England before his boat was wrecked and he was killed. He was awarded the CBE.

Malcolm CAMPBELL

Motor Racing
(Sir) Malcolm Campbell. b. 11 Mar 1885 Chislehurst, London. d. 31 Dec 1948 Reigate, Surrey.

A pilot in World War I, he had started flying in 1909, raced motorcycles from 1906 and started motor racing in 1910. He called his cars *Bluebird* after a play by Maeterlinck he had seen in 1912. Following a successful racing career he turned to pursuing the world land speed record which he improved nine times, taking it from 235.21 km/h *146.16 mph* in 1924 to 484.6 km/h *301.13 mph* in 1935. He was the first man to exceed 150, 250 and 300 mph on land and was knighted in 1931.

In 1937 he wrested the world water speed record from the American Gar Wood with a speed of 208.4 km/h *129.5 mph* on Lake Maggiore, Italy. The following year he improved this record to 210.67 km/h *130.91 mph* on Lake Hallwil, Switzerland, and in 1939 made a third improvement to the record with a speed of 228.10 km/h *141.74 mph*. His son Donald (qv) also set both land and water speed records; they were two of only three men to hold both records simultaneously.

Ollie CAMPBELL

Rugby Union
Seamus Oliver Campbell. b. 3 Mar 1954 Dublin.

Scoring 217 points in 22 matches 1976-84, Campbell was Ireland's leading points scorer in international rugby until Michael Kiernan (qv) surpassed his total in 1988. He broke the Irish points scoring record of 14 points in an international with 19 (five penalties and two conversions) against Australia in 1979 and he scored 21 points to improve the record with one dropped goal and six penalties against Scotland in 1982. Although this record has since been beaten, his 52 points in the 1983 season remains an Irish record for a championship season.

Campbell won international honours as a fly-half and as centre and after touring Australia with Ireland in 1979, he went with the British Lions to South Africa in 1980 and New Zealand in 1983, playing in 7 internationals (20 points). He was the top scorer for the Lions on both tours. Educated at Belvedere College, he played for Old Belvedere and Leinster, and today holds a senior appointment in the textile industry.

Mike CAMPBELL-LAMERTON

Rugby Union
Michael John Campbell-Lamerton. b. 1 Aug 1933 Malta.

Overseas service as a regular Army officer delayed his entry into international rugby and he did not win the first of his 23 Scottish caps (1961-6) until he was 27 years old. Standing 1.94m *6 ft 4 ½in* and weighing almost 113kg *250 lbs* his physique served him well against the rugged opposition encountered on two tours with the British Lions. In South Africa in 1962 he played in all four Tests but his second tour, when he captained the Lions to Australia and New Zealand in 1966, proved a disappointment. After victory in both Tests against Australia, the Lions encountered one of the great All Blacks teams and lost the series 0-4.

Although proving a popular, diplomatic and inspiring captain Campbell-Lamerton felt that his form did not always justify his selection for the major matches and he stood down for two Tests.

He played for Halifax, London Scottish and the Army and is now the bursar of Balliol College, Oxford. His son, **Jeremy** (b. 21 Feb 1959 Gibraltar), played in the Scottish pack in the 1987 World Cup in New Zealand.

George CAMSELL

Football
George Henry Camsell. b. 27 Nov 1902 Framwellgate Moor, nr. Durham. d. 7 Mar 1966 Middlesbrough.

A former pit boy, he signed as a professional with Durham City in 1924 and transferred to Middlesbrough the following year. A high-scoring centre-forward his 59 goals in the 1926/7 season set a new League scoring record and helped Middlesbrough to the Second Division title. They were their relegated after just one season in the First Division but bounced straight back to win promotion again in 1929. In 444 League appearances for Durham City and Middlesbrough, he scored a total of 344 goals and was capped nine times by England between 1929 and 1936. After retiring as a player during World War II he remained at Middlesbrough in a variety of administrative capacities and Brian Clough (qv) was one of the many who benefitted from his coaching.

Morny CANNON

Horse Racing
Herbert Mornington Cannon. b. 21 May 1873 Stockbridge, Hampshire. d. 1 Jun 1962 Hove, East Sussex.

The son of Tom Cannon (qv), he was champion jockey in England 1891-2, 1894-7, with a peak of 182 winners in 1892. He won six Classics, including the Triple Crown on *Flying Fox* in 1899. He was a natural horseman and a great judge of pace, but he refused to adopt the crouching style when that was introduced at the turn of the century. His first winner came the day before his 14th birthday in 1887, and he was champion while still a teenager. He gave up riding in 1907.

Tom CANNON

Horse Racing
Thomas Cannon. b. 23 Apr 1846 Eton, Berkshire. d. 13 July 1917 Stockbridge, Hampshire.

Regarded as a graceful horseman and skilful jockey and renowned for his gentle handling of two-year-olds, especially fillies, and for being scrupulously honest, Tom Cannon rode 1544 winners in his career, including 13 Classics between 1866 and 1889. He rode his first winner in 1860 and he was champion jockey in 1872 with 87 winners. Having taken over the Danebury stables from his father-in-law, John Day, he trained *Busybody* to win the 1000 Guineas and Oaks in 1884.

Joseph Cannon (1849-1933), younger brother of Thomas, rode three Classics winners, as did his son **Noel** (1897-1959) and Mornington's brother **Kempton** (1879-1951). Lester Piggott was a great-grandson of Thomas Cannon, whose daughter Margaret married Ernest Piggott.

Geoff CAPES

Athletics, Shot
Geoffrey Lewis Capes. b. 21 Aug 1949 Holbeach, Lincolnshire.

Britain's greatest shot putter, he ranked as Britain's No. 1 from 1971 to 1980 and world No. 1 in 1975, and was unbeaten by a British putter from 1970. He could have remained there for a further decade but opted to be a professional strong man with great success at such competitions as television's World Strongest Man, which he won twice as well as three British strongest man titles, and he was six times World Highland Games champion.

Tall at 1.97m *6 ft 5 ½ in* and hugely powerful at around 135kg *21 stone* but very athletic, this former police officer set 17 British records at the shot, from 19.56m in 1972 to 21.68 in 1980, the most for any event as well as eleven indoor records and his major championships record included: 4th 1970, 1st 1974 and 1978 at the Commonwealth Games; 3rd 1974 Europeans; 1st

1974 and 1976, 2nd 1975, 1977 and 1979, 3rd 1978 at the European Indoors; 6th 1976 and 5th 1980 at the Olympic Games. In 1978 he was not allowed to contest the European final for allegedly manhandling an official. He was the European Cup Final winner in 1975, AAA champion outdoors 1972-3 and 1975-9 and indoors 1971-2, 1974-5 and 1977-8 and UK champion 1977-9. He had won AAA junior titles in 1966 and 1967. From 67 internationals 1969-80 he achieved a record 35 individual event wins.

He was also a fine discus thrower, with a best of 58.34m in 1973 with 5th place at the 1974 Commonwealth Games. Coached by Stuart Storey from 1964, he competed for Birchfield Harriers and the Borough of Enfield Harriers.

He bred budgerigars. His daughter Emma was WAAA intermediate shot champion in 1990 and son Lewis plays American Football for the London Monarchs.

Johnny CAREY (Ireland)

FOOTBALL
John Joseph Carey. b. 23 Feb 1919 Dublin.

A player of remarkable versatility, Carey won international honours in six different positions. Joining Manchester United as a 17-year-old in 1936 he remained at Old Trafford until 1953 and scored 17 goals in 306 appearances. He was a member of the team which defeated Blackpool 4-2 to win the FA Cup in 1948 and were League Champions in 1951/2.

As an international, he played 29 times for Ireland and 9 times for Northern Ireland (including 2 Victory Internationals). He captained the Rest of Europe against Great Britain at Hampden Park in 1947 and was Footballer of the Year in 1949. Initially an inside forward, he later moved to wing half and then to full back before becoming a wing half again; he occasionally played in other positions and was a competent substitute goalkeeper. Although lacking pace his intelligent distribution of the ball made him one of the outstanding full backs of his generation.

When he retired in 1953, he became manager of Blackburn Rovers and took them back into the First Division in 1958. He moved on to Everton, Leyton Orient and Nottingham Forest before returning to Blackburn in 1969. After Rovers dropped to the Third Division for the first time in their history in 1971, he was replaced.

Will CARLING

Rugby Union
William David Charles Carling. b. 12 Dec 1965 Bradford-on-Avon, Wiltshire.

Having made his England senior debut in 1988 Carling was appointed captain within the year, at the age of 22, and quickly established himself as England's most successful leader. A strong running centre, he played a major role in the successive Grand Slam victories in 1991-2 and again in 1995. He has been easily the most successful captain in international rugby, leading England to 37 wins in 48 games to the end of March 1995, but he was sacked in May 1995 for making derogatory remarks about RFU administrators, who he called 'old farts'. That ill-considered reaction by the RFU was soon shown to be unacceptable, as the whole England World Cup squad backed their captain, and two days later he was reinstated as captain, subject to certain conditions. The Cup matches, with England reaching the semi-finals, took his record to 40 wins in 53 games. Carling also holds the record as England's most capped centre (60), scoring 11 tries.

He was spoken of as a possible captain of the 1989 Lions tour to Australia but was unable to tour due to a leg injury and, although he was selected for the tour to New Zealand in 1993, Gavin Hastings was preferred as captain. Carling played in just the first of the three Tests on that tour.

After attending Sedbergh and Durham University (on an Army scholarship), Carling played for the Harlequins, but resigned his Army commission to devote more time to rugby. He was awarded the OBE in 1992. He now runs his own management training and personal development company.

Sandy CARMICHAEL

Rugby Union
Alexander Bennett Carmichael. b. 2 Feb 1944 Glasgow.

Carmichael was the first Scottish player to win 50 caps and the first prop, from any country, to achieve this total. He toured twice with the British Lions, to New Zealand in 1971 and to South Africa in 1974, but failed to win a place in the Test team. His first tour was cut short when he received such severe facial injuries in the match against Canterbury that he had to fly home. Educated at Loretto, he played for the West of Scotland and the Barbarians and his international career lasted from 1967 to 1978. He was awarded the MBE.

Denys CARNILL

Hockey
Denys John Carnill. b. 11 Mar 1926 Hampstead, London.

After winning a bronze medal at the 1952 Olympics, Carnill captained the GB team at the 1956 and 1960 Games and was the first British hockey player to take part in three Olympic Games. Unrivalled as a left-back, he won 45 caps for England and 27 for GB. After attending Hitchin GS he went up to Oxford and won his Blue 1949-51. He also played cricket for the University and Hertfordshire but failed to win a Blue at the second sport.

Arthur CARR

Cricket
Arthur William Carr. b. 21 May 1893 Mickleham, Surrey. d. 7 Feb 1963 West Witton, North Yorkshire.

A forthright captain of Nottinghamshire from 1919 to 1934, including taking them to the County Championship in 1929, he was a powerful batsman who did not achieve much success in his 11 Tests. Much the best of his 11 seasons over 1000 runs was 1925 when he scored 2338 runs at 51.95, and a year later he was appointed England captain for the series against Australia. After four draws he was replaced by Percy Chapman (qv) for the final Test, but he led England again in two Tests against South Africa in 1929. His vigorous support of Harold Larwood and Bill Voce (qqv) and 'bodyline' bowling tactics led to his dismissal as Notts captain in December 1934. Despite much popular support he did not play again for the county.
11 Tests 1922-9: 237 runs at 19.75, HS 63; 3 catches.
First-class 1910-35: 21,051 runs at 31.56, 45 100s HS 206; 31 wickets at 37.09, BB 3-14; 393 catches, 1 stumping.

Harry CARR

Horse Racing
William Henry Carr. b. 30 Nov 1916 Clifton, nr Penrith, Cumbria. d. 19 Oct 1985 Bury St Edmunds, Suffolk.

For 18 years stable jockey to Capt. Cecil Boyd-Rochfort (qv), Carr was appointed as jockey to King George VI in 1947, in which year he ride 81 winners, and he continued to ride for Queen Elizabeth II. His greatest success was surely that of riding *Meld* to the fillies' triple crown in 1955. To these Classics successes he added the Derby on *Parthia* in 1959 and two more St Legers.
He was apprenticed to Robert Armstrong, for whom his father was travelling head lad, and after riding his first winner in 1933 rode mostly in India before the War. He retired at the end of 1964 and then managed his stud near Newmarket.

Joe CARR (Ireland)

Golf
Joseph Boynton Carr. b. 18 Feb 1922 Dublin.

Carr played in a record ten Walker Cup ties 1947-67, missing only that of 1965, when he was non-playing captain. He had also been captain in 1963. He played in the Eisenhower Trophy, the World Amateur Team Championship, on the first two occasions it was held, 1958 and 1960, and for Ireland in the Home International series each year 1947-69.
A long hitter but a poor putter, he was the Amateur Champion in 1953, 1958 and

1960 and runner-up in 1968. In his third win in 1960 he beat Bob Cochran 8 & 7 in the final. He also won the Irish Amateur six times, 1954, 1957, 1963-5 and 1967, was a semi-finalist in the 1961 US Amateur Championship and was leading amateur in the Open in 1958 and 1963. He was captain of the Royal and Ancient 1991/2.

His sons Roderick and John have both played for Ireland and Roddy played in the Walker Cup in 1971.

Willie CARSON

Horse Racing
William Hunter Fisher Carson. b. 16 Nov 1942 Stirling.

On 22 May 1990, Carson became the fourth jockey to ride 3000 winners in Britain. He was the first Scot to be champion jockey, winning five times, in 1972-3, 1978, 1980 and 1983.

He started his career as an apprentice with Gerald Armstrong in Yorkshire in 1957, moving to Gerald's son Sam at Newmarket at the end of the 1962 season, soon after his first winning ride, at Catterick on 19 Jul 1962.

It was not until 1972, however, that he rode his first Classic winner, *High Top* in the 2000 Guineas, but by his win on *Erhaab* in the 1994 Derby (his 26th ride in the race) he had ridden 17 Classics winners in England: 4 each at Derby, Oaks and 2000 Guineas, 3 St Leger and 2 at 1000 Guineas. He had a career total of 3637 winners in Britain to the end of 1994, with more than 100 winners each year from 1971 to 1993, except for 1984, with successive peaks of 145 in 1971, 163 in 1973, 182 in 1978 and 187 in 1990. In 1990 he set a prize money record in Britain of £2,903,976.

He met with particular success from 1977 when he became first jockey to Major Dick Hern, and for him rode the Derby winners *Troy* in 1979 and *Henbit* in 1980. He considers *Nashwan*, his third Derby winner (1989), to have been the best horse that he has ever ridden.

A most determined rider, his cheerful personality and infectiously cackling laugh were brought to the widest audience when he regularly took part on the BBC's *Question of Sport*. He was awarded the OBE in 1983.

Raich CARTER

Football
Horatio Stratton Carter. b. 21 Dec 1913 Hendon, Sunderland. d. 9 Oct 1994 Willerby, nr Hull.

Capped six times before World War II and seven times afterwards, Carter's 13-year international career 1934-47 was the longest of any England inside-right.

After playing for England Schoolboys in 1927 and 1928, he signed as a professional for Sunderland in 1931 and captained the team which won the Football League in 1936 and the FA Cup in 1937. After appearing as a guest player for Derby County during World War II, he signed for them in December 1945 and won a second FA Cup winners' medal in 1946. In March 1948 he moved to Hull City, where as player-manager he took them to the Third Division (North) title in 1949. During a brief spell with Cork Athletic he won an FA of Ireland Cup winners' medal in 1953 at the age of 40. He moved on to manage Leeds and guided them into the First Division by 1956, and later managed Mansfield 1960-3 and Middlesbrough 1963-6.

He was probably at his best during the war years when he played between Stanley Matthews (right-wing) and Tommy Lawton (centre-forward) in the unofficial internationals; he played in 17 in all, scoring 18 goals. Undoubtedly, his finest peacetime performance came in the 1946 FA Cup Final when his brilliant understanding with Peter Doherty (qv) at inside-left led to a 4-1 victory for Derby. Quite a small man (1.70m, 64kg), but a powerful marksman with superb ball control and distribution as well as a fine turn of pace, he ranks as one of the greatest inside-forwards. He was also an accomplished cricketer and played three first-class matches for Derbyshire in 1946.

Joyce & Nancy CAVE

Squash
Joyce I Cave. b. 1909.

Nancy F Cave. b. 1903. Later Mrs N Evans.

The Cave sisters completely dominated the early years of competitive women's squash in Britain. From the first women's championship in 1922 up to 1932 one or both were finalists and each won the final three times, Joyce (1922, 1924, 1928) and Nancy (1923, 1929-30). Nancy was runner-up six times and Joyce twice. They met three times in the final with Joyce winning twice. Both sisters had passed their peak by the time the Wolfe-Noel Cup was introduced but Nancy played in the first match against the USA in 1933. The following year she became the first chairman of the Women's SRA.

The advantage of having a private court at their home was confirmed by the fact that a third sister was a semi-finalist (losing to Nancy) at the first championships in 1922.

Madge CAVE - see SYERS

Victor CAZELET

Squash
Victor Alexander Cazelet. b. 27 Dec 1897 London. d. 4 Jul 1943 Gibraltar.

After schooling at Eton, Cazelet won an MC serving with the Life Guards before going up to Oxford where he won Blues for real tennis, lawn tennis and rackets. He also represented the University at squash and ultimately this was to prove his best game. He reached the final of the Amateur Championship for six consecutive years 1925-30, winning the title four times, 1925, 1927, 1929-30. He also won the Canadian Amateur in 1926.

Elected Conservative MP for Chippenham in 1924, he served as liason officer between the British Government and General Sikorski, the Prime Minister of Poland and Commander-in-Chief of the Free Polish forces, during World War II. Both Cazelet and Sikorski were killed when their plane crashed shortly after taking off from Gibraltar.

Henry CECIL

Horse Racing
Henry Richard Amherst Cecil. b. 11 Jan 1943 near Aberdeen.

Cecil was the leading trainer in Britain ten times between 1976 and 1993; in 1985 he was the first to achieve season's winnings of over £1 million and in 1987 broke a record which had stood for 120 years with a total of 180 winners (from 446 starts) and record first-prize money of £1,896,689. He had over 100 winners 13 times between 1978 and 1992, with previous best totals of 109 in 1978, 128 in 1979 and 132 in 1985.

After attending agricultural college and working in Europe and the USA, he was assistant trainer to his step-father Sir Cecil Boyd-Rochfort (qv) 1964-8, before starting training at Freemason Lodge, Newmarket in 1969. In 1976 he moved to Warren Place, previously used by his father-in-law Noel Murless (qv). His first Classics winner was *Bolkonski* in the 1975 2000 Guineas and his first Derby winner *Slip Anchor* in 1985, in which year he won four of the five Classics, as *Oh So Sharp* took the fillies' triple crown.

Sue CHALLIS – see SHOTTON

Craig CHALMERS

Rugby Union
Craig Minto Chalmers. b. 15 Oct 1968 Galashiels, Borders.

With 46 international caps to the end of the 1995 World Cup, Chalmers has passed John Rutherford's record for a Scottish fly-half. In those games he has scored 126 points (4 tries, 8 dropped goals, 7 conversions, 24 penalties). But for a loss of form in the 1993/4 season, when he was dropped after the match against Wales, he would be futher ahead. He played for Scottish Schools, under-18, under-19 and under-21 before his first senior cap for Scotland in 1989. He scored a try and dropped goal on his debut, and toured Australia with the British Lions that summer, playing in the first Test before being replaced by Rob Andrew (qv) for the remainder of the series. Generally expected to be the first choice at fly-half for the 1993 Lions tour to New Zealand he was put out of contention by a double break of his right arm in the match against England. A fine all round player, he has scored many points for his club, Melrose, and for Scotland through his talent as a drop goal specialist.

Jo CHAMBERLAIN

Cricket
Joanne Chamberlain. b. 1969. Now Mrs Jordan.

Chamberlain will long be remembered for her match-winning performance when England won the World Cup in 1993. She scored 38 runs from 33 deliveries and then ran out New Zealand's leading batsman, Debbie Hockley, with a direct hit from extra cover; she also took a wicket with her left-arm quick bowling. She first played for Engand in 1984 at the age of 18, and established a 7th wicket partnership record of 110 with Karen Smithies against Australia at Hove.
6 Tests 1984-92: 113 runs at 16.14, HS 59; 20 wickets at 22.90.
34 One-day Ints 1987-93: 401 runs at 23.58; HS 47*; 42 wickets at 15.95, BB 7-8; 15 catches.

John CHAMBERS

Administration
John Graham Chambers. b. 12 Feb 1841 Llanelli, Carmarthenshire. d. 4 Mar 1883 Earl's Court, London.

After rowing for Cambridge in the Boat race 1862-3, Chambers won the 7 mile walk at the AAC Championships in 1866, but his influence as an administrator far exceeded any mark he made as a competitor. He was educated in France before Eton and Cambridge, and there was scarcely any sport in Britain which did not benefit from his influence. He founded the Inter-Varsity Sports, staged the FA Cup final in 1873, and instituted amatcur championships in billiards, boxing, cycling and wrestling. He devised the Queensberry rules for boxing and re-wrote the rules for billiards, yet still found time to edit a

national newspaper, coach the Cambridge crew to four successive Boat Race wins, and row beside Captain Webb (qv) when he swam the Channel. He also managed the Lillie Bridge sports ground.
This almost unbelievable frenzy of activity came partly as a result of having to earn his living after his father, a wealthy Welsh landowner, made some unwise investments. Whatever the motive, the contribution of Chambers to British sport was immense. Sadly the prodigious workload took its toll and he died at the early age of 42.

Mrs Lambert CHAMBERS – see
DOUGLASS

Bob CHAMPION

Horse Racing
Robert Champion. b. 4 Jun 1948 North Yorkshire.

The story of Bob Champion's Grand National victory on *Aldaniti* in 1981 two years after cancer had been diagnosed and he had undergone harrowing chemotherapy treatment delighted and inspired the nation. His life was immortalised in the film *Champions*, in which he was played by John Hurt.
Champion had joined Toby Balding's stable in 1967 and won on his first ride as a pro in 1968. In 1973 he moved to ride for Josh Gifford (qv) and had his best year in 1977/8 with 56 winners. He is now a trainer at Newmarket. He was awarded the MBE.

Mick CHANNON

Football
Michael Roger Channon. b. 28 Nov 1948 Orcheston, Wiltshire.

A forceful attacking player and a powerful striker, Channon scored a record 182 goals in 511 appearances during two separate spells with Southampton. He first signed for the Hampshire club in 1965, winning an FA Cup winners' medal in 1976 before moving to Manchester City the following year. After three seasons with City he returned to Southampton but in 1982 he moved to Newcastle United and then Bristol Rovers before signing for Norwich City, his third club in one season. He played for Norwich when they won the League Cup in 1985 and then finished his career with Portsmouth 1985-6. He was capped 46 times by England 1972-7, scoring 21 international goals.

From 1990 he has been a racehorse trainer, with 65 horses in his care in 1995. He is also the owner of a chain of shops, and has been called on to give his expert opinions on television football broadcasts.

Herbert CHAPMAN

Football
Herbert Chapman. b. 19 Jan 1878 Kiveton Park, Sheffield. d. 6 Jan 1934 Hendon, London.

Chapman was a man who raised the profession of football manager to new heights. He created teams at both Huddersfield Town and Arsenal that won three consecutive English League titles.

Having trained as a mining engineer, he signed as a professional footballer for Northampton in 1901, moving to Notts County in 1903 and Tottenham Hotspur 1905, before returning to Northampton as player-manager in 1907. He took over as secretary-manager of Leeds City in 1912. His glory days started when he took over at Huddersfield in 1921, leading them to win the FA Cup in 1922 and to start their run of League titles 1924-6. In 1925 he moved to Arsenal, and under his managership, until his death in office in 1934, they were the leading team in the country. An authoritative figure,Chapman was also a great innovator, tactically and technically.

Percy CHAPMAN

Cricket
Arthur Percy Frank Chapman. b. 3 Sep 1900 Reading, Berkshire. d. 16 Sep 1961 Alton Hospital, Hampshire.

In 1926 the debonair Chapman was appointed to the England captaincy for the 5th Test at The Oval; England won and the Ashes were regained. He led England to three innings victories over the West Indies

in 1928 and to wins in all four Tests that he played against Australia in 1928/9. A win in the first Test against Australia in 1930 meant that he had won his first nine Tests as captain and the hard-hitting left-handed middle-order batsman and brilliant fielder, especially in the gully, became a public hero. However after two draws and a loss and although he had made his one Test century in the 2nd Test, he lost his place as his batting was thought to be too unpredictable, and Bob Wyatt (qv) took over as captain for the final Test of that series. He led the England team against South Africa in 1930/1, but had no success and that was the end of his Test career.

He had scored prolifically at Uppingham School and made a century on his first-class debut for Oxford University in 1920 with a century also in the University match of 1922. He made his Test debut in 1924, although his county cricket to that point had been with the minor county of Berkshire, before joining Kent, whom he captained irregularly from 1931 to 1936.

His most remarkable feat of scoring was his innings of 260 in just over three hours for Kent against Lancashire at Maidstone in 1927. Coming together with the score 70-5 he put on 284 runs in 2 $\frac{1}{2}$ hours with Geoffrey Legge. In this, his best season, he scored 1387 runs at 66.04.

26 Tests 1924-31: 925 runs at 28.90, 1 100 HS 121; 32 catches.
First-class 1920-38: 16,309 runs at 31.97, 27 100s HS 260; 22 wickets at 41.86, BB 5-40; 356 catches.

Vera CHAPMAN

Hockey
Vera Chapman. b. 1930 Kingston-upon-Thames, London.

An outstanding forward, Chapman scored 71 goals in 66 internationals for England. Making her debut against Wales in 1948 she was, apart from a spell in the reserves in 1950-1, a regular choice for England until her retirement in 1961, when she was captain. She toured with the England team to South Africa 1954, Australia 1956, Germany 1958 and Netherlands 1959.

From Tiffin Girls' School she went to a PE

College in Liverpool and became a teacher although she had to resign, at least once, in order to go on an England tour. On retiring from international hockey she studied as a missionary and in 1962 went to Pakistan to teach in a Church Missionary Society School. Her sister, **Beryl**, played in goal for England on 18 occasions 1951-3 and 1962.

John CHARLES

Football
William John Charles. b. 27 Dec 1931 Cwmdu, nr Swansea. *21/2/04*

Winning the first of his 38 caps in 1950 shortly after his 18th birthday he was then the youngest ever Welsh international. During his years in Italy he was not always available for international selection, otherwise he would have been capped far more often as his international career continued until 1964. Having played three games for Swansea Town 'A' team, he was signed as an amateur by Leeds United when only 15, making his League debut at 17. He initially played at centre-half but in 1951 made a successful switch to centre-forward. He scored 42 League goals in 1953/4 and his goalscoring abilities were a major factor in Leeds' promotion to the First Division in 1956 and the following season, after he had topped the First Division scorers with 38 goals, he was transferred to Juventus for a British record transfer fee of £65,000. He helped Juventus win the Italian Cup twice and the League three times and for them scored 93 goals in 155 appearances. In August 1962 Charles returned to Leeds, but after playing in 11 matches he joined Roma. His return to Italy was equally brief as after only 10 games he signed for Cardiff City and then after a further 8 games he retired from first-class football and became player-manager of Hereford United and later Merthyr Town.

Blessed with a magnificent physique, he scored many goals with his head but he also had a fierce shot and was an excellent distributor of the ball. During his five years in Italian football he never lost his reputation for fine sportsmanship and was known to the fans as the 'Gentle Giant'.

His brother **Mel** (b. 14 May 1935 Swansea) played 31 internationals for Wales 1955-62, with six goals, including a Welsh record four against Ireland in 1962.

Bobby CHARLTON

Football
Robert Charlton. b. 11 Oct 1937 Ashington, Northumberland.

After signing for Manchester United as an amateur in 1953 he turned professional the following year and remained with the club for virtually his entire playing career. The eight-year contract he signed with United in 1968 is the longest in League history. His total of 106 caps (1958-70) stood as an England record until beaten by Bobby Moore (qv) in 1973. He played in every forward position except outside-right, and his total of 49 goals remains an England record. A survivor of the Munich air disaster he played with his elder brother, Jack (qv), in England's 1966 winning World Cup team and was voted Footballer of the Year for both Europe and England that year. He was awarded the OBE in 1969, the CBE in 1974 and was knighted in 1994.

At club level he scored 198 goals in 606 League appearances for Manchester United and helped them win the European Cup 1968, the FA Cup 1963 and the Football League 1957, 1965 and 1967. After retiring in 1973 he became manager of Preston North End and played for them in 1974/5 (8 goals in 38 League games). He later served briefly as a director of Wigan Athletic and in 1984 was appointed a director of Manchester United. He now runs a football coaching school.

His powerful, accurate shooting, particularly from long range, was the hallmark of his game but his fine all-round skills made him one of the most admired players of his generation.

Jack CHARLTON

Football
John Charlton. b. 8 May 1935 Ashington, Northumberland.

Although he signed professional forms for

Leeds United in 1952, he did not win his first England cap until 1965 when he was almost 30. He remained with Leeds throughout his career, scoring 95 goals in 772 games for them. He won the last of his 35 England caps in 1970 and retired three years later. At centre-half he was a stalwart of England's World Cup winning side in 1966 and helped Leeds to a host of honours: League Division Two 1964, Division One 1969, League Cup 1968, FA Cup 1972 and the Inter-Cities Fairs Cup 1968 and 1971. In 1967 he was voted Footballer of the Year.

Between 1973 and 1985 he served as manager of Middlesbrough (twice), Sheffield Wednesday, and Newcastle United. In February 1986 he took over as manager of Ireland, steering them to their best ever success in international competition. After his team reached the quarter-finals of the 1994 World Cup he became one of only six people ever to be awarded honorary Irish citizenship. He has also hosted a popular TV programme on angling. He was awarded the OBE in 1974.

Dave CHARNLEY

Boxing
David F Charnley. b. 10 Oct 1935
Dartford, Kent.

During a notable amateur career he was the 1954 ABA featherweight champion, beating Dick McTaggart (qv) inside a round in the final, and a bronze medallist at the Commonwealth Games that year. As a professional, he fought as a lightweight winning the British (1957), Empire (1959) and European (1960) titles. He made unsuccessful attempts in 1959 and 1961 to take the world title from Joe Brown (USA), but in 1963 beat Brown when he was no longer champion. Charnley, who was a southpaw, lost his Empire title in 1962, forfeited his European crown the following year, but retired as the undefeated British champion in 1965. He became a wealthy property dealer.
Career record 1954-65: 61 contests. Won 48 (30 KO), Drew 1, Lost 12.

Chris CHATAWAY

Athletics
(Rt Hon. Sir) Christopher John Chataway.
b. 31 Jan 1931 Chelsea, London.

The 'Red Fox' was a charismatic athlete who went on to distinguished careers in several fields. He was a friend and Oxford colleague of Roger Bannister (qv), whom he helped to the first sub-four minute mile in 1954. Two months later he was 2nd in the AAA 3 miles, sharing the world record with winner Fred Green, before going on to beat Green to win the Empire Games 3 miles. He took the silver medal behind Vladimir Kuts (USSR) in the European 5000m, running 14:08.8 to the world record of 13:56.6 by Kuts. In an epic race under the floodlights of the White City in October 1954, both men smashed that record as Chataway gained his revenge and just won 13:51.6 to 13:51.7. Fittingly he ended that year by being voted the first BBC Sports Personality of the Year.

In Olympic 5000m finals Chataway led for much of the last lap in 1952 but fell after being passed by Emil Zátopek (Cs) and staggered home in 5th place; he was 11th in 1956. He was AAA 3 miles champion in 1952 and 1955, when he ran a world record 13:23.2. He set British records also at 2000m 5:09.4 (1955), 3000m 8:06.2 (1954) and 2 miles 8:41.0 (1954) and had other best times: 1500m 3:43.6 (1955), 1 mile 3:59.8 (1955).

On 25 Sep 1955 he became the first newscaster on Independent Television and he was a Conservative MP 1959-66 and 1969-74, with ministerial positions from 1970-4 before retiring from politics to further a business career. He was managing director of Orion Bank 1974-88 and since then has been chairman of the Civil Aviation Authority. he was knighted in 1995 for his services to the aviation industry.

Leslie CHEAPE

Polo
Leslie St Clair Cheape. b. 5 Oct 1882
Scotland. d. 23 Apr 1916 Egypt.

England's top polo player, he was an Army captain when he played for England in the

Westchester Cup against the USA in 1911 and 1913 and when he led them to victory in 1914. He was killed in action against the Turks in 1916.

Susan CHEESEBOROUGH

Gymnastics
Susan Cheeseborough. b. 9 Sep 1959.

Having competed for Britain at the 1976 Olympic Games, Cheeseborough succeeded Avril Lennox (qv) as British champion in 1978, in which year she led the English team to team silver at the Commonwealth Games. Then, at the World Championships she became only the third British woman to earn the International Gymnastics Federation award.

Her father, **Albert** (b. 17 Jan 1935), played soccer for Burnley, Leicester, Port Vale and Mansfield Town over a professional career from 1951 to 1966 and was an England Under-23 international.

Frank CHESTER

Cricket
Frank Chester. b. 20 Jan 1895 Bushey, Herts. d. 8 Apr 1957 Bushey.

Described by Don Bradman as the 'greatest umpire under who I played', Chester raised umpiring to a new peak of excellence. He pioneered the habit of bending low over the wicket when the bowler delivered the ball.

He was a highly promising cricketer who scored 1773 runs at 23.95, with four 100s, highest 178*, and took 81 wickets at 31.61 as a teenager for Worcestershire 1912-14. At 17 he had been the youngest century maker in English first-class cricket. However he lost his right arm at Salonika on Army service in World War I, so took up umpiring and was appointed to the first-class list in 1922.

When he retired in 1955 he had stood in over 1000 first-class matches, including 48 Tests 1924-55, for many years the umpiring record.

Sam CHIFNEY

Horse Racing
Samuel Chifney. b. 1753 Norfolk. d. 8 Jan 1807 Fleet Prison, London, to which he had been committed for debt.

He brought new skills and tactics to jockeyship, often saving his horses for a late swoop. Apprenticed in 1770 to Foxe's stable in Newmarket, he was the first jockey to win the Derby and Oaks double in the same year, 1789, and rode three more Oaks winners. After being employed to ride the Prince of Wales's horses he was involved in scandal in 1791 when *Escape* finished last in a race at Newmarket at 2-1 on. The Prince retired from the Turf and Chifney was strongly suspected of pulling the horse. A dandy, his lack of modesty was shown by his biography entitled *Genius Genuine*.

His eldest son **William** (1784-14 Oct 1862) trained five Classics winners, and, profiting from many betting coups, bought Warren House at Newmarket. Later he had to sell it to pay his debts. Another son **Samuel** Jnr (1786-1854) was also a talented jockey, and rode the winners of nine Classics between 1807 and 1843.

Joe CHILDS

Horse Racing
Joseph Childs. b. 1884 Chantilly, France. d. 5 Feb 1958 Emsworth, Hampshire.

Having had his first winner in 1900, he rode 59 winners in 1901 when apprenticed to Thomas Jennings Jnr. He rode in France for a while, with 75 winners there in 1908 and 90 in 1909, and it was not until 1912 that he had his first Classics success in England, on *Mirska* in the Oaks. From then until 1933 he rode 15 Classics winners in all: 4 each of the Oaks and St Leger, 3 of the Derby and 2 each of both 1000 and 2000 Guineas, and was first jockey for King George V 1925-35. Tall for a jockey and strong-willed, he usually played a waiting game. On retirement he took an interest in a greyhound racing stadium in Portsmouth and ran a small stud at Nazeing, Essex.

His father rode in France and he had four

brothers who were also jockeys Albert, Arthur, Charles and Henry, with Charles riding the winner of a wartime St Leger in 1916.

Martin CHIVERS

Football
Martin Harcourt Chivers. b. 27 Apr 1945 Southampton.

A centre-forward of imposing physique with a fine scoring record, Chivers was signed by Southampton in 1962 from a local amateur club and scored 97 League goals before moving to Tottenham in 1968 for a then record £125,000. He enjoyed his best years at Spurs, scoring 118 goals in 278 League games and helping the club to victories in the Football League Cup (1971, 1973) and the UEFA Cup (1972). Capped 17 times by England at Under-23 level, he later won 24 full England caps 1971-3, scoring 13 goals. From Tottenham he went to Servette (Geneva) in 1976 after which he was briefly associated with Norwich, Brighton & Hove Albion, Dorchester and Barnet. He is now a licencee.

Linford CHRISTIE

Athletics
Linford Christie. b. 2 Apr 1960 St. Andrews, Jamaica.

A late starter as a sprinter, Christie narrowly missed Olympic selection in 1984, but thereafter worked hard to reach the peak of sprinting excellence in his 30s. In 1988 he had a triumphant Olympic Games with four UK records, winning silver medals at 100m in 9.97 and at sprint relay, and at 200m in 20.09. In 1992 he won the Olympic gold medal at 100m in 9.96 to become by four years the oldest ever winner at this event. A year later he sealed his position as an all-time great by winning the World title in a time of 9.87, just 0.01 off the world record.

Christie, coached throughout his career by Ron Roddan at Thames Valley Harriers, burst through to international prominence in 1986 with gold medals in the European Indoor 200m and outdoor 100m (bronze at

sprint relay), and silver in the Commonwealth 100m. In 1987 he was originally 4th in the World 100m, but was awarded the bronze medal when Ben Johnson (Can) was disqualified. He was European champion at 100m again in 1990, when he added a relay silver and 200m bronze and won Commonwealth gold at both 100m and relay. Indoors he was European champion at 60m in 1988 and 1990, when he ran a European record time of 6.51, and in 1991 he won World Indoor silver medals at both 60m and 200m. In 1994 he retained both European and Commonwealth 100m titles and in 1995 set his first world record, indoors at 200m (20.25) and improved his European indoor 60m record to 6.47.

Linford Christie - season's bests		
Year	100m	200m
1977	10.9	23.2
1978		22.5
1979	10.7/10.6w	21.89/21.8
1980	10.73/10.6/10.5w	22.0/21.4w
1981	10.85/10.7	21.6/21.70i
1982	10.50	21.38/21.2
1983	10.46/10.4	21.71i/21.31w
1984	10.44/10.31	21.0/21.44
1985	10.42/10.20w	21.37i
1986	10.04	20.51
1987	10.03	20.48
1988	9.97	20.09
1989	10.10/10.08w	20.51
1990	10.02/9.93w	20.33
1991	9.92/9.90w	20.43
1992	9.96	20.25
1993	9.87	20.39/20.19w
1994	9.91	20.67/20.56i.

His 23 major championships medals (ten gold) is a British male record as is his 25 national titles, and he also won the World Cup 100m in 1989, 1992 and 1994. With a triple in 1994 and 1995, and Cup records at both 100m and 200m in 1995, he has won a record nine individual (unbeaten) and four relay races in the European Cup 1987-95. He was awarded the MBE in 1990, and was Sports Writers Association British Sportsman of the Year 1992 and 1993. His home track, the West London Stadium, was renamed in his honour in October 1993.

Douglas CLARK

Rugby League
Douglas Clark. b. 2 May 1891
Ellenborough, Cumbria. d. 1 Feb 1951
Birkby, Huddersfield, West Yorkshire.

A loose forward of immense strength, Clark was also well known as a wrestler. He first played for the amateur club Brookland Rovers before signing for Huddersfield in 1909. During the 1914 tour of Australia he was one of the heroes of the famous 'Rorke's Drift Test' when Great Britain, although reduced to only ten men, held on to win 14-6 and clinch the series. For most of the match Clark played with a broken thumb and collar bone. Severely gassed during the war, he was discharged with a 95% disability but made a second tour of Australasia in 1920. Nine of his 11 Great Britain caps came during the 1914 and 1920 tours of Australia and New Zealand. He played in three winning Challenge Cup and five Championship final teams.

Gillian CLARK

Badminton
Gillian Margaret Clark. b. 2 Sep 1961
Baghdad, Iraq.

Clark won a record 12 Commonwealth medals at badminton, including six golds: team 1982, 1986, 1990, 1994; women's doubles 1986, mixed doubles 1994; three silver: women's doubles 1982, 1990 and 1994; three bronze: singles 1982 and 1986, mixed doubles 1990.
Championship honours in her long career started with three All-England Under-18 titles 1978-9 and the European junior doubles in 1979. Having made her senior England debut in 1981, she won two World Championship bronzes: women's doubles 1983 and mixed doubles 1993, and four European titles: women's doubles 1982, 1984 and 1986 and mixed doubles 1988 (with a silver and two bronze medals). At the 1992 Olympics she was a quarter-finalist at women's doubles with Julie Bradbury. She won nine English National doubles titles: women's 1987-90, and 1992-3 and mixed 1983, 1990 and

1993, before retiring with a record 145 England international appearances, 1980-94. She chairs the International Badminton Players' Federation.

Jim CLARK

Motor Racing
James Clark. b. 14 Mar 1936 Kilmany, Fife. d. 7 Apr 1968 Hockenheim, Germany.

World drivers' champion in 1963 and 1965, he beat Juan-Manuel Fangio's record with 25 Grand Prix wins in his career, including a record seven wins in a year in 1963. He totalled 274 points from his 72 races 1960-8.
The son of a Scottish sheep farmer, he began racing in 1956, when he had several class wins in a Sunbeam. He progressed rapidly, with 12 wins in 20 starts in a D-type Jaguar in 1958 and great success in Lotus Elite and Jaguar cars in 1959, before making his move into single-seater racing. He made his World Championship debut in 1960 for Lotus, for whom he drove for the rest of his career. His first win was at Pau in 1961 and in addition to his two world titles, he was 2nd in 1962 and 3rd in 1964 and 1967.
He competed in many types of racing, winning the Indianapolis 500 in 1965, having shaken the Americans by taking 2nd place in a rear-engined Lotus-Ford there in 1963. He was killed at Hockenheim when his Formula Two Lotus left the track and hit a tree in the opening round of the European F2 Championship.
A great, natural driver, he was highly consistent, always seeming in total control of his car, bringing an unprecedented level of technical perfection to driving.

Roger CLARK

Rallying
Roger Clark. b. 5 Aug 1939.

For a decade Clark dominated British rallying, and was twice the winner of the RAC Rally - in 1972 and 1976 as well as winning four British championships. His 1972 RAC win with Tony Mason was the first British victory at the event since 1959. He made his name driving his own Mini-

Cooper before signing for Ford in 1966. He won the Tulip and Acropolis rallies in 1968 but did not often make the Ford A team for World Championship races, although he had many successes in Britain. A fast, but very safe driver, he had been a talented all-round sportsman, including swimming for his county. He retired from the world rallying championship 1980, and since then has concentrated on historic rallies, but he returned to drive in the Vauxhall Rally of Wales 1995 with his son Matthew, both in Subaru cars.

William CLARKE

Cricket
William Clarke. b. 24 Dec 1798 Nottingham. d. 25 August 1856 Wandsworth, London.

In 1846 Clarke founded the All England XI, a team of many of the finest cricketers in England who travelled the country playing against local sides. The side broke up in 1852 as some of the players thought that Clarke kept too much of the profit to himself and the dissidents started a rival team – the United All-England XI. The two teams continued to tour, but the quality of each was obviously not as great as the original. The teams met in a great match at Lord's in 1856 and this fixture was maintained until 1869. From this era, the pioneering work of taking cricket around the country done, the structure of county cricket that we know today began to emerge.
In 1837 Clarke had married the widow who kept the Trent Bridge Inn at Nottingham and with her developed the ground.
First-class 1826-55: 2133 runs at 10.35, HS 75; 795 wickets, BB 9-29; 55 catches.

Ronnie CLAYTON

Boxing
Ronald Clayton. b. 9 Feb 1923 Blackpool, Lancashire.

Clayton was one of only six men to win two Lonsdale Belts outright. After turning professional in 1941 he won the Empire and European featherweight title in 1947 by outpointing Al Phillips in a contest which was also for the vacant British title. He lost his European title to Ray Famechon (Fra) in 1948, his Empire title to Roy Ankrah (Gold Coast) in 1951 and, finally, his British title to Sammy McCarthy in 1954 when he was forced to retire at the end of the eighth round. After this bout, Clayton retired because of persistent eye trouble. His sparkling style and sportsmanlike behaviour made him one of the most popular fighters of his time
Career record 1941-54: 113 contests. Won 79 (47 KO), Drew 8, Lost 26.

Ray CLEMENCE

Football
Raymond Neal Clemence. b. 5 Aug 1948 Skegness, Lincs.

Although a contemporary of England's most capped goalkeeper, Peter Shilton (qv), Clemence still won 61 caps 1972-83.
After starting as an amateur with Notts County, he signed as a professional with Scunthorpe before moving to Liverpool in 1967. Although he did not make his League debut for the Merseyside club until almost three years later, he went on to win a host of honours as part of Liverpool's highly organised defence. He won three European Cup winners' medals and two UEFA Cup winners' medals and, with Clemence in goal, Liverpool won the League championship five times and the FA Cup and the Football League Cup once each.
In 1981 he was transferred to Tottenham and in 1982 he won a second FA Cup winners' medal. On 7 Sep 1985 he became the second British footballer (after fellow-goalkeeper Pat Jennings) to make 1000 senior appearances, was awarded the MBE in 1987 soon after passing Jennings' record of 1098 matches, and retired in 1988 with a total of 1119, including 665 for Liverpool, 337 for Tottenham and 50 for Scunthorpe. He took on coaching duties at Tottenham and is now general manager of Barnet. He also works regularly on TV.

Brian CLOSE

Cricket
Dennis Brian Close. b. 24 Feb 1931
Rawdon, Leeds.

Against New Zealand in 1949 Close became the youngest ever England Test cricketer at 18 years 149 days and in that season the youngest ever to achieve the double of 1000 runs and 100 wickets. He never quite fulfilled his youthful promise as an off-spin bowler and hard-hitting left-handed batsman, but was turned to on many occasions by England, especially when someone with his great fortitude was needed to stand up to fast bowlers. He was also an outstandingly brave close-to-the-wicket fielder.

His Test career was full of gaps, but he was a popular hero when he came into a demoralised team to lead them to victory in the final Test against the West Indies in 1966. That was the first of six wins in his seven matches as captain, as he continued most successfully against India and Pakistan in 1967. He was then dropped after using time-wasting tactics in a county match for Yorkshire, whom he led very successfully from 1963-70 in which time they won four Championships. After falling out with his native county, he went to Somerset, whom he captained 1972-7. In 1972 he captained England again, in the three one-day internationals against Australia as Ray Illingworth (qv) was injured, and in 1976 he was recalled, at the age of 45, to the England team to take on the West Indies pace bowlers; he battled on to score 166 runs averaging 33.20 in three matches.

The title of his autobiography *I Don't Bruise Easily* admirably summed up his qualities. He played a few games of League football for Arsenal and Bradford City in 1952. He was awarded the CBE.

22 Tests 1949-76: 887 runs at 25.34, HS 70; 18 wickets at 29.55, BB 4-35; 24 catches.
3 One-day Ints 1972: 49 runs at 16.33, HS 43; 1 catch.
First-class 1949-86: 34,994 runs at 33.26, 52 100s HS 198; 1171 wickets at 26.42, BB 8-41; 813 catches, 1 stumping.

Brian CLOUGH

Football
Brian Howard Clough. b. 21 Mar 1935
Middlesbrough.

Clough only played twice for England (in 1959), but before his playing career was ended by serious injury at the age of 29 he had established the highest ever goals per game average in the Football League. He totalled 251 goals in 274 games as a centre-forward; 197 for Middlesbrough 1955-61 and 54 for Sunderland 1961-4; all but the last three of these games were in the Second Division.

He became an inspirational and highly successful manager in his own unique style, initially in partnership with Peter Taylor, with whom he had played at Middlesbrough. Starting with Hartlepool United 1965-7, they moved to Derby County 1967-73, steering them to the Second Division title in 1969 and to become League champions in 1972. After brief spells with Brighton 1973-4 and 44 days with Leeds United (without Taylor) in 1974, he was manager of Nottingham Forest from 1975 to his retirement in 1993 (with Taylor 1976-82). Under Clough, who was awarded the OBE in 1991, Forest were League champions and League Cup winners in 1978, European Cup and League Cup winners in 1979, European Super Cup and European Cup winners in 1980 and League Cup winners in 1989 and 1990.

His son **Nigel** (b. 19 Mar 1966) played for him at Nottingham Forest and played 14 times for England 1989-93. He was transferred to Liverpool in June 1993 for reported fee of £2.275 million.

Marion COAKES - see Marion MOULD

John COBB

Motor Racing
John Rhodes Cobb. b. 2 Dec 1899 Esher, Surrey. d. 29 Sep 1952 Loch Ness, Highland.

Cobb broke the world land speed record three times in his Railton Mobil Special, with speeds of 563.58 km/h *350.20 mph* in 1938, 595.02 km/h *369.74 mph* in 1939 and 634.37 km/h *394.19 mph* in 1947. He was the first man to exceed 400 mph on land, reaching 648.7 km/h *403.1 mph* on a one-way run in 1947. He was awarded the Segrave Trophy in 1947.

A big man who with his careful, methodical approach, was a perfect test driver, he preferred to race big cars. His first race win was in 1925, and he set many records at Brooklands, including the outer circuit lap record at 215.43 km/h. At one time he held every world record from 1 hour to 24 hours. He was a fur broker by profession.

He was killed when attempting the world water speed record on Loch Ness in his jet-engined *Crusader*, after becoming the first man to exceed 200 mph on water. His first run averaged 332.95 km/h *206.89 mph* for a mile with a peak speed of about 385 km/h *240 mph*.

Don COCKELL

Boxing
Donald John Cockell. b. 22 Sep 1928 Battersea, London. d. 18 Jul 1983 Leatherhead, Surrey.

A former blacksmith, he turned professional in 1946 and won the British light-heavyweight title four years later, adding the European title in 1951, before losing the crown to Randolph Turpin (qv) in 1952. Faced with weight problems, he immediately moved up to the heavyweight division and within a year, after a final eliminator against Tommy Farr (qv), a surprise win over Johnny Williams gave him the British and Empire titles. He went on to defeat some of the best American heavyweights and in May 1955 he became the first Briton to challenge for the world heavyweight title since Farr fought Joe Louis in 1937. In San Francisco, Cockell had the misfortune to meet Rocky Marciano (USA) at his best and although the contest was stopped in the ninth round, the fight was memorable for Cockell's courageous display in the face of a barrage of foul blows which would have seen Marciano disqualified by an impartial referee. This virtually marked the end Cockell's career and after defeats by two boxers of no particular talent he retired in

1956 as the undefeated holder of the British and Empire heavyweight title. Career record 1946-56: 80 contests. Won 65 (37 KO), Drew 1, Lost 14.

John COCKETT

Hockey
John Ashley Cockett. b. 23 Dec 1927 Broadstairs, Kent.

On leaving Aldenham School, he went up to Cambridge where he won Blues for cricket (1951) and hockey (1949-51). As a midfield player he won 37 caps for England at hockey and his then record 18 matches for GB included the Olympic Games of 1952 (bronze medal) and 1956. After leaving University, he played for a variety of clubs including Cambridge University Wanderers, Chelmsford, Cheltenham and Edgbaston. In the summers, he continued to play cricket for Buckinghamshire and represented the Minor Counties against the Australian tourists in 1953. For many years he was a schoolmaster at Felsted.

Sebastian COE

Athletics
Sebastian Newbold Coe. b. 29 Sep 1956 Chiswick, London.

The complete middle distance runner, Coe is Britain's most prolific world record setter, with nine outdoors and three indoors. His bests at 800m (1:41.73) and 1000m (2:12.18) in 1981 remain unsurpassed more than a decade later. After taking the silver medal for 800m behind his great rival Steve Ovett (qv) he won the Olympic 1500m title in 1980. Four years later he repeated the silver at 800m and then retained his 1500m title, having made a wonderful recovery from serious illness in 1983.

After placing 3rd in the European Junior 1500m in 1975, his first major title was the European Indoor 800m in 1977, and his first world record was 800m in 1:42.40 at Oslo on 5 Jul 1979. Twelve days later at the same venue he set the 1 mile record with 3:48.95, improving his personal best by a remarkable 8.72 secs. He set further

The Great British Middle-distance Trio - Best Times Season by Season								
SEBASTIAN COE			**STEVE OVETT**			**STEVE CRAM**		
800m	1500m	1 mile	800m	1500m	1 mile	800m	1500m	1 mile
1970	4:31.8		2:00.0	4:10.7				
1971	2:08.4	4:18.0		1:55.3				
1972	1:59.9	4:05.9		1:52.5	4:01.5			
1973	1:56.0	3:55.0		1:47.34	3:44.8	4:00.0		4:31.5
1974				1:45.76	3:46.2	3:59.4	2:11.0	4:22.3
1975	1:53.8	3:45.2		1:46.09	3:39.5	3:57.00	2:07.1	4:13.9
1976	1:47.7	3:42.67	3:58.35	1:45.44	3:37.89		1:59.7	4:07.1
1977	1:44.95		3:57.67	1:48.31	3:34.45	3:54.69	1:56.3	3:47.7
1978	1:43.97		4:02.17	1:44.09	3:35.59	3:52.8	1:53.5	3:40.09	3:57.43
1979	1:42.33	3:32.03	3:48.95	1:44.91	3:32.11	3:49.57	1:48.5	3:42.5	3:57.03
1980	1:44.7	3:32.19		1:45.40	3:31.36	3:48.8	1:48.41	3:34.74	3:53.8
1981	1:41.73	3:31.95	3:47.33	1:46.40	3:31.57	3:48.40	1:46.29	3:34.81	3:49.95
1982	1:44.48	3:39.1	3:59.5	1:46.08	3:38.48		1:44.45	3:33.66	3:49.90
1983	1:43.80	3:35.17	3:52.93	1:45.25	3:30.77	3:50.49	1:43.61	3:31.66	3:52.56
1984	1:43.64	3:32.39	3:54.6	1:44.81	3:34.50		1:46.0	3:33.13	3:49.65
1985	1:43.07	3:32.13	3:49.22		3:37.74	3:55.01	1:42.88	3:29.67	3:46.32
1986	1:44,10	3:29.77			3:33.78	3:52.99	1:43.19	3:30.15	3:48.31
1987	1:46.18				3:36.43	3:57.03	1:45.31	3:31.43	3:50.08
1988	1:43.93	3:35.72		1:48.88	3:36.90	3:58.71	1:43.42	3:30.95	3:48.85
1989	1:43.38	3:34.05		1:48.16	3:37.40	3:59.66	1:46.37	3:35.3	3:51.58
1990	1:47.24				3:45.33			3:33.03	3:53.99
1991							1:50.36	3:34.18	3:52.11
1992							1:51.1	3:42.24	3:56.7
1993								3:35.63	3:52.17
1994							1:50.3	3:42.8	

records of 3:48.53 and 3:47.33 in 1981. At 1500m he ran a world record 3:32.03 at Zürich in 1979, before losing the record to Ovett.

A title that gave him as much pleasure as his Olympic successes was the European gold at 800m in 1986, for at that, perhaps his best distance, he had been favourite in both 1978 and 1982, and yet had to settle for bronze and silver respectively. He had had to withdraw from the 1986 Commonwealth Games through viral illness, so his return to fitness was all the more welcome and he went on to add the European silver behind Steve Cram (qv) at 1500m, and to miss the 1500m world record narrowly at Rieti, when he ran his best ever time of 3:29.77.

He raced the longer distance less often but was undefeated in a 1500m or 1 mile final from 14 Sep 1976 to 24 Jun 1983. Controversially omitted from the 1988 Olympic team after failing in the trials through illness, he was 2nd to Abdi Bile in the 1989 World Cup 1500m, but ended his career with a disappointing 6th place in the 1990 Commonwealth Games.

Other best time: 400m 46.87 (1979).

An economics graduate of Loughborough University, Coe served as vice-chairman of the Sports Council 1986-9 and was elected as Conservative MP for Falmouth and Camborne in 1992. Voted BBC Sports Personality of the Year 1979, he was awarded the MBE in 1982 and the OBE in 1990.

In 1990 he married **Nicola McIrvine**, who earlier that year had ridden *Middle Road* to win the Badminton three-day event.

Eamonn COGHLAN (Ireland)

Athletics

Eamonn Christopher Coghlan. b. 21 Nov 1952 Drimnagh, Dublin.

Coghlan followed in the great tradition set by Ron Delany (qv) by becoming the 'Chairman of the Boards' - the king of indoor middle distance running - in the USA, where he studied at Villanova

University, Pennsylvania. He won 52 of his 70 races at 1500m or 1 mile 1974-87, including win streaks of 15 in 1978-80 and 14 in 1983-5. He won a record seven Millrose Miles and set six world indoor records: 1500m 3:35.6 (1981), 1 mile 3:55.0 and 3:52.6 (1979), 3:50.6 (1981) and after coming back from a damaged Achilles tendon in 1982 the first sub 3:50-time indoors with 3:49.78 (1983); 2000m 4:54.07 (1987). He also had an indoor 2 miles best of 8:20.84 in 1985.

After Olympic 4ths at 1500m 1976 and 5000m 1980, 2nd 1978 European 1500m, he won the world 5000m in devastating style in 1983. He was European Indoor champion at 1500m in 1979 and won the World Cup 5000m in 1981. After that several injuries caused him to miss much of the outdoor seasons. He won the AAA 1500m 1979, 1981, four NCAA 1500m/1M titles indoors and out 1975-6 and 11 Irish titles 1974-83: 5 each at 800m and 1500m, 1 at 5000m.

He set 15 Irish records outdoors between 1975 and 1983 with a European mile record of 3:53.3 in 1975 and he ran on Ireland's 4 x 1M world best in 1985. Outdoor bests: 800m 1:47.8 (1977), 1000m 2:20.2 (1977), 1500m 3:36.2 (1983), 1M 3:51.59 (1983), 2000m 4:57.66 (1983), 3000m 7:37.60 (1980), 2M 8:25.8 (1978), 5000m 13:19.13 (1981), 10,000m 28:19.3 (1986), marathon 2:25:13 (1991). Having worked for several years for the Irish Tourist Board he became chief executive of the Irish athletics federation in 1990. On 20 Feb 1994 he became the first over-40-year-old to run a four minute-mile, with 3:58.15 indoors at Boston.

Maurice COLCLOUGH

Rugby Union
Maurice John Colclough. b. 2 Sep 1953 Oxford.

With 25 England caps 1978-86 and eight Test appearances for the British Lions, he was one of the great British locks of his era. On his first Lions tour to South Africa in 1980 he was not initially rated as a candidate for the Test side but his hard scrummaging and line-out skills earned him a place in the team for all four Tests.

He only made his second Lions tour to New Zealand in 1983 after a late fitness test and again he played in all four Tests.

In many of his early matches for England and on his first Lions tour he partnered Bill Beaumont (qv) in the second-row and together they made a major contribution to England's 1980 Grand Slam. Although the Lions lost all four Tests in New Zealand in 1983, Colclough exacted a measure of revenge later in the year when he scored the decisive try at Twickenham to give England their first home win against the All Blacks in 47 years.

He played for Wasps and Swansea and for a while for Angoulême (France), where he managed a leisure centre. Today, he owns a restaurant in Swansea.

Neil COLES

Golf
Neil Chapman Coles. b. 26 Sep 1934 London.

A much respected and consistently successful golfer, he won 28 European tournaments from 1961 to 1982. He was the leading money winner in 1964 and won the Vardon Trophy in 1963 and 1970. He was in the top 12 in the Order of Merit each year 1961-80 with four more years either side in the top 20. In his 50s he was a formidable senior player, winning his fourth PGA Senior title in five years in 1989, and became chairman of the PGA European tour's board of directors.

He turned pro at 16, but it took him several years to reach the top, an important stepping stone being winning the British Assistants title in 1956. He was beaten 2 &1 by Arnold Palmer in the final of the first World Match Play Championship in 1964 and won the PGA Match Play in 1964, 1965 and 1973 as well as being runner-up three times. Other important wins included the Dunlop Masters 1966. In the Open his best placings were 2nd in 1973 and 3rd in 1961. His Ryder Cup record was 12 wins, 21 losses and 7 halves in eight ties 1961-77; his total of 40 matches remains the all-time record for either team. Awarded the MBE, he became chairman of the European Tour.

Cecilia COLLEDGE

Figure Skating
Magdalena Cecilia Colledge. b. 28 Nov 1920 Hampstead, London.

Colledge was world figure skating champion, six times British champion and the youngest ever British Olympic competitor. The daughter of a Wimpole Street specialist, she was inspired to take up skating after watching Sonja Henie (Nor) win her second world title at the Ice Club, Westminster in 1928. Her parents arranged lessons with the renowned Jacques Gerschwiler and in January 1932 she placed second to Megan Taylor (qv) at the British Championships. The following month she went to Lake Placid, USA for the Winter Olympics and at the age of 11 years 76 days set a record, which still stands, of being the youngest female Olympic competitor from any country in any sport. She was 2nd in the European Championships that year and went on to win six British Championships 1935-8 (two in 1937) and 1946. After finishing 2nd to Sonja Henie at both the 1935 Worlds and the 1936 Olympics, she won the World title in 1937 and the European each year 1937-9. In 1938 she lost her World title to Megan Taylor, her teammate at the 1932 and 1936 Olympics.
After serving with the forces as a driver with the Mechanised Transport Corps during the war, she turned professional in July 1946 and in 1951 emigrated to America where, for more than 25 years, she was attached to the prestigious Skating Club of Boston.

Charlie COLLIER

Motorcycling
Charles Richard Collier. d. 28 Aug 1954 Plumstead, London.

With his elder brother **Harry** (d. 1944) he was responsible for the development and success of the Matchless machines. They began manufacturing them with their father Harry A Collier in Plumstead in 1893 and on these machines Charlie set four world speed records from 80.24 mph *129.13 km/h* in 1910 to 91.23 mph *146.82*

km/h in 1911. Charlie represented Britain in International Cup races in Europe and when the Isle of man TT races started in 1907 he was the first ever winner of the single cylinder class. In 1909 Harry recorded the first ever lap of the course in over 50 mph on his way to TT victory, and Charlie won in 1910. Charlie died in his managing director's office at Plumstead in 1954.

Bobby COLLINS

Football
Robert Young Collins. b. 16 Feb 1931 Govanhill, Glasgow.

Initially an outside-right with Celtic, he was a key figure in their successes in the Scottish Cup 1951, Scottish League Cup 1957 and 1958, and Scottish League 1954, and scored 81 goals in 220 games for them. In 1958 he was transferred to Everton, where he had had a trial as a teenager, and then to Leeds four years later and at both clubs he took on the role of a midfield general, scoring 42 goals in 133 games for Everton and 25 in 167 for Leeds. A non-stop, hard-tackling, aggressive competitor, he was named Player of the Year in 1965, when Leeds failed by the narrowest of margins to clinch the double after they lost the League on goal average and the FA Cup in extra time. In the same season Collins regained his place in the Scotland team after an interval of six years and won the last three of his 31 caps, 1950-65. His great year sadly ended when he broke his leg in October in a Fairs Cup match in Turin, but he recovered to join Bury in 1967 and help them win promotion to the Second Division the following year. Spells with Morton and then in Australia followed before he returned home in 1972 to play a few games with Oldham, after which he held managerial or coaching appointments with a number of clubs.

Peter COLLINS

Motor Racing
Peter John Collins. b. 8 Nov 1931 Kidderminster, Worcs. d. 3 Aug 1958 Nürnberg, Germany.

A brilliant driver, Collins became the then second youngest ever winner of a Formula One Grand Prix with the Belgian GP in 1956. He also won the next race, the French GP and had three 2nd places that year, his first for Ferrari, to finish 3rd in a closely contested driver's championship behind his team-mate Juan-Manuel Fangio (Arg) and Sterling Moss (qv). He had a modest 1957 season, but after sports car wins in the Buenos Aires 1000 km and Sebring 12 hours with Phil Hill (USA), he won the British Grand Prix for Ferrari at Silverstone.

Regarded as not only one of the fastest drivers, but also one of the safest and a fine sportsman, tragedy struck in the next race as he crashed at over 100 mph in the German Grand Prix and was thrown out of the car. He died in hospital soon afterwards from severe head injuries.

His father Patrick ran a motor dealership in Kidderminster, and Peter had started racing in 500 cc cars in 1949. His first major race win was the 1952 Goodwood Nine Hours with Pat Griffith. With Sterling Moss he won the Targa Florio in a Mercedes in 1955 and was 2nd in the 1956 Le Mans 24-hours.

Peter COLLINS

Speedway
Spencer Peter Collins. b. 24 Mar 1954 Urmston, Manchester.

In a remarkable 1973 season he established himself as one of the world's leading riders at an unusually early age. He started his career as a 17-year-old with Rochdale in 1971, moving to the Belle Vue senior team the following year. In 1973, when still only 19, he scored maximum points for Britain when they won the World Team Championship. In 1974 he became the first English rider to win the European Championships and in 1976 he won the World Individual Championship, the first British winner since Peter Craven (qv) 14 years earlier. In eight world final appearances he scored 71 points. He was a member of the winning British team five times, 1973-5, 1977 and 1980 and is also the most successful British rider in the World Pairs, winning four times with different partners, Malcolm Simmons in 1977, David Jessup in 1980, Kenny Carter in 1983 and Chris Morton in 1984. He rode 136 times for England and British Lions and in 16 seasons at Belle Vue scored 3865 points from 403 league matches. He won his first motorcycle race at 16 and was British 350cc grass-track champion in 1971 and 1972. He was British Junior speedway champion 1973, British League Riders champion 1974 and 1975, and British champion 1979.

Alf COMMON

Football
Alfred Common. b. 25 May 1880 Sunderland. d. 3 Apr 1946 Darlington.

The most highly valued player of his time, he was the subject of both the first £500 and the first four figure transfer fee. He moved from Sheffield United to Sunderland for £520 in 1904 and from Sunderland to Middlesbrough for £1,000 the following year. From Sunderland he went to Woolwich Arsenal (1910) and then to Preston North End (1912). He won an FA Cup winners' medal with Sheffield United in 1902 and was capped three times by England 1904-06, playing twice at inside-right and once at centre-forward. He became a licencee in Darlington after leaving football.

Archie COMPSTON

Golf
Archibald Edward Wones Compston. b. 14 Jan 1893 Penn, Wolverhampton. d. 8 Aug 1962 Northwood, London.

A very tall and strong golfer, Compston twice came close to breaking the run of ten successive American wins in the Open Championship between 1924 and 1933. He was joint 2nd with Ted Ray in 1925, beaten by one stroke by Jim Barnes, and 3rd in 1928 behind Walter Hagen and Gene Sarazen. He also had a great chance in 1930, but after a third round of 68 to lead the field by one, he fell away badly with a final round of 82 and ended joint 6th. He won the PGA Championship in

1927 and beat Hagen by the amazing score of 18 & 17 over 72 holes in 1928 for a stake of £500. Playing in the Ryder Cups of 1927, 1929 and 1931, he won just one and halved one of his six matches.

He was an intrepid gambler and won a celebrated court case against the Inland Revenue concerning his winnings. He was also a notable teacher of golf, including the Prince of Wales amongst his pupils.

Denis COMPTON

Cricket and Football
Denis Charles Scott Compton. b. 23 May 1918 Hendon, London.

Compton wasa brilliant right-handed batsman and unorthodox slow left-arm bowler. He received his county cap for Middlesex in 1936, when at 18 he was the youngest ever to score 1000 runs in his debut season. He was England vice-captain on the tour to Australia in 1950/1 and Middlesex joint captain with Bill Edrich (qv) in 1951-2. His 300 v North-Eastern Transvaal at Benoni 3-4 Dec 1948, made in 181 minutes, is the fastest ever triple century.

In 1947 he set English season's record figures unlikely ever to be broken, of 3816 runs (av. 90.85) and 18 centuries, four of them in the Test series with South Africa. He charmed and thrilled large crowds with his dashing strokeplay. A year later a knee injury incurred at football flared up and his mobility throughout the rest of his career was often severely impaired. At soccer he played outside-left for Arsenal, gaining an FA Cup winners' medal in 1950 after the League title in 1947/8, and he won 12 wartime England international caps (two goals).

A batting genius, he brought sparkle to the cricket and soccer fields of post-war England, and was undoubtedly the most popular sportsman of the era. He was *Daily Express* Sportsman of the Year 1947 and 1948. Astutely managed by Bagenal Harvey, he was one of the first professional sportsmen to build on their appeal, most notably through his Brylcreem advertisements. Awarded the CBE for services to cricket 1958, he has written several books,

worked as a journalist, PR consultant and advertising agency director.

78 Tests 1937-57: 5807 runs at 50.06; 17 100s HS 278; 25 wickets at 56.40, BB 5-70; 49 catches.

First-class 1936-64: 38,942 runs at 51.85, 123 100s HS 300; 622 wickets at 32.27, BB 7-36; 415 catches.

His elder brother **Leslie** Harry Compton (1912-84) kept wicket for Middlesex 1938-56 and, was also an Arsenal footballer, first at centre-forward, then full-back and finally at centre-half. He played twice for England at soccer at the age of 38 in 1950, his country's oldest debutant. He had, however played in five wartime internationals. Both Les and Denis played for the County cricket champions of 1947 and League football champions of 1947-8.

Keith CONNOR

Athletics, Triple Jump
Keith Leroy Connor. b. 16 Sep 1957 Anguilla.

Connor confirmed his status as Britain's greatest ever triple jumper, when he ranked as world's number one in 1982. In that year he won both Commonwealth and European titles and the NCAA title for Southern Methodist University in the USA with 17.57. This mark, set at the high altitude of Provo, Utah improved the British and Commonwealth record of 17.16 that he had set in 1980 and remains unbroken 13 years later. At the time it was also a European record.

His first British record had been set with 16.76 at the 1978 Commonwealth Games where he won his first gold medal with a wind assisted 17.21. In other major championships at the Europeans he was 2nd indoors and 6th outdoors in 1978, at the Olympics, 4th in 1980 and 3rd in 1984, also winning a bronze at the 1981 World University Games. He was AAA champion indoors and out in 1978 and UK champion in 1978 and 1980. He set a world indoor record with 17.31 when he won the NCAA indoor title in 1981 and he retained this title in 1982. His long jump best was 7.71 indoors in 1981.

Born in the West Indies, he came to Britain with his family at the age of six. Coached by his schoolmaster Ted King, he won the English Schools intermediate title in his first year at the event in 1974 and he was AAA junior champion in 1976.

John CONROY

Hockey
John Valentine Conroy. b. 27 Nov 1928 India. d. 9 Nov 1985 Liverpool

Born into a large Anglo-Indian family when his father was serving with the British Army in India, Conroy only took up hockey seriously when he settled in England and joined the Army himself shortly after the war. After some impressive performances with service teams he joined Mid-Surrey HC in 1950 and made his international debut two years later. A brilliant and skilful inside-forward, he won 32 caps (30 goals) for England 1952-60 and 23 caps (13 goals) for GB 1952-9, including Olympic appearances in 1952 (bronze medal) and 1956. These totals would have undoubtedly been higher had he not spent 1957 in Canada. He also played for Hounslow and St. Annes and he collapsed and died at the age of 57 while playing in a junior club match.

John CONTEH

Boxing
John Anthony Conteh. b. 27 May 1951 Liverpool.

After a brilliant amateur career during which he won the 1970 Commonwealth Games gold medal at middleweight and ABA titles at middleweight 1970 and light-heavy 1971, he turned professional. He beat Rüdiger Schmidtke (Ger) for the European light-heavyweight title and then beat Chris Finnegan (qv) for the British and Commonwealth title in 1973 and in 1974 won the WBC World crown with a points victory over Jorge Ahumada (Arg). He made three successful defences but these were his only fights in 3 ½ years before he was stripped of his title in 1977 for refusing to meet his contractual obligations to defend against Miguel Ceullo (Arg). He made three attempts to regain his World title, losing firstly to Mate Parlov (Yug) in 1978 and then he was defeated twice by Matt Saad Muhammed (USA) in 1979 and 1980. In the early part of his career he was hailed as the most talented British boxer for many years but he never totally fulfilled his earlier promise. This was due, in part, to recurring hand injuries but his unsettled relationship with his managers was also a significant factor. He showed his all-round ability by winning the all-sport British Superstars TV competition in 1974.
Career record 1971-80: 39 contests. Won 34 (24 KO), Drew 1, Lost 4.

Kathy COOK

Athletics
Kathryn Jane Cook. b. 3 May 1960 Winchester. née Smallwood.

By far Britain's biggest medal winner (23) ever at major Games and finest all-round woman sprinter, she never failed to win a sprint relay medal from 1977 to the 1986 Commonwealth Games. She set British records at all sprints: 100m 11.10 for 2nd in the 1981 World Cup; four at 200m from 22.70 in 1979 to 22.13 for the 1982 European silver, and UK & Commonwealth 400m records of 50.46 in 1982 and a brilliant 49.43 for the Olympic bronze in 1984. She also set a world 300m best of 35.46 in 1984. Troubled by a serious hamstring injury from 1985, she found it difficult to return to her best, but won four medals at the 1986 Commonwealth Games.
Her full medal collection: Olympics (3): 1980 2nd 4 x 100m, 1984 3rd 400m & 4 x 100m. Worlds (2): 1983 2nd 4 x 100m, 3rd 200m. Europeans (3): 1978 2nd 4 x 100m, 1982 2nd 200m & 4 x 100m. Commonwealth (7): 1978 1st 4 x 100m, 1982 1st 4 x 100m & 2nd 200m, 1986 1st 4 x 100m, 2nd 200m & 4 x 400m, 3rd 400m. European Juniors (3): 1977: 3rd 100m, 200m, 4 x 100m. World Student Games (5): 1979 2nd 100m, 200m, 4 x 100m, 1981 1st 200m, 2nd 4 x 100m. National titles: UK 100m 1983; 200m 1980, 1983, 1985-6; WAAA 100m 1978, 1980, 1983-4;

200m 1978-80, 1982, 1984-5; 400m 1986; English Schools 200m 1977-8. A member of Wolverhampton & Bilston AC and graduate of West London Institute, she was awarded the MBE in 1986.

She married **Garry Cook** (10 Jan 1958 Wednesbury, W. Midlands), who was a top-class 800m runner (best of 1:44.55 in 1984) and 2nd at the 1979 World Student Games and a fine 400m relay runner with medals: gold 1982 Commonwealth, silver 1982 Europeans and 1984 Olympics, bronze 1983 Worlds. He ran on the British teams that set a world record for 4 x 800m relay in 1982 and a European 4 x 400m record 1984.

Charlotte COOPER

Tennis
Charlotte Reinagle Cooper. b. 22 Sep 1870 Ealing, London. d. 10 Oct 1966 Helensburgh, Argyll and Bute. Later Mrs Sterry.

After winning three Wimbledon singles, 1895-6 and 1898, as Miss Cooper, she won two further titles, 1901 and 1908, following her marriage to Alfred Sterry in January 1901. At the time of her fifth victory in 1908 she was aged 37 years 282 days and is the oldest winner of the women's singles. She also won the All England mixed doubles with Laurie Doherty (qv) in 1901 and 1902 before the event was given full championship status.

Away from Wimbledon, she won two singles (1895, 1898) and four mixed doubles titles at the Irish Championships and also won the 1898 Welsh and 1899 Scottish singles. She also won two gold medals (singles, mixed doubles) at the 1900 Olympic Games to become the first woman from any country to win an Olympic title.

Her daughter, **Gwen**, was a Wightman Cup player in 1927 and her son, **Rex**, served for many years as vice-chairman of the All England Club. One of the longest-lived of all champions, she attended the Wimbledon 75th anniversary celebrations in 1961 when in her 91st year and she died in Scotland aged 96.

Henry COOPER

Boxing
Henry William Cooper. b. 3 May 1934 Bellingham, London.

Cooper held the British and Commonwealth professional heavyweight titles from 1959 to 1970 and was also thrice European champion at that weight. He set a record with his three Lonsdale belts, won in 1961, 1964 and 1967.

He was a skilful boxer with a powerful left hook, but his biggest fault was that he cut easily, leading to his nickname, 'Bleeding 'Enry'. Perhaps Cooper's greatest hour came in a losing cause. In 1963 he floored Muhammad Ali (USA) in the fourth round of a non-title fight, only the bell saving Ali. However in round five, Cooper was cut and the fight had to be stopped.

Henry, who had won ABA light-heavyweight titles in 1952 and 1953, and his twin brother George (who fought as Jim Cooper as there was another George) signed up as pro boxers in 1954 with Jim Wicks, who managed Henry throughout his career until he retired in 1971 after losing his British, Commonwealth and European titles to Joe Bugner (qv).

Henry had lost his first three title fights, all in 1957, to Joe Erskine twice for the British title, and to Ingemar Johansson (Swe) for the European title, but persevered to gain the British title when he beat Brian London on points in January 1959.

Awarded the OBE in 1969, Cooper was hugely popular in Britain and has retained that celebrity status to this day. He was twice voted as BBC Sports Personality of the Year (1967 and 1970).

Career record 1954-71: 55 contests. Won 40 (27), Drew 1, Lost 14.

John COOPER

Athletics, Hurdling
John Hugh Cooper. b. 18 Dec 1940 Bromyard, Herefordshire. d. 3 Mar 1974 in the Paris air crash.

A most tenacious competitor, the peak of Cooper's career was when he took silver medals at both 400m hurdles and in the 4 x 400m relay at the 1964 Olympics. In the former he set British records in each round - 50.5 (50.58 auto-timing) in his heat, 50.4 (50.40) in the semi and 50.1 in the final, won by Rex Cawley (USA) in 49.6. He only had a best flat time of 47.9 for 440y but he ran a marvellous 400m relay leg of 45.5.

A member of Birchfield Harriers, his first important title was the English Schools intermediate triple jump in 1957. He started hurdling in 1960 and made rapid improvement in 1961, breaking into world class with British records of 51.0 and 50.5 at 400m hurdles in 1963. He competed at his second Olympics in 1968, making the 400m hurdles semi-final and made 22 international appearances for Britain 1961-9. Formerly a schoolteacher, at the time of his death, returning from the England – France rugby match, he was a marketing manager for Adidas.

Joyce COOPER

Swimming
Margaret Joyce Cooper. b. 18 Apr 1909 Sri Lanka (then Ceylon). Later Mrs Badcock.

At the first Empire Games in 1930, Cooper won three of the four individual women's events: 100y and 400y freestyle and 100y backstroke and a fourth gold at the relay, when her sister Doreen was also a member of the team. She was the winner of four Olympic medals: silver at 4 x 100m relay and bronze at 100m freestyle and backstroke in 1928, followed by a relay bronze in 1932, when she was 4th at 400m freestyle and 6th at 100m backstroke. At the Europeans she took a relay gold with the 100m freestyle silver in 1927, and three silver, 400m free, 100m backstroke and relay, with bronze at 100m free in 1931. She won 19 ASA titles: freestyle: 100y 1929, 1931-2; 220y 1927-9, 1931-2; 440y 1928-32, long distance 1930-3, 150y backstroke 1929, 1931.

She married **John** Charles **Badcock** (b. 17 Jan 1903 West Ham, London. d. 29 May 1976 Petersfield, Hampshire), known as 'Felix' in 1934. A rower, he won Olympic gold at coxless fours in 1932 and silver at eights in 1928.

Their eldest son, also named Felix, rowed for England at the 1958 Commonwealth Games and their younger son David won his rowing Blue at Oxford that same year.

Malcolm COOPER

Shooting
Malcolm Douglas Cooper, b. 20 Dec 1947 Camberley, Surrey.

Cooper was the winner of two Olympic gold medals, six World Championships and four Commonwealth Games titles. He first took up shooting as a schoolboy in New Zealand where his father was stationed as a lieutenant in the Royal Navy. Following his return to England he developed into one of the world's finest marksmen. After a relatively undistinguished performance at the 1972 and 1976 Olympics he missed the 1980 Games because of the boycott, but in both 1984 and 1988 he was Olympic champion in the small bore rifle, three positions. His Commonwealth titles came at small bore rifle: prone pairs 1982, 3 positions pairs 1982 and 1986, 3 positions 1986.

His host of other outstanding performances include gold medals at each of the five World Championships held between 1978 and 1990: free rifle 1978, 1982, 1986 (3 x 40 and 3 x 20), 1990 (3 x 40); standard rifle 1986. Particularly notable were the 1985 Europeans where he won all five individual events and the 1986 Worlds where he set five world records. His world record of 587 for 3 x 20 shots with a standrd rifle at 300m in 1989 still stands six years later.

His wife **Sarah** (b. 23 Mar 1949 Kettering, Northants) was a member of the Olympic shooting team in 1988 and together they won the small bore rifle, pairs, at the 1986 Commonwealth Games.

Steve COPPELL

Football
Stephen James Coppell. b. 9 Jul 1955 Liverpool.

An accomplished player in the midfield or as a forward he spent a season with Tranmere Rovers while a still a student at Liverpool University. In 1975 he was transferred to Manchester United and remained with the club until his career was ended by injury in 1983. With United he won an FA Cup winners' medal in 1977 and was a finalist in 1976 and 1979. He was also a finalist in the League Cup in 1983 and was capped 42 times by England 1976-83, scoring 7 goals.

After he had been forced to give up playing because of a recurrent knee injury, at the age of 29 he became the League's youngest manager, of Crystal Palace. He stayed there from 1984 to 1993, and was then chief executive of the League Managers' Association 1993-5.

Cyril CORBALLY (Ireland)

Croquet
Cyril Corbally. b. c.1880 Ireland. d. 1946 Ireland.

The most successful croquet player of all-time until the arrival of Humphrey Hicks (qv), Corbally won the Open Championship at his first attempt in 1902 and was only defeated twice in the six other Opens in which he played until 1913. He also won the mixed doubles in 1903 and 1911 and with his brother Herbert the men's doubles in 1913.

He was one of the greatest of an early school of Irish players who introduced the centre-stance to England, which quickly and virtually permanently replaced the side-stance favoured by the Victorian English players. Corbally only came to England twice after the war, winning the men's championship in 1926, but on his second visit in 1934 he only played in provincial tournaments. For someone who suffered from ill health as a young man and had been advised to take up croquet as a form of 'gentle exercise', he showed a remarkable aptitude for the game and his record of five Open championship wins (1902-03, 1906, 1908, 1913) was not beaten until Hicks scored his sixth victory in 1950.

Richard CORSIE

Bowls
Richard Corsie. b. 27 Nov 1966 Edinburgh.

At the world outdoor championships in 1992 he won the pairs for Scotland with Alex Marshall with a team gold and a silver medal in the singles, and has been especially successful at the World Indoor Championship, where he won the singles in 1989, 1991 and 1993 and the doubles with Marshall in 1995. He was beaten in the singles final in 1992. At his third Commonwealth Games he won the singles in 1994, having won bronze medals in 1986 and 1990. His first important success was the Scottish junior title in 1983 and a year later he made his senior international debut and won the British junior title. A postman, in 1995 he succeeded David Bryant (qv) as chairman of the World Bowls Players Association.

Edmond COTTER

Croquet
Edmond Patrick Charles Cotter. b. 24 Sep 1904.

Although he had played croquet as a boy, he did not take up the game seriously until 1947 when he was aged 43. In 1949 he won the President's Cup at his first attempt and repeated his victory five times in the next 11 years. He also won the Open Championship in 1955, 1958 and 1962, the men's championship four times, 1952, 1954, 1963 and 1969; the mixed in 1951 and, with John Solomon, he won the Open doubles ten times between 1949 and 1969.

His game, which was based on an attacking approach, was a welcome development after the defensive attitude which had become prevalent in the game since the war. Cotter was also a scratch golfer but in addition to his sporting talents he brought a fine brain to the game. He was a classics master at St Paul's School, an international bridge player and the compiler of the crossword puzzle in the *Financial Times*.

Fran COTTON

Rugby Union
Francis Edward Cotton. b. 3 Jan 1947 Wigan, Gt. Manchester.

Making his England debut in 1971, he went on to become England's most capped prop before poor health ended his career in 1981 with 31 caps to his credit. He toured with the British Lions to South Africa in 1974 and New Zealand in 1977 and only missed one of the eight Tests over the two tours. On his third Lions' tour to South Africa in 1980 he was afflicted with severe chest pains and it was thought his life was in danger. He recovered sufficiently to regain his place in the England team against Wales in 1981 but recurrent leg infections soon brought about his final retirement. A forceful personality and inspiring leader with Loughborough Colleges and Coventry, he led the North-West Counties to victory over the All Blacks in 1972. He also captained England and the Lions in some of their Provincial matches. His father was a rugby league international.

Henry COTTON

Golf
Thomas Henry Cotton. b. 26 Jan 1907 Holmes Chapel, Cheshire. d. 22 Dec 1987 London.

After the Americans became dominant in golf in the early part of the 20th century, only Henry Cotton really challenged this until the 1980s. He won the British Open three times, 1934, 1937 and 1948; in 1937 defeating a field that contained the whole US Ryder Cup team. He played on three Ryder Cup squads, captained the team in 1947 (as well as the team that did not play in 1939 due to the declaration of the war) and was non-playing captain in 1953. He won two and lost four of his six Ryder Cup matches. He was PGA Match Play champion in 1932, 1940 and 1946. With Walter Hagen (USA) and Bobby Locke (SAf), he was one of the first three professionals to be accorded honorary membership by the Royal & Ancient Golf Club.
Cotton will always be remembered for the round of 65 which he shot in winning the 1934 Open at Sandwich which inspired the popular golf ball, the 'Dunlop 65'. He made only sporadic trips to the United States, winning only one tournament on their PGA Tour.
After leaving school he had three assistant-

ships before becoming a full professional in 1926. At the end of his playing career Cotton became a well-known golf pundit, journalist and course architect and settled in Portugal. He was awarded the MBE in 1946, and shortly before his death heard that he was to be knighted in the 1988 New Year's Honours List.

Robin COUSINS

Figure Skating
Robin John Cousins. b. 17 Aug 1957 Bristol.

Having placed 10th behind John Curry in 1976, Cousins became only the second British male to win an Olympic figure skating gold medal in 1980. A superb display of free skating gave him a narrow victory over Jan Hoffman (GDR), but Hoffman got his revenge at the World Championships and a World title was the one honour which eluded Cousins, as he had won a bronze medal in 1978 and silver in 1979. In 1980 he also won the European title and was awarded the MBE and was voted BBC Sports Personality of the Year. He was British champion each year 1976-9. The son of a former Millwall goalkeeper, he combined his skating activities with his studies at Bristol but after his Olympic victory he turned professional and in 1989 was appointed head of coaching at a new advanced training centre in southern California.

Ronnie COVE-SMITH

Rugby Union
(Dr) Ronald Cove-Smith. b. 26 Nov 1899 Edmonton, London. d. 9 Mar 1988 Brighton. East Sussex.

A lock-forward with Old Merchant Taylors he was capped 29 times by England and was on the losing side in only five of those matches. He captained the British Lions in South Africa in 1924 and led England to a Grand Slam win in 1928. After holding a commission in the Grenadier Guards during the war he went up to Cambridge and won his blue in 1919-21; in his third year he captained Cambridge in the first University Match to be played at

Twickenham. He also represented Cambridge at swimming and water polo. After University he enjoyed a distinguished career in medicine.

Fred COVEY

Real Tennis
G. Frederick Covey.

After unsuccessfully challenging 'Punch' Fairs (qv) for the world real tennis championship in 1910, he beat Fairs for the title two years later, but then lost the crown to the multi-millionaire American amateur, Jay Gould, in Philadelphia in 1914. However, Covey resumed his position as world champion when Gould relinquished the title the following year. Covey then defended his title against three challenges before losing to Pierre Etchebaster (Fra) in 1928.

In 1907 he was appointed as head professional when Lady Wentworth opened her new court at Crabbet Park, West Sussex.

Colin COWDREY

Cricket   4/12/2000
(Sir) Michael Colin Cowdrey. b. 24 Dec 1932 Pulumala, Ooatacamund, India.

Undoubtedly a great batsman, elegant with all the strokes, Cowdrey was so determined that he was flown out to Australia after three years out of Test cricket at the age of 42 to face Lillee and Thomson at their fiercest when the England batting was falling away before them. And yet he did not quite satisfy his admirers when sometimes his batting became over-introspective, as if he could not quite come to terms with his own genius.

That genius was obvious from his earliest days when he went straight into the Tonbridge team at the age of 13 and was the youngest schoolboy ever to play in a Lord's match. He lost his youthful ability as a leg-break bowler, but immediately after leaving Oxford University he made his Test debut against Australia in 1954/5 to rave reviews, with a hundred in his third Test. Over the next 20 years he passed the records of Wally Hammond (qv) for most runs for England and catches in Test cricket.

He captained England in 27 Tests 1959-69, but never in Australia despite making six tours there. He was one of the longest serving of county captains, leading Kent from 1957-71. He made 1000 runs in a season 27 times, in South Africa, Australia and West Indies as well as 21 in England, with a peak of 2039 at 63.42 in 1965.

In 1952 he lost in the final of the amateur rackets championships. Awarded the CBE 1972, he was president of the MCC in 1986/7 and chairman of the ICC for several years to 1993. He was knighted for his services to cricket in 1992. His son **Christopher** (b. 20 Oct 1957) played in six Tests for England 1984-8, the last as captain, and three one-day internationals 1985, and another son **Graham** (b. 27 Jun 1964) also plays for Kent.

His second wife is the racehorse trainer **Lady Herries of Terregles** (b. 12 Jun 1938), the eldest daughter of the 16th Duke of Norfolk. She trains *Celtic Swing*, rated in 1994 as the best two-year-old and in 1995 the winner of the French Derby.

114 Tests 1954-75: 7624 runs at 44.06, 22 100s HS 182; 120 catches.
1 One-day Int 1971: 1 run.
First-class 1950-76: 42,719 runs at 42.89, 107 100s HS 307; 65 wickets at 51.21, BB 4-22; 638 catches.

Mark COX

Tennis
Mark Cox. b. 5 Jul 1943 Leicester.

Educated at Millfield and Cambridge University, he had an outstanding career as an amateur the highlight of which was the defeat of two of the greatest professionals (Pancho Gonzalez (USA) and Roy Emerson (Aus)) at the 1968 British Hard Court Championships, the world's first Open tournament. Although he did not win the Hard Court title that year, he was to do so in 1970 shortly after he had turned professional. He made his international debut in the King's Cup in 1963 and reached the quarter-finals of the singles of the 1966 US, 1967 Australian and 1973 South African Opens. He was also a semi-finalist in the men's doubles with Alan Mills at Wimbledon in 1966.

A left-handed player, he was ranked as British No.1, a then record six times, between 1968 and 1976 and in 1980, at the age of 37, he was still ranked among the top ten in Britain. He had a fine Davis Cup record, 1967-79, winning 23 out of 35 rubbers (15/21 singles, 8/14 doubles). He was awarded the MBE in 1979 and is now a coach and TV commentator.

Steve CRAM

Athletics
Stephen Cram. b. 14 Oct 1960 Gateshead, Tyne and Wear.

Cram achieved a unique treble at 1500m with Commonwealth, European and World titles 1982-3, before returning from injury to take the 1984 Olympic silver medal. He had run on the UK team that set a world record at 4 x 800m relay in 1982, but first entered the world record lists as an individual in 1985, when he ran three records in 19 days: at 1500m 3:29.67, 1 mile 3:46.32 and 2000m 4:51.39, times which remained his best.

He set a world age-17 mile best with 3:57.43 in 1978 and in that year made his championships debut at the Commonwealth Games. The next year he won the European Junior title at 3000m and in 1980 was 8th in the Olympic 1500m.

In 1986 Cram became the third man to win the Commonwealth 800m/1500m double when he looked unbeatable, the supreme middle-distance runner, and then won gold (1500m) and bronze (800m) at the Europeans. Since then he increasingly suffered from calf and other leg injuries. At his third Europeans he was 5th at 1500m in 1990, and he won seven national senior titles: AAA 1500m 1981-3, 800m 1984, 1986, 1988; UK 5000m 1989. Voted BBC Sports Personality of the Year 1983, he was awarded the MBE in 1986.

Other bests: 800m 1:42.88 (1985), 1000m 2:12.88 (1985), 3000m 7:43.1 (1983), 2M 8:14.93 (1983), 5000m 13:28.58 (1989).
For season-by-season progress - see Sebastian Coe.

Peter CRAVEN

Speedway
Peter Theodore Craven. b. 21 Jun 1934 Liverpool. d. 24 Sep 1963 Edinburgh.

World champion in 1955 and 1962, Craven was the only English rider to win two world titles - although Welshman Freddie Williams (qv) had been a double winner in 1950 and 1953. In ten consecutive championships 1954-63 Craven scored 96 points in all. His career was cut short at the age of 29 when he died from injuries sustained during a crash in Edinburgh. He started in the minor leagues with Liverpool and Fleetwood before beginning a ten-year association with First Division Belle Vue. He was one of the most spectacular and popular of the post-war riders and was still in the top flight when he met his premature death.

Jack CRAWFORD

Cricket
John Neville Crawford. b. 1 Dec 1886 Coulsdon, London. d. 2 May 1963 Epsom, Surrey.

A hugely talented cricketer was lost prematurely to the Test arena when following a dispute with his county, Surrey, Crawford went to Australia to become a schoolmaster in Adelaide.

He made his first-class debut for Surrey in August 1904, when he still had another year at school at Repton, and was an instant success, taking 44 wickets at 16.93 that year to finish top of the national bowling averages. Soon after leaving school he went with the MCC to South Africa and, while still a teenager, played in all five Tests on the 1905/6 series. In 1906 he became the youngest cricketer to achieve the double, repeated that feat in 1907 and was only two wickets short in 1908. In Australia he helped South Australia to win the Sheffield Shield twice before moving to New Zealand to coach Otago in 1914. He showed what might have been by playing a few matches for Surrey in 1919, taking third in the national averages with 488 runs at 61.00. He was a hard-hitting middle-order batsman and a most accurate medium-pace off-break bowler.

His father the Rev. John C Crawford (1849-1935) played for Kent 1872-7, and his brother Vivian **Frank** Shergold Crawford (1879-1922), was a very exciting batsman, who scored 1340 runs for Whitgift School in 1897,and also played for Surrey (1896-1902) before moving to Leicestershire, when he was appointed their secretary in 1903. Frank had the distinction of making the biggest hit in first-class cricket, 160 yards hit-to-pitch at Bristol in 1900. He emigrated to Ceylon and captained them against the MCC in 1911/12. Another brother Reginald T (1882-1945) also played for Leicestershire. 12 Tests 1905-8: 469 runs at 22.33, HS 74; 39 wickets at 29.48, BB 5-48; 13 catches. First-class 1904-21: 9488 runs at 32.60, 15 100s HS 232; 815 wickets at 20.66, BB 8-24; 162 catches.

Pat CRERAND

Football
Patrick Timothy Crerand. b. 19 Feb 1939 Glasgow.

A constructive wing-half and intelligent analyst of the game, Crerand played a major part in helping Manchester United to win the FA Cup in 1963 and the Football League in 1965 and 1967. He had been signed in 1963 for £55,000 from Celtic, with whom he started an international career for Scotland that brought him 16 caps 1961-5.

He was noted for his fiery temper and during his career he was sent off six times, including once when playing for Scotland. When his playing days were over he stayed with Manchester United as a member of their coaching staff and in 1976 took over as manager of Northampton Town. The appointment only lasted six months and he left the game to become PRO to a Manchester engineering firm.

Warney CRESSWELL

Football
Warneford Cresswell. b. 5 Nov 1897 South Shields, Tyne and Wear. d. 20 Oct 1973 South Shields.

Cresswell was a classic full-back who could play with equal facility on either flank. An England schoolboy international in 1911, he assisted a number of Scottish clubs during World War I before joining the army and becoming a prisoner of war. After the war he signed for South Shields in 1919, moving to Sunderland in 1922 and then to Everton in 1927 where he stayed for the remainder of his playing career.

He won his first cap in 1921 while with South Shields, four more with Sunderland and his final two caps with Everton. While he was with the Merseyside club they won the League in 1928 and the FA Cup in 1933. On retiring in 1936 he served briefly as coach and manager of Port Vale before taking over as manager of Northampton Town until he rejoined the forces on the outbreak of war.

Julian CREUS

Weightlifting
Julian Creus. b. 30 Jun 1917 Lancashire.

After winning international honours as a bantamweight in 1939, he served in the Merchant Navy throughout the war, after which he built up a remarkable record for consistency. He won the British featherweight title for nine successive years, 1945-53, and added a tenth title in 1956. His Olympic silver medal as a bantamweight in 1948 has been matched only by Louis Martin (qv) among British lifters in recent times. In the featherweight division he also won bronze at the World Championships 1950-1, and silver at the Europeans 1950-1 and Empire Games 1950.

Britain's finest wightlifter of the immediate post-war era, Creus emigrated to Australia when he retired from the sport.

Norwood CRIPPS

Real Tennis and Rackets
Norwood A R Cripps.

Cripps was the winner of a record ten British Open doubles titles at real tennis. After winning the inaugural title with Ronald Hughes in 1971, he won three times with Charles Swallow and took his last six titles partnering the Old Wykehamist amateur, Alan Lovell. He also won the British Open singles in 1971 and 1973. Although never quite as successful at rackets, he was the British professional champion six times, 1977-9, 1981-3. He succeeded Jim Dear (qv) as senior professional at Queen's Club and then took over from Dear at Eton College in 1979.

Beryl CROCKFORD - see MITCHELL

June CROFT

Swimming
June Alexandra Croft. b. 17 Jun 1963
Ashton in Makerfield, Gt. Manchester

From 1979 to 1989 Croft won eight ASA national titles and 16 ASA short-course titles. At freestyle she set a Commonwealth long course record of 56.60 for 100m in 1982, four British records at 200m in 1981-2 to her Commonwealth record 1:59.74 in 1982, and one at 400m in 1982. She also set 16 British short-course freestyle records: eight at 100m to 55.16 in 1982, four at 200m to 1:57.15 in 1982 and four at 400m to 4:04.93 in 1984. She was Commonwealth champion at 100m and 200m freestyle in 1982, with a third gold at 4 x 100m freestyle, a silver at 4 x 100m medley and bronze at 400m, but was disappointed only to place 7th at 200m and 400m at the Worlds that year, having gone into the championships as the fastest in the world at 200m. At the Olympic Games she won a silver medal at 4 x100m medley in 1980 and bronze at 400m freestyle in her best ever time of 4:11.49 in 1984, with 6th at 200m 1980 and both 100m and 200m in 1984. She swam for Wigan Wasps.

Bob CROMPTON

Football
Robert Crompton. b. 26 Sep 1879
Blackburn, Lancashire. d. 15 Mar 1941
Blackburn.

Unchallenged for the position of England's right-back from 1902 to 1914, he won a total of 41 caps which stood as an England record until beaten by Billy Wright (qv) in 1952. He joined Blackburn Rovers in 1896 and remained with the club until his retirement in 1920 which, at the time, was the record for the time spent by a player with one club. Crompton won Football League championship medals in 1912 and 1914, and played 17 times for the League in representative matches.

A year after his retirement he was appointed a director of Blackburn and served as team manager 1926-31. In 1935 he accepted the job as manager of Bournemouth & Boscombe Athletic but stayed less than a year and from 1938 until his death he was honorary manager of his old club. His physical strength enabled him to play a robust game to great effect and he was a master of the shoulder charge. Despite his style he was known as a scrupulously fair player. He was q plumber by trade.

Johnny CRONSHEY

Speed Skating
John Dennis Cronshey. b. 7 Jul 1926
Brentford.

Over a period of 12 years 1947-58 he only took part in the World Championship six times and on one of these occasions (1949) he competed under the auspices of the International Skating Union as he was engaged at the time in one of his many disputes with the British authorities. In 1951 he became the only British speed skater to win a medal at the World Championships when a superb series of performances in the 500m (3rd), 1500m (11th), 5000m (2nd) and 10,000m (3rd) gave him second place overall. Despite this success, he disappointed in his two Olympic appearances, his best performances being 11th place in the 5000m (1948) and 10,000m (1956). He missed the 1952 Olympics as he was, once again, at loggerheads with the British authorities.

Due to the lack of facilities at home, he lived and trained abroad for a number of years and had he not been quite such a 'rebel' he would have had the opportunity to seek many more Championship honours. During his career he broke every British record.

Lee CROOKS

Rugby League
Lee Crooks. b. 18 Sep 1963 Castleford, West Yorkshire.

Signed as a 17-year-old from the amateur ranks by Hull in 1980, Crooks captained the first ever GB Colts tour to Australia in 1982. He also won a Challenge Cup winners' medal in May that year and in October he won his first GB cap against Australia. At the age of 19 years 42 days he was, at the time, the youngest forward ever to be capped.

After summer spells with Western Suburbs and Balmain in Australia he was transferred to Leeds in 1987 for a then record fee of £172,500 and in 1990 he moved to Castleford helping then to win the Regal Trophy in 1994. He has won 17 GB caps (plus 2 as a substitute) 1982-94 and has toured three times with the British Lions (1984, 1988, 1992) and only an injury, which kept him out of the Test side on the 1988 tour, prevented him from adding to his total of international appearances. For a prop-forward, he has exceptional ball handling skills and he is also a reliable place kicker.

Tim CROOKS

Rowing
Timothy John Crooks. b. 12 May 1949.

A versatile oarsman, Crooks finished 5th in the double sculls at the 1972 Olympics and then won a silver medal in the eights in 1976. He also won a silver in the eights at the 1974 World Championships with 4th places in the coxed fours in 1975 and quadruple sculls in 1977. At home he won the Goblets at Henley in 1971, the Diamonds, 1977-8 and the Wingfield Sculls 1979-80. He showed his all-round ability by winning the all-sport British Superstars TV competition in 1977.

Harold CUDMORE (Ireland)

Yachting
Harold Cudmore. b. 21 Apr 1944.

Cudmore has become well established as one of the world's foremost match-racing helmsmen, achieving outstanding success in the Congressional Cup, as he was the winning helmsman in the UK event in 1978, 1980-2 and 1984-5, and the US event in 1986.

He represented Ireland at the 1972 Olympics in the Flying Dutchman class. Making his name in dinghy sailing, he won the Half Ton Cup in 1976 and won all five events for the One Ton Cup in 1981 in *Jusine III*. He was overall skipper of *White Crusader*, the British challenger for the America's Cup 1986/7 and skippered the winning British Admiral's Cup team in 1989.

Retaining his America's Cup connection, he was adviser and coach for the winning US boat America 3 in 1992, and in 1995 advised the French challenger.

Stan CULLIS

Football
Stanley Cullis. b. 25 Oct 1916 Ellesmere Port, Cheshire. *28/2/2001*

Cullis was one of England's finest centre-halves, although his career was curtailed by World War II. He made his debut for Wolverhampton Wanderers in 1934 and remained loyal to the club throughout his career. He won 12 England caps 1937-9, and played in the 1939 FA Cup final when Wolves surprisingly lost to Portsmouth. He made 20 appearances for England in wartime internationals and although he won no further full caps after the war he continued to play for Wolves until 1947, when he was appointed the club's assistant manager.

Many of the honours that eluded him during his playing days came his way during his long period as manager of Wolves, from 1948 to 1964. Under his guidance the club won the FA Cup twice (1949, 1960) and were League champions three times (1954, 1958-9).

Surprisingly sacked by Wolves in 1964, he was manager of Birmingham City 1965-70, after which he became a businessman in Wolverhampton and served on the Midland Sports Council.

Arthur CUMMING

Figure Skating
Arthur Warren Jack Cumming. b. 8 May 1889 Marylebone, London. d. 8 May 1914 Hammersmith, London.

His free flowing, rhythmic movements provided the foundation from which all modern free-skating programmes have developed and he is one of the most influential figures in the evolution of the sport. His unique artistic style was based on the Russian Ballet and he had numerous talks with their producer and director, Serge Diaghilev, when the Russians visited London.

After finishing 2nd in the pattern-skating event at the 1908 Olympic Games, he adopted his new style and placed 2nd at the British Championships in 1910 before taking the title in 1912 and 1914. At the World Championships he finished 5th in the singles in 1912 and 7th in the pairs 1912-3 partnering the Hon. Mrs Arthur Cadogan. Sadly he never fulfilled his potential as he was killed in a car accident on Hammersmith Bridge after celebrating his 25th birthday.

John CURRIE

Rugby Union
John David Currie. b. 3 May 1932 Clifton, Bristol. d. 8 Dec 1990 Leicester.

Currie and David Marques (qv) formed one of England's great second-row pairings. They both made their international debuts against Wales in 1956 and went on to play together in 22 consecutive internationals before Marques retired in 1961. During this period, England won the Grand Slam in 1957, the Triple Crown in 1960 and lost only four matches. Currie won three further caps in 1962 partnering Vic Harding.

An Oxford Blue 1954-7, he won the majority of his caps with the Harlequins but the last three came after he had moved to Bristol. An accomplished cricketer, he played nine first class matches for Oxford without winning his Blue and he played once for Somerset.

He served as chairman of the Harlequins

1980-8, and also as an England selector. He died after suffering a heart attack while driving from his Buckinghamshire home to Loughborough during a blizzard.

Joan CURRY

Squash and Tennis
Patricia Joan Curry. b. 10 Oct 1920, Sidmouth, Devon. Later Mrs G E Hughesman.

Curry was British squash champion and a Wightman Cup tennis player. As a promising tennis player, she qualified for Wimbledon in 1939 but lack of opportunities during the war years led her to take up squash and in her first tournament appearance she won the Ladies' Open at Queen's Club in 1946. She went on to win the British squash title three times, 1947-9, before losing to Janet Morgan (qv) in the next three finals, 1950-2.

On resuming her tennis career after the war, she was a Wimbledon singles quarter-finalist in 1946 and played in the Wightman Cup in 1946 and 1950, although she lost both her singles matches. In 1950 she doubled up by also uniquely representing GB v USA at squash in the Wolfe-Noel Cup. She was the British Hard Court singles champion 1949-50 and the British Covered Court champion in the singles 1949 and the doubles 1948 and 1950.

John CURRY

Figure Skating
John Anthony Curry. b. 9 Sep 1949 Birmingham. d. 15 Apr 1994 Binton, Warwickshire.

The first Englishman to win an Olympic figure-skating title, Curry's originality and elegance revitalised the sport in Britain. After winning the British Junior Championship in 1967 he won his first senior title in 1970. Steadily improving performances in the World and European Championships and 11th place at the 1972 Olympics led to invaluable sponsorship from the American millionaire, Ed Moser. This enabled him to train under the renowned coach Carlo Fassi in ideal conditions in Colorado. The benefits were soon apparent and in 1975 he placed 2nd in the European and 3rd in the World Championships. He won the European title in 1976 and then gave a superbly artistic performance to take the Olympic gold medal. He quickly consolidated his position by winning the World title and then turned professional and was able to negotiate a highly lucrative contract.

He produced and starred in a successful ice show but he never forgot his early financial hardships and was a generous supporter of the National Skating Association. He was voted BBC Sports Personality of the Year and awarded the OBE in 1976. He appeared professionally as a dancer in *Brigadoon* and as a Shakespearean actor, and died of an AIDS-related illness.

David CUTLER

Bowls
David J Cutler. b. 1 Aug 1954 Redruth, Cornwall.

At the age of 18 in 1972 he became the youngest ever winner of an English title, with the triples, having started bowling at the age of 14. Two years later, 1974, he won the national junior singles title. Between 1974 and 1984, bowling for St Austell, Cornwall, he won five major EBA titles, including the English singles in 1979. He made his debut for England in an outdoor international in 1975 and won numerous caps, both indoors and outdoors, up to 1988. He is the owner of a bowls equipment business and part-time civil servant in Plymouth.

Kenny DALGLISH

Football
Kenneth Mathieson Dalglish. b. 4 Mar 1951 Dalmarnock, Glasgow.

A player of prodigious talent, Dalglish has been equally successful as a manager. Joining Celtic in 1970 he helped them to win nine major titles: the Scottish Cup (1972, 1974-5, 1977), Scottish League (1972-4, 1977) and Scottish League Cup (1975).

After ten years he moved to Liverpool in 1977 for the then British record fee of

£440,000. His successes in major competitions were continued at Anfield and he was a member of the team which won the European Cup (1978, 1981, 1984), the FA Cup 1986, the Football League six times (1979-80, 1982-4, 1986) and the League Cup for four consecutive years 1981-4. He followed 112 League goals at Celtic with 118 for Liverpool and is the only man to have scored 100 goals in both the English and Scottish Leagues.

In June 1985 he was appointed as player-manager at Liverpool and in his first season led the club to the League and Cup double. He repeated the League championship success in 1988 and 1990. He made his last League appearance in May 1989 and in February 1991 he shocked the football world by suddenly resigning, but he came back into the game in October when he took over as manager of Blackburn Rovers, helping them win promotion from Division Two in 1991/2, to 2nd place in 1993/4 and first in 1994/5 in the Premier League. He thus joined Herbert Chapman and Brian Clough (qqv) as the only men to have managed more than one club to win the championship. In June 1995 he became Blackburn's Director of Football, with his assistant Ray Harford taking over as team manager.

Dalglish won a record 102 Scottish caps 1971-86, and equalled Denis Law's scoring record of 30 goals for Scotland.

He was awarded the MBE in 1985 and he was both Player of the Year (Writers' 1979, 1983, PFA 1983) and Manager of the Year (1986, 1988, 1990, 1995). One of the greatest of all British forwards, he will be remembered for his determined and incisive finishing when in the opponents' goal area.

Fred DALY

Golf
Frederick Daly b. 11 Oct 1911 Portrush, Co. Antrim. d. 18 Nov 1990.

In 1947 Daly won the Open by one shot to become the first ever Irish winner. In that year he went on to win the PGA Match Play, a title he won again in 1948 and 1952. He was also 2nd in the Open in

1948, joint 3rd in 1950, joint 4th in 1951 and 3rd in 1952. He was the first Irishman ever to play for Britain in the Ryder Cup, in which he played in the four ties 1947-53 with a record of three wins, four losses and one half.

He learned the game as a caddie at Portrush and became the professional at Mahee Golf Cup at the age of 17, achieving his first important success with the Ulster Professional Championship in 1936. He went on to win this title a further ten times to 1958 and he was Irish Professional champion in 1940, 1946 and 1952. For 30 years, from 1944, he was the professional at the Balmoral Club in Belfast.

Fred DARLING

Horse Racing
Frederick Darling. b. 15 May 1884 Beckhampton, Wiltshire. d. 9 June 1953 Beckhampton.

He was leading trainer in Britain six times: 1926, 1933, 1940-2 and in his last season of 1947, and trained 19 Classics winners, including seven of the Derby, tying the record. Darling came from a notable racing family; his great-grandfather Sam had ridden the winner of the St Leger in 1833, his father Sam (1852-1921) was a successful trainer with seven Classics winners, and his elder brother Sam (1881-1967) also trained at Newmarket.

Fred was an apprentice jockey to his father before taking out a trainer's licence in 1907. After training in Germany he took over his father's stables at Beckhampton in 1913 and trained there for 33 years. He produced his first Classics winner when *Hurry On* won the 1916 St Leger and his best horses included the 1942 Triple Crown winner *Sun Chariot* and *Tudor Minstrel*. He was a fierce disciplinarian, totally dedicated to his job.

Bernard DARWIN

Golf
Bernard Richard Meirion Darwin. b. 7 Sep 1876 Downe, nr Bromley, Kent. d. 18 Oct 1961 Denton, East Sussex

Darwin was widely respected as the greatest writer and authority on the game of golf and a most distinguished essayist. He was the first golf correspondent for *The Times*, for whom he wrote from 1919 until 1953, and he also wrote for *Country Life* until shortly before his death.

No mean player himself, he was a semi-finalist in the Amateur Championship, in which he made 25 appearances, in 1909 and 1921, and won a Walker Cup singles in 1922 when, covering the match for *The Times*, he was called in to replace the sick British captain, Robert Harris. He played for England against Scotland eight times between 1902 and 1924 and was captain of the Royal and Ancient in 1934/5.

The grandson of anthropologist Charles Darwin and son of Sir Francis Darwin FRS, he practised law on leaving Cambridge University before deciding on a life writing about golf from 1907. Hewas awarded the CBE in 1937 for his services to literature and sport.

Chris DAVIDGE

Rowing
Christopher Guy Vere Davidge. b. 5 Nov 1929 Northampton.

After stroking the Eton boat in 1948 to their first victory in the Ladies' Plate at Henley for 27 years, he went up to Oxford and stroked the University boat as a freshman in 1949 when they narrowly lost to Cambridge. He missed the 1950 race through jaundice and in 1951 Oxford sank at the start, losing the re-row two days later, but the following year he finally stroked Oxford to victory.

He was a competitor at the Olympic Games in 1952 (4th coxless pairs), 1956 (eights) and 1960 (5th coxless fours) and attended the next four Games as a coach. At the 1962 Commonwealth Games he won gold in the coxless fours and a bronze in the eights and in the European Championships he won the coxless pairs in 1957 after winning a bronze in 1954. At Henley he won the Goblets 1957-8 and 1963 and the double sculls in 1959.

Vice chairman of the Commonwealth Games Council for England, he was deputy team manager in 1970 for the

England team at the Commonwealth Games, general team manager in 1974 and deputy team commandant in 1986 and 1990. He works as a Lloyds underwriter, was awarded the OBE in 1982 and was President of the ARA 1975-85.

Bob DAVIES

Horse Racing
Bertram Robert Davies. b. 14 May 1946 Shrewsbury, Shropshire.

The highlights of his career as a jumps jockey came when he shared the NH jockeys' title with Terry Biddlecombe (qv) in 1968/9 with 77 winners and when he won the title with 91 winners in 1969/70 and with 89 in 1971/2. He also had 91 winners in 1975/6, five behind the winner, John Francome (qv) and in his career 1966-82 rode 911 winners. In 1978 he won the Grand National on *Lucius*.

He rode as an amateur from 1962 to 1967 and had his first winner in 1966. He obtained a degree in agriculture from Wye College in 1967 before turning professional. He married Terry Biddlecombe's sister, Susan.

Gerald DAVIES

Rugby Union
Thomas Gerald Reames Davies. b. 7 Feb 1945 Llansaint, Carmarthenshire.

A fast, elusive runner, Davies was one of the most exciting backs of any era. Winning 11 caps at centre and 35 on the wing, he shared with Gareth Edwards (qv) the Welsh record for the most international tries (20, before surpassed by Ieuan Evans), with a further three for the British Lions.

From Queen Elizabeth GS, Carmarthen he went to Loughborough College and then to Cambridge University where he won his Blue 1968-70. In 1970 he withdrew from international rugby to concentrate on his finals at Cambridge but on his return the following year he helped Wales to the Grand Slam and then played for Cardiff, London Welsh and the Barbarians.

On the 1968 Lions tour of South Africa injury restricted his Test appearances to one match, but he was at his best on the 1971 tour of Australia and New Zealand when he played in all four Tests. He declined invitations to tour South Africa in 1974 and New Zealand in 1977. He is now the rugby correspondent of *The Times*.

Jonathan DAVIES

Rugby Union and Rugby League
Jonathan Davies. b. 24 Oct 1962 Trimsaran, Carmarthenshire.

One of the very few players to became legends at both codes of rugby football, Davies is now rated by some as the greatest rugby player of the day in either code. As a stand-off with Llanelli he won 27 Welsh union caps 1985-8, helping his country to the Triple Crown in 1988 and scoring a record 13 drop goals, before signing for league club Widnes in January 1989. The transfer made the headlines as one of the biggest sporting stories of the year and Davies made an immediate impact at this game, where he became a utility back, rather than a specialist stand-off. He scored 1000 points in just 109 matches and only fellow Welsh rugby union international, Lewis Jones (qv) of Leeds, had ever reached that milestone in fewer matches (104).

Davies toured Australia with GB in 1990 and scored 342 points (30 tries, 112 goals) for Widnes in 1991 to set a club scoring record for one season and was voted the rugby league Player of the Year in 1991 and 1994. At the end of 1991 he played in Australia in the closed season and in 1993 he moved to Warrington. Some thought that his jink, dummy and sidestep, the trademarks of great Welsh fly-halves, would not stand up to the rigours of the league game but Davies proved to be quite capable of handling the more physical aspects of the code. His 10 goals in GB's 72-6 victory over France in April 1993 removed any doubt as to ability to adapt to the league game and his genius was shown to best effect with a brilliant try to set up Britain's great win over Australia in October 1994. To then he had won 12 GB caps (plus one as a replacement), kicking 49 goals. He was awarded the MBE in 1995.

Laura DAVIES

Golf
Laura Jane Davies b. 5 Oct 1963 Coventry.

A prodigious striker of a golf ball, but also a fine putter, Davies had won 36 tournaments, including 11 in the USA around the world by June 1995, by when she had become firmly established as the world number one. In 1994 she became the first European golfer to head the money list for the LPGA tour in the USA and worldwide she won eight tournaments, uniquely on five tours: three in the US, two in Europe, one in Japan, one in Asia (Thailand), and ending the year with the Australian Ladies' Masters.

The winner of the Surrey Girls' title in 1982 and the English Ladies' intermediate title in 1983, she played on the Curtis Cup team in 1984, when she beat the noted American Anne Sander. She turned professional in 1985, meeting with such immediate success that she was top of the order of merit on the European tour. A year later she won the British Open and was again the European tour top money-winner in 1986. In 1987 she became the first British golfer to win the US Women's Open and, joining the US tour, had two victories in her first season of 1988, but did not play there regularly enough until 1994 to break into the top ten. Then, however, she burst through to end up just ahead of Beth Daniel (USA) with season's figures of $687,201 to take her LPGA career figure to $1,685,657.

She led the European tour for a third time in 1992 after losing 42 lb *19 kg* in weight. She played for the European Team in the Solheim Cup in 1990, 1992 and 1994, with a record of six wins and three losses; her three wins in 1992 played a major part in inspiring the European success. She was awarded the MBE in 1988.

Lynn DAVIES

Athletics
Lynn Davies. b. 20 May 1942 Nantymoel, Bridgend.

'Lynn the Leap' was gold medallist at the long jump at the 1964 Olympics, 1966 Europeans and 1966 and 1970 Commonwealth Games. His confidence destroyed by Bob Beamon's epic jump, he was only 9th in the 1968 Olympics, but he came back to win the 1969 European silver and to take part again in the Olympics in 1972, when he did not qualify for the final. Also in the Europeans he was 4th in 1971 and 12th in 1962 outdoors, and was 1st in 1967 and 2nd in 1969 indoors. He was AAA champion five times outdoors and three times indoors. His eight UK records were headed by his best jump of 8.23m *27ft* at Berne on 30 Jun 1968. He made 43 international appearances for the UK from 1962, when he made his debut at the European Championships (11th at long jump). That year he was also 4th in the Commonwealth long jump.

Coached and inspired by Ron Pickering, he was a most tenacious competitor and a great ambassador for sport. Davies later became technical director of Canadian athletics (1973-6) and British team manager before taking up a broadcasting career with BBC Wales.

Other bests: 100y 9.5 (1964), 100m 10.4 (1967), triple jump 15.43m (1962).

Mervyn DAVIES

Rugby Union
Thomas Mervyn Davies. b. 9 Dec 1946 Swansea.

With 38 caps for Wales in consecutive matches (1969-76) and eight for the British Lions (1971, 1974) he was at the time of his retirement the world's most capped No. 8.

A member of the Welsh team which won the Five Nations Championships five times between 1969 and 1976, he went on two British Lions' tours during this period, playing in all four Tests in New Zealand 1971 and in South Africa 1974. The Lions won both series and his superb play led to him being generally recognised as the outstanding No. 8 in world rugby. On his return from South Africa he took over the captaincy of a disjointed Welsh side and led them to the Grand Slam in 1976. A clear favourite to lead the Lions in New Zealand in 1977, his career was ended when he suffered a brain haemorrhage in the 1976 Welsh Cup semi-final. Apart from a brief spell with London Welsh, when he was teaching in England, he remained loyal to Swansea and captained the club in his final season.

His father played for Wales in a Victory International in 1946.

Mike DAVIES

Tennis
Michael Grenfell Davies. b. 3 Jan 1936 Swansea.

Davies was one of the few top class players from Wales. He won the British Covered Court singles in 1958 and the Hard Court singles in 1960, when was also runner-up in the Wimbledon doubles partnering Bobby Wilson (qv).

Between 1955 and 1960 he built a fine Davis Cup record (15/22 singles: 9/15 doubles) in 16 ties. His playing career was cut short when he became a professional administrator with WCT.

Phil DAVIES

Rugby Union
Phllip Thomas Davies. b. 19 Oct 1963 Seven Sisters, Neath and Port Talbot.

Winning 45 caps 1985-95,Davies is the most capped Welsh forward of all-time. Essentially a back-row specialist, although sometimes playing at lock, he captained Llanelli 1987-90. Formerly a police officer and financial consultant, he now runs his own packaging business.

Sharron DAVIES

Swimming
Sharron Elizabeth Davies. b. 1 Nov 1962 Plymouth. Married to Derek Redmond.

The tall Davies was the golden girl of British swimming when she won the Olympic silver medal at 400m individual medley in 1980, in a time that remained the UK record 15 years later. She had been, at the age of 13, the youngest member of the 1976 British Olympic team. progressing to become the 400m IM European bronze medallist in 1977 and Commonwealth champion at 200m

and 400m individual medley in 1978. That year, when she won a swimming scholarship to Kelly College, she also won World silver medals at both 4 x 100m relays and was 6th at 400m IM. After a nearly nine-year retirement, in which she had worked on radio and television as well as making celebrity appearances, she returned in 1989, regained her national title at 200m IM, and made the British team for the European Championships. In 1992 she improved the UK short-course medley records that she had set in 1980.

Her British records have been: freestyle: 200m 2:04.11 (1978), two 400m to 4:18.59 (1979), 800m 8:58.87 (1978); backstroke: four 200m to 2:19.30 (1978); IM: five at 200m to 2:17.31 (1980), four at 400m to 4:46.83 (1980). Short-course: one 100m butterfly, two at each of 100m, 400m and 800m freestyle, 100m backstroke; three at 200m free, 200m back, five 200m IM to 2:13.41 (1992), six at 400m IM to 4:42.24 (1992). Also 100m medley 1:03.27 (1992). ASA national champion at freestyle: 100m 1978, 200m & 400m 1977-9, 800m 1978; 200m back 1976-8, 50m butterfly 1992, 200m IM 1976-80, 1989, 1992; 400m IM 1976-80, as well as 15 short-course titles. She was awarded the MBE in 1993.

Her husband **Derek** Anthony **Redmond** (b. 3 Sep 1965 Bletchley, Northants) ran British records for 400m at 44.82 in 1985 and 44.50 in 1987. The latter was in the semi-finals of the World Championships, at which he was 5th in the final before a silver medal with the British record-setting team in the 4 x 400m. Four years later he ran a brilliant 44.15 leg for the British team that won the World title in another record time. He was 4th at 400m and won relay gold at the 1986 Europeans and was AAA 400m champion in 1991, but his careeer was sadly blighted by injuries, most poignantly when his father helped him off the track with a torn hamstring in the 1992 Olympic semi-finals.

Terry DAVIES

Rugby Union
Terence John Davies. b. 24 Sep 1933 Llwynhendy, nr Llanelli, Carmarthenshire.

Capped 21 times as full-back by Wales 1953-61, he kicked 50 points (7 conversions, 12 penalty goals). He toured Australia and New Zealand with the British Lions in 1959 and, with 72 points in nine appearances, he was the leading scorer on the New Zealand leg of the tour where he played in the second and fourth Tests. As an 18-year-old he played for Swansea against the 1951 South Africans but he later joined Llanelli. He is the joint proprietor of a saw mill with his brother, Leonard, who toured Canada with the Barbarians in 1957.

W.J.A. DAVIES

Rugby Union
William John Abbott Davies. b. 21 Jun 1890 Pembroke. d. 26 Apr 1967 Teddington, London.

For US Portsmouth, Royal Navy and England, 'Dave' Davies and Cyril Kershaw (qv) had few rivals as a half-back pairing. They were partners in the England team a record 14 times and in their four seasons together, England won the International Championship twice and shared it once. Davies captained England in 11 of his 22 internationals 1913-23, and held the record as England's most capped fly-half until 1989 when the record passed to Rob Andrew (qv). The only time he was on the losing side in an international was on his debut against South Africa in 1913. He was noted for his left-footed drop kicks and elusive running.

A regular naval officer, he was awarded the OBE in 1919 for his work with the naval constructor corps.

DAVIN Brothers (Ireland)

Athletics
Maurice Davin. b. 29 Jun 1842 Carrick-on-Suir, Co. Tipperary. d. Jun 1927.

Thomas Davin. b. 1852 Carrick-on-Suir. d. 1949.

Patrick Davin. b. 4 Jun 1857 Carrick-on-Suir. d. 1890.

The Davins were three remarkably talented Irish brothers, who were all world record

holders. Tom was the first to post a world best with 5 ft 10 $1/4$ in *1.785m* for high jump in 1873, and Pat improved the family and world record to 6 ft 2 $3/4$ in *1.90m* in 1880 before twice setting a world long jump record of 23 ft 2 in *7.06m* within a fortnight in 1883. Maurice set world records at both shot and hammer (7 ft circle) at the 1881 AAA Championships, and with Pat winning the high jump and long jump, the brothers won every field event, except the pole vault at these Championships.

Between them the brothers also won 30 Irish titles. Pat led the way with 16 between 1878 and 1883: five each at 120y hurdles and high jump, four at long jump, and one each at 100y and shot.

Tom and Pat qualified as solicitors, while Maurice took over the family farm and river boat business. In the turbulent early years of organised athletics in Ireland, Maurice was a steadying influence and was elected the first president of the Gaelic Athletic Association in 1884.

Fred DAVIS

Snooker D *14/4/98*
Fred Davis. b. 14 Feb 1913 Whittingham Moor, near Chesterfield, Derbyshire.

He played billiards and snooker at the highest level for more than 60 years, from winning the national Under-16 billiards title in 1929 to ending his professional career in 1990. He succeeded his elder brother Joe as world snooker champion in 1948, and the following year became the first professional to defeat Joe on level terms. He was also world snooker champion in 1949 and from 1951-6, having been beaten in the final in 1940 and 1947. He won the Professional Match-play championship for the first five (1952-6) of its six years as the world's top tournament. When he emulated his brother by winning and later retaining the world professional billiards title in 1980, he became the oldest ever world champion at any sport.

His other major titles: UK pro billiards 1951, *News of the World* snooker 1958-9, Australian Open snooker 1960. He was awarded the OBE in 1977.

Howard DAVIS

Hockey
Francis Howard Vincent Davis. b. 24 Sep 1932 Breseley, Shropshire.

Between 1956 and 1964, Davis won 40 caps for England and, a then record, 41 caps for Great Britain, and captained both teams from the centre-half position. His international career included three appearances at the Olympic Games 1956-64.

On leaving Felsted School, he joined the North Stafford Club in 1950 and apart from a period of National Service, when he represented the Army and the Combined Services, he remained with the club until his retirement.

Joe DAVIS

Billiards and Snooker
Joseph Davis. b. 15 Apr 1901 Whitwell, Derbyshire. d. 10 Jul 1978 Hampshire.

Supreme at snooker and second only to Walter Lindrum (Aus) at billiards, Joe Davis is the only man to have held the world title at both games simultaneously. He learned to play in his father's public house and first qualified for the World Championship in 1922 when he lost to Tom Newman (qv) in the final. He was again beaten by Newman in the final on his second and third appearances in 1926 and 1927, but finally became the world billiards champion the following year and retained the title until beaten by Walter Lindrum in 1933. His best championship break, without the aid of repetitive sequences, was 2,052 in 1930.

In 1926, two years before becoming the world billiards champion, he won the world snooker title and remained unbeaten at that game until 1955. His name became synonymous with the game and he was so superior to the rest of the world that he retired from championship play after winning the world title for the 15th time in 1946. In 1955 he became the first man to make a maximum break of 147 under championship conditions and between 1928 and 1965 he compiled 687 century breaks.

More than any man, he was responsible for turning snooker into a world game and his personality and business acumen brought considerable financial benefit both to himself and to the game in general. He was awarded the OBE in 1963.

Steve DAVIS

Snooker
Steve Davis. b. 22 Aug 1957 Plumstead, London.

Davis was the dominant snooker player of the 1980s, when with flawless technique he won 22 ranking tournaments compared to the next best of five (Ray Reardon) and was world champion in 1981, 1983-4 and 1987-9, runner-up twice and once a semi-finalist. His other major titles have included the British Open in 1981-2, 1984, 1986 and 1993; the UK Open 1980-1 and 1984-7; Benson & Hedges Masters 1982 and 1988. He also has a record four World Cup appearances on the winning team, for England 1981, 1983, 1988-9.

He was awarded the MBE in 1988, in which year he was BBC Sports Personality of the Year.

After winning the British junior title at billiards in 1976, he turned professional in 1978 and under the careful guidance of Barry Hearn soon made his mark. In 1980 he beat the defending champion Terry Griffiths (qv) in the second round of the World Championship, before winning his first title the following year.

In the 1990s he hit, by his standards, a poor patch, and he went 27 months without winning a ranking tournament until two in early 1992. He hit a low-point with a loss to Peter Ebdon in the 1992 World Championship first round, then had to wait another year for a tournament win until he beat Stephen Hendry (qv) in the final of the European Open in 1993. He followed that with his seventh win in the B&H Irish Masters, his 66th professional tournament victory and briefly regained his provisional world top ranking in March 1994 until Hendry regained it by beating him in the World semi-final. In January 1995 he won his 70th professional tournament from 93 finals, including 28 ranking events.

Eugene DAVY (Ireland)

Rugby Union
Eugene O'Donnell Davy. b. 26 Jul 1904 Dublin.

As fly-half or centre, Davy was a regular member of the Irish side for a decade. Between 1925 and 1934 he won 34 caps and against Scotland at Murrayfield in 1930 he scored three tries in the first half; this remained an Irish record until 1991 when Brian Robinson crossed the line four times in the World Cup match against Zimbabwe.

Davy was a member of the Lansdowne club's brilliant three-quarter which was selected in its entirety for three successive internationals in 1931-2. A stockbroker, he served as President of the Irish RU in 1967.

Alison DAWES

Equestrianism, Show Jumping
Alison Selina Dawes b. 14 Mar 1946 Sutton Coldfield, West Midlands. née Westwood.

Riding *The Maverick* Alison won bronze medals at the first World ladies' individual championship in 1965 and at the 1969 European Ladies', improving to silver in 1971, after her marriage. She was also British ladies' champion in 1972, won the Queen Elizabeth II Cup in 1969 and 1973 (shared with Ann Moore (qv)), and the Hickstead Jumping Derby in 1968 and 1973.

John DAWES

Rugby Union
Sydney John Dawes. b. 29 Jun 1940 Chapel of Ease, Caerphilly.

A shrewd tactical centre, Dawes won 22 caps for Wales 1964-71. In 1971 he led Wales to the Grand Slam and at the end of the season he became the first Welshman to be honoured with the captaincy of the Lions for the tour of New Zealand. Under his leadership the Lions became the only British side to win a Test series in New Zealand. He retired from the international game at the end of the tour but returned to captain the Barbarians to a memorable victory against New Zealand in 1973.

When he finally gave up playing, he maintained his interest in the game notably as coach of the Welsh national team and the 1977 Lions. He was awarded the OBE for his services to the game.

While at Loughborough College, he won many University representative honours and most of his club rugby was with London Welsh who became one of the most exciting teams in the country under his leadership.

Mat DAWSON

Horse Racing
Mathew Dawson. b 9 Jan 1820 Gullane, East Lothian d. 18 Aug 1898 Newmarket.

A great Scottish trainer, Dawson produced 28 Classics winners: six each of the 1000 Guineas, Derby and St Leger and five each of the 2000 Guineas and Oaks. His greatest horse was, however, not a Classics winner, *St Simon*. He was apprenticed to his father, George, at Stamford Hall, East Lothian, and at 18, prior to training on his own account, became head lad for his brother **Thomas** (1809-80), who trained at Middleton from 1830 and had five Classics winners.

His younger brothers **John** and **Joseph** trained four and five Classics winners respectively. In 1885 Mathew handed over his Heath House stable at Newmarket to his nephew **George** (c.1853-1913), who added ten Classics wins to the family tally, but Mathew continued to train and won four Classics for Lord Rosebery in 1884-5.
A bluff man, always immaculately dressed, he was widely respected, and had a contempt for heavy betting. He was one of the first trainers to run a private stable, at Newmarket, rather than train privately for a specific owner.

Ronnie DAWSON (Ireland)

Rugby Union
Alfred Ronald Dawson. b. 5 Jun 1932 Dublin.

Dawson was an outstanding leader who captained the 1959 British Lions in Australasia after winning only nine of his

27 Irish caps 1958-64. As hooker for Dublin Wanderers and Leinster he made his international debut against Australia in 1958 when he scored a try in Ireland's first-ever win against a touring side. After missing much of the 1960 season due to a broken leg, he captained the Barbarians to victory over the South Africans in 1961. On retirement, he became a successful coach and accompanied the 1968 Lions to South Africa as assistant manager. An architect by profession, he served as Barbarians committee member and was elected to the International Rugby Board in 1974.

John DAY

Horse Racing
John Barham Day. b. 1793 Houghton Down, Hampshire. d. 21 Mar 1860.

Known, sarcastically, as 'Honest John Day' he was a most successful lightweight jockey, riding 16 Classics winners between 1826 and 1841: five each of the 1000 Guineas and Oaks, four of the 2000 Guineas and two of the St Leger. From 1835 he trained at Danebury in Hampshire, with seven Classics successes, three each of the 1000 and 2000 Guineas and one of the Oaks. A heavy gambler, he and his family were much involved in many of the scandals which plagued the racing world in the 19th century.

One son **John Day Jnr** (1819-93), who eventually took over the Danebury stables, rode the winner of the 2000 Guineas in 1844 and as a trainer had 12 Classics successes 1846-69: four each of the 1000 and 2000 Guineas and two each of the Derby and Oaks. Another son **William** Henry Day (1823-1908) trained three Classics winners.

Christopher DEAN

Ice skating
Christopher Colin Dean. b. 27 Jul 1958 Nottingham.

His partnership with Jayne Torvill (qv) produced some legendary performances in ice dancing. They joined forces in 1975 after both had achieved some success with previous partners and they won the first of a record six successive British titles three years later. After placing 5th at the 1980 Olympics they established themselves as performers of the highest class by winning the World and European Championships in 1981. After successfully defending both titles in 1982, they won their third successive World title in 1983 after missing the Europeans because of injury.

Their performance at the 1984 Olympics in Sarajevo will go down in history as one of the greatest sporting exhibitions of all-time. Their brilliant interpretation of Ravel's *Bolero* drew a six (the maximum score) from each of the nine judges for artistic presentation and their total of 12 sixes for the entire competition broke all previous records. It seemed at the time that this performance was the ultimate, but four weeks later the judges awarded them a total of 13 sixes to secure their fourth consecutive World title. They had earlier won their third European title and at the end of the year were voted BBC Sports Personality of the Year. Throughout their career they received a record total of 136 sixes. They then turned professional and were a huge success with their ice show.

Dean was awarded the MBE in 1981. He was married in 1991-3 to the French-Canadian Isabelle Duchesnay (b. 18 Dec 1963) who with her brother Paul (b. 31 Jul 1961) won the 1991 world ice dance title and silver medals at the 1992 Olympics. With the readmittance of professionals to competitive skating, Torvill and Dean made a triumphant comeback in 1994, winning first the British ice dance title and then the European, although the latter rather luckily. They skated beautifully at the Olympics but had to settle for bronze medals as the judges preferred the styles of their younger Russian rivals.

Dixie DEAN

Football
William Ralph Dean. b. 21 Jan 1907 Birkenhead, Merseyside. d. 1 Mar 1980 Liverpool.

Dean was a robust, high-scoring centre-forward who was renowned for the power and direction of his heading. Joining Everton from Tranmere Rovers in 1925, he stayed at Goodison Park until 1938, and scored 473 goals in 502 first-class matches (379 in 437 League matches). His greatest season was 1927/8 when he scored 60 goals in 39 League matches to set a record which still stands. That year he also scored 22 goals in other competitions to bring his season's total to 82.

The previous season he had claimed 12 goals in his first international season, uniquely scoring in each of his first five matches for England. In total he scored 18 times in his 16 international matches 1927-32. While he was with Everton they won the Football League in 1928 and 1932, and the FA Cup in 1933. In 1938 he moved to Notts County but played only nine games before transferring to Sligo Rovers where he helped the club to the final of the FA of Ireland Cup (1939).

Dean, who was nicknamed 'Dixie' because of his swarthy complexion, retired on the outbreak of war and was a licensee in Chester until overtaken by ill-health in 1964. He died at Goodison Park after an Everton v Liverpool match and the death of this football legend was mourned far beyond Merseyside.

Colin DEANS

Rugby Union
Colin Thomas Deans. b. 3 May 1955 Hawick, Borders.

Like his father he was the hooker for Hawick. With 52 caps 1978-87, he was the world's most capped hooker when he retired and he also shared the record as Scotland's most capped player with his Hawick team-mate, Jim Renwick (qv). After winning his first cap in 1978 he only missed two internationals, both through injury. He was a member of Scotland's Grand Slam team of 1984. Chosen for the British Lions 1983 tour of New Zealand he was unfortunate that the Lions captain, Ciaran Fitzgerald (qv), was also a hooker and although Deans was clearly a better player, Fitzgerald played as hooker in every Test - all four of which were lost. He was awarded the MBE 1988.

Jim DEAR

Racket Sports
James Patrick St George Dear. b. 17 Mar 1910 Fulham, London. d. 7 Nov 1981 Eton, Berkshire.

The only man to have been British Open champion at rackets, real tennis and squash, Dear added world titles at the first two. A pupil of the great Peter Latham (qv), he started as a ball boy at Queen's Club in 1924 before becoming, at the age of 17, an apprentice professional at Prince's Club. Initially he excelled as a squash player, losing challenges for the British Open to Amr Bey (Egy) for three successive years, 1935-7, before taking the title in 1938. He lost it to Mahmoud Karim (Egy) in the last Open held on a challenge basis in 1946. He became the outstanding rackets and real tennis player of his generation, taking the British Open title at real tennis in 1938 and 1954, and at rackets in 1946, 1951 and 1960.

In 1947 he beat Kenneth Chantler (Can) for the vacant world rackets title, retaining it until beaten by Geoffrey Atkins in 1954. He unsuccessfully challenged Pierre Etchebaster for the world real tennis crown in 1948, but when Etchebaster retired in 1955 Dear beat Albert 'Jack' Johnson (USA) for the vacant title. Johnson made a successful challenge in 1957 and Dear never regained the title. He was a notable coach at Eton, Queen's Club, Wellington College and the New York Racquet Club. Although not an exceptionally hard hitter, he was a master of the angles and change of pace and he used the drop shot to great effect at all the sports. He was awarded the MBE in 1960.

Charles de BEAUMONT

Fencing
Charles Louis Leopold Alfred de Beaumont. b. 5 May 1902 Liverpool. d. 7 Jul 1972 London.

A successful competitor, de Beaumont was also an influential administrator. After winning his Blue at Cambridge in 1923 he later became the first man to win the AFA épée title for three successive years, 1936-8, and he was champion for a fourth time in 1953. After making his debut at the World Championships in 1931, he competed in three Olympic Games (1936, 1948, 1952) and at the Commonwealth Games he won gold medals in the individual épée and the sabre team event in 1950 and the épée team event in 1954 when, at the age of 52, he became the oldest ever Commonwealth Games fencing champion. In 1930 he was appointed the British representative on the International Fencing Federation and he was Hon. Secretary of the AFA from 1936 until 1956 after which he served as President. He was awarded the MBE while serving as Wing Commander with the RAF in World War II and the OBE in 1959 for his services to fencing. He completed his three-volume historical work *Modern British Fencing* in 1966.

Phil DeFREITAS

Cricket
Phillip Anthony Jason DeFreitas b. 18 Feb 1966 Scotts Head, Dominica.

DeFreitas has lived in England since 1976 and was educated at Willesden High School with his England colleague Chris Lewis. He made his debut for Leicestershire in 1985 and took 94 wickets and scored 645 runs in his first full season in 1986. Such success as a fast-medium bowler, coupled with brilliant fielding and batting which included a flamboyant century in 106 minutes against Kent, meant that he was selected for England's tour to Australia in 1986/7, when he made his Test debut. Initially proving more successful in one-day internationals than in Tests, he seemed to have lost his way somewhat and left Leicestershire to join Lancashire in 1989. He was omitted from the 1990/1 tour to Australia, but did well when summoned as a replacement and flourished in the 1991 series against West Indies with 22 wickets at 20.77. Since then, however, except for 21 wickets at 21.47 in three Tests against New Zealand in 1994, he has not quite consolidated his position in the England team. He changed counties again when he joined Derbyshire in 1994. He remains an effective bowler, especially

when not striving for extra pace, but his batting, which was seen at its best in a brilliant 88 against Australia at Adelaide in 1995, has all too often disappointed. He is capable of all the shots, but has yet to achieve any consistency in making useful scores at international level.

43 Tests 1986-95: 910 runs at 14.91, HS 88; 138 wickets at 33.22, BB 7-70; 14 catches.

93 One-day Ints 1987-95: 566 runs at 15.29, HS 49*; 105 wickets at 32.39, BB 4-35; 26 catches.

First-class 1985-95: 6016 runs at 22.03, 6 100s HS 113; 711 wickets at 28.15, BB 7-21; 68 catches.

Jimmy DELANEY

Football
James Delaney. b. 3 Sep 1914 Cleland, Lanarkshire. d. 26 Sep 1989.

Delaney was a speedy right-winger who enjoyed an exceptionally long career. He joined Celtic in 1933 and ended his playing days with Elgin City in 1957. With Celtic, he played on the team which won the Scottish Cup in 1937 and the Scottish League 1936 and 1938. He also won nine Scottish caps from 1936 before moving to Manchester United in 1946, where he won four further caps and an FA Cup winners' medal in 1948.

From Manchester, he went to Aberdeen and then Falkirk after which he enjoyed some successful years in Ireland. Uniquely he won a Cup winners medal in England, Scotland and Northern Ireland (Derry City, 1954) and he was also a losing Cup finalist in Ireland (Cork Athletic, 1956). His son **Pat** played for Motherwell 1958-66.

Ron DELANY (Ireland)

Athletics
Ronald Michael Delany. b. 6 Mar 1935 Arlow, Co. Wicklow.

Delany was the surprise Olympic champion at 1500m in 1956, when he set a new Olympic record of 3:41.2, after covering the last 300m in 38.8, an unprecedented time. He had run his first four-minute mile with 3:59.0 earlier in the year. He was a master of the sprint finish, especially adept at indoor running, and undefeated throughout his career in 40 indoor races in the USA 1956-9, including 34 at the 1 mile. These included three world indoor mile records, 4:03.4 in 1958 and 4:02.5 and 4:01.4 in 1959 and four successive AAU titles 1956-9.

He first came to prominence by winning the first of four successive Irish 880y titles in 1954. This gained him selection for the European Championships where he improved his pb to 1:51.8 and 1:50.2 in qualifying for the final in which he placed 8th. A month later he accepted a scholarship to Villanova University in the USA, and for them won the NCAA 1500m 1956 and mile 1957-8 and the 880y in 1958. His first Irish records came in 1955 at 880y (1:50.0), 1500m (3:49.9) and 1 mile (4:05.8). His best for 880y was 1:47.8 in 1957 and at 1 mile he ran 3:57.5 in 3rd place to Herb Elliott's world record 3:54.5 at Dublin in 1958.

Lawrence DEMMY

Ice Dance
Lawrence Demmy. b. 7 Nov 1931
Manchester.

Partnering Joan Westwood (qv), his victory in the unofficial World championships in 1951 was followed by four consecutive official World titles (1952-5). They also won the European title in 1954 and 1955. After their fifth World victory, he retired to concentrate on his business interests, but he remained an influential figure in the sport being appointed Chairman of the ISU Ice Dance Committee in 1971 and First Vice-President of the ISU in 1994. He was awarded the MBE.

Jack 'Nonpareil' DEMPSEY (Ireland)

Boxing
né John Kelly. b. 15 Dec 1862 Curragh, Co. Kildare, Ireland. d. 2 Nov 1895 Portland, Oregon, USA.

Irish-born, Dempsey went to Brooklyn as a child and began his ring career as a wrestler. After taking up boxing he claimed the World lightweight champi-

onship in 1882 and after moving up to the middleweight class he knocked out George Fulljames (USA) in 22 rounds in 1884 to become the first undisputed world champion of the division under Queensberry Rules. Dempsey retained his title until January 1891 when, after he had taken heavy punishment from Bob Fitzsimmons (qv), the referee stopped the contest after 15 rounds.

Career record 1883-91: 78 contests. Won 48 (25 KO), Drew 7, Lost 3, No decision 17, No contest 3.

Mike DENNESS

Cricket
Michael Henry Denness. b. 1 Dec 1940
Bellshill, North Lanarkshire.

Although his confidence as England captain was all but destroyed by the fearsome fast bowling of Dennis Lillee and Jeff Thomson in Australia in 1974/5, Denness was a determined and intelligent leader. An elegant stroke-maker and fine cover fielder, after playing for Scotland as a schoolboy, he joined Kent in 1962 and led them with much success from 1972 to 1976. After being controversially relieved of the captaincy, he joined Essex and played for them until 1980, helping them to their first championship in 1979.

After just one Test for England in 1969 he was vice-captain to Tony Lewis in India in 1972/3 and became the first Scotsman to captain England when he succeeded Ray Illingworth (qv) as captain for the West Indies tour in 1974. After dropping himself for the 4th Test on that Australian tour, he returned to score 188 in the final Test, although without having to face Jeff Thomson, and he led England to the semifinal of the World Cup in 1975 before again finding the Australian pace men too much in the Test series that followed. His record as captain was six wins and five defeats in his 19 matches in charge. He had been an outstanding fly-half as a rugby player at Ayr Academy.

28 Tests 1969-75: 1667 runs at 39.69, 4 100s HS 188; 28 catches.
12 One-day Ints 1973-5: 264 runs at 29.33, HS 66; 1 catch.

First-class 1959-80: 25,886 runs at 33.48, 33 100s HS 195; 2 wickets at 31.00, BB 1-7; 411 catches.

Doreen DENNY

Ice Dance
Doreen Diana Denny. b. 28 Jan 1941 Staines, Surrey. Later Mrs Canepa, Mrs McSalka and Mrs Routon.

Partnering Courtney Jones (qv), Doreen Demmy won three British and European titles (1959-61) and two World titles (1959-60). They would almost certainly have won their third consecutive World title in 1961 but the Championships were cancelled following the loss of the US team in an air crash.

Her first marriage (1961) to Italian ice dancer, Gianfranco Canepa, ended in divorce and she then married (1966) an American, McSalka, and her third marriage (1981) was to another American, Routon.

Rob DERBYSHIRE

Swimming and Water Polo
John Henry 'Rob' Derbyshire. b. 29 Nov 1878 Manchester. d. 30 Jul 1938 Forge Baslow, Derbyshire.

After winning a gold medal at the 1900 Olympics for water polo, Derbyshire won a silver for 4 x 250m relay in 1906 and another gold for 4 x 200m in 1908. His best individual placing at 100m at three Games 1906-12 was 5th in 1906. In 1907 he became the first British swimmer to break the minute barrier for 100y and he won ten ASA titles: 100y 1898-1901, 1903-04; 220y 1898, 1901, 1903; 880y 1897. He became a baths manager in Manchester and London.

Lord DESBOROUGH

Administration
William Henry Grenfell, Lord Desborough. b. 30 Oct 1855 London. d. 9 Jan 1945 London.

A notable all-round sportsman in his youth, he ran at 3 miles for Oxford v Cambridge in 1876 and rowed in the Boat Race 1876-7. He swam twice across the Niagara Falls, stroked an eight across the English Channel, climbed the Matterhorn three times by different routes and won an Olympic silver medal for fencing (épée team 1906). He later proved equally energetic and versatile as an administrator, serving as president of the MCC, the AAA, the Royal Life Saving Society, the AFA, LTA, National Amateur Wrestling Association and British Olympic Association. With Charles Herbert (1846-1924) he was the first Briton to be elected a member of the IOC. No other individual has come close to matching such a contribution. At one time he served on 115 sporting and civil committees simultaneously.

He entered parliament in 1880, was elevated to the peerage in 1905 and in 1921 declined the offer of the Governor-Generalship of Canada. He became a Knight of the Garter.

Frank DEVLIN (Ireland)

Badminton
Joseph Francis Devlin. b. 16 Jan 1900 Dublin. d. 27 Oct 1988 Clane, Co. Kildare.

The best badminton player of his era, Devlin won successive All-England singles titles 1925-9, with a sixth win in 1931. He also won seven men's doubles, the first with George Sautter (Eng) in 1922 and the rest with his compatriot 'Curly' Mack(qv); and five mixed doubles, the first two with the top tennis player Kitty McKane (see Godfree). In 1931 he became a teaching professional initially at Winnipeg in Canada, then after a tour of Australasia and Malaysia he settled in the USA, in New York and then Baltimore. At the age of 12, he lost half a heel due to osteomyelitis, but while lying in bed spent hours hitting a shuttle against the wall; this developed his powerful and supple wrist.

His daughters **Susan** (later Peard) and **Judith** (b. 22 Oct 1935, later Hashman) were both outstanding players for the USA. Judy became the most successful woman badminton player in the history of the All-England Championships, with ten singles titles, 1954, 1957-8, 1960-4 and 1966-7. She also won seven women's doubles titles, once with Tonny Holst-Christensen

(Den) and six with Susan.That is a record for one pair, and the sisters also won a record ten US women's doubles titles together.

A formidably determined match player, Judy won a record 12 US women's singles titles, 1954, 1956-63, 1965-7, 12 women's doubles and 8 mixed doubles. She helped the USA to three wins in five Uber Cup series, but having lived in England from 1960 she played for them in 1970-2. In 1978 she was appointed England team manager and coach, although that was short-lived as she came into dispute with the Badminton Association. A fine all-rounder, she represented the US at junior level at tennis and was a member of the US lacrosse team for five years.

Susan was a member of the US Uber Cup team 1957-62 and of the Irish team 1963-9. She directed badminton coaching for school children in Ireland 1960-84.

Nilla de WHARTON BURR

Archery
Petronilla de Wharton Burr.

'Nilla' was the only British woman to win the World individual archery title twice. After taking her first title in Stockholm in 1946, she placed 3rd in Prague in 1947 before regaining the title in 1948, when the Championships were held in the grounds of Dulwich College. She was also a member of the winning team in 1946 and 1949 and her total of four World Championship gold medals has only been matched by Louise Nettleton (qv) among British lady archers. At the 1949 Championships she was the top-scorer at every distance setting several world records. She was twice British National champion, 1947-8.

The wife of the Headmaster of a Sussex prep school, she was a keen violinist and maintained that similar strength and dexterity of the fingers was required for both her sporting and musical interests.

Ted DEXTER

Cricket
Edward Ralph Dexter. b. 15 May 1935 Milan, Italy.

'Lord Ted' was a splendid, authoritative batsman, whose powerful straight driving was a particular feature of his game. His great natural talent was also shown in his lively medium-fast bowling and fine fielding, and he was a top-class golfer.

His command made him an obvious choice as captain and he led Cambridge University 1958, Sussex 1960-5 and England (in 30 Tests) 1961-4 as well as being the last captain of the Gentlemen against the Players. Yet he was an unenterprising captain, whose interest in the game often seemed to dull. His majestic innings of 70 against the West Indies at Lord's in 1963 showed him at his best, but he also showed his character with match-saving innings against Australia of 180 in 1961 and 174 in 8 hours in 1964.

In 1964 he stood unsuccessfully for Parliament against Jim Callaghan in Cardiff and retired from cricket the following year. He was persuaded to return three years later and made 203* for Sussex in his first innings. That earned him a Test recall for two matches against Australia. He ran a successful PR company and commentated on TV before being a controversial chairman of the England cricket committee in 1989-93.

62 Tests 1958-68: 4502 runs at 47.89, 9 100s HS 205; 66 wickets at 34.93, BB 4-10; 29 catches.
First-class 1956-68: 21,150 runs at 40.75, 51 100s HS 205; 419 wickets at 29.92, BB 7-24; 233 catches.

Jimmy DICKINSON

Football
James William Dickinson. b. 24 Apr 1925 Alton, Hampshire. d. 8 November 1982 Alton.

His 764 League appearances for one club stood as a record until 1980. He played his first game for Portsmouth as an amateur in 1943 and made his final appearance on his 40th birthday in 1965. He was virtually an automatic choice for England from 1949 to 1956, winning 45 caps at left-half and 3 at right-half when he changed flanks to accommodate the youthful Duncan Edwards (qv). He seemed assured of further international honours until he switched to centre-half for Portsmouth, although he knew he could not command a regular England place in that position. Towards the end of his career in club football he played at left-back. Dickinson played for Portsmouth in the First, Second and Third Divisions of the Football League and was a stalwart of the team which won the First Division title in 1949 and 1950.

Following his retirement in 1965, Dickinson continued to serve the club as public relations officer, scout, secretary and finally as manager from April 1977 to May 1979 when he retired on medical advice. He was the epitome of an ideal club player and was never once cautioned by the referee throughout his lengthy career. In recognition of his fine example he was awarded the MBE in 1964.

Michael DICKINSON

Horse Racing
Michael William Dickinson. b. 3 Feb 1950 Gisburn, Lancashire.

In a meteoric career, Dickinson was champion in three of his four years as a National Hunt trainer, setting a record of 120 winners (from 259 runners) in 1982/3, including the unique feat of saddling the first five horses in the Cheltenham Gold Cup on 17 Mar 1983: *Bregawn, Captain John, Wayward Lad, Silver Buck* and *Ashley House.*.

Formerly a top jockey, he took over the stables of his father **Tony** (b. 6 Aug 1915, d. 25 Jun 1991) at Harewood, West Yorkshire in 1980. In 1984 he handed over to his mother, **Monica**, and became private trainer for Robert Sangster on the flat at Manton in Wiltshire. Despite producing the most modern training centre in Britain, he achieved a mere four successes in his first year of 1986 and was sacked by Sangster in November that year. He then left to train in Maryland, USA.

The family trained six winners of the King George VI Chase between 1978 and 1986: *Gay Spartan* 1978, *Silver Buck* 1979-80 and *Wayward Lad* 1982-3, 1985.

Jimmy DIMMOCK

Football
James Henry Dimmock. b. 5 Dec 1900 Tottenham, London. d. 23 Dec 1972 Enfield, London.

Signing for Tottenham Hotspur in 1919, Dimmock was a key member of the great Spurs team which won promotion to the First Division in 1920 and the FA Cup in 1921. During the 1920s, England called on no less than 15 different players to fill the left-wing position and during this unsettled period Jimmy Dimmock was capped three times, first against Scotland in 1921 with his other two caps coming five years later in 1926.

He left Tottenham in 1931 and after brief spells with Thames, Clapton Orient and Ashford (Kent) he retired from the game after which he worked in the road haulage business.

John DISLEY

Athletics
John Ivor Disley. b. 20 Nov 1928 Corris, Caernarfonshire and Merrionethshire.

Coached by Geoff Dyson (qv), Disley became Britain's first world-class steeplechaser for 15 years when he set four British records at 2 miles and five at 3000m, in the former taking the record from 10:12.6 in 1950 to 9:44.0 in 1952 and the latter from 9:18.4 in 1950 to 8:44.2 in 1955. He smashed through the 9-minute barrier at the 1952 Olympics, when he improved from 9:11.8 to 8:59.59 in the heats and to 8:51.94 for the bronze medal in the final. Four years later he entered the Games as Britain's No.1, and nearly matched his best with 8:44,6, but with that he was sixth in the final won by his teammate Chris Brasher (qv).

Disley was AAA champion in 1952, 1955 and 1957. He ran for London AC and was a schoolmaster in his running days. He was a member of the International Orienteering Federation 1972-8 and was a leading pioneer of the sport in Britain. He was awarded the CBE in 1979 for his work in outdoor education, he was vice-chairman of the Sports Council 1974-82. He is a director of the London Marathon.

His numerous Welsh records on the flat included bests of 1500m 3:53.4 (1956), 1 mile 4:05.4 (1958), 2000m 5:10.9 (1955), 3000m 8:09.6 (1957), 2 miles 8:43.8 (1957), 5000m 14:13.2 (1957).

In 1958 he married **Sylvia Cheeseman** (b. 19 May 1929), who set British records at 100y 11.0 (1951) and 220y 24.5 (1949), won silver and bronze medals in relay races at the 1950 Empire Games and relay bronze at the 1952 Olympics, and was WAAA champion at 100m 1949 and 200m/220y 1946-9 and 1951-2.

Charles DIXON

Tennis
Charles Percy Dixon. b. 7 Feb 1873 Grantham, Lincs. d. 29 Apr 1939 West Norwood, London.

Although he first reached the final of the All-Comers' singles at Wimbledon in 1901, he didn't enjoy any major successes until he reached the veteran stage. In 1912, at the age of 39, he won the Wimbledon doubles with Roper Barrett (qv), the Australian doubles with James Parke (qv), the Olympic mixed doubles (indoors) with Edith Hannam and concluded a memorable year by captaining the team which recaptured the Davis Cup from Australasia. In 1913, at the age of 40, he successfully defended his Wimbledon doubles title with Roper Barrett.

Educated at Haileybury and Clare College, Cambridge before becoming a solicitor, he won a Blue for rackets but, surprisingly, not for lawn tennis. He was also a scratch golfer and his sporting talents were shared by his brother, **John** Augur Dixon (1861-1931), who captained Nottinghamshire at cricket 1889-99 and won an England cap at soccer, playing as a forward for Notts County.

Colin DIXON

Rugby League
Colin Dixon. b. 3 Dec 1943 Cardiff.

In a career spanning more than 20 years with Halifax, Salford and Hull Kingston Rovers, he played a total of 713 games (plus 25 as substitute), a total only exceeded by Jim Sullivan and Gus Risman (qqv). Joining Halifax in 1961 as a centre he later used his speed to good effect in the second row. In 1968 he transferred to Salford for a record £12,000 (plus a player exchange) and was a member of the team which won the League in 1974 and 1976. After winning a host of other honours at Salford he moved to Hull Kingston Rovers in 1980 and in 1982 he returned to his first club, Halifax, where he served as coach for two years.

He toured twice with GB (1972, 1974) winning 12 caps (plus two as a replacement) and he represented his native Wales 10 times.

Freddie DIXON

Motorcycling
Frederick William Dixon. b. Stockton-on-Tees, Durham 1892. d. 3 May 1957 Battersea, London.

Having first raced around the Isle of Man in 1912, Dixon achieved star status in the island's TT races in the 1920s. He was runner-up in the Senior TT in 1921 on an Indian machine and in 1923 won the first sidecar race in a Douglas outfit as well as placing 3rd in the Senior. Four years later he achieved the unique feat of being the only rider to win both a solo and a sidecar TT by winning the Junior TT on an HRD. A gifted engineer, he retired from motorcycle racing in 1929 and raced cars in the 1930s, being particularly successful in Rileys.

Karen DIXON

Equestrianism, Three-day Event
Karen Elizabeth Dixon. b. 17 Sep 1964 Newcastle-upon-Tyne. née Straker.

The European junior three-day event champion in 1982, Dixon has become a consistently successful rider. She was taught to ride by her mother Elaine, who became an internatonal instructor. With the British team she won silver medals at the 1988 Olympics and 1990 Worlds and won both team gold and individual bronze medals at the 1991 Europeans and 1994 Worlds. At the 1992 Olympics she was 6th in the individual event and she was British champion in 1994. She married the son of Robin Dixon (qv).

Robin DIXON

Bobsleigh
(Hon.) Thomas Robin Valerian Dixon. b. 21 Apr 1935 London.

The heir of Lord Glentoran won gold for Britain at two-man bobsleigh with partner Tony Nash (qv) at the 1964 Games at Innsbruck, Austria. They (Tony as driver and Robin as brakeman) had been 3rd at the World Championships in 1963, went on to win the world title in 1965 and were 5th at the 1968 Olympics. They also formed half of the four-man team that were 4th at the 1963 Worlds. Dixon has a family seat at Doagh, Co. Antrim and having served in the Grenadier Guards, has been managing director of Redland of Northern Ireland since 1972. He became president of the British Bobsleigh Association and has served on the Northern Ireland Sports Council. He was awarded the MBE in 1969 and the CBE in 1992.

Tommy DOCHERTY

Football
Thomas Henderson Docherty. b. 24 Apr 1928 Glasgow.

A robust right-half who won 25 Scottish caps (8 as captain), 1951-8, Docherty was ultimately better known as a high profile manager.
He began his professional playing career with Glasgow Celtic in 1948 but the following year he was signed by Preston North End where he stayed until 1957, making 324 League appearances. In 1958 he moved to Arsenal before going to Chelsea, initially as a player-coach, in February 1961. Later that year he became chief coach and in January 1962 manager. Chelsea were relegated that year but his drive helped them back into the First Division the next year and to win the League Cup in 1965 before their first Wembley FA Cup final in 1967. He left Chelsea in October 1967, moving in quick succession to Rotherham, Queen's Park

Rangers, Sydney Olympic (Australia), Preston North End, South Melbourne (Australia), Wolverhampton Wanderers and non-league Altrincham.
While he took three teams to FA Cup finals: Chelsea (1967) and Manchester United (1976, 1977), he was also in charge when Rotherham, Aston Villa and Manchester United were relegated.

Lottie DOD

Tennis
Charlotte Dod. b. 24 Sep 1871 Bebington, Merseyside. d. 27 Jun 1960 Sway, Hampshire.

Dod was an all-rounder of prodigious talent who was never beaten in five appearances at Wimbledon, winning the singles in 1887-8 and 1891-3. She was aged 15 yrs 285 days when she first won in 1887 and she remains, to this day, the youngest-ever Wimbledon champion.
In 1892 she won the All-England mixed doubles with her brother Anthony before the event reached full championships status. Throughout her career she only lost five open singles before retiring from competitive tennis, aged only 21, after the 1893 Wimbledon. She then turned to other sports and played hockey for England in 1899-1900 and won the British women's golf championship in 1904 after being a semi-finalist in 1898 and 1899. She was also won a silver medal for archery at the 1908 Olympic Games.

Willie DOD

Archery
William Dod. b. 18 Jul 1867 Lower Bebington, Merseyside. d. 8 Oct 1954 Earl's Court, London.

The son of a wealthy cotton broker, Dod was able to devote ample time to his sporting interests and in 1908, on his 41st birthday, he became the only British male archer ever to win an Olympic gold medal. He later won the Grand National title (British Championship) in 1909 and 1911, after which he gave up archery and devoted his time to golf. Although never showing the sporting versatility of his younger sister, Lottie (qv), he played off scratch and won the South of Ireland Championship in 1901 and reached the fourth round of the British Amateur in 1912.

Laurie DOHERTY

Tennis
Hugh Laurence Doherty. b. 8 Oct 1875 Wimbledon, London. d. 21 Aug 1919 Broadstairs, Kent.

Hugh was the younger of two brothers who dominated world tennis at the turn of the century. On leaving Westminster School, he attended Trinity College, Cambridge, winning his Blue from 1896-8. The Doherty brothers were one of the most formidable doubles teams in history. They won the Wimbledon doubles eight times 1897-1901 and 1903-05, with the first two victories coming while Laurie was still at Cambridge. They also won the US title in 1902 and 1903, the Olympic title in 1900, and were unbeaten in the five Davis Cup doubles they played together.

Laurie also won all seven singles that he played in the Davis Cup between 1902 and 1906. He won the All-Comers' singles at Wimbledon in 1898 but lost to Reggie in the Challenge Round. He later won the title for five years in succession 1902-06. He was Olympic champion in 1900 and in 1903 became the first overseas player to win the US Championships.

He was renowned for his speed around the court and with his smash and volley he was an unusually aggressive player for his era. After poor health forced him to give up the game in 1906, he concentrated on golf and played several times in the Amateur Championship. War service in the RNVR further damaged his health and he died a year after the war ended.

Peter DOHERTY

Football
Peter Dermont Doherty. b. 5 Jun 1913 Magherafelt, Co. Derry. d. 6 Apr 1990 Fleetwood, Lancashire.

Doherty was rated by many as the greatest-ever Irish player and during his peak years

the finest inside-forward in Britain. A former bus conductor, he signed for Glentoran in 1932, moving to Blackpool the following year where he won the first of his 16 caps for Northern Ireland in 1935. He went to Manchester City in 1936 and in his first full season won a League Championship medal, scoring 30 goals. After service abroad, he guested for Derby County at the end of the war and joined them full-time in 1945. With Doherty at inside-left and the brilliant Raich Carter (qv) at inside-right, Derby won the FA Cup in 1946 but half-way through the next season Doherty was on the move again and went to Huddersfield Town. Three years later he was appointed player-manager of Doncaster Rovers and, after winning his final international cap in 1950, he was appointed manager of Northern Ireland, taking them to the 1958 World Cup finals after they had eliminated Italy and Portugal.

He gave up playing in 1953 having scored 197 goals in 403 league games and after a brief spell as manager of Bristol City he became a scout, assistant or manager for various clubs. He left football altogether after a career which was marred to a great extent by his acerbic off-field attitude - he left Manchester City, Huddersfield and Doncaster because of disputes with the management. Had he been able to curb this side of his character he would undoubtedly have won more than 16 caps over a 15-year period.

Reggie DOHERTY

Tennis
Reginald Frank Doherty. b. 14 Oct 1872 Wimbledon, London. d. 29 Dec 1910 Kensington London.

After winning the Wimbledon singles from 1897 to 1900, Doherty lost to Wentworth Gore (qv) in the 1901 Challenge Round after his doctor had forbidden him to play. His younger brother, Laurie (qv), then won the title from 1902 to 1906 and, apart from this lapse in 1901, the brothers dominated the Wimbledon singles for a full decade. Like his brother, he was educated at Westminster and Trinity College, Cambridge and they won many major doubles titles together. His ground strokes, particularly on the backhand, provided a perfect complement to his brother's more aggressive style. In eight Davis Cup rubbers (3 singles, 5 doubles) the only match he lost was his singles against William Larned (USA) in 1903. Despite warnings about his health, he continued to play in selected tournaments after his last appearance at Wimbledon in 1906. After winning both the singles and the doubles (with George Hillyard) at the 1909 South African Championships he died the following year. Gates at the south-east entrance to Wimbledon were named after the brothers.

Basil D'OLIVEIRA

Cricket
Basil Lewis D'Oliveira. b. 4 Oct 1931 Signal Hill, Cape Town, South Africa.

A prodigious player in Cape Coloured cricket in South Africa, D'Oliveira was prevented by Apartheid from making his mark at first-class level. He was, however, encouraged by John Arlott to come to England, where he started by playing for Middleton in the Central Lancashire League. He showed that he could make the transition to the highest grade on two Commonwealth tours and, despite being well into his 30s, was persuaded by Tom Graveney (qv) to join Worcestershire in 1964. Thus began a happy career with the county, playing until the age of 48 in 1980, and coaching thereafter.

He graced the English game with his calm authority and was an outstanding success as a Test cricketer from making his debut at 34, a hard-hitting middle-order batsman who exerted great power from a very short backlift, and an accurate medium-paced seamer.

His original omission from the England team selected to tour South Africa in 1968 was itself a disgrace, but when he was eventually added to replace the injured Tom Cartwright, a selection surely essential after he had scored 158 in the final Test against Australia that summer, he was not allowed to come by the South Africans and the tour was cancelled. Amid all the controversy his quiet dignity was greatly admired. He was awarded the OBE in 1969.

His son **Damian** (b. 19 Oct 1960) played for first-class cricket for Worcestershire from 1982 to 1994.

44 Tests 1966-72: 2484 runs at 40.06, 5 100s HS 158; 47 wickets at 39.55, BB 3-46; 29 catches.
4 One-day Ints 1971-2: 30 runs at 10.00, HS 17; 3 wickets at 46.66, BB 1-19; 1 catch.
First-class 1961-80: 18,919 runs at 39.57, 43 100s HS 227; 548 wickets at 27.41, BB 6-29; 211 catches.

Mal DONAGHY

Football
Malachy Martin Donaghy. b. 13 Sep 1957 Larne, Co. Antrim.

In making 410 League appearances for Luton Town, Donaghy remarkably missed only six League games in nine years 1978-87. A model of consistency, he formed the backbone of both the Luton and Northern Ireland teams' defence, earning 91 caps for his country from 1980, making him second only to Pat Jennings in the all-time lists.

A versatile player who could play anywhere across the back four and also in midfield, he began his career with the Irish Club, Larne, and after signing for Luton Town in 1978, he had 11 seasons with the club before moving to Manchester United in 1988. During his five seasons at Old Trafford he failed to command a regular first team place and in 1992-4 he played for Chelsea.

He was sent off in Ireland's World Cup match against Spain in 1982.

Walter DONALDSON

Snooker
Walter Weir Wilson Donaldson. b. 2 Feb 1907 Coatbridge, North Lanarkshire. d. 24 May 1973 Newport Pagnell, Buckinghamshire.

The first man to succeed Joe Davis (qv) as world snooker champion, Donaldson beat Fred Davis (qv) to take the title in 1947. After losing the rematch in 1948 he regained the title in 1950. He was beaten by Fred

Davis in the final of the Professional Match-play Championship in its first three years, 1952-4, and then retired from competitive play, having been a professional from the age of 16. He had been the first British Boys champion at billiards in 1922 and won his first Scottish title in 1928.

Steve DONOGHUE

Horse Racing
Steven Donoghue. b. 8 Nov 1884 Warrington, Cheshire. d. 23 Mar 1945 London.

The idol of the racing public in England in the 1920s, Donoghue was champion jockey for ten successive years, 1914-23, riding over 100 winners in a season five times, with a peak of 143 in 1920. He rode 14 Classics winners between 1915 and 1937, including six Derby winners, with a record three in succession 1921-3.

He struggled to gain a foothold in racing, and after an apprenticeship with John Porter (qv) he went to France, where he rode his first winner in 1905. After success in Ireland, where he was champion in 1908, he returned to England in 1911 as first jockey to Atty Persse (qv), for whom he rode his first great horse *The Tetrarch* in 1913. Later in his career he rode *Brown Jack* to win the Queen Alexandra Stakes at Ascot each year from 1929 to 1934. After his 1000 Guineas and Oaks double on *Exhibitionist* in 1937 he retired, having ridden 1845 winners. He trained for a while, but did not meet with much success. A charming man, he had great courage and showed his horsemanship with his balance and superb hands. Due to an accident early in his career he rode in a more upright position than was usual.

Wade DOOLEY

Rugby Union
Wade Anthony Dooley. b. 2 Oct 1957 Warrington, Cheshire.

Initially a rugby league player like his father, Dooley turned to the union code at the age of 18 where his height made him a formidable line-out specialist. First capped in 1985, he played 55 times for England and on his retirement from the interna-tional game in 1993 he held the record as England's most capped lock. During his later games for England his second row partnership with Paul Ackford (qv) was particularly effective and they played together in two Tests during the 1989 British Lions tour of Australia.

A Lancashire policeman, he played for Fylde and Preston Grasshoppers.

Derek DOUGAN

Football
Derek Alexander Dougan. b. 20 Jan 1938 Belfast

Dougan was a centre-forward whose extrovert personality and goal-scoring abilities made him a favourite of the crowd at his many clubs. Signed by Portsmouth from Distillery in 1957 he then played for Blackburn Rovers, Aston Villa, Peterborough United and Leicester City before finally settling at Wolverhampton Wanderers in 1966. He stayed with Wolves for nine seasons and commanded a regular first team place until his retirement in 1974 at the age of 36.

For his six English clubs he played a total of 546 games (258 for Wolves) and scored 219 goals (93 for Wolves). He was on the losing side in the 1960 FA Cup final (Blackburn) and the 1972 UEFA Cup (Wolves), but was finally on the winning team in the 1974 League Cup. First capped by Northern Ireland in 1958, he won his 43rd and final cap 15 years later. On his retirement he served as chairman of the Professional Footballers Association and built a successful career in radio and television.

Bryan DOUGLAS

Football
Bryan Douglas. b. 27 May 1934 Blackburn.

Unusually, Douglas spent his entire senior career with one club, that of his home town Blackburn. During his 19 years with the Rovers he scored 102 goals in 438 League games. Between 1957 and 1963 he won 36 England caps, scoring 11 goals. A small man, at outside-right or inside-forward his unorthodox play and brilliant ball control made him a great favourite with the crowd.

Desmond DOUGLAS

Table Tennis
Desmond Hugh Douglas. b. 20 Jul 1955
Kingston, Jamaica.

Douglas was a winner of a record 26 titles at the English Closed Championships, including a record 11 men's singles (1976, 1979-87, 1990), 11 men's doubles and 4 mixed doubles. He was the English Open singles in 1980 and 1984 and was unbeaten by a British player in singles for nine years until Alan Cooke beat him in 1986. He turned professional in 1977 and played in the Bundesliga in Germany for PSV Borussia Düsseldorf 1977-85.
With Linda Jarvis he was beaten in the final of the 1980 European mixed doubles and he was a member of the British team that was beaten in the final of the European Championships in 1988, when he also played for Britain at the Olympic Games. He was Commonwealth champion at singles and with the winning England team in 1985, and achieved his greatest success by winning the European Top 12 tournament in 1987, in which year he was awarded the MBE.
After five years out of the international team he returned to play well for Britain at the 1995 World championships.

Johnny DOUGLAS

Cricket and Boxing
John William Henry Tyler Douglas. b. 3 Sep 1882 Clapton, London. d. 19 Dec 1930 off Læso, Denmark.

Douglas was an obdurate right-handed batsman and skilful fast-medium bowler, with pronounced late swing either way. He completed the double five times in English seasons – in the last prewar season of 1914, and on the resumption of play in 1919-21 and in 1923. He twice more took over 100 wickets and exceeded 1000 runs in all ten times between 1906 and 1927. He was a born leader and captained England in 18 of his 23 Tests, from his first when he deputised for Pelham Warner (qv) in 1911, and Essex from 1911 to 1928.
He won an England amateur cap for soccer, and in 1908 won the Olympic title for middleweight boxing. He was pre-sented with his gold medal by his father, who was then president of the Amateur Boxing Association. Douglas lost his life with his father when the boat in which they were returning from Finland sank following a collision and both were drowned.
23 Tests 1911-25: 962 runs at 29.15, 1 100 HS 119; 45 wickets at 33.02, BB 5-46; 9 catches.
First-class 1901-30: 24,531 runs at 27.90, 26 100s HS 210*; 1893 wickets at 23.32, BB 9-47; 364 catches.

Dorothea DOUGLASS

Tennis
Dorothea Katharine Douglass. b. 3 Sep 1878 Ealing, London. d. 7 Jan 1960 Kensington, London. Later Mrs Lambert Chambers.

The winner of seven Wimbledon singles championships between 1903 and 1914, she narrowly missed an eighth title when she held two match points against Suzanne Lenglen (Fra) in the 1919 Challenge Round. The following year she again met Lenglen in the Challenge Round but at the age of 41 was overwhelmed by the 21-year-old.
The daughter of an Ealing vicar, Douglass won the Wimbledon singles, 1903-04 and 1906, and following her marriage to Robert Lambert Chambers in April 1907 she won four more titles 1910-11 and 1913-14. She was also a winner of the women's doubles (1903, 1907) and the mixed doubles (1906, 1908, 1910) at Wimbledon before they became full championship events. She won her doubles in the 1925 Wightman Cup and played again in 1926 aged 47; two years later, as she approached her 49th birthday, she made her final challenge at Wimbledon in the women's doubles. In 1928 she became a professional coach. She was also a fine badminton player, who won the All England women's doubles in 1903 and the mixed doubles the following year, and she played hockey for Middlesex.
The finest British player of the pre-World War I era, her strength was her forehand. Although a semi-permanent wrist injury restricted her power, she used an angled cross-court shot to great effect.

Dai DOWER

Boxing
David William Dower. b. 20 Jun 1933
Abercynon, Rhondda Cynon Taff.

The ABA flyweight champion and an
Olympic quarter-finalist in 1952, Dower
turned professional the following year and
in 1954 won the Empire flyweight title by
outpointing Jake Tuli (SAf). He then took
the vacant British title in February 1955
and later in the year held the European title
for seven months. In 1957 he met Pascual
Pérez (Arg), the 1948 Olympic gold medallist, for the world title in Buenos Aires. The
Welshman, who was a weak puncher, was
knocked out in the first round and relinquished his British and Empire titles
shortly afterwards.
Career record 1953-7: 37 contests. Won 34
(14 KO), Lost 3.

Terry DOWNES

Boxing
Terence Richard Downes. b. 9 May 1936
Paddington, London.

London-born, Downes went to America at
the age of 15 when his family settled in
Baltimore. After joining the US Marines
he won the All-Services title and took part
in the 1956 US Olympic Trials before his
cockney origin was discovered. He turned
professional on his return to England the
following year and won the British middleweight title within 17 months of joining
the paid ranks. He lost the title to John
McCormack on a foul in 1958, but regained
his crown in a return match two months
later. He remained the champion until 1962,
when he was deprived of his title for refusing to defend it against McCormack within
a given time.
An aggressive, crowd-pleasing fighter he
had a tendency to cut easily and this
resulted in the referee stopping the contest
after seven rounds in his first world title
fight against Paul Pender (USA) in 1961.
Later in the year Downes took the world
title when Pender retired after nine rounds,
but in their third contest in Boston in 1962
the American reclaimed the title. This was
Downes' final challenge for the world

middleweight crown, but in 1964 he took
on Willie Pastrano (USA) for the world
light-heavyweight title and after losing in
11 rounds he retired. In partnership with
his manager, Sam Burns, he built a successful bookmaking business.
Career record 1957-65: 44 contests. Won
35 (28 KO), Lost 9.

John DOYLE (Ireland)

Hurling
John Doyle. b. 1930 Holycross, Thurles,
Co. Tipperary.

In 1992 Doyle became just the third player
to be elected to the Hurling Hall of Fame.
In his senior career as a corner-back and
half-back with Tipperary from 1949 to
1967 he won eight all-Ireland hurling
titles, 1949-51, 1958, 1961-2 and 1964-5,
from ten finals. He also won 11 National
League medals with the county. With
Munster in the Interprovincial Championships he won five Railway Cup medals.
Later he was elected to the Dáil Éireann
and subsequently became a member of the
Senate.

Tony DOYLE

Cycling
Anthony Paul Doyle. b. 19 May 1958
Hampton Court, London.

Britain's most successful pursuit rider
between the days of Hugh Porter and Chris
Boardman (qqv), Doyle also earned a formidable reputation as a six-day racer on
the European circuit. A keen track rider
from the age of 14, he took a bronze medal
in the British junior 3km pursuit in 1975
and two years later won the British 4km
pursuit title for the first time, winning
again in 1978 and 1979, when he also won
national amateur titles at points and madison. In 1978 he won individual and team
pursuit bronze at the Commonwealth
Games and he competed at the Olympic
Games in 1980, when the British team
became the first to record a sub 4:20 time
for 4km. They ended out of the medals,
however, and Doyle turned pro straight
afterwards. He immediately won the
national 5km pursuit title, which he was to

win again in 1981-2 and 1986-8, and within a couple of months he added the world title.

Doyle went on to a distinguished record in the World Championships, with a further pursuit win in 1986, when his semi-final time of 5:40.339 was the fastest ever recorded. He was 2nd in 1984, 1985 and 1988, 3rd 1987 and 4th 1982 and 1983. He was also 2nd in the points championship in 1987 and was European madison champion in 1984-5, 1987, 1989 and 1990, adding the omnium title in 1988-9. He was national champion at madison in 1993 and in 1994 he returned to Commonwealth Games action with a medal at team pursuit. For his services to cycling he was awarded the MBE in 1988.

Ted DRAKE

Football
Edward Joseph Drake. b. 16 Aug 1912 Southampton. d. 30 May 1995.

Drake was a robust, attacking centre-forward whose direct approach was typical of his era. He signed for Southampton in 1931 and when he went to Highbury in 1934 he played a major role in the successes of the great Arsenal team of the mid-1930s. Renowned for his powerful shot, he scored a record 42 League goals in his first season with Arsenal and the following year he scored all the goals in Arsenal's 7-1 victory over Aston Villa to tie the Division I record. It is said that that he only had eight shots at goal and that the eighth hit the bar! In 1935 he was the top scorer in the League with 43 goals and he helped Arsenal to the League Championship in 1935 and 1938 and scored the winning goal in the 1936 FA Cup final.

Injuries restricted his number of England caps to five 1934-8, and a spinal injury brought about his retirement in 1945 with a record of 171 goals in 239 League appearances, after which he held managerial appointments at Hendon, Reading and, from 1952-61, Chelsea, who he led to the 1955 League Championship. He was assistant manager at Barcelona in 1970 and later a full-time scout for Fulham, whose president he became. He played cricket for Hampshire 1931-6, scoring 219 runs and taking 4 wickets in first-class matches, and his son, **Bob** (b. 7 Sep 1943) played full-back for Fulham in the 1960s.

Tom DREAPER (Ireland)

Horse Racing
Thomas William Dreaper. b. 28 Sep 1898. d. 28 Apr 1975 Killsallaghan, Co. Dublin.

It will no doubt be as the trainer of the great *Arkle* that Tom Dreaper will best be remembered. However for 25 years before *Arkle* came on the scene he had produced many fine steeplechasers from his stables at Greenogue, Kilsallaghan, Co. Dublin. His first great horse had been *Prince Regent*, the 1946 Cheltenham Gold Cup winner, who was in his prime during World War II, and from *Prince Regent* in 1942 to *Flyingbolt* in 1966 he sent out ten different horses to win the Irish Grand National, winning for seven successive years 1960-6. Many of his triumphs were shared by Pat Taaffe (qv), his stable jockey from 1950. Dreaper rode as an amateur jockey from 1922 to 1940.

His son James Thomas Russell '**Jim**' (b. 30 Jan 1951) was a successful amateur rider and now trains at the Greenogue stables. He was leading National Hunt trainer in Ireland in his first five seasons in charge at Kilsallaghan and won the Irish Grand National four times in those years, including with *Brown Lad* 1975-6 and 1978, as well the Cheltenham Gold Cup with *Ten Up* in 1975.

Leslie DRIFFIELD

Billiards
Leslie Driffield. b. 1912.

The owner of a Leeds iron foundry, Driffield won the English Amateur Billiards Championship eight times 1952-4, 1957-9, 1962 and 1967 and was World Amateur champion in 1952 and 1967. He turned professional in 1969, as much as anything because the world professional title was the only major one he had yet to win, and duly succeeded in that quest in 1971.

Jim DRISCOLL

Boxing
James Driscoll. b. 15 Dec 1880 Cardiff. d. 30 Jan 1925 Cardiff.

A master of the classic straight left and gifted with superb defensive skills he is regarded as possibly the most talented of all British boxers and was known as 'Peerless Jim'. In 1907 he took the British featherweight title from Joe Bowker and with three successful defences he was the first outright winner of a Lonsdale Belt in the featherweight division. He relinquished his British title following a draw with Owen Moran in 1913 and he also held at various times the Empire and Europe crowns and the British version of the World title. In 1909 he went to New York where he met the generally recognised world champion, Abe Attell (USA), over 10 rounds. Driscoll completely outboxed the American but it was a 'no decision' bout and the Welshman never got the chance of a return match with the world title at stake, although he was unbeaten in 11 contests in America. His attempted comeback after World War I was short-lived and he died of consumption.
Career record 1899-1913: 71 contests. Won 52, Drew 6, Lost 3, No decision 10.

Des DRUMMOND

Rugby League
Desmond Lloyd Drummond. b. 17 Jun 1958 Jamaica.

Drummond's exceptional speed, allied with his strength as a juduoka, made him one of the most effective wingers of his time. He was signed by Leigh from their junior ranks and in 1982 he helped them to only their second ever League title; their previous success had been in 1906. He was voted Young Player of the Year in 1981 and 1982.
During his ten seasons with Leigh he won 22 caps for GB but a dispute with the club led to him being out of the game for a season before joining Warrington in 1987 with whom he won two further GB caps. He toured with the 1984 Lions and was selected for a second tour in 1988 but he lost his place as a result of disciplinary action following a dispute with a spectator during a match at Widnes.

Anneli DRUMMOND-HAY

Equestrianism, Three-day Event
Elizabeth Ann Drummond-Hay. b. 4 Aug 1937 Dorset. Now Mrs Wucherphennig.

Riding *Merely-A-Monarch*, whom she had bought as a three-year-old, she won the Burghley three-day event in 1961 and Badminton in 1962. However as women were at the time barred from the Olympic Games at that discipline, she and *Merely-A-Monarch* turned to show jumping and after 3rd place in 1963 won the European title in 1968, with 2nd place in 1969. They had had to miss the 1964 Olympics, however, as the great horse had health problems for a couple of years. At the World Ladies' Championship they tied for 2nd place with Marion Mould (qv) in 1970. The combination added to their trophies with the Queen Elizabeth II Cup in 1970, and Anneli won the British and Italian Jumping Derbys on *Xanthos* in 1969. *Merely-A-Monarch* retired in 1971 and died at the age of 25 in 1980.
Anneli, who was the grand-daughter of the Duke of Hamilton, married the South African show jumper Errol Wucherphennig in February 1972 and retired from international competition.

Andy DUCAT

Football and Cricket
Andrew Ducat. b. 16 Feb 1886 Brixton, London. d. 23 Jul 1942 St John's Wood, London.

Ducat was one of only 12 players to have been capped by England at both football and cricket. Signed from Southend Athletic by Woolwich Arsenal in 1905, he won three England caps as an attacking right-half in 1910 before moving to Aston Villa in 1912. He captained Villa when they won the 1920 FA Cup and won three further England caps in 1920. After playing for Fulham 1921-2, he became their manager for two years and was then reinstated as an amateur and played occasionally for the Casuals.

As a cricketer he joined the Oval staff in 1906 and in all passed 1000 runs in a first-class season 14 times with eight double centuries for Surrey. In 1920 his exhilarating batting and courage against fast bowling brought him 1695 runs at 52.96, and he played in one Test v Australia in 1921 when he scored 3 and 2. His most prolific season came in 1930 when he scored 2067 runs at 49.21. He retired from first-class cricket at the end of the 1931 season after which he spent five years as coach at Eton before becoming a sporting journalist He died of a heart attack while batting (29 not out) in a wartime match for the Home Guard against Surrey and Sussex at Lord's.

First-class cricket 1906-31: 23,373 runs at 38.63, 52 100s HS 306*; 21 wickets at 43.00, BB 3-12; 205 catches.

David DUCKHAM

Rugby Union
David John Duckham. b. 28 Jun 1946 Coventry.

Duckham was one of the most exciting runners seen in British rugby in recent years. A wonderful attacking player either in the centre or on the wing, he played for Coventry and England in both positions and on the wing for the British Lions in three Tests during their 1971 tour of New Zealand. One of his finest performances came on this tour when he scored five first-half tries and added a sixth in the second half in the provincial match against West Coast-Buller. Capped 36 times by England 1969-76, he was on the winning side in only 10 matches. He scored 10 international tries and in addition to his attacking flair he was superb in defence.

George DUCKWORTH

Cricket
George Duckworth. b. 9 May 1901 Warrington, Cheshire. d. 5 Jan 1966 Warrington.

A most agile and aggressive wicket-keeper, Duckworth could surely have played more than 24 Test matches but for Leslie Ames (qv) being a far better bats-man. A stalwart of the Lancashire team that won the county championship five times between 1926 and 1934, he developed his skills against both the pace of Ted McDonald and the spin of Cecil Parkin (qv) and Richard Tyldesley. In 1928 he took 107 dismissals (76 caught and 31 stumped), a season's total surpassed at the time only by Ames. Short and square, he was renowned for his loud and piercing appeals.

He played for a season for Cheshire in the Minor Counties, wrote and broadcast on cricket amongst various activities and managed three Commonwealth tours to the Indian sub-continent between 1949 and 1954, succeeding Bill Ferguson as England's scorer and baggage-master.

24 Tests 1924-36: 234 runs at 14.62, HS 39*; 45 catches, 15 stumpings.

First-class 1923-47: 4945 runs at 14.58, HS 75; 753 catches, 343 stumpings.

Mary DUGGAN

Cricket
Mary Beatrice Duggan. b. 7 Nov 1925 Worcester. d. 10 Mar 1973 Blackheath, London.

Duggan was the leading wicket-taker in women's Test cricket, with 77 wickets at 13.49 in her 17 Tests for England 1948-63. She was a left-arm medium-fast swing bowler in her early career and later a spin bowler, and captained England 1957-63. She achieved her best Test bowling performance at St Kilda's Cricket Ground, Melbourne in February 1958, when she took 7-6 in 14.5 overs, including 11 maidens, against Australia. This was one of five times that she took five or more wickets in a Test innings. She also scored 662 runs at 24.51, including two 100s, in Tests, and was the first woman to score a century and take five wickets in the same Test, 108 and 6-55 from 40 overs against New Zealand at Christchurch in 1957. In 1962 Duggan and Ruth Prideaux became the first women to be awarded the MCC Advanced Coaching Certificate.

She was elected president of the Women's Cricket Association in 1972, and was vice-principal of Dartford College of PE.

Willie DUGGAN (Ireland)

Rugby Union
William Patrick Duggan. b. 12 Mar 1950
Kilkenny.

A back-row forward of imposing physique from Blackrock College and Leinster, 39 of Duggan's 41 caps for Ireland 1975-84 were at No. 8 and on his retirement he was the most-capped Irish player in that position. He developed considerably as a player during Ireland's 1976 tour of New Zealand and on his return to New Zealand the following year with the 1977 British Lions he was the only Irishman in the party to play in all four Tests. He works as an electrical contractor.

Geoff DUKE

Motor Cycling
Geoffrey E. Duke. b. 29 Mar 1923 St Helens, Merseyside.

The motor cycling hero of the 1950s, Duke is considered to be the first of the modern-style racers. He won six world titles: riding for Norton at both 350cc and 500cc in 1951 and at 350cc in 1952, and for Gilera at 500cc in 1953-5. In all he won 22 500cc races and 11 350cc races, and was awarded the OBE after his feat of winning both titles in 1951. He helped to change the traditional racing attire as he got a tailor in his native St Helens to make one-piece leathers for him, giving reduced wind resistance. A supremely stylish and skilful rider, he had a special 'feel' for his machines.

His interest in the sport was kindled by a visit to the Isle of Man in 1939, and during the War he instructed army motor cycle despatch riders. His competitive career began as a member of the BSA trials team and he made his road racing debut at the age of 26 in 1948 on a 350cc Norton in the Manx Grand Prix. He won his first senior TT on the Isle of Man in 1950, won again in 1951 and 1955, and also won the junior race in 1951-2. He briefly, but unsuccessfully, switched to motor racing for Aston Martin in 1953. Gilera quit racing in 1957, and after declining success Duke retired in 1960.

George DUNCAN

Golf
George Duncan. b. 16 Sep 1883 Methlick, Aberdeenshire. d. 15 Jan 1964.

In 1920 at Deal, Duncan set a course record of 71 in the third round and followed it with a 72 to come from 13 strokes behind Abe Mitchell to win the Open Championship. Two years later he was runner-up to Walter Hagen (USA), his brilliant final round of 69 leaving him just one shot adrift. He had previously had six top ten finishes in 1906-14. He won the *News of the World* Matchplay title in 1913 and was beaten in the finals of 1910 and 1919. He also won the French Open in 1913 and 1927.

A superb iron player, he played in the first three Ryder Cups, 1927, 1929 and 1931, and won his two singles matches but lost all three foursomes. In 1929 he was captain and beat his opposite number, Walter Hagen, the great American's only Cup defeat in ten matches. He played for Scotland against England over a 30-year span 1906-36.

Always immaculate, and often playing in a bow tie, he called his autobiography *Golf at the Gallop* in recognition of his exceptionally fast play. He had a superb, natural swing and was both a long hitter and a fine putter.

Beginning as a caddie at the Old Links in Aberdeen, where he turned down an offer to play professional football, he became the professional at Stonehaven and later at Hanger Hill, Ealing and at Mere, amongst others. His son Ian was also a professional golfer.

Joey DUNLOP

Motor Cycling
William Joseph Dunlop. b. 25 Feb 1952
Ballymoney, Co. Antrim. *D 2/7/20*

Dunlop has become the most successful rider in Isle of Man TT races, with a record 17 TT race wins 1977-94, and a record 29 wins on the Isle of Man road circuit at Castletown. He also won a record five Formula One world titles, 1982-6 (2nd 1987-8 and 1990). He equalled Mike Hailwood's record of 14 Isle of Man TT wins in 1992 and passed it in 1993. He emulated another of Hailwood's records with three wins in a year, at Senior, Junior and Formula One in both 1985 and 1988. He was Formula One winner each year 1983-8 and his other TT wins included: Jubilee 1977, Classic 1980 and 1987, Senior 1987, Junior 1993-4. He set the TT lap record of 190.66 km/h *118.48 mph* on a Honda in 1984. A pub landlord in Co. Antrim, who began racing in 1970, he was awarded the MBE in 1986. His brother **Robert** won the 125cc TT in 1989 and 250cc in 1991.

Richard DUNWOODY

Horse Racing
Thomas Richard Dunwoody. b. Comber, Co. Down 18 Jan 1964.

A fine horseman, Dunwoody quickly established himself as a leading National Hunt jockey. He rode his first winner in 1983 and was 3rd in the amateur championship in 1983/4. Turning professional, he was runner-up to Peter Scudamore (qv) in the jockeys' championship in 1989/90 with 102 winners, 1990/1 with 127 and 1991/2 with 137. He succeeded the latter as chief jockey for Martin Pipe (qv) and as champion in 1992/3 with 173 winners and season's record prize money of £1,088,320. At the end of the season he was awarded the MBE.
In 1993/4 he had an epic dash for the championship with Adrian Maguire (qv), with the title not decided until the last day of the season, Dunwoody triumphing with 198 winners from 891 rides. His 1000th winner in Britain came on 30 Jan 1994 and by the end of the year he had ridden 1107 in all. He accumulated winners at an even faster rate in 1994/5, reaching his century on 29 December, more than a month earlier than the previous year, but at the end of May ended his two-year tenure as first jockey to Pipe in order to ride more often in Ireland and at Saratoga, New York. He rode *Desert Orchid* to several of his major race victories, and also won the Grand National on *West Tip* in 1986 and on *Minnehoma* in 1994, the Cheltenham Gold Cup on *Charter Party* in 1988 and the Champion Hurdle on *Kribensis* in 1990.

Jo DURIE

Tennis
Joanna Mary Durie. b. 27 Jul 1960 Bristol.

After winning British Junior titles on all three surfaces, grass, hard court and indoors in 1976, Durie developed into Britain's leading player of recent years. In 1981 she recovered from a back operation to reach the last 16 at Wimbledon, French and Australian Opens and she succeeded Virginia Wade (qv) as British No. 1 in 1982, also achieving that position in 1983-4, 1986 and 1990-2. She enjoyed her best year as a singles players in 1983 when she was a semi-finalist at the French and US Championships, a quarter-finalist at the Australian and was ranked No. 6 in the world at the year end. Her major victories came in the Wimbledon mixed doubles in 1987 and the Australian mixed in 1991.
A stalwart of the Wightman Cup team, she played in 10 ties (1979, 1981-9) but won only 2 out of 15 singles and 2 out of 10 doubles matches. She has also been a Federation Cup regular playing in 32 rubbers 1981-95 and in 1989 she was a member of the team which won the European Cup. She won the British National singles seven times, 1983-4, 1986-7 and 1990-2, and the doubles nine times, 1983-7 and 1989-90 with Anne Hobbs, 1991-2 with Clare Wood. She was the second British woman player, after Virginia Wade (qv), to win $1 million in prize money.
She had several operations on her knees and declared while playing at Wimbledon in 1995, her 18th appearance at the Championships, that it would be her last year.

Geoff DYSON

Athletics
Geoffrey Harry George Dyson. b. 22 Jun 1914 Camberwell, London. d. 5 Feb 1981 Winchester, Hampshire.

A good all-round athlete in pre-war days, with a 120y hurdles best of 14.8 in 1938, Dyson was appointed the AAA's Chief Coach in 1947, the first ever such appointment apart from a brief stint by Walter Knox (Can) in 1914. Dyson, who had started coaching at Loughborough in 1935, was an inspiration to a generation of athletes, taking his enthusiasm and lectures on the mechanical principles applied to athletics to thousands of people on his nationwide tours of schools and colleges. His *Mechanics of Athletics* became the standard work in its field.

He personally coached many of Britain's top athletes of the 1940s and 1950s at a wide range of disciplines, marrying one of his first star pupils Maureen Gardner (qv). However, he had many disagreements with officialdom in the years ahead of the recognition of the importance of coaches, and he resigned from the AAA in 1961.

He was national director of the Royal Canadian Legion's sports training plan 1963-8 and returned to England in 1968 when he became director of Physical Education at Winchester College.

George EASTHAM

Football
George Edward Eastham. b. 23 Sep 1936 Blackpool.

Eastham and his father **George** Richard Eastham (b. 13 Aug 1914 Blackpool), who played once for England, as an inside-right, in 1935 when with Bolton Wanderers and who later managed Accrington Stanley, are the only father and son to have been capped by England at football and both later become club managers.

A creative inside-right, George Jnr began his professional career with Newcastle United in 1956, moved to Arsenal after four seasons and then went to Stoke City in 1966 and scored the winning goal in the League Cup final in 1972.

Apart from a short spell in South Africa, he stayed with Stoke until his retirement in 1975 and he served briefly as club manager in 1977-8.

Although capped 19 times by England 1963-6 (scoring 2 goals), he will be best remembered for his High Court action while with Newcastle in 1963 which resulted in the ruling that the 'retain and transfer' system was an unreasonable restraint of trade. He was awarded the OBE in 1973.

Pat EDDERY (Ireland)

Horse Racing
Patrick James John Eddery. b. 18 Mar 1952 Newbridge, Co. Galway.

In 1974 Eddery became the youngest champion jockey for 50 years, and won again in 1975-7, 1986, 1988-90 and 1993. In 1990, with 209, he became the first jockey to ride more than 200 winners in a season in Britain for 38 years, and in 1991 he became the fifth jockey to ride 3000 winners in a career in Britain.

Pat was apprenticed to Frenchie Nicholson (qv) at Cheltenham, and his first winner was in 1969, *Alvaro* at Salisbury. He was champion apprentice in 1971 with 71 winners and became first jockey to Peter Walwyn (qv) in 1972. In 1974 he rode *Polygamy* in the Oaks, the first of his 11 English Classics winners to 1994. To that he has added nine Irish Classics winners, three winners of the French Derby and four of the Prix de l'Arc de Triomphe. He rode a total of 3574 winners in Britain to the end of 1994, with over 100 each year from 1973 to 1994, except in 1982. For eight years, 1986-93, he was retained to ride for Prince Khaled Abdulla. That relationship started in great style with *Dancing Brave* on whom Eddery won the King George VI and Queen Elizabeth Stakes and the Prix de l'Arc de Triomph in 1986. Earlier the greatest horse that Eddery rode was probably *Grundy*, on whom he won English and Irish Derbys and the King George in 1975.

His father **Jimmy** had been Irish champion jockey seven times and won the 1955 Irish Derby, and his brothers Paul (b. 14 Jul 1963) and David (b. 4 Apr 1966) are also riders. His wife Carolyn is the daughter of the great jockey Manny Mercer (qv).

Liz EDGAR

Equestrianism, Show Jumping
Elizabeth Edgar. b. 28 May 1943. née Broome.

The sister of David Broome (qv) she has a record five wins in the Queen Elizabeth II Cup, on *Everest Wallaby* in 1977, *Everest Forever* in 1979, 1981 and 1982, and *Everest Rapier* 1986. She had been a member of the winning British team at the 1960 European Junior Championships and was British open show jumping champion in 1964 and ladies' champion in 1964, 1975 and 1982.

She married **Ted Edgar** (b. 10 Oct 1935), who was British show jumping champion in 1957 and won the King George V Gold Cup on *Uncle Max* in 1969 and who became a leading show-jumping trainer.

Phil EDMONDS

Cricket
Philippe-Henri Edmonds. b. 8 Mar 1951 Lusaka, Zambia.

A top-class left-arm bowler, and very much his own man, he never quite fulfilled his cricketing promise, particularly as a batsman, although he is a highly successful entrepreneur and chairman of Middlesex Holdings, a company dealing in non-ferrous metals.

With a model action from a good height 1.87m 6 ft 1½ in he was an aggressive bowler as well as a brilliant close field. With an English father and Belgian mother, he came to England from Zambia as a teenager and gained his Blue at Cambridge University 1971-3 (captain 1973), also getting close to one at rugby. He then became an integral part of the successful Middlesex team, combining superbly with off-spinner John Emburey (qv), even though he could never quite get on the right wavelength with his captain Mike Brearley (qv). He took 5-25 in the first innings of his first Test against Australia in 1975 and had his best analysis of 7-66 in his fourth Test, against Pakistan in 1978, but was rarely an England regular until 1984-7. He retired at the end of the 1987 season, but returned for one match for Middlesex in 1992, when he stepped out of his Rolls Royce to show all his skills in taking 4-48.

His wife Frances is an author and journalist, who wrote two witty chronicles of Phil's last two tours.

51 Tests 1975-87: 875 runs at 17.50, HS 64; 125 wickets at 34.18, BB 7-66; 42 catches.

29 One-day Ints 1977-87: 116 runs at 10.54, HS 20; 26 wickets at 37.11, BB 3-39; 6 catches.

First-class 1971-92: 7651 runs at 18.93, 3 100s HS 142; 1246 wickets at 25.66, BB 8-53; 345 catches.

Bill EDRICH

Cricket
William John Edrich. b. 26 Mar 1916 Lingwood, Norfolk. d. 24 Apr 1986 Chesham, Buckinghamshire.

The golden summer of 1947 was lit by the genius of Denis Compton (qv), but also by his Middlesex and England team-mate Bill Edrich, whose 3539 runs (av. 80.43) has been exceeded only by Compton's 3816. Edrich's rich promise was immediately evident with the minor county Norfolk, for whom he made his debut at the age of 16 against All-India in 1932 and was awarded his county cap a year later. He went to Lord's in 1934 and made his first-class debut that year, but he continued to play for Norfolk until 1936. Then fully qualified for Middlesex he made 2154 runs at 44.87 in his first full season in first-class cricket in 1937. After a very successful tour with Lionel Tennyson's team to India in 1937/8, he started 1938 with 1000 runs before the end of May and his selection for England followed. At first he met with little success at the highest level, only 67 runs in 6 innings against Australia, but the selectors persevered with him and their trust was eventually rewarded with his breakthrough 219 in the 'Timeless Test' in Durban in the final Test of the 1938/9 series against South Africa. His DFC, awarded for his war-time service as a squadron leader in the RAF, mirrored his bravery and determination as a batsman, and he gave great service to England after the War, while living life to the full, although he was dropped from the England side 1950-3, initially for alleged ill-discipline. He was a magnificent player against fast bowling, particularly strong on the on-side, and was also for several years a tearaway fast bowler. In his great year of 1947 he also took 67 wickets of 22.58, having done even better in 1946 with 73 at 19.28. Joint captain of Middlesex with Compton in 1951-2 and sole captain 1953-7, on leaving the first-class game in 1958 he returned to play for Norfolk until he was 55, leading them with much distinction. He also played League football as a speedy left winger for Norwich City and Tottenham Hotspur until a serious ankle injury cut short his career at this sport.

His three brothers Eric, Geoffrey and Brian all played first-class cricket. **Eric** (1914-93) as wicket-keeper/batsman for Lancashire 1946-8, **Geoffrey** (b. 13 Jul 1918) as middle-order batsman for Lancashire 1946-58 (15,600 runs at 34.82 in first-class cricket), and **Brian** (b. 18 Aug 1922) as middle-order batsman and off-spin bowler for Kent 1947-53 and and Glamorgan 1954-6.

39 Tests 1938-55: 2440 runs at 40.00, 6 100s HS 219; 41 wickets at 41.29, BB 4-68; 39 catches.

First-class 1934-58: 36,965 runs at 42.39, 86 100s HS 267*; 479 wickets at 33.31, BB 7-48; 526 catches, 1 stumping.

John EDRICH

Cricket
John Hugh Edrich. b. 21 Jun 1937 Blofield, Norfolk.

Edrich followed his older cousin Bill as a splendidly determined batsman and gully fielder for England. He was a left-handed opener who played for Surrey, captaining the county 1973-7 and also taking over the England captaincy as deputy in one Test for Mike Denness (qv) in 1975. He reached his peak in 1965 when he scored a majestic 310* against New Zealand at Headingley, hitting a Test record 57 boundaries (5 sixes, 52 fours). Scoring over 1000 runs each year 1959-77 (plus twice overseas), he had a peak of 2482 at 51.70 in 1962, one of six years over 2000, averaging over 60 in 1965 (2319 at 62.67) and 2969 (2238 at 69.93). Like Bill he played for Norfolk on either side of his first-class career. He was awarded the MBE. In 1995 he was appointed England batting adviser.

77 Tests 1963-76: 5138 runs at 43.54, 12 100s HS 310*; 43 catches.

7 One-day Ints 1971-5: 223 runs at 37.16, HS 90.

First-class 1956-78: 39,790 runs at 45.47, 103 100s HS 310*; 311 catches.

Duncan EDWARDS

Football
Duncan Edwards. b. 1 Oct 1936 Dudley, West Midlands. d. 21 Feb 1958 Munich, Germany.

Edwards was a teenage prodigy whose brilliant career was ended when he died from injuries received in the Munich air disaster. He won nine caps for England Schoolboys 1950-2, and made his debut for Manchester United as a 16-year-old amateur in April 1953. Two years later, almost to the day, he won the first of his 18 England caps: aged 18 years 183 days he is England's fourth youngest ever international.

In 1956 and 1957 he helped Manchester United win the Football League. In 1957 they were also FA Cup finalists and reached the semi-finals of the European Cup in their first venture into Continental competition. In February 1958 Edwards played his last match for United in Belgrade and two weeks later he met his tragic death at the age of 21. He was rated as the complete player and during his relatively brief career he established himself as one of the greatest wing-halves.

Gareth EDWARDS

Rugby Union
Gareth Owen Edwards. b. 12 Jul 1947 Gwaun-cae-Gurwen, Swansea.

After winning his first cap for Wales as a 19-year-old against France in 1967, the Cardiff scrum-half never missed a match for Wales, playing 53 consecutive internationals until his last against France in 1978. In only his fifth international, against Scotland in 1968, he was appointed, at the age of 20 years 7 months, the youngest player ever to captain Wales. He toured with the British Lions to South Africa in 1968 and 1974 and New Zealand in 1971, playing in a total of 10 Tests on the three tours. His partnership with fly-half Barry John (qv) was the foundation of many successes for Cardiff, Wales and the Lions.

His 53 caps (13 as captain) stood as a Welsh record until beaten by J.P.R.Williams (qv) in 1981, but remains the record for a scrum-half and his record 20 tries for Wales was equalled by Gerald Davies (qv) but has since been surpassed by Ieuan Evans (qv). In 1975 he was awarded the MBE for his services to the game.

While at Millfield School he set a British junior record for 200y hurdles of 22.4 in the heats of the 1956 English Schools Championships, and he became an accomplished angler achieving a British record with his 20.58 kg *45 lb 6 oz* pike in 1990.

Jonathan EDWARDS

Athletics, Triple Jump
Jonathan David Edwards. b. 10 May 1966 London.

A vicar's son, as a committed Christian, Edwards would not compete on Sundays, thus passing the chance of competing in the 1991 World Championships, but he changed his mind in 1993. This proved fortunate as the qualifying round of the triple jump at the World Championships was on a Sunday. He progressed safely to the final, where he took the bronze medal. Two years later he produced the greatest display of triple jumping ever seen, and again on a Sunday. This came at the European Cup at Villeneuve d'Ascq, near Lille in France, when, with a wind just over the legal limit of 2 m/s he produced the first triple jumps ever over 60 ft *18.29m*. His series was 17.90w, 18.43w (+2.4), 17.72 with a legal wind to add 14 cm to his British record, and 18.39w (+3.7). The previous longest ever jump was 18.20 (+5.2 wind) by Willie Banks (USA) at Indianapolis in 1988 and the world record is 17.97. The next Sunday, at Gateshead, he was again over 18m, but excess wind ruled out his 18.03 jump. However, he added British records at 17.72 and 17.74.

Despite having to pass the AAA Championships due to an ankle injury, the world record came two days later, when at Salamanca on 18 July he jumped 17.98, with a 'legal' wind of 1.8 m/s.

English Schools champion in 1984, Edwards first jumped 16m in 1986 and progressed rapidly to become the best triple jumper in Britain by 1989, when he burst into world class. He jumped over 17m first with 17.07w at Vigo in June, then 17.28 to win at the World Cup. In 1990 his form was affected by an injured right ankle, but he won the Commonwealth silver medal, a feat he repeated in 1994, when he was also 6th at the Europeans. He competed at the 1988 and 1992 Olympics, but did not make the final and was UK champion in 1989 and 1992, and AAA in 1989 and 1994. He started the 1995 outdoor season with a British record 17.58 for the triple jump, having achieved a wind-aided best of 17.70 in 1993. His long jump best: 7.41 and 7.45w (1992). A physics graduate from Durham University, he has been coached for many years by Carl Johnson and competes for Gateshead Harriers.

'Jumbo' EDWARDS

Rowing
Hugh Robert Arthur Edwards. b. 17 Nov 1906 Woodstock, Oxfordshire. d. 21 Dec 1972 Southampton, Hampshire.

Edwards was a double gold medallist at the 1932 Olympic Games, the last British rower to achieve such a feat. He first won the coxless pairs with Lewis Clive and then was a member of the winning coxless fours team, coming in as a late substitute due to Thomas Tyler's illness.

He won gold medals at eights and coxless fours at the 1930 Empire Games and had also shown the strength suggested by his nickname with three wins in one day at the Henley Royal Regatta in 1931, eights, coxless fours and pairs. He rowed for Oxford twice in the Boat Race, in 1926 and again in 1930, when he had returned to university. Although he did not row in a winning boat he achieved a great reputation as coach of winning Oxford boats in the post-war years. After being commissioned into the RAF in 1931 he became a well-known racing pilot, and during the war won the AFC in 1943 and DFC in 1944 before retiring as a Group Captain in 1946. His sons **David** and **John** won silver medals in the Welsh coxless fours at the 1962 Commonwealth Games.

Margaret EDWARDS

Swimming
Margaret Edwards. b. 28 Mar 1939.

The backstroke rivalry between Judy Grinham (qv) and Margaret Edwards was a highlight of British swimming in the late 1950s. Edwards was 3rd when Grinham won the Olympic 100m in 1956, just a few months after being in a plaster cast due to a slipped disk, and set her first world record for 110y with 1:13.5 in Blackpool in 1957. She set further world records at 1:12.4 and 1:12.3 at Cardiff in 1958, the second in a heat of the Empire Games, only to have Grinham improve this to 1:11.9 in the final when Edwards was second at 1:12.6. Edwards set seven British records in all at 110y from 1:14.0 in 1954 to 1:11.7 in 1969, was also runner-up to Grinham at the 1958 Europeans and won ASA titles at 110y backstroke in 1959 and 1961.

Shaun EDWARDS

Rugby League
Shaun Edwards. b. 17 Oct 1966 Wigan, Gt. Manchester.

After captaining England Schoolboys at both league and union codes, Edwards signed as a professional on his 17th birthday and soon repaid the world record fee for a schoolboy of £35,000 which Wigan had paid for his services. In 1984, at 17 years 201 days, he became the youngest player ever to appear in a Challenge Cup final; the following season when he played against France at the age of 18 years 135 days he was, at the time, Britain's youngest ever international. In 1988, when still only 21, he became the youngest-ever captain of a winning Challenge Cup team when Wigan beat Halifax at Wembley. By 1995 he had played in 41 consecutive winning Challenge Cup games for Wigan as the all-conquering team won the Cup for eight successive years. Adding his first final in 1984, when Wigan lost, and a win in 1985, he has set records of appearing in ten Challenge Cup finals and of playing on the winning team nine times. He has a record 37 winners' or runners-up medals in major competitions for Wigan 1983-95.
His first international honours came as a full-back and, although he was usually selected as a stand-off, he also played for Great Britain as a scrum-half. He has scored 15 tries in 35 Tests to October 1994, although the total would undoubtedly have been greater had he not returned from the 1988 tour of Papua New Guinea and Australia after being injured in the first game. He was awarded the Man of Steel trophy as rugby league's top personality in 1990. Having already captained Britain twice, against France in 1990 and 1992, he was appointed to succeed Gary Schofield (qv) as captain in 1994 against Australia, but was sent off for a high tackle in his first match.

Joe EGAN

Rugby League
Joseph Egan. b. 19 Mar 1919 Wigan, Lancashire.

After signing for Wigan as a full-back in 1937, World War II deprived Egan of his best playing years but he developed into the outstanding hooker of the post-war era. He won 14 caps for Great Britain and toured Australia and New Zealand in 1946 and 1950. He led Wigan to victory in the 1948 Challenge Cup and after 13 years with the club moved to Leigh as player-coach in 1950. After he gave up playing in 1956, he returned to Wigan as coach and later moved to Widnes. In seven seasons as a coach he took his teams to the Challenge Cup final four times. Wigan won the trophy in 1958 and 1959 and were the losing finalists in 1961, and Widnes were the winners in 1964.

Verona ELDER

Athletics
Verona Marolin Elder. b. 5 Apr 1953 Wolverhampton. née Bernard.

In her international career from 1971 to 1983, Elder made a record 73 appearances for Britain, mostly at 400m, and she is now the British team manager. She achieved special eminence indoors, with three European gold medals at 400m (1973, 1975, 1979) as well as silver 1977 and bronze 1981, and a record eight WAAA indoor titles at 400m 1972-3, 1975-7, 1979, 1981-2, adding the 800m in 1978. She set British indoor records at

53.04 and 52.68 in her first two European wins. Outdoors, she won Commonwealth gold at 4 x 400m and silver at 400m in both 1974 and 1978, and WAAA titles at 400m in 1972 and 1976-7. She ran on the British team that set a world record for 4 x 200m in 1977 and set two British 400m records with 52.1 in 1973 and 51.94 in 1974, improving her best to 51.4 in 1976. She also ran a world indoor best of 1:29.0 for 600m in 1974. She was awarded the MBE in 1983.

Other best times: 100m 11.7 (1973), 200m 23.29 (1978), 800m 2:03.18 (1979), 400m hurdles 57.07 (1983).

Vic ELFORD

Rallying and Motor Racing
Victor Elford. b. 10 Jun 1935 Peckham, London.

Elford achieved a rare success for Britain in the Monte Carlo Rally in 1968, when with co-driver David Stone he drove a Porsche 911T to victory. He had won the GT category of the European Championship in 1967, when he won the German, Tulip and Geneva rallies and in 1968 he also won the Targo Floria, Daytona 24-hours and Nürburgring 1000 km in Porsche sports cars as well as driving for Cooper in the Formula One World Championship. He was 4th in his first race, the French GP, but never bettered that in 13 GP starts. He had a serious crash in 1969 at the German GP which effectively ended his Grand Prix career, apart from one race in 1971.

He started rallying as a navigator, progressing to drive for Standard Triumph and then spent three years as a Ford works driver from 1964 before joining Porsche in 1967.

Alf ELLABY

Rugby League
Alfred Ellaby. b. 24 Nov 1902 St Helens, Merseyside. d. 29 Sep 1993.

One of the greatest of all wingers, he had speed, acceleration. deception and, most importantly. devastating finishing power. During two spells at St Helens (1926-34, 1937-9) and one at Wigan (1935-6) he scored a total of 446 tries in club, repre-

sentative and international matches, a record which remained unbeaten until bettered by Australian Brian Bevan. Other scoring feats by Alf Ellaby included topping the League try-scoring list three times (1927-8, 1930) and scoring 31 hat tricks for St Helens.

Capped 13 times by GB 1928-33, he toured Australia in 1928 and 1932, scoring 41 tries in only 28 appearances over the two tours and topping the Lions scoring list in both years.

Douglas ELLIOT

Rugby Union
W I Douglas Elliot. b. 18 Apr 1923 Stow, Midlothian.

A farmer who played for Edinburgh Academicals, Elliot was a regular member of the Scottish team in the years immediately following World War II. Winning 29 caps 1947-54 he was, at the time, Scotland's most capped flanker.

Helen ELLIOT

Table tennis
Helen Elliot. b. 20 Jan 1927 Edinburgh. Later Mrs Hamilton.

Elliott won world titles at women's doubles in 1949 with Gizi Farkas (Hun) and in 1950 with Dora Beregi (Eng) and had also been runner-up with Beregi in 1948. She partnered Viktor Barna in 1951 and Aubrey Simons in 1955 to win English Open mixed doubles titles.

Launceston ELLIOT

Weightlifting
Launceston Elliot. b. 9 Jun 1874 India. d. 8 Aug 1930 Melbourne, Australia.

Elliot was Britain's first Olympic champion. He took up weightlifting on his return to England from India, where his father was a magistrate, and at the age of 16 was a pupil of the professional strongman, Eugen Sandow. At the first modern Olympics of 1896, he won the one-handed lift and placed 2nd in the two-handed event in addition to competing in the 100m sprint, rope-climbing and wrestling. A magnificent all-round athlete, he also took part in the discus at the 1900 Olympics, when the omission of weightlifting from the programme prevented him from defending his title. He later turned professional and toured widely with a successful music hall act. On retiring he farmed for a while in England before settling in Australia.

Charlie ELLIOTT

Horse Racing
Edward Charles Elliott. b. 3 Oct 1904 Newmarket, Suffolk. d. 6 Jan 1979 London.

A natural and stylish jockey, he ended Steve Donoghue's (qv) run of ten years as champion jockey by tying with him (89 winners) in 1923 and then became champion himself in 1924 with 106 winners while still apprenticed to Jack Jarvis (qv). He won on his first two mounts in 1921, and between 1923 and 1949 he rode the winners of 14 English Classicss, and also raced a lot in France where from 1929 he rode for Marcel Boussac, for whom he rode four winners of the French Derby and three of the Prix de l'Arc de Triomphe. Elliott also had much success as a jockey for Boussac in England in the late 1940s and also trained for him 1953-7, before returning to train at Newmarket, where he had come from a local racing family, until his retirement in 1963.

Geoff ELLIOTT

Pole vault
Geoffrey Michael Elliott. b. 7 Apr 1931 Ilford, London.

Britain's top pole vaulter and decathlete of the 1950s, Elliott won the AAA junior high jump and pole vault in 1948 and, coached by Geoff Dyson (qv), in his first international season of 1950 he set a British decathlon record for 11th place at the European Championships. He improved that in 1951 and in 1952, when his score for 9th at the Olympic Games equates to 6398 points on the current tables. From then, however, he concentrated mostly on the pole vault, and from 1952 to 1959 set 16 British records, starting at 4.11m and ending with five at 4.30m. He was Commonwealth vault champion in 1954 and 1958, and AAA in 1952-3 and 1955. He competed for Woodford Green AC.

Peter ELLIOTT

Athletics
Peter Elliott. b. 9 Oct 1962 Rawmarsh, Rotherham.

Desperately unlucky with injuries which have severely affected his career, Elliott reached the top of world middle distance running for an all-too-brief spell during which he was a brilliant winner of the 1990 Commonwealth Games 1500m title. Later that year, when favourite for the European title, he was brought down in his heat. He was allowed to run in the final by the Jury of Appeal, but the controversy over this undoubtedly affected him and he came 4th. He first came through as a determined front runner and won cross-country and 800m English Schools titles at junior level in 1977, and intermediate in 1979. He was national youths cross-country champion in 1980 and in 1981 was 4th in the European Junior 800m. At this distance in 1983 he was 2nd at the European Indoors, and a magnificent 4th at the World Championships. In 1984 he became the first British athlete to beat Seb Coe (qv) at 1500m since 1976, when the choice was between the two of them for the final place to join Steve Cram (qv) and Steve Ovett (qv) on the Olympic team. Coe was rightly preferred and went on to retain his title, while the unlucky Elliott, after getting through two rounds, was unable to take his place through injury in the 800m semi-finals.

Injuries caused him to miss nearly all of the 1985 season, but in 1986 his series of good races at 800m included 3rd in the Commonwealth Games and a win in the Grand Prix final. He ended 1987 in great form with the World silver medal at 800m and personal bests at 1500m and 2000m and in 1988 ran magnificently at the Olympics despite a groin injury to be 2nd at 1500m and 4th at 800m. He won the European Cup 1500m in 1991 but had to withdraw through injury from the World Championships.

Formerly a joiner with British Steel, he won the UK 800m in 1983-4 and 1986, and 3000m 1991; and the AAA 800m 1982 and 1987, 1500m 1984 and 1988. On the road he won Fifth Avenue Mile, New York 1987, 1989-90, the last in 3:47.83 (slightly downhill). He ran on the British team that set a world record for 4 x 800m in 1982 and set a world indoor 1500m record of 3:34.20 in 1990, with three more British indoor records: 1500m 3:37.9 (1988), 1M: 3:53.70 (1988) and 3:52.02 (1990).

Best times: 400m 48.2 (1984), 600m 1:16.6 (1983), 1000m 2:16.30 (1990), 1500m 3:32.69 (1990), 1 mile 3:49.20 (1988), 2000m 4:52.82 (1987), 3000m 8:07.51 (1991). He was awarded the MBE in 1990.

Shay ELLIOTT (Ireland)

Cycling
Seamus Elliott. b. 4 Jun 1934 Dublin. d. 1971.

Initially a leading Irish amateur, who set a world indoor record for 10 km from a standing start of 13:36.0 in 1955, Elliott was the winner of the first 100 miles professsional road race held on the Isle of Man in 1959. He later took up residence in Paris and competed successfully on the Continent. He won the Het Volk in 1959 and after finishing 2nd in the Tour de l'Oise in 1963 he was the winner in 1965. He competed in the Tour de France five times, and in 1963 he led the race for six days, being both the first rider from the British Isles to wear the yellow jersey and still the man to waer it for the longest period. He took the lead at the end of the second stage and won the 4th stage. He was found dead, with a shotgun beside him in 1971.

Keith ELWELL

Rugby League
Keith Elwell. b. 12 Feb 1950 Widnes, Cheshire.

Elwell played a record 239 consecutive games as hooker for Widnes between May 1977 and September 1982.
His decision to withdraw from the England team against France in 1981 in order to maintain his unbroken sequence of club appearances affected his international prospects and he only played three times for Great Britain and twice for England. Between 1972 and 1985 he won 28 winners' or runners-up medals in major competitions. He is one of only three men to have played in seven Challenge Cup finals and was on the winning side four times, 1975, 1979, 1981 and 1984.

John EMBUREY

Cricket
John Ernest Emburey. b. 20 Aug 1952 Peckham, London.

A highly respected off-break bowler, Emburey was generally England's first choice spinner in the 1980s, returning to play a couple of Tests in 1993, although he had a three-year ban from being one of the England rebels to tour South Africa in 1982.
Tall at 1.88m *6 ft 2 in* and with an easy action, his record does perhaps less than justice to his skills, but his highest number of wickets in a series was 19 against Australia in 1985. In an age of using spinners as containers he perhaps tended to bowl too defensively, but such ability proved most valuable in one-day cricket. He was 25 when he became a regular for Middlesex, having being kept out of the team by Fred Titmus (qv), but took 81 wickets at 18.37 in his first full season in 1977 and made his Test debut a year later. His best year was 1983 when he took 103 wickets at 17.88 and also made a season's best 782 runs with his highly unorthodox but effective batting. In the 1980s he formed the best county spin partnership with left-armer Phil Edmonds (qv) and he has remained a top bowler at county level into the mid-1990s. In the year of four captains he led England in two Tests against the West Indies in 1988.

63 Tests 1978-93: 1705 runs at 22.73, HS 75; 147 wickets at 37.85, BB 7-78; 33 catches.
61 One-day Ints 1980-93: 501 runs at 15.30, HS 49*; 76 wickets at 30.86, BB 4-37; 25 catches.
First-class 1973-94: 11,395 runs at 23.59, 7 100s HS 133; 1503 wickets at 25.91, BB 8-40; 434 catches.

Wayne ENSTONE

Rugby Fives
Geoffrey Wayne Enstone. b. 12 Jun 1951 Stockport.

Introduced to the game of rugby fives by his father at the age of 14, Enstone has dominated the game for more than 20 years. In that time he has won the National Singles title a record 21 times, 1973-8 and 1980-94 and National Doubles a record 11 times, with John East 1975-9, with Steve Ashton 1986 and with Neil Roberts 1991-5. The one man to interrupt his singles streak was David Hepdon in 1979 and it was 14 years before Enstone suffered another defeat in any tournament, eventually losing to Rick Carr in the West of England event in 1993.
Enstone is head of sports science at Stockport College and plays for Manchester YMCA.

Carl ERHARDT

Ice Hockey
Carl Alfred Erhardt. b. 15 Feb 1897 Beckenham, London. d. 3 May 1988 Bromley, London.

Erhardt was an inspiring captain of the winning British team at the 1936 Olympic Games and, at the age of 39, the oldest ice hockey player ever to win an Olympic gold medal.
He learned the game at school in Switzerland, Austria and Germany and on his return to England he initially played for the Prince's Club before joining Streatham. After retirement, he coached the 1948 Olympic team, was a referee at the 1950 World championships and after many years service as an official he was elected a life vice-president of the British Ice Hockey Association. He was also a founder member and the first president of the British Water Ski Federation.

Chris EUBANK

Boxing
Christopher Livingstone Eubank. b. 8 Aug 1966 Dulwich, London.

Eubank began his professional career in America in 1985 but after five fights in Atlantic City he returned to England two years later and by 1990 had won both the WBC and the WBO versions of the world middleweight championship. He successfully defended his WBC title twice and his WBO crown three times before taking the vacant WBO World super-middleweight title in 1991. His opponent in the bout to decide who should succeed the great Thomas Hearns (USA) as the champion was the unfortunate Michael Watson who, having looked a likely winner for most of the fight, was caught by Eubank in the penultimate round and sustained permanent brain damage.
After this tragedy, Eubank considered his own future in the ring but, after taking a break, he decided to carry on fighting and he successfully defended his title 15 times, although he was fortunate to draw with Ray Close in May 1993, until he lost his title to Steve Collins in March 1995, his first defeat after 44 pro fights. Many of his challengers were of modest calibre, some apparently chosen to satisfy the demands of his lucrative television deal, firstly with ITV and from 1994 with BSkyB, rather than for their capabilities as World Championship contenders.
An arrogant, complex character, he has never been a true favourite of the British sporting public despite his impressive record in the ring.

Bobby EVANS

Football
Robert Evans. b. 16 Jul 1927 Glasgow.

A hard-tackling half-back, Evans's resolute play earned him a place in the Scottish team for more than ten years. Initially a right-half he later moved to centre-half and when he retired from international football in 1968 only George Young (qv) had bettered his total of 48 Scottish caps 1948-60. His peak years were spent with Glasgow Celtic with whom he won winners' medals in the Scottish Cup (1951, 1954), the Scottish League Cup (1957, 1958) and the Scottish League (1954).
In 1960 he moved to Chelsea but after one

season was given a free transfer to Newport County, where he acted as player-manager, after which he spent time with Morton, Third Lanark and Raith Rovers. He was voted Scottish 'Player of the Year' in 1953.

Eric EVANS

Rugby Union
Eric Evans. b. 1 Feb 1921 Droylsden, Manchester. d. 12 Jan 1991 Stockport.

After attending Loughborough College 1939-42 and serving as a Sergeant in the Border Regiment, Evans joined Sale immediately after the war. Although he made his England debut against Australia in 1948 as a loose-head prop, he soon established a reputation as an outstanding hooker, although not winning a regular place in the team until 1953. Evans went on to win 30 caps - just one short of Wavell Wakefield's England record - and made his final international appearance in 1958 at the age of 37.

Having proved himself as an inspiring leader for Lancashire, for whom he made 105 appearances, he captained England 13 times from 1956. In 1957 he led England to their first Grand Slam since 1928 and England were again unbeaten in 1958. Originally a school teacher, he was later an industrial relations officer and was appointed an England selector in 1963.

Godfrey EVANS

Cricket
Thomas Godfrey Evans. b. 18 Aug 1920 Finchley, London. *D 3/5/99*

Evans was an automatic choice for England as wicket-keeper in the 12 years after World War II. A genial and extrovert character, he was always in the action, but his showmanship was matched by his brilliance. He made his Kent debut in 1939, but then had to wait until 1946 for his first full season, taking over the England 'keeping in the final Test of that summer. He was a hard-hitting batsman, and it was totally out of character when he set the all-time record by remaining at the crease for 97 minutes without scoring against

Australia in 1947. In contrast he scored 98 before lunch on the way to his second Test century against India in 1952.

He passed Bert Oldfield's record number of dismissals (130) in Test cricket in 1954 and went on to be the first to 200 dismissals and the first to 2000 runs and 200 dismissals. At his retirement he had played in a record 91 Tests. Four times he passed 1000 runs in a first-class season, with a peak of 1613 in 1952, and in 1947 he was close to the elusive 'wicketkeeper's double' with 1110 runs and 93 dismissals. He was awarded the CBE in 1960.

91 Tests 1946-59: 2439 runs at 20.69, 2 100s HS 104; 173 catches, 46 stumpings.
First-class 1939-69: 14,882 runs at 21.22, 7 100s HS 144; 2 wickets; 816 catches, 250 stumpings.

Ieuan EVANS

Rugby Union
Ieuan Cenydd Evans. b. 21 Mar 1964 Capel Dewi, Carmarthenshire.

A speedy, elusive runner in the best tradition of the great Welsh wingers, Evans made his international debut in 1987 and, although he missed the 1989/90 and part of the 1994/5 international seasons due to injury, he has won 54 caps to the end of the 1995 World Cup. His appointment as captain for the 1993/4 season did much to revive the flagging fortunes of Welsh rugby and when he led his country for the 19th time against Spain in 1994 he beat the record set by Arthur Gould (qv) in the 1890s. Evans has captained Wales 27 times and his total of 23 tries is also a Welsh record.

He played in all three Tests on the 1989 British Lions tour of Australia and his try in the third Test, following a defensive lapse by David Campese (Aus), clinched the series for the tourists. His second Lions tour was to New Zealand in 1993 when he again played in all three Tests. One of the most gifted players in present day rugby, he played originally for Carmarthen Quins and then for Llanelli from 1984.

His sister **Non** is a Welsh international at 100m hurdles.

Mal EVANS

Bowls
Maldwyn L Evans. b. 8 Nov 1937 Rhondda.

Evans became the first Welshman to become world champion at bowls, as he won the singles at Worthing in 1972. At the first World Championships in 1966 he had beaten David Bryant (qv) 21-18, but the latter went on to win the title while he came 4th. In 1972 he thrashed Bryant 21-6 on his way to victory.

A schoolmaster from Tonypandy, he represented the Gelli Park bowling club, in Rhondda Cynon Taff, and also contested the third World Championships in 1976. He won the Gibson-Watt Cup for the Welsh Open singles three times, 1964, 1966-7, and although he never won the Welsh singles titles, took the pairs in 1966 and 1967 with his elder brother **Gwyn** Evans (b. 15 Aug 1931).

George EYSTON

Motor Racing
(Capt.) George Edward Thomas Eyston. b. 28 Jun 1897 Bampton, Oxfordshire. d. 11 Jun 1979 West Orange, New Jersey, USA.

Eyston set three world land speed records in his *Thunderbolt* at Bonneville Salt Flats in Utah, 502.436 km/h *312.199 mph* in 1937, 556.002 km/h *345.484 mph* and 575.330 km/h *357.493 mph* in 1938, and many other speed records in cars of all sizes between 1926 and 1954. He was awarded the Segrave Trophy in 1937.

A skilled engineer, he raced motorcycles before and after his distinguished service in World War I, in which he won the MC. He went up to Cambridge University in 1919 and took up car racing from 1923. Also a fine rower and yachtsman, he was awarded the OBE in 1948.

Marquess of EXETER - see Lord BURGHLEY

George FAIRBAIRN

Rugby League
George A Fairbairn. b. 25 Jul 1954 Peebles, Borders.

Joining Wigan from the Scottish Rugby Union club Kelso in 1974, Fairbairn won 14 caps for Great Britain at full-back before moving to Hull Kingston Rovers in 1981 for a record fee of £72,500. He won a further three caps with the Humberside club where, in his first season, he kicked 166 goals - 20 more than Neil Fox's (qv) previous club record. In his career 1974-90 he kicked 1306 goals, including 594 goals for Wigan and 573 for Hull KR.

Surprisingly omitted from the 1979 Lions touring party, he flew out as a replacement for the injured Tommy Martyn and played in five Tests. In his 17 appearances for GB, 1977-82, he kicked 44 goals and scored 91 points. He won the Man of Steel award in 1980. He coached at Hull from 1991.

Nicola FAIRBROTHER

Judo
Nicola Kim Fairbrother. b. 14 May 1970 Henley-on-Thames, Oxfordshire.

The world title at the 56 kg category in 1993 was the culmination of a relentless sweep to the top for Fairbrother. She started her sporting career as a gymnast (her mother was an international coach) but, after breaking an arm falling off the beam, began judo at the age of eight. She won the silver in 1986 and gold in 1987 at the European Juniors, going on to be senior champion in 1992 and 1993 after bronze in 1990, and was British Open champion in 1990 and 1993, with the 1991 world bronze and 1992 Olympic silver medals. In 1994 she took the European silver medal, but lost her title when penalised due to holding inside her own jacket, but she regained the title on her 25th birthday in 1995.

Punch FAIRS

Real Tennis
Cecil James Fairs. b. 1874 Chelsea, London. d. Chelsea.

Fairs was the only man ever to defeat Peter Latham (qv) in a championship match at real tennis or rackets. After failing to wrest the World real tennis title from Latham in 1904, he was successful in his challenge the following year. Latham regained the title in 1907, Fairs then took the title off Edward Johnson in 1908 and after a successful defence against Fred Covey in 1910 he lost the title to Covey in 1912.

The son of the World rackets champion of 1876-8, **H.B.Fairs**, Punch learned the game at the Prince's Club where he developed his fluent stroke play and superb 'drop service' under the guidance of former World champion, Charles Saunders. In 1915 he went to America to take over Clarence McKay's new private court on Long Island.

Nick FALDO

Golf

Nicholas Alexander Faldo. b. 18 Jul 1957 Welwyn Garden City, Hertfordshire.

Nick Faldo established a position in the early 1990s as the finest golfer in the world, with a great record in the majors. Having been an England boys and youth international and English Amateur and British Youths champion of 1975, he turned professional in 1976, coming 8th on the European money list in 1977 and 3rd in 1978 when he won his first major tournament, the PGA Championship. He won that title again in 1980-1 and in 1989.

Faldo took time out to remodel his swing under the direction of David Leadbetter, but by the late 1980s his steady play had brought him to the top of the world's players. In 1990 he came very close to contending for the Grand Slam of golf. He won the US Masters for the second successive year and the British Open (as he had done in 1987) and between those two, he came within a lipped-out 15-foot putt of tying for the US Open championship at Medinah, having to settle for 3rd equal.

A big man at 1.91m *6 ft 3 in* he won the World Matchplay in 1989 and 1992, and that same year with his third British Open and the Johnny Walker World Championship he had worldwide earnings of £1,558,978, a world record. He was also runner-up in the World Matchplay in 1983, 1988 and 1993. In 1993 he played superbly at the British Open, equalling the tournament record with a 63 in the 2nd round, but had to settle for 2nd place, on his 36th birthday, as his aggregate of 269 left him two shots behind Greg Norman (Aus). He had a frustrating 1994 but ended the year with a win over many of the world's best at the Million Dollar Challenge in Sun City, following 2nd places there in 1983-4 and 1987.

In 1995 he determined to concentrate on the US tour, but despite a good start there, did not fare well in the first two majors of the year.

From 1977 to 1993 Faldo played in nine Ryder Cups, tying Seve Ballesteros (Spa) for a European record 19 wins, with 13 losses and 4 halves. The leading money-winner in 1983 and 1992, his career European tour earnings are a record £3,988,568 with 28 wins 1976-94. He has also added $2,800,256 from the US PGA tour from 1981 to June 1995, with three wins. He was awarded the MBE in 1988, and was voted BBC Sports Personality of the Year 1989 and the Sports Writers Sportsman of the Year 1987, 1989 and 1990.

Tom FARNDON

Speedway

Thomas Farndon. b. 1909 Coventry. d. 30 Aug 1935 London.

With some of the finest speedway riding ever seen at the time, Farndon won the premier event of 1933, the 'Star' Championship. Considered the best rider in the world at the time, he would have been a favourite for the 1935 championship, but was critically injured in a collision with his teammate Ron Johnson at New Cross the previous evening and died in hospital the day after the meeting. Riding for New Cross he won the London Riders' Championship and the Match Race Championship in both 1934 and 1935. He took up racing in his native Coventry in 1929 and reached the top flight after joining Crystal Palace in 1931, from when he was a regular member of the England Test team.

Ken FARNES

Cricket

Kenneth Farnes. b. 8 Jul 1911 Leytonstone, London. d. 20 Oct 1941 Chipping Warden, Northamptonshire.

His death on flying training as an RAF pilot officer in the war was a severe blow for English cricket, for he was the fastest bowler in world cricket immediately before the war and achieving much success in Tests. After leaving Cambridge University, where he gained his Blue in 1931-3, his appearances for Essex were restricted by his teaching duties at Worksop College, but he twice took over 100 wickets in a season, 113 at 18.38 in 1933 and 107 at 18.84 in 1938.

He tended to be erratic, but at his best this big man (1.95m *6 ft 5 in* tall and 98kg) was a formidable bowler. His 8-43 for the Gentleman against the Players in 1938 came from some of the fastest bowling ever seen at Lord's.

15 Tests 1934-9: 58 runs at 4.83, HS 20; 60 wickets at 28.65, BB 6-96; 1 catch.
First-class 1930-9: 1182 runs at 8.32, HS 97*; 690 wickets at 21.45, BB 8-38; 84 catches.

Judy FARR

Walking
Judith Undine Farr. b. 24 Jan 1942 Poole, Dorset. née Woodsford.

Competing years before women's walking events became part of the international programme, Farr won a record nine successive WAAA walks titles, at 1.5 miles 1962-8 and 2500m 1969-70. She seemed well on her way to a tenth but was disqualified with a lap to go in 1971. Her total of wins was 10 as she had also won in 1960 and in all she placed in the first three 17 times in 16 years at the various WAAA distances for track walks.

She set several British records on the track between 1964 and 1969, although most of her best times came later: 1M 7:36.2 (1965), 1.5M 12:06.8 (1964), 3000m 14:13.0 (1979), 5000m 24:37.7 (1977), 10,000m 50:46.0 (1978). Road 5km 24:21 (1978).

Tommy FARR

Boxing
Thomas George Farr. b. 12 Mar 1914 Clydach Vale, Rhondda Cynon Taff. d. 1 Mar 1986 Shoreham, West Sussex.

After some years as a middleweight and light-heavyweight (Welsh champion 1933-5) it was only when he moved up to the heavyweight division that Farr was recognised as one of Britain's most talented boxers. After beating Ben Foord to take the British heavyweight title in March 1937, he outpointed Max Baer (USA) and then knocked out the formidable Walter Neusel (Ger) in the third round before leaving for America and his legendary world title bout against Joe Louis in New York on 30 Aug 1937. Partisan British journalists claimed victory for Farr, although more realistic assessments showed Louis as a comfortable winner on points. There is, however, no doubt that Farr fought magnificently and, at the time, was one of only three men to have gone 15 rounds with Louis.

The Welshman stayed on in the USA hoping for a re-match but, after being the victim of a disgraceful decision in his bout with Jim Braddock (USA), he lost heart and was defeated in his other three American fights. On his return home he found that he had been stripped of his British title because of his absence abroad and he engaged in only four more rather inconsequential fights before retiring. In 1950, at the age of 36, he decided to make a comeback and was defeated only four times in 15 fights before he was stopped in eight rounds by Don Cockell (qv) in March 1953 after which he retired permanently. He used his crouching style and brilliant ringcraft to great effect and although he lacked the punching power of a world champion he is rated as one of greatest British heavyweights of modern times.

Career record: 125 Contests. Won 80, Drew 13, Lost 30, No decision 2.

Jimmy FARRELL (Ireland)

Rugby Union
James Leo Farrell. b. 7 Aug 1903. d. 24 Oct 1979 Cirencester, Glos.

A versatile and superbly fit forward from Bective Rangers who won international honours as a lock, flanker and prop, Farrell won 29 caps 1926-32 and was a member of the Irish team which shared the International Championship in 1926 and

1927 and of first Irish team to win at Murrayfield (1926) and Twickenham (1929). These fine performances earned him a place on the 1930 British Lions tour where he played in the second row in all four Tests in New Zealand and as a prop in the one Test against Australia.

Max FAULKNER

Golf
Max Faulkner. b. 29 Jul 1916 Bexhill, East Sussex.

The colourful (as a personality and sartorially) Faulkner won the 1951 Open title by two shots from the Argentinian Tony Cerda; this proved to be the last time that there was a British winner until Tony Jacklin (qv) in 1969. Faulkner had been joint 6th in 1949 and joint 5th in 1950, but was to have no more top six finishes. His best other wins were the Dunlop Masters 1951 and PGA Match Play 1953 and he continued to play with success into his 50s as he won the Portuguese Open in 1968 and the Seniors title in 1968 and 1970, when he retired to concentrate on fishing.
His father, Gustavus, the professional at Pennard Golf Club in South Wales, who was once 2nd in the Welsh Open, encouraged his son, who became a pro in 1933. Faulkner had to wait until after the war for any important successes and made his first Ryder Cup appearance in 1947. His record in his five Cups to 1957 was, however. disappointing as he won just one, with Jimmy Adams in 1949, and lost the other seven of his eight matches.
Faulkner was a beautiful striker of the ball, a powerful long driver and also had a sure touch as a putter.

Penny FELLOWS – see LUMLEY

Percy FENDER

Cricket
Percy George Herbert Fender. b. 22 Aug 1892 Balham, London. d. 15 Jun 1985 Exeter.

Fender was perhaps too much his own man for the selectors' taste and surprisingly played only five Tests, despite consistent all-round form, and was never asked to be England captain, a role in which many feel he would have been outstanding. However, he was a most enterprising and able leader of Surrey, whom he captained from 1921 to 1931. He had first played for Sussex 1910-13, making his Surrey debut in 1914. He was a forceful middle-order batsman, a medium-paced leg-break bowler and a marvellous slip fielder. He achieved the double six times, exceeding 1000 runs nine times and taking over 100 wickets seven times, with bests of 1625 at 33.16 in 1929 and 178 at 19.98 in 1923. His century in 35 minutes against Northampton in 1920 was a world record that has not been bettered against honest bowling. He spent his career in the wine trade and also wrote extensively about the game, covering several MCC tours for newspapers.
13 Tests 1920-9: 380 runs at 19.00, HS 60; 29 wickets at 40.86, BB 5-90; 14 catches.
First-class 1910-35: 19,034 runs at 26.65, 21 100s HS 185; 1894 wickets at 25.05, BB 8-24; 600 catches.

Alex FERGUSON

Football
Alexander Ferguson. b. 31 Dec 1941 Govan, Glasgow

With Aberdeen and Manchester United, Fergusone has become a hugely successful manager. With Aberdeen 1978-86 he won the Scotttish Championship three times, the Scottish Cup four times, Scottish League Cup once with the European Cup Winners' Cup and Super Cup in 1983. With United he won trophies in successive seasons from the 1990 FA Cup: 1991 Cup Winners' Cup, 1992 League Cup, 1993 Championships, 1994 the double of Championship and FA Cup. He was awarded the OBE 1985, CBE 1995.
He played for Scotland at schoolboy and youth level before joining Queen's Park in 1957, later playing for St Johnstone, Dunfermline and Rangers. He began his managerial career with East Stirling in 1974, but left after three months for St Mirren, whom he took to the Second Division title in his first season,

Joe FERGUSON

Rugby League
Joseph Ferguson.

From 1900 to 1922 Ferguson was a county player at rugby league, an amazing record of durability for a forward. He played 15 times for Lancashire 1900-05 and then 31 times for his native Cumberland 1906-22. Between 1899 and 1923 he played in 682 first-class fixtures, including a record for a forward of 677 games; he scored 66 tries and 582 goals for 1362 points.

He was principally a hooker, but had a few games as full back, playing for Oldham throughout his career. He led Oldham to victory in the last two of five consecutive Championship finals they contested from 1906/07 and 1910/11, but they lost in the Challenge Cup finals of 1907 and 1912. He played for England in internationals contested at 12-, 13- and 15-a-side, captaining them to victory over New Zealand in 1908 and Wales in 1909. He had, however, to turn down the invitation to go on Great Britain's first tour of Australia in 1910 for business reasons.

Liz FERRIS

Diving
Elizabeth Anne Esther Ferris. b. 19 Nov 1940 Bridgwater, Somerset.

Ferris won an Olympic bronze medal for springboard diving in 1960, the first Olympic medal by a British woman diver for 40 years. She made her international debut at 16, and at springboard won the World Student Games title in 1961, was ASA champion in 1960 and 1962, and at the Commonwealth Games of 1958 and 1962 won bronze and silver medals respectively. She retired from diving in 1964 to concentrate on completing her medical studies, although she still swam for London University.

A doctor and sports medicine specialist, she has been a leading proponent of the role of women in sport and was a founder of 'Olympians', a society for all British Olympic competitors.

Sam FERRIS

Marathon
Samuel Ferris. b. 29 Aug 1900 Dromore, Co. Down, N. Ireland. d. 21 Mar 1980 Torbay, Devon.

Ferris, an RAF mechanic from 1918 to 1950 and member from the age of 16 of Shettleston Harriers in Glasgow, achieved a record eight wins in the Poly marathon, 1925-9 and 1931-3, a great record at such a demanding event. He made his marathon debut with 2nd to his great rival Dunky Wright in 1924, but was never subsequently beaten in the race. With his wins in 1925-7 Ferris won the first three AAA marathon titles, his time in 1925 of 2:35:58.2 being a British record. He improved that record when winning at Liverpool to 2:35:27 in 1927 and 2:33:00 in 1928.

At the Olympic Games, Ferris was 5th in 1924, 8th in 1928 and a rapidly closing 2nd in 1932, when he finished in his best ever time of 2:31:55, much fresher than the winner Juan Carlos Zabala (Arg) 2:31:36. Ferris was 2nd in the 1930 Empire Games marathon and in his career won 12 of his 19 marathons. He also ran for Ireland in the International Cross-country Championship 1925-7. On retirement from the RAF, he reported on road running and was a great supporter of the sport despite suffering from Parkinson's Disease for the last 19 years of his life.

James FIGG

Boxing
James Figg. b. c.1695 Thame, Oxfordshire. d. 8 Dec 1734 London.

Figg was generally reckoned to be the first recognised world heavyweight champion at the old prize ring methods of fighting.

He became widely known in 1719 as an all-round athlete in such sports as quarterstaff, cudgel fighting and small backsword, but he was best known as a fighter. Figg was considered the world bare-knuckle champion from 1719 until 1734 when George Taylor claimed the title. Figg was also well known as a teacher of boxing, setting up booths in many local fairs to ply his trade.

Don FINLAY

Athletics, Hurdling
Donald Osborne Finlay. b. 27 May 1909
Christchurch, Dorset. d. 18 Apr 1970 Gt.
Missenden, Bucks.

Finlay had a highly distinguished 20-year
career as an international athlete, from his
debut at long jump against France in 1929
to his win against France in 1949 in a
national record time for 120y hurdles in
14.4. He lost only twice in 18 international
dual meets, to his team-mates Lord Burghley
(qv) v France in 1931 and to John Thornton
v Germany in 1937. His first success at a
major championships was when he split
the Americans to take the Olympic bronze
medal at 110m hurdles in 1932; four years
later he won the silver medal. At the sprint
hurdles he won the Empire Games title in
1934 and the European title in 1938 and
won a record seven successive AAA titles
1932-8. A regular officer in the RAF, he
returned to competition after the war and
won an eighth AAA title in 1949 at the age
of 40, having fallen when leading in his
heat at the 1948 Olympics. In 1950 he was
4th at the Empire Games.
He set five British records from 14.5 in
1936 to 14.3 in 1938 and also ran the
110m hurdles in 14.1 at Stockholm in
1937. This was not accepted as a record
due to alleged wind assistance, although a
photograph of the race shows a flag hanging motionless.
He was an accomplished all-rounder with
other bests including high jump 1.83
(1938) and long jump 6.96 (1938). He also
played three war-time games for Spurs at
soccer in 1942/3. He retired from the RAF
with the rank of Group Captain, winning
the DFC and AFC as a fighter pilot in
World War II. Severe injuries in a motor
accident were the ultimate cause of his
death.

Chris FINNEGAN

Boxing
Christopher Martin Finnegan. b. 5 Jun
1944 Uxbridge, London.

After being ruled out of the 1968 ABA
semi-finals because of a cut eye, the southpaw boxer was a surprise choice for the
Olympic team. In Mexico City he survived
two desperately close decisions to take the
gold medal and become Britain's first
Olympic middleweight champion since Harry
Mallin (qv) in 1924. On turning professional
he won the British, Commonwealth and
European light-heavyweight titles and in
1972 he challenged Bob Foster (USA) for
the World crown but lost on a 14th round
KO. He soon lost his European title and
then John Conteh (qv) deprived him of his
British and Commonwealth titles, but he
regained his British crown by defeating
Johnny Frankham in 1975, before being
forced to retire the following year due to a
detached retina in his right eye. He was
awarded the MBE after winning his
Olympic gold medal in 1968, since when
no other British boxer has won an Olympic
title.
His brother **Kevin** (b. 18 Apr 1948) won
the British middleweight title on three separate occasions (1974, 1977, 1979) and
was the European champion (1980). Chris
and Kevin were the first pair of brothers to
win Londale belts outright.
Career record 1968-76: 37 contests. Won
29 (16 KO), Drew 1, Lost 7.

Tom FINNEY

Football
Thomas Finney. b. 5 April 1922 Preston,
Lancashire.

A high-scoring winger of exceptional ability, Finney also won international honours
as a centre-forward. After playing for
Preston North End in the 1941 wartime
Cup Final his career was interrupted by
service in the 8th Army in North Africa
and it was not until 1946 that he played his
first League game for Preston. One month
later he made his international debut at
outside-left against Scotland and went on
to win 76 caps for England to 1958, missing a further 11 caps through injury. At the
time, only Billy Wright (qv), who was in
the same team as Finney in all but two of
his internationals, had played more times
for England.
Finney won 40 caps at outside-right, 33 at
outside-left and 3 as centre-forward, scor-

ing on his debut in each position. His total of 30 goals for England stood as a record for a number of years.

He remained with Preston throughout his career, scoring a record 187 goals in 433 League matches between 1946 and 1960, and he served as president of the club in 1975-6. Voted Footballer of the Year in 1954 and 1957, he was awarded the OBE in 1961 and the CBE in 1992. Finney owns an electrical and plumbing contracting firm in his home town.

Allison FISHER

Snooker
Allison Fisher. b. 24 Feb 1968 Cheshunt, Hertfordshire.

Fisher was the women's world champion at snooker seven times: 1985-6, 1988-9, 1991 and 1993-4. She won the UK Women's Open for the first five years that it was staged, 1986-90, and became the first woman professional to compete against men in 1990. In 1991 she won the World and World masters mixed doubles titles with Steve Davis (qv). In 1992, at the Dubai Duty Free Classic, she recorded the highest break by a woman, 133, in a professional competition and that year also won the British Open title at billiards.

Bob FITZSIMMONS (UK/USA)

BOXING
Robert Fitzsimmons. b. 26 May 1863 Helston, Cornwall, d. 22 Oct 1917 Chicago, Illinois.

Fitzsimmons was the first man to win three world titles and the only English-born professional world heavyweight champion. He grew up in New Zealand where he was apprenticed as a blacksmith. He was spotted winning a local contest by the renowned visiting fighter Jem Mace, who encouraged him to begin a professional career, and won his first world title as a middleweight in 1891 when he knocked out Jack 'The Nonpareil' Dempsey. He then set his sights on the heavyweight crown and annexed that title by knocking out Jim Corbett (USA) in 14 rounds in Carson City in 1897. At 75kg *165lb* he remains the lightest ever champion. Fitzsimmons, by then a naturalised American, lost the title in his first defence in 1899 to Jim Jeffries (USA). He also lost a re-match to Jeffries in 1902, but in 1903 added his third world title, claiming the recently created light-heavyweight crown by defeating George Gardner (USA). He lost that title in 1905 but boxed until 1914, when he was 52 years old.

Nearly bald from an early age apart from sparse tufts of ginger hair, which gave rise to his nickname of 'Ruby Robert', he had spindly legs but a very powerful upper body.

Career record: 49 Contests. Won 40 (32), Lost 9.

Nat FLATMAN

Horse Racing
Elnathan Flatman. b. 1810 Holton St Mary, Suffolk. d. 20 Aug 1860 Newmarket.

Champion jockey in England for 13 successive seasons, 1840-52, Flatman set six progressive records for most winners in a season from 50 in 1840 to 104 in 1848. An honest and dependable jockey, he rode 10 Classics winners between 1835 and 1857. He was apprenticed to William Cooper at Newmarket in 1825. His career was ended by a heavy fall in 1859.

Keith FLETCHER

Cricket
Keith William Robert Fletcher. b. 20 May 1944 Worcester.

'The Gnome' captained Essex from 1974 to 1985 and again in 1988. Under his leadership Essex not only won their first honours but dominated county cricket in the 1980s with eight trophies, including three Championships and he was the first captain to win all four domestic competitions. He had his final season in the first team in 1988 but remained in charge of the second team nurturing a string of talented players. In 1992 he left his beloved county to succeed Micky Stewart as England team manager. Three years later, after a depressing series of results - 5 wins, 15 losses and 6 draws in his 26 Tests as manager - he was relieved of his five-year appointment. That was all too similar to his experience as England captain. After five years out of the Test team he had been recalled to succeed Mike Brearley (qv), but Fletcher's team had played in a very tedious series in India and Sri Lanka in 1981/2 and, after only one of his seven matches in charge was won, he was summarily dismissed by Peter May (qv). In the early 1970s his sound technique brought him much success for England. He exceeded 1000 runs in an English season 20 times, 1963-73 and 1976-84. He was awarded the OBE in 1985.

59 Tests 1968-82: 3272 runs at 39.90, 7 100s HS 216; 2 wickets at 96.50, BB 1-6; 54 catches.

24 One-day Ints 1971-82: 757 runs at 39.84, 1 100 HS 131; 4 catches.

First-class 1962-83: 33,957 runs at 38.63, 59 100s HS 228*; 50 wickets at 44.48, BB 5-41; 564 catches.

Ron FLOCKHART

Motor Racing
William Ronald Flockhart. b. 16 Jun 1923 Edinburgh. d. 12 Apr 1962 Australia.

After progressing from motorcycles to cars, Flockhart came to prominence in Formula Libre races in 1953. From 1954 he raced occasionally in Formula One, mostly for BRM although his best finish was 3rd in the 1956 Italian GP in a Connaught. In sports car racing he won the Le Mans 24-hour race in both 1956 and 1957 in Jaguars, the first success being with Ninian Sanderson and the second with Ivor Bueb.

He turned to aviation, but was killed when his aeroplane broke up while he was practising in Australia for a London-to-Sydney record attempt.

Ron FLOWERS

Football
Ronald Flowers. b. 28 Jul 1934 Edlington, nr. Doncaster, South Yorkshire.

An attacking left-half who signed as a professional for Wolverhampton Wanderers in 1951, Flowers remained loyal to the club throughout virtually all his playing career. He played 467 games for Wolves between 1952 and 1966, winning an FA Cup winners' medal (1960) and three League Championship medals (1954, 1958-9), forming a most effective Wolves half-back line-up with internationals Eddie Clamp and Bill Slater (qv). Between 1955 and 1966 Flowers won 49 England caps 1955-66. When he finally left Wolverhampton, he spent two seasons (1967-8) with Northampton Town before moving to non-league Telford United as player-coach.

Brian FLYNN

Football
Brian Flynn. b. 12 Oct 1955 Port Talbot, Neath and Port Talbot.

Flynn, a tenacious midfield player, was capped 66 times for Wales between 1974 and 1984, just two short of the then record held by Ivor Allchurch (qv). His professional career (1972-91) was notable for the frequency with which he changed clubs. He had three separate spells at Burnley, two at Doncaster Rovers and he also played for Leeds, Cardiff, Bury, Limerick and Wrexham, where he became manager in 1989.

Carl FOGARTY

Motorcycling
Carl George Fogarty. b. 1 Jul 1965 Blackburn. Lancashire.

TT Formula One world champion each year 1988-90, riding Hondas, Fogarty became, with Terry Rymer, Britain's first world endurance champion for Kawasaki in 1992, and Britain's first world superbike champion in 1994 for Ducati, having been 2nd in 1993. By halfway through the 1995 season he seemed well on the way to retaining his title.

On the Isle of Man he won the Newcomer Manx Grand Prix in 1985 and won the Senior TT and Formula One riding Hondas in 1990, with a TT lap record at 198.92 kmh *123.61 mph* on a Honda in 1992.

Bernard FORD

Ice Skating
Bernard Albert Ford. b. 27 Sep 1947
London.

World, European and British ice dance champion for four consecutive years, 1966-9, Ford's partnership with Diane Towler (qv) brought a new dimension to the sport. Coached by Gladys Hogg, the world's foremost instructor, their exciting and daring style to music, which was initially thought to be unsuitable for ice dancing, was in sharp contrast to the impeccable elegance and footwork which was the characteristic of previous British champions. Their innovative talents established them as the greatest of all ice dancers until the arrival of Torvill and Dean (qqv). They relinquished their amateur status in 1969 to coach at Streatham and were both awarded the MBE. Despite their coaching activities they maintained their competitive interest and won the World Professional Championship at Wembley in 1969.

Horace FORD

Archery
Horace Alfred Ford. b. 1822 London. d. 24 Jun 1880 Bath.

The greatest British archer of the 19th century, Ford won 12 Grand National titles, 11 of them consecutively from 1849 to 1859, with a final championship in 1867. In 1857 he scored 1251 points for the Double York Round, which was a British record for that competition, shot in two directions at any open meeting, until 1960. This was done with traditional long-bow and wooden arrows. He was a Glamorgan colliery owner and was the author of *Archery: its theory and practice* which was first published in 1856 and which remains a classic.

Trevor FORD

Football
Trevor Ford. b. 1 Oct 1923 Swansea.

After war service with the Royal Artillery, Ford made an immediate impact as one of the best centre-forwards of the post-war era. An aggressive, bustling player and a noted charger of goalkeepers, he played in a 'wartime' international in 1946 and won his first full cap with Swansea Town in 1947, but moved to Aston Villa before the end of that season. He then joined Sunderland in 1950 but was happier when he returned to Wales and Cardiff City in 1954. His disparaging views of officialdom, expressed in his autobiography published in 1957, resulted in his suspension during which he spent three successful years in Holland with PSV Eindhoven. He won 38 caps for Wales 1946-56, and with 23 international goals he shared the Welsh scoring record with Ivor Allchurch (qv), before Ian Rush (qv) took over. In the Football League he scored 177 goals from 349 matches.

George FORDHAM

Horse Racing
George Fordham. b. 24 Sep 1837 Cambridge. d. 11 Oct 1887 Slough, Berkshire.

Easily the top jockey of his generation, Fordham passed Nat Flatman's record with progressive totals for winners in a year of 108 in 1856, 118 in 1859, 146 in 1860 and 166 in 1862, as he was champion jockey 14 times, 1855-63, 1865, 1867-9, 1871, with a career total of 2587 winners, 1851-84. He retired in 1875, but due to failure of investments was forced to return to riding in 1878. From then until 1884 he rode a further 482 winners, and brought his total of Classics winners to 16, including his first Derby in 1879.
Although he grew stronger, he weighed just 54 lb when he started his successful riding career, apprenticed to Richard Drewitt. Known as 'The Demon', he rode with shorter leathers than contemporary jockeys and was renowned for keeping his mounts balanced and for his honesty.

Brendan FOSTER

Athletics
Brendan Foster. b. 12 Jan 1948 Hebburn, Tyne and Wear.

In the 1970s Foster became Britain's most successful distance runner. At 1500m he won Commonwealth 1970 and European 1971 bronze medals and was 5th at the 1972 Olympics, before steadily moving up in distance. He set world records for 2 miles, 8:13.68 in 1972, and for 3000m, 7:35.2 at the opening of the Gateshead track in 1974. His greatest victory was in the 1974 European 5000m when he destroyed the field with a 60.2 eighth lap, running a championship best 13:17.21 despite hot and humid conditions. Earlier in the year he had just lost in an epic duel to Ben Jipcho (Ken) in the Commonwealth 5000m, setting a British record of 13:14.6 (he was also 7th at 1500m). He won the European Cup 5000m in 1973 and 1975, and at the end of that year made the fastest ever debut at 10,000m, 27:45.43, to win at the Coke meeting at Crystal Palace. The following year he was weakened by illness and had to settle for the Olympic bronze at this distance; following this with 5th at 5000m, after setting an Olympic record 13:20.34 in his heat.

A member of Gateshead Harriers, and chemistry graduate of Sussex University, he won AAA titles at 5000m in 1973-4 and 1976, and in 1978 added the 10,000m, when he ran a world record time of 27:30.3. He went on to win the Commonwealth title at 10,000m and the bronze at 5000m, but this took the edge off his running so that three weeks later he was 4th in the European 10km, although running 27:32.65, in the fastest ever mass finish. In 1979 he won his third European Cup title, at 10,000m, but was below his best in his final major race, 11th at the 1980 Olympics. He also set British records at 1500m 3:37.64 (1974) and 2000m 5:02.93 (1975) and had other bests of 1 mile 3:55.9 (1972) and marathon 2:15:49 (1980).

Voted BBC Sports Personality of the Year 1974 and awarded the MBE in 1976, he has become a successful athletics promoter, notably in the North-East of England, businessman, managing director of Nova International, and a TV commentator for the BBC.

Frank FOSTER

Cricket
Francis Rowbotham Foster. b. 31 Jan 1889 Deritend, Birmingham. d. 3 May 1958 Northampton.

Foster's first-class cricket career was brief, as a wartime motor-cycle accident left him lame, but his new ball partnership with Sidney Barnes in Australia in 1911/12 will long be remembered as they played the leading part in enabling England to win the series 4-1. After an extraordinary 1911 season in which at 22 he did the double and led Warwickshire to the County Championship, he took 32 wickets at 21.62 in the five Tests 'down under'. He was descibed by *Wisden* as 'the very personification of youthful energy.' He generated good pace off a short run with a beautifully easy left-arm action, and was a most aggressive batsman, who scored 305* for Warwickshire v Worcestershire in 1914, when he achieved his second double. He also took 100 wickets in 1910 and 1912.

11 Tests 1911-2: 330 runs at 23.57, HS 71; 45 wickets at 20.57, BB 6-91; 11 catches.
First-class 1908-14: 6548 runs at 26.61, 7 100s HS 305*; 718 wickets at 20.72, BB 9-118; 121 catches.

Harry FOSTER

Rackets and Cricket
Henry Knollys Foster. b. 30 Oct 1873 Malvern, Worcs. d. 23 Jun 1950 Aconbury, Kingsthorne, Herefordshire.

Foster was one of the greatest rackets players of all-time and the eldest of seven brothers who all played cricket for Worcestershire.

Educated at Malvern, he won the Public Schools rackets championship (doubles) in 1892 with his brother Bill (1874-1958), and when he went up to Oxford he played against Cambridge 1893-6 and also won a cricket Blue in the last three years. While at Oxford, he won the first of seven consecutive Amateur Singles rackets championships in 1894 with an eighth title coming in 1904. He also won the Amateur Doubles seven times (1894, 1896-1900,

1903) and completely dominated the game for a full decade.

He played cricket for Worcestershire from 1899 to 1925 and captained the county for many years (1901-10, 1913), exceeding 1000 runs in a season eight times, but his brother 'Tip' (qv) was the best cricketer in this remarkable family.

First class cricket 1894-1925: 17,154 runs at 34.10, 29 100s HS 216; 15 wickets at 29.60, BB 3-63; 206 catches.

Jimmy FOSTER

Ice Hockey
James Foster. b. 13 Sep 1905 Glasgow.

Scottish-born, Foster went to Canada as a child and became one of the world's greatest goalkeepers. In his prime he had no equals in the amateur game and few, if any, among the professionals. While with Moncton Hawks, he became the first goalkeeper to register two straight shut-outs in Allan Cup finals (1931-2) and he once held the Canadian record of playing for 417 minutes without having a score against him. He enhanced his considerable reputation at the 1936 Olympics by conceding only three goals in seven matches for the winning British team. One of the controversial Canadian-based players on the British Olympic team, Foster remained in England until the outbreak of war, playing for Richmond Hawks and Harringay Greyhounds before returning to Canada.

Mark FOSTER

Swimming
Mark Andrew Foster. b. 12 May 1970 Billericay, Essex.

A sprinter par excellence, Foster won the World short-course title at 50m freestyle in December 1993 (with bronze at 4 x100m medley), having set a world record for this event at 21.60 in February that year. At the Commonwealth Games he won bronze medals at 4 x 100m freestyle in 1986 and at 50m in 1990, but then retired. disillusioned with swimming, and notorious for his escapades.

He returned 18 months later with a more determined attitude and since then has been in world class. At 50m freestyle he was 6th at the 1992 Olympics and at the 1994 Worlds and won the 1994 Commonwealth title. He also won bronze in the European medley relay in 1993.

He began his international career in 1985 and won his first senior national title in 1986. He has set numerous British records, including long-course 50m bests of freestyle 22.43 (1992) and butterfly 24.68 (1995), and three short-course world records for 50m butterfly 23.72 and 23.68 (1994), 23.55 (1995).

ASA 50m titles: freestyle 1986-8, 1992; butterfly 1992-3; short-course freestyle 1986-7, butterfly 1993; 100m butterfly 1987.

'Tip' FOSTER and FOSTER family

Cricket
Reginald Erskine Foster. b. 16 Apr 1878 Malvern, Worcestershire. d. 13 May 1914 Kensington, London.

'Tip' Foster uniquely captained England at both cricket (against South Africa) and (against Wales) at soccer, at which he won five England caps as an inside forward 1900-02. His 171 for Oxford against Cambridge in 1900 was then the highest ever in the annual match and the following week he scored a century in each innings for the Gentlemen against the Players. In 1899 he scored 141 and 106 for Worcestershire against Hampshire, while his brother Bill made 140 and 172* at the other end. All that was topped by his dazzling innings, marked by devastating cutting, at Sydney in 1903 when he made 287 for England against Australia, a record for the Ashes series for many years, on his Test debut.

Apart from that winter tour he was unable to devote himself to full-time cricket and although he captained England in 1907 he had to refuse the invitation to take the MCC team to Australia in 1907/08. In his last full season of 1901 he had scored 2128 runs at 50.66 in his usual rapid and delightful style. He was also a sure slip fielder and also played for Oxford against Cambridge at golf and racquets. His career was cut short by diabetes and he died at the age of 36.

8 Tests 1903-7: 602 runs at 46.30, 1 100 HS 287; 13 catches.

First-class 1897-1912: 9076 runs at 41.82, 22 100s HS 287; 25 wickets at 46.12, BB 3-54; 179 catches.

His father Henry Foster was awarded his cricket colours at Winchester at the age of 14, but was unable to afford to play the game at Clare College, Cambridge. He took holy orders and was a housemaster at Malvern College. His wife Sophia was a good games player and their seven sons all played cricket for Worcestershire, though only a maximum of four in any one match. Tip was the third oldest, the others in order were:

Harry (qv), the greatest rackets player of his era.

Bill (Wilfrid Lionel, 1874-1958), who scored 1041 runs at 34.70 in 1899, his only full season as he was a regular soldier (he won the DSC in Somaliland), was a fine golfer and who won the amateur doubles at rackets with Harry in 1898 and with Basil in 1907. He was awarded the CBE for his fund-raising in World War I.

Basil Samuel (1882-1959) who won the singles championship at rackets in 1912-13 and the doubles five times between 1903 and 1913 with four partners including Harry (1903) and Bill, and became a well-known actor on the London stage. He played occasional first-class cricket for Worcestershire and Middlesex.

Geoffrey Norman (1884-1971), who scored 6600 runs at 28.32 in first-class cricket and who also played for England at soccer.

Maurice Kirshaw (1889-1940), who scored 8295 runs at 28.70 and was Worcestershire captain 1923-5.

'Johnnie' Neville John Acland (1890-1978), who won the 1908 public schools' rackets title with brother Maurice.

There were also four girls, three of whom showed much talent for games.

Freddie FOX

Horse Racing
Frederick Sydney Fox. b. Feb 1888 Durrington, Wiltshire. d. 12 Dec 1945 Frilford cross-roads between Wantage and Oxford, Berkshire.

Apprenticed to Frederick Pratt at Lambourn, Fox rode his first winner in 1907. He rode in Austria and Germany in 1912-13 before returning to Britain where he became a most popular jockey. After placing 2nd in the jockey's championship with 116 winners in 1929, he interrupted the sequence of wins by Gordon Richards (qv) by becoming champion in 1930 with 129 winners. He was also runner-up in 1926 (74) and 1934 (132). In his career he rode six Classics winners; two each of the Derby and 2000 Guineas and one each of the 1000 Guineas and St Leger. At the time of his death in a car accident he was chief racing correspondent for the *News of the World* and also a Justice of the Peace.

Jim FOX

Modern Pentathlon
Jeremy Robert Fox. b. 19 Apr 1961 Pewsey, Wiltshire.

Jim Fox achieved the best ever placing by a British modern pentathlete with 4th place at the 1972 Olympic Games and at his fourth Games in 1976 helped Britain to win the team gold medal. He had been 29th in 1964 and 8th in 1968. At that time he was a sergeant in the REME, and having been persuaded to delay his retirement he also delayed applying for a commission for several years. In 1975 he was third in the World Championships, the first Briton ever to place in the top three, and by then he had won a record ten British titles, 1963, 1965-8 and 1970-4. He was awarded first the MBE, then the OBE for his services to the sport.

Neil FOX

Rugby League
Neil Fox. b. 4 May 1939 Sharlston, West Yorkshire.

With a total 6220 points in 828 matches 1956-79 he is the most prolific scorer of all-time. Although he scored 358 tries, his phenomenal scoring feats were based on his left-footed goal kicking abilities and during his career he kicked 2575 goals at club, county and international level.

He made his debut for Wakefield Trinity in

1956 and won all his 29 Great Britain caps with the club, where he stayed to 1974. He also played briefly for Bradford Northern, Hull Kingston Rovers, York, Bramley and Huddersfield. As a member of Wakefield's winning Challenge Cup team in 1960, he set an individual scoring record for a Wembley final of 20 points (7 goals; 2 tries). Two years later he dropped three goals and scored one try in the Challenge Cup final against Huddersfield and was awarded the Lance Todd Trophy as Man of the Match.

He used his powerful physique to good effect in the centre but in the latter part of his career he played as a forward. After retirement he coached Underbank amateurs and at Huddersfield 1977-8, and was awarded the MBE in 1983 for his services to the sport.

Richard FOX

Canoeing
Richard Munro Fox. b. 5 Jun 1960 Winsford, Cheshire.

The winner of a record five world titles for canoe slalom in the K1 class, 1981, 1983, 1985, 1989 and 1993, Fox also won five team gold medals at the biennial championships, each year 1981-7 and in 1993, and the World Cup 1988-9 and 1991. He was one of the favourites for gold when canoe slalom was reintroduced to the Olympic Games in 1992 after a 20-year absence, but had to settle for 4th place. He is a marketing consultant and was awarded the MBE in 1986.

His sister Rachel (now Crosbee) was the British champion in 1992 and his wife **Myriam Jérusalmi** (Fra) (b. 24 Oct 1961) was the women's world champion at canoe slalom K1 in 1989 and 1993, and runner-up in 1987. She also won team gold medals with the French team in 1983, 1985, 1989, 1991 and 1993, and was the World Cup winner each year 1989-91.

Dick FRANCIS

Horse Racing
Richard Stanley Francis. b. 31 Oct 1920 Coedcanlas, Pembrokeshire.

Champion National Hunt jockey in 1953/4 with 76 winners, Dick Francis's best remembered ride may well be one that did not win. On the Queen Mother's *Devon Loch* he was leading the 1956 Grand National when, for no clear reason his mount, full of running, fell on the flat some 50 yards from the finish. Having been a flying officer in the RAF 1940-5, Francis rode his first winner as an amateur in the 1946/7 season and was a professional jumps jockey from 1948. He retired in 1957 after 345 winners, following a bad fall at Newbury, to become racing correspondent of the *Sunday Express* 1957-73 and a well-known and successful writer of more than 30 thrillers.

Gerry FRANCIS

Football
Gerald Charles James Francis. b. 6 Dec 1951 Hammersmith, London.

A complete midfield player and natural leader, Francis won six England Under-23 caps and 12 full international caps 1974-6. He was appointed England captain at the age of 23 by Don Revie (qv) in 1975, but his international career was cut short by a back injury while at Queen's Park Rangers, for whom he had signed as a pro in 1969. He played for Crystal Palace 1979-81, then back to QPR in 1981 before playing for Coventry City, Exeter City, Cardiff, Swansea, Portsmouth, Wimbledon and Bristol Rovers. He was also manager at Exeter 1983-4 and of Bristol Rovers 1987-91, taking them to the Third Division title in 1989/90. He then returned to QPR as manager for three years before succeeding Ossie Ardiles (Arg) at Tottenham Hotspur in 1994.

Trevor FRANCIS

Football
Trevor John Francis. b. 19 Apr 1954 Plymouth, Devon.

Francis was a richly talented forward whose exceptional goal-scoring abilities fully justified his large transfer fees. Signing as a professional with Birmingham City in 1971, he scored four goals for them in a 4-

0 win over Bolton Wanderers on 20 Feb 1971, at 16 the youngest ever to do so in a Football League match. He became Britain's first £1 million player when he was transferred to Nottingham Forest in 1978, scoring the winning goal for them in the European Cup final of 1979. When he moved to Manchester City in 1981 the transfer fee was again £1 million. In 1982 a further large fee took him to Italy, where he spent six years with Sampdoria (Genoa) and Atalanta (Bergamo).

On his return to Britain in 1987 he signed for Rangers where he won a Scottish League Cup winners' medal (as a substitute) in 1988 before moving as player-manager first to Queen's Park Rangers 1988-90 and then to Sheffield Wednesday where he was manager from 1991 to 1995. Between 1971 and 1994 he played in a total of 503 League games (including 18 in the Scottish League). Rather surprisingly he was not capped by England until 1977 but, despite missing a number of games through injury, he went on to win 52 caps in an international career that ended in 1986, scoring 12 goals.

John FRANCOME

Horse Racing
John Francome. b. 13 Dec 1952 Swindon, Wiltshire.

A marvellous horseman, Francome passed Stan Mellor's record total of winners under National Hunt rules, totalling 1138 winners from 5072 mounts over jumps from 1970 to 1985. He was champion jockey seven times, in 1975/6, 1978/9 and each year from 1980/1 to 1984/5, tying with Peter Scudamore (qv) in 1981/2; his most wins in a season was 131 in 1983/4.

He first rode at the age of four, and achieved much success in gymkhanas, becoming a British show jumping international in 1969, in which year he joined the stable of Fred Winter (qv), for whom he was first jockey 1975-85. He won on his first NH ride, a 3 miles hurdles race at Worcester on 2 Dec 1970. He rode *Midnight Court* to win the Cheltenham Gold Cup in 1978 and *Sea Pigeon* to win the Champion Hurdle in 1981. Awarded the MBE in 1986, he is now a writer and TV commentator.

Neil FRANKLIN

Football
Cornelius Franklin. b. 24 Jan 1922 Stoke-on-Trent.

Franklin was a superbly talented centre-half. who succeeded Stan Cullis (qv) in the England team during the war, playing in 10 consecutive wartime internationals 1945-6. When full internationals were resumed he held his place for 27 consecutive matches 1946-50.

He joined Stoke City shortly before the war but his career was effectively ended when he flew to Colombia in 1950 to join the Santa Fé club in Bogotá. Promises of rich rewards were never fulfilled and within two months he was back in England. Neither England nor Stoke City showed any further interest, so he was transferred to Hull City, then Crewe and finally Stockport before disappearing into the obscurity of non-League football. He reappeared as manager of Colchester in 1963, but after five years he left football completely and became a licensee in Oswaldtwistle.

Angus FRASER

Cricket
Angus Robert Charles Fraser. b. 8 Aug 1965 Billinge, Merseyside.

'Gus' Fraser is proving a stalwart member of the England pace bowling attack. With five wickets in the first innings of the 2nd Test aginst the West Indies on his home ground at Lord's in June 1995 he passed 100 wickets in Tests in his 25th match and played a vital role in England's epic victory.

He had seemed out of favour with England manager Ray Illingworth (qv), and originally been omitted from the 1994/5 tour to Australia, but showed on his recall that he was at last recapturing the from that he had shown prior to his chronic hip injury three years earlier. Having made his Middlesex debut in 1984, he progressed to take 80 wickets at 19.38 in 1988 and 92 at 20.22 in 1989. From his Test début against Australia in 1989 to 1991 he had bowled consistently well for England with his disciplined pace bowling, but he played very little in the summer of 1991 or in 1992.

24 Tests 1989-95: 233 runs at 7.76, HS 29; 99 wickets at 27.86, BB 8-75; 6 catches.

33 One-day Ints 1989-95: 80 runs at 10.00, HS 38*; 38 wickets at 29.79, BB 4-22; 1 catch.

First-class 1984-95: 1562 runs at 11.31, HS 92; 500 wickets at 26.30, BB 8-75; 32 catches.

His brother Alastair played for Middlesex and Essex 1986-92.

Tich FREEMAN

Cricket
Alfred Percy Freeman. b. 17 May 1888 Lewisham, London. d. 28 Jan 1965 Bearsted, Kent.

With his slow leg-spin bowling, Freeman captured an enormous haul of wickets for Kent in the 1920s and 1930s. He was 26 when he made his debut in 1914 and missed four seasons due to the war so it was not until he was 32 in 1920 that he began playing regularly. Every year from 1920 to 1934 he took over 100 wickets in a season, and after his all-time record of 304 at 18.05 in 1928, took over 200 every year to his penultimate year of 1935.

He took all 10 wickets in an innings three times and twice took 17 wickets in a match. Just 1.58m *5 ft 2 in* all, he was most impressively accurate for a bowler of his type.

He only played 12 times for England and only twice against Australia, so although his Test figures were nowhere near as impressive as his county ones, his worth at the highest level was not fully explored.

12 Tests 1924-9: 154 runs at 14.00, HS 50*; 66 wickets at 25.86, BB 7-71; 4 catches.

First-class 1914-36: 4961 runs at 9.50, HS 66; 3776 wickets at 18.42, BB 10-53; 238 catches, 1 stumping.

His elder brother John (1883-1958) played for Essex from 1905 to 1928.

Frederick FRITH

Motorcycling
Frederick Lee Frith. b. 1910 Grimsby. d. 25 May 1988 Louth, Lincolnshire..

A stylish rider, Frith's contribution to sport was recognised when, on his retirement to run his motorcycle business in Grimsby in 1949, he became the first motorcycle racer to be awarded the OBE.

In his last season he won the inaugural world championship at 350cc, winning all five races in the series on Velocettes. He also won the Junior TT on the Isle of Man, adding to his earlier Junior successes in 1936 and 1948. That first Junior win had been in his first TT race, and he was also 3rd in the Senior in 1936. He did even better in 1937 when he won the Senior, during which he achieved the first ever 90mph lap on the Island circuit, and was 2nd in the Junior. He was also 3rd in the Senior in 1938 and 1939 and in the Junior in 1938. His career had begun with grass-track racing in the 1920s and in 1930, riding a Velocette, he was 3rd in the first Manx GP. Having won the Junior Manx GP in 1935 on a Norton, he joined their works team in 1936 and achieved his seven first three placings in the TT races of 1936-9 on their machines.

Charles FRY

Cricket
Charles Burgess Fry. b. 25 Apr 1872 West Croydon, Londony. d. 7 Sep 1956 Hampstead, London.

Renaissance man, C.B.Fry's brilliance at all pursuits seemed to know no limits. England cricket captain in six Test matches in 1912 (won 4. drawn 2), he would have led the team more often had he been available for tours. He set a world long jump record with 7.17m on 4 Mar 1893 and three times won that event for Oxford University v Cambridge. He also won his Blue for soccer, at which he played for England in 1901 and for Southampton in the 1902 FA Cup final; and he would have won one for rugby too but for injury. He played cricket for Sussex 1894-1908 (captain 1904-8), and occasionally for Hampshire 1909-21. His greatest season was 1901, when he scored 3147 runs (av. 78.67), including 13 hundreds of which his last six were in successive innings, still a record. He was a fast-medium bowler, but was called for throwing in 1898. A first-class honours graduate in classics, he failed to be elected for parliament, although he stood several times as a Liberal, but after World War I he was India's representative at the League of Nations. He also declined an offer to be King of Albania. An avid conversationalist, broadcaster and author, he edited boys' magazines and directed his naval training ship *Mercury* with his martinet wife from 1909.

26 Tests 1896-1912: 1223 runs at 32.18, 2 100s HS 144; 17 catches.

First-class 1892-1921: 30,886 runs at 50.22, 94 100s HS 258*; 166 wickets at 29.34, BB 6-78; 240 catches.

Robert FULFORD

Croquet
Robert Ian Fulford. b. 26 Aug 1969 Colchester, Essex.

The world's top croquet player, Fulford won the world title in 1990, 1992 and 1994, and was runner-up in 1995 and a semi-finalist in 1991. Having won the President's Cup in 1989, he made his international debut when Britain won the MacRobertson Shield in 1990, and was again in the winning team in 1993. He won the British Under-19 title in 1986-7 and was men's champion in 1990, won the Open singles in 1991-2 and the Open doubles with Chris Clarke each year 1990-3. He coaches at the Chattooga Club, North Carolina, USA.

Arthur FULTON

Shooting
Arthur George Fulton b. 16 Sep 1887 London. d. 26 Jan 1972 Brookwood, Surrey.

With three generations winning the King's or Queen's Prize at Bisley, the Fulton family holds a unique place in British shooting. **George** (1859-1944) was the first winner, in 1888; his son Arthur won in

1912, 1926 and 1931, and his grandson **Robin** (b. 27 Feb 1917) was the winner in 1958. Arthur is the only man ever to have won the Prize three times and he came desperately close to a fourth victory in 1914 when he tied with Sgt J L Dewar, but lost in the shoot-off. He appeared in the final 'hundred' a record 28 times.

After winning an Olympic silver medal in the military rifle team event at both the 1908 and 1912 Olympics, he was awarded the DCM for his sniping exploits in France during World War I. In 1959 he was awarded the MBE for his services to shooting.

His father, George, gave up his work as a engraver and used his prize money to set up in business as a gunsmith. Arthur spent his working life in this business, which continues to thrive.

Carl FURRER

Trampolining
Carl Furrer.

Furrer was world champion at synchronised pairs with Stewart Matthews in 1980 and British individual champion each year 1981-4. He also won the World Cup individual title in 1980-1 and 1983.

Davina GALICA

Skiing
Davina Mary Galica. b. 13 Aug 1944 Watford, Herts.

A top woman skier, she was 8th in 1968 and 7th in 1972 at the Olympics at giant slalom. This was her most successful discipline, although she was also a most courageous and determined downhill racer. She had also competed in 1964 and 28 years later, although at a demonstration sport, returned to the Olympic arena in 1992 to take part at speed skiing. In 1993 she set the British women's speed skiing record at 200.667 km/h *124.689 mph* at Les Arcs in France.

In between her skiing feats she tried sedan/saloon car racing and was 4th in the 1976 F5000 series. She also raced at Formula One, but in three attempts 1976-8 failed to qualify for Grand Prix races.

Bernard GALLACHER

Golf
Bernard Gallacher. b. 9 Feb 1949 Bathgate, West Lothian.

Gallacher, a tough competitor with a great reputation at match play, had 13 European tour victories from 1969 to 1984. In 1969, his second season as a pro he became the youngest ever winner of the Vardon Trophy and headed the money list. That was a feat he never again achieved, but he had six more top ten placings with a best of 3rd in 1974.
In 1967 he won the Scottish Amateur stroke-play title before turning professional. In 1969 he became the then youngest ever Ryder Cup player at 20, and won his first game, a foursomes with Maurice Bembridge against the Americans Lee Trevino and Ken Still. He went on to play in eight Ryder Cups to 1983, with a record of 13 wins, 13 losses and 5 halves, and succeeded Tony Jacklin (qv) as non-playing captain for the ties of 1991 and 1993, after assisting him in the three previous ties.
He also played for Scotland in the World Cup five times between 1969 and 1983. His major wins included the Dunlop Masters of 1974 and 1975, Spanish Open 1977 and French Open 1979. He became club professional at Wentworth.

Hughie GALLACHER

Football
Hugh Kilpatrick Gallacher. b. 2 February 1903 Bellshill, North Lanarkshire. d. 11 June 1957 Low Fell, Tyne and Wear.

Gallacher was the greatest centre-forward of his era and possibly the greatest Scottish player of all-time in that position. Starting his professional career with Airdrieonians in 1921, he moved to Newcastle in 1925 and then played for Chelsea 1930-4, Derby County 1934-6, Notts County 1936-8, Grimsby Town 1938 and Gateshead 1938-9. During his 21 seasons in League football he scored 387 goals in 543 matches for seven different clubs. For Scotland he scored 22 times in 20 matches, including a Scottish record of 5 goals against Northern Ireland in 1929. One of his finest interna-tional performances came at Wembley in 1928 when, although he failed to score, he was in the Scottish line-up whose 5-1 defeat of England earned them immortality as the 'Wembley Wizards'.
Although short in stature (1.66m tall) he scored many of his goals with his head. A mercurial player with superb ball control, he won a Scottish Cup winners' medal with Airdrie in 1924 and he was with Newcastle when they won the Football League in 1927. From a humble back-ground, he found it difficult to cope with the fame and money which his football tal-ents brought him. His problems with alcohol increased over the years and the day before he was due to appear in court for ill-treating his daughter he threw him-self in front of an express train.

Frank GALLAGHER

Rugby League
Frank Gallagher. b. 1895. d. 1966.

A loose forward noted for his constructive attacking play, Gallagher was with Dewsbury when chosen for the 1920 Lions tour but had moved to Batley before tour-ing again in 1924. He won 12 Test caps and spent the last two seasons of his career with Leeds.

Christine GALLIE

Judo
Christine Gallie. b. 1946. née Child.

The highest rated British woman judo player, at 6th Dan, Gallie won a record six British titles: heavyweight 1971-5 and the Open division in 1973.

Maureen GARDNER

Athletics, Hurdling
Maureen Angela Jane Gardner. b. 12 Nov 1928 Oxford. d. 2 Sep 1974 North Stoneham, Hampshire.

Gardner won the Olympic silver medal at 80m hurdles in 1948, her time of 11.2, a new British record, and the same time as that of the winner, Fanny Blankers-Koen (Hol). She was still a teenager and it was only her second season of hurdling, after her coach Geoff Dyson (qv), whom she married six weeks after the Olympics, had advised her to switch from sprinting. She set four British records in 1947 and one in 1948 at 11.5, before her Olympic break-through. She won the WAAA 100m on the flat in 1946 and four times at 80m hurdles, 1947-8 and 1950-1. In 1950 she ran her fastest ever time, a wind-assisted 11.1 and was again runner-up to Blankers-Koen at the 1950 Europeans. She retired before the 1952 Olympics and returned to her first love to run a ballet school.

Best flat times: 100y 11.1, 100m 12.1, 220y 25.3 (all 1947).

Nora GARDNER – see PERRY

Philomena GARVEY (Ireland)

Golf
Philomena K Garvey. b. 26 Apr 1927 Drogheda, Co. Louth.

Garvey was the winner of the Ladies' British Open Amateur Championship in 1957, and also runner-up four times, 1946, 1953, 1960 and 1963. She played in the Curtis Cup six times between 1948 and 1960, winning two matches, losing eight and halving one. She turned professional in 1964 but was later reinstated as an amateur and won the Irish Ladies' Amateur title a record 15 times, 1946-8, 1950-1, 1953-5, 1957-60, 1962-3 and 1970.

Paul GASCOIGNE

Football
Paul John Gascoigne. b. 27 May 1967 Dunston, Gateshead.

The most talked-about footballer at the start of the 1990s, as a midfield player he was the inspiration of the England team at the 1990 World Cup, at which he was voted Best Young Player in the Tournament. Later he was voted BBC Sports Personality of the Year.

He joined Newcastle United as an apprentice in 1982 and captained their team to victory in the FA Youth Cup in 1985, in which year he made his Football League debut. He played for England Under-21s in

1987 and signed for Tottenham Hotspur for a British record fee of £2 million in July 1988, after scoring 22 goals in 106 League and Cup appearances for Newcastle. He made his England debut in September 1988 and was voted PFA Young Footballer of the Year. His career was severely threatened by ruptured cruciate ligaments in his right knee due to his own horrendous tackle in the 1991 Cup Final. With this and a further fracture of the same knee in October 1991 he was out of action for 16 months. The Italian league club Lazio had offered £8 million for him, but that fee was eventually cut to £5.5 million when Gascoigne finally signed in June 1992.

Despite not regaining full fitness, he made a triumphant return to the England side in the final months of 1992, but his career was again halted when he broke his right leg in training in April 1994. He only played 44 matches in three seasons with Lazio. Headstrong and controversial, he undoubtedly has a brilliant talent with a great sense of balance and position, although 'Gazza' mania in the media threatened to get out of hand at one stage. His resilience has been shown by his fight back against injuries and he returned to play for England in June 1995 prior to a transfer to Glasgow Rangers. He has scored six goals in his 32 internationals.

Mike GATTING

Cricket
Michael William Gatting. b. 6 Jun 1957 Kingsbury, London.

Gatting made his Test debut at 20 in 1977, but took a long time to make his mark. Finally, after consistently averaging over 50 for year after year in county cricket with pugnacious and exciting batting, he broke through on the tour to India in 1984/5, making his maiden century in his 31st Test and 54th innings, and scoring 207 three Tests later. He went on to considerable batting success until 1987, although his form declined in Tests thereafter. He captained England 23 times including success in the Ashes series against Australia in 1986/7, but after losing the captaincy after a series of incidents, he led a 'rebel' tour to South Africa in 1989/90, which meant a three-year Test ban. He returned to Tests in 1993, and after missing out for a year was recalled to the England team to tour Australia in 1994/5. He played in all the Tests, and after poor form and only retaining his place due to the numerous injuries to his teammates, he scored his tenth Test century in the 4th Test, his 78th. His previous Test century had been in his 58th. At the end of the tour he announced his retirement from Test cricket.

Awarded the OBE in 1987, he has captained Middlesex since 1983, playing a major role in their Championship successes of 1985, 1990 and 1993 (having played on four earlier county championship teams) and four one-day trophies. He has exceeded 1000 runs in 17 seasons, including once overseas, and over 2000 three times, with a peak of 2257 at 68.39 in 1984. He averaged over 50 in 13 of the 14 English seasons 1981-94, managing 47.30 in his worst year of 1988, and was over 60 six times.

His brother **Steve** (b. 29 May 1959) played League football as a defender for Arsenal, Brighton and Charlton Athletic from 1978.
79 Tests 1977-95: 4409 runs at 35.55, 10 100s HS 207; 4 wickets at 79.25, BB 1-14; 59 catches.
92 One-day Ints 1977-95: 2095 runs at 38.36, 8 100s HS 115*; 10 wickets at 33.60, BB 3-32; 22 catches.
First-class 1975-95: 32,317 runs at 50.57, 83 100s HS 258; 156 wickets at 29.43, BB 5-34; 428 catches.

Kenneth GEE

Rugby League
Kenneth Gee. b. 23 Sep 1916 Wigan, Gt. Manchester. d. 17 April 1989 Wigan.

Gee was an uncompromising prop forward of impressive physique. After signing for Wigan in 1933 he waited two seasons for a place in the first team but soon established himself as an indispensable member of the pack. He played 33 times for England, won 17 caps for Great Britain and toured Australasia in 1946 and 1950. In many of his international appearances he played alongside his club-mate Joe Egan (qv), the Wigan hooker, and their combined strength and understanding of each other's play provided a formidable scrummage base. Unusually for a forward, Gee was also a talented goal kicker, his best season being in 1949/50 when he kicked 133 goals.

Walter GEORGE

Athletics
Walter Goodall George. b. 9 Sep 1858 Calne, Wiltshire. d. 4 Jun 1943 Mitcham, London.

As an amateur George set numerous world records at distances from 1000y, 2:18.0 (1881) to 18,555m in 1 hour (1884), with other bests including $^3/_4$ mile 3:08 $^3/_4$ (1882); 1 mile 4:18.4; 2 miles 9:17.4; 3 miles 14:39; 6 miles 30:21 $^1/_2$; 10,000m 31:40 and 10 miles 51:20 (all in 1884). He uniquely won AAA titles at four events, 880y, 1M, 4M and 10M in both 1882 and 1884, the first three events on the same day, and he also won the 1 and 4 miles in 1880 and the National cross-country in 1882 and 1884.

George turned professional in 1885 for his great series of races against William Cummings, highlighted by his win at 1 mile in 1886 in 4:12 $^3/_4$, a time that was not bettered by an amateur until 1915, although George himself was reported to have run 4:10.2 in a time trial in 1885. He also ran several series of match races against Lawrence Myers (USA), winning two out of three races as an amateur in 1882, but losing all five in 1886-7.

George's brother **Alfred**, ten years his junior, won one AAA and three AAU titles.

Mike GIBSON

Rugby Union
Cameron Michael Henderson Gibson. b. 3 Dec 1942 Belfast

Gibson was universally recognised as one of the greatest centres of all time.

Beginning his career with Campbell College, he later played for Trinity College, Dublin, Cambridge University, North of Ireland FC and the Barbarians. He won 69 caps for Ireland 1964-79, establishing what was then the record as the world's most capped player. Although winning 25 caps as a fly-half and four on the wing he will remembered as the complete centre.

He and Willie John McBride (qv) are the only players to go on five British Lions tours. Gibson played in all four Tests for the Lions in New Zealand in 1966 and 1971 and South Africa in 1968, but did not play in the Tests against South Africa in 1974 or New Zealand in 1977. A Belfast solicitor by profession, he was awarded the MBE for his services to the game.

Josh GIFFORD

Horse Racing
Joshua Thomas Gifford. b. 3 Aug 1941
Huntingdon.

Champion National Hunt jockey four time (1962/3, 1963/4, 1966/7 and 1967/8), Gifford had a top figure of 122 winners in 1966/7. Under NH rules between 1959 and 1970 he rode a total of 643 winners. He gained his trainer's licence in 1970 and trains at The Downs, Findon, West Sussex, where he took over from Ryan Price (qv), for whom he had been first jockey. He trained *Aldaniti* to win the 1981 Grand National and his besy year has been 1987/8 with 91 winners.

He started riding on the flat from 1951, apprenticed to Sam Armstrong, and had his first winner 14 days before his 15th birthday. After 51 winners on the flat, increased weight pushed him to jumping from 1959. He was awarded the OBE in 1989.

Gifford married show-jumper Althea Roger-Smith. His younger brother **Macer** rode *Larbawn* to victory in the 1968 Whitbread Gold Cup and his daughter **Kristina** won team gold for Britain in the 1994 three-day event world championships.

Norman GIFFORD

Cricket
Norman Gifford. b. 30 Mar 1940
Ulverstone, Cumbria.

Perhaps the peak of Gifford's three decades in first-class cricket came when he led England in two matches in Sharjah in 1985 - at 44 years 61 days he is the oldest ever one-day international captain. This came 22 years after he was the Man of the Match in the first Lord's one-day final, when he took 4-33 for Worcestershire in their unavailing attempt to best Sussex in the Gillette Cup Final.

A fine left-arm spinner and a determined tail-end batman who chipped in with useful innings, he played for Worcestershire from 1960 to 1982, captaining them from 1971-80, including to the County Championship of 1974, having earlier played on their winning teams in 1964 and 1965. He then joined Warwickshire and captained them 1985-7. The best of his four 100-wicket hauls was in his second season, 133 wickets at 19.66 in 1961. After two Tests in 1964 he played 13 more times for England 1971-3 but he had to contend with the great Derek Underwood (qv) for a place.

He went on to be assistant manager on several England tours from 1982/3 and is now cricket manager at Sussex. He was awarded the MBE in 1979.

15 Tests 1964-73: 179 runs at 16.27, HS 25*; 33 wickets at 31.09, BB 5-55; 8 catches.

2 One-day Ints 1985: 0 runs; 4 wickets at 12.50, BB 4-23; 1 catch.

First-class 1960-88: 7047 runs at 13.02, HS 89; 2068 wickets at 23.56, BB 8-28; 319 catches.

Ryan GIGGS

Football
Ryan Joseph Giggs. b. 29 Nov 1973
Cardiff.

The youngest player ever to play for Wales at just 17 years and 332 days in 1991, Giggs has already established himself as one of the great talents of the modern game, dazzling defences with his pacy, skilful runs and accurate crosses. A product of the Manchester United youth team, he made his first team debut on the left wing in 1990/1. He was the PFA Young Player of the Year in 1992 and 1993, the first player to win this award twice, as Manchester United won the League Cup in 1992, League Championship in 1993-4, and the double with the FA Cup in 1994. Giggs already has three superb international goals to his credit from 13 caps for Wales to March 1995, many of which were gained as substitute. A dynamic and direct attacker, he can play as striker or on either wing.

Jack GILES

Squash
John Henry Giles.

Giles was winner of the UK Closed Professional squash championship the first ten years the event was held (1954-63), after which he relinquished the title undefeated.

After serving an apprenticeship at Prince's and the Public Schools Club he became the professional at the Manchester Tennis and Racquets Club from 1941-9. A brief spell at Canford School followed, after which he went to Abbeydale Park SRC, before being appointed to the RAC in 1956 where he remained for the rest of his playing career. He was awarded the MBE.

Johnny GILES (Ireland)

Football
Michael John Giles. b. 6 Jan 1940 Cabra, Dublin.

In a long international career from 1959 to 1979 Giles won 59 caps for the Republic of Ireland. Although he won an FA Cup winners' medal in 1963 for Manchester United, for whom he made his Football League debut in 1959, it was as a reject that he was persuaded by Don Revie (qv) to join Leeds United. There he flourished; he joined as a right-winger but, having helped them win promotion from the Second Division in 1963/4, switched to inside-left to replace Bobby Collins (qv) after the latter broke his leg in October 1965.

Giles, a deep-thinking player, alongside Billy Bremner (qv) in midfield, played a vital part in helping Leeds to win the League title in 1969 and 1974, the League Cup 1968, FA Cup 1972 and Fairs Cup 1968 and 1971. He became an ace at delivering accurate long ball passes and his cool temperament made him a formidable

penalty taker. He scored 115 goals in 525 games for Leeds, moving to become player-manager of West Bromwich Albion 1975-7 and of Shamrock Rovers 1977-8. He was manager of the Republic of Ireland team 1973-80.

Gillian GILKS

Badminton
Gillian M Gilks. née Perrin. b. 20 Jun 1950 Epsom, Surrey.

The most successful woman badminton player in Europe in the 1970s, Gilks had special success at doubles with a record 10 European titles, four women's and six mixed at the biennial championships between 1972 and 1986. She was also European singles champion in 1974 and 1976, and took five European silver medals. At the All-England Championships she was singles champion in 1976 and 1978, took three women's doubles with different partners and five mixed doubles titles, three with Derek Talbot (qv) and two with Martin Dew. At the Commonwealth Games of 1974 she won the treble of women's singles and both doubles, having won three silver medals in 1970.

Her most successful World Championships were the first, in 1977, when she won silver medals at singles, beaten by Lena Köppen (Den), and at mixed doubles, partnering Talbot; she added bronze medals in 1983 and 1987. She also won the mixed doubles with Talbot at the 1972 Olympics when badminton was a demonstration sport, and in all won 27 English national titles between 1968 and 1988, 9 singles, 7 women's doubles and 12 mixed doubles.

She had a long and distinguished career from winning the All-England under-15 singles at the age of 12 and her first senior international at 16, and made a record number of 111 international appearances for England, although that might have been even higher but for several brushes with the badminton authorities. She was awarded the MBE in 1976 and elected Sportswoman of the Year by the British Sports Writers in 1974 and 1976. She also won the first televised women's Superstars competition in 1977.

Billy GILLESPIE

Football
William Gillespie. b. 6 Aug 1892 Ballintrae,
Co. Derry. d. 2 Jul 1981 Bexley, London.

A prematurely bald inside-left, Gillespie's
total of 25 caps for Northern Ireland 1913-
27 would have been far greater had it not
been for the interruption caused by World
War I. On his international debut he scored
both Ireland's goals in their first ever win
over England.
Initially, he failed to make an impression
in English football when he signed for
Leeds United but on moving to Sheffield
United he proved himself as one of the
great inside-forwards of his day. He played
more than 500 games for Sheffield and
captained them to their FA Cup win in
1925. For most of his career he played
with a silver plate in his leg following a
compound fracture in 1914. On retirement
he returned to Ireland to manage Derry.

Arthur GILLIGAN

Cricket
Arthur Edward Robert Gilligan. b. 23 Dec
1894 Denmark Hill, London. d. 5 Sep
1976 Pulborough, West Sussex.

In 1924 Gilligan was appointed England
captain for the series against South Africa.
He started sensationally, as he and his
Sussex team-mate Maurice Tate (qv)
bowled out South Africa for 30 in 48 minutes, Gilligan 6-7 and Tate 4-12; and he
added 5-83 in the 2nd innings to ensure
England's innings victory. This followed
matches in which he and Tate had dismissed Surrey for 53 and Middlesex for
41, and after the Test he scored 112 in an
hour and half for the Gentlemen against
the Players. In the previous innings, however, Gilligan was badly hurt when hit
over the heart by a lifting ball while batting and was never again able to bowl so
lethally fast.
He had played two Tests against South
Africa in 1922/3 and went on to take the
England team to Australia in 1924/5, but
that was the end of his Test career, having
won four of his nine matches in charge.
His best year was 1923 when he scored

1183 runs and took 163 wickets at 17.50
and he also took over 100 wickets in 1922
and 1924. He was MCC president in
1967/8 and a radio commentator for the
BBC. He was also a prominent golfer and
was president of the English Golf Union.
11 Tests 1922-5: 209 runs at 16.07, HS 39*;
36 wickets at 29.05, BB 6-7; 3 catches.
First-class 1919-32: 9140 runs at 20.08, 12
100s HS 144; 868 wickets at 23.20, BB 8-
25; 180 catches.
Two brothers also played first-class
cricket. **Frank** Gilligan (1893-1960)
played for Oxford University and Essex
1919-29 before emigrating to New
Zealand
Alfred Herbert **Harold** Gilligan (1896-
1978) played as a stylish middle-order
batsman and leg-spin bowler for Sussex
1919-31. He captained England in four
Tests in New Zealand in 1930, scoring 71
runs at 17.75, when he took over due to
Arthur's ill health. In first-class record was
8873 runs at 17.96 and 115 wickets at 33.66.
His daughter married Peter May (qv).

Nick GILLINGHAM

Swimming
Nicholas Gillingham. b. 22 Jan 1967
Walsall, West Midlands

Gillingham followed the great British
breaststroke swimming tradition by winning the European 200m title in 1989,
1991 and 1993 (2nd 100m, 3rd medley
relay), the World short-course title in 1993
(in a European record 2:07.91), and the
Commonwealth gold in 1994. At 200m at
the Olympic Games he won a silver in
1988 and a bronze in 1992 and Commonwealth bronze in 1986 and 1990. At the
World Championships he took the bronze
at 200m in 1991 and was 4th in 1994. He
also won a world short-course bronze at 4
x 100m medley, with 4th at 100m in 1993.
He won seven successive national titles at
200m 1987-93 and the 100m 1992-3. He
was awarded the MBE in 1993.
Best times: Breaststroke: UK records:
100m 1:01.33 (1992), 200m six from
2:14.58 in 1988 to 2:11.29 in 1992. Short-
course world records for 200m 2:08.15 and
2:07.93 in 1991.

Mary GLEN HAIG

Fencing
(Dame) Mary Alison Glen Haig. b. 18 Jul 1918. née James.

After winning the British Ladies' foil championship in 1948 and 1950, Glen Haig finished as runner-up no less than eight times, losing to Gillian Sheen (qv) in 1951-6 and 1960 and to Margaret Stafford in 1959. She was a four-time Olympian (1948-60) and at the Commonwealth Games she won a gold medal in the individual foil in 1950 and 1954 and a bronze medal in 1958. A distinguished administrator she served as President of the AFA and the British Ladies' Fencing Union, was a member of the Sports Council 1966-82, and was elected a member of the International Olympic Committee in 1982. She was awarded the MBE in 1971, the CBE in 1977 and was appointed Dame Commander of the British Empire in 1993.

Tom GODDARD

Cricket
Thomas William John Goddard. b. 1 Oct 1900 Gloucester. d. 22 May 1966 Gloucester.

Given Goddard's great first-class record and huge reputation as an off-spinner, it seems amazing that he played in only eight Tests - except that off-spin was less well regarded in his day than leg spin, in the 1930s he was up against left-armer Hedley Verity (qv) and after the war he must have been thought too old.
Standing 1.90m *6 ft 3 in*, with huge hands, he started at Gloucestershire as a fast bowler, but met with little success, so he took 1928 out to learn to bowl medium-paced off-spin on the MCC staff. He returned to Gloucester with such success that he took 184 wickets at 16.38 in 1929, and was over 100 wickets each year from then to 1939 and again after the war from 1946-50. Indeed he exceeded 150 wickets ten times and was four times over 200: 200 at 20.36 in 1935, 248 at 16.76 in 1937, 200 at 14.86 in 1939 and 238 at 17.30 in 1947. He headed the national averages in 1947 and 1949 despite being in his late 40s. He

took six hat-tricks, the second best ever figure, including one for England against South Africa in 1938, and in 1939 he took 17 wickets in one day, for Gloucester v Kent, to equal the world record.
8 Tests 1930-39: 13 runs at 6.50, HS 8; 22 wickets at 26.72, BB 6-29; 3 catches.
First-class 1922-52: 5234 runs at 9.39, HS 71; 2979 wickets at 19.84, BB 10-113; 313 catches.

Kitty GODFREE

Tennis
Kathleen Godfree. b. 7 May 1896 Bayswater, London. d. 19 Jun 1992 London. née McKane.

One of the world's outstanding players of the early 1920s, McKane was a worthy successor to Dorothea Lambert Chambers (see Douglass) as the British No. 1. She first entered Wimbledon in 1919 and reached the final four years later where she lost to Suzanne Lenglen. She was singles champion in 1924 beating Helen Wills (USA), who was making her Wimbledon debut, in a classic final. This was the only defeat that Wills-Moody suffered in nine appearances at Wimbledon
In 1926 McKane married Leslie Godfree (qv) while on a tennis tour to South Africa and then, while Kitty won her second singles title after losing to Lenglen in the 1925 semi-finals, they became the only married couple ever to win the Wimbledon mixed doubles. As Miss McKane she had earlier won the mixed doubles at Wimbledon in 1924 and the US Championships in 1925. In the women's doubles she was the US champion in 1923 and 1927, the World Hard Court champion in 1923 and an Olympic gold medallist in 1920. At the Olympic Games of 1920 and 1924 she won five medals (1 gold, 2 silver, 2 bronze) – a record for a woman tennis player. She played in the first Wightman Cup in 1923 and made her seventh and final appearance in 1934. In her career at the Wimbledon Championships she won 112 of her 147 matches.
At badminton she won four All-England singles titles 1920-2 and 1924, the women's doubles with her sister Margaret

in 1921 and 1924, and the mixed with Frank Devlin (qv) in 1924-5. She was also a member of the English lacrosse team in 1918.

Leslie GODFREE

Tennis
Leslie Allison Godfree. b. 27 Apr 1885 Brighton, East Sussex. d. 17 Nov 1971 Richmond, London.

Prior to winning the Wimbledon mixed doubles with his wife in 1926 (see above), he won the men's doubles in 1923 with Randolph Lycett (qv). A member of the Davis Cup team 1923-7 and captain in 1924, he played only in the doubles and won six of his eleven matches. He had the distinction of hitting the first ball on the new Wimbledon centre court in 1922.

Albert GOLDTHORPE

Rugby League
Albert Edward Goldthorpe. b. c. 1872. d. 8 Jan 1943 Leeds.

Goldthorpe was a prodigious kicker; more than 200 of his total of almost 1,000 goals came from drop kicks. In 1907/8 he was captain of Hunslet when they became the first side to win all four Cups, and in this season he became the first player to kick 100 goals in a season with 101. He had set previous records with 66 in 1897/8 and 67 in 1898/9. After retirement he joined the Hunslet committee and was appointed secretary-manager in 1924.

Harry GOLOMBEK

Chess
Harry Golombek. b. 1 Mar 1911 London. d. 7 Jan 1995.

The doyen of British chess journalists and chess correspondent of *The Times* from 1945 to 1985, he was a key figure in the resurgence of chess standards in Britain by the end of his life, doing much to encourage young players and to raise the profile of the game. His peak success as a player came with his wins in the British Championship of 1947, 1949 and 1955 and

when he became, in 1951, the first Englishman to qualify for the inter-zonal stage of the World Championship. He had won the London Boys' title in 1929 and represented Britain in the World Team championships of 1935, 1937 and 1939, and for a further six Olympiads, to 1962, after the war, in which he served as a code-breaker at Bletchley Park.

He was a philologist at King's College, London. he qualified as an International Master in 1950 and was made an Emeritus Grand Master in 1985. For many years he was the English delegate to the annual FIDE congress, he served for over 30 years on the FIDE rules commission, and he wrote and edited many standard works on the game. He was awarded the OBE in 1966, the first to be so awarded for services to chess.

Graham GOOCH

Cricket
Graham Alan Gooch. b. 23 Jul 1953 Leytonstone, London.

A powerful batsman, Gooch reached his peak as England captain with scores of 333 and 123 (a record Test match aggregate) against India at Lord's in 1990. That year he also became the first player to score over 1000 Test runs in an English summer (306 v New Zealand, 752 at 125.33 v India) and became only the fifth player ever to average over 100 in an English first-class season, as his 2746 runs at 101.70 was the highest since 1961.

He made his Test debut in 1975, but had to wait until 1978 for a second chance, from when he established himself as an England regular, except for a three-year ban after he had captained an English 'rebel' tour to South Africa in 1982. After captaining England twice in 1988, he returned to the job in 1990 and led the team by the personal example of his magnificent batting, although often it seemed with no great tactical acumen. He resigned after England lost four of the first five Tests of the Ashes series in 1993, with an overall Test record of 10 wins in his 34 matches as captain. He did, however continue to bat marvellously well in that series, with 673 runs at 56.08

in the six Tests. In perhaps one tour too many he announced his retirement from Test cricket during the 1994/5 series against Australia.

He has played for Essex from 1973, captaining them in 1986-7 and 1989-94. With them he has won six county championships (1979, 1983-4, 1986, 1991-2) as well as the Sunday League in 1984 and 1985. To the end of the 1994 season he holds the runs records for all three English one-day competitions: 7906 in the Sunday League, including the record score of 176 in 1983; 2383 in the Gillette/NatWest Cup; and 4934 (to end 1995) in the Benson & Hedges Cup, including the record score of 198* in 1982. In 1994, when he exceeded 1000 runs in a season for the 19th time (five over 2000), he passed 40,000 runs in first-class cricket, including 12 double centuries. He is also a useful medium-pace swing bowler. He was awarded the OBE in 1991.

118 Tests 1975-95: 8900 runs at 42.58, 20 100s HS 333; 23 wickets at 46.47, BB 3-39; 103 catches.

125 One-day Ints 1976-95: 4290 runs at 36.98, 8 100s HS 142; 36 wickets at 42.11, BB 3-19; 45 catches.

First-class 1973-95: 40,859 runs at 48.93, 113 100s HS 333; 238 wickets at 34.81, BB 7-14; 513 catches.

Duncan GOODHEW

Swimming
Duncan Alexander Goodhew. b. 27 May 1957 Marylebone, London.

At the 1980 Olympic Games Goodhew, left bald due to an accident, won the gold medal at 100m breaststroke in 1:03.44, just outside the British record of 1:03.31 he had set earlier in the year, He also took Olympic bronze at medley relay and was 6th at the 200m breaststroke. His 200m best was 2:19.07 in 1980, and his short-course bests were British records of 1.01.83 for 100m and 2:16.88 in 1980.

At his first Olympics in 1976, when still a student at Millfield School, he had been 7th at 100m and in 1978 he won three silver medals at the Commonwealth Games, 100m and 200m breaststroke and medley relay, and was 4th in both individual events with bronze at medley relay at the World Championships.

He was ASA champion at both 100m and 200m each year 1978-80, also winning both short-course titles in 1980.

Andy GOODWAY

Rugby League
Andrew Goodway. b. 6 Jun 1961 Castleford, West Yorkshire.

After winning 11 Great Britain caps with Oldham, Goodway moved to Wigan in July 1985 for £65,000, then a record fee for a forward, and won a further 12 caps with his new club for a total of 23 in 1983-90. He moved to Leeds in 1992 and returned to Oldham 1993, becoming their coach the following year.

He made an impressive international debut against France in 1983, scoring a try from the second row. His robust play, however, frequently failed to meet with the approval of the referee.

Elenor GORDON

Swimming
Helen Orr Gordon. b. 10 May 1934 Hamilton, South Lanarkshire. Later Mrs McKay.

The outstanding Scottish woman swimmer of the 1950s, she won the Commonwealth 220y breaststroke in 1950 and 1954 and at medley relay bronze in 1950 and gold in 1954. She made her British international debut at the 1947 European Championships and competed at three Olympics 1948-56, with the high point being her bronze at 200m breaststroke in 1952, followed by 6th at that event in 1956. She was ASA champion at 200y 1950-2 and 220y 1955-6 and was Scottish champion each year 1947-57. At 220y breaststroke she set three British records, with a best of 2:57.4 in 1956.

Mary GORDON-WATSON

Equestrianism, Three-day event
Mary Diana Gordon-Watson. b. 3 Apr 1948 Blandford, Dorset.

Gordon-Watson's father's horse *Cornishman V* had been ridden by Richard Meade (qv) when he won the Olympic three-day event team gold in 1968, as Mary lost her chance of competing there through injury. Mary, however, rode *Cornishman* when she won the individual three-day event title at the 1969 European Championships, took team and individual gold at the 1970 World Championships and team golds at the 1971 Europeans and 1972 Olympics. After her retirement she became an equestrian teacher and a member of the British selection committee. She was awarded the MBE.

Wentworth GORE

Tennis
Arthur William Charles Gore. b. 2 Jan 1868 Lyndhurst, Hampshire. d. 1 Dec 1928 Kensington, London.

A player of remarkable durability, Gore competed at every Wimbledon over a span of 39 years and 35 Championships 1888-1927, winning 121 of his total of 182 there. He won the singles three times, 1901, 1908 and 1909, and the men's doubles in 1909. He is the only player to have won a singles title over the age of 40, in 1908 and at 41 years 182 days in 1909, and in 1912 at 44, he added the distinction of being the oldest Wimbledon singles finalist when he lost to Tony Wilding in the Challenge Round.
Wentworth Gore played in the first British Davis Cup team at Boston in 1900 and reached the semi-finals of the US championships that year. He played again in the Davis Cup in 1907 and 1912. Other successes included gold medals in the men's singles and men's doubles at the 1908 Olympics. An outstanding baseline player with a strong forehand, his speed around the court allowed him to protect his extremely vulnerable backhand.

Darren GOUGH

Cricket
Darren Gough b. 18 Sep 1970 Monk Bretton, nr Barnsley, South Yorkshire.

Although he can hardly yet be accorded all-time great status, Gough has excited the cricketing public more than any other young England player since Ian Botham. Having received his Yorkshire county cap in 1993, he made his international debut in the one-day international against New Zealand in May 1994, dismissing Martin Crowe with the sixth ball of his first over. Six weeks later he made his Test debut, taking six wickets in the match with his fast-medium bowling and making a splendid 65 in his one innings. After 11 wickets in three Tests against South Africa and an exhilarating display of hitting to galvanise the England team at The Oval, he took 20 wickets in three Tests in Australia. In the Third Test at Sydney he led a stirring England recovery, hitting 51 off 56 balls in England's first innings and followed that with 6-49 to dismiss Australia for 116. He then had to return home through injury, and has proved susceptible to a series of problems in his short career, but he has been resilient enough to bounce back on each occasion.
7 Tests 1994-5: 244 runs at 34.85, HS 65; 37 wickets at 26.78, BB 6-49; 4 catches.
10 One-day Ints 1994-5: 78 runs at 15.60, HS 45; 17 wickets at 20.58, BB 5-44; 2 catches.
First-class 1989-95: 1242 runs at 16.56, HS 72; 249 wickets at 30.08, BB 7-42; 18 catches.

Richard GOUGH

Football
Charles Richard Gough. b. 5 Apr 1962 Stockholm, Sweden.

An assured and dominant centre-back, Gough earned 61 Scotland caps from 1982 until his retirement from international football in 1993, having scored a commendable six goals from defence.
The son of a Scottish father and a Swedish mother, he attended Witz University in South Africa before signing for Dundee United in 1980. Playing at right-back or as a central defender he played a large part in their championship winning team of 1982/3 and helped them to the final of both the Scottish Cup and Scottish League Cup in 1985. He moved in 1986 to Tottenham

Hotspur and quickly became captain but after missing out on an FA Cup winners' medal in a dramatic 1987 final, he was tempted back to Scotland with Rangers, who he led to win seven league titles in succession to 1995, as well as five League Cup and two Scottish Cup trophies.

His father, **Charles** (b. 21 May 1939, Glasgow), played for Charlton Athletic in the 1960s.

Arthur GOULD

Rugby Union
Arthur Joseph Gould. b. 10 Oct 1864 Newport. d. 2 Jan 1919 Newport.

An outstanding leader, nicknamed 'Monkey' for his agility, Gould captained Wales a record 18 times in 27 international appearances between 1885 and 1897. He led Wales to their first Triple Crown in 1893 and at the time of his retirement he was Wales' most capped player. His retirement was marked by the Welsh RU with the gift of a house which resulted in Ireland and Scotland refusing to play Wales in 1897 as they considered this an act of professionalism. Gould was appointed to the committee of the Welsh RU in 1897 and became a selector the following year.

He was one of six brothers who all played for Newport and three of whom were capped by Wales. He was twice placed in the AAA 120y hurdles and used his speed to great effect as a full back or in the centre.

David GOWER

Cricket
David Ivon Gower. b. 1 Apr 1957 Tunbridge Wells, Kent.

A sublime left-handed batsman, Gower charmed cricket watchers with his batting for many years, but was churlishly dropped by the England selectors after playing with considerable success in 1990-1. He never scored the mass of runs in first-class cricket of many other great batsmen, but significantly his average was much higher in Tests than in other matches.

An incident in which he borrowed an aeroplane and 'buzzed' his colleagues seemed more important to them than his batting. Recalled, however, in 1992 he averaged 50 in three Tests against Pakistan and passed Geoffrey Boycott (qv) as England's leading run-scorer in Test cricket. There was then a national outcry over his non-selection for the winter tour to India. Despite that, and continued failures by English batsmen, he was again overlooked in 1993 in favour of younger players, and at the end of that season he announced his retirement from first-class cricket to become cricket correspondent of the *Sunday Express*.

Gower made his first-class debut for Leicestershire in 1975, playing for them until 1989, captain 1984-6. He then switched to play for Hampshire. He started a law degree course, but gave that up to concentrate on cricket.

His class was swiftly recognised and he made his Test debut at the age of 21. He averaged over 50 in three of his first four series, and scored 200* against India at Edgbaston in 1979. Between 1982 and 1989 he captained England 32 times but was not a great success, apart from a 2-1 win over India in 1984/5 followed by a 3-1 win in 1985 against Australia, in which Gower himself had his most successful series with 732 runs at 81.33, including his Test highest of 215 at Edgbaston. When he made his 100th Test appearance for England in 1988 he was, at 31, four years younger than anyone else to achieve that feat. He was awarded the OBE in 1992.

117 Tests 1978-92: 8231 runs at 44.25, 18 100s HS 215; 74 catches.
114 One-day Ints 1978-91: 3170 runs at 30.77, 7 100s HS 158; 44 catches.
First-class 1975-93: 26,339 runs at 40.09, 53 100s HS 228; 280 catches, 1 stumping.

Lily GOWER

Croquet
Lilias Mary Gower. b. 1877. d. 29 Jul 1959 West Kensington, London. Later Mrs Beaton.

Gowe was the first great woman croquet player and the first lady to win the Open Championship. She learned her tactics entirely from an instructional book and her tournament debut at Budleigh Salterton in 1898, when she beat the defending champion, was the first time she had ever played on a full-sized court and the first time she had even seen a first-class game. After this astonishing start, she won the first of her three successive victories in the women's championship the following year. A fourth victory came many years later when, as Mrs Beaton, she took the title in 1928.

She was the equal of most of her male contemporaries and in 1905 she became the first woman to win the Open title, beating **Reginald** Charles John **Beaton** (b. 5 Aug 1870), whom she married later in the year, in the final. Her husband was Open champion in 1904 and 1907 and together they won the doubles championship in 1904, 1906-7 and 1920.

Edward GRACE

Cricket
Edward Mills Grace. b. 28 Nov 1841 Downend, Bristol. d. 20 May 1911 Thornbury, Gloucestershire.

'The Coroner', W.G.'s elder brother, and also a doctor, was the best batsman in England before W.G. took over, and also a fine athlete, who was an early triple jump record holder.

His nickname came because he was coroner for West Gloucestershire. He had a priceless ability and the eye to hit the ball where the fielders were not, by whatever method, and was first a right-arm fast round-arm bowler, reverting later to slow lobs. In 1862 he scored 192* and took ten wickets in an innings for MCC v Gentlemen of Kent. With his brothers W.G. and Fred he played in the first ever Test in England in 1880. He was secretary of Gloucestershire CC from 1871 to 1909.

1 Test 1880: 36 runs at 18.00, HS 36; 1 catch.

First-class 1870-95: 10,025 runs at 18.66, 5 100s HS 192*; 305 wickets at 20.37, BB 10-69; 369 catches, 1 stumping.

His brother George **Fred**erick Grace (b. 13 Dec 1850 Downend), a middle-order batsman and fast bowler. died of congestion of the lungs following a severe cold just two weeks after the 1880 Test.

W.G. GRACE

Cricket
Dr William Gilbert Grace. b. 18 Jul 1848 Downend, Bristol. d. 23 Oct 1915 Mottingham, Kent.

'The Champion' bestrode cricket for 40 years, taking it from a rural pursuit into a national sport, as he himself became the best known figure in the land; a figure that changed over the years from the athletic young man who made an immediate impact as a teenager to the portly giant who played his last Test at the age of 50 and made his last first-class appearance in 1908.

His run-scoring dwarfed his contemporaries. In 1871 when he became the first player to exceed 2000 runs in a season and made a record ten centuries, his total of 2739 runs was at an average of 78.25, while the next best averaged 37.66. He again exceeded 2000 in 1876, 1887 and, just when some thought his powers were declining, again in 1895 and 1896. He made the first ever first-class triple century, 344 for MCC v Kent in 1876, and followed that a few days later with 316 for Gloucs v Yorkshire.

In his early days he was also by far the best all-rounder in the country, bowling slow round-arm deliveries, with a best season of 191 wickets (av. 12.94) in 1875. He did the double of 1000 runs and 100 wickets eight times, and in 1873 and 1876 became the first to achieve 2000 runs and 100 wickets. He was also a magnificent catcher, whose career total has been surpassed only by Frank Woolley.

W.G. was often seen at his best in the Gentlemen v Players matches, transforming the fortunes of the Gentlemen, for whom he scored 6008 runs including 15 100s, and took 271 wickets. He played for Gloucestershire 1868-99 (captain 1870-98) and then ran the London County team 1900-04.

He qualified as a doctor, but left his practice to locums whenever there was cricket to be played. In his youth he was also a fine athlete. In August 1866 WG achieved a unique double when he scored 224*, then the highest ever first-class score, for England v Surrey at the Oval, but missed the second day of the match to run at the

W.G. GRACE in First-class Cricket						
Year	Runs	Ave.	HS	100s	Wkts	Ave.
1865	189	26.71	48	0	290	13.40
1866	581	52.81	224*	2	31	13.35
1867	154	30.80	75	0	39	7.51
1868	625	56.81	134*	3	49	(14.29)
	588	*65.33*			*44*	*14.52*
1869	1320	57.39	180	6	73	17.19
	1320	*52.86*	*180*	*6*	*73*	*16.28*
1870	1808	54.78	215	5	50	15.64
1871	2739	78.25	268	10	79	17.02
1872	1561	53.82	170*	6	68	(11.87
	1485	*57.11*			*56*	*12.10*
1873	2139	71.30	192*	7	106	12.94
	1805	*72.20*			*75*	*14.57*
1874	1664	52.00	179	8	140	12.71
1875	1498	32.56	152	3	191	12.94
1876	2622	62.42	344	7	129	19.05
					130	*18.90*
1877	1474	39.83	261	2	179	12.79
1878	1151	28.77	116	1	152	14.50
1879	993	38.19	123	3	113	13.19
	880	*35.20*			*2 105*	*13.46*
1880	951	39.62	152	2	84	17.61
1881	917	38.20	182	2	57	18.00
	792	*37.14*			*45*	*19.53*
1882	975	26.35	88	0	101	17.36
1883	1352	34.66	112	1	94	22.09
1884	1361	34.02	116*	3	82	21.48
1885	1688	43.28	221*	4	117	18.79
1886	1846	35.50	170	4	122	19.99
1887	2062	54.26	183*	6	97	21.42
1888	1886	32.51	215	4	93	18.18
1889	1396	32.46	154	3	44	23.18
1890	1476	28.38	109*	1	61	19.39
1891	771	19.76	72*	0	58	16.77
1891/2	448	44.80	159*	1	5	26.80
1892	1055	31.02	99	)	31	30.90
1893	1609	35.75	128	1	22	38.81
1894	1293	29.38	196	3	29	25.24
1895	2346	51.00	288	9	16	32.93
1896	2135	42.70	301	4	52	24.01
1897	1532	39.28	131	4	56	22.17
1898	1513	42.02	168	3	36	25.41
1899	515	23.40	78	0	20	24.10
1900	1277	42.56	126	3	32	30.28
1901	1007	32.48	132	1	51	21.78
1902	1187	37.09	131	2	46	23.34
1903	593	22.80	150	1	10	47.90
1904	637	25.48	166	1	21	32.71
1905	250	19.23	71	0	7	54.71
1906	241	26.77	74	0	13	20.61
1907	19	9.50	16	0	-	
1908	40	20/00	25	0	0	

first National Olympic Association meeting at Crystal Palace, where he won the 440y hurdles. At a slower pace, in 1903 he was elected the first president of the English Bowling Association. His brother Edward (qv) preceded him as the leading batsman in England and both Edward and another brother Fred played with W.G. in the first Test match ever played in England, against Australia at The Oval in 1880. In that match W.G. scored 152, the first century by an England batsman in Tests.

He captained England in his last 13 Tests from the age of 40.

22 Tests 1880-99: 1098 runs at 32.29, 2 100s HS 170; 9 wickets at 26.22, BB 2-12; 39 catches.

First-class 1865-1908: 54,896 runs at 39.55, 126 100s HS 344; 2876 wickets at 17.92, BB 10-49; 887 catches, 5 stumpings.

The definition of a first-class match was not precise in the 19th century, and figures for Grace varied, both as to the matches included and to the accuracy of their compilation. Listed left is his season-by-season record, based on the traditional figures, but also showing in italics revised ones according to the list of first-class matches compiled by the Association of Cricket Statisticians (ACS), where the variance is significant.

Bowling averages in brackets are for when some matches were excluded due to the runs conceded not being known, the wickets figures include all matches.

George GRAHAM

Football
George Graham. b. 30 Nov 1944
Bargeddie, North Lanarkshire.

A much travelled player, after working on the ground staff at Aston Villa, Graham signed as a professional with the club in 1961. He subsequently played for Chelsea, Arsenal, Manchester United, Portsmouth and Crystal Palace, as well as in California in 1978. For Chelsea he scored 46 goals in 102 games and for Arsenal he scored 59 in 227 appearances between 1966 and 1972, taking winner's medals in the Inter Cities' Fairs Cup in 1970 and the FA Cup and Football League in 1971.

A stylish and effective striker, although not particularly fast, he won 12 caps for Scotland 1971-3. On his retirement in 1980 he coached at Queen's Park Rangers before being appointed manager of Millwall in 1982. His successes at Millwall led to him returning to Highbury as manager of Arsenal in 1986 where he guided the club to the League title in 1988/9 and 1990/1, the Football League Cup and FA Cup in 1993 and the European Cup Winners' Cup in 1994 before he was forced to resign in February 1995 due to allegations of financial improprieties.

A Football Association commission of inquiry found him guilty of misconduct and banned him from the game for a year..

Dalton GRANT

Athletics, High Jump
Dalton Grant. b. 8 Apr 1966 London.

Grant is a man who has time after time risen (literally) to the big occasion. Typical examples of his ability came in 1991 when, from a season's best of 2.20m, he won the European Cup with 2.30. Then he showed further moderate form until the World Championships in Tokyo, where he entered at 2.31, 1 cm above his year's best, cleared that, passed 2.34 and then cleared 2.36 for 4th place. This was his ninth British high jump record outdoors from 2.29 in 1988, the last three also being Commonwealth records. He also set four British indoor records in 1989 to 2.35, equalling the Commonwealth record, and after Steve Smith (qv) had taken over as record holder improved his best to 2.37 indoors in 1994 to win the European Indoor title.

After ranking 5th, 4th, 3rd and 2nd each year 1984-7, he became Britain's No.1 in 1988 and his great season in 1989, when he was 4th in the World Indoors, 2nd in the European Indoors, 1st at the European Cup and 2nd at the World Cup, meant that he became the first British high jumper to be ranked in the world's top ten since Alan Paterson (qv) in 1950.

His best Olympic placing has been 7th equal in 1988 and at the Commonwealth Games he was 7th in 1986, 2nd in 1990 and 5th in 1994. He was AAA champion in 1989 and 1990 and UK in 1990-1 and 1993.

Tom GRAVENEY

Cricket
Thomas William Graveney. b. 16 Jun 1927
Riding Mill, Northumberland.

Graveney was a majestically elegant batsman, who, although his class was apparent from when he made his Test debut in 1951, for some years did not prove as successful in Tests as perhaps he should have. That may have been due to some distrust of his abilities when more work-a-day qualities were appreciated. He did not play in Tests between 1959 and 1962. Then he averaged 100.25 in a four-Test series against Pakistan, but after faring less well against Australia in 1962/3 he was again dropped and did not reappear until 1966.

He had played for Gloucestershire 1948-60, but left the county after losing the captaincy (1959-60). He moved to Worcestershire, and there found the best form of his career. He helped them to their first ever championship in 1964, and captained them in 1968-70. Somewhat belatedly the England selectors recognised his marvellous consistency and recalled him to the Test side at the age of 39 in 1966, when he averaged 76.50 in four matches against the West Indies. For the next three years he excelled for England, until he lost his place due to a petty squabble over activity on the rest day of a Test match. He captained England once against Australia in 1968.

He scored over 1000 runs in a season 22 times, including twice overseas, and over 2000 seven times, with a peak of 2397 in 1956 and was also a safe close fielder.. He was awarded the OBE. His brother Ken (b. 16 Dec 1924) captained Gloucestershire in 1963-4 and Ken's son David (b. 2 Jan 1953) has since captained Gloucestershire and Durham.

79 Tests 1951-69: 4882 runs at 44.38, 11 100s HS 258; 1 wicket; 80 catches.

First-class 1948-72: 47,793 runs at 44.92, 122 100s HS 258; 80 wickets at 37.96, BB 5-28; 550 catches, 1 stumping.

Jimmy GREAVES

Football
James Peter Greaves. b. 20 Feb 1940
Poplar, London.

A mercurial inside-forward with an extraordinary flair for goalscoring, Greaves played for Chelsea 1957-61, AC Milan 1961, Tottenham Hotspur 1961-70 and West Ham United 1970-1, and scored on his debut for each club. He also scored in his first games for England and for the England Under-23 team. He scored a record 357 goals in 517 matches in the First Division and was the leading scorer in the Division for six seasons. A further 55 goals in FA Cup ties, 44 for England (including a record six hat-tricks), and many more in representative matches, made him one of the most exciting and entertaining players of his era.

His finest years came while he was with Tottenham who he joined after a brief, unhappy spell in Italy with AC Milan. He played a vital role in the team which won the FA Cup in 1962 and 1967, and the European Cup-Winners' Cup in 1963. He played 57 times for England 1959-67, 42 while with Spurs, but his greatest disappointment was that he was left out of the team for the closing stages of the 1966 World Cup. Only Bobby Charlton and Gary Lineker (qqv), who played in many more matches, have scored more goals for England.

Immediately following his retirement in May 1971, he had little involvement in football, preferring to concentrate on his varied business interests, but he later made occasional appearances for Chelmsford and Barnet. Having overcome alcoholism, he has now found his metier as a TV personality.

Lucinda GREEN

Equestrianism, Three-day event
Lucinda Jane Green. b. 7 Nov 1953
London. née Prior-Palmer.

Green was an outstanding three-day eventer who achieved a record six Badminton victories. Her first was in 1973 on *Be Fair*, whom her parents had bought her as a 15th birthday present, and the others were: *Wide Awake* 1976, *George* 1977, *Killaire* 1979, *Regal Realm* 1983 and *Beagle Bay* 1984. She was European Champion on *Be Fair* in 1975 and on *George* in 1977, and World champion on *Regal Realm* in 1982, when she also won a team gold. She also won at Burghley in 1977 and 1981.

She competed at two Olympics; in 1976 when *Be Fair* broke down in his last competition, and in 1984 when she was 6th individually and took a team silver. With the British team she boycotted the 1980 Games. She was awarded the MBE in 1978, and married the Australian rider David Green (b. 28 Feb 1960) in 1981. David competed for Australia at the 1988 Olympics.

Her first international appearance was in 1971 when she was a member of the winning British team at the European Junior Championships. A natural cross-country rider, she worked hard at becoming equally proficient at show jumping and dressage. She was Sports Writers Sportswoman of the Year 1975.

Tommy GREEN

Walking
Thomas William Green. b. 30 Mar 1894
Fareham, Hampshire. d. 29 Mar 1975
Eastleigh, Hampshire.

The surprise Olympic champion at 50 km walk in 1936, Green was also, at 38, the oldest ever winner of the event. He nearly made the team four years later, as well, but missed by a place when he was 4th in the RWA Championship.

Due to rickets he was unable to walk until he was five years old, but he joined the Army in 1906, having falsified his age. However, he was invalided out four years later when a horse fell on him; he also suffered wounds and gassing on his return to the Army in World War I. He was then encouraged to start walking and in 1926 won the first race that he contested, after which he joined Belgrave Harriers. He won the London to Brighton race four times, 1929-31 and 1933 and the inaugural RWA Championship at 50km in 1930 in what remained his best ever time, 4:35:36. He was runner-up in the RWA 20 miles in 1932 and 1933.

Harry GREGG

Football
Harold Gregg. b. 25 Oct 1932 Magherafelt, Co. Derry.

Signed in 1952 by Doncaster Rovers from the Irish club, Dundalk, he was capped nine times as Northern Ireland's goalkeeper before moving to Manchester United in 1957 for £23,500, then a record fee for a goalkeeper. While at Old Trafford he brought his total of Irish caps up to 24 (1954-63), and showed himself to be one of the world's finest goalkeepers in the 1958 World Cup, before his international career ended in unusual circumstances. A survivor of the Munich air disaster, he had an understandable aversion to flying, and he was dropped by Northern Ireland when he refused to fly to Madrid for an international against Spain.

During his ten years with Manchester United he made 210 League appearances and kept goal when they won the FA Cup and League Championship double in 1963. In 1966 he was transferred to Stoke City but only played two games for them before retiring. He was for a while manager of Shrewsbury Town. He was awarded the MBE in 1995.

Andy GREGORY

Rugby League
Andrew Gregory. b. 10 Aug 1961 Wigan, Gt. Manchester.

Gregory was a tough, aggressive scrum-half who joined Widnes in 1979 and later moved to Warrington, Wigan, Leeds and Salford (from 1993). The only player to appear in eight Challenge Cup finals, he was on the winning side a record seven times; with Widnes in 1981 and 1984 and with Wigan in 1988-92. He played for three winning clubs of the Premiership Trophy: Widnes 1982 and 1983, Warrington 1986 and Wigan 1987. His only disappointment was with Widnes in 1982, when they lost to Hull after a replay. He played in four series against Australia but was on the losing side each time.

Short (1.63m *5 ft 4 in*) but powerfully built, he made his international debut against France in 1981 and went on to win 24 caps (plus one appearance as a substitute) to 1992.

Colin GREGORY

Tennis
(Dr) John Colin Gregory. b. 28 Jul 1903 Beverley, East Yorkshire. d. 10 Sep 1959 Wimbledon, London.

After apparently reaching the end of his Davis Cup career in 1930, he later became the non-playing captain of the British team and in 1952, at the age of 48, he nominated himself to play in a vital doubles match against Yugoslavia. Gregory and his partner, Tony Mottram (qv), were the winners in five sets and Gregory is the oldest player ever to win a Davis Cup rubber. Between 1926 and 1952 he played 15 Davis Cup ties (13/21 singles, 8/9 doubles). In 1929 he won the Australian singles and was a finalist with Ian Collins in the men's doubles at Wimbledon losing in five sets to Americans, Wilmer Allison and John van Ryan. In the Wimbledon singles, he was a quarter-finalist in 1926 and 1930. He was chairman of the All England Club, 1955-9.

John GREIG

Football
John Greig. b. 11 Sep 1942 Edinburgh.

A hard-tackling wing-half, Greig made 857 first team appearances for Rangers during one of the Glasgow club's greatest eras. With Greig usually playing at left-half, and latterly as captain, they won the European Cup-Winners' Cup (1972), the Scottish Cup (1963-4, 1966, 1973, 1976, 1978), the Scottish League Cup (1964-5, 1978) and the Scottish League (1963-4, 1975-6, 1978). He also won 44 caps for Scotland between 1964 and 1976, captain on several occasions, and was voted Scottish Player of the Year in 1966 and 1976.
Joining Rangers in 1960 he remained loyal to the club throughout his career and when he announced his retirement in May 1978 he was appointed manager later in the month, a position he held until 1983. He was awarded the MBE in 1977.

Tony GREIG

Cricket
Anthony William Greig. b. 6 Oct 1946 Queenstown, South Africa.

Greig will be remembered as the leading aid to Kerry Packer (Aus) in recruiting players for World Series Cricket. He was at the time a highly successful captain of England, who inspired a series win in India in 1976/7. The revelation of his World Series preparations brought him much abuse, notably from those who had never been comfortable with the fact that a South African born man could become England captain, and he lost the captaincy although he played under Mike Brearley (qv) in 1977 before the Packer series began. He continued to be a leading figure in the Packer organisation and a TV commentator in Australia.
Such notoriety distracts attention from the fact that he had a superb temperament for Test cricket, achieving notable success as a middle-order batsman and a medium pace or off-break bowler, and instilling great spirit into a flagging England side. Born of a Scottish father and South African mother, he qualified to play for Sussex at the age of 20, and captained them in 1973-7. He made

his England debut against the Rest of the World in 1970 and was the tallest player at 2.02m *6 ft 7 ½in* to play for England.
His brother **Ian** (b. 8 Dec 1955) played in two Tests for England in 1982 and played for Cambridge University 1977-9, Sussex 1980-5 and Surrey as captain 1987-91.
58 Tests 1972-7: 3599 runs at 40.43, 8 100s HS 143; 141 wickets at 32.20, BB 8-86; 87 catches.
22 One-day Ints 1972-7: 269 runs at 16.81, HS 48; 19 wickets at 32.57, BB 4-45; 7 catches.
First-class 1965-78: 16,660 runs at 31.19, 26 100s HS 226; 856 wickets at 28.85, BB 8-25; 345 catches.

Billy GRIFFITH

Cricket
Stewart Cathie Griffith. b. 16 Jun 1914 Wandsworth, London. d. 7 Apr 1993 Felpham, West Sussex.

A fine wicket-keeper, Griffith went into the record books, when, pressed into service as a makeshift opener, he score 140 on his Test debut against the West Indies in 1948. He had played in all five 'Victory' Tests in 1945 and he also played two Tests as vice-captain in South Africa in 1948/9 before retiring to become cricket correspondent of the *Sunday Times* for two years. He then became one of two assistant secretaries of the MCC and ten years later secretary, serving with much charm in that office 1962-74, a time of great change for the game; he was also MCC President 1979/80. He prepared the 1980 code of the Laws of Cricket.
He was awarded the DFC as a glider pilot in the War and the CBE for his services to cricket. He had won his Blue at Cambridge in 1935 and played one match for Surrey in 1934 before making his Sussex debut in 1937, while a master at his old school of Dulwich. He was Sussex captain in 1946 and secretary until 1950.
3 Tests 1948-9: 157 runs at 31.40, 1 100 HS 140; 5 catches.
First-class 1934-54: 4846 runs at 16.42, 3 100s HS 140; 328 catches, 80 stumpings.
His son **Mike** (b. 25 Nov 1943) played hockey for England and captained Sussex at cricket 1968-72.

Terry GRIFFITHS

Snooker
Terence Martin Griffiths. b. 16 Oct 1947
Llanelli, Carmarthenshire.

Winner of the World Professional title at his first attempt in 1979, Griffiths has not won again but has remained one of the world's best with his steady, deliberate play. He was Welsh Amateur champion in 1975 and won the English Amateur in 1977 and 1978 before turning professional. He helped Wales win the World Cup in 1979 and 1980, and in 1980 won the Benson & Hedges Masters. In 1982 he won the Mercantile Credit Classic and the UK Open, but did not reach another World semi-final until 1988, when he was beaten by Steve Davis (qv) in the final.
While not recapturing such an exalted position in the game, he has remained a leading professional player, with a most consistent record into the mid-1990s.

Arthur GRIMSDELL

Football
Arthur Grimsdell. b. 23 Mar 1894
Watford, Herts. d. 12 Mar 1963 Watford.

Grimsdell was an unorthodox left-half noted for his relentless attacking play. After playing for Watford as an amateur, he turned professional in 1911 before moving to Tottenham the following year. In 1920 he won the first of his six England caps and led Tottenham to the Second Division title. Utilising his attacking style to the full, he scored 14 goals in their successful League campaign, a record for a half-back. Under Grimsdell's inspiring captaincy, Tottenham finished as runners-up in their first season in the First Division and won the FA Cup that year, 1921. After a brief spell with Clapton Orient 1929-30, he retired to run his sports shop in Watford but returned to football in 1945 when he became a director of Watford FC. A fine cricketer, he kept wicket for Hertfordshire for 25 years (1922-47) and played one first-class match.

Judy GRINHAM

Swimming
Judith Brenda Grinham. b. 5 Mar 1939
Hampstead, London. Later Mrs Rowley,
now Mrs Roe.

In 1956 when she won the Olympic 100m backstroke she became Britain's first swimming gold medallist for 36 years. In so doing she set an initial long-course world record of 1:12.9, adding further records at 110y (and the shorter 100m) with 1:11.9 in 1958 when she won the Commonwealth Games title. There, in Cardiff, she also won a gold medal on England's world record-breaking medley relay team and took a bronze in the freestyle relay. She achieved a unique hat-trick by adding the European backstroke title that year, and also won a silver at freestyle relay and bronzes at 100m freestyle and medley relay. She was ASA champion at 110y backstroke in 1955-6, 1958, and at freestyle 220y 1957 and 110y 1958.
She swam for the Hampstead Ladies SC, where she was coached by Reg Laxton. After her retirement in March 1959 she wrote for the *Daily Express*. In 1960 she married the hockey journalist Patrick Rowley. She coached swimming and in 1977 began work for Dr Barnardo's, becoming their national training officer.

George GUNN

Cricket
George Gunn. b. 13 Jun 1879 Hucknall
Torkard, Notts. d. 29 Jun 1958 Cuckfield,
Sussex.

In his long career he scored over 35,000 runs, yet that figure could well have been higher but for his somewhat eccentric attitude. That may well also have cost him the chance of playing more Tests, for he played only once (in 1909) in England despite his fine record. On his Test debut in 1907 he made 119 and 74 against Australia, and although he did not live up to that, the fact that he announced his intentions to do something special on his 50th birthday and then scored 164 for Notts v Worcester showed his genius. At that age he played four Tests for England in the West Indies in 1930, after a record interval of 17 years and 316 days since his previous selection. He relished fast bowling. 15 Tests 1907-30: 1120 runs at 40.00, 2 100s HS 122*; 15 catches.

First-class 1902-32: 35,208 runs at 35.96, 62 100s HS 220; 66 wickets at 35.68, BB 5-50; 473 catches.

His uncle William 'Billy' (1858-1921) played 11 Tests for England 1887-99 scoring 392 runs at 21.77, HS 102*, and had a first-class career record of 25,691 runs at 33.02; and his brother John (1876-1963) played six Tests for England 1901-05, scoring 85 runs at 10.62 and taking 18 wickets at 21.50, with a first-class career record of 24,557 runs at 33.18 and 1242 wickets at 24.52. In 1931 George and his son George V Gunn both scored centuries for Nottinghamshire v Warwickshire, a unique feat in the first-class game.

Sally GUNNELL

Athletics
Sally Jane Janet Gunnell b. 29 Jul 1966 Chigwell, Essex.Now Mrs Bigg.

Olympic champion at 400m hurdles in 1992, Gunnell added the World title in 1993, when she ran a world record (and her eighth British record) time of 52.74, with Sandra Farmer-Patrick (USA), 2nd in 52.79, also under the old world record. Gunnell also won bronze medals for 4 x 400m with the British team at both these events. Well established as the world's No.1, Gunnell added the European 400m hurdles title in 1994 as well as Commonwealth golds at 400m hurdles and 4 x 400m. She thus became the first woman athlete to hold the big four major titles in athletics.

Gunnell's first national titles were at long jump: WAAA junior 1980, intermediate 1981. After UK age records, 15-17 at heptathlon and 16-17 at 100m hurdles, she emerged as the UK number one at the latter event, winning the Commonwealth gold, in 1986. She moved up to the 400m hurdles in 1988, improving very rapidly to set four British records from 55.40 to 54.03 when 5th at the Olympics. She also ran a British record of 12.82 for 100m hurdles. In 1989 she won the European Indoor

400m and in 1990 won Commonwealth gold medals at 400m hurdles and 4 x 400m relay and a silver at 100m hurdles. In 1991 she improved her British record for 400m hurdles with 53.78 and 53.62 and took the World silver medal. At 400m hurdles she also won the European Cup in 1993 and 1994 and the World Cup in 1994. Her national titles: UK 100mh 1986, WAAA 100mh 1986-9 and 1991-3, 400mh 1988, indoor 200m 1987, 400m 1988. Sports Writers Association British Sportswoman of the Year each year 1992-4. She married 800m runner Jon Bigg in 1992.

Other bests: 100m 11.83 (1990), 11.8 (1987), 11.79w (1986); 200m 23.30 (1993), 300m 36.44 (1993), 400m 51.04 (1994), 800m 2:08.36i (1991), 60mh 8.27i (1990), high jump 1.67 (1983), long jump 6.08 (1983), shot 11.18 (1984), heptathlon 5493 (1984).

Jeremy GUSCOTT

Rugby Union
Jeremy Clayton Guscott. b. 7 Jul 1965 Bath.

An elusive and incisive attacking centre, Guscott scored tries on his debut for both England and the British Lions. Beginning with the mini-section at Bath, he rose through the ranks to command a regular place in the Club's 1st XV and marked his international debut against Romania in 1989 with a hat-trick of tries. After his England team-mate, Will Carling (qv), dropped out because of injury he joined the Lions for their tour to Australia later in the year and played in two Tests. On his second Lions tour to New Zealand in 1993 he played in all three Tests.

He was a member of the England team which won successive Grand Slams 1991-2 before his career was interrupted by injury causing him to miss the 1993/4 season. He returned to club rugby in the early part of the following season and immediately reclaimed his international place and helped England to another Grand Slam, although without, perhaps, compltely recapturing his former brilliance. He has won 39 caps for England to the end of the 1995 World Cup.

Jimmy GUTHRIE

Motorcycling
A James Guthrie. b. 1897 Hawick, Borders. d. Aug. 1937 Germany.

From 1920 to 1937 Guthrie rode for Norton with great success, highlights including his world 1-hour record of 183.613 km *114.092 miles* at the Montlhéry track in France in 1935 and his European championship in 1936. He first appearance in Isle of Man TT races was in 1923 and after 2nd in the 1927 senior his first win came on an AJS at lightweight in 1930. He went on to win the double at Junior and Senior in 1934, adding further wins for Norton with the Junior in 1935 and 1937 and the Senior in 1936. In 1935 he thought he had won the double for a second time, and was originally announced as the winner, only to discover that he had lost the Senior by a mere four seconds to Stanley Woods (qv). Within a mile of the finish, when well in the lead, of the 1937 German Grand Prix he crashed at the last corner and died shortly afterwards. In 1939 a memorial to him was unveiled on the Isle of Man course at the spot where he retired in his last TT in 1937.

Schofield HAIGH

Cricket
Schofield Haigh. b. 19 Mar 1871 Berry Brow, Huddersfield, West Yorkshire. d. 27 Feb 1921 Lockwood, North Yorkshire.

With George Hirst and Wilfred Rhodes (qqv), Haigh formed the heart of a formidable Yorkshire bowling attack. Eight county championships were won during his Yorkshire career. His pace was generally medium-fast, but he was capable of bowling very quick off breaks. He took over 100 wickets in 11 seasons, with a best of 174 at 14.59 in 1906, and he did the double in 1904. He later coached at Winchester College.
11 Tests 1898-1912: 113 runs at 7.53; HS 25; 24 wickets at 25.91, BB 6-11; 8 catches.
First-class 1895-1913: 11,715 runs at 18.65, 4 100s HS 159; 2012 wickets at 15.94, BB 9-25; 298 catches.

Mike HAILWOOD

Motor Cycling and Motor Racing
Stanley Michael Bailey Hailwood. b. 2 Apr 1940 Oxford. d. 23 Mar 1981 Birmingham.

The supreme motorcyclist of the early 1960s, one of the most exciting periods in the history of the sport, 'Mike the Bike' is many experts' choice as the greatest of all-time. He became the youngest ever world champion in 1961 at 250cc, and won further world titles at 500cc 1962-5 and at both 250cc and 350cc, 1966-7. After switching to motor racing, he returned to win the motorcycling Formula One world title in 1978.
Hailwood was started in his motorcycling career by his father Stan, a wealthy motorcycle dealer in Oxford, at the age of 17 in 1957 on a 125cc MV. Four years later he was world champion. He won a total of 76 Grand Prix races between 1961 and 1967, displaying consummate skill and natural ability by winning on different bikes: 2 at 125cc, 21 at 250cc, 16 at 350cc and 37 at 500cc, mostly for MV Augusta and Honda, including a record 19 in one year, 1966. He set a record which stood until 1993 with 14 wins in Isle of Man TT races between 1961 and 1979, winning three events in one year in both 1961 and 1967. He was awarded the MBE in 1968.
On four wheels he met with less success as he did not win a Formula One Grand Prix, but he scored 29 world championship points in 50 races 1971-4, with a best place of 2nd in the 1971 Italian GP driving a Surtees-Ford. He won the European Formula Two title in 1972. In 1973 he was awarded the George Medal for rescuing Clay Regazzoni (Swi) from his blazing Ferrari at Kyalami. He died in a car accident in Birmingham.

Peter HAINING

Rowing
Peter Moir Haining. b.3 Apr 1962 St Andrews.

He began rowing as a boy with the Loch Lomond RC and his career prospered with the introduction of lightweight classes. In 1986 he won a Commonwealth gold medal in the lightweight fours and in 1992 he stroked the British crew in the quadruple sculls at the Barcelona Olympics. He then concentrated on lightweight sculling and won the world single sculls in 1993 and 1994. At previous World Championships he had earned silver medals at lightweight coxless fours 1986-7 and bronze with the eight in 1990.

He won the Scullers' Head in 1993 and 1994 and in that year set course records both for this race, 19:53.4, and when winning the Wingfield Sculls in 19:58. He also won the Thames World Sculling Challenge in 1994 and retained the Wingfield Sculls in 1995. He was awarded the MBE in 1995.

Jack HALE

Swimming
Jack Irwin Hale. b. 5 Jun 1922 Hull.

In the immediate post-war years Hale was Britain's most successful male swimmer with ASA tiles at freestyle: 220y 1947-8, 440y, 880y and 1 mile 1946-8. He was also long distance champion either side of the war, 1939 and 1947, and in 1954 he took the 220y butterfly title.

At the 1948 Olympics he was 7th at 400m and at the Commonwealth Games in 1950 he won a gold medal on the English 4 x 100m medley relay team with a bronze at 4 x 220y freestyle. He set British records for freestyle with 2:12.8 for 220y (1952), 4:46.2 for 440y (1948) and 21:33.2 for 1 mile (1947) with three at 220y butterfly in 1953-4 with a best of 2:30.0.

Darren HALL

Badminton
Darren James Hall. b. 25 Oct 1965 Walthamstow, London.

The nephew of Ray Stevens (qv), Hall won a record seven English national men's singles titles in ten successive finals 1985-94. His greatest triumph was perhaps his win over Morten Frost (Den) to win the European title in 1988. Two years later he lost in the final to his compatriot Steve Baddeley (qv). At the 1990 Commonwealth Games he won a team gold and singles bronze. He made his way successfully through junior ranks with English under-15 titles at singles and both doubles in 1981 and was junior champion in 1983 and 1984, as well as winning a team gold at the 1983 European Juniors.

John HALL

Rugby Union
Jonathan Peter Hall. b. 15 Mar 1962 Bath.

Hall was a stalwart of Bath Football Club during their great years of dominance of English club rugby from 1981 until his retirement at the end of the 1994/5 season. He had to miss the 1995 Pilkington Cup Final through injury, but he went up to receive the Cup for Bath's 9th win in 12 seasons from 1984, and his club also won six League Championships.

A flanker, he was described by Jack Rowell, Bath's coach until he took over the England job in 1994, as one of the players of all-time in English rugby history, so it is therefore a surprise that he did not receive more than 21 internationals caps from his England debut in 1984. This was partially due to injuries.

Willie HALL

Football
George William Hall. b. 12 Mar 1912 Newark, Notts. d. 22 May 1967 Newark.

Although Hall once captured the headlines with a sensational scoring feat, his real value as an inside forward was as a playmaker. Joining Tottenham Hotspur from Notts County in 1932 he won 10 England caps 1933-9, and in the match against Northern Ireland in 1938 he scored five goals in succession, the first three within the space of four minutes. He made his international debut as an inside-left but won his other caps as an inside-right partnering Stanley Matthews (qv) in eight of the nine remaining internationals. Major club honours eluded him and only two of his nine playing seasons were in the First Division. He retired through injury in 1944 and his managerial career (Clapton Orient and Chingford) was dogged by ill health. During the war years he had both legs amputated after a severe attack of thrombosis and although he recovered sufficiently to become a licensee, he remained in poor health until his death.

Ian HALLAM

Cycling
Ian Hallam. b. 24 Nov 1948 Basford, Nottingham.

A Nottingham dental surgeon, Hallam was a three-time Olympian competing in both the individual and team pursuit in 1968, 1972 and 1976 and winning a bronze medal in the team event on the last two occasions.
In the individual pursuit he was a gold medallist at the 1970 Commonwealth Games and shortly afterwards won a silver at the World Championships. He again won a silver at the 1973 World Championships but this time in the team pursuit, and at the 1974 Commonwealth Games he won gold in both the individual and team pursuit and bronze in the 1000m time trial and the 10 miles. After turning professional he set a British record for 5km (standing start) and between 1969 and 1982 he won a record 25 British titles. His British records included bests for unpaced standing start of: 5km 6:20.9 (1979), 10km 13:18.3 (1981), 20km 26:503 (1981). He was awarded the MBE.

Steve HALLARD

Archery
Steven Leslie Hallard. b. 22 Feb 1965 Rugby, Warwickshire.

The leading British archer of recent years and an international from 1981, Hallard won an individual silver medal at the 1989 World Championships and team bronze at the 1988 and 1992 Olympics. He has won eight British titles to 1994, and set numerous British scoring records, including bests of 1318 and 2616 for single and double FITA rounds, and 1192 and 2356 single and double York rounds. A design draughtsman by profession, he is a member of the Dunlop Archers.

Jim HALLIDAY

Weightlifting
James Halliday. b. 19 Jan 1918 Farnworth, Gt. Manchester.

After being on the verge of British championships honours prior to World War II, Halliday fulfilled his promise after the war despite spending almost four years in a Japanese prison camp.
He won the British middleweight title five times, 1948-50, 1952 and 1954, and was a bronze medallist in the lightweight division at the 1948 Olympic Games. He again represented Britain at the 1952 Games. At the Empire (Commonwealth) Games he won the lightweight title in 1950 and at middleweight in 1954.

Nellie HALSTEAD

Athletics
Nellie Halstead. b. 19 Sep 1910 Bury, Gt. Manchester. d. Nov 1991.

Halstead excelled at a wide range of distances. She set women's world records for 220y at 25.2 in 1930 and 100y at 11.0 in 1931, while her most astonishing achievement came at 440y. She had twice run a world record time of 58.8 in 1931, but in the 1932 WAAAs took two seconds off that time with 56.8, a time that no woman surpassed even at the slightly shorter distance of 400m until 1950.
She set an unratified world record of 2:15.6 for 800m to win the WAAA title in 1935 and her full list of WAAA titles was: 100y 1931, 220y 1930-2, 200m 1934, 440y 1931-2, 400m 1933, 1937; 800m 1935, 1938. She also took bronze medals in the Women's World Games 200m 1930, Olympic 4 x 100m 1932 and Empire Games 220y 1934, when she also won relay gold and silver.
Her 'sister' **Edith** (b. 7 Sep 1907) set three British women's javelin records 1931-3, with a best of 35.22m, and was WAAA champion in 1932 and 1934, but the name on 'her' birth certificate was changed in 1943 to Edwin. Eddie later married and fathered several children.

Wyndham HALSWELLE

Athletics
Wyndham Halswelle. b. 30 May 1882
Mayfair, London. d. 31 Mar 1915 Neuve
Chapelle, France.

Halswelle has the unique achievement of winning an Olympic athletics gold medal in a walkover. He was 2nd at 400m and 3rd at 800m in the 1906 Games and was the favourite for the title in London in 1908, having run a world record of 31.2 for 300y and 440y in 48.4 in Glasgow a few weeks earlier. The 48.4 lasted as a British record until 1934 and a Scottish native record for 50 years. He won his heat and improved the Olympic 400m record to 48.4 in winning his semi. Halswelle faced three Americans in the final, which was not run in lanes, and was baulked by John Carpenter (USA) who ran diagonally from the inside down the finishing straight. A post-race inquiry ordered a re-run with Carpenter disqualified, this time in 'strings', but the other Americans refused to race and Halswelle simply ran over the distance on his own in 50.0 secs. The incident soured Halswelle's attitude to the sport and he retired after a farewell race at the Rangers Sports.
On Army service with the Highland Light Infantry in South Africa, Halswelle, who had shown promise at Charterhouse School, soon came to the fore, winning Scottish titles at 100y 1906-07, 220y 1906-08, 440y 1905-06, 1908, and 880y 1906, including all four events in one afternoon in 1906, and the AAA 440y in 1905-06 and 1908. Captain Halswelle by killed by a sniper's bullet at the Front in 1915.

Jill HAMMERSLEY

Table Tennis
Jill Patricia Hammersley. b. 6 Dec 1951
Carshalton, London. née Shirley. Later
Mrs Parker.

She won a record seven women's singles titles in the English Closed Championships, 1973-6, 1978-9 and 1981, and played for England on a record 413 occasions, 1967-83. In the European Championships at the women's singles she won in 1976 and was runner-up in 1978, and won the women's doubles in 1976. She was awarded the MBE.

Walter HAMMOND

Cricket
Walter Reginald Hammond. b. 19 Jun 1903
Dover, Kent. d. 1 Jul 1965 Durban, South
Africa.

The greatest England batsman of his generation, Hammond set a record for most runs in Test cricket, passing Jack Hobbs' total of 5410 in 1937 and going on to be the first to score 6000 and 7000 runs. With 336 not out in 318 minutes against New Zealand in 1933, he set the then highest Test score, and having scored 227 in the first of the two Tests, his 563.00 is the highest ever average for a Test series. His feat of leading the English first-class averages for eight successive seasons, 1933-9 and 1946, has never been matched. He was also a magnificent all-rounder, a fine medium-fast bowler, and an incomparable slip fielder with a season's record 78 catches in 1928, which included a world record ten catches in a match, for Gloucestershire v Surrey at Cheltenham when he also made a hundred in each innings. He was also the first fielder to hold 100 catches in Test cricket.
He made his Gloucestershire debut in 1920 but was prevented from playing for them regularly in his early years due to being born in Kent, and he then missed the 1926 season through serious illness. Thereafter he swept all before him and broke into the England team, where he became the dominant force. In 1928/9 against Australia he set a series record of 905 runs at 113.12 in the five Tests. He changed status from professional to amateur and became England's captain in 1938; he also captained Gloucestershire in 1939 and 1946. Twelve times he exceeded 2000 runs in a season, with three years over 3000 and a peak of 3323 at 67.81 in 1933. He scored his 100th first-class century at 31, the youngest ever to reach this milestone. His 36 career double centuries is exceeded only by Don Bradman (Aus). He settled in South Africa after his retirement.

				Walter Hammond in Test Cricket					
Year	v	Tests	Runs	Ave.	HS	Wkts	Ave.	BB	Catches
1927-8	SAf	5	321	40./12	90	15	26.60	5-36	6
1928	WI	3	111	63	-	3	34.33	1-20	9
1928-9	Aus	5	905	113.12	251	5	57.40	3-53	1
1929	SAf	4	352	58.66	138*	1	95.00	1-19	2
1930	Aus	5	306	34.00	113	5	60.40	2-24	5
1930-1	SAf	5	517	64.62	136*	9	26.66	4-63	9
1931	NZ	3	169	56.33	100*	2	34.00	1-8	5
1932	Ind	1	47	23.50	35	3	8.00	3-9	2
1932-3	Aus	5	440	55.00	112	9	32.33	3-21	6
1933	NZ	2	563	563.00	336*	0			2
1933	WI	3	74	24.66	34	0			4
1934	Aus	5	162	20.25	43	5	72.80	3-111	12
1935	WI	4	175	25.00	47	0			4
1935	SAf	5	389	64.83	87*	6	24.33	2-8	7
1936	Ind	2	389	194.50	217	1	94.00	1-19	2
1936-7	Aus	5	468	58.50	231*	12	25.08	5-57	5
1937	NZ	3	204	51.00	104	4	25.25	2-19	1
1938	Aus	4	403	67.16	240	0			8
1938-9	SAf	5	609	87.00	181	3	53.66	1-11	6
1939	WI	3	279	55.80	138	-			5
1946	Ind	3	119	39.66	69	0			2
1946-7	Aus	4	168	21.00	37	-			6
1947	NZ	1	79	79.00	79	-			1

85 Tests 1927-47: 7249 runs at 58.45, 22 100s HS 336*; 83 wickets at 37.83, BB 5-36; 110 catches.
First-class 1920-51: 50,551 runs at 56.10, 167 100s HS 336*; 732 wickets at 30.58, BB 9-23; 819 catches, 3 stumpings.

Tommy HAMPSON

Athletics
Thomas Hampson. b. 28 Oct 1907 Clapham, London. d. 4 Sep 1965 Stevenage, Hertfordshire.

Hampson only gained his athletics Blue in his final year at Oxford, and was last against Cambridge at 880y in 1929, but soon improved to top class and made his international debut later that year. In 1930 he won the first of three successive AAA titles at 880y in an English Native record time of 1:53.2, improving to 1:52.4 in winning the Empire Games title by 20 yards. He set his sights on the 1932 Olympic title at 800m, and fulfilled his dream with a perfect race, maintaining an even paced schedule, so that despite being 15m behind Phil Edwards (Can) at 400m, he came through to win in a world record time of 1:49.7. Five days later he collected a silver medal at 4 x 400m relay, running his leg in 47.6.

He was successively a schoolteacher, education officer in the RAF, and social welfare officer.

Tony HAND

Ice Hockey
Anthony Hand. b. 15 Aug 1967 Edinburgh.

Hand is undoubtedly the best ice hockey player produced in Britain and the only British born and bred player ever to be drafted by a Canadian NHL team. In 1986 he was drafted by the Edmonton Oilers but preferred to stay in his native Scotland. Playing for Murrayfield (now Edinburgh) Racers, latterly as captain, he holds the record as the highest scorer in the British Premier League with 2136 points (875 goals, 1261 assists) in 449 games to the end of the 1994/5 season.

His brother **Paul** also plays defence for the same club and both are GB internationals.

Ellery HANLEY

Rugby League
Ellery Hanley. b. 27 Mar 1961 Leeds.

Gifted and versatile and equally talented as a forward or a back, the uncompromising Hanley has been a great leader as a rugby league player. He won 35 caps (plus one appearance as a substitute) in four different positions; stand-off, centre, wing and loose forward up to his retirement from internationals in 1993, scoring 20 tries and captaining Britain in 19 of these matches. He was signed by Bradford Northern from a Leeds amateur club in 1978 but did not play a full Division I match for three years. Once established as a first-team player, he set a variety of records. His 55 tries in the 1984/5 season was the highest ever by anyone other than a winger, and after his transfer to Wigan for a record fee of £150,000 in 1985 his record breaking continued. In his first season with Wigan he scored 63 tries, again a record for a non-winger, and 30 of these came from the loose forward position, which was yet another record.

On the 1984 tour of Australia he scored 12 tries in 17 matches as a winger, and on the 1988 tour he became the first black player to captain Great Britain. The highlight of the tour was a victory in the Third Test which was Great Britain's first win over Australia for ten seasons. His outstanding achievements were acknowledged when he was awarded the MBE in 1990. After a brilliant career with Wigan, which included captaining them to three successive Challenge Cup Final wins 1989-91, he moved to Leeds in September 1991 as player-coach-captain and led them to the Challenge Cup finals in 1994 and 1995, where they lost to Wigan. He was appointed coach to the Great Britain team in 1994. He won the Man of Steel award as the rugby league personality of the year on a record three occasions, 1985, 1987 and 1989 and in his career 1978-94 scored 387 tries (plus c.40 1994/5).

Alan HANSEN

Football
Alan David Hansen. b. 13 Jun 1955 New Sauchie, Clackmannan.

Signed by Liverpool from Partick Thistle in 1977, he played a vital role in the Merseyside club's successes of the 1980s. He was a member of the teams which won the European Cup (1978, 1981, 1984), the FA Cup (1986, 1989), the Football League Cup (1981, 1983-4) and the Football League (1979-80, 1982-4, 1986, 1988, 1990) and he captained the side when they won the 'double' in 1986.

A stylish central defender, he was a natural athlete and represented Scotland at Under-18 level at golf, squash and volleyball - although, surprisingly, not at football. He won just 26 Scottish caps 1979-87 and is now an astute and highly respected summariser on television. His elder brother, **John** (b. 3 Feb 1950) played in two internationals, both as substitute, for Scotland in 1972.

Eddie HAPGOOD

Football
Edris Albert Hapgood. b. 24 Sep 1908 Bristol. d. 20 Apr 1973 Leamington Spa, Warwicks.

A left-back with a rock solid defence, Hapgood captained Arsenal and England with notable success. Signed from non-League Kettering by Arsenal in 1927 he was a stalwart of the team which won the League five times (1931, 1933-5, 1938) and the FA Cup twice (1930, 1936) in addition to being losing Cup finalists in 1932

He won 30 England caps 1933-9 and in 13 of these internationals his Arsenal team mate, George Male, played alongside him at right-back. Hapgood also played in 13 wartime internationals before retiring in 1944. He went on to managerial jobs with a variety of clubs, his final position being with Bath City but, as with his previous clubs, the relationship ended in unhappy circumstances. He then became a tennis coach and later took a job as warden of a hostel for apprentices with the Atomic Energy Authority. The hostel closed in 1970 and one of England's greatest full-backs died two years later, deeply saddened that there had been no job for him in football in his later years.

Sarah HARDCASTLE

Swimming
Sarah Lucy Hardcastle. b. 9 Apr 1969
Chelmsford, Essex.

As a 15 year-old she won silver (at 400m) and bronze (at 800m) at the 1984 Olympic Games in British records of 4:10.27 and 8:32.60. She went on improve both records when winning gold medals at the 1986 Commonwealth Games with 4:07.68 and 8:24.77, both times still standing nine years later and the latter also a European record, as well as taking silver at 4 x 200m freestyle and bronze at 400m individual medley. That year she also won the World 400m bronze. She then retired, but came back in 1993, taking a bronze in the European 4 x 200m freestyle, with 8th place at 400m and 6th at 800m. In 1994 she won a Commonwealth Games bronze at 400m and was 5th at 800m.

She had won the European Junior titles at 400m and 800m in 1982 after 2nd at 800m in 1981, was 5th in the 1982 Commonwealth 400m, and took the European senior bronze at 800m in 1983 and silver at 400m in 1985.

ASA senior champion (long-course) at 400m and 800m 1984, 1986 and 1993, 400m 1994, 400m individual medley 1983 and 1986; short-course: 400m 1985-6, 1994. Best times: UK freestyle records: 1500m 16:43.95 (1985) and 16:39.46 (1994). Short-course 800m 8:23.96 (1993).

Phylis HARDING

Swimming
Phylis May Harding. b. 15 Dec 1907
Wandsworth, London.

Her long career included a record for a British swimmer of four Olympic Games 1924-36, successively 2nd, unplaced, 4th and 7th at 100m backstroke. She was 3rd at 100y in the first Empire Games in 1930 and won the title in 1934, with a silver at medley relay, and at the Europeans was 3rd in 1927 and 1931 and 4th in 1934. Surprisingly she won only two ASA backstroke titles, 1935 and 1936. In 1932 she set a world record for 100m backstroke at 1:18.6.

Alan HARDISTY

Rugby League
Alan Hardisty. b. 12 Jul 1941 Pontefract, West Yorkshire.

As stand-off for Castleford and GB (12 internationals 1964-70) he influenced many matches with his speed off the mark and superb generalship. His 206 tries for Castleford (1958-71) still stands as a club record. Having skippered Castleford to two successive Challenge Cup victories (1969-70) he was allowed a free transfer to Leeds in recognition of his services to Castleford. Although nearing the end of his career, his experience proved invaluable to Leeds and in 1972 he took them to the Challenge Cup final and to victory in the League Championship final.

He later embarked on a coaching career and was associated with Dewsbury, Halifax and Ryedale-York but only stayed a few months at each club.

Joe HARDSTAFF

Cricket
Joseph Hardstaff. b. 3 Jul 1911
Nuncargate, Notts. d. 1 Jan 1990
Worksop, Notts.

An elegant and accomplished batsman and a magnificent outfielder, Hardstaff was an England regular on either side of World War II, but who lost many of his best years because of it. He established his place in the Notts side in 1934 with 1817 runs at 40.17, and from there exceeded 1000 runs in 13 successive seasons in England to 1952, with 2540 at 57.72 in 1937, 2396 at 64.75 in 1947 and 2251 at 72.61 to top the first-class averages in 1949. He made his Test debut in 1935 and after two centuries against New Zealand in 1937. made 169* in the Oval Test in 1938, adding 215 for the sixth wicket with Len Hutton (qv), who made the record Test score of 364. He made his highest Tests score, 205*, against India at Lord's in 1946. He also played for Auckland in New Zealand 1948-50, which, at the time, caused discussion as to whether this affected his county qualification.

23 Tests 1935-48: 1636 runs at 46.74; 4

100s HS 205*; 9 catches.

First-class 1930-55: 31,847 runs at 44.35, 83 100s HS 266; 36 wickets at 59.47, BB 4-43; 123 catches.

His father, also **Joe** (b. 9 Nov 1882 Kirkby-in-Ashfield, Notts. d. 2 Apr 1947 Nuncargate, Notts) played all five Tests for England on the 1907/8 tour to Australia, scoring 311 runs at 31.10. Although not selected again for England he scored 17,146 runs at 31.34 in his first-class career 1902-26 and he was a highly respected umpire, although he had to stand down from officiating in Tests once his son gained his place in the team. Three generations of first-class players were achieved when Joe Jnr's son Joseph (b. 28 Feb 1935) played two matches in 1961-2; he became an air vice-marshal and is now secretary of Middlesex CCC.

Sam HARDY

Football

Sam Hardy. b. 26 Aug 1883 Newbold, Chesterfield, Derbyshire. d. 24 Oct 1966 Chesterfield.

Considered by many to be the greatest of all goal keepers, Hardy was signed from Chesterfield by Liverpool in 1905 and helped them win the Second and First Division titles in successive seasons. After moving to Aston Villa in 1912 he was twice on the winning side in the FA Cup final (1913, 1920) and after the war he was signed by Nottingham Forest where, although nearing the age of 40, he helped them to the Second Division title in 1922.

Unspectacular, with a fine positional sense he played in goal for England 21 times 1907-20, winning his last cap at the age of 36. When he finally retired in 1925 he had made 549 League appearances for his four clubs. In retirement, he owned and ran a hotel in his native Chesterfield.

Dusty HARE

Rugby Union

William Henry Hare. b. 29 Nov 1952 Newark, Notts.

Hare was the scorer of a world record 7337 points in first-class matches from 1971 to 1989, comprising 1800 for Nottingham, 4427 for Leicester, 240 for England, 88 for the British Lions and 782 in other representative matches. He set new records with 44 points in the 1984 season's International Championship and for the most points in a Championship match with 19 against France in 1983. Although these records have now been surpassed, Dusty Hare remains one of the most reliable full-backs ever to represent England. Capped 25 times between 1974 and 1984, he only failed to score in his first two international matches, and on his retirement he was England's most capped full-back and at the time also leading scorer. Despite these impressive performances and his general all-round reliability, he was not a fixture in the England XV and was dropped five times during his international career. He toured New Zealand with the 1983 British Lions but failed to win a Test place.

Despite the demands made on his time as a farmer, he found time to play cricket in the summer and made 10 first-class appearances for Nottingham 1971-7. He was awarded the MBE 1989. For 15 months in 1992-3 he was Nottingham's first Director of Coaching.

Ernie HARPER

Marathon

Ernest Harper. b. 2 Aug 1902 Chesterfield, Derbyshire. d. 1979 Australia.

A three-time Olympian, Harpere was 4th at cross-country and 5th at 10,000m in 1924, 22nd at marathon in 1928 and took the marathon silver medal in 1936 in his best ever time of 2:31:23.2.

He achieved a record seven placings in the first three in the English National cross-country, which he won in 1927 and 1929 and represented England for nine successive years in the International 1923-31, winning in 1926 and 2nd in 1924. He won the AAA 10 miles in 1923, 1926-7 and 1929 and his track bests included world records at 25,000m (1:23:45.8 in 1929) and 2 hours (33,653m in 1932); also 52:04.7 for 10 miles in 1926.

Lord HARRIS

Cricket
Sir George Robert Canning Harris (4th Lord Harris). b. 3 Feb 1851 St Anne's, Trinidad. d. 24 Mar 1932 Belmont, Faversham, Kent.

A commanding figure in the world of cricket, Harris was a fearless upholder of the laws of the game; his authority helped to stamp out the throwing which was blighting the game in the 1880s. Educated at Eton and Oxford University, where he won his Blue in 1871-2 and 1874, he played for Kent from the age of 16 in 1870 to the age of 60 years 151 days in 1911, which makes him the oldest ever first-class cricketer in England. He was Kent's captain 1875-89, secretary 1875-80 and a committee member most of his life. He was hugely influential in the MCC, of which he was a Trustee 1906-16 and Hon. Treasurer from 1916 to his death in 1932; he was also President in 1895.
An attacking middle-order batsman and fast round-arm bowler, he played in four Tests for England, captaining the team on each occasion. He managed to play much cricket despite his political responsibilities, which included appointments as under-secretary for India and then for War. He was Governor of Bombay 1890-5 and was appointed GCSI, GCIE, CB.
4 Tests 1878-84: 145 runs at 29.00; HS 52; 2 catches.
First-class 1871-1911: 9990 runs at 26.85, 11 100s HS 176; 5 wickets at 25.11, BB 5-57; 190 catches.

Martin HARRIS

Swimming
Martin Clifford Harris. b. 21 May 1969 Bow, London.

At the 1994 Commonwealth Games, Harris won the 100m backstroke with bronze in the 4 x 100m medley relay. From 1990 he set 38 national backstroke records to his long-course bests of 55.00 for 100m in 1995. In 1993 he won a silver medal at 100m at the world short-course championships in a British record 53.93 and took bronze medals at 100m and medley relay at the Europeans, with 8th at 100m in the 1994 World Championships.
He won ASA long-courese backstroke titles: 50m 1991-4, 100m 1990-4, and at short-course he won all three backstroke titles, 50m (25.07), 100m (53.15) and 200m (1:56.65) in British record times in December 1994. He also holds all the world masters records for backstroke in both short- and long-course pools.

Reg HARRIS

Cycling
Reginald Hargreaves Harris. b. 31 Mar 1920 Bury, Gt. Manchester. d. 22 Jun 1992 Macclesfield, Cheshire.

Britain's greatest ever track sprint cyclist, Harris began track racing in 1936 and was a member of the British World Championships team on the outbreak of World War II. In 1947 he won the world amateur title, but at the 1948 Olympics he was hampered by a recently broken arm, having earlier made a remarkable recovery from a broken neck, and won only silvers in the individual and tandem sprint races, followed by 3rd in the World Championships. He then turned pro and became the first sprinter to win a world professional championship at his first attempt, going on to four sprint titles, 1949-51 and 1954, and to place 2nd in 1956 and 3rd in 1953. As a professional he set two world records for the unpaced kilometre from a standing start outdoors, with 1:09.8 in 1949 and 1:08.6 in 1952, which stood for over 21 years. He also set three indoor records at 1km with a best of 1:08.0 in 1957. Seventeen years after his retirement in 1957, after which he was awarded the OBE, he made an amazing return to racing in 1974, and won the British sprint championship.

Tommy HARRIS

Rugby League
Thomas Harris. b. 5 Jun 1927.

For a hooker, the transition from rugby union to rugby league is, because of the quite different technique, more difficult than for players in other positions but

Tommy Harris, a former union hooker with Newbridge, made the move to Hull with conspicuous success. With 25 caps (1954-60) he became the most capped league hooker of all time and in 1960, while helping Hull defeat Wakefield Trinity in the Challenge Cup final, he became the only hooker ever to win the Lance Todd Trophy. He toured Australia and New Zealand with the Lions in 1954 and 1958 and is one of a handful of hookers to have toured twice with Great Britain.

At home, he remained loyal to Hull throughout his career making 444 appearances 1949-62, and scoring 69 tries.

Donna HARTLEY

Athletics
Donna-Marie Louise Hartley. b. I May 1955 Southampton. née Murray. Later Mrs Knut.

Hartley was the golden girl of British athletics in the 1970s. A member of Southampton AAC, and coached by Mike Smith, she first competed at a major championships at the age of 17, reaching the semis of the Olympic Games 200m in 1972. She was 7th at 200m and won a sprint relay bronze at the 1973 European Juniors, before taking up the 400m seriously in 1974. Her greatest success came in 1978 when she won gold medals at 400m and 4 x 400m at the Commonwealth Games, and in that year she was 6th in the European 400m. At the Olympics she was a 400m quarter-finalist in 1976 and won a relay bronze medal in 1980.

She won the WAAA 200m in 1972 and 400m 1975 and the UK 400m 1977. She ran on the British team which set a world record for 4 x 200m in 1977 and set British records at 200m 22.75 (1978), 300m 36.2 (1974) and 400m 51.77 (1974), 51.28 (1975) and 51.2 (1978). Other bests: 100m 11.46 (1975), 800m 2:07.8 (1976).

In 1977 she married **Bill Hartley** (b. 27 Jun 1950), who in 1974 placed 6th at 400m hurdles and won a relay silver at the Commonwealth Games and won a 4 x 400m relay gold at the European Championships. He ran his best 400m hurdles time, 49.65, to win the 1975 AAA title, and he also won UK titles in 1978 and 1981. After that marriage was dissolved Donna married comedian Bobby Knut.

Eddie HARTY (Ireland)

Horse Racing
Edward Patrick Harty. b. 10 Jun 1937.

Harty is the only man to have contested the Olympic three-day event, placing 9th in 1960, and to have ridden the winner of the Grand National, which he did on *Highland Wedding* in 1969. His mother came from an American horse racing and polo-playing family, his father, Capt. Cyril Harty, trained the winner of the 1944 Irish Grand National and was an international show jumper, and his brothers Buster and John rode in Ireland.

He started at show jumping at the age of seven in 1944 and rode his first winner under National Hunt rules at the age of 16 in 1953. He worked for two years in the USA as a catttle rancher before his career, 1961-72, as a professional National Hunt rider. He took out a trainer's licence in 1972 and is now a bloodstock agent, trainer and farmer in Co. Kildare.

Len HARVEY

Boxing
Leonard Austin Harvey. b. 11 Jul 1907 Stoke Climsland, nr. Callington, Cornwall. d. 28 Nov 1976 Holloway, London.

One of Britain's most talented boxers between the wars, Harvey won the British and Empire titles at middleweight, light-heavyweight and heavyweight. He also challenged for the NBA version of the world middleweight crown in 1932 but was outpointed by Marcel Thil (Fra), and in 1936 he fought John Lewis (USA) for the undisputed world light-heavyweight title but was again outpointed over 15 rounds.

He started as a pro fighter before his 13th birthday and had his first eight-round fight at 14. By 18 he had grown to be a welterweight and had his first title fight, a draw against Harry Mason. He won his first

British title at middleweight in 1929, and between 1928 and 1939 Jock McAvoy and Jack Petersen were the only British boxers to gain a decision over him, although he beat both fighters on other occasions. He lost his title to McAvoy in 1933, but two months later he took the light-heavyweight crown and at the end of the year beat Petersen to add that of heavyweight. Petersen beat him to recapture the latter in 1934 but Harvey won it again in 1938 after he also regained his light-heavyweight title by beating McAvoy.

He had his last fight in June 1942 when he lost his British and Empire light-heavyweight titles to Freddie Mills (qv) and was knocked out for the only time in his career. He retired at the end of the year and relinquished his British and Empire heavyweight titles. Although lacking a significant punch, his skill and tactical awareness made him one of the most admired boxers of his generation. Some sources show that he took part in 418 professional contests, but his official career record (below) credits him with 133 fights.

Career record 1920-42: 133 contests. Won 111 (51 KO), Drew 9, Lost 13.

Gavin HASTINGS

Rugby Union
Andrew Gavin Hastings. b. 3 Jan 1962 Edinburgh.

Hastings succeeded Andy Irvine (qv) as Scotland's record points scorer in international rugby. When he retired following the 1995 World Cup he had scored 689 points in 62 matches for Scotland, including a world record 227 in World Cup matches. He added a further 28 in three games for the British Lions against Australia in 1989 and 38 in three against New Zealand in 1993.

Captain of Scottish Schools in 1980 and Cambridge Blue in 1984-6 (captain 1985-6), his club rugby has been with London Scottish and Watsonians. He made his senior debut for Scotland as full back in 1986 with his brother Scott in the centre; he scored 18 points in that match and set a record for the International Championship series with 52 points in the season. In 1987 he set a Scottish scoring record with 27 points in a match against Romania, 2 tries, 8 conversions and one penalty goal. In Scotland's four maches of the 1995 World Cup he scored 104 points, smashing his previous record with 44 points in the opening match against the Ivory Coast, and following that with 31 against Tonga to become the top scorer in World Cup history.

A charismatic figure and powerful player, he was appointed Scotland's captain for 1993 and then as captain of the Lions touring team to New Zealand. By profession he is a sports marketing executive.

Scott HASTINGS

Rugby Union
Scott Hastings. b. 4 Dec 1964 Edinburgh.

After making his international debut in 1986 both Scott and his brother **Gavin** both won their 50th cap for Scotland in the same match (v France 1994). At centre, wing or full-back, his incisive running and devastating tackling earned him a place on the British Lions tour of Australia in 1989 where he played in two of the three Tests. Both Scott and Gavin played in the second Test and this was the first time that two Scottish brothers had played together for the Lions in a Test match. He again toured with the Lions in 1993 but his early return with a fractured cheek bone kept him out of the reckoning for a Test place.

For Scotland he partnered **Sean** Raymond Patrick **Lineen** (b. 25 Dec 1961, Auckland, NZ) in the centre 28 times, a world record for an international centre three-quarter pairing. After being dropped for the opening matches of the 1995 Five Nations Championship he replaced the injured Ian Jardine in the match against Wales and won his 53rd cap in the next match to pass Jim Renwick's record as Scotland's most capped three-quarter. By the end of the 1995 World Cup he had 57 caps, scoring 9 tries. He has played for Watsonians from 1982 and also played for Northern while he was at Newcastle Poly.

Jack HATFIELD

Swimming
John Gatenby Hatfield. b. 15 Aug 1893
Middlesbrough, North Yorkshire. d. 30
Mar 1965 Middlesbrough.

The most prolific English national champion, Hatfield won 36 ASA titles in his career from 1912 to 1931: 220y 1912-13, 1922, 1925; 440y 1912-13, 1924, 1927; 500y 1912-13, 1921-3; 880y 1912-13, 1921-5; 1 mile 1912-14, 1921-24, 1929-30; long distance 1913-14, 1921, 1923-4, 1929, 1931. He set four world records: 300y 3:26.4 (1913), 400m 5:21.6 (1912), 500y 6:02.8 (1913), 500m 6:56.8 (1912).
He competed at the four Olympic Games 1912-28, placing 2nd to George Hodgson (Can) at 400m and 1500m in 1912 and 5th and 4th at these events in 1924. He also took a bronze medal at 4 x 200m in 1912 and competed at water polo in 1928.

Gina HATHORN

Skiing
Georgina Melissa Hathorn. b. 6 Jul 1949
Andover, Hampshire. Later Mrs Sopwith.

At the 1968 Olympics Hathorn was 4th in the slalom, just three-hundredths of a second slower than the bronze medal time. That is the closest that any British skier has come to an Olympic skiing medal. She equalled the record for most British ladies' titles with four, 1966, 1968-70.
She had been British junior champion at the age of 12 and also competed in the Winter Olympics in 1964 and 1972 and the nearest she came to her success of 1968 was 11th place in the 1972 downhill. She was British champion in 1966 and 1968-70.
She married Thomas Sopwith, son of aviation pioneer and yachtsman Tommy Sopwith (qv).

Gary HAVELOCK

Speedway
Robert Gary Havelock. b. 4 Nov 1966
Eaglescliffe, Co. Durham.

He won the British final of the World Championship in 1991 and in 1992, in which year he went on to become world champion. He had been British Under-21 champion and also the National League grand slam champion in 1986, then moving from Middlesbrough to Bradford.

Arthur HAVERS

Golf
Arthur Gladstone Havers. b. 10 Sep 1898
Norwich. d. 27 Nov 1980 Haslemere,
Surrey.

The Open champion of 1923 by one shot from Walter Hagen (USA), he had shown great ability while a youth, with a Royal Norwich Golf Club record of 68 at the age of 15 and qualifying for the 1914 Open.
After war service in the RAF, he tied for 7th in the 1920 Open and was 4th in 1921. On a visit to America in 1924 he beat the great Bobby Jones (USA) 2 & 1 over 36 holes and Gene Sarazen (USA) 5 & 4 over 72 holes. He played in the Ryder Cups of 1927, 1931 and 1933, with a record of three wins and three losses in his six matches; his two wins in 1933 helped Britain to victory.
A long hitter, he remained a force, particularly in match play for many years. He was professional at West Lancashire GC, then Sandy Lodge and Moor Park, Hertfordshire.

(Lord) Martin HAWKE

Cricket
(Lord) Martin Bladen Hawke. b. 16 Aug
1860 Willingham Rectory, Gainsborough,
Lincolnshire. d. 10 Oct 1938 Edinburgh.

Taking over the Yorkshire captaincy in 1883, while still at Cambridge University, where he won his Blue in 1882, 1883 and 1885, he led the county until 1910. He was Yorkshire's president from 1898 to his death and not only controlled their affairs but with his strict discipline and dedication made them the powerhouse of English cricket. He was also a power at the MCC, serving as president 1914-19 and treasurer 1932-8. Although a forceful middle-order batsman, he was not a great cricketer, but played in five Tests for England, four of them as captain, on the tours that he took to South Africa in 1895/6 and 1898/9.

5 Tests 1895-9: 55 runs at 7.85; HS 30; 3 catches.
First-class 1882-1911: 16,749 runs at 20.15, 13 100s HS 166; 209 catches.

Mike HAWTHORN

Motor Racing
John Michael Hawthorn. b. 10 Apr 1929 Mexborough, South Yorkshire. d. 27 Jan 1959 near Guildford, Surrey.

In 1958 Hawthorn became the first British world motor-racing champion. In his Grand Prix career, 1952-8, he won three of his 45 races, with 127.64 points.
Trained as an engineer, Mike started racing with his father Leslie, who owned a garage, with a Riley Imp in 1951. The following year he won two Irish trophy races in a Riley Sprite, moved up to Formula Two racing, and was 4th at Spa in his first Grand Prix drive in a Cooper-Bristol. He was 4th in the World Championship both that year and in 1953 for Ferrari, when he became the first British driver to win the French Grand Prix for 30 years. He progressed to 3rd place in 1954, but that year his father was killed in a car accident.
Mike met with much press criticism in the mid 1950s, including over his involvement in the 1955 Le Mans tragedy, which deeply affected him. He won that Le Mans race (with Ivor Bueb), but both 1955 and 1956 were unsuccessful years in the World Championship, in which he drove a variety of cars, He improved in 1957 to 4th for Ferrari, and then beat Stirling Moss (qv) by one point for the title in 1958. He then announced his retirement to concentrate on his garage business, but that was short lived, as he was killed in a road accident when his Jaguar went out of control on the Hog's Back in Surrey in 1959.

Ann HAYDON – see JONES

Seamus HAYES (Ireland)

Equestrianism. Show Jumping
Seamus Brendan Hayes. b. 5 Nov 1924. d. 30 Oct 1989.

Having come to England in 1946, he was British champion at show jumping each year 1948-50. He then returned to Dublin as a civilian instructor to the Irish army team, for which his father Major General Liam Hayes had bought many top show jumpers in the 1930s. He won the first Hickstead Jumping Derby in 1961 on *Goodbye III*, winning again in 1964.

Johnny HAYNES

Football
John Norman Haynes. b. 17 Oct 1934 Kentish Town, London. *18/10/05*

An inside-forward with an exceptionally long and accurate pass, he was one of the great stars of the 1950s, becoming the first £100 a week player in Britain. In his early days he was noted for his goalscoring abilities but later played a deeper game. He was the first player to represent England at all five international levels - Schoolboy, Youth, Under-23, 'B' and senior.
Joining the Fulham groundstaff as a schoolboy in 1950, he turned professional two years later and stayed with the club until 1970 when he went to South Africa on a free transfer. He played more than 700 games for Fulham and would almost certainly have won domestic honours had he chosen to play for a more fashionable club. He missed a whole season after being seriously injured in a car crash in August 1962. This ended his international career in which he was capped 56 times between 1954 and 1962, captain 22 times, scoring 18 goals.

Tom HAYWARD

Cricket
Thomas Walter Hayward. b. 29 Mar 1871 Cambridge. d. 19 Jul 1939 Cambridge.

Hayward was a prolific scorer in county cricket and the second man, after W.G. Grace (qv), to score 100 hundreds. From 1895 to 1914 he scored over 1000 runs every year, with ten seasons over 2000 and peaks of 3170 at 54.65 in 1904 and 3518 at 66.37 in 1906. The latter figure has been exceeded only by Denis Compton and Bill Edrich (qqv) in 1947. Initially batting at No. 3, he opened from 1900, forming formidable partnerships with Bobby Abel (qv) and then Jack Hobbs (qv), with whom he put on 40 century stands for Surrey. In his early days he also bowled quickish off-breaks and in 1897 achieved the double with 114 wickets and 1368 runs. He was an England regular for more than a decade, scoring centuries against Australia in the 4th and 5th Tests in 1899.

35 Tests 1896-1909: 1999 runs at 34.46, 3 100s HS 137; 14 wickets at 36.71, BB 4-22; 19 catches.

First-class 1893-1914: 43,551 runs at 41.79, 104 100s HS 315*; 481 wickets at 22.95, BB 8-89; 492 catches.

His father and grandfather, both Daniel, played for Cambridgeshire and Surrey and his uncle **Thomas** (1835-76) was renowned as one of the top batsmen of the 1860s.

Mike HAZELWOOD

Water Skiing
Michael Hazelwood. b. 14 Apr 1958 Heckington, Lincolnshire.

Hazelwood was the greatest water skier ever produced in the United Kingdom. He began skiing at age eight and made the British team when he was only 15. He reached the top in 1977 when he was the first European to win the Moomba Masters and the first Briton to become World over-all champion. He won further World titles at his forté, jumping, in 1979 and 1981 and achieved the first 60m jump in 1981, improving the world record to 61.9m *203 ft* in 1986.

Four times Hazelwood was the US Masters overall champion, 1978-81, and he won a record nine European overall titles, 1976-83 and 1986, and seven British titles 1974, 1976-9, 1981 and 1983. He was awarded the MBE.

Donald HEALEY

Rallying
Donald Mitchell Healey. b. 3 Jul 1898 Perranporth, Cornwall. d. 15 Jan 1988 Plymouth.

On leaving school he was apprenticed to Sopwith Aviation and was a fighter pilot in World War I before a serious crash led to his transfer to the Aircraft Inspection Authority. A talented rally driver from the 1920s, he had his first big win with the Monte Carlo in a 4.5 litre Invicta in 1931. He went on to 2nd place in that race in 1932, 3rd in 1934 and 8th in 1936. By then he was technical director of Triumph (1934-9) and his fellow directors encouraged him to leave the hazardous driving behind.

With Riley he helped to conceive the family of sports cars Riley Imp to Sprite, and from 1946 he headed the production of cars bearing his name. Austin-Healey cars went on to world renown. From 1973 he was chairman of Jensen Motors. He served in the RAF in both World Wars and was awarded the CBE in 1973.

Jack (J.T.) HEARNE

Cricket
John Thomas Hearne. b. 3 May 1867 Chalfont St Giles, Bucks. d. 17 Apr 1944 Chalfont St Giles.

For 35 years J.T.Hearne gave exceptional service to Middlesex as a lively medium-paced bowler and a useful batsman. He took over 100 wickets in a season 15 times, and three years over 200: 212 at 16.47 in 1893, 257 at 14.28 in 1896 and 222 at 14.05 in 1898, and is one of only four bowlers to have taken over 3000 wickets in his first-class career. In 1899 he took a Test hat-trick for England against Australia at Leeds although, surprisingly, he played in only one more Test after this. He became a notable coach and, most unusually at the time for a professional, he was elected to the Middlesex committee..

12 Tests 1892-9: 126 runs at 9.00, HS 40; 49 wickets at 22.08, BB 6-41; 4 catches.

First-class 1888-1923: 7205 runs at 11.98, HS 71; 3061 wickets at 17.75, BB 9-32; 426 catches.

Jack (J.W.) HEARNE

Cricket
John William Hearne. b. 11 Feb 1891 Hillingdon, London. d. 14 Sep 1965 West Drayton, London.

'Young Jack', a distant cousin of

J.T.Hearne (qv), compiled a most impressive all-round record in first-class cricket for Middlesex, although his Test performances were generally more modest. Ill health, accidents and the fact that World War I came at the peak of his career, held him back. In his second Test, against Australia in 1911/12, he became, at 20 years 324 days, England's youngest Test centurion until Denis Compton (qv) in 1938.

He was an elegant middle-order batsman, and a fast scorer in the early part of his career, and a skilful leg break bowler, most effective with his googlies in the 1911-14 period. He scored 11 double centuries for Middlesex and exceeded 1000 runs in a season 19 times, with four years over 2000, and did the double five times. Hs best years were either side of the war, 2116 runs at 60.45 and 123 wickets at 22.69 in 1914, and 2148 at 55.07 and 142 at 17.83 in 1920. He retired to run a sports shop in Ealing and to coach. His brothers Herbert and Walter played first-class cricket for Kent.

24 Tests 1911-26: 806 runs at 26.00; 1 100 HS 114; 30 wickets at 48.73, BB 5-49; 13 catches.

First-class 1909-36: 37,252 runs at 40.98, 96 100s HS 285*; 1839 wickets at 24.42, BB 9-61; 348 catches.

Basil HEATLEY

Marathon
Benjamin Basil Heatley. b. 25 Dec 1933 Kenilworth, Warwickshire.

Heatley won the AAA 10 miles in 1960 in a British record 48:18.4 and in 1961 in a world record 47:47.0. Earlier in 1961 he had won both National and International cross-country championships. He also won the National in 1960 and 1963 and in the International from 1957 to 1960 he placed successively 2nd, 9th, 4th, 4th. He had been Midland marathon champion in 1956 and 1957, and returned to this event in 1963 with 2nd at the AAS and a win in the Kosice Marathon. In 1964 he improved his track bests to 13:22.8 for 3 miles and 27:57.0 for 6 miles, but did even better at the marathon, setting a world best time of 2:13:55 to win the Poly marathon in June and going on to take the Olympic silver medal in Tokyo, two places ahead of his Coventry Godiva team-mate Brian Kilby (qv). He then retired and in more recent years has been a British team manager.

Other best times: 1 mile 4:09.6 (1962), 3000m 8:13.2 (1961), 2 miles 8:46.0 (1963), 5000m 13:57.2 (1963), 10,000m 28:55.8 (1963)

Peter HEATLY

Diving
(Sir) Peter Heatly. b. 9 Jun 1924 Edinburgh.

Having been Scottish swimming champion at 440y and 880y freestyle in 1946, Heatly turned to diving with immediate success. At the Olympic Games, after 5th at highboard in 1948, he competed again in 1952, but was controversially omitted from the team in 1956. He was Commonwealth champion at highboard in 1950 and 1958, with a bronze in 1954, while at springboard he won in 1954 and took the silver in 1950. He also won the European bronze in 1954, after only making the final in the 12th and last qualifying spot. He won 10 ASA titles: highboard 1949-51 and 1957, 3m springboard 1948-50, 1m springboard 1949-51; and 27 Scottish diving titles: highboard 1947, 1949-51 and 1953-8, 3m springboard 1946-51 and 1953-7, 1m springboard 1951-6.

A distinguished engineer, he has also devoted much time to sports administration. He was vice-chairman of the Organising Committee of the 1970 Commonwealth Games and chairman of the Commonwealth Games Federation 1982-90, with the second Games at Edinburgh in 1986 during his term of office. He was chairman of the Scottish Sports Council 1975-87. In 1971 he was awarded the CBE for his services to sport and knighted in 1990.

Gerry HELME

Rugby League
Gerry Helme.

Helme was the first man to win the Lance Todd Trophy twice, paying for the winners, Warrington, in 1950 and 1954. He played 12 internationals for Britain 1948-54 and played in 442 games for Warrington 1945-57.

David HEMERY

Athletics
David Peter Hemery. b. 18 Jul 1944
Cirencester, Gloucestershire.

Hemery was Olympic champion at 400m hurdles in 1968, winning by a huge margin to smash the world record with 48.12; the pervious record had been 48.94. That year he was voted BBC Sports Personality of the Year. Amazingly he only contested the event in four seasons. He first ran it in 1965 when he had a best of 52.8 for 440y hurdles, improving to 51.8 in 1966. After his epic 1968 season, in which he ran five British records at 440y hurdles and five more at 400m hurdles, he did not run the event again until 1972. Then he won the bronze medal at the Olympics, as well as a silver in the 4 x 400m relay.

He had started as a high hurdler and set six British records at 110m/120y hurdles with a best of 13.6 in 1969 (and 13.72 on automatic timing in 1970), winning the Commonwealth title in 1966 and 1970, the World Student Games in 1970 and taking the European silver in 1969. He won the NCAA 400mh in 1968 and the AAA 110mh 1966 and 400mh 1968 and 1972. He also competed for Britain at the decathlon (best of 6893 points).

His family had moved to Boston, USA when he was 12, returning six years later. Having started a banking career he went back to the USA in 1964, to Boston University, where he was coached by Billy Smith. With Smith's aid and that of his English coach Fred Housden he became a supreme stylist. His great strength and disciplined preparation were shown further by his success in the all-sport Superstars competitions (British champion 1973 and 1976) after his retirement from athletics in 1972. He was awarded the MBE in 1969. Since his retirement he has worked in Britain and the USA as a coach and performance consultant.

Noel HENDERSON

Rugby Union
Noel Joseph Henderson. b. 10 Aug 1928
Drumahoe, Co. Derry.

Virtually an automatic selection for the Irish side for more than a decade, he won 40 caps 1949-59, and was never out of favour with the selectors; only injury prevented him from adding to his impressive tally of international appearances. A strong attacking runner and a fearless tackler, he won 35 caps as a centre before moving to full-back for his last five internationals. He also made one Test appearance for the British Lions when he replaced the injured Ken Jones on the wing in the third Test against New Zealand in 1950. He captained Ireland 10 times and also represented his country at badminton.

Patsy HENDREN

Cricket
Elias Henry Hendren. b. 5 Feb 1889
Turnham Green, London. d. 4 Oct 1962
Tooting Bec, London.

The third most prolific batsman ever in first-class cricket, Hendren played for Middlesex for 30 years and most successfully for England, especially from the mid-1920s, although by then well into his 30s. He was also a brilliant fielder, excelling in the deep. A short, strong man, he became a hero in the West Indies in 1930 with his devastating batting when he scored 693 runs at 115.50 in the Tests and 1765 at 135.76 in first-class games, and for his humorous banter with the crowds.

He scored over 2000 runs in 15 seasons: 1920-9, 1931-4 and 1936, including over 3000 three times: 3010 at 77.17 in 1923, 3311 at 70.44 in 1928 and 3186 at 56.89 in 1933. He was also a good wing forward at soccer, playing for Brentford, Queens Park Rangers, Manchester City and Coventry, and in a 1919 'Victory' international against Wales. After retirement from playing he coached at Harrow School and then for Sussex before four years, and was then Middlesex scorer 1952-60.

51 Tests 1920-35: 3525 runs at 47.63, 7 100s HS 205*; 1 wicket; 33 catches.

First-class 1907-38: 57,611 runs at 50.80, 170 100s (22 over 200) HS 301*; 47 wickets at 54.76, BB 5-43; 754 catches.

Stephen HENDRY

Snooker
Stephen Gordon Hendry. b. 13 Jan 1969 Edinburgh.

Hendry succeeded Steve Davis (qv) as the world's top snooker player and has become clearly the greatest. His career earnings of £4,156,975 after his fourth successive world title in 1995 have now passed Davis and he has won 52 professional titles (22 in rankings tournaments). In 1990 he became World champion, at 21 years 106 days the youngest ever, then he beat Jimmy White in the world final each year 1992-4. In 1992 he trailed 8-14, but astonishingly came through to win 18-14 and, after a clear win in 1993, won a third title after an epic 18-17 match in 1994. In 1995, when he beat Nigel Bond in the final, he scored a record 12 century breaks and had a maximum 147 against White in his semi-final.
His other major tournament wins include: UK Open 1989-90, Benson & Hedges Masters 1989-93, European Open 1993-4 and British Open 1988, 1991 and 1994. He reached new standards of excellence in winning the last, as in his 10-5 win in the final over Ken Doherty he scored a record seven century breaks in one day; his 12 in the tournament (since matched, see above) beat his record of ten in the Sky Sports International at Plymouth in 1993. This also took his total of century breaks in professional competition to 264, already 30 ahead of Steve Davis, the next best. In 1990-1 his consistency brought him 36 successive unbeaten matches in ranking tournaments, and in the semi-final of the UK Open in 1993 against John Parrott (qv) he scored 447 points in succession without his opponent potting a ball.
Hendry started playing at the age of 12, won the British Under-16 title in 1983 and a year later, at 15, became the youngest ever Scottish amateur champion. He retained that title in 1985 and then turned professional. In 1986 he won his first

Scottish professional title and in 1987 became the youngest ever winner of a ranking tournament, beating Dennis Taylor (qv) 10-7 to win the Rothmans Grand Prix. He was awarded the MBE in 1993.

Dick HERN

Horse Racing
(Major) William Richard Hern. b. 20 Jan 1921 Holford, Somerset.

Hern was leading trainer in Britain four times, 1962, 1972, 1980 and 1983. He was formerly an amateur rider at point-to-points 1938-56, and was assistant trainer to Major Michael Pope 1952-7, before taking over as private trainer to Lionel Holliday at Newmarket. In 1962 he took over Bob Colling's stables at West Ilsley, but had to leave there in the late 1980s and now trains near Lambourn.
His 16 Classics successes 1962-95 have included six winners of the St Leger, from his first with *Hethersett* in 1962, three each of the Oaks and the Derby, two each of the 1000 and 2000 Guineas. His greatest horse was *Brigadier Gerard*. He was awarded the CVO in 1980.

Maurice HERRIOTT

Athletics
Maurice Herriott. b. 8 Oct 1939 Great Wyrley, Staffordshire.

Herriott won a record eight AAA titles at 3000m steeplechase, 1959, 1961-7, and set six British records, from 8:40.4 in 1963 to 8:32.4 in Tokyo 1964, when he won the Olympic silver medal behind Gaston Roelants (Bel).
A member of Sparkhill Harriers, he first emerged by winning the AAA junior 1 mile steeplechase title in 1957, winning again in 1958 when the distance changed to 1500m. That year he ran two unofficial world junior records for 3000m steeplechase. A motor-cycle fitter, he represented Britain in 32 internationals from 1959 to 1968, when he ran at his second Olympics, and was also 8th at the 1966 Europeans. At the Commonwealth Games he was 2nd in 1962 and 4th in 1966 at the steeplechase for England. The British Athletics Writers

elected him as British male athlete of the year in 1963 and 1965.

Best flat times: 1 mile 4:07.4 (1966), 3000m 8:08.0 (1966), 2 miles 8:47.8 (1964), 5000m 14:15.6 (1963).

David HEWITT

Rugby Union
David Hewitt. b. 9 Sep 1939 Belfast.

A brilliant but sometimes inconsistent three-quarter, Hewitt never quite fulfilled his potential to be a truly great player. Born into a rugby playing family, his father, **Thomas** (b. 12 Mar 1905, d. Jul 1991) and two cousins played for Ireland. He won 18 caps for Ireland (1958-65) and went on two tours with the British Lions. On his first tour in 1959, he played in two Tests against Australia and three against New Zealand and in South Africa in 1962 he played only in the final Test after injuries had restricted his appearances earlier in the tour.

Although his game was sometimes flawed by his reluctance to pass the ball, or to pass erratically when he did, these deficiencies were fully compensated for by his superb goal-kicking. On his debut for the Lions against Australia in 1959, he kicked two penalties, added two conversions in the second Test and then kicked a penalty in the first Test against New Zealand. He also scored a try in the third Test against the All Blacks.

He qualified as a solicitor from Queen's University, Belfast and later played for Instonians.

Brian HEWSON

Athletics
Brian Stanford Hewson. b. 4 Apr 1933 Croydon, London.

Having been 2nd to Herb Elliott (Aus) at 880y and a poor 8th in the mile at the 1958 Commonwealth Games, it was a surprise when the selectors chose him for the 1500m rather than the 800m at the following European Championship. Their decision was justified, however, as Hewson set a British record of 3:41.1 in his heat and produced a brilliant finishing burst to take the title in 3:41.9. A consistent international runner, scoring 83 points out of a possible 106 in dual meetings, he had also taken the Commonwealth 880y silver medal in 1954 and was 5th in the 1956 Olympic 1500m. He set a European 880y record of 1:47.8 in 1958, British records for 1000m at 2:19.9 (1956) and 2:19.2 (1958), and ran on the England team that set a world record for 4 x 1mile in 1958.

Other best times: 800m 1:47.0 (1958), 1 mile 3:58.9 (1958). He was AAA champion at 880y in 1954 and 1958-9 and at 1 mile in 1955 and 1957 and had won the junior 880y in 1951. A persistent leg injury ended his career in 1960.

Rachel HEYHOE FLINT

Cricket
Rachel Heyhoe. b. 11 Jun 1939 Bilston, West Midlands. Mrs Flint.

With 1594 runs at 45.54 in 22 matches from 1960 to 1979 (1814 at 51.82 in 25 matches including 3 unofficial matches v Jamaica 1971), Hayhoe Flint is the leading run-scorer in women's Test cricket, and she was unbeaten as England captain 1966-77. She hit four Test centuries, with a highest score of 179 against Australia in 1976. In 1963 against Australia she hit the first six in a women's Test. She also took 3 wickets and held 13 catches in Tests. In one-day internationals she scored 643 runs at an average of 58.45, with a top score of 114, and captained England to victory in the first women's World Cup in 1973.

Her strong, charming personality and media awareness brought the women's game to public attention. She also played for England four times as a goalkeeper at hockey in 1964 and county squash for Staffordshire.

On her marriage to Derrick Flint in 1971 she added his name to hers. She was awarded the MBE in 1973. Formerly a PE teacher she became a journalist, sports editor of the *Wolverhampton Chronicle* 1973, and public relations executive.

Harry HIBBS

Football
Henry Edward Hibbs. b. 27 May 1906
Wilnecote, Staffs. d. 23 Apr 1984 Hatfield,
Herts.

Since Sam Hardy (qv) won his last cap in 1920, England tried no less that 21 different goalkeepers in 46 internationals before Harry Hibbs won his first cap in 1929. With his unspectacular but thoroughly reliable style he was very much in the same mould as Hardy and he went on to win 25 caps to 1936, then a record for an England goalkeeper. He played for Birmingham throughout his career but despite his talents they met with little success; during Hibbs' years with the club their best performance was as losing FA Cup finalists in 1931.

Hibbs retired in 1940 and after some years as manager of Walsall (1944-51) he drifted into non-League football before disappearing from the game.

Graeme HICK

Cricket
Graeme Ashley Hick. b. 23 May 1966
Harare, Zimbabwe

A tall (1.91m *6 ft 3 in*), natural games player Hick has been the most prolific century scorer in first-class cricket over the past decade, with the power to destroy bowling attacks. His Test career, long delayed while he took seven years to qualify to play for England, took a while to develop, but by 1993, when he topped both batting and bowling averages (with his under-utilised off-breaks) in the Tests in India, he had largely overcome his growing uncertainties and his success had begun to match his county cricket record. He passed 2000 runs in Test cricket in the 2nd Test against the West Indies in 1995. He is also an excellent fielder, excelling either with a very safe pair of hands in the slips or as an outfield with a powerful throw.

Hick first visited England at the age of 17 with a junior Zimbabwe hockey team and, with his home country, for whom he made his first-class debut in 1983, some years

away from Test status, came to England to play in 1984 on a scholarship originally to work on the Lord's ground staff, but soon joining Worcestershire. In his first full season in 1985 he scored 1265 runs at 52.70 in first-class matches, improving to 2004 at 64.64 in 1986, at 20 the youngest player ever to score over 2000 runs in a season, and he has averaged over 50 each year since then apart from his poor year in 1991, when he made his Test debut most uncertainly against the West Indies.

He had been the youngest member of Zimbabwe's World Cup squad in 1983 and withdrew from their ICC Trophy squad in 1986 in order not to jeopardise his England qualifying. In 1988 he made the second highest ever score in Britain, 405* against Somerset, and his first-class record was 2713 runs at 77.51 and in 1990 2347 runs at 90.26. He has also played for Northern Districts in New Zealand 1987-9 and for Queensland, Australia in 1990/1.

32 Tests 1991-5: 1933 runs at 35.79; 2 100s HS 178; 19 wickets at 51.21, BB 4-126; 50 catches.

47 One-day Ints 1991-5: 1571 runs at 39.27, 1 100 HS 105*; 13 wickets at 37.07, BB 3-41; 25 catches.

First-class 1983-95: 24,001 runs at 57.41, 80 100s HS 405*; 178 wickets at 42.07, BB 5-37; 347 catches.

Humphrey HICKS

Croquet
Humphrey Osmond Hicks. b. 20 May 1904
Esher, Surrey. d. 9 Jun 1986 Colyton,
Devon.

Hicks was rhe dominant figure in world croquet until the arrival of John Solomon (qv). Although his early career was curtailed by illness, he reached the final of the 1930 Open Championship and won the title in 1932 and 1939. After the war he was the Open champion five more times between 1947 and 1952, failing to win the title only in 1951. He also won the men's championship nine times between 1930 and 1966, the President's Cup five times (1947-8, 1951, 1954 and 1961), the men's Open doubles seven times and the mixed doubles four times. His total of 27

Championship victories remained a record until surpassed by Solomon.

He played for the Budleigh Salterton club and is rated as one of the greatest players of all time. Before the handicap limit was fixed at minus 5 he held the lowest ever handicap of minus 5.5.

Edward HIDE

Horse Racing
Edward William George Hide. b. 12 Apr 1937 Ludlow, Shropshire.

Hide rode 2591 winners in his riding career in Britain, 1950-85, with his first winner in 1951 and over 100 for the first time in 1957, when he had 131. He was also over 100 in 1958-9, 1972-4, 1976-7 and 1980-1, with a peak of 137 in 1974. His father, William (1907-89), was a trainer, and Edward began his career with him, becoming champion apprentice in 1954 (53 winners) and 1956 (75). Mostly based in the north, although with a spell at Newmarket, he had six Classics winners, from St Legers on *Cantelo* in 1959 to *Julio Mariner* in 1978, and he won the 1973 Derby on *Morston*. He now runs a small stud farm near York.

His brother **Tony** (b. 13 May 1939) was a jockey from 1954 to 1968 and later a trainer in Italy and England, and Tony's son **Philip** Hide had his first major success as a National Hunt jockey when he rode *Bradbury Star* to win the 1994 Mackeson Gold Cup.

Molly HIDE

Cricket
Mary Edith Hide. b. 24 Oct 1913 Shanghai, China.

Hide's career was interrupted by World War II but she played in 15 Tests for England between 1934 and 1954 and was captain 1937-54. She was a fluent bat, scoring 872 runs in Tests at an average of 36.33 including two 100s, 141* for England v The Rest in 1952, and 63 and 124* in the third Test against Australia at Sydney in 1948. As a spin bowler she took 36 wickets at 15.25, with Test best bowling performances being 5-5 v New

Zealand in 1935 and 5-20 v Australia 1937.

Her second-wicket partnership of 235 (made in 142 minutes) v New Zealand at Christchurch in 1934 remains a Test record; Hide scored 110 and Betty Snowball (qv) 189. She played county cricket for Surrey 1936-54 and, having obtained a degree in agriculture from Reading University, ran the family farm in Haslemere, Surrey.

Alex HIGGINS

Snooker
Alexander Higgins. b. 18 Mar 1949 Belfast.

The fiery, controversial Higgins took the snooker world by storm in 1972 when he won at his first attempt at the World Professional Championships, at 23 then the youngest ever winner of the title. He was the biggest attraction in snooker, but did not win the title again until 1982 in an emotional final against Ray Reardon (qv). His other major tournament wins include: British Gold Cup 1980, UK Open 1983, Benson & Hedges Masters 1978 and 1981. After winning the Irish title in 1983 he went six years without a tournament win until regaining the Irish title in 1989, although he had helped Ireland to win the World Cup in 1985-7. Also in 1989 he won the B & H Irish Masters.

His often churlish behaviour brought him increasingly into trouble and he suffered bans from the game. At his peak, though, he was a brilliant, fast player and a great entertainer.

Mick HIGGINS (Ireland)

Gaelic Football
Michael Higgins. b. 1922 New York, USA.

He played senior football with Cavan 1942-53 and won his first all-Ireland football medal in Cavan's historic win over Kerry in the 1947 final, which was played at the Polo Grounds in New York. He captained Cavan to their last all-Ireland victory in 1952, but continued at club level until 1958. He won two Railway Cup medals with Ulster in the Interprovincial Championship of 1947 and 1950 and was elected to the Hall of Fame in 1989.

Billy HIGGS

Horse Racing
William Arnold Higgs. b. 8 Feb 1880
London. d. 12 Dec 1958 Hatton,
Warwickshire.

Higgs was champion jockey by a big
margin in both 1906 (149 winners) and
1907 (146), when he rode his one Classics
winner in the 1000 Guineas. He also
exceeded the century in 3rd place each
year with 107 in 1905, 124 in 1908 and
101 in 1909. In his short riding career
'Farmer' Higgs rode 1002 winners, but
was less successful as a trainer 1923-40.

Albert HILL

Athletics
Albert George Hill. b. 24 Mar 1889
Southwark, London. d. 8 Jan 1969 Canada.

In 1920 Hill won both 800m (in a British
record 1:53.4) and 1500m at the Olympic
Games as well as taking a silver medal for
the 3000m team race. This triumph came
ten years after he had won his first AAA
title - at 4 miles in 1909. A railwayman,
little was heard of him until, after chang-
ing clubs from Gainsford to Polytechnic
Harriers, he was 2nd in the AAA 880y in
1914. After serving as a wireless operator
in France he won both 880y and 1 mile at
the first postwar AAA Championships in
1919, and then equalled the British record
of 4:16.8 for 1 mile. He improved that
mile record to 4:13.8 (1.2 sec. outside the
world record) in winning the 1921 AAA
title. He then became a coach, his most
notable pupil being Sydney Wooderson
(qv), and emigrated to Canada in 1947.

Damon HILL

Motor Racing
Damon Graham Devereux Hill. b. 17 Sep
1960 Hampstead, London.

The son of Graham Hill (qv), Damon took
a while to break into Formula One, but
when he succeeded Nigel Mansell (qv) on
the Williams team he quickly established
himself as one of the top drivers, winning
for the first time at Budapest on 15 Aug
1993, and then also winning the next two

Grand Prix races. In 1994 he had an epic
struggle for the championship with
Michael Schumacher (Ger). Hill had six
Grand Prix victories and had narrowed the
lead of his German rival to just one point
going into the final race, the Australian
Grand Prix. There Hill was forced to retire
when Schumacher crashed and then veered
back into Hill's car, which was in close
pursuit.He was voted BBC Sports
Personality of the Year 1994. In just over
three seasons, by 2 July 1995, Hill has
scored 195 points from 41 races, with 11
wins.

Hill had started racing motorbikes, moving
into cars with Formula Ford in 1983,
achieving his first important successes in
F3 in 1987-8. From 1989 to 1991 he raced
in F3000, before being taking on by
Williams as a test driver. He had a try at
Formula One in 1992 with Brabham, but
only qualified twice in eight tries.

Graham HILL

Motor Racing
Norman Graham Hill. b. 15 Feb 1929
Hampstead, London. d. 29 Nov 1975 in a
plane crash at Arkley, North London.

A hugely popular driver, Hill was world
motor racing champion in 1962 and 1968,
and runner-up 1963-5. He was the only
driver to have also won the Indianapolis
500 (1966) and Le Mans 24-hour race
(1972).

He started driving late, buying his first car
at the age of 24, and began work for Lotus
as a racing mechanic in 1954. He made his
Grand Prix debut for them in 1958 and by
his retirement in 1975 had driven in a
record 176 championship races of which
he won 14, totalling 289 points. He drove
for Lotus 1958-9 and 1966-70, BRM
1960-6 with his first win in the 1962 Dutch
GP, Brabham 1971-2, Shadow and Lola
1973-5. He won that tough race, the
Monaco Grand Prix, five times in seven
years 1963-9. His son Damon Hill (qv) has
followed as a top driver.

In 1953 he had stroked London Rowing
Club's eight to victory in the Grand
Challenge Cup at Henley.

Mick HILL

Athletics, Javelin
Michael Christopher Hill. b. 22 Oct 1964
Leeds.

Hill has won three Commonwealth silver medals for the javelin. The first in 1986 came when he was 21 years old. From there he made rapid improvement to top international standards and in 1987 was ranked 6th in the world as he achieved consistency over 80 metres, and set three UK all-comers records before his Commonwealth record 85.24 in Stockholm. He ended the year troubled by knee and shoulder injuries, but returned to form in 1989 after an operation to remove a bone growth in his knee and he had a further operation on his left knee in March 1990.

He has remained in world class, with a best throw of 86.94 in 1993, but in British terms he has been overshadowed by Steve Backley (qv) to whom he was runner-up at the Commonwealth Games of 1990 and 1994.

At the World Championships he was 7th in 1987, 5th in 1991 and 3rd in 1993, and at the Europeans 8th in 1986, 4th in 1990 and 6th in 1994. His best Olympic placing is 11th in 1992. He was UK champion in 1985-7, and 1992-3, and AAA in 1987, 1990-1 and 1994. A sports science graduate from Carnegie College, he competes for Leeds City and is coached by John Trower.

Ron HILL

Marathon
(Dr) Ronald Hill. b. 21 Sep 1938
Accrington, Lancashire.

The enthusiasm and dedication for running shown by Ron Hill is clearly demonstrated by his amazing record of having trained every day for over 30 years from 1964, covering well over 200,000 km. To May 1994 he has finished 114 marathons, all under 2:52, in 55 countries. Having made his British international debut in 1962, when he did not finish the European marathon, his first major marathon win was the Poly in 1964, and he achieved peak success at the marathon with wins at

the 1969 Europeans and 1970 Commonwealth Games, adding European 3rd in 1971 and at the Olympics 18th in 1964 and 6th in 1972. In both 1964 and 1968 he was English National cross-country champion and 2nd in the International race. On the track he was 5th in the 1966 Commonwealth 6 miles and a brave 7th in the 1968 Olympic 10,000m at high altitude in Mexico City. He set four world records: twice at 10 miles in 1968: 47:02.2 and 46:44.0, and at 15 miles (1:12:48.2) and 25,000m (1:25:22.6) in 1965. He also set British records at 6 miles, 27:49.90 to win the 1963 AAA title, and with 58:39.0 for 20,000m and 20,472m in 1 hour in 1968. Further AAA titles came at 10 miles 1965-9 and marathon 1969, 1971-2. His two British bests at the marathon came in 1970, 2:10:30 to win at Boston and 2:09:28 in Edinburgh to take the Commonwealth title.

A chemistry graduate of Manchester University, specialising in textiles, he built up a successful sports goods business bearing his name. His two-volume autobiography *The Long Hard Road* presents the most detailed study of a long-distance runner.

Other best times: 3000m 8:11.8 (1963), 2 miles 8:41.0 (1965), 3 miles 13:27.2 (1967), 5000m 14:00.6 (1969), 6 miles 27:25.94 (1966), 10,000m 28:38.98 (1969), 30,000m 1:32:17.0 (1970).

Bob HILLER

Rugby Union
Robert Hiller. b. 14 Oct 1942 Woking, Surrey.

Winning 19 caps (1968-72), Hiller was, at the time, England's most capped full-back and he captained his country seven times. He scored in every international and his total of 138 points was then an England record. He toured with the British Lions to South Africa (1968) and Australia and New Zealand (1971) but did not play in a Test on either tour.

At Oxford he won Blues for rugby (1965) and for cricket (1966) as a fast-medium bowler and on leaving university he played for Harlequins.

Blanche HILLYARD – see BINGLEY

Harold HILTON

Golf

Harold Horsfall Hilton. b. 12 Jan 1869
West Kirby, near Hoylake, Merseyside. d.
5 Mar 1942 Westcote, Oxford.

An amateur throughout his career, who
learned the game at the Royal Liverpool
Golf Club, Hilton was the Open champion
in 1892 and 1897 and winner of the
Amateur Championship four times, 1900-
01, 1911 and 1913. His first win came after
he had been beaten in the final three times,
in 1891-2 and 1896. He was also Irish
Amateur champion four times, 1897,
1900-02 and American Amateur champion
in 1911, thus becoming the first man and
only Briton to win both US and British
amateur titles. In that year he nearly
achieved a great treble, as he led the
British Open with three holes to play, but
lost by one stroke.
Just 1.62m *5 ft 4 in* tall, he was still able to
hit the ball with great power. He became
the first editor of *Golf Monthly* and later
editor of *Golf Illustrated*.

Julian HIPWOOD

Polo

Julian Brian Hipwood. b. 23 Jun 1946
Pakistan.

A professional polo player from 1964 and
England captain 1971-6 and 1978-91. He
was the first player to achieve World Cup
wins for five successive years 1980-4 and
twice a British Open winner. Julian
Hipwood, generally playing at the front,
and his brother **Howard** (b. 24 Mar 1950),
a massively consistent hitter, best at no. 3
or 4, have been the highest rated British
players of recent years, both achieving a
top handicap of nine.

George HIRST

Cricket

George Herbert Hirst. b. 7 Sep 1871
Kirkheaton, West Yorkshire. d. 10 May 1954
Ludley, Huddersfield, West Yorkshire.

The Yorkshire pair of Wilfred Rhodes (qv)
and George Hirst were unbeatable as all-
rounders. In 1906 Hirst achieved the
unique feat of scoring 2000 runs (2385 at
45.86) and taking 200 wickets (208 at
16.50) in a first-class season. That was one
of 14 doubles (1000/100) that he obtained,
including a record 11 in succession 1903-
13, and in two more of those he scored
over 2000 runs, with a high of 2501 at
54.36 in 1904. In 1906 for Yorkshire
against Somerset he achieved a feat which
remains unique in first-class cricket of
scoring a hundred in each innings and five
wickets twice with 111, 117*, 6-70 and 5-45.
A middle-order forcing right-handed batsman, a left-arm medium-fast inswing
bowler and a magnificent fielder, he was
surprisingly not very effective in Tests,
with his best series against Australia in
1903/4 when he scored 217 runs and took
15 wickets, but was hugely popular. He
later coached at Eton College for 18 years.
24 Tests 1897-1909: 790 runs at 22.57, HS
85; 59 wickets at 30.00, BB 5-48; 18
catches.
First-class 1891-1929: 36,323 runs at
34.13, 60 100s HS 341; 2739 wickets at
18.72, BB 9-24; 604 catches.

Steve HISLOP

Motorcycling

Steven Hislop. b. 11 Jan 1962 Hawick,
Borders.

Hislop emulated Mike Hailwood and Joey
Dunlop (qqv) by twice winning three TT
races on the Isle of Man in the same year,
with the Senior, Formula One and 600cc in
both 1989 and 1991. He also won the
Senior TT in 1992 and both Senior and
Formula One in 1994 and has a career total
of 11 TT race victories 1987-94. His career
on the island had started with 2nd in the
Newcomers Manx Grand Prix in 1983 and
his first win was at Formula Two 350cc in
1987 on a Yamaha, after which his successes were for Honda.

Barry HOBAN

Cycling

Peter Barry Hoban. b. 5 Feb 1940
Northern Ireland.

As an amateur, he won the British pursuit
title in 1960 and competed in the team pur-

suit at the Olympics that year. He later achieved great success as a professional in Continental road races and in 10 starts (1967-75, 1978) in the Tour de France he was a stage winner eight times, a record for a British rider. His best final placing was 33rd in 1968. He won the Frankfurt Grand Prix in 1966, finished 2nd in the Paris-Tours 1967 and 3rd in the Liège-Bastogne-Liège 1969 and the Paris-Roubaix 1972.

Jack HOBBS

Cricket
(Sir) John Berry Hobbs. b. 16 Dec 1882 Cambridge. d. 21 Dec 1963 Hove, East Sussex.

'The Master' was the supreme English batsman, a great cover fielder and a wonderful man. He set records which may never be surpassed with 61,237 runs and 197 centuries (or 199 on a more accurate, but non-traditional assessment) in first-class cricket. But he was not especially interested in runs for the sake of runs, and it was the sheer quality that made him such a delight and so dependable for Surrey and England.

He exceeded 1000 runs in 26 seasons (24 in England and 2 in South Africa), with a record 17 over 2000 and once over 3000, 3024 at 70.32 in 1925, when he set the record (passed by Denis Compton in 1947) of 16 centuries in the season. He scored an amazing 98 of his first-class centuries after the age of 40, and remained a must for England from 1907 until he was 47 in 1930; he remains the oldest Test centurion for his 142 against Australia at 46 years 82 days in 1929. He formed notable opening partnerships with Tom Hayward and Andy Sandham (qqv) for Surrey, and with these men he made 40 and 66 century partnerships respectively. Then for England he opened principally with Wilfred Rhodes and Herbert Sutcliffe (26 century partnerships, including 15 in Tests). Hobbs was the first batsman to reach 4000 runs (1926) and 5000 runs (1929) in Test cricket.

He played for Cambridgeshire before making his Surrey debut in 1905 and then made 155 in his first Championship match

and was immediately presented with his county cap. In 1953 he became the first professional to be knighted for services to cricket.
61 Tests 1907-30: 5410 runs at 56.94, 15 100s HS 211; 1 wicket; 17 catches.
First-class 1905-34: 61,237 runs at 50.65, 197 100s HS 316*; 107 wickets at 25.00, BB 7-56; 339 catches.

Liz HOBBS

Water Skiing
Elizabeth Hobbs. b. 14 May 1960 St Albans, Herts.

Hobbs was the world women's ski-racing champion of 1981 and 1984. She first water skied at the age of nine while on a Spanish holiday and won her first British title in 1976 at the end of her first year on the circuit. She retained that title in the following two years and was then 5th in the inaugural world ski-racing championships in 1979. In 1982 she set a women's world speed record on Lake Windermere and won the first official European Championships. After a terrible crash in the British Championships of 1984 she came back to regain the European title in 1986. She was awarded the MBE in the 1986 New Year Honours.

Glenn HODDLE

Football
Glenn Hoddle. b. 27 Oct 1957 Hayes, London.

Hoddle was a naturally gifted, elegant, mid-field player whose undoubted talents were often overlooked by the England selectors. His critics claimed that he was not prepared to take on his share of defensive work but his supporters maintained that any such deficiency was outweighed by his brilliant attacking skills. Signing as professional for Tottenham Hotspur in 1975 he helped them win the FA Cup in 1981 and 1982 and the UEFA Cup 1984 and scored 106 goals in 484 league and cup games for them. By the time Spurs were losing finalists in the 1987 FA Cup it was clear that Hoddle's game had lost some of its edge but on moving to Monaco he showed all his old flair and helped the club to the French League Championship in 1988. He also won his 53rd and final England cap (from 1979, with 8 goals) in 1988 before a knee injury put him out of the game. He returned in 1991 to become player-manager at Swindon Town and in 1993 he took over at Chelsea, where he led them to the FA Cup final in his first year in charge. He was PFA Young Footballer of the Year 1980.

Carole HODGES

Cricket
Carole Anne Hodges. b. 1 Sep 1959 Blackpool.

After a decade as England's leading all-rounder she retired with a Test record of 1164 runs at 40.13 from 18 Tests, having made her highest score, 158*, in her first series against New Zealand in 1984, 23 wickets at 29.47 with her accurate off-spin bowling, and, as an exceptional close fielder, an England record 25 catches. In her last season she played a leading part in England's World Cup triumph in 1993, scoring 334 runs at 47.71 in the tournament including a match-winning 105* in 141 balls against Australia and 45 in the final against New Zealand, and taking a hat-trick against Denmark. She captained England in 1986 and is the most capped England player, with 47 one-day internationals (1982-93) to add to her 18 Tests and an overall record of 2237 runs at 36.08, including 4 centuries (HS 113), 81 wickets at 19.16 and a record 47 catches. She captained Lancashire and Cheshire and helped Wakefield to three League and Cup doubles and another League win in her last five seasons. She married a farmer in 1993.

Martin HODGSON

Rugby League
Martin Hodgson. b. 26 Mar 1909. d. 19 July 1991 Salford, Manchester.

In an era of outstanding British forwards he was rated as one of the greatest. A strong attacking runner and devastating cover tackler, he was also a fine goal kicker. Playing in the Swinton second-row,

he won 16 GB caps (1929-37), toured Australia twice (1932, 1936) and is the only forward to have played in five Test series against Australia. For Swinton, Cumbria and Great Britain he played against the Australians a total of 12 times and was never once on the losing side. On his second tour with the Lions in 1936 he kicked 65 goals and his name is still in the record books for his prodigious goal for Swinton against Rochdale on 13 April 1940. The ball travelled just 9 inches short of 78 yards which remains the world record for the longest goal ever kicked.

Margaret HOHMANN – see KELLY

Jack HOLDEN

Marathon
John Thomas Holden. b. 13 Mar 1907 Bilston, West Midlands.

Before World War II Holden compiled a great record in the International Cross-country Championships, winning the race a record four times, 1933-5 and 1939, including by a record 56 second margin in 1934. He was also 2nd in 1932 and 1936 and had ten top ten placings, including his postwar appearance, 6th in 1946. He won the English National in 1938-9 and 1946.

After the war he turned to marathons and in 1950 won five of them, taking both Commonwealth and European titles, and becoming the oldest medallist at each. He was 42 years 335 days when he won the former, despite running the last eight miles barefoot after his shoes split and having to fight off the attentions of a Great Dane with two miles to go. The latter came at 43 years 163 days. A month earlier he had run his fastest time of 2:31:03.4 in winning his fourth successive AAA title and earlier his third successive Poly marathon.

On the track he was AAA champion at 6 miles each year 1933-5 and 4 miles in 1934 and had best times of 3 miles 14:33.8 (1936), 6 miles 30:26.7 (1932), 10 miles 52:21.4 (1934).

Jane HOLDERNESS-RODDAM – see BULLEN

Virginia HOLGATE – see LENG

Andrea HOLMES

Trampolining
Andrea Holmes. b. 2 Jan 1970.

Holmes made her international debut at the 1982 World Championships at 12 years 131 days, the youngest ever British international and went on to become world champion at synchronised pairs with Lorraine Lyon in 1992 and runner-up in the individual event four times, 1986, 1988, 1990 and 1994. At the European Championships she was individual champion in 1983 (shared with Sue Shotton (qv)), 1985 and 1991, and winner at synchronised pairs in 1983, followed by four third placings. She was the World Cup individual winner in 1984-5, 1987, 1991 and 1994 and British individual champion overall 1983, 1987 (shared), 1986-9 and 1994.

Cyril HOLMES

Rugby Union and Athletics
Cyril Butler Holmes. b. 11 Jan 1915 Bolton, Lancashire.

A top-class sprinter, Holmes is one of the fastest men ever to play international rugby. A winger with the Manchester club, he scored a try on his England debut in the 1947 Calcutta Cup and closed his brief international career (3 caps) by playing against France and Ireland in 1948. As a rugby player, he will be best remembered for the try he scored when the Barbarians beat the Australian tourists 9-6 in 1948.
As a sprinter he set British records for 100y, 9.7, and 220y, 21.2, when he won Empire Games titles at Sydney in 1938, adding a silver medal when he anchored the England 4 x 110y relay team. He also ran a British record for 100m 10.6 in 1937 and improved to 10.5 in 1939, with a wind-assisted best of 10.4 in 1937.
He competed at the 1936 Olympic Games and was a triple gold medallist (100m, 200m and relay) at the 1937 World University Games. He was AAA champion at 100y in 1937 and 220y in 1939 and indoors at 70y in 1936 and 1937

Kelly HOLMES

Athletics
Kelly Holmes. b. 19 Apr 1970 Pembury, Kent

Holmes had been one of the top young runners in Britain in the mid-1980s, winning the English Schools junior 1500m title in 1984 and competing as a junior international in 1977. But then, having joined the army at 18, hardly competed for the next four years. She came back in 1992 and broke into world class in 1993, when she won AAA and UK titles at 800m and broke two minutes for the first time.
In 1994 she improved her best time at 1500m from 4:17.3 to 4:01.41 and at this new distance won the Commonwealth title, the European silver medal, and she was 2nd in the European Cup and 3rd in the World Cup. Improving futher in 1995, she won the 1500m for Britain at the European Cup, and a series of wins in international races and an English record 1:57.56 for 800m to win the AAA title gave every hope for major honours to come. Other best times: 400m 54.7 (1994), 1000m 2:37.29 (1993), 3000m 9:07.7 (1995). A physical training instructor, she has also been army judo champion and played for them at volleyball.

Percy HOLMES

Cricket
Percy Holmes. b. 25 Nov 1886 Oakes, Huddersfield, Yorkshire. d. 3 Sep 1971 Marsh, Huddersfield.

From 1919 to 1932 Holmes and Sutcliffe were Yorkshire's openers; together they shared 69 century partnerships for the first wicket, the culmination of which was their record stand of 555 against Essex at Leyton in 1932 when Holmes was 44. They also opened together in six of the seven Tests that Holmes played for England, a figure that of course would have been much higher but for the fact that Jack Hobbs and Herbert Sutcliffe (qqv) were the England openers. Holmes, an attacking right-handed batsman and an outstanding slip fielder, was 26 when he made his first-class debut and then lost much of his early career due to World War I. He made two treble centuries for Yorkshire and ten other scores over 200. He made over 1000 runs in a season in South Africa 1927/8 and in England each year 1919-32, and over 2000 seven times with a peak of 2453 at 57.04 in 1925.

7 Tests 1921-32: 357 runs at 27.46; HS 88; 3 catches.

First-class 1913-33: 30,573 runs at 42.11, 67 100s HS 315*; 2 wickets at 92.50, BB 1-5; 336 catches.

Terry HOLMES

Rugby Union
Terence David Holmes. b. 10 Mar 1957 Cardiff.

After winning a record number of Welsh youth caps over a three-year period, Holmes made 195 appearances for Cardiff at scrum-half. He won 25 Welsh caps 1978-85, and scored nine international tries. He would undoubtedly have won more caps had it not been for injury.

He toured with the British Lions to South Africa 1980 and New Zealand 1983, and played in the first Test against New Zealand but during the game he suffered a severe injury and was unable to play again on the tour. A tough, strong tackler he was well suited to Rugby League and in December 1985 he signed as a professional with Bradford Northern but a succession of shoulder injuries led to his retirement two years later.

Lloyd HONEYGHAN

Boxing
Lloyd Honeyghan. b. 22 Apr 1960 St Elizabeth, Jamaica.

Born in Jamaica, Honeyghan made his professional debut in London in 1980. He won the British welterweight title in 1983 and the Commonwealth and European titles in 1985 and he went on to become the World champion, achieving in September 1986 the rare distinction, for a British boxer, of winning a World title fight in America. In Atlantic City, his opponent, Don Curry (USA), recognised as pound-for-pound the best boxer in the

world, retired after six rounds and Honeyghan became the undisputed World welterweight champion. He was voted as British Sportsman of the Year 1986 by the Sports Writers'. He made just one defence of the IBF version of the title, beating Johnny Bumphus (USA) in two rounds in February 1987, but was far more active when the WBC title was at stake. After two successful defences he lost the title to Jorge Vaca (Mexico) in October 1987, but in his next fight he won the re-match with Vaca to regain the title. After one more defence, he lost to Marlon Starling (USA) in February 1989 and one year later he failed to regain the title when the referee stopped the contest in the third round of his bout against Mark Breland (USA).

Although he never again challenged for the WBC title he was the undefeated WBA, IBF, British, Commonwealth and European welterweight champion. Moving up a division, he won the Commonwealth light-middleweight title in January 1993, but after a successful defence in February 1994 was stripped of the title in July.

Career record 1980 - March 1994: 47 contests. Won 43, Lost 4.

Maurice HOPE

Boxing
Maurice Hope. b. 6 Dec 1951 Antigua.

Hope was one of many fine boxers from the West Indies who achieved success after settling in England. In 1972 he was an Olympic quarter-finalist at welterweight. As a light-middleweight, he was the undefeated British (1974-7), Commonwealth (1976-9) and European (1976-8) champion and he was also the World title-holder. He first challenged for the WBC crown in March 1977 but narrowly failed to take the title following a draw with Eckhard Dagge (Ger).

Hope had to wait two more years for another chance at the World title, but he took it well forcing Rocky Mattioli (Italy) to retire after eight rounds in front of a partisan crowd in San Remo, Italy. Three successful defences of the title followed before he was KO'd in the 12th round by Wilfred Benitez (USA) in Atlantic City in

May 1981. In 1982 he failed in a bid for the European title.

Career record 1973-82: 35 contests. Won 30 (24 KO), Drew 1, Lost 4.

Thelma HOPKINS

Athletics, High Jump
Thelma Elizabeth Hopkins. b. 16 Mar 1936 Hull. Later Mrs McClernon.

Born in England and raised in Belfast, Hopkinsset a world record for the high jump at 1.74m in 1956 before going on to take an Olympic silver medal. Coached by the Australian Franz Stampfl, she was 4th as a 16 year-old in the 1952 Olympic high jump and in 1954 won both Empire and European titles at high jump, adding a long jump silver at the Empire Games. At subsequent Empire/ Commonwealth Games she was 8th at high jump and 7th at long jump in 1958, and 9th and 6th in 1962.

She set a British record for the pentathlon with 4289 points when winning the Northern Irish title in 1955 and later improved her best to 4379 points (1954 tables) in 1961, in which year she was 3rd at both 80m hurdles and high jump at the World Student Games. Other bests: 80m hurdles 11.2 (1964), long jump 6.11m and 6.12m wind-aided (1956). She was WAAA champion at high jump 1955 and 1957, long jump 1955 and 80m hurdles 1957.

She was also a brilliant forward at hockey, winning 40 caps for Ireland, and was also an Irish squash international. Educated at Queen's University, Belfast and Ulster College, she became a PE teacher.

Paddy HOPKIRK (Ireland)

Rallying
Patrick Hopkirk. b. 1933.

By the end of the 1960s Hopkirk was probably the world's best-known rally driver He won a Coupe d'Argent on the Alpine Rally which resulted from Coupes gained with a Triumph TRS in 1956, a Sunbeam Rapier in 1959 and a Mini Cooper in 1965. He started the great successes of the Mini Cooper S by winning the Monte Carlo Rally (with Henry Liddon) in 1964 and also won the Acropolis Rally and the Alpine Rally in 1967. He won the Circuit of Ireland a record five times, with a Triumph TR3 in 1958, Sunbeam Rapiers in 1961-2 and Mini Coopers 1965 and 1967.

British Leyland (formerly BMC) decided to curtail their rallying activities at the end of 1968, so that was the end of the Mini Cooper era, but they retained the jovial Irishman to drive for them in long-distance races, such as the 1968 London to Sydney marathon, in which he was 2nd.

Denis HORGAN (Ireland)

Shot
Denis Horgan. b. 18 May 1871 Fermoyle, near Banteer, Co. Cork. d. 2 Jun 1922 Crookstown, Co. Cork.

Horgan still holds the British record for the most AAA titles in a single event, winning the shot put 13 times between 1893 and 1912. He also won the American title in 1900 and won 17 Irish titles at the 16 lb shot, as well as 11 at other weights. He set seven world records (from a 7ft square, rather than the circle which was introduced to international competition in 1904) from 1894 to his 14.88m *48 ft 10 in* in 1904, a distance no British athlete bettered until 1949 and an Irish record until 1950. He would surely have won an Olympic title, but he competed for the first time in 1908 when he was past his peak and took the silver medal.

In 1905 he had left Ireland for the USA, and there in 1907, as a policeman in New York, he had been savagely beaten to the point of death, with his skull broken by a shovel. He was pensioned off from the police force and returned to Ireland. He recovered remarkably, so that by the summer of 1908 he was able to regain his AAA title and secure a place on the British Olympic team.

A sturdy man of 1.78m *5 ft 10 in* tall and a useful jumper in his youth, his weight increased from 75kg in 1893 to 108kg in 1908. He was said to warm up by consuming a dozen eggs in a pint of sherry. Best hammer throw 42.12m (1909).

Albert HORNBY

Cricket and Rugby Union
Albert Neilson Hornby. b. 10 Feb 1847
Blackburn, Lancashire. d. 17 Dec 1925
Nantwich, Cheshire.

'Monkey' Hornby was the first double international at cricket and rugby union. He had nine caps for England at rugby, 1877-82, and played for Preston Grasshoppers and Manchester. He was also the first man to captain England at both sports, both in 1882, at rugby against Scotland and at cricket against Australia at The Oval. Having made his Test debut in 1879, he also captained England in his third Test in 1884 and was Lancashire captain 1880-93 and 1897-8, transforming them into a formidable team and taking them to the County Championship in 1881 and 1897.

Hornby, who first played at Lord's for Harrow against Eton, was a fine fielder and an attacking batsman, in contrast to his Lancashire opening partner, the stonewaller Dick Barlow; together they inspired Francis Thompson's verse which included the phrase 'O my Hornby and my Barlow long ago'.

On 14 Jul 1873 Hornby set a record for first-class cricket with 10 runs from a single hit, for Lancashire v Surrey at The Oval. He also played football for Blackburn Rovers and in later life was devoted to hunting. His son Albert (1877-1952) captained Lancashire at cricket from 1908 to 1914.

3 Tests 1878-84: 21 runs at 3.50; HS 9.
First-class 1867-99: 16,109 runs at 24.07, 16 100s HS 188; 11 wickets at 23.45, BB 4-40; 313 catches, 3 stumpings.

Bill HOSKYNS

Fencing
William Henry Furse Hoskyns. b. 19 Mar 1931 London.

A courageous left-hander he was national junior champion at foil and épée and 3rd at sabre while a student at Oxford University. He was AFA champion at épée 1956-8 and 1967, foil 1959, 1964 and 1970; sabre 1966, to become only the second man to win AFA titles with all three weapons.

With a victory in the individual épée in 1958 he became the first British male fencer to win the World title. He also finished as runner-up 1965 and won a second silver medal in the team event. At the Olympic Games he won silver medals in the épée team (1960) and the épée individual (1964) and he shares with Alan Jay (qv) the distinction of being one of only two British males to have won an Olympic medal in an individual fencing event. He also shares with the swimmer and water polo player, Paul Radmilovic (qv), the record for a British male of competing in six Olympic Games (1956-76). At three Commonwealth Games (1958, 1966, 1970) he won four individual (épée 1958, 1966, 1970; sabre 1958) and five team gold medals and one silver. During his best years he farmed in Somerset and, although he was deprived of the top-class competition available in London, he was the outstanding British fencer of his generation. He was awarded the MBE.

Ray HOUGHTON

Football
Raymond James Houghton. b. 9 Jan 1962 Glasgow.

Although Scottish born, he has won 64 caps for Ireland in the midfield from 1986 to June 1995. He first signed as a professional for West Ham but after just one first team appearance as a substitute in 1982 he moved to Fulham where he stayed four seasons. He then played for Oxford United 1985-7, Liverpool 1987-92, Aston Villa 1992-5 and Crystal Palace 1995. While he was with Oxford they won the League Cup in 1986 (he scored the second goal) and he helped Liverpool to two wins in the FA Cup final, 1989 and 1992, and to the League Championship twice 1988 and 1990.

Bonzo HOWLAND

Shot
Robert Leslie Howland. b. 25 Mar 1905 Berkhamsted, Herts. d. 7 Mar 1986 Saffron Walden, Essex.

Britain's top shot putter of the 1930s,

Howland took the British record from 14.02 in 1929 to 14.86 in 1935. Twice AAA indoor champion, 1935 and 1938, he did not win an outdoor title, being runner-up to an overseas athlete nine times between 1929 and 1939. He was also second at the Empire Games of 1930 and 1934 and competed once at the Olympics, in 1928.

A classical scholar and Cambridge Blue 1925-8, winning in his last three years, he became a don at his old university and a renowned lecturer on the ancient world.

Philip HUBBLE

Swimming

Philip Hubble. b. 19 Jul 1960 Beaconsfield, Bucks.

Having won silver medals for 200m butterfly at the 1980 Olympics and 1981 Europeans, Hubble had his greatest success at the 1982 Commonwealth Games, where he won the 200m butterfly and took four silver medals: 100m butterfly and all three relays. In 1978 he was 3rd at 200m and 5th at 100m at the Commonwealth Games.

A determined competitor, he set his first British records in 1979 with 55.52 for 100m and 2:01.28 for 200m butterfly, improving at the longer event to a Commonwealth record 2:00.21 in 1981. He was ASA butterfly champion at 100m in 1979-80 and 1982 and at 200m 1976, 1978, 1980 and 1981-2 and also won at 200m freestyle in 1980 and 1983.

He went to the University of Calgary in Canada.

Brian HUGGETT

Golf

Brian George Charles Huggett. b. 18 Nov 1936 Porthcawl, Bridgend.

A most determined and resolute golfer, the Welshman won the Vardon Trophy in 1968 and achieved 17 tournament victories in Europe 1962-78, including the Dunlop Masters in 1970, the PGA Championship 1967 and the PGA Match Play in 1968. His best placings in the Open were joint 2nd in 1965 and joint 3rd in 1962. He represented Wales nine times in the World

Cup and was a stalwart of the Ryder Cup team, winning nine, losing ten and halving six of his 25 matches in six ties between 1963 and 1975. He was non-playing captain in 1977. His abiding memory of the Ryder Cup was his 5-ft putt on the final green to halve his match with Billy Casper in 1969, thinking that this would bring the Cup to Britain, but it did not quite do that, for the last pair Jacklin and Nicklaus halved their match and the Cup was tied for the first time.

He turned professional in 1951 and won the British Assistants championship in 1958. He was awarded the MBE in 1978.

His father was professional at Porthcawl and Neath.

Emlyn HUGHES

Football

Emlyn Walter Hughes. b. 28 Aug 1947 Barrow-in-Furness, Cumbria.

A talented and personable midfield player, Hughes proved an ideal captain for Liverpool and England. First signing as a professional for Blackpool in 1964, he was transferred to Liverpool for £65,000 in 1967 and won a host of honours with the Merseyside club: European Cup (1977, 1978), UEFA Cup (1973, 1976), FA Cup (1974), and League Championship (1973, 1976, 1977, 1979).

The only major trophy that eluded him was the League Cup, but after moving to Wolverhampton Wanderers in 1979 he added a winner's medal for this competition to his collection in 1980. He won 62 England caps 1969-80 while with Liverpool and Wolves after which he moved on to Rotherham United, Hull City, Mansfield Town and Swansea. He was the Football Writers Player of the Year in 1977.

He was awarded the OBE in 1980 and later had a successful career in television. His father was a Rugby League international, his brother and uncle played the game professionally and his aunt played hockey for England.

Mark HUGHES

Football
Leslie Mark Hughes. b. 1 Nov 1963 Wrexham.

Hughes left the Welsh village of Ruabon to join Manchester United at the age of 14, and played a major part in enabling United to win the Premier League in 1993 and to the league and cup double in 1994. He scored the two goals that took them to victory over Barcelona in the final of the 1991 European Cup-Winners' Cup.

He left United for an unhappy spell abroad with Barcelona in 1986-8 and a short period on loan to Bayern Munich, once playing for them as a substitute in the evening of a day (11 Nov 1987) in which he had played for Wales against Czechoslovakia in Prague. He returned to Manchester with such success that he was PFA Footballer of the Year 1989 and 1991, having won the Young Footballer award in 1985. Prior to the 1994 double he had played on the winning FA Cup teams of 1985 and 1990 (when he scored two goals), the European Cup Winners' Cup team of 1991 and the League Cup in 1992. With his explosive shooting, especially on the volley, Hughes has earned a reputation for spectacular goals.

A powerful and volatile player, he has earned 56 caps for Wales from 1984 to April 1995, scoring 12 goals. In June 1995 he was transferred to Chelsea for £1.5 million, signing a three-year contract.

Norman HUGHES

Hockey
Norman Hughes. b. 30 Sep 1952 Nantwich, Cheshire.

Hughes was the first player to win 100 caps for England. He reached this landmark against Spain in 1986 and won five further caps that year before retiring from the international game. Playing at midfield or forward, he captained England and GB for whom he was capped 26 times. He won a silver medal at the World Cup 1986 and bronze medals at the Olympic Games 1984 and the European Cup 1978. After attending Crewe County GS and Leeds University, he played for Wakefield and worked as a marketing manager for Dunlop Slazenger International. He is now a leading coach.

Pat HUGHES

Tennis
George Patrick Hughes. b. 21 Dec 1902 Sutton Coldfield, West Midlands.

An outstanding doubles player, Hughes was a member of four winning Davis Cup teams, 1933-6. Between 1929 and 1936 he played in 21 Cup ties (2/2 singles, 13/20 doubles).

In the major Championships he won the French (1933) and the Australian (1934) doubles with Fred Perry (qv) and Wimbledon (1936) with Charles Tuckey. He won all three titles at the 1931 Italian Championships and took the men's doubles for a second time the following year. Apart from his win in Italy, his best singles performance was to reach the semi-finals at the French Championships and the finals of the British Hard Court Championships in 1931. He was also a quarter-finalist at Wimbledon in 1931 and 1933.

After his playing career ended he became the editor of the *Lawn Tennis Almanack*.

Joe HULME

Football
Joseph Harold Anthony Hulme. b. 26 Aug 1904 Stafford. d. 27 Sep 1991 Winchmore Hill, London.

A winger of exceptional speed, Hulme played in a record five Wembley FA Cup finals and won nine England caps 1927-33. After playing for York City and Blackburn Rovers he was signed by Arsenal in 1926 where he developed into an outstanding winger. His partnership with Alex James (qv) was particularly effective and they played a major role in Arsenal winning the FA Cup in 1930 and 1936 and the League championship 1931. Hulme was also on the losing side in the FA Cup in 1927 and 1932 and he played in a then record fifth Wembley final in 1938 shortly after he had joined Huddersfield. He retired at the end of the season with a record of 113 goals in

414 League appearances, but returned to the game during the war when he joined the administrative staff at Tottenham Hotspur, firstly as assistant secretary and latterly as manager 1945-9, after which he worked as a sports journalist until his retirement in 1965.

He also played cricket for Middlesex 1929-39, with a first-class record of 8103 runs at 26.56 and 12 centuries, highest 143, and 89 wickets at 36.40 as a medium-paced bowler, with 110 catches. He scored over 1000 runs in a season three times and was noted for his dazzling footwork and his speed between the wickets.

Donald HUME

Badminton
Donald Charles Hume. b. 6 Sep 1907 Hackney, London. d. 3 May 1986 Brighton.

During a long career he won 24 caps for England 1928-48, and won the All-England singles in 1930. A hard-hitting, agile player he was at his best in the doubles, winning the All-England men's doubles with Raymond White four times, 1932-5, and the mixed with Betty Uber (qv) four times, 1933-6.

Bernard HUNT

Golf
Bernard John Hunt. b. 2 Feb 1930 Atherstone, Warwicks.

A consistently successful golfer in the 1950s and 1960s, he won the Vardon Trophy for the lowest stroke average in 1958, 1960 and 1965. His 24 European tournament wins between 1953 and 1973 included the Dunlop Masters 1963 and 1965 and the Opens of Belgium 1957, Germany 1961 and France 1967, but his best placings in the British Open were 3rd in 1960 and 4th in 1964.

A Ryder Cup regular, he played in eight ties 1953-69, with a record of 6 wins, 16 losses and 6 halves, and he was non-playing captain in 1973 and 1975. He also represented England in the World Cup seven times, 1958-60, 1962-4 and 1968. For many years professional at Foxhills, Ottershaw, Surrey, he had a short, tidy swing and was an excellent putter. He was elected captain of the PGA in 1995. He was awarded the MBE.

His father was a professional golfer and his brother **Geoffrey** Michael **Hunt** (b. 28 Dec 1935 Atherstone) won the Assistants Championship in 1953 and 1963 and played in the 1963 Ryder Cup; Bernard and Geoffrey were only the second pair of brothers to play in this fixture.

James HUNT

Motor Racing
James Simon Wallis Hunt. b. 29 Aug 1947 Belmont, London. d. 15 Jun 1993 Wimbledon, London.

World motor racing champion in 1976, Hunt drove in Formula One for Hesketh 1973-5 and McLaren 1976-9, winning 10 Grand Prix races, six in 1976, and 179 points from 92 starts in his career. He was a natural athlete, excelling at many sports, and overcame a poor reputation as 'Hunt the Shunt' to reach the top, which ensured great popularity for this extrovert, glamorous, arrogant but intelligent driver.

He raced in Formula Ford in 1968-9, then turned to Formula Three, where he teamed up with Lord Alexander Hesketh in 1972. The latter gave him his chance at Formula One in 1973 and by the time that Hesketh had to pull out of this expensive world, Hunt had made his name and he won the world title in the dramatic year of 1976. His first GP win was at Zandvoort in 1975, when he was 4th in the championship. After his retirement he became a BBC television commentator on motor racing.

Roger HUNT

Football
Roger Hunt. b. 20 Jul 1938 Golborne, Gt. Manchester.

Hunt was a powerful and determined inside-right in England's 1966 World Cup winning team. Signed by Liverpool from a local club in 1958 he spent his best years with the Merseyside club and was their most prolific scorer with 245 league goals (a record since surpassed by Ian Rush). He was with Liverpool when they won the

Football League (1964, 1966) and the FA Cup (1965) and, after moving to Bolton Wanderers in 1969, he retired in 1972 and devoted his time to the family haulage business. He played 34 times for England 1962-9.

Geoff HURST

Football
Geoffrey Charles Hurst. b. 8 Dec 1941 Ashton-under-Lyne, Gt. Manchester.

As a relative unknown, his three goals in the 1966 World Cup final brought him instant fame. This was only his eighth international and he is the only player to have scored a hat-trick in a World Cup final. He went on to win 49 caps and score 24 goals as England's centre-forward 1966-72. He signed as a professional with West Ham in 1959 and was initially a wing-half, but he only played in eight League matches in his first two seasons.

His career really took off when his manager, Ron Greenwood, moved him up front and in successive years he earned winners' medals in the FA Cup 1964, European Cup-Winners' Cup 1965 and World Cup 1966. He stayed with West Ham for 13 seasons scoring 180 goals in 410 League matches, but because of crowd abuse at Upton Park he moved to Stoke City in 1972 and then to West Bromwich Albion three years later. His final seasons were spent with Cork Celtic and Telford United as player-manager before spending 18 months as the manager of Chelsea. His days at Stamford Bridge marked the end of his active involvement with football and he pursued his various business interests. A fine club cricketer, he played once for Essex in 1962.

Tim HUTCHINGS

Athletics
Timothy Hilton Hutchings. b. 4 Dec 1958 London.

Having won the AAA indoor 1500m title, Hutchings ran in the 1978 Commonwealth Games for England as a teenager and was 10th at 1500m. In 1982 he won the UK 1500m. Moving up to 5000m he ran mar-

vellously well to place 4th and smash his personal best with 13:11.50 at the 1984 Olympics, and in 1986 took bronze medals at both Commonwealth Games and European Championships, after 14th and 7th respectively at those events in 1982. He was also 7th in the World 5000m in 1987.

In 1989 he moved up again, to 10,000m at which he was second in the AAAs and European Cup; he also improved his five-year-old 3000m best to 7:43.03. He was selected at 10,000m but withdrew from the European Championships team in 1990 due to groin strain and injuries prevented him from further successes. He had perhaps his greatest success at cross-country, with 2nd places in the World Championships in 1984 and 1989 and wins in the National in 1983 and 1986.

A graduate of Loughborough University, he now works as a consultant and television commentator, mostly for Eurosport. In 1987 he married **Sharon McPeake** (b. 22 Jun 1962 Ballymena), who was the 1986 Commonwealth Games high jump silver medallist for Northern Ireland with her best ever jump of 1.90m.

Other best times: 800m 1:51.8 (1977), 1000m 2:22.6 (1982), 1500m 3:38.06 (1984), 1 mile 3:54.53 (1982), 2000m 5:00.37 (1983), 2 miles 8:15.53 (1986), 10,000m 28:07.57 (1990).

Horace HUTCHINSON

Golf
Horatio Gordon Hutchinson. b. 16 May 1859 London. d. 28 Jul 1932 London.

Hutchinson was the Amateur champion of 1886 and 1887, after being runner-up in the first ever championship in 1885. He was a semi-finalist in 1896, 1901 and 1904, but poor health prevented him from achieving greater success as a player. He became the leading golfing writer of his day, and his *Golf* in the Badminton Library series is a classic on the game. In 1908 he became the first Englishman to captain the Royal and Ancient Golf Club at St Andrews.

Len HUTTON

Cricket
(Sir) Leonard Hutton. b. 23 Jun 1916
Fulneck, Pudsey, West Yorkshire. d. 6 Sep
1990 Kingston-upon-Thames, London.

A complete batsman on all types of wickets, Hutton's greatness was all the more amazing for the fact that he made a full recovery from a wartime accident which shortened his left arm by two inches.
He made his Test debut just three days after his 21st birthday against New Zealand in 1937. He scored 0 and 1 in that match but made 100 in the first innings of the next Test. A year later, at the age of 22, he compiled the highest ever Test score with his 364 against Australia at The Oval. Fourteen years later he became the first professional to captain England, and in all led his country in 23 Tests (with an 11-4 win-loss record), the high spots being the regaining of the Ashes in 1953 and their retention in 1954/5.
From 1937 to 1953 he averaged at least 48 in every English season, with a peak in 1949 when he scored 3429 runs at 68.58 and made a record number of runs for any month, 1294 in June. He averaged over 60 in 1938-9, 1947-9 and 1952-3. His mastery was especially shown on the 1950/1 tour of Australia when he scored 533 runs in the Tests at an average of 88.83, compared to the next best Englishman at 38.77, and in the West Indies in 1953/4 when he scored 677 runs in Tests at 96.71. He was also a very fine close fielder and a useful leg spinner in his early days.
He was the first professional to be elected to membership of the MCC during a playing career and the second (in 1956) to be knighted for services to the game.
79 Tests 1907-30: 6971 runs at 56.67, 19 100s HS 364; 3 wickets at 77.33; 57 catches.
First-class 1934-60: 40,140 runs at 55.51, 129 100s HS 364; 173 wickets at 29.51, BB 6-76; 400 catches.
His son **Richard** (b. 6 Sep 1942) played in five Tests for England as an all-rounder, with a Test record of 219 runs at 36.50 and 9 wickets at 28.55 and in first-class cricket 7561 runs at 21.48 and 625 wickets at 24.01 at fast-medium.

Dorothy HYMAN

Athletics
Dorothy Hyman. b. 9 May 1941 Cudworth, South Yorkshire.

From 1957 to 1963 Hyman competed with great distinction as Britain's best ever woman sprinter. She had started sprinting at the age of 13 and in 1956 won English Schools and WAAA junior titles. In 1957 she was WAAA intermediate champion and made her international debut. She won Commonwealth gold medals with the England sprint relay team in 1958 (with a world record) and at both 100y and 220y in 1962, when she added a relay silver. After a relay silver in 1958 she was European champion at 100m and second at 200m with a relay bronze in 1962.
At the Olympics she was 2nd at 100m and 3rd at 200m in 1960, but was held back by injury in 1964 and did well to make the 100m final and take a bronze medal in the relay. WAAA champion at 100m and 200m in 1959-60 and 1962-3, she retired somewhat prematurely and was prevented from resuming her career due to the then rules of amateurism, because she had received the proceeds of her biography. However, she ran again domestically in 1969, when she was WAAA champion at 200m and helped a talented squad of women sprinters from her Dorothy Hyman Track Club.
She ran British records for 100y at 10.6 in 1962 and 1964, for 100m eight times from 11.6 in 1960 to 11.3 twice in 1963, for 200m six from 23.8 in 1960 to 23.2 in 1963, and for 220y three to 23.7 in 1963. She was voted BBC Sports Personality of the Year 1963.

Derek IBBOTSON

Athletics
George Derek Ibbotson. b. 17 Jun 1932 Huddersfield.

Running for Longwood Harriers, he had been Yorkshire junior mile champion 1949-51. After RAF service he shot into world class in 1955, when he was 2nd to Chris Chataway (qv) in the AAA 3 miles. A year later he beat Chataway to win that title and later won the Olympic bronze at 5000m. A great favourite of the British public, 'Ibbo' reached the peak of his fame in 1957. In the midst of a hectic programme of some 70 races that year he set a European record for the mile with 3:58.4, then a month later retained his AAA 3 miles title in a British record 13:20.8 and six days later, on 19 Jul 1957, took the world mile record with 3:57.2 at the White City Stadium to improve John Landy's 1954 time by 0.7 sec; en route he set a British record for 1500m at 3:41.9. He never quite recaptured such form and was 10th and 8th at 3 miles in the Commonwealth Games of 1958 and 1962. He ran on the England team that set a world record for 4 x 1mile in 1958. Indoors he won AAA titles at 2 miles in 1962 and 1965, when he ran a British indoor record time of 8:42.6.

Other best times: 880y 1:52.2 (1958), 2000m 5:12.8 (1955), 3000m 8:00.0 (1959), 2 miles 8:41.2 (1957), 5000m 13:54.4 (1956), 6 miles 28:52.0 (1955).

His first wife **Madeline** (née Wooller, b. 31 Dec 1935 Twickenham), who later married Jonah Barrington (qv), was second in the WAAA 1 mile in 1962 and 1963 and won the national cross-country in 1963 and 1964.

Raymond ILLINGWORTH

Cricket
Raymond Illingworth. b. 8 Jun 1932 Pudsey, West Yorkshire.

For long a canny and accurate off-break bowler and useful middle-order batsman, Illingworth reached the peak of his career after he had left his native county of Yorkshire and become captain of Leicestershire. After just a few matches there he took over as captain of England in 1969 when Colin Cowdrey (qv) was injured. He met with immediate success over the West Indies and produced the best batting of his life, including a century in the 2nd Test. From then until 1973 he proved to be a highly respected captain, achieving a record of 12 wins, 5 losses and 14 draws in his 31 Tests in charge. He retired as captain of Leicestershire after the 1978 season, but

returned first to manage and then to captain Yorkshire at the age of 50 in 1982-3. That was not a success, but that embattled county's members were left to reflect on what might have been if they had held on to this redoubtable player and tactician after 1968. Yorkshire won the Championship seven times during Illingworth's 16 full seasons with them up to and including his last of 1968, but have not done so since. He become a TV commentator on the game, before taking over the role of chairman of the England Test selectors in 1993, adding that of team manager as well in 1995. He achieved the double of 1000 runs and 100 wickets six times between 1957 and 1964. He was awarded the CBE in 1973.

61 Tests 1958-73: 1836 runs at 23.24, 2 100s HS 113; 122 wickets at 31.20, BB 6-29; 45 catches.

3 One-day Ints 1971-3: 5 runs at 2.50, HS 4; 4 wickets at 21.00, BB 3-50; 1 catch.

First-class 1951-83: 24,134 runs at 28.06, 22 100s HS 162; 2072 wickets at 20.28, BB 9-42; 446 catches.

Paul INCE

Football
Paul Emerson Carlyle Ince. b. 21 Oct 1967 Ilford, London.

From the West Ham Youth squad, Ince graduated to the League team in 1986/7 where he spent four seasons before being transferred to Manchester United for £1.9 million in 1989. At Old Trafford he helped United to many triumphs: the FA Cup 1990 and 1994, European Cup Winners' Cup 1991, League Cup 1992 and the League Championship 1993-4. Capped at Youth, Under-21 and 'B' levels he made his full international debut in 1993 and that year in the US Cup he became the first black player to captain England. To 1994 he has won 15 caps (scoring 2 goals). In June 1995 he was transferred to Internazionale, Milan for £7 million. Having calmed a fiery temperament, he has matured into a fine motivational player who adds weight to both defence and attack with his strong tackling and running off the ball. He is a cousin of boxer Nigel Benn (qv).

Melbourne INMAN

Billiards
Melbourne Inman. b. 15 Jul 1878
Brentford, London. d. 11 Aug 1951
Farnborough, Bromley, London.

A six-time winner of the world professional billiards championship, Inman lost the title by default. Initially a marker at a Twickenham club, he began his professional career as a 16-year-old and was declared the world champion in 1908 when the Billiards Association decided to nominate a champion in an effort to revive the championship which had been in abeyance since 1903. He went on to win the title again in 1909, 1912-14 and 1919 but during this period he lost in the final to H.W.Stevenson (qv) in 1910 and 1911.

After beating Stevenson for the 1919 championship he declined to defend his title in 1920 as he felt that the champion should not be required to play through the preliminary rounds. He never recaptured the title but still featured prominently in the championship until 1930.

He was a superb match player who combined a mastery of safety play with an ability to make large breaks and he once held the world record with a break of 894. He toured the world twice, was a keen racehorse owner and was one of the most popular and successful sportsmen of his generation.

Innes IRELAND

Motor Racing
Robert McGregor Innes Ireland. b. 12 Jun 1930 Kirkudbright, Dumfries & Galloway. d. 22 Oct 1993 Reading, Berkshire

A throw-back to a previous age, Ireland brought a flamboyant attitude to the world of racing; a proud Scotsman, he was determined to enjoy his sport. A seemingly fearless driver, the son of a veterinary surgeon, he started racing while doing his national service. He followed this by going into partnership in a garage business in Aldershot. He quickly made his mark and was signed by Colin Chapman for Lotus in 1959. He made an impressive Grand Prix debut with 4th at Zandvoort. In 1960 he had two 2nd places and ended 1961 with his first win, in the US GP. Ireland was then replaced on the Lotus team by Jim Clark (qv) and had no Formula One successes in later years, mostly with the UDT-Laystall team which became the British Racing Partnership. His overall Formula One record was 1 win and 47 points from 50 starts 1959-66. He became the sports editor of *Autocar* in 1967, and in 1992 was elected president of the British Racing Drivers' Club.

Andy IRVINE

Rugby Union
Andrew Robertson Irvine. b. 16 Sep 1951 Edinburgh.

A brilliant attacking full-back, Irvine's elusive running was also recognised at the highest level by his selection on the wing for the British Lions. He is Scotland's most capped full-back with 47 appearances and also played four times on the wing. In his 60 matches (51 for Scotland, 9 for the Lions) he scored a then world record total of 301 points (273 Wales, 28 Lions). He toured three times with the British Lions, playing twice on the wing against South Africa in 1974, at full-back in all four Tests against New Zealand in 1977, and at full-back in three Tests against South Africa in 1980.

His adventurous running added much to the game, although his dedication to attack sometimes exposed defensive weakness.

Sam IRVING

Football
Samuel Johnstone Irving. b. 28 Aug 1893 Belfast. d. 17 Jan 1969 Dundee.

A forceful, attacking inside-forward or wing-half, he won 18 caps for Northern Ireland between 1924 and 1931 while with Dundee United, Cardiff City and Chelsea. He won an FA Cup winners' medal with Cardiff in 1927 and after he moved to Chelsea in 1928, at the age of 34, he helped them back into the First Division in 1930. In 1932 he moved to Bristol Rovers where he ended his playing career.

Bill IVY

Motor Cycling
William David Ivy. b. 27 Aug 1942 Kent. d. 12 Jul 1969 Sachsenring, GDR.

From 1959 he raced British machines, becoming a full-time professional in 1965, when he won his first British title. He shot to world recognition when he signed in 1966 for Yamaha, for whom he was world champion at 125cc in 1967. On the Isle of Man he won TT races at 125cc in 1966 and 250cc 1968, and in 1968 he became the first man to lap the TT course at over 100 mph *160.9 km/h* on a 125cc machine.

A small man at 1.60m and 60kg, he was a flamboyant and hugely popular character. He had a major dispute in 1968 with his team mate Phil Read (qv), who beat him to the world titles at 125cc and 250cc, following which he announced his retirement, but he came back in 1969 to ride for Yawa. He was killed that year while practising for the East German Grand Prix.

David JACK

Football
David Bone Nightingale Jack. b. 3 Apr 1899 Bolton, Gt. Manchester. d. 10 Sep 1958 London.

An inside-forward with superb ball skills and an exceptional goal-scoring talent, Jack started his career with Plymouth Argyle, where his father was manager, but after one season he returned to his home town where he signed for Bolton Wanderers. With Bolton he won two FA Cup winners' medals, scoring the first-ever goal in a Wembley Cup final in 1923, and the only goal in the 1926 final.

At the age of 30, he was signed by Arsenal for £10,890 - the first five figure fee and nearly double the previous transfer record - and with the London club he won a third FA Cup winners' medal in 1930 and was a losing finalist in 1932. He also won three League Championship medals, 1931, 1933-4. In a career total of more than 500 League appearances, he scored nearly 300 goals.

Despite his successes at club level, he only won nine England caps, 1924-32, although this was almost certainly due to his indi-vidualistic character rather than any lack of actual playing ability. He retired in 1934 and was successively manager of Southend 1939-40, Middlesbrough 1944-52 and Shelbourne 1953-5. During the war years he managed Sunderland greyhound stadium.

His father **Bob** (b. 4 Apr 1876 Alloa, d. 6 May 1943 Southend) was a leading player for Bolton before he became the first professional player at Southend, first playing for them in 1903. He was their secretary-manger until his death and led them into the Football League in 1920 and also played bowls for England. His son **David** (1925-90) was a football writer for newspapers in England and Australia.

Tony JACKLIN

Golf
Anthony Jacklin. b. 7 Jul 1944 Scunthorpe, Lincolnshire.

Jacklin was one of the most influential British golfers, and the first great one since Henry Cotton (qv) in the 1930s. Although his time as a truly great player was fleeting, he restored the image of British golf by becoming the first European player of his era to win a US tournament, at Jacksonville in 1968, winning the British Open in 1969 (3rd in 1971-2) and the US Open by seven strokes in 1970. He had 13 victories on the European Tour, including the Dunlop Masters in 1967 and 1973, and three on the US PGA tour.

After his competitive career went into decline, Jacklin was Ryder Cup captain from 1983 to 1989, inspiring winning European squads in 1985, 1987 and 1989. He played 35 matches in seven Cup appearances 1967-79, winning 13, losing 14 and halving 8. In 1969 he was part of great drama at Royal Birkdale. At that time the US had won the last five ties and 12 of the last 13, but Jacklin defeated Jack Nicklaus 4 & 3 on the last morning to keep Britain close. In the deciding match, also against Nicklaus, Jacklin holed a long birdie putt on 17 to get square. He then tied the match by halving Nicklaus on the last green. He also played for England in the World Cups of 1966, 1970-2.

He was awarded the OBE 1970 and CBE 1990. On turning 50 he joined the US Seniors' tour in 1994, when he won one tournament and earned $221,834 for 37th place in the money list!

Brian JACKS

Judo
Brian Albert Thomas Jacks. b. 5 Oct 1946 London.

Introduced to judo by his father Albert, Jacks became Britain's most famous player. He took up the sport at the age of 11 and was London schoolboys' champion in 1960. He went to Japan to learn the skills of the sport in 1961, returning to be European junior champion in 1964 and 1965. At the Olympic Games judo was first included in 1964 and Jacks competed as a lightweight. The sport was not contested in 1968, but Jacks won a bronze medal at middleweight (82kg) in 1972 and competed again in 1976.

His first major championship medals had been bronzes at the 1966 Europeans and 1967 Worlds and he won the European middleweight title in 1970. He was British middleweight champion each year 1973-6 and at 86kg in 1978.

His supreme all-round fitness helped him to an even wider audience at the multisport television Superstars programmes, at which he won the British title in 1978 and 1979 and the European in 1978, when he tied with Dutch hockey player Ties Kruize, and in 1979.

Alec JACKSON

Football
Alexander Skinner Jackson. b. 12 May 1905 Renton, Dumbarton and Clydebank. d. 15 Nov 1946 Cairo, Egypt.

Although winning only 17 caps, he is acknowledged as probably the greatest Scottish right-winger. He was at his brilliant best with three goals for the 'Wembley Wizards' in Scotland's 5-1 victory over England in 1928. After playing for junior clubs in Dumbarton he emigrated to the United States while still a teenager, but returned home to join Aberdeen in 1923. In his first full season he was capped three times and attracted the attention of various English clubs, and in 1925 Herbert Chapman (qv) signed him for Huddersfield Town. Within a year he had won a League Championship medal and he helped Huddersfield to the FA Cup final in 1928 and 1930 where they were the losing finalists in both years.

In September 1930, Alec Jackson went south to Chelsea, but he failed to show his earlier brilliance. He lost his place in the Scottish team and stayed only two seasons at Stamford Bridge before a dispute with the management led to his joining the unknown non-League club, Ashton Nationals. The short-lived Lancashire club soon ran into financial problems and were unable to meet their commitments to Jackson who generously helped them by tearing up his contract and retiring to manage a pub. He later played very briefly for Margate and for Nice in France, but his career effectively ended at the age of 27 when he played his last League game for Chelsea. He was killed in a car accident in Egypt while serving as a major in the army.

Arnold (Strode-) JACKSON

Athletics
Arnold Nugent Strode (Strode-) Jackson. b. 5 Apr 1891 Addlestone, Surrey. d. 13 Nov 1972 Oxford.

A talented all-round sportsman at Malvern College, Jackson won the mile for Oxford in the Varsity match each year 1912-14, and his first victory was just enough to earn him selection for the Olympic Games. In Stockholm he became the surprise winner of the 1500m title in a British record time of 3:56.8, his giant strides taking him past the favourites in the last 30m. He never bothered to enter the AAA Championships and in all he only had some half a dozen top class races. In World War I he became, at 27, the youngest brigadier in the British Army, winning the DSO and three bars, one of only seven officers to be so honoured.

In 1919 he adopted Strode as an additional surname, although retaining it also as a forename. He was a member of the British peace delegation to the Paris Peace Conference and was awarded the CBE for his services before settling in America in 1921, becoming a US citizen in 1945, although he later returned to England.

He was the nephew of **Clement N Jackson** (b. 2 Apr 1846 India. d. 28 Oct 1924), who ran a world record for 120y hurdles, 16.0 in 1865, and who, as Treasurer of Oxford athletics and rugby clubs, played a leading part in building university sport. He was Hon. Treasurer of the AAA from its foundation in 1880 until 1910.

Colin JACKSON

Athletics
Colin Ray Jackson. b. 18 Feb 1967 Cardiff.

After a brilliant junior career, Jackson made an immediate impact in senior ranks as a sprint hurdler, and was the world's best by 1992, although then he came only 7th in the Olympics after sustaining an injury in the second round. In 1993 he was second to his training companion, the Canadian Mark McKoy (who got away with a blatant flying start), in the World Indoor 60m hurdles, but won his first world title at 110m hurdles in the summer at Stuttgart in great style, taking 0.01 off the world record with his time of 12.91. In 1994 he was by far the world's best, being unbeaten at 60m hurdles indoors at which he first tied the world record at 7.36 and then smashed it with 7.30, and outdoors at 110m hurdles, in which he ran 11 times under 13.10 (including two wind assisted), by far the highest number ever, and won gold medals at both Europeans and Commonwealth Games. He won a unique double with both 60m flat and 60m hurdles at the 1994 European Indoors.

At 110m hurdles he was 2nd to his great rival Jon Ridgeon (qv) in the 1985 European Juniors, won the World Junior title and was 2nd in the Commonwealth Games in 1986, was 3rd in the 1987 Worlds, 2nd in the 1988 Olympics, and won both Commonwealth and European titles in 1990. He won the European Cup in 1989, 1991 and 1993 and the World Cup

in 1992. From 1988 to 1993 he set eight Commonwealth and seven European records from 13.23 to 12.91 at 110mh. He also ran a Commonwealth and European record time of 7.41 for 60m hurdles in 1989 and a world best time of 22.63 for 200m hurdles in 1991. At 60m hurdles indoors he won the World silver in 1989 and 1993, European silver 1987 and gold 1989.

A versatile talent, his first two serious long jump competitions were in Welsh internationals, when he improved his best from 7.13m to 7.58w to 7.96w! He was Sports Writers Association British sportsman of the year 1994 and awarded the MBE in 1990.

Other best times: 60m 6.49i (1994), 100m 10.29 (1990), 200m 21.19/21.0 (1988), 21.18w (1989); 50mh 6.48i (1992).

Les JACKSON

Cricket
Herbert Leslie Jackson. b. Whitwell, Derbyshire 5 Apr 1921.

Les Jackson and Cliff Gladwin formed a great new-ball partnership for Deryshire from the late 1940s to 1958. From a mining family, Jackson made his debut on one game in 1948 and broke through to top class with 120 wickets in 1949, when he was also selected for a Test against New Zealand. From then to 1962 he took at least 100 wickets in 10 seasons, with a peak of 160 at 13.61 in 1960 and heading the first-class averages in 1953 and 1958, when his average of 10.99 (from 143 wickets) was the lowest by a centurion since 1894.

He was a master bowler and although it was an era of great strength of English fast bowling, it is nonetheless extarordinary that it was not until 1961, at the age of 40, that he was again asked to play for England. After 1963 he retired to play league cricket very successfully for a decade.

2 Tests 1949-61: 15 runs at 15.00; HS 8; 7 wickets at 22.14, BB 2-26; 1 catch.
First-class 1947-63: 2083 runs at 6.19, HS 39*; 1733 wickets at 17.36, BB 9-17; 136 catches.

Peter JACKSON

Rugby Union
Peter Barrie Jackson. b. 22 Sep 1930
Birmingham.

Jackson was an unorthodox winger who could score from the most unlikely positions. In 20 matches for England he scored six tries, none more memorable than the one against Australia in 1958 which gave England victory in the final minutes of the game.
He first played in an England Trial in 1950 when he was still with Old Edwardians, but did not win his first cap until 1956 by which time he was playing for Coventry. After winning 15 caps he lost his England place after the 1959 season and in the next three years 1960-2 he only played in one international, but in 1963, at the age of 33, he was recalled to the team and played in all four matches when England won the International Championship. On the 1959 British Lions tour he played in both Tests against Australia and in three of the four Tests against New Zealand.
His exciting and deceptive running seemed admirably suited to the style of play espoused by the Barbarians but surprisingly he never played for this famous touring side.

Stanley JACKSON

Cricket
(Rt Hon. Sir) Francis Stanley Jackson. b. 21 Nov 1870 Chapel Allerton, West Yorkshire. d. 9 Mar 1947 Knightsbridge, London.

'Jacker' was a great natural cricketer, a classic batsman, great cover fielder and astute medium-pace bowler who showed supreme ability to rise to the big occasion. He did that most notably in 1905 when he captained England to a 2-0 win with three draws against Australia and personally dominated the series, winning the toss in each match and heading both batting and bowling averages with 492 runs at 70.28 and 13 wickets at 15.46.
Such success came despite the fact that his business career permitted him only one full season with Yorkshire in 1898, when he scored 1566 runs and took 104 wickets. He captained Cambridge University for two years and toured India with Lord Hawke's team in 1892/3, but thereafter did not have the time for touring.
A Conservative MP from 1915-26 and chairman of the party from 1923, he subsequently became Governor of Bengal, and was awarded the GCSI and GCIE. He was President of the MCC 1921.
20 Tests 1893-1905: 1415 runs at 48.79, 5 100s HS 144*; 24 wickets at 33.29, BB 5-52; 10 catches.
First-class 1890-1907: 15,901 runs at 33.83, 31 100s HS 160; 774 wickets at 20.37, BB 8-54; 195 catches.

Alex JAMES

Football
Alexander Wilson James. b. 14 Sep 1901 Mossend, North Lanarkshire. d. 1 Jun 1953 London.

Beginning his career in senior football with Raith Rovers in 1922, James moved to Preston North End after three years and in 1929 he was transferred to Arsenal. At Highbury, Herbert Chapman (qv) used him in a deep-lying role and he developed into one of the finest schemers the game has known. While he was with Arsenal they won the League four times (1931, 1933-5) and the FA Cup twice (1930, 1936).
Surprisingly, he won only eight Scottish caps - four with Preston and four with Arsenal - but this was due to his disagreements with the selectors and certainly not to any lack of ability. Before Chapman changed his style of play, James was an orthodox goal-scoring inside-forward – while with Raith Rovers and Preston North End he scored 80 goals in 257 appearances - but significantly he only scored 26 times in 231 matches for Arsenal. He retired in June 1937 and coached briefly in Poland. After the war he was on the coaching staff at Highbury.
With his baggy shorts he was the subject of many cartoons and caricatures and was one of the best-known sportsmen in Britain between the wars.

Carwyn JAMES

Rugby Union
Carwyn Rees James. b. 2 Nov 1929
Cefneithin, Carmarthenshire. d. 10 Jan
1983 Amsterdam.

As a contemporary of the great Cliff Morgan (qv), his international opportunities were limited. He won his first cap at fly-half in 1958 when he dropped a goal to help Wales beat Australia 9-3 and his second and final cap came against France later that season when he played in the centre, outside Morgan.

Despite his modest international playing career, James had a major influence on the game as a coach. Because of personal differences with the Welsh RU he never coached the national side, but proved his undoubted worth when he was appointed coach to the 1971 Lions in New Zealand. His brilliant tactical thinking and quiet but inspiring leadership guided the Lions to victory in the series. Other coaching successes included the victories of both Llanelli and the Barbarians over the 1972 All Blacks. He later coached in Italy where he did much to enhance the knowledge and capabilities of the emerging players.

On retiring from coaching, he became a highly respected journalist, author and TV commentator.

Mark JAMES

Golf
Mark Hugh James. b. 28 Oct 1953
Manchester.

A boy international in 1971 and English Amateur Champion in 1974, he played on the 1975 Walker Cup team before turning professional at the end of that year. In his first season as a pro he finished 5th in the Open with a final round of 66. He improved to 4th in 1979 (when he achieved his highest position, 3rd, on the European Order of Merit) and to equal 3rd in 1981 and his leading wins include the Irish Open 1979 and 1980, English Open 1989 and 1990 and British Masters 1990. His reputation as a tough match player has helped him to a regular place in the Ryder Cup, in which he has a record of 7 wins,

14 losses and 1 half in six ties 1977-93. His best tie was in 1989, after he had worked hard on remodelling his swing, when his three wins in four matches were vital in enabling Europe to draw with the USA.

He used to be regarded as somewhat tempestuous and had several brushes with the authorities, but is now well respected and a director of the European tour.

European tour winnings 1976-94: £2,252,769.

Andrew JAMESON

Swimming
Andrew David Jameson. b. 19 Feb 1965
Thornton Cleveleys, Lancashire.

In 1986 at the Commonwealth Games Jameson won the 100m butterfly in 54.07, with silver at 4 x 100m medley and bronze at 100m and 4 x 100m freestyle. At the 1982 Commonwealth Games he had been 4th at 200m and 6th at 100m backstroke. He improved his British record to 53.67 in a heat before taking the 1986 World bronze medal and to 53.49 in a heat before winning the 1987 European title (2nd 1985). He won an Olympic bronze medal at 100m butterfly in 1988, having been 5th in 1984. He was also World Student Games champion at 100m freestyle and butterfly in 1987 and won the American 100m butterfly title in 1988 while studying at Arizona State University.

National titles: long-course 100m freestyle and butterfly 1988; short-course 100m butterfly 1982. British long-course records 1984-8: 100m freestyle: four to 50.57 (1988); 50m butterfly: four to 25.00 (1988), 100m butterfly: 11 to 53.30 (1988).

Tommy JAMESON (Ireland)

Squash
Tom Ormsby Jameson. b. 4 Apr 1892
Clonsilla, Co. Dublin. d. 6 Feb 1965 Dún
Laoghaire, Co. Dublin.

After leaving Harrow, Jameson was commissioned into the Rifle Brigade serving in World War I and West Africa and it was not until his regiment returned home in 1919 that he had the chance to display his talents as a fine all-round sportsman. He played cricket for Hampshire (1919-32) and Ireland (1926-8) as a middle-order batsman and leg break and googly bowler. He was the winner of the first two Amateur Squash Championships 1922-3, was the runner-up for the Amateur Rackets singles title in 1924 and he also won the Army rackets title three times, 1922-4.

First class cricket 1919-38: 4675 runs at 26.56, 5 100s HS 133; 252 wickets at 24.03, BB 7-92; 102 catches.

Christine JANES – see TRUMAN

Douglas JARDINE

Cricket
Douglas Robert Jardine. b. 23 Oct 1900 Bombay, India. d. 18 Jun 1958 Montreux, Switzerland.

Amid the controversy of the England tour to Australia in 1932/3, which Jardine captained, and in which he encouraged his fast bowlers to use 'Bodyline' tactics, the fact that he was a middle-order batsman of the highest class is often forgotten. After Winchester, Jardine played for Oxford University 1920-3 and Surrey 1921-33, captaining them in 1932-3. His classic batting was matched by his iron will, and he displayed that to full effect as England captain in 15 Tests between 1931 and 1933, with an unmatched 9-1 win-loss record. Never playing regular county cricket and stopping in his prime at the age of 33, his best seasons were when he led the first-class averages in 1927, 1002 runs at 91.09 and 1928, 1133 at 87.15.

His father Malcolm (1869-1947) was an Oxford Blue for four years, scoring 140 in the 1892 University match, who became Advocate-General of Bombay.

22 Tests 1928-34: 1296 runs at 48.00, 1 100 HS 127; 26 catches.

First-class 1920-48: 14,848 runs at 46.84, 35 100s HS 214; 48 wickets at 31.10, BB 6-28; 188 catches.

Keith JARRETT

Rugby Union and League
Keith Stanley Jarrett. b. 18 May 1948 Newport.

Jarrett, who played his club rugby for Newport, made his international debut for Wales at rugby union at the age of 18 and leapt into the headlines with 19 points as full-back in this match against England. He won a further nine caps as a centre and full-back and also went on the 1968 Lions tour of South Africa before switching to league, signing professional forms for Barrow in 1969. Although he played twice for the Welsh Rugby League team, he never won a GB cap.

He played two first-class cricket matches for Glamorgan in 1967, and his father, Harold, had played cricket for Warwickshire and Glamorgan.

Tony JARRETT

Athletics, Hurdling
Anthony Alexander Jarrett. b. 13 Aug 1968 Enfield, London.

But for Colin Jackson (qv), Jarrett would undoubtedly be acclaimed as one of Britain's sporting superstars. As it is the Haringey man is a magnificent athlete, with a brilliant international record.

With his European Junior gold in 1987, he became the third British athlete to win a major junior title at 110m hurdles in successive seasons. He lined up beside the other two, Colin Jackson and Jon Ridgeon (qv), in the Olympic final in 1988 and was 6th. He also demonstrated his sprinting prowess with relay gold medals at the European Juniors and in the 1989 and 1993 European Cups and the 1994 World Cup. It was at the latter that he won his first big international race, after a splendid series of performances: Olympics 4th 1992, World bronze at both hurdles and relay in 1991 and silvers at both events in 1993; European silver 1990 and bronze 1994; Commonwealth silver 1990 and 1994. Indoors at 60m hurdles he took the European silver in 1990 and world bronze in 1995. He was UK champion at 110m hurdles in 1987 and 1988. He has set four English records at 110m hurdles to the 13.00 that he ran in the 1993 World Championships behind Jackson. Other best times: 100m 10.55 (1993), 10.42w (1987); 200m 20.50 (1995), indoor 60mh 7.42 (1995), 200mh 22.77w (1991).

Jack JARVIS

Horse Racing
(Sir) John Layton Jarvis. b. 28 Dec 1887. d.
19 Dec 1968 Newmarket, Suffolk.

The third son of William Arthur Jarvis
(1852-1921), to whom he was apprenticed
at Newmarket, Jack Jarvis became a most
distinguished trainer and was knighted for
his services to racing in 1967. He rode 121
winners on the flat from his first in 1902
until becoming too heavy in 1909. He rode
a little over jumps and after five years as
assistant to his father became a private
trainer before taking a lease on the Park
Lodge Stable in 1919. Between 1923 and
1953 he sent out the winners of nine
Classics, six of them for Lord Rosebery,
with whose family both he and his father
had a long association. He was leading
trainer in 1939, 1951 and 1953.

His elder brother **William** Rose **Jarvis**
(1885-1943) trained the winners of three
Classics and William's sons **Basil** and
William Joseph **Ryan Jarvis** (b. 19 Nov
1913 Newmarket, d. 25 Jun 1991) were
also notable trainers.

John JARVIS

Swimming
John Arthur Jarvis. b. 24 Feb 1872
Leicester. d. 9 May 1933 St Pancras,
London.

The self-styled 'Amateur Swimming
Champion of the World' took two Olympic
gold medals in 1900, swimming down-
stream in the River Seine in Paris, by huge
margins, winning the 1000m in 13:40.2 by
a margin of 1:13.2 and the 4000m in
58:24.0, nearly 11 minutes ahead of the
runner-up. In 1906 he added a 2nd place at
1 mile and two 3rd places, 400m and 4 x
250m relay. He set many world best times,
having developed, with his professional
rival Joey Nuttall, a special kick, known as
the Jarvis-Nuttall kick for his right overarm sidestroke.

He won numerous long-distance swimming events and 24 ASA titles: 440y 1898
and 1900, 500y and 880y 1898-1901, 1
mile 1897-1902, long distance 1898-1904
and 1906. He was also the plunging cham-

pion in 1904 and a water polo international
1894-1904. After retirement from competition he devoted himself to promoting
lifesaving techniques, and was known as
Professor Jarvis.

Allan JAY

Fencing
Allan Louis Neville Jay. b. 30 Jun 1931
London. né Goldstone.

With four individual medals at major
championships, Jay is Britain's most successful fencer at international level. At the
World Championships, with the foil he
won gold 1959 and bronze 1957 and with
the épée silver in 1959, when only a single
hit prevented him from winning a second
gold medal. He also won silver with the
épée at the 1960 Olympic Games.

After leaving Cheltenham College, he emigrated to Australia with his parents and at
the age of 19 he was a member of the
Australian team which won the gold
medals in the épée team event at the 1950
Commonwealth Games. Shortly afterwards he returned to England to enter St
Edmund Hall, Oxford and following his
graduation in 1954 he pursued a career as
a solicitor.

After his initial success with Australia he
won seven more Commonwealth gold
medals representing England. He competed at five Olympic Games 1952-68, and
at the AFA Championships he won the
épée three times (1952, 1959-60), was 2nd
five times 1954-8, and also won the foil
once, 1963, with five runners-up places He
was later the manager of three British
Olympic fencing teams 1984-92 and he
was awarded the MBE in 1970 for his services to the sport.

Dickie JEEPS

Rugby Union
Richard Eric Gautrey Jeeps. b. 25 Nov
1931 Willingham, Cambridgeshire.

A solid, reliable player, Jeeps went on the
1955 British Lions tour of South Africa as
third choice scrum-half although not yet
capped by England. The quality of his service to fly-half Cliff Morgan (qv) earned

him a place in all four Tests. He toured again with the Lions to Australia and New Zealand in 1959 and South Africa in 1962, playing in a total of 13 Tests which stood as a record until beaten by Willie John McBride (qv).

On his return from his initial visit to South Africa, Jeeps won his first England cap against Wales in 1956 but was immediately dropped and did not command a regular place in the England team until the following season. He went on to win 24 caps before his retirement in 1962 and he captained England in the last 13 matches of his international career.

From school he played for Cambridge City for one season before moving to Northampton in 1949. He also appeared regularly for London Counties and Eastern Counties. After retirement he served as an England selector and was President of the RFU in 1976-7. He was awarded the CBE in 1977 and was Chairman of the Sports Council from 1978-85.

John JEFFREY

Rugby Union
John Jeffrey. b. 25 Mar 1959 Kelso, Borders.

First capped by Scotland in 1984, he did not command a regular place in the international team until 1986. Once established in the Scottish XV, his aggressive back-row play earned him 40 caps until his retirement in 1991. His 11 international tries is a record for a Scottish forward. He toured Australia with the British Lions in 1989 but did not play in a Test match and the following season he played a major role in Scotland's Grand Slam.

A Kelso farmer, he played for the local club throughout his career and when he gave up playing he appeared regularly on TV, providing expert summaries on the international rugby scene.

Albert JENKINS

Rugby Union
Albert Edward Jenkins. b. 11 Mar 1895 Llanelli, Carmarthenshire. d. 7 Oct 1953 Llanelli.

One of the greatest Welsh centres of the 1920s, Jenkins surprisingly only won 14 caps in nine years, 1920-8. He scored four tries and three dropped goals for Wales in addition to kicking seven conversions and three penalties. He played for Llanelli throughout his career, captaining the club for three seasons and in 1923 he captained Wales against Ireland.

David JENKINS

Athletics
David Andrew Jenkins. b. 25 May 1952 Pointe-à-Pitre, Trinidad.

Jenkins showed his awesome talent when becoming the youngest ever European individual event winner in taking 400m in 1971 at 19 years and 80 days in a British record time of 45.45 from the outside lane. Despite a decade as Britain's outstanding one-lap runner, he never quite fulfilled his potential although he was undoubtedly a great relay runner, and a sad postscript to his career came with his conviction for drugs dealing in the USA in 1987. He later admitted that he had used anabolic steroids himself intermittently from the end of 1975. He improved the British record at 400m four times to 44.95, in winning the American title in 1975, a year in which he also won the European Cup 400m. That set him up as an Olympic favourite for 1976, but he disappointed with 7th, a placing he repeated at the 1980 Games. He had been a semi-finalist in 1972, when he won a relay silver medal. At the Europeans he added 2nd at 400m and relay gold in 1974 and a relay silver in 1982, and at the Commonwealth Games he was 4th at 400m and 7th at 200m in 1974 and won a 4 x 100m gold for Scotland in 1978.

He had been AAA youth champion at 200m and 400m in 1968 and junior champion at 100m and 400m in 1969 and won a record six senior 400m titles 1971-6. He was also UK 400m champion in 1980. He also set British records at 200m, 20.66 (1973) and hand-timed 20.3 (1972), 300m 32.44 (1975) and 600m 1:15.6 (1974), with a 100m best of 10.1 (1972). In his 36 British internationals 1969-81 he won a record 44 races (25 individual and 19 relay).

His brother **Roger** (b. 30 Sep 1955) was 5th at 400m with a 4 x 400m bronze medal at the 1973 European Juniors, won the 1974 AAA Junior 400m and ran at the 1974 Europeans and 1978 Commonwealth Games. His best 400m time was 46.49 (1975).

Neil JENKINS

Rugby Union
Neil Roger Jenkins. b. 8 Jul 1971 Church Village, Rhondda Cynon Taff.

The Pontypridd fly-half has become renowned for the accuracy of his place kicking at club and international level, and indeed for the care and time he takes. In his 36 games for Wales from 1991 to the 1995 World Cup he has scored 399 points and has replaced Paul Thorburn (qv) as the leading Welsh points' scorer; among players from the four Home Unions, only Gavin Hastings (qv) has scored more points. Before winning his full international cap, he represented Wales at Youth, Under-21 and 'B' levels. In five years of club rugby to 1995 he scored over 1000 points, with many tries to add to his goals.

Vivian JENKINS

Rugby Union
Vivian Gordon James Jenkins. b. 2 Nov 1911 Port Talbot, Neath and Port Talbot.

An Oxford Blue at rugby (1930-32) and cricket (1933), Jenkins later captained London Welsh (1936-7) at rugby and played cricket for Glamorgan (1931-7). Although playing in the centre for Oxford he won his 14 Welsh caps (1933-9) as a full-back and his try against Ireland in 1934 was the first ever scored by a Welsh full-back in an international. Selected as vice-captain for the 1938 British Lions tour of South Africa, he was restricted by injury to the first match of the series. After a career as a schoolmaster, he became a full-time and highly respected journalist as rugby correspondent for the *Sunday Times*..

Pat JENNINGS

Football
Patrick Anthony Jennings. b. 12 Jun 1945 Newry, Co. Down.

Jennings was an outstanding goalkeeper and Northern Ireland's most capped player. Beginning his career with Newry Town in his native Ireland, he joined Watford in 1963 but within a year moved to Tottenham where he spent 13 seasons before making a surprise move to Arsenal in 1977. While with Spurs he won winner's medal in the FA Cup 1967, League Cup 1971 and 1973, and a UEFA Cup 1972. In 1973 he was voted Footballer of the Year. With Arsenal he won a second FA Cup winners' medal in 1979. He returned to Tottenham in 1993 as a member of the coaching staff.
A superbly efficient but unspectacular player, he was possibly the best keeper in the world at his peak and for many years had no rival for his position in Northern Ireland's team. Making his international debut in 1964, he retired after the 1986 World Cup having won a then world record 119 caps and with a total of 1098 first-class appearances. He was awarded the MBE in 1976 and the OBE in 1987.

Gilbert JESSOP

Cricket
Gilbert Laird Jessop. b. 19 May 1874 Cheltenham, Glos. d. 11 May 1955 Fordington, Dorset.

Jessop was cricket's most outstanding fast scorer, and throughout his career he maintained remarkable rate, achieving many records. His five 200s were made at a rate of just under 100 runs an hour, while in the Hastings Festival of 1907 he made 191 in an hour and a half.
However, 'The Croucher' was far from just a slogger and he was also a candidate as the greatest fielder of his era, with unerring accuracy in throwing from the covers, as well as a fast bowler. He was a fine all-round sportsman, and captained Cambridge University in his final year 1899 and Gloucestershire 1900-12. The best aggregate of his 14 seasons at over 1000 runs was 2323 at 40.75 in 1901, and

he twice achieved the double, with over 100 wickets in 1897 and 1900 (when he also scored 2210 runs). Typically his one Test century, against Australia at The Oval in 1902, was 104 out of 139 made off 76 balls in 75 minutes, still the fastest ever for England, taking hs team to victory. His best ever score of 286 for Gloucestershire v Sussex at Hove on 1 Jun 1903 was made out of 335 in under three hours; his 200 in 120 minutes remains the fastest ever double century by an Englishman.

18 Tests 1899-1912: 569 runs at 21.88, 1 100 HS 104; 24 wickets at 33.29, BB 4-68; 11 catches.

First-class 1894-1914: 26,698 runs at 32.64, 53 100s HS 286; 873 wickets at 22.80, BB 8-29; 463 catches.

His son the Rev Gilbert Jessop also played first-class cricket.

Barry JOHN

Rugby Union
Barry John. b. 6 Jan 1945 Cefneithen, Carmarthenshire.

With his jink, swerve, sidestep and mastery of the drop-kick, John was the archetypal Welsh fly-half, but his superlative skills were admired far beyond Welsh boundaries and even the demanding New Zealand crowds joined in calling him 'The King'.

Beginning his senior career with Llanelli, he moved on to Cardiff where he teamed up with scrum-half Gareth Edwards (qv). After being capped twice in 1966 he only established a regular place in the Welsh team after he first partnered Edwards internationally in 1967. In all but the first two of John's 25 appearances for Wales he partnered Edwards, and all five of his Tests for the British Lions were in partnership with his clubmate. He set many scoring records, which would undoubtedly have been improved on had he not decided to retire at the early age of 27.

Bob JOHN

Football
Robert Frederick John. b. 3 Feb 1899 Barry, Vale of Glamorgan. d. 17 Jul 1982 Barry.

John was left-half in the great Arsenal team of the 1930s which won the Football League (1931, 1933 and 1934), the FA Cup (1930) and were twice losing finalists in the FA Cup (1927, 1932). Although essentially a half-back, he was versatile and adaptable, playing a number of times at full-back and at outside-left in the 1932 FA Cup final. Between 1922 and 1937 he made 421 League appearances for Arsenal which stood as a club record until 1974. After making his debut for Wales in 1922, while still playing in the reserves at Highbury, he went on to win 15 caps until his retirement in 1936 when he became a coach at West Ham until 1939. During the war he worked in Barry Docks but after the war ended he was associated with Torquay United, Crystal Palace and Cardiff City in various coaching and administrative capacities.

Derek JOHNSON

Athletics
Derek James Neville Johnson. b. 5 Jan 1933 London.

Johnson displayed his immense talent early, running a British age-17 best of 48.8 to win the AAA junior 440y in 1950. He improved his best to an English Native record 47.9 in 1954 and to 47.7 in 1958, but it was at 800m that he achieved his greatest distinction. In 1954 he won the Empire Games 880y, with a second gold medal as his 46.9 final leg took the British 4 x 440y team to victory, and set a British record of 1:47.4 when 4th in the European 800m. In 1956 he took the Olympic silver medal when narrowly beaten in a great 800m race by Tom Courtney (USA), and he further improved the British record to 1:46.9 and 1:46.6 in 1957. In 1958 he won a silver medal on the British 4 x 440y team at the Empire Games, but after running 3:42.9 for 1500m in 1959 contracted tuberculosis and spent a year in a sanatorium. He displayed great tenacity in shaking off the illness and returning to run 800m in 1:50.0 in 1963.

Other best times: 1000m 2:20.4 (1956), 1 mile 4:05.0 (1957), 440y hurdles 53.7 (1956), 3000m steeplechase 9:16.8

(1957).A graduate of Oxford University, he became the leading figure in the International Athletes Club and the South of England AAA.

James JOHNSON

Figure Skating
James Henry Johnson. b. 1874 Chorlton, Cheshire. d. 15 Nov 1921 London.

In 1908 James Johnson and his wife, Phyllis, won silver medals in the pairs at the World Championships and the Olympic Games and they went on to win the World Championship (1909, 1912). They remain the only British couple ever to win the World pairs title twice. They were also the British champions in 1914.
As a director of a Wigan colliery he enjoyed ample means and lived in London in order to pursue his passion for skating. Sadly, his career was curtailed by ill health and he died at the early age of 46.

Joe JOHNSON

Snooker
Joe Johnson. b. 29 Jul 1952 Bradford.

In 1978 Johnson was runner-up for the world amateur title just after making an official world record break for an amateur with 140 in the final of an event televised by Tyne Tees television. He turned professional a year later and made his way in the pro ranks. It was, nonetheless, a considerable surprise when his first big tournament win came in 1986 with the biggest of them all as he defeated Steve Davis 18-12 to take the Embassy World Championship. Until then his best performance had been in the 1983 Professional Players Tournament, where he lost 8-9 to Tony Knowles in the final. In 1987 he won the Scottish Masters and again reached the world final, although this time Davis won 18-14. He had been British junior champion in 1972.

Phyllis JOHNSON

Figure Skating
Phyllis Wyatt Johnson. b. – Dec 1886. d. 2 Dec 1967 Tunbridge Wells, Kent. née Squire, later Mrs Waite.

In addition to her successes in the pairs with her husband, James (qv), Phyllis Johnson was a notable performer in the singles. As Miss Squire, she placed 2nd in the British championship and after her marriage she was a three-time medallist at the World Championships placing 2nd in 1913 and 3rd in 1912 and 1914. At the 1921 British Championships, which were open to both men and women, she finished first but the official title was awarded to Kenneth Beaumont who was the leading male competitor.
After her husband had given up the sport because of ill health, she partnered Basil Williams and at the 1920 Olympic Games after she had placed 4th in the singles, they won the bronze medals in the Pairs.

Ralph JOHNSON

Fencing
William Ralph Johnson. b. 3 Jun 1948 London.

With six AFA épée titles (1968, 1982, 1984-5, 1987, 1990) he equalled the record of Teddy Bourne (qv) and holds the record for the longest span of titles, 22 years. He competed in four Olympic Games (1968-84) and won a gold medal in the épée team event at the 1970 Commonwealth Games. He is a solicitor.

Tebbs Lloyd JOHNSON

Walking
Terence 'Tebbs' Lloyd Johnson. b. 7 Apr 1900 Melton Mowbray, Leics. d. 26 Dec 1984 Coventry.

By taking bronze at the 50km walk in 1948, when he was 48 years 115 days, Johnson became the oldest ever Olympic medallist at athletics. A year later he became the oldest national walking champion taking the RWA 50km, 18 years after he had first won this title, which he also won in 1934, and 22 years after his first RWA title, the 20 miles in 1927, a title he won again in 1931 and 1934. His span of placings in the first three at national championships is a record 28 years from his 3rd in 1923 to 2nd in 1951, both at 20 miles. Johnson also competed at the 1936

Olympics, 17th at 50 km. He became a national coach.

Best times: 20km 1:37:55.4 (1934), 50km 4:36:02 (1948).

Trish JOHNSON

Golf
Patricia Johnson b. 17 Jan 1966 Bristol.

After a fine amateur career, Johnson has competed with much success in the USA with a notably sharp short game. In 1993 she not only won four events on the European tour, but became the first European to win two successive tournaments in the USA on her way to 10th place on the money list.

As an amateur she was English Ladies' amateur champion and stroke-play champion in 1985, and in 1986 was the top points scorer on either side in the Curtis Cup and also played for England in the World Cup, in which she was 3rd. She turned professional and in 1987 was the top newcomer on the European tour, winning three times. She was the Order of Merit leader in 1990 and played on the Solheim Cup teams of 1990, 1992 and 1994, with a disappointing record of one win, one half and seven losses.

Harry JOHNSTON

Football
Henry Johnston. b. 26 Sep 1919 Droylsden. Manchester. d. 12 Oct 1973.

After signing for Blackpool as an amateur in 1935 he turned professional the following year and remained with the club until his retirement in 1955. A calm and constructive half-back, he was at his best immediately after World War II winning ten England caps 1946-53 and leading Blackpool to three FA Cup finals. After losing at Wembley in 1948 and 1951 they finally won the trophy in 1953. An inspiring club captain, he was voted Footballer of the Year in 1951. Following his retirement, he was manager of Reading 1955-63 and later returned to Blackpool as chief scout and caretaker manager.

Margaret JOHNSTON (Ireland)

Bowls
Margaret Johnston. b. 2 May 1943 Londonderry.

A nurse by profession, Johnston started bowling on a short mat in 1964 and outdoors in 1979. That year, competing for Ballymoney, she reached the final of the Irish singles and she won her first national title with the Irish fours in 1983, taking both singles and pairs a year later. In 1985 she won the British Isles titles at both pairs and singles.

Reaching top world class, at the World Championships she won the pairs with Phyllis Nolan for Ireland in 1988, and in 1992 not only retained her title but also won the singles. She won a Commonwealth Games singles bronze in 1990 and was World Indoor champion in 1988 and 1989 and lost in the final in 1991. She was awarded the MBE 1991.

Ann JONES

Tennis
Adrianne Shirley Jones. née Haydon. b. 7 Oct 1938 Birmingham.

The first left-hander to win the women's singles at Wimbledon, Jones took the singles and also won the mixed doubles in 1969, when she was voted BBC Sports Personality of the Year. She had previously been a singles finalist in 1967 and a semifinalist on six other occasions, and had won the junior title in 1956. Her other major victories came at the French Championships where she won the singles 1961 and 1966 and the women's doubles 1963, 1968-9. She was a member of 13 Wightman Cup teams (1957-67, 1971, 1975) winning 16 (10 singles, 6 doubles) of her 32 rubbers. In the Federation Cup she played in 18 ties, winning 21 (10 singles, 11 doubles) of her 34 rubbers.

Initially, Ann Haydon was an outstanding table tennis player, representing England 69 times and she reached five World finals but was runner-up on each occasion: singles 1956, women's doubles 1953 and 1956, and mixed doubles 1955-6. She was English junior champion three times in the singles 1953, 1955-6 and won the English Open doubles with Diane Rowe in 1956.

In August 1962 she married 'Pip' Jones, a Birmingham businessman, and following her retirement from the game she became a leading administrator.

Bryn JONES

Football
Brynmor Jones. b. 2 Feb 1912 Pentard, Merthyr. d. 18 Oct 1985 Wood Green, London.

After playing for a variety of non-league clubs, he was signed by Wolves in 1933 and some fine performances at inside-forward led to his transfer to Arsenal in 1938 for a then record fee of £14,000. The attendant publicity, which included questions asked in the House of Commons about the "outrageous" state of transfer fees, affected his play and just as Arsenal were beginning to get a return on their investment war was declared. Jones stayed at Highbury until 1949 and won 17 Welsh caps 1935-48, with a further eight wartime internationals. He then moved to Norwich but retired from the game on health grounds 18 months later. This was the end of his active involvement with the game and he took a newsagent's shop at Stoke Newington, near the Arsenal ground.

Cliff JONES

Football
Clifford William Jones. b. 7 Feb 1935 Swansea.

The son of Welsh international, Ivor (1899-1974), and the nephew of Bryn (1912-85), Jones fully lived up to his distinguished pedigree. His dazzling speed on the wing and his spectacular headed goals made him both popular with the crowd and feared by opposing defences.

After winning Welsh international honours at schoolboy and youth level he signed for Swansea in 1952, winning his first full cap in 1954 before moving to Tottenham in 1958 for £25,000, then a record fee for a winger. A broken leg in pre-season training delayed his debut for Spurs but once fit he became a regular member of possibly

the greatest team in the club's history. They won the League Championship in 1961, the FA Cup in 1961-2 and 1967, and the European Cup Winners' Cup in 1963. Jones was only a substitute for the 1967 Cup Final and, although not called on to play, he became the first substitute to win an FA Cup winners' medal. After making more than 300 League appearances for Tottenham, he was given a free transfer as a reward for his services to the club to Fulham, where he won the last of his 59 Welsh caps in 1968. At the time, only his teammate for Swansea and Wales, Ivor Allchurch (qv) had won more.

In 1970 he retired from League football but sadly a failed business venture cost him all the money he had earned at Tottenham and he found it necessary to continue with a number of non-League clubs. In turn, he played for King's Lynn, Wealdstone, Bedford Town and Cambridge City before finally finishing his playing days with Wingate in the Athenian League. For a while he returned to sheet metal working, a trade to which he had been apprenticed before becoming a professional footballer, but eventually he found more fitting and congenial employment and he became a sports master at a London school.

Cliff JONES

Rugby Union
William Clifford Jones. b. 12 Mar 1914 Porth, Rhondda Cynon Taff. d. 27 Nov 1990 Bonvilston, Vale of Glamorgan.

Jones was a brilliant fly-half whose scintillating attacking play brought the best out of the great Welsh three-quarter line of the 1930s. His understanding with centre Wilf Wooller was particularly effective and they played some superb rugby together for Cardiff, Cambridge University, Barbarians and Wales. He was capped 13 times (1934-8) and was one of the Welsh team that beat the All Blacks 13-12 in 1935. He won a Blue in each of his three years at Cambridge (1933-5) and later qualified as a barrister. His playing career was ended by injury but he served as a Welsh selector from 1956-78 and as President of the

Welsh Rugby Union during the Centenary year of 1981. He was awarded the OBE.

Courtney JONES

Ice Dance

Courtney John Lyndhurst Jones. b. 30 April 1933 Poole, Dorset.

Jones was the winner of four successive world ice dance titles with two different partners, in 1957-8 with June Markham and in 1959-60 with Doreen Denny (qv). Like other British champions of the time he received greater recognition abroad than he did at home. Denny and Jones won three British and European titles, 1959-61, and they would almost certainly have won their third (and Jones' fifth) world title in 1961 but the championships were cancelled following the loss of the entire US team in an air crash.

Jones retired in 1961 when his partner turned professional, but he returned in 1963 when, with Peri Horne, a former Olympic figure skater, they introduced two new dances which soon became internationally accepted. A freelance fashion designer, he has been President of the National Ice Skating Association from 1992 and was awarded the MBE 1980 and the OBE in 1989 for his services to the sport.

Ivor JONES

Rugby Union

Ivor Edgwad Jones. b. 10 Dec 1901 Loughor, Swansea. d. 16 Nov 1982 Swansea.

A furnaceman in a South Wales steelworks, he was on the losing side in his first two internationals for Wales in 1924 and had to wait until 1927 before winning his third cap. Once he had regained his place he won his last 14 caps in consecutive matches and captained Wales three times. Although losing his place in the Welsh XV he was invited to tour South Africa with the 1924 British Lions but declined the honour.

He later went to Australia and New Zealand with the 1930 Lions where his performances are rated among the best ever seen from a British Lion of any era. An immensely versatile player, he played everywhere in the backs, except fly-half, at some stage of the tour. But in all five Tests he made a massive contribution as a loose forward although he deputised as scrum-half in the second Test after Paul Murray was injured.

Despite his brilliant play with the Lions he was never again selected for Wales although he was outstanding with Llanelli for another five seasons, scoring more than 1200 points in his career with the club. He captained Llanelli against the visiting All Blacks in 1935 and his omission from the national team astounded the New Zealanders. There is little doubt that he was the victim of intransigent Welsh rugby politics. Whatever the differences, they were eventually forgiven or forgotten and after the war Ivor Jones served as a Welsh selector, delegate to the International Board (1962-5) and as President of the Welsh Rugby Union (1968-9). He was awarded the CBE for his services to the game.

Jack JONES

Rugby Union

John Phillips Jones. b. 2 Mar 1886 Pontypool, Torfaen. d. 19 Mar 1951 Llantarnam, Torfaen.

Jones was a direct running centre or winger with an excellent eye for scoring opportunities either for himself or, by perfectly timed passes, for his team-mates. He went on the Anglo-Welsh tour of New Zealand in 1908, where he played in all three Tests, before he had been capped by Wales. On his return he won the first of his 14 Welsh caps with four of his six international tries coming in successive matches in 1909-10: France (2 tries), Ireland (1t) and France (1t).

On the full British Lions of South Africa in 1910 he again played in all three Tests, leading the tourists to victory in the first Test when he took over the captaincy from the injured Tom Smyth. He began his career with Pontypool before moving to Newport, but after the war he returned to Pontypool and, at the age of 33, he was recalled to Welsh side for two matches in

1920. Two of his brothers also played for Wales, **David** (1881-1936) and **James** (1883-1964), each winning one cap.

Joey JONES

Football
Joseph Patrick Jones. b. 4 Mar 1955 Llandudno, Aberconwy and Colwyn.

Winning 72 caps between 1975 and 1986, Jones became the most capped Welsh player of all time, a record taken from him by Peter Nicholas and then Neville Southall (qv). Joining Wrexham from school in 1973 he moved to Liverpool after two years where he played a key role as full-back in the side that won the European Cup 1977, the Football League 1976-7, and were runners-up in the FA Cup 1977. In 1978 he went back to Wrexham and then signed for Chelsea in 1982. After he had helped them regain First Division status the following year he moved on to Huddersfield in 1985.

Almost inevitably, after two seasons with Huddersfield he returned to Wrexham once again and ended his playing days with the club where he began his somewhat nomadic career. Despite his League and Cup successes and his abundance of international honours he remains an underrated player, but a most dedicated one.

Jonathan JONES

Powerboating
Jonathan Jones. b. 1967.

Jones was the world champion at powerboating in formula two 1986 and 1989 and at the revised specfication formula one in 1991. He was runner-up for the world title in 1994. In 1985 the Harmsworth trophy was contested by two-boat national teams at Formula Two for outboard engines, and he won in January and December.

Ken JONES

Rugby Union
Kenneth Jeffrey Jones. b. 30 Dec 1921 Blaenavon, Torfaen.

An Olympic sprinter, Jones used his speed to great effect on the wing for Newport and Wales. Between 1947 and 1957 he won 44 Welsh caps – 43 of them in successive matches – and he played for the British Lions in three Tests in New Zealand in 1950. For Wales he scored 17 tries and 16 for the Lions, including two in Tests.

Although speed was a vital part of his game, he also possessed a deceptive swerve and a solid defence. At the time of his retirement his total of 47 international caps (including 3 for the Lions) was a record in world rugby. In athletics he was 3rd at 220y and 6th at 100y in the 1954 Empire Games; semi-finalist at 100m and sprint relay silver medallist in the 1948 Olympics; and Welsh champion seven times at 100y and eight times at 220y between 1946 and 1954. Best times: 100y 9.8 (1949), 100m 10.6 (1948), 200m 21.7 (1949). He was awarded the MBE.

Lewis JONES

Rugby League
Benjamin Lewis Jones. b. 11 Apr 1931 Gorseinon, Swansea.

Capped 10 times by Wales from his debut as an 18 year-old in 1950 and twice by the British Lions as a rugby union player, he caused a surprise by signing professional forms for Leeds in November 1952 for the then record fee of £6,000. Although a fractured arm, sustained within two months of his switching codes, delayed his impact on the League game, he went on to set many scoring records, including 278 points on the 1954 British tour of Australia, and a season's record 496 points (194 goals, 36 tries) in 1956/7. This included a British Test record 21 points on his home debut against France on 26 Jan 1957.

After playing 15 times for Great Britain (66 goals, 147 points) he left for Australia in 1964 and at the age of 33 became the player-coach with Wentworthville in Sydney. He was equally at home as a stand-off, centre, full-back or winger and with his sidestep, jink, dummy and change of pace he was the archetypal Welsh three-quarter.

His elder brothers were also good rugby

players, Cliff at fullback for Neath, Swansea and Llanelli before the war, and Alan, a lock forward, captained Llanelli in 1952/3.

Mandy JONES

Cycling
Amanda Jones. b. 24 Mar 1962.

From 1980 to 1982 Jones, who competed for the West Pennine Club of Rochdale, burst across the women's cycling scene. At unpaced standing start she set a British record for 3000m in 1980 at 4:10.8. Then on 30 June 1981 at Leicester she set all the British records from 1 km to the hour: 1km 1:21.2, 3km 4:05.1, 5km 6:52.4, 10km 14:01.1, 20km 28:31.3 and 41.322 km in the hour. She was 3rd in the 1980 World road race championship, but was bitterly disappointed not to medal in 1981. She bounced back, however, and having won her third successive national pursuit title on 31 Jul 1982, came back on to the track at Leicester two hours later to set a world record for 5000m of 6:41.75 and take her British 3km record to under 4 minutes, with 3:59.701 (although she had recorded 3:56.376 in a pursuit race). She sealed a great year by winning the world road race title at Leicester.

She was national road race champion in 1983, when she was also 4th in the World road race, and at 25 miles in 1990-1.

Robert JONES

Rugby Union
Robert Nicholas Jones. b. 10 Nov 1965 Trebanos, Swansea.

After making his debut in 1986, Jones missed only one international in the next five seasons and his understanding with fly-half Jonathan Davies (qv), whom he partnered in 22 internationals, was the redeeming feature of some mediocre Welsh performances at the time.

He captained both Swansea and Wales and was at his best on the 1989 Lions tour of Australia. Playing in all three Tests, his acerbic duels with Australian scrum-half, Nick Farr-Jones, reflected the robust nature of the Test series which, with Robert Jones marginally taking the honours in his personal duel, the Lions won 2-1.

An outstanding kicker for position in attack, he was dropped by Wales for the final game of the 1993 Five Nations Championship, although many hold the view that he lost his place prematurely. Despite this loss of confidence by the Welsh selectors, he was chosen as a replacement for the injured Scot, Gary Armstrong, on the 1993 Lions tour although he didn't play in the Tests in New Zealand. He was recalled to the Welsh team for the match against France at the start of the 1995 Five Nations Championship and in the next match against England he became one of only three Welshman to win 50 caps. By the end of the 1995 World Cup he had taken his total to 54. He is the son-in-law of **Clive Rowlands** (b. 14 May 1938) who won 14 caps as the Welsh scrum-half 1963-5.

Steve JONES

Marathon
Stephen Henry Jones. b. 4 Aug 1955 Tredegar, Blaenau Gwent.

With a useful track racing pedigree behind him, Jones moved sensationally into the limelight by winning the 1984 Chicago marathon in the world's best ever time, 2:08:05. He had dropped out at Chicago in 1983 at his only previous attempt at the event. In 1984 he had earlier been 3rd at the World Cross-country and at 10,000m won AAA titles on track and road and placed 8th at the Olympics. He consolidated his status with marathon wins at London (2:08:16) and Chicago (2:07:13) in 1985 after Carlos Lopes (Por) had improved the world's best time to 2:07:12 at Rotterdam.

Jones ran a UK half-marathon best, 60:59, when second to Mike Musyoki (Ken) in the 1986 Great North Run and he won his first major championships medal at 10,000m at the Edinburgh Commonwealth Games, but after leading the European marathon by two minutes struggled home suffering from dehydration. He returned in 1987 to place 2nd in the Boston marathon, but was injured in a fall in the UK 10,000m and missed the World Championships. Ninth in the 1988 Boston, he then left his job as a corporal air frame technician in the Royal Air Force (in which he had served for 20 years) and returned to form to win the New York marathon in 2:08:20, but that proved to be his last sub 2:10 time. He was 4th at the 1990 Commonwealth Games marathon. He now lives in Boulder, Colorado.

On the track he set Welsh records at 5000m 13:18.6 (1982) and 10,000m 27:39.14 (1983) and had made his British international debut at the 3000m steeplechase at which his best was 8:32.00 (1980).

Other best times: 1500m 3:42.3 (1982), 1 mile 4:00.6 (1980), 3000m 7:49.80 (1984), 2 miles 8:26.71 (1980).

Jo JORDAN – see CHAMBERLAIN

Tony JORDAN

Badminton
Anthony Derek Jordan. b. 12 Jun 1934 Birmingham.

An All-England junior triple champion in 1952, he went on to become a stalwart of the British game. He was the first man to win 100 caps (97 consecutively) for England from his international debut at 17 in 1951 to 1970, and he played in seven Thomas Cup series. He won the All-England mixed doubles four times, 1956, 1958, 1964, 1968, with three different partners and at the English National Championships 1964-70 he won five doubles titles (four men's, one mixed), having earlier won three singles, five men's doubles and four mixed doubles titles at the English Invitation Tournament 1954-63. He also won the mixed doubles with Sue Whetnall at the first European Championships in 1968 and at the Commonwealth Games he won a mixed doubles silver medal in 1966. He was awarded the MBE for his services to the game in 1970.

David JUDGE (Ireland)

Hockey
Harold David Judge. b. 19 Jan 1936 Dublin.

A full-back with Three Rock Rovers, Judge's 124 international caps (1957-78) was an Irish record, although since surpassed by William McDonnell and Stephen Martin (qqv). He also won 15 caps for Great Britain, including five matches at the 1964 Olympics and he captained both GB and Ireland.

Peter KANE

Boxing
né Peter Cain. b. 29 Apr 1918 Heywood, Gt. Manchester. d. 23 Jul 1991 Leigh, Gt. Manchester.

Initially a fairground fighter, Kane took out a professional licence as soon as he reached the age of 16 and soon established a reputation as a devastating puncher. He won 23 of his first 27 professional bouts by a KO and by October 1937 he had earned a fight with fellow-Scotsman, Benny Lynch (qv), for the World and British flyweight title. Lynch won by a KO in the 13th round but he failed to make the weight in a return match five months later and the non-title bout, which replaced the scheduled world championship fight, resulted in a draw.

Kane finally took the world title in 1938 by outpointing Jackie Jurich (USA) after which he usually fought as a bantamweight. After some difficulty, he made the weight to defend his world flyweight title in 1943 but was knocked out in the first round by Jackie Paterson, yet another superb Scottish flyweight. Kane immediately returned to the bantamweight division and held the European title from 1947-8.

Career record 1932-43: 109 contests. Won 98 (58 KO), Drew 7, Lost 3, No contest 1.

Vince KARALIUS

Rugby League
Vince Karalius. b. 15 Oct 1932 Widnes, Cheshire.

A player of impressive strength, his voracious appetite for the physical side of the game earned him the nickname 'Wild Bull of the Pampas'. He also had excellent ball handling skills and was the ideal loose-forward. Signed by St Helens from the amateur game in 1951 he led them to victory in the Challenge Cup final in 1961 and after moving to Widnes he won his second Cup winners' medal, again as captain, in 1964.

Winning 10 caps with Widnes and two with St Helens, he was at his best on the 1958 tour of Australia and New Zealand where he played in all five Tests and was a clear winner of the physical confrontation with the Australian 'hard men'. In the second Test he took over as stand-off, after captain Alan Prescott (qv) broke his arm, and his devastating tackling and charging attacks provided much of the inspiration which enabled GB to level the series before winning the final Test.

After retirement from the game he built up the scrap business that he had started with his brother. The sale of this enabled him to retire in considerable comfort, but before and after that he coached the Widnes teams that won the 1975 and 1984 Challenge Cups.

Ronnie KAVENAGH (Ireland)

Rugby Union
James Ronald Kavenagh. b. 21 Jan 1931 Dublin.

An exceptionally tough and durable loose forward, Kavenagh made his international debut against France in 1953 and closed his career in 1962 after winning 35 Irish caps. He was, at the time, Ireland's most capped forward but he was surprisingly passed over for the Lions tours in both 1955 and 1959. His brother, **Patrick** (b. 2 Sep 1929 Dublin), also won two caps for Ireland (1952, 1954). Both played for Dublin Wanderers and both also represented Ireland at water polo.

Moss KEANE (Ireland)

Rugby Union
Maurice Ignatius Keane. b. 27 Jul 1948 Currow, Co. Kerry.

Although not outstanding in any particular aspect of the game, Keane's all-round abilities as a hard-working forward won him 51 caps for Ireland 1974-84. He was only on the winning side in 17 of these matches but Ireland won the Five Nations Championship in 1974 and 1982 and shared the title in 1983. Called up for the British Lions tour of New Zealand in 1977 after Geoff Wheel failed a fitness test, he played in one Test. A former Gaelic footballer, he was the first to win international rugby union honours after the eligibility rules were changed.

Roy KEANE (Ireland)

Football
Roy Maurice Keane. b. 10 Aug 1971 Cork.

Signed by Nottingham Forest from the Irish club Cobh Ramblers in 1990, Keane was transferred to Manchester United in 1993 for a then British transfer record of £3.75 million and was a key member of the team which took the League and Cup double in 1994. A strong-running and energetic midfield player he played for Ireland in the 1994 World Cup finals and has won a total of 28 caps 1991-5, with one goal.

Kevin KEEGAN

Football
Joseph Kevin Keegan. b. 14 Feb 1951 Armthorpe, nr Doncaster, South Yorkshire.

Outstanding as a forward or in midfield, Keegan epitomised the modern player who reaped rich financial rewards from his skills. Signing as an apprentice for Scunthorpe United in 1967, he became a full professional 12 months later and in 1971 moved to Liverpool where he played on the winning team in the FA Cup 1974, the European Cup 1977, the UEFA Cup 1973 and 1976, and the Football League, 1973, 1976-7. In the summer of 1977 he left Liverpool for SV Hamburg and helped them to the Bundesliga title in 1979 and to the final of the European Cup in 1980. He returned to England to join Southampton in 1980 and after two years at the Dell he moved to Newcastle United where he remained until his retirement in May 1984. He returned there as manager in 1992 with immediate success as they won Division One in 1992/3 and were third in the Premier League 1993/4.

He won 63 caps for England 1972-82, and captained the team on many occasions. He was equally adept at scoring or creating goals and it is testimony to his great talent that he won five Footballer of the Year awards: European 1978-9 (only the second player, after Johan Cruyff (Hol), to win this award in successive years), English 1976 and 1982, and West German 1978. He was awarded the OBE in 1982.

Peter KEENAN

Boxing
Peter Keenan. b. 8 Aug 1928 Anderston, Glasgow.

Keenan is one of only six fighters to have won two Lonsdale Belts outright. A Scottish ABA flyweight champion, he fought as a bantamweight on turning professional, winning the British title in May 1951 and the European title four months later. In January 1952 he met Vic Toweel (SAf) for the World title but lost on points and later in the year he lost his European title.
In June 1963 he regained his European crown but lost both his British and European titles in October when a surprise defeat by John Kelly put paid to his chances of a second challenge for the World title. The titles continued to change hands when Keenan beat Kelly in a return bout, but then in January 1959 Freddie Gilroy took over as champion with an 11th round victory over Keenan who immediately announced his retirement from the ring at the end of the fight.
Career record 1948-59: 66 contests. Won 54 (23 KO), Drew 1, Lost 11.

Paul KELLEWAY

Horse Racing
Paul Anthony Kelleway. b. 31 Aug 1940 London.

As a jumps jockey, Kelleway rode *What A Myth* to victory in the Whitbread Gold Cup in 1966 and the Cheltenham Gold Cup in 1969 and he won the Champion Hurdle on *Bula* in 1971 and 1972. He rode 48 winners in his best season of 1970/1. He took a trainers' licence in 1977 and trains at Newmarket.

His daughter **Gay** Marie Kelleway (b. 19 Dec 1963 Cranleigh, Surrey) was the champion female jockey each year 1983-5, having been top amateur in 1982. She became the first lady to ride a winner at Royal Ascot, and has trained in New Zealand from 1988 and then in England from 1991.

Bob KELLY

Football
Robert Kelly. b. 16 Nov 1893 Ashton-in-Makerfield, Gt. Manchester. d. 22 Sep 1969 Fylde, Lancashire.

Adept at beating the opposition with his dribbling skills or with his elusive swerve, Kelly was equally at home at inside- or outside-right. To these attributes he added a deadly shot in either foot and was one of the most talented forwards of his generation. After signing for Burnley in 1913 he stayed with the club until 1925 when he went to Sunderland for a then record fee of £6,550. Moves to Huddersfield (1927), Preston North End (1932) and Carlisle (1935) followed before he took over as manager of Stockport County 1936-9. After the war he was the trainer for Sporting Club de Portugal and the manager of Barry Town.
He was capped 14 times by England 1920-8, helped Burnley to the League Championship in 1921 and for Huddersfield he was twice on the losing side in the FA Cup final, 1928 and 1930.

Margaret KELLY - HOHMANN

Swimming
Margaret Mary Kelly. b. 22 Sep 1956 Liverpool. Later Mrs Hohmann.

In 1988 Margaret Hohmann, mother of a two-year-old boy, came back to compete at the Olympic Games, eight years after she had retired, having won an Olympic silver medal at the medley relay and placed 4th at 100m breaststroke in Moscow in 1980. She had been 7th at both 100m and 200m at the 1976 Olympics. In 1989 she broke 70 seconds for the 100m breaststroke for the first time, with a short course 69.68 and also broke her British short-course record for 50m with 32.30. She had set three British short-course 100m breaststroke records in 1978-80 and six at 200m from 1976 to 2:32.62 in 1980. In long-course pools she set British breaststroke records: nine at 100m from 1:15.48 in 1975 to 1:11.73 in 1978 and five at 200m from 2:42.13 in 1975 to 2:36.98 in 1978, improving her best times to 1:11.48 and 2:36.46 in 1980.

Kelly joined Bootle Swimming Club in 1966 and later swam for Wigan Wasps. In 1978 she won Commonwealth silver medals at 100m and medley relay and bronze at 200m, and a World bronze at 100m (5th at 200m).

ASA long-course champion at 100m 1975-80, 200m 1975, 1977-8, 1980; short-course 100m/110y 1976-80 and 1987, 200m/220y 1976, 1979-80. She was awarded the MBE in 1979.

Sean KELLY (Ireland)

Cycling
John James Kelly. b. 24 May 1956 Curraghduff, Co. Waterford.

Kelly was ranked as world No.1 cyclist in the computer rankings from October 1984 to May 1989. This was based mainly on his wins in the one-day classics, of which he won 12 in his career from a total of 193 wins in his professional career from 1977 to 1994. He won 32 races in 1984 and 29 in 1986 and became the first World Cup series winner in 1989. He was not as formidable in the major tours because he was only an average climber, and his biggest disappointment was his inability to win the Tour de France, although he was points winner a record four times (1982-3, 1985, 1989), his best placing being 4th in 1985 and he had five stage wins 1978-82 as well as wearing the yellow jersey for one day in 1983. His greatest success has come in the Paris-Nice stage race, which he won for an amazing seven consecutive years 1982-8. He had first made an impression with the All-Ireland junior road race titles of 1972 and 1973.

Other major victories: Vuelta à España 1988 (and points jersey 1980, 1985-6, 1988); Tour de Suisse 1983; Milan-San Remo 1986, 1992; Ghent-Wevelgem 1988; Paris-Roubaix 1984, 1986; Liège-Bastogne-Liège 1984, 1989; Grand Prix de Nations 1986; Paris-Tours 1984; Tour of Lombardy 1983, 1985, 1991.

Jack KELSEY

Football
John Alfred Kelsey. b. 19 Nov 1929 Llansamlet, nr Swansea. d. Mar 1992.

Regarded by many as the best ever Welsh goalkeeper, Kelsey made 41 out of a possible 44 international appearances for them 1954-62. His career was then ended prematurely when he received a severe back injury against Brazil. He made 327 League appearances for Arsenal 1949-62, with a Championship winners' medal in 1953. He stayed with Arsenal, running their shop, and retiring in 1989 as their commercial manager.

Howard KENDALL

Football
Howard Kendall. b. 22 May 1946 Ryton, Tyne and Wear.

A talented midfield player, Kendall won Schoolboy, Youth and Under-23 honours for England and played for Preston North End in the 1964 FA Cup Final at 17 years 345 days, the youngest-ever player to appear in a Wembley final. Following the auspicious start to his career it is surprising that he never went on to win a full England cap.

He spent five seasons with Preston North End before moving to Everton in 1967 where he was on the losing side in the FA Cup final for a second time in 1968, but he won a League Championship medal in 1970. From Everton he moved on to Birmingham City in 1974 and Stoke City before becoming a successful player-manager at Blackburn Rovers in 1979. He returned to Everton as a full-time manager in 1981, leading them to League titles (1985, 1987), the FA Cup (1984) and the European Cup Winners' Cup (1985). In 1987 he took over as manager of Athletic Bilbao (Spain) and then went to Manchester City before returning to Everton for a less successful spell in 1990-3. He managed Xanthi in Greece, and was briefly manager of Notts County, Jan - Apr 1995.

John KENDALL-CARPENTER

Rugby Union
John MacGregor Kendall-Carpenter. b. 25 Sep 1925 Cardiff. d. 23 May 1990 Wellington, Somerset.

Kendall-Carpenter was an inspirational leader, who won 23 caps for England 1949-54 as a prop or No. 8. Headmaster of Wellington School, Somerset for 17 years, he died suddenly in his last term before his planned retirement to concentrate on his position as chairman of organising committee for the second Rugby Football World Cup. After war service in the Fleet Air Arm he went up to Oxford, where he won his Blue each year 1948-50, captaining the side in his final year. He also captained the Cornwall, Bath and Penzance and Newlyn teams, as well as Engand. He taught geography at Clifton College for ten years from 1951 before appointments as headmaster of successively Cranbrook, Eastbourne College and Wellington. His brilliant try at Murrayfield 1952 was used for 20 years as part of the opening montage for Gaumont-British newsreels. He was president of the RFU in 1980/1 and was awarded the CBE in 1989.

Alec KENNEDY

Cricket
Alexander Stuart Kennedy. b. 24 Jan 1891 Edinburgh. d. 15 Nov 1959 Hythe, Southampton.

Kennedy took over 100 wickets in a season 15 times between 1912 and 1932, with a best total of 205 at 16.80 in 1922. Each year 1920-2 he made over 1100 runs and took over 180 wickets, and he also did the double in 1928 and 1930. The Hampshire stalwart was a middle-order or opening batsman and a right-arm medium pace swing bowler. His best performance was 10-37 for the Players v the Gentlemen at The Oval in 1927.
5 Tests 1922-3: 93 runs at 15.50; HS 41*; 31 wickets at 19.32, BB 5-76; 5 catches.

First-class 1907-36: 16,586 runs at 18.53, 10 100s HS 163*; 2874 wickets at 21.23, BB 10-37; 530 catches.

Ken KENNEDY

Rugby Union
Kenneth William Kennedy. b. 10 May 1941 Rochester, Kent.

Winning 45 caps for Ireland and four for the British Lions (1965-75), Kennedy was the most capped hooker in world rugby when he retired after 11 seasons in the Irish scrum.
On the 1966 Lions tour of Australia and New Zealand he played in four Tests and because of injury he missed almost certain selection for the 1968 Lions in South Africa. Although available he was not chosen for the Lions in New Zealand in 1971, but in 1974, to the surprise of many, he was called up for the tour to South Africa. Although he failed to oust Bobby Windsor (qv) from the Test team he made a major contribution to the success of the mid-week team. While in Ireland, he played for Queen's University but after qualifying as a doctor he settled in Kent and joined London Irish.

Sean KERLY

Hockey
Sean Robin Kerly. b. 29 Jan 1960 Tankerton, Kent.

With 64 goals in 99 appearances, Kerly is the top goalscorer for Great Britain. He also played 73 times for England (45 goals) and won a further 20 England caps in indoor internationals. He made his international debut against Poland in 1981 and after winning a bronze medal at the 1984 Olympics he won gold in 1988. At his third Games in 1992 the GB team were not among the medal winners. Other successes included a silver medal in the 1986 World Cup and in the European Cup he won silver in 1987 and bronze in 1991. A powerful striker, he played at centre-forward for Southgate, Kent, Middlesex and the South before announcing his retirement after the 1992 Olympics. He was awarded the MBE in 1993.

Cecil KERSHAW

Rugby Union
Cecil Ashworth Kershaw. b. 3 Feb 1895. d.
1 Nov 1972 Worthing, West Sussex.

As scrum-half, Kershaw formed a legendary partnership with W.J.A.Davies (qv). In the 14 internationals they played together they were never on the losing side. Kershaw won only two caps without Davies as his partner and England lost both matches (v Wales 1920 and 1922).
Both Davies and Kershaw enjoyed distinguished naval careers and most of their playing days were spent together with US Portsmouth. When not utilising his speedy long pass, Kershaw linked with his loose forwards and unlike current scrum-halves he seldom kicked for position.
A champion fencer, he twice represented Britain at the Olympic Games, 1920-24.

Thomas KIELY (Ireland)

Athletics
Thomas Francis Kiely. b. 25 Aug 1869
Ballyneal, Co. Tipperary. d. 6 Nov 1951
Dublin.

Kiely was the Olympic champion in 1904 at the all-around ten-event title, the precursor of the decathlon. He declined sponsorship from the English authorities because it would have entailed his representing Great Britain, and he travelled to the USA at his own expense. Actually it was not until 1954 that the IOC rectified the previous mistake of not officially recognising him as champion.
A native of Ballyneal, Co. Tipperary and nephew of Maurice Davin (qv), he won a total of 53 Irish titles, including 18 at the hammer, after initially excelling as a triple jumper and hurdler. On one day, 10 Sep 1892, he won a record seven Gaelic AA titles. He won the US all-around title in 1904 and again in 1906 and won five AAA hammer titles. He was a farmer in Ballyneal.

Michael KIERNAN

Rugby Union
Michael Joseph Kiernan. b. 17 Jan 1961
Cork.

An international centre and winger from the Dolphin club in southwest Ireland, he scored a record 308 points for Ireland in 43 matches 1982-91. As a contemporary of the great goal-kicker, Ollie Campbell, Kiernan did not take on that role for Ireland until his 11th international match. In those first 11 matches he scored two tries, thus giving him an even more impressive record of scoring 302 points in his remaining 33 internationals.
In 1986 he kicked 7 conversions in the match against Romania and he kicked a total of 62 penalties during his international career. He played in the centre in three Tests on the 1983 British Lions tour of New Zealand but the goal-kicking duties remained with his Irish colleague, Ollie Campbell (qv). An Irish Schools international in 1979, he was a good sprinter with a 200m best of 21.41 (1981). He is the nephew of Tom Kiernan (qv).

Tom KIERNAN (Ireland)

Rugby Union
Thomas Joseph Kiernan. b. 7 Jan 1939
Cork.

While playing at centre for Cork Constitution, Kiernan was surprisingly chosen as full-back by Ireland, and immediately proved an outstanding success in his new position, going on to win 54 caps for Ireland (1960-73) and play in five Tests for the British Lions.
Although Ireland only won once in Kiernan's first 10 matches, he impressed sufficiently to win a place with the 1962 Lions in South Africa. He played in only one Test but he returned to South Africa as captain of the 1968 Lions. His 17 points in the first Test and 35 points in the series (of the 38 scored by the Lions) were then British records. Apart from Kiernan's 11 penalty goals, the only other score by the Lions in the entire Test series was a try by Willie John McBride (qv) – which Kiernan converted.
Although he retired 20 years ago, he is Ireland's most capped full-back and his record of captaining his country 24 times also remains unbeaten. After his playing days were over he became a highly successful coach for Munster and Ireland.

Brian KILBY

Marathon
Brian Leonard Kilby. b. 26 Feb 1938
Coventry.

Kilby made his marathon debut in 1960, when he was second in the Poly Marathon and won the first of a record five successive AAA titles, but had a poor run at the Olympics for 29th. He had a brilliant year in 1962 when he won his three marathons to take the AAA, Commonwealth and European titles. In 1963 he smashed the British record set by Jim Peters in 1954, running 2:14:43 in the Welsh Championship at Port Talbot, and in 1964 was 4th at the Olympic Games, but did not finish the final marathon of his career at the 1966 Commonwealth Games. Running for Coventry Godiva Harriers, he was Midland 6 miles champion in 1965.
Best track times: 3 miles 13:39.6 (1963), 6 miles 27:53.0 (1963), 10 miles 49:07.0 (1962), 1 hour 19,474m (1962).

Lord KILLANIN (Ireland)

Administration
(Sir) Michael Morris, Lord Killanin. b. 30 Jul 1914 London.

Lord Killanin, also a distinguished journalist and filmmaker, was elected President of the Irish Olympic Council in 1950. Two years later he became a member of the International Olympic Committee (IOC). He became a member of the Executive Board in 1967 and vice-president in 1968, and succeeded Avery Brundage to become the sixth President of the IOC, 1972-80. His presidency was memorable for his innovation and the modernisation of the Olympic Games, particularly through the difficult years of boycotts at Montreal and Moscow. At the 83rd session of the IOC in Moscow in 1980 he was awarded the gold medal of the Olympic Order, the highest accolade available for Olympism. He has received many honorary degrees and awards in Ireland and abroad.
His father, Lieutenant-Colonel George Henry Morris, a member of the Irish Guards, died in action in France only one month after Michael Morris was born.

Morris was educated in England at Eton, at the Sorbonne in Paris, and then at Magdalene College, Cambridge. He was diplomatic and political correspondent for the *Daily Mail* and the *Sunday Dispatch*, having earlier worked for the *Daily Express*, before serving in the World War II. Then he was a Brigade-Major of the 30th Armoured Brigade in the British Army and was awarded the MBE. After the war he took up his family seat in Spiddal, Co. Galway, where his family had been residents since the 14th century; Lord Killanin's grandfather was Lord Chief Justice of Ireland in 1885. In 1945 he married Sheila Dunlop, whose father, Henry Wallace Doveton Dunlop had founded the Irish Champion Athletic Club and the Lansdowne Road Rugby grounds.
Lord Killanin has written several works including *My Olympic Years* and *My Ireland* and has edited the *Shell Guide to Ireland* with Michael Duignan. He also worked with the filmmaker John Ford in his Irish productions, including *The Quiet Man, The Rising of the Moon* and *The Playboy of the Western World*.
One of his sons, the Hon. Michael Francis Lee **'Mouse' Morris** (b. 4 Apr 1951) rode *Billycan* to win the Irish Grand National in 1977 and is a leading National Hunt trainer in Ireland.

Michael KINANE (Ireland)

Horse Racing
Michael Joseph Kinane. b. 22 Jun 1959 Co. Tipperary.

Irish champion jockey ten times between 1984 and 1994; in 1993 he reached 100 winners in the year in record time and ended with 115 winners, passing his own previous record of 113 in 1988. His first winner was at Leopardstown in 1975, and, apprenticed to Liam Browne, he was champion apprentice in 1978. His first Irish Classics success was the 2000 Guineas in 1982, and he won that race again in 1986, the 1000 Guineas in 1988, Oaks 1989 and the St Leger in 1993-4 (both on *Vintage Crop*). His first English Classics successes came with the 1990 2000 Guineas (*Tirol*) and the 1993 Derby

(*Commander-in-Chief*). In 1989 he won the Prix de l'Arc de Triomphe on *Carroll House* and in November 1993 he rode *Vintage Crop* to the first ever victory in the Melbourne Cup in Australia by a horse trained in Europe.

In 1994 he was signed to ride for Sheikh Mohammed in major races, when not needed by Dermot Weld (qv).

His father **Tommy** rode *Monksfield* to win the Champion Hurdle in 1978.

Jeff KING

Horse Racing
Jeffrey Stephen King. b. 6 Jul 1941 Teignmouth, Devon.

Apprenticed for three years with Sir Gordon Richards (qv), King rode his first winner in 1960 and then joined Bob Turnell's stable. His best season was with 66 winners in 1971/2 and in his career to 1981, wheh he took up training, he rode 710 winners. Acclaimed by his fellow professionals for his all-round riding ability, he was unfortunate not to win one of the very top races.

Norman KING

Bowls
Norman King. b. 7 Aug 1914 Sunderland.

After taking up bowls in 1942, King first achieved international honours in 1954, won the EBA singles in 1957 and the following year was a gold medallist in the fours at the Commonwealth Games. In 1970 he won a second Commonwealth gold in the pairs and at the 1972 World Championships, at the age of 57, he won a gold in the fours.

Thelma and Leonie KINGSBURY

Badminton
Thelma Kingsbury. b.12 Jan 1911. Later Mrs C W Welcome.

Leonie May Kingsbury. b.25 Jan 1909. Later Mrs H Middlemost.

As daughters of the 1908 Olympic cycling gold medallist, Clarence Brickwood Kingsbury, the sisters from Hampshire had a fine sporting pedigree. Thelma, a tall, athletic, hard-hitting left-hander, lost to her sister in the All-England singles final in 1934 but later won the title twice, 1936-7. She also won the doubles with Marjorie Bell (later Henderson) each year 1933-6, and in 1937 she won the mixed doubles. The following year she played as a professional in America, where she later settled, winning the US Open singles in 1941 and the doubles with Janet Wright in 1941 and 1947-50. She also won the Senior US Open Ladies' doubles in 1958.

Leonie also won the All-England singles twice, 1932, 1934, but didn't match the successes of her sister as a doubles player. However, like Thelma, she also settled abroad and after taking up residence in South Africa she represented her adopted country internationally.

Lord KINNAIRD

Football
Arthur Fitzgerald Kinnaird. b. 16 Feb 1847 Kensington, London. d. 30 Jan 1923 London.

A brilliant all-round sportsman, Kinnaird was one of the legendary figures from the early days of organised football. He played in a record nine FA Cup finals and was on the winning side five times: for Wanderers in 1873 and 1877-8, and for Old Etonians 1879 and 1882. He was also a losing finalist in 1875-76, 1881 and 1883 and was capped by Scotland in their first-ever international against England in 1873.

From Eton he went up to Cambridge where he represented the University at football, fives, real tennis and swimming. Despite his playing successes, his real contribution to the game was as an administrator. First elected to the FA committee as a representative of the Old Etonians in the 1868/9 season, he was appointed treasurer in 1877 and was president in 1890. His contribution to the game was immeasurable, as he led the way in codifying the rules, oversaw the birth of professionalism and by birth and rank was able to speak for the sport in high places. Universally popular, he remained as the FA President up until his death and in his

33 years in office he did more than any other single individual to fashion the game as we know it today.

Bill KITCHEN

Speedway
William Kitchen. b. 7 Dec 1908 Lancaster. d. 20 May 1994.

Equal 5th in the world championship of 1938, when he rode for Belle Vue, Kitchen had to wait until after the war for his next chance of honours and was past his best by the time the World Championship was re-introduced in 1949. Riding for Wembley, whom he captained, however, he had been runner-up to Tommy Price and Jack Parker (qqv) respectively in the top event of 1946 and 1947, the British Riders' Championship.

Having served an apprenticeship in motor engineering, he had competed at all forms of motorcycle sport, including TT, hill climbing, scrambles and reliability trials, before taking up speedway in 1933. Within a few weeks he was selected as a reserve for England's Test team and rode four times for England in Tests that year. In the course of one day in 1933 he was the winner of a 100 mile sand race at Southport and then won all his speedway races for Belle Vue in the evening.

Billy KNIGHT

Tennis
William Arthur Knight. b. 12 Nov 1935 Northampton.

A hard-hitting left-hander, Knight was the British Junior singles champion in 1952 and again in 1953 when he also won the Boys' singles at Wimbledon. He later won the British Hard Court singles (1958, 1963-4), the Covered Court singles (1960) and the German singles (1959). He also won the mixed doubles at the 1959 French Championships. In the Davis Cup he played in 21 ties between 1955 and 1960 (21/34 singles, 6/9 doubles). He captained the British Davis Cup team in 1991-5.

Alan KNOTT

Cricket
Alan Philip Eric Knott. b. 9 Apr 1946 Belvedere, London.

One of the greatest of wicket-keepers, Knott was surely the greatest wicket-keeper/batsman, with the ability to bat at his best at the highest level. Supremely fit, and renowned for his on-field callisthenics, he made a record 65 consecutive appearances for England 1968-77 before going to play World Series cricket, adding another six Tests on his return in 1980-1. He followed in the great Kent wicket-keeping tradition and perhaps exceeded even Godfrey Evans (qv) in ability. Against Australia 1970/1 he set an English record with 24 dismissals in a series, and in his 78th Test he passed Evans' record 220 dismissals (from 91 Tests). He is the only wicket-keeper to score 4000 runs and take 200 dismissals in Test cricket. He twice exceeded 1000 runs in a first-class season, with a best of 1209 at 41.68 in 1971 and his highest tally of dismissals in a season was 98 in 1967. He was originally taken on to the Kent staff as a batsman keen to bowl off-breaks.

95 Tests 1967-81: 4389 runs at 32.75, 5 100s HS 135; 250 catches, 19 stumpings.
20 One-day Ints 1971-7: 200 runs at 20.00, HS 50; 15 catches, 1 stumping.
First-class 1964-85: 18,105 runs at 29.63, 17 100s HS 156; 2 wickets; 1211 catches, 133 stumpings.

Charles KORTRIGHT

Cricket
Charles Jesse Kortright. b. 9 Jan 1871 Ingatestone, Essex. d. 12 Dec 1952 South Weald, Essex.

Although he never played for England the Essex amateur was thought at the time to have been the fastest bowler that ever lived. He was also a good middle-order batsman. His best seasons were 1898 when he took 96 wickets at 19.19 and 1895, 76 at 15.83.

First-class 1894-1907: 4404 runs at 17.61, 2 100s HS 131; 489 wickets at 21.05, BB 8-57; 176 catches.

Jackie KYLE

Rugby Union
John Wilson Kyle. b. 30 Jan 1926 Belfast.

First capped in 1947 while a medical student at Queen's University, Belfast, Kyle went on to play 46 times for Ireland and in six Tests for the British Lions on the 1950 tour of Australia and New Zealand. On his retirement in 1958 he was the world's most capped player and still enjoys the distinction of being Ireland's most capped fly-half. A notable feature of his international career was that in his 11 matches against Scotland, he was on the winning side each time.

A fly-half in the classic mould and ragarded as Ireland's greatest player in that position, he was a well-balanced, athletic player whose brilliant attacking skills were matched by his solid defence. He played for Belfast Royal Academy and Queen's University.

On leaving the international rugby scene he became a doctor in Malaysia and later moved to Zimbabwe as a medical missionary. He was awarded the OBE.

Maeve KYLE (Ireland)

Hockey and athletics
Maeve Esther Enid Kyle. b. 6 Oct 1928 Kilkenny. née Shankey.

In 1956 Maeve Kyle became the first woman to compete for Ireland in the Olympics when she ran in the 100m and 200m, but then and in Rome in 1960 did not progress beyond the heats. At her third Olympics in Tokyo 1964 she fared better, making the semi-finals of 400m and 800m. She won a record 41 titles at Irish and Northern Irish championships between 1955 and 1975, and undoubtedly would have won more had there been more organised athletics in her younger days. She achieved her best international result with the European Indoor bronze at 400m in 1966 and was 6th in the outdoor European 400m in 1962.

She set numerous Irish records from a 5.33m long jump in 1944 to 29.0 for 200m hurdles in 1969 with best performances: 100y 10.8 (1964), 220y 25.5 (1960), 440y 54.9 (1962), 800m 2:10.6 (1962), long jump 5.56m (1966). She set numerous world age bests in her 40s and 50s after she had retired from hockey, at which she won a record 58 caps for Ireland as a winger.

A graduate of Dublin University, she built up the Ballymena Ladies club with her husband, leading coach Sean Kyle, and became a top administrator, with her responsibilities including being honorary secretary of the Northern Ireland WAAA in 1969, and a member of the Northern Ireland and Irish Sports Councils.

Her great uncle Professor **Harry Thrift** (1882-1958) was capped 18 times for Ireland at rugby union as a winger and her daughter Shauna won Northern Ireland titles at 100m hurdles in 1971 and 1973 and 200mh 1973.

Roy LAIDLAW

Rugby Union
Roy James Laidlaw. b. 5 Oct 1953 Jedburgh, Borders.

After being selected as a reserve 13 times Laidlaw finally won his first cap at the age of 26 in 1980 and went on to win 47 caps as scrum-half, so that on his retirement in 1988 he was Scotland's most capped player in that position. He played for Scotland in 31 consecutive matches and his fine understanding with fly-half John Rutherford (qv) led to them playing together 35 times, a world record for a half-back pairing; they made a major contribution to Scotland's Grand Slam in 1984.

He captained Scotland several times and toured six times for Scotland and once for the British Lions. With the Lions in New Zealand in 1983 he came on as a replacement for the injured Terry Holmes (qv) in the first Test and held his place for the rest of the series. The injury to Holmes placed a heavy work load on Laidlaw who was called on to play in 11 of the first 14 tour matches and the fact that he had to play behind a beaten pack in the Tests added to the tourists' problems.

He remained with second division Jedforest throughout his international career.

Jim LAKER

Cricket
James Charles Laker. b. 9 Feb 1922
Frizinghall, Bradford, West Yorkshire. d.
23 Apr 1986 Putney, London.

Laker's peak as a great off-spin bowler undoubtedly came in the 1956 Test series against Australia when he took 46 wickets in the series at an average of 9.60. In an astonishing display in the 4th Test at Old Trafford in July he took 9-37 and 10-53, figures all the more amazing for the fact that his Surrey spin partner Tony Lock (qv) bowled 69 overs in the match for just one wicket. This is the only instance of more than 17 wickets in a first-class match and the only instance of all ten wickets in a Test innings. Laker had also taken 10-88 for Surrey against the Australians earlier in the season. At the end of this momentous year he was voted BBC Sports Personality of the Year.

He had first played for England on the 1948 tour to the West Indies, and had taken 18 wickets in the Tests, but he played curiously little for England over the next four or five years, even though he took 8 wickets for 2 runs in a Test Trial at Bradford in 1950. He was, however, a regular from 1956 to 1959 and ended his test career with 17 wickets at 10.17 against New Zealand in 1958 and 15 at 21.20 in Australia in 1958/9. For Surrey he was a vital member of their matchless championship winning teams of 1952-8, and after his retirement in 1959 came back to play for Essex 1962-4. He took over 100 wickets in a season 11 times, each year 1948-58, with a best total of 166 at 15.32 in 1950. Tall and strong, he had a model action and was a master of his craft. He was also a useful lower-order batsman. Although his 1960 autobiography *Over to Me* caused ill-feeling, he became a much respected TV commentator.

46 Tests 1948-59: 676 runs at 14.08, HS 63; 193 wickets at 21.24, BB 10-53; 12 catches.

First-class 1946-65: 7304 runs at 16.60, 2 100s HS 113; 1944 wickets at 18.41, BB 10-53; 270 catches.

Jim Laker's Match – 19 wickets

England v Australia at Old Trafford, Manchester, on 26-31 July 1956.
England 459 (David Sheppard 113, Peter Richardson 104, Colin Cowdrey 80, Godfrey Evans 47, Peter May 43) won by an innings and 170 runs.

AUSTRALIA

Colin McDonald	c Lock b Laker	32	c Oakman b Laker	89
Jim Burke	c Cowdrey b Lock	22	c Lock b Laker	33
Neil Harvey	b Laker	0	c Cowdrey b Laker	0
Ian Craig	lbw b Laker	8	lbw b Laker	38
Keith Miller	c Oakman b Laker	6	b Laker	0
Ken Mackay	c Oakman b Laker	0	c Oakman b Laker	0
Ron Archer	st Evans b Laker	6	c Oakman b Laker	0
Richie Benaud	c Statham b Laker	0	b Laker	18
Ray Lindwall	not out	6	c Lock b Laker	8
Len Maddocks	b Laker	4	lbw b Laker	2
Ian Johnson	b Laker	0	not out	1
Extras		0		16
		84		**205**

England bowling figures

	O	M	R	W		O	M	R	W
Brian Statham	6	3	6	0		16	10	15	0
Trevor Bailey	4	3	4	0		20	8	31	0
Jim Laker	16.4	4	37	9		51.2	23	53	10
Tony Lock	14	3	37	1		55	30	69	0
Alan Oakman						8	3	21	0

O – overs, M – maidens, R – runs, W – wickets

Allan LAMB

Cricket
Allan Joseph Lamb. b. 20 Jun 1954
Langebaanweg, Western Cape, South
Africa.

Lamb made his first-class debut for Western
Province in 1972/3 and, with South Africa
banned from Test cricket, took advantage
of the fact that both his parents were British
(emigrating to South Africa in the 1940s)
to qualify for England. He came to play
with Northamptonshire in 1978 and met
with immediate success with batting of the
highest quality. He scored 1747 runs at 67.19
in 1979, topped the first-class averages
with 1797 at 66.55 in 1980 and exceeded
2000 runs (2049 at 60.26) in 1981. Such
form ensured him a Test place as soon as
he was eligible and he duly made his debut
in 1982.

He established himself as a determined
middle-order batsman, whose pugnacious
attack turned the course of many matches
and was particularly effective in one-day
internationals. Against the mighty West
Indian attack in 1984 he scored centuries
in three successive Tests.

In 1988 he played for Orange Free State in
South Africa, and made the highest ever
innings in the Currie Cup of 294. He was
appointed Northamptonshire captain in 1989
and captained England in 3 Tests 1990-1,
as deputy for the injured Graham Gooch
(qv), making a century against the West
Indies in the first of these at Bridgetown.

He lost his Test place in 1992 but continued to challenge for reinstatement over the
next couple of years with consistently successful county form. He led Northants to
the NatWest Trophy in 1992.

79 Tests 1982-92: 4656 runs at 36.09, 14
100s HS 142; 75 catches.
122 One-day Ints 1982-92: 4010 runs at
39.31, 4 100s HS 118; 31 catches.
First-class 1972-94: 31,131 runs at 48.64,
86 100s HS 294; 8 wickets at 24.87, BB 2-
29; 353 catches.

Dorothea LAMBERT-CHAMBERS – see
DOUGLASS

Eric LANGTON

Speedway
Eric Langton. b. 1907 Leeds.

Langton, who led the Belle Vue team to
League and Cup honours, won the 'Star'
Championship in 1932 and was runner-up
in 1934, in the years when this event was
the season's premier event prior to the
establishment of the World Championship
in 1936. He was runner-up to Lionel Van
Praag (Aus), who beat him by a mere bike
length in a run-off for the first world final.
He won the British Match-race Championship
in 1932 after Jack Parker (qv) crashed in the
challenge match, but Langton declined to
defend his title in 1933. Before taking up
speedway he was an outstanding trials rider.

Sonia LANNAMAN

Athletics
Sonia May Lannaman. b. 24 Mar 1956
Aston, Birmingham. Now Mrs Garmston.

A sprint prodigy who showed exceptional
talent from the age of 13, Lannaman went
on to have a long career at the top. She
competed at the 1972 Olympics as a 16-
year-old, and the following year won the
European Junior 100m, with a sprint relay
bronze. In 1974 she won a Commonwealth
relay silver medal and in 1976 a European
Indoor silver medal at 60m. Her greatest
triumphs came in 1977, when she was 2nd
at both 100m and 200m in the European
Cup and at 100m in the World Cup to rank
2nd in the world at both events, and at the
1978 Commonwealth Games where she
won gold medals at 100m and sprint relay
and silver at 200m. At the Europeans in
1978 she was 8th at 100m, although winning a relay silver. She won a relay bronze,
with 8th at 200m at the 1980 Olympics,
and in her final major championships won
a relay gold at the 1982 Commonwealth
Games.

After winning WAAA junior titles at 100m
in 1969 and 1970 and 200m 1970, she was
senior champion at 100m in 1977 and 200m
in 1977 and 1981, with the WAAA 60m in
1971 and 1974 and the UK 100m and 200m
in 1977 and 1978. She was awarded the
MBE in 1979.

Best times: 100m 11.20 (1980) and 10.93w (1977), hand timed 11.1 (1980), 10.8w (1976); 200m British record 22.58 (1980); indoors 50m 6.2 (1971), 60m 7.25 (1976).

Ethel LARCOMBE

Tennis
Ethel Warneford Larcombe. b. 8 Jun 1879 Islington, London. d. 10 Aug 1965 Budleigh Salterton, Devon. née Thompson.

Winner of the Wimbledon singles (1912), the doubles (1904-5) and the mixed doubles (1903-4, 1912, 1914), Larcombe was the last Wimbledon singles champion to serve underarm. Her first four doubles victories were as Miss Thompson before her marriage in 1906 to Dudley Larcombe, later secretary of the All England Club 1925-39.

At the Scottish Championships she won all three titles in 1910 and 1912 and the singles and doubles in 1911 and at the Irish Championships she won the singles and mixed doubles in 1912. She played at Wimbledon for the last time in 1919 when, at the age of 40, she lost to Suzanne Lenglen (Fra) in the first round and in 1922 she became a professional coach.

George LARNER

Walking
George Edward Larner. b. 7 Mar 1875 Langley, Berkshire. d. 4 Mar 1949 Brighton, East Sussex.

Larner became the Olympic walking champion at 3500m and 10 miles in 1908. He only took up race walking as a sport at the age of 28 in 1903, but won both AAA track walking titles, at 2 miles and 7 miles, in both 1904 and 1905. In this period he also set nine world records, but then decided to retire as he could not fit in the necessary training with his job as a Brighton policeman. However his Chief Constable was persuaded to allow him time to prepare for the 1908 Games and he re-appeared after a two-year absence. He was disqualified in his first race, the 1908 AAA 7 miles, but then won his third 2 miles title and had his two Olympic triumphs in July. He then retired again but

returned to win the AAA 7 miles in 1911. He became a leading race walking judge. Between 1904 and 1908 he set the following world records: 2M 13:11.4, 3M 20:25.8, 4M 27:14.0, 5M 36:00.2, 6M 43:26.2, 7M 50:50.8, 8M 58:18.4, 9M 1:07:37.8, 10M 1:15:57.4, 1 Hour 13,275m. These times remained British records for many years, with his 2 miles mark not matched by a British walker until Stan Vickers (qv) did so in 1960 and his mile best of 6:26 until Paul Nihill (qv) did so in 1970.

Harold LARWOOD

Cricket
Harold Larwood. b. 14 Nov 1904 Nuncargate, Nottinghamshire.

Larwood was the scourge of Australia on the 'Bodyline' tour of 1932/3. His hostile fast bowling, 33 wickets at 19.51, did much to win the series for England. Ridiculously he was made the scapegoat for the controversy that the bodyline form of attack generated, and he never again played for England, and indeed his county career with Nottinghamshire ended when he was only 33. His innings of 98 in 135 minutes in his last Test was at the time the highest ever by a 'night-watchman'.

Although of only medium height (1.72m 5'8"), he generated intense pace, with his superb action and long arms. He took over 100 wickets in a season eight times between 1926 and 1936, headed by 162 at 12.86 in 1932. He also headed the first-class averages in 1927: 100 at 16.95, 1928: 138 at 14.51, 1931: 129 at 12.03 and 1936: 119 at 12.97.

In 1950 he sold his confectionery shop in Blackpool and emigrated to settle happily in Australia. In 1993 he was belatedly awarded the MBE, a fitting reward, no doubt influenced by a cricket-loving prime minister in John Major.

21 Tests 1926-33: 485 runs at 19.40, HS 98; 178 wickets at 28.41, BB 6-32; 15 catches.

First-class 1924-38: 7290 runs at 19.91, 3 100s HS 102*; 1427 wickets at 17.51, BB 9-41; 234 catches.

Peter LATHAM

Rackets and Real Tennis
Peter Walker Latham. b. 18 May 1865
Manchester. d. 27 Nov 1953 Chiswick,
London.

The only man to hold the world title for
rackets and real tennis simultaneously,
Latham was the leading player of court
games in the latter part of the 19th century.
He first challenged for the world rackets
title in 1887 beating the reigning champion, Joseph Gray, and after defeating four
challengers he resigned the title in 1902.
In 1895 he successfully challenged Charles
Saunders for the world real tennis title and
retained it against challenges from Tom
Petitt (USA) in 1898 and 'Punch' Fairs
(qv) in 1904. The following year, Fairs
was successful in his challenge and this
was the only championship match that
Latham ever lost at either game. In 1907
he recaptured the title from Fairs.
Beginning his career as an 11-year-old at
the Manchester Racquet Club, Latham
went on to become head professional at
Queen's Club in 1888. In 1901 he accepted
a post as the private professional to Sir
Charles Rose, but in 1916 returned to
Queen's, where he taught many future
champions.
Although Jock Soutar (USA) at rackets
and Jay Gould (USA) at real tennis might
be rated his equal in their individual fields,
no player in history could match his skills
at both games.

Denis LAW

Football
Denis Law. b. 24 Feb 1940 Aberdeen.

Law was one of the greatest inside-forwards of the post-war era. After signing
amateur forms for Huddersfield in 1955,
he turned professional two years later and
then moved to Manchester City in 1960.
After little more than a year he went to
Torino but he did not settle in Italy and
quickly returned to join Manchester
United, with whom he won an FA Cup
winners' medal 1963 and Football League
championship medals in 1965 and 1967.
he scored five hat-tricks for United in

European cup competitions. He was voted
European Footballer of the Year in 1964.
He made his international debut in 1958 at
the age of 18, when he was still with
Huddersfield, and went on to win 55 caps
for Scotland before retiring after the 1974
World Cup finals.
A deadly shot when the ball was on the
ground, he also scored many goals with
soaring headers despite being only 1.75m
5 ft 9 in tall. After his golden years at
Manchester United, Denis Law returned to
Manchester City for one final season after
which he developed a career as a radio and
TV commentator.

Herbert LAWFORD

Tennis
Herbert Fortescue Lawford. b. 15 May
1851 Bayswater, London. d. 20 Apr 1925
Dess, Aberdeenshire.

A large man with a powerful baseline
game, Lawford first played at Wimbledon
in 1878 and in 12 appearances he lost
seven times to one or other of the Renshaw
twins (qv). From 1884-6 he won the All
Comers' singles but lost each time to
William Renshaw in the Challenge Round,
but in 1887 William Renshaw did not
defend his title and Lawford finally won
the title when he defeated Ernest Renshaw
in five sets in the All Comers' final.

Ivan LAWLER

Canoeing
Ivan Lawler. b. 19 Nov 1966 Addlestone,
Surrey.

Lawler has been Britain's most successful
competitor at canoe marathon World
Championships, winning at K1 in 1992
and at K2 with Graham Burns in 1994, following silver medals with Burns at K2 in
1988 and 1990. In the World Cup for
canoe marathon Burns and Lawler were
4th in 1986, 2nd in 1987 and winners in
1989 and 1991, before Lawler won the K1
event in 1993. At sprint canoe racing
Lawler, accompanied by Grayson Bourne,
won a silver medal in 1989 and gold in
1990 at K2 10,000m, thus becoming the
only British canoeist to have been a world

champion at two disciplines. He also competed at the Olympic Games of 1988 and 1992. Currently a student at the London School of Osteopathy, Lawler has been unbeaten in domestic competition since 1986.

Joe LAWSON

Horse Racing
Joseph Lawson. b. 1881 Boldon Gint, nr Marsden, Tyne and Wear. d. 20 May 1964 Newmarket.

Having ridden for a few years, Lawson joined Alec Taylor's stables at Manton, Wiltshire, where he remained for 49 years, taking over from Taylor (qv) in 1927. In 1947 he moved to Newmarket, where he bought the Carlburg stable from Charles Waugh and trained there until his retirement in 1957. From 1929 he sent out the winners of 12 Classics, with the last being *Never Say Die* to win the Derby and St Leger in 1954.

Barbara LAWTON

Athletics, High Jump
Barbara Jean Lawton. b. 28 Oct 1949 Farnham, Surrey. née Inkpen.

She set nine British high jump records outdoors from 1.765m in 1969 to 1.87 in 1973, as well as four indoors. Her best international results were winning the Commonwealth gold in 1974 and European silver in 1971, while at the Olympic Games she was 13th in 1968 and 4th in 1972. She was WAAA champion outdoors in 1967-9 and indoors in 1969-70 and 1973. She had a long jump best of 6.33 indoors in 1970 and won the 1967 WAAA indoor title.

She married **Carl Lawton** (b. 20 Jan 1948), who was a British international walker.

Tommy LAWTON

Football
Thomas Lawton. b. 6 Oct 1919 Bolton, Gt. Manchester.

Lawton was a strongly built centre-forward whose powerful shooting and strength in the air proved invaluable to the Everton and England attack. He signed as a professional for Burnley on his 17th birthday and four days later, against Tottenham, became the youngest player ever to score a hat-trick in the Football League. After only three months he moved to Everton where he took over from the legendary Dixie Dean (qv), and in the last two pre-war seasons Lawton was the top scorer in the First Division, winning a League Championship medal in 1939.

He was the top goalscorer (337 goals in major matches) in wartime football, when he appeared as a guest for a variety of clubs and scored 24 goals in 23 wartime internationals. He signed for Chelsea in 1945 for the first post-war season and moved to Notts County two years later. He won the last four of his international caps while playing for the Third Division side. He had earlier won 8 caps with Everton, 11 with Chelsea and in his 23 games for England, 1938-48, he scored 22 goals.

After leaving Notts County in 1952 he played for Brentford, Arsenal and Kettering Town and held a variety of managerial posts.

Martine LE MOIGNAN

Squash
Martine Le Moignan. b. 28 Oct 1962 Guernsey.

After winning the British Under-21 title in 1980, Le Moignan made her international debut for England that year and has since win a record number of England caps.

In 1981 she was runner-up at the World junior championships and at the senior championships she won four team gold medals (1985, 1987, 1989-90) and the individual champion in 1989, which she followed by being a semi-finalist in 1990 and 1992. She was a three-time winner (1984, 1988, 1991) at the English Ladies' Championships and has played on most of the England teams which have dominated the European Championships 1982-92. She was awarded the MBE in 1990.

Johnny LEACH

Table Tennis
John Alfred Leach. b. 20 Nov 1922
London.

Leach was the last Englishman to win the World singles title at table tennis, which he did in 1949 and 1951. He was also three times runner-up in the men's doubles (1947, 1952-3) and once in the mixed doubles (1952).

He learned the game at the Romford YMCA and while serving with the RAF, and with a technique which was built on a solid defence he developed into the most consistent British player in the immediate post-war years. Surprisingly he never won the singles at the English Open, his best being runner-up in 1953, though he won the men's doubles in 1951 and 1953 and the mixed doubles in 1950, 1952, 1954 and 1956. He won 152 caps for England and was a member of the winning Swaythling Cup team in 1953.

After retirement he continued as non-playing captain of the British team and gave a great deal of time to coaching, being particularly involved in the development of young players. He was awarded the MBE in 1966 for services to the game.

Con and Pat LEAHY (Ireland)

Athletics, High Jump
Cornelius Leahy. b. 27 Apr 1876
Charleville, Cregane, Co. Cork. d. 1921
USA.

Patrick Joseph Leahy b. 20 Jul 1877
Charleville, Cregane, Co. Cork. d. 1926
USA.

There were seven Leahy brothers who were all excellent athletes. At the Olympic Games Pat Leahy was 2nd at high jump, 3rd at long jump and 4th at triple jump in 1900, and Con won the high jump and was 2nd in the triple jump in 1906 and was 2nd at high jump in 1908. At the high jump Pat took the Irish AAA title 1897-1900, the Gaelic AA in 1897-8 and AAA 1898-9 as well as the Irish and Gaelic long jump titles in 1903. Con won the Gaelic high jump 1901-05, Irish 1902-08, AAA 1905-08 and AAU of America 1907, as well as

the Irish long jump 1904-06 and both Irish and Gaelic triple jump in 1902. Con and Pat emigrated to the USA in 1909.

Best performancess: high jump - Con 1.94 (1904), Pat 1.95 and an unrecognised 1.97 (1898); long jump - Con 7.21 (1902), Pat 7.29 (1902); triple jump - Con 15.00 (1904) and 15.06 (1900) with 2 hops and a jump, Pat 15.15 (1901) with 2 hops and a jump.

Of the other brothers, Tim high jumped 1.92 for the best in the world in 1910, and Joe was one of very few men of those days who could beat 7m in the long jump.

Diane LEATHER

Athletics
Diane Susan Leather. b. 7 Jan 1933 Streetly, West Midlands. Later Mrs Charles.

Just 23 days after Roger Bannister (qv) became the first man to run a mile under four minutes, Diane Leather became the first woman to break the 5 minute barrier, with 4:59.6 at Birmingham on 29 May 1954. Distance running for women was in its infancy and women did not run such distances in international championships until 15 years later, but Leather set five world bests for the mile, from 5:02.6 in 1953, only a year after she had started running seriously, to 4:45.0 in 1955, via 5:00.2 and 4:59.6 in 1954 and 4:50.8 in 1955.

She set three ratified world records: 2:09.0 at 880y in 1954 and two at 3 x 880y relay, and ran a world best 56.6 for 440y in 1954 and two world bests at 1500m, 4:30.0 and 4:29.7 in 1957 (and an unofficial 4:22.2 in her final world record mile), with six British records at 800m, culminating in 2:06.6 when she won the European silver medal in 1958. She also won the 1954 European silver medal, but was past her best when the 800m was reintroduced to the Olympics in 1960, and went out in the heats. She was WAAA champion at 880y 1954-5 and 1957 and at 1 mile in 1956-7 and won the national cross-country title each year 1953-6. Her first win came very soon after she had joined Birchfield Harriers to get fit for hockey. Trained as a micro-analyst at chemistry, she was coached by Dorette Nelson Neal.

Judy LEDEN

Hang Gliding
Judy Leden. b. 23 Dec 1959 London. Later Mrs Gardner.

Having started hang gliding in 1979, Leden won the first two world titles, in 1987 and 1991, was European champion in 1986 and British champion 1983 and 1988-92. She set women's world records for straight line distance in 1983 and 1990 and for distance over a triangular course (114.1 km) in 1991.

At paragliding she set a women's world record for straight line distance (128.5 km) in 1992, further world records in 1994, and won the world title in 1995. Awarded the MBE in 1989, she married Trevor Gardner in 1990.

Francis LEE

Football
Francis Henry Lee. b. 29 Apr 1944 Westhoughton, Gt. Manchester.

Lee made his Football League debut at the age of 16 for Bolton Wanderers against Manchester City, whom he joined seven years later. His skills as a striker helped City to win the League in 1968, the FA Cup in 1969 and the League Cup and European Cup Winners Cup (scoring from a penalty) in 1970. He began as an outside-right, but his power and strong right-footed shot made him a considerable goalscorer, once converting 13 penalties in a season.

Although he played for the England youth team, he was not selected at Under-23 level and had to wait until he was 24 for his first senior international. He made an immediate impact with his positive approach, although he had a relatively modest World Cup in 1970. He scored 10 goals in his 27 England appearances 1968-72. He moved on to Derby County and played for their League winning team in 1975.

He became a racehorse trainer, based in Cheshire, taking out a licence for National Hunt in 1984 and on the flat in 1987. He is also a very successful businessman, and is now chairman of his old club, Manchester City.

George LEE

Gliding
Douglas George Lee. b. 7 Nov 1945.

Lee has been Britain's most successful gliding pilot at the World Championships, winning three successive titles at the Open category, in 1976, 1978 and 1981. At that time he was serving as a Flight Lieutenant in the RAF, flying Phantoms. He now flies Boeing 747s as a Captain with Cathay Pacific, operating out of Hong Kong.

Michael LEE

Speedway
Michael Andrew Lee. b. 11 Dec 1958 Cambridge.

World speedway champion in 1980 and long-track champion in 1981, Lee was a member of the winning English team in the World Team Championship in 1977 and 1980. British champion 1977-8, he had been a highly promising 4th on his first appearance in a world final in 1977 at the age of 18, and 3rd in 1979, after winning the first Commonwealth final. He then rode for Kings Lynn. Moving on to Poole he was 3rd in the 1983 World Championship.

Sidney LEE

Billiards
Sydney Raphael Lee. b. 24 Apr 1910 Wandsworth, London. d. 10 Nov 1988 Holsworthy, Devon.

After being beaten in the final by Laurie Steeples in 1931, Lee became the world amateur billiards champion in 1933. He had been a child prodigy and was a school-boy champion in 1925. In 1929 he was runner-up in the English amateur billiards championship and he won this title each year from 1931 to 1934, after which he turned professional. Sadly for him, billiards went into decline shortly thereafter and the world championships were not held between 1934 and 1951, his prime years. He was never as successful at snooker, although he was runner-up in the *Daily Mail* tournament in 1940. He was, however, the first snooker player to be seen on television, in a demonstration from Alexandra Palace in 1936. He was resident professional at Burroughes Hall in London and an expert coach of many top players.

His brother **Benny** was the English speed roller-skating champion at 880y, mile and 5 miles in 1924 and 1925.

Alice LEGH

Archery
Alice Blanche Legh. b. 1855. d. 3 Jan 1948 Pitchcombe, Stroud, Gloucestershire.

The greatest woman archer from the British Isles, Legh won her first Grand National championship in 1881. For the next four years she took a back seat to her mother, who won the title four times consecutively, but Alice then took over. Between 1886 and 1922 she won 22 more championships, making 23 in all. This included runs of eight, 1902-09, and seven, 1886-92, in succession. She elected not to compete in the 1908 Olympic archery contests, held in London, which were won by fellow British archer Sybil 'Queenie' Newall (qv), but the following week at Oxford she defeated Newall by the huge margin of 151 points.

Cecil LEITCH

Golf
Charlotte Cecilia Pitcairn Leitch. b. 13 Apr 1891 Silloth, Cumbria. d. 16 Sep 1977 London.

A great English amateur, Leitch shares the record of four British Ladies' titles, 1914, 1920-1 and 1926, with Joyce Wethered (qv). It is likely she would have set unmatched records had she not had to compete in the same era as Wethered. Leitch won the Canadian championship in 1921 by 17 & 15, the largest margin of victory in any final of a national championship.

She was a semi-finalist in the British Ladies' Championship in 1908 at 17, and won the first of five French titles in 1912. In 1914 she won the English, French and British Ladies' and repeated that treble when they were first contested after the war, with the English in 1919 and the other two in 1920. She won further French titles

in 1921 and 1924. She was an outspoken character and her strong, attacking play mirrored her personality.

Her sisters **Mary** and **Edith** were also top-class golfers. Edith (Mrs Guedalla) won the English Ladies' Amateur Championship in 1927 and was an English international from 1908 to 1933.

Richard LEMAN

Hockey
Richard Alexander Leman. b. 13 Jul 1959 East Grinstead, West Sussex.

Leman was an Olympic gold medallist and England's most capped player at hockey. Making his England debut against Ireland in 1980 he went on to win a record 158 caps (106 outdoor, 52 indoor). He also represented Great Britain 70 times, so that when he retired after the 1990 World Cup he had amassed a total of 228 international selections. He won a gold medal at the 1988 Olympics, silver at the 1986 World Cup and 1987 European Cup, and a bronze at the 1984 Olympics. A forward or midfield player, he played for East Grinstead, West Sussex and the South after leaving Gresham's School.

Virginia LENG

Equestrianism, Three-day Event.
Virginia Helen Antoinette Leng. b. 1 Feb 1955 Malta. née Holgate, now Mrs Elliott.

'Ginny' has been a highly successful three-day eventer. Riding *Priceless* she won the 1985 European and 1986 World individual titles, and had team golds in the 1981 and 1985 Europeans and 1982 and 1986 Worlds. She went on to further European individual and team golds in 1987 on *Night Cap* and in 1989 on *Master Craftsman*. She won Badminton in 1985, 1989 and 1993, Burghley in 1983-4 and 1986 and was British champion in 1987 and 1993. At the Olympic Games she won team silver and individual bronze in both 1984 and 1988.

Born in Malta, where her father was serving in the Royal Marines, she was brought up in Cyprus, Canada, Singapore and the Philippines before her family settled in

Devon when she was 16. She began riding at age three and her first international victory was in 1973 when she rode *Dubonnet* to the European Junior title. In 1977 she broke her left arm in 23 places, but made a gallant return. She made the 1980 British Olympic team but the equestrians did not go to Moscow. She was Sports Writers' Sportswoman of the Year 1985 and married Michael Elliott on 1 October 1993.

Donal LENIHAN

Rugby Union
Donal Gerard Lenihan. b. 12 Sep 1959 Cork.

Leniham was capped 52 times (1981-92) and only Willie John McBride (qv) has played at lock more times for Ireland. A hard-working forward for Cork Constitution and Munster he is one of the few Irishmen to have played for his country at schools, Under-23, 'B' and full international level. A brilliant leader, he captained Ireland in the 1987 World Cup and for the next two seasons and after a brief interval, when alternative captains were tried, he resumed the captaincy in 1990 but he missed the following season because of injury.
An original selection for the 1983 British Lions tour to New Zealand, he was forced to withdraw through injury but he later flew out as a replacement for the injured Bob Norster (qv). He also went to Australia with the 1989 Lions but did not play in a Test on either tour.

Avril LENNOX

Gymnastics
Avril Johnston Clegg Lennox. b. 26 Apr 1956.

Lennox was Britain's most successful gymnast of the 1970s until her career was cut short by a persistent ankle injury at the age of 21. She was British champion four times, each year 1974-7, representing Charles Keene College, and also winning 13 individual apparatus titles. At the 1976 Olympics she was 35th overall.

Jason LEONARD

Rugby Union
Jason Leonard. né Horey. b. 14 Aug 1968 Barking, London.

One of the best loose-head props of recent years, he showed on the 1993 Lions tour of New Zealand that he was equally effective at tight-head. After being capped by England Colts while playing for Barking, he joined Saracens and then moved to Harlequins in 1990, winning his first full England cap on the tour of Argentina that year. In New Zealand with the Lions in 1993 he played in the second and third Tests and at home he became England's most capped prop when he played his 38th consecutive game in England's front-row against Scotland in 1995. His run of consecutive games ended at 40 when he was rested during the World Cup, but by the end of the tournament he had taken his number of Egland caps to 43.

Alan LERWILL

Athletics, Long Jump
Alan Leslie Lerwill. b. 15 Nov 1946 Portsmouth.

Although somewhat overshadowed by Lynn Davies (qv), Lerwill who only started jumping in 1966 when passing an athletics track on the way to the pub, was a top-class jumper, who won the Commonwealth title in 1974, after 3rd place in 1970. A student at Borough Road College before becoming a teacher, he won the World Universities title in 1970 and was 7th at the 1972 Olympics, after competing also in 1968. He was AAA champion outdoors in 1970, 1972 and 1974-5 and indoors in 1973, He had a personal best of 7.98 (1974), although with wind assistance he jumped 8.15m in 1972. A highly talented all-round sportsman, he set a British high jump record with 2.10m in 1973 and had triple jump bests of 16.10m and 16.21w in 1971.
Now a teacher at Felsted School in Essex, and a coach, his son Tom won the English Schools 800m tityle in 1995.

Sheila LERWILL

Athletics, High Jump
Sheila W Alexander b. 16 Aug 1928
London. Later Mrs Lerwill.

Lerwill beat the eight year-old world high jump record of Fanny Blankers-Koen (Hol) with a jump of 5 ft 7 $^{5}/_{8}$ *1.718m* at the 1951 WAAA Championships. A year earlier she won the European title and also set her first British record at 5 ft 6 $^{5}/_{8}$ in *1.692m*. In 1952 she won the Olympic silver medal. A Surrey county netball player, 1.70m tall, she did not start athletics until after she had left school at 18. With a best of 5 ft 1 in *1.55m* she went to George Pallett for coaching in December 1947. Under his guidance she worked hard to master the straddle technique, at which she was a pioneer among women jumpers. She was WAAA champion four times, 1950-1 and 1953-4

Simon LESSING

Triathlon
Simon Christopher Lessing. b. 12 Feb 1971 Cape Town, South Africa.

Lessing was world champion in 1993 and winner at the Goodwill Games in 1995, his eighth consecutive triathlon victory. The nephew of the novelist Doris Lessing, he was South African champion in 1988, and coming to Britain won the European junior and senior titles in 1991, retaining the latter in 1993 after 2nd in 1992. He was British champion in 1992.

John LEVER

Cricket
John Kenneth Lever. b. 24 Feb 1949 Stepney, London.

A marvellously consistent and dedicated left-arm fast-medium swing bowler for Essex, Lever might easily have played more than he did for England. He achieved his best batting and bowling performances in Test cricket in his very first match, scoring 53 and taking 7-53 and 3-24 to play a major part in England's win over India at Delhi in 1976; the first English player to score a 50 and take 10 wickets on debut.

He helped Essex to four County Championships and five limited-overs trophies and in an age of reduced first-class opportunities excelled to pass 100 wickets in a season four times, 106 in 1978-9 and 1983 and a best of 116 in 1984. He suffered a 3-year Test ban for playing in South Africa with the England 'rebels' in 1982, but returned to the Test team in 1986. With a very strong throw and great fitness, he was a fine outfielder. He was awarded the MBE in 1990.
21 Tests 1976-86: 306 runs at 11.76; HS 53; 73 wickets at 26.72, BB 7-46; 11 catches.
22 One-day Ints 1976-82: 56 runs at 8.00; HS 27*; 24 wickets at 29.70, BB 4-29; 6 catches.
First-class 1967-89: 3678 runs at 10.53, HS 91; 1722 wickets at 24.25, BB 8-27; 187 catches.

Geoff LEWIS

Horse Racing
Geoffrey Lewis. b. 21 Dec 1935 Talgarth, Powys.

As a flat race jockey Lewis rode over 100 winners in a season four times, with peaks when he was second to Lester Piggott (qv) in the jockeys' championship with 146 in 1969 and with 135 in 1970. He joined Ron Smyth's stable at Epsom and rode his first winner in 1953. He became stable jockey to Peter Hastings-Bass and then for Ian Balding, who trained the great *Mill Reef*, who Lewis rode to win the Derby and the Arc in 1971. In that year Lewis became number one jockey for Noel Murless (qv), for whom he rode the Oaks winner in 1971 and 1973. He took his list of Classics winners to five with one win in each of the Guineas.

He retired from riding in 1979, having ridden 1863 winners, and took out a trainers' licence the following year, based at Epsom.

Lennox LEWIS

Boxing
Lennox Claudius Lewis. b. 2 Sep 1965 West Ham, London.

Lewis is the only British-born world heavyweight champion this century. At the age of nine he emigrated to Canada where he had a brilliant record as an amateur, winning gold medals as a super-heavyweight at the 1983 World Junior Championships, the 1986 Commonwealth Games and the 1988 Olympics. On turning professional in 1989 he returned to England and after winning the European heavyweight crown in 1990 he took the British title the following year and the Commonwealth title in 1992. Later in 1992 he disposed of the formidable Canadian, Razor Ruddock, in two rounds in a final eliminator for the WBC title and the manner of his victory led the reigning champion, Riddick Bowe (USA), to relinquish his title rather than defend it against Lewis.

Having become WBC champion by default, Lewis successfully defended his title against Tony Tucker (USA) and Frank Bruno in 1993 and Phil Jackson (USA) in 1994, but he suffered his first-ever defeat as a professional later in the year when he lost his world title to Oliver McCall (USA).

Career record 1989-95: 27 contests. Won 26 (22 KO), Lost 1.

Ted 'Kid' LEWIS

Boxing
Ted 'Kid' Lewis. né Gershon Medeloff. b. 24 Oct 1894 Aldgate, London. d. 20 Oct 1970 London.

Lewis is usually considered, pound-for-pound, the greatest fighter ever produced in the UK. He began his professional career when he was only 14 and just before his 19th birthday won the British and European featherweight titles. He then went to the United States, where he had a whirlwind career, with 100 fights in five years. He had 20 fights against Jack Britton (USA), against whom his record was won 3, lost 5, drawn 1 and no decision 11, and who he outpointed to become the undisputed world welterweight champion in 1915. He held that title until 1919, when he was beaten by Britton.

Returning to England, in 1920 he beat Johnny Basham for the British, Empire and European welterweight titles, the first two of which he held until 1924. He had his last fight in 1929 - a win against Basham.

Career record: 283 Contests. Won 215 (71), Lost 44, Drawn 24.

Maurice LEYLAND

Cricket
Maurice Leyland. b. 20 Jul 1900 Newpark, Harrogate, North Yorkshire. d. 1 Jan 1967 Scotton Banks, Harrogate.

Leyland was an outstanding left-handed middle-order batsman, who scored over 1000 runs in 17 successive seasons 1923-39, with over 2000 in 1930 and 1933-4. His unorthodox slow left-arm bowling was also most useful for Yorkshire. He was an invaluable member of the England team virtually throughout the 1930s, and produced his best against Australia, scoring 137 and 53 in his first Test against them, the 5th Test of the 1928/9 tour, scoring 478 runs at 68.28 including three centuries in 1934, 441 at 55.12 in 1936/7 and although not selected until the The Oval Test in 1938, then scored 187, adding 382 for the 2nd wicket with Len Hutton (qv). In 1946 he helped Yorkshire to win the 12th championship while he played for them and he was Yorkshire's coach 1951-63.

41 Tests 1928-38: 2764 runs at 46.06, 9 100s HS 187; 6 wickets at 97.50, BB 3-91; 13 catches.
First-class 1920-48: 33,660 runs at 40.50, 80 100s HS 263; 466 wickets at 29.31, BB 8-63; 246 catches.

Billy LIDDELL

Football
William Beveridge Liddell. b. 10 Jan 1922 Townhill, nr Dunfermline, Fife. *3/7/2001*

Universally rated as one of the great players of all time, Liddell was strong, fast and fearless. Although essentially a left-winger, he often played on the opposite wing or at centre-forward where his 'two-footed' ability led to numerous scoring records. Signing for Liverpool in 1939, the start of his career was delayed by the war and it was not until 1946 that he made his

League debut. Apart from war-time guest appearances for a variety of clubs, he remained loyal to Liverpool and on his retirement in 1961 he had scored 229 goals in 537 appearances.

After eight wartime internationals, he won 28 caps for Scotland 1946-55 and a League Championship medal with Liverpool in 1947. Throughout his time at the club he worked in an accountant's office and always remained a part-time footballer. After retirement he became an assistant bursar at Liverpool University, in addition to serving the City as a youth worker, lay preacher and justice of the peace.

Eric LIDDELL

Athletics and Rugby
Eric Henry Liddell. b. 16 Jan 1902 Tianjin, China. d. 21 Feb 1945 Weixin, China.

The film *Chariots of Fire* was based on the story of the 1924 Olympic gold medallists Eric Liddell and Harold Abrahams (qv). Liddell's gold was at 400m, at which he set an Olympic and European record of 47.6, which remained the British record until 1936. He had gone into the Games with a best (for 440y) of 49.6, his winning time at the 1924 AAAs, improving to 48.2 in the semi-final. He also took the Olympic bronze medal at 200m, but had concentrated on the 400m rather than the 100m due to the fact that the latter was held on a Sunday.

At Scottish championships he won the 100y and 220y for five successive years 1921-5, completing trebles with Edinburgh University's mile relay team 1921-3 and by winning the 440y in 1924 and 1925, adding a fourth success at the mile relay in 1925. He was AAA champion at 100y and 220y in 1923, running his personal best times of 9.7 (which lasted as a British record for 35 years) and 21.6.

A fine all-round sportsman, he won seven caps for Scotland on the wing at rugby football in 1922-3. In 1925 he returned to China to join his father as a missionary and died there after two years of internment in a Japanese concentration camp.

Dick LILLEY

Cricket
Arthur Frederick Augustus Lilley. b. 28 Nov 1866 Holloway Head, Birmingham. d. 17 Nov 1929 Brislington, Bristol.

Lilley was England's best wicket-keeper in the early days of the century, a regular in the Test team for 13 years. His method was undemonstrative and reliable and he was also a fine, forcing batsman, exceeding 1000 runs in a season three times, with a peak of 1399 in 1895. Having made his first-class debut for North v South in 1891 he played for Warwickshire 1894-1911.

35 Tests 1896-1909: 903 runs at 20.52; HS 84; 1 wicket at 23.00, BB 1-23; 70 catches, 22 stumpings.

First-class 1894-1911: 15,597 runs at 26.30, 16 100s HS 171; 41 wickets at 36.21, BB 6-46; 717 catches, 194 stumpings.

James LILLYWHITE Jr.

Cricket
James Lillywhite Jr. b. 23 Feb 1842 Westhampnett, West Sussex. d. 25 Oct 1929 Westerton, Chichester, West Sussex.

Lillywhite was England's first Test captain, although those matches against Australia in 1877, when he organised and managed the team, came when he was 35 and had for long been one of the best bowlers in England, playing for Sussex from 1862, when he took 9-29 against the MCC on his debut. He had his biggest total of wickets with 110 at 13.36 in 1873. He was a very accurate medium-paced left-arm bowler, and also a useful batsman. In all he was concerned with the organisation of five tours to Australia, four in conjunction with Alfred Shaw and Arthur Shrewsbury (qqv). The last, in 1887/8, was unfortunately a financial disaster and that was the end of such speculative ventures by English professionals.

2 Tests 1876-7: 16 runs at 8.00; HS 10; 8 wickets at 15.75, BB 4-70; 1 catch.

First-class 1862-83: 5523 runs at 14.30, 2 100s HS 126*; 1210 wickets at 15.23, BB 10-129; 109 catches.

His uncle was **William Lillywhite** (1792-

1850), known as the 'Nonpareil', a leading cricketer of his day and largely responsible for developing round-arm bowling, and his cousins **James snr** (1825-82) and **John** (1826-74) played for Sussex and Middlesex. John went on the first overseas tour with the All England Team to Canada and the USA 1859, organised by his father **Fred** (1792-1854). James took over responsibility for the cricket annual which John had managed.

Peter LINE

Bowls
Peter A. Line. b. 13 Oct 1930 Southampton.

An outstanding skip and superb singles player, Line was EBA singles champion in 1961 and 1964, won the pairs gold in 1970 and silver in 1974 at the Commonwealth Games and the fours gold in 1972 and bronze in 1976 at the World Championships. As well as many outdoor tournament wins to the British Isles triples in 1986, his indoor successes include the EIBA fours in 1970, British Isles fours 1971 and EIBA mixed fours 1982. A draughtsman by profession, he played for Banister Park and Hampshire, making his international debut in 1955.

His wife **Wendy** (b. 24 Jul 1935 Hampshire, formerly Mrs Clarke) did not take up bowls until she was 40, but she has won the English singles (1982), triples (1985) and fours (1981) and British Isles triples (1985) with a gold medal in the women's singles at the 1986 Commonwealth Games.

Gary LINEKER

Football
Gary Winston Lineker. b. 30 Nov 1960 Leicester.

A high-scoring marksman, Lineker played for Leicester 1978-85, Everton 1985-6, Barcelona 1986-9 and Tottenham 1989-92 before signing a lucrative contract to play in Japan for Grampus Eight of Nagoya. By then he had scored 322 goals in 631 senior games. He scored 48 goals in 80 appearances for England 1984-92, just one goal

short of Bobby Charlton's record for England. He also proved to be a fine captain. In 1986 with six goals including a hat-trick against Turkey he was the top scorer in the World Cup and, having also been top scorer in the First Division in 1985/6 with 40 goals, was voted Player of the Year by both the football writers (as he was again in 1992) and his fellow players. In 1990 a further four goals brought his World Cup total to 10 to make him the top British scorer in the competition.

Despite his fine international record, he won few honours at home; he helped Leicester to the Second Division title in 1980 and was an FA Cup finalist with Everton in 1986. With Barcelona, who paid £2.3 million for him, he won a Spanish Cup winners' medal in 1988 and the European Cup Winners' Cup in 1989. With Tottenham in 1991 he at last won an FA Cup winners' medal. Persistent injuries restricted his appearances in Japan and he announced his retirement in September 1994.

His major strengths were his superb acceleration, fine positional play and an ability to turn half-chances into goals. Above all he showed an appetite for the game that many of his contemporaries seemed to lack. Articulate and with an attractive manner, he is much in demand as a TV authority on the game. He was awarded the OBE 1992.

League appearances/goals: Leicester 194/45, Everton 41/30, Tottenham 105/67.

Judy LIVERMORE – see SIMPSON

Harry LLEWELLYN

Equestrianism, Show Jumping
(Sir) Henry Morton Llewellyn. b. 18 Jul 1911 Merthyr Tydfil.

Educated at Oundle and Trinity College, Cambridge, Llewellyn was a successful amateur steeplechase jockey prior to World War II, placing 2nd on his father's horse *Ego* in the 1936 Grand National.

At show jumping he won the Olympic individual bronze in 1948 and the team gold in 1952, riding his famous horse *Foxhunter* (1940-59), whom he had bought in 1947, and on whom he won 78 international events, including the King George V Gold Cup in 1948, 1950 and 1953, and the British Championship in 1953. *Foxhunter*'s clear round on the last day of the 1952 Games ensured Britain of its only gold medal at Helsinki.

During the war, Llewellyn saw action in Italy and Normandy and was awarded an OBE in 1944 by Field Marshal Montgomery for working as his liaison officer.

Llewellyn then took up a career in the business world of Wales, which eventually led to his being knighted in 1977, having received the CBE in 1953. In 1978 he succeeded to the Baronetcy upon the death of his older brother. He was chairman of the Sports Council for Wales 1971-81.

Willie LLEWELLYN

Rugby Union
William Morris Llewellyn. b. 1 Jan 1878 Tonypandy, Rhondda Cynon Taff. d. 22 Mar 1973 Pontyclun, Cardiff.

Llewellyn was one of greatest stars in the early days of Welsh rugby. First capped against England in 1899 he scored four tries which remains the record for an international debut and he went on to score 16 tries in his 20 games on the wing for Wales 1899-1905. On the Great Britain tour of Australasia in 1904 he played on the wing in the three Tests against Australia (4 tries) but moved to the centre for the one Test against New Zealand.

He played most of his club rugby in Wales for Newport and captained London Welsh 1900-03 while studying pharmacy. A national hero, his chemist's shop was left untouched during the Tonypandy riots of 1910. When he died at the age of 95 he was the last surviving member of the Welsh side that beat the 1905 All Blacks.

Emrys LLOYD

Fencing
John Emrys Lloyd. b. 8 Sep 1908. d. 28 Jun 1987 Henley-on-Thames.

Educated at Winchester and King's College, Cambridge where he won his Blue (1925-8), Lloyd won the first of his record seven AFA foil titles, 1928, 1930-3,

1937-8 while still at university. He competed at four Olympic Games 1932-52 and won two individual bronze medals at the World Championships, 1931 and 1933.

A London solicitor, he was awarded the OBE while serving with the RAF in World War II and he married the daughter of Philip Doyne (1886-1959) who competed as a fencer at three Olympic Games 1920-8. He was President of the AFA 1974-8.

John LLOYD

Tennis
John Michael Lloyd. b. 27 Aug 1954 Leigh-on-Sea, Essex.

One of three tennis playing brothers from Essex, John formed the doubles pairing with brother David in the Davis Cup match v France in 1976 and they were the first brothers to represent Britain in the Cup since the Dohertys (qv) in 1906. Between 1974 and 1984, John played in 21 Davis Cup ties (won 15/32 singles: 9/14 doubles) and played a major part in taking Britain to the final in 1978 where they lost 4-1 to USA in Palm Springs. A talented player, he later regretted not working hard enough to make the world's top ten as a singles player, but he is the last British man to have reached the final of a men's grand slam event, the 1977 Australian Open. There he lost to Vitas Gerulaitis (USA) in five sets.

He formed an effective mixed doubles partnership with Wendy Turnbull (Aus) and together they won the French title in 1982 and Wimbledon in 1983-4. With David he reached the semi-final of the men's doubles at Wimbledon in 1973. In 1979 he married Wimbledon singles champion Chris Evert (USA), but they were divorced in 1987.

David Alan **Lloyd** (b. 3 Jan 1948) was a determined fighter in Davis Cup matches 1972-80, with a record of no wins from 4 singles but 9 of 15 doubles. He has built up a highly successful chain of tennis and indoor sports centres; the company was floated on the stock market in 1994, and by 1995 had a market value of £115 million. In January 1995 David was appointed team captain and John coach to the British

Davis Cup team. The third brother, Anthony, also partnered John in major doubles events.

Tony LOCK

Cricket
Graham Anthony Richard Lock. b. 5 Jul 1929 Limpsfield, Surrey. d. 30 Mar 1995 Perth, Western Australia.

An aggressive left-arm medium-paced spin bowler, Lock was capable of very fast balls, though with a doubtful action for which he was no-balled for throwing in five matches, eventually causing him to re-model it. Having done so, with great courage and dedication, in 1960 he continued to enjoy much success. He formed a great spin partnership with Jim Laker (qv) for both England from 1952 and Surrey, for whom he was a regular from 1949 to 1963, enjoying great success with their Championship winning teams 1952-8.

He took 100 wickets in a season each year 1951-62, with a peak of 216 at 14.39 in 1955, the last occasion on which a bowler took over 200 wickets in a season. After being surprisingly omitted from the England team to tour Australia he played nine seasons for Western Australia from 1962/3, all but the first as their inspirational captain as well as coach, and led them to the Sheffield Shield in 1967/8, just the second time they had won this competition. He also played for Leicestershire for three seasons 1965-7, and again took 100 wickets when he captained them in both 1966 and 1967.

He was a brilliant close fielder, perhaps the best ever leg-slip, and his career total of 830 catches is the third highest of all time. He made the highest score of his career in his last Test innings, against the West Indies in 1968.

49 Tests 1952-68: 742 runs at 13.74, HS 89; 174 wickets at 25.58, BB 7-35; 59 catches
First-class 1946-71: 10,342 runs at 15.88, HS 89; 2844 wickets at 19.23, BB 10-54; 830 catches.

Margaret LOCKWOOD – see BECK

William LOCKWOOD

Cricket
William Henry Lockwood. b. 25 Mar 1868 Old Radford, Notts. b. 26 Apr 1932 Radford, Notts.

Lockwood formed a formidable pace attack for Surrey with Tom Richardson (qv), helping Surrey to six County Championships in the 1890s. His subtle change of pace made him especially dangerous, and he was also a good middle-order batsman, achieving the double in 1899 and 1900. The best of his seven seasons taking over 100 wickets were with 151, 150 and 150 wickets in the three years 1892-4.

His Test career started well with 14 wickets in two matches against Australia in 1893, but after a poor tour in 1894/5 his form so declined and drinking so increased that he dropped out of the Surrey team, taking just 1 wicket in 1897. He bounced back in 1898, took 7-71 for England in the first innings of the final Test of 1899, and ended his Test career with three five-wicket hauls in the last two Tests of 1902. He had played five matches for Nottinghamshire in 1886-7 and returned there to play club cricket after 1904.

12 Tests 1893-1902: 231 runs at 17.76; HS 52*; 43 wickets at 20.55, BB 7-71; 4 catches.
First-class 1886-1904: 10,673 runs at 21.96, 15 100s HS 165; 1376 wickets at 18.34, BB 9-59; 140 catches.

Nat LOFTHOUSE

Football
Nathaniel Lofthouse. b. 27 Aug 1925 Bolton, Gt. Manchester.

Lofthouse was a vigorous, bustling centre-forward who was thought by some to be excessively physical in his approach. Whatever his style it was certainly effective. Signing amateur forms for Bolton Wanderers in 1939, he turned professional during the war and remained loyal to the club throughout his career. Scoring twice on his England debut v Yugoslavia in 1950 his international career ended in 1958 after he had won 33 caps and equalled Tom Finney's England scoring record of 30 goals. He was nicknamed 'The Lion of Vienna', from his game against Austria when he scored twice and hit the woodwork twice in 1952. He also scored six goals for the Football League against the Irish League in a 7-1 win in 1952.

For Bolton, he scored in every round of the 1953 FA Cup, including the final, which Blackpool won after a late rally inspired by Stanley Matthews (qv). At the end of the season Lofthouse was voted Player of the Year by the Football Writers Association. After topping the First Division scoring list in 1956, he scored both goals in Bolton's win over Manchester United in the 1958 FA Cup final. When his career was ended by injury in 1960 he had scored 285 goals in 503 appearances for Bolton Wanderers. He remained at the club in a variety of capacities, including that of manager, and in 1986 he was appointed its president. He was awarded the OBE in 1994.

George LOHMANN

Cricket
George Alfred Lohmann. b. 2 Jun 1865 Kensington, London. d. 1 Dec 1901 Matjiesfontein, Western Cape, South Africa.

Lohmann has by far the best average of any bowler taking 25 or more wickets in Test cricket, and his strike rate, with a wicket every 34 balls, is also a record. He had a short career with Surrey and England, which was ended by ill-health, but took over 140 wickets each year 1885-92, with 200-wicket hauls each year 1888-90. He was also an exceptional slip fielder.

After two years out of action, 1883-4, having contracted tuberculosis, he returned for two years 1895-6 and had extraordinary success on the matting wickets of South Africa, taking 35 wickets at 5.80 in the three Tests 1895/6: 7-38 and 8-7, 9-28 and 3-43, 7-42 and 1-45. The 9-28 was the first ever 9-wicket take in Test cricket and the 8-7 remains unparalleled. At that time he held the record for most wickets in Tests and on 4 Mar 1896 he was the first to reach 100. He managed the 1901 South African team in England.

18 Tests 1886-96: 213 runs at 8.87, HS 62*; 112 wickets at 10.75, BB 9-28; 28 catches.
First-class 1884-98: 7247 runs at 18.68, 3 100s HS 115; 1841 wickets at 13.74, BB 9-28; 337 catches.

Liz LONG

Swimming
Elizabeth Carole Long b. 30 Jul 1946.

In 1965 Long set European records at 200m freestyle with 2:16.2 and 2:16.1 and was voted England's swimmer of the year. At the Commonwealth Games she won bronze medals at 440y and 4 x 100y in 1962 and at the Olympics was 6th at 400m in 1964. She was ASA champion at 220y 1964-5 and 440y 1960, 1962-5.

Henry LONGHURST

Golf
Henry Carpenter Longhurst. b. 18 Mar 1909 Bronham, Bedfordshire. d. 21 Jul 1978 Hassocks, West Sussex.

A brilliant writer on golf, principally for *The Sunday Times*, whose correspondent he was from 1932 to 1977, Longhurst became the voice of the game on BBC Television and indeed worldwide. His humour, sense of timing, economy of words and distinctive voice allied to vast knowledge of the game made him virtually irreplaceable. He wrote 12 books, including his autobiography. He was awarded the CBE in 1972 for his services to golf.

As an amateur player he had captained Cambridge University and won the German Open Amateur title in 1936. He served as a Conservative Member of Parliament for Acton from 1943 to 1945.

Anita LONSBROUGH

Swimming
Anita Lonsbrough. b. 10 Aug 1941 York. Later Mrs Porter.

Lonsbrough was simultaneously Olympic, European and Commonwealth champion at breaststroke swimming. She set two world records for 200m, 2:50.3 in 1959 and 2:49.5 when winning the 1960 Olympic title, and two at 220y in 1962.

A member of the Huddersfield Borough Club, she only started at the breaststroke nine months before winning her first title at the 1958 Empire Games. There she won the 220y and a second gold on England's world record-setting medley relay team. In 1962 she won both Commonwealth 110y and 220y breaststroke titles and added a silver at the medley relay. At the Europeans she had been 2nd at 200m breaststroke and bronze medallist at medley relay in 1958, and won silver at 400m individual medley and bronze at medley relay as well as her 200m gold in 1962 despite illness and injury prior to those championships. She ended her career at the 1964 Olympics, where she was 7th at 400m IM.

She was ASA champion at 220y breaststroke 1958-62, 440y IM 1963-4, 220y freestyle 1963. Other best times: 400m IM 5:30.5 and 440y IM 5:33.6 in 1964.

She was voted Sportswoman of the year in two polls in Britain in both 1960 and 1962, and BBC Sports Personality of the Year 1962, and awarded the MBE 1963, the first swimmer to be so honoured. For many years she has written on swimming for the *Daily Telegraph* and the *Sunday Telegraph* and commentated for BBC Radio. She is married to cyclist Hugh Porter (qv).

Cyril LOWE

Rugby Union
Cyril Nelson 'Kit' Lowe. b. 7 Oct 1891 Holbeach, Lincs. d. 6 Feb 1983 Chobham, Surrey.

Scoring 18 tries in 25 consecutive international appearances between 1913 and 1923. Lowe was England's leading try scorer until Rory Underwood (qv) bettered his record in 1990. This remarkable record was achieved despite the fact that he failed to score in each of the five matches in his first international season of 1913.

On leaving Dulwich College he went up to Cambridge University where he won his Blue in 1911-13. During the war he was an ace fighter pilot, winning the DFC and MC

and rising to the rank of Group Captain. Having played for England nine times in 1913-14 he won a further 16 caps after the war and, briefly, held the record as England's most capped player. Individually, 1914 was his best season as he scored three tries against Scotland and France and two against Wales, and that total of 8 tries in one Championship season remains an England record. In his six international seasons England won the Grand Slam four times.

Douglas LOWE

Athletics
Douglas Gordon Arthur Lowe. b. 7 Aug 1902 Manchester. d. 30 Mar 1981 Cranbrook, Kent.

Lowe was the first athlete to retain his Olympic 800m title as he won in 1924 and 1928, on both occasions setting British records at 1:52.4 and 1:51.8 respectively. After the 1928 Games he improved that record to 1:51.2. He also anchored the British 4 x 400m team that was 5th at the 1928 Games.

He was AAA champion at both 440y and 880y in 1927 and 1928 and set a world record for 600y with 1:10.4 in 1926. While at Pembroke College, Cambridge he won a Blue for soccer as well as for athletics, at which he won the 880y 1922-4 and mile 1924 against Oxford. He was Hon. Secretary of the AAA from 1931 to 1938, and became a leading barrister and QC. Other best times: 440y 48.8 (1927), 1500m 3:57.0 (1924), 1 mile 4:21.0 (1925).

John LOWE

Darts
John Lowe. b. 21 Jul 1945 Clay Cross, Derbyshire.

Formerly a joiner, Lowe has been one of the top players since he won his first major title, the World Masters in 1976. He won that title again in 1980 and won the World Cup singles in 1981 and 1991. He has played on seven winning England teams in the latter tournament from 1979 to 1991. He lost to Leighton Rees (qv) in the final of the first World Professional Championship in 1978, but won the title the following year and also in 1987 and 1993, being runner-up in 1981-2, 1985 and 1988.

On 13 Oct 1984 Lowe won £102,000 for achieving the first 501 scored with the minimum nine darts in a major event. This was in the quarter-finals of the first World Matchplay Championship at Slough; he went on to win the final. He won the British Open in 1977 and 1988, the British Matchplay in 1978 and 1986, the *News of the World* Championship in 1981, and with Bob Anderson (qv) the first World Pairs title in 1986. He is chairman of the World Professional Darts Players Association.

Laddie LUCAS

Golf
Percy Belgrave Lucas. b. 2 Sep 1915 Sandwich Bay, Kent.

The first notable left-handed golfer, Lucas played for Britain in the Walker Cup in 1947, having been selected but not playing in 1936, and was non-playing captain in 1949. He was the British Boys champion in 1933 and leading amateur in the Open in 1935.

A distinguished fighter ace in World War II, he was decorated with the DSO and bar and the DFC. MP for Brentford and Chiswick 1950-9, he was Chairman of the Greyhound Racing Association, a member of the Sports Council 1971-83, and built up a golf driving range business with John Jacobs. He was awarded the CBE in 1981.

Muriel LUCAS

Badminton
Muriel Lucas. Later Mrs King Adams.

The most successful player in the early days of the All-England Badminton Championships, Lucas's total of 17 titles remains unbeaten by a woman. She was singles champion in 1902, 1905 and 1907-10, won the women's doubles 10 times in 12 years between the first championships in 1899 and 1910 with four different partners, and the mixed doubles with Norman Wood in 1908.

Linda LUDGROVE

Swimming
Linda Kay Ludgrove. b. 8 Sep 1947 Greenwich, London. Later Mrs Lillo.

At 15 years 80 days Ludgrove was the youngest champion at the 1962 Commonwealth Games when she won the 110y backstroke, having set a world record 1:10.9 in a heat. She went on to win the 220y title as well, twice setting a world record time of 2:36.2 with a silver in the medley relay. Four years later she retained both titles, with a Games record 1:09.0 in a 110y heat and a world record 2:28.5 to win the 220y and she helped England to a world record time in the medley relay for her fifth Commonwealth gold.

At European Championships she won a silver at 100m backstroke in 1966 with medley relay bronze medals in 1962 and 1966, and at the 1964 Olympics was 6th at 100m. She won ASA backstroke titles at 110y 1962-4 and 1966-7 and at 220y in 1964 and 1966-7. She was voted Sportswoman of the Year in 1966 by the Sports Writers' Association.

Margot LUMB

Squash
Margot E Lumb. b. 1913. Later Mrs H W L Gordon.

With five consecutive victories (1935-9) Lumb was the most successful home player in the British Women's Championships until the arrival of Janet Morgan (qv). During the five years she won the title she didn't lose a single game until her fourth Championship, when Betty Cooke managed to win a game (9-6) in the 1938 semi-final. She also won the US title in 1935 and represented GB v USA in the Wolfe-Noel Cup a record five times between 1934 and 1950. Her last appearance in 1950, aged 37, was as Mrs Gordon after which she settled in South Africa, where her husband was working. She also played tennis against the USA as a member of the Wightman Cup team in 1937-8. A hard-hitting left-hander, she relied on the pace of shot and her speed about the court and she seldom became involved in lengthy rallies.

Penny LUMLEY

Real Tennis
Penelope Christine Lumley. b. 13 May 1963 Frinton, Essex. née Fellows.

Penny Fellows won the world singles title at real tennis in 1989, retained the title in 1991, having married Colin Lumley, and regained it in 1995. In 1993 she won the world doubles title with Charlotte Cornwallis. At the British Open Championships she won the singles in 1988, 1991 and 1993 and the doubles in 1991 with Alex Garside. Before taking up real tennis she was a county standard lawn tennis player.

Arnold, Harry and Peter LUNN

Skiing
Sir Henry Simpson Lunn. b. 30 Jul 1859 Horncastle, Lincs. d. 18 Mar 1939 Marylebone, London.

Sir Arnold Lunn. b. 18 Apr 1888 Madras, India. d. 2 Jun 1974 London.

Peter Northcote Lunn. b. 15 Nov 1914 London.

Henry Lunn, who had been a Methodist missionary in India, organised an ecumenical conference at Grindelwald in Switzerland in January 1892. Encouraged by the success of this meeting he organised another in the summer of 1892 and found that with such organisation of people's travel he could make a profit; thus started Lunn's Tours. Wishing to keep his staff occupied in the winter he tried the experiment of taking a party to Chamonix in 1898/9 for winter sports, including his 10-year-old son **Arnold**. He further developed this, to attract the upper classes, by founding the Public Schools Alpine Sports Club in 1902-3 and organising the first ski race. From those beginnings, by British tourists, has developed the whole Alpine skiing industry.

After World War I Arnold, dissatisfied with downhill racing, introduced the modern slalom as a test of turning technique as well as courage and speed, with the first contest at Mürren in 1922. With Hannes Schneider he devised the Arlberg-

Kandahar ski racing competition and this was first staged in 1928. His rules for downhill and slalom racing were recognised by the FIS in 1930.

Arnold Lunn, who was knighted in 1953 for his services to skiing and to Anglo-Swiss relations, was the author of over 50 books, and his son, **Peter**, also became a distinguished writer on skiing, having captained the British skiing team at the 1936 Olympics, where he placed 15th in the downhill, 13th slalom and 12th combined. At successive world championships 1934-6 he was 9th at slalom, 10th downhill and 9th downhill. He served in the diplomatic service and was awarded the OBE in 1951 and CMG in 1957.

Gladys LUNN

Athletics
Gladys Annie Lunn. b. 1 Jun 1908 King's Norton, Birmingham. d. 3 Jan 1988 Great Barr GC, Birmingham.

Often known as 'Sally' after the well-known teacake 'Sally Lunn' of her era, she was a great pioneer of women's athletics. In 1925 she achieved her first world best time with 2:24.8 for 880y, a record she improved in 1930 to 2:18.2 when she won the first of five WAAA titles at 880y or 800m. That win came just after her international debut against Germany and she went on to win the 1930 World Games title at 800m. She was also WAAA champion at 880 yards in 1931-2, 1934 and 1937, at javelin in 1937 and at 1 mile in 1936 and 1937, in both of which races she ran world best times, 5:23.0 and 5:17.0 respectively. She ran a third mile best of 5:20.9 in between these wins, and set official world records at 1000m with 3:04.4 in 1931 and 3:00.6 in 1934.

At the women's World Games in London in 1934 she was 3rd in the 800m in a time estimated at a British record 2:17.0. Zdenka Koubková of Czechoslovakia smashed the world record with 2:12.4, but it later transpired that 'she' was a man, and the world record is now accepted as having been set by the runner-up Märtha Wretman (Swe) in an estimated 2:15.2. At the javelin Lunn set three British records and had a best performance of 36.40m for the bronze medal at the 1938 Empire Games, where she was the English women's team captain. She had won both the 880y and javelin at the 1934 Empire Games. At cross-country she was both national and international champion in 1931 and 1932. A stalwart member of Birchfield Harriers, she became president of the Midland Counties WAAA in 1947. A proficient golfer, she died while playing on her favourite course.

Randolph LYCETT

Tennis
Randolph Lycett. b. 27 Aug 1886 Birmingham. d. 9 Feb 1935 Jersey.

Born in England, Lycett learned his tennis in Australia, where he spent much of his early life, and in 1911 he declined an offer to represent Australasia in the Davis Cup. After the war he represented Britain in the Cup in three ties in 1921 and 1923, (4/8 singles, 2/7 doubles). Having won the Australian doubles in 1905 and 1911, he was the winner at Wimbledon for three successive years 1921-3 with three different partners. He was also a three-time winner of the mixed doubles with Elizabeth Ryan (USA) at Wimbledon 1919, 1921 and 1923.

Joe LYDON

Rugby League
Joseph Lydon. b. 26 Nov 1963 Wigan, Gt. Manchester.

Lydon was a deceptive and speedy runner who excelled at centre, wing or full-back. As a 19-year-old he scored a try on his international debut against France in 1983 and went on to win 23 caps (plus 7 appearances as a substitute) 1983-92. Beginning his career with Widnes, with whom he won the Premiership in 1983 and the Challenge Cup 1984, he moved to Wigan in 1985 for a then world record fee of £100,000. He played in further Challenge Cup winning teams for Wigan each year 1988-90 and 1992, and helped them win the Premiership 1987, 1992 and 1994, the John Player Special Trophy 1987 and

Regal Trophy 1989-90 and 1993. He won the Man of Steel award as the rugby league personality of the year in 1984. During the summer of 1987 he played for Eastern Suburbs, Sydney.
He had toured Zimbabwe with the English Schools rugby union team in 1982. He now also works as a TV commentator.

Sandy LYLE

Golf
Alexander Walter Barr Lyle. b. 9 Feb 1958 Shrewsbury.

Known for his prodigious length off the tee, Lyle was one of the top golfers in the world in the 1980s, and with Nick Faldo (qv) was responsible for the restoration of British golfing prestige.
He was a boy international from 1972 and British Youths champion in 1977, when he played in the Walker Cup before turning professional. In 1979 he won the Scandinavian and European Opens and made his Ryder Cup debut. He won the British Open in 1985, and had a great year in 1988 when he won the US Masters and World Matchplay and was voted Sports Writers Sportsman of the Year. Thereafter he slumped somewhat and failed to make the Ryder Cup teams, so that his record 1979-87 reads seven wins, nine losses and two halves in five ties. In 1992 he was back, however, to win the Volvo Masters and rank 8th on the European money earnings. His career European Tour earnings are £2,252,867 with 18 wins 1977-94, having been leading money-winner in 1979, 1982 and 1985 and Vardon Trophy winner 1979-80 and 1985. He has five wins on the US PGA tour. He was awarded the MBE in 1987.
His father was the professional at Hawkstone Park, Shropshire.

Andrea LYNCH

Athletics
Andrea Joan Caron Lynch. b. 24 Nov 1962 Barbados. Later Mrs Saunders.

Lynch vied with Sonia Lannaman for most of the 1970s for the title of Britian's top woman sprinter and represented Britain 39 times 1970-8. She came to the fore with a

European Junior silver medal at 100m in 1970 and in winning English Schools titles at 100m 1970 and 200m 1971. In 1972 she was an Olympic semi-finalist at 100m and a year later set her first British record for 100m at 11.2. She improved that to 11.1 in 1974 and 1975 and to 10.9 when she won the 1977 USTFF title while at Long Beach State.

At 100m she was ranked 3rd in the world in 1974, when she won silver medals at 100m and 4 x 100m relay at the Commonwealth Games and European bronze at 100m, and 2nd in 1975 when she was 2nd in the European Cup 100m. She was 7th in the 1976 Olympic 100m and ended her championships career with 2nd at 100m and 3rd 200m at the 1977 World University Games. Indoors at 60m she was 2nd in 1974 and 1st in 1975 at the European Indoors, on each occasion running a British record time of 7.17. She won the WAAA 100m in 1973 and 1975-6 and the indoor 60m in 1973 and 1976. Her 200m best times: 23.15 and 22.90w (1975).

She married the Canadian 400m runner Brian Saunders, who had a best time of 45.68 in 1977.

Benny LYNCH

Boxing
Benjamin Lynch. b. 2 Apr 1913 Clydesdale, Glasgow. d. 6 Aug 1946 Glasgow.

Lynch was a superbly talented flyweight whose devastating punch earned him a world title after only four years of professional fighting. In September 1935 he floored defending NBA world champion, Jackie Brown, ten times within the first two rounds before the referee stopped the contest. At the time, the Americans recognised Small Montana (Phi) as the world champion, but Lynch defeated him on points in January 1937 to become the undisputed champion and later in the year he defended his title with a 13th round KO over Peter Kane (qv) after one of the most thrilling flyweight contests ever seen in a British ring. By this time his addiction to alcohol was becoming increasingly apparent and Lynch failed to make the weight limit for a world title defence against

Jackie Jurich (USA) in June 1938; although he knocked out the Californian in the 12th round of the non-title fight which replaced the scheduled bout, he forfeited his world title. Four months later he had his last fight when, in woeful physical condition, he was knocked out in three rounds by the Romanian, Aurel Toma. After a meteoric rise to the top the tragic decline of Benny Lynch was equally rapid. Driven by the need to support his craving for alcohol, he was reduced to pawning his trophies and fighting in booths and he was found dead in a gutter aged only 33.

Career record 1931-8: 110 contests. Won 82, Drew 15, Lost 13.

Jack LYNCH (Ireland)

Hurling
John Lynch. b. 15 Aug 1917 Blackpool, Co. Cork.

While he achieved his greatest eminence as Taoiseach (prime minister) of Ireland, 1966-73 and 1977-9, Jack Lynch was a redoubtable exponent of Gaelic sports. He became the first player to win all-Ireland medals at both hurling (1941-4 and 1946) and Gaelic football 1945; thus winning with Cork at one or the other sport for six successive years.

He made his debut in the Cork senior hurling side in 1935 and captained them in an all-Ireland final for the first time in 1939. As he played on the losing side in 1947 he is the only player to have taken part in seven successive all-Ireland finals. He also won three national League medals and three Railway Cup medals. He became a Fianna Fáil MP in 1948.

Liz LYNCH – see McCOLGAN

Hon. Alfred LYTTELTON

Cricket
Rt. Hon. Alfred Lyttelton KC. b. 7 Feb 1857 London. d. 5 Jul 1913 Marylebone, London.

An enterprising batsman and outstanding wicket-keeper, the feat for which Lyttelton will be best remembered is that of taking four wickets for 19 runs with lobs while still wearing his pads for England at The Oval against Australia in 1884! That was his last Test and from the age of 28 he concentrated on his work as a barrister. Son of the 4th Lord Lyttelton, he was a brilliant all-round sportsman, who represented Cambridge University at real tennis, racquets and athletics as well as his four years in the cricket team, and played for England at soccer in 1877 after playing for Old Etonians in the 1876 Cup Final. He was an MP from 1895 to his death at 56 following a operation.

4 Tests 1880-4: 94 runs at 15.66; HS 31; 4 wickets at 4.75, BB 4-19; 2 catches.

First-class 1876-1887: 4429 runs at 27.85, 7 100s HS 181; 4 wickets at 43.00, BB 4-19; 134 catches, 70 stumpings.

Five of his brothers played first-class cricket and one, Edward (1955-1942) also played for England at soccer.

Jack McAULIFFE (Ireland)

Boxing
Jack McAuliffe. b. 26 Mar 1866 Cork, Ireland. d. 5 Nov 1937 Forest Hills, New York, USA.

Irish-born, McAuliffe's parents emigrated to Brooklyn when he was a child and he grew up to be one the greatest fighters in America. In a career which lasted some 12 years, he was the world lightweight champion at the end of the bare knuckle days and the beginning of the gloved era. When Jack 'Nonpareil' Dempsey (qv) gave up his world lightweight title he nominated McAuliffe as his successor and the Irish-American's first world title fight was against the British champion, Jem Carney, in Revere, USA on 16 November 1887. After 74 rounds (sic) the bout was declared a draw following an invasion of the ring by McAuliffe's supporters who, mindful of their wagers, realised that their hero was about to be knocked out. After this close call, McAuliffe was never seriously troubled again. In defence of his World title he knocked out Bill Dacey (USA) in 1888 and Billy Myer (USA) in 1892 before he retired in 1896, having been unbeaten throughout his career. After he gave up boxing he went on the stage.

Career record 1884-97: 36 contests. Won 31 (21 KO), Drew 5.

Jock McAVOY

Boxing
né Joseph Bamford. b. 20 Nov 1908 Burnley, Lancashire. d. 20 Nov 1971 Partington, Gt. Manchester.

McAvoy was one of the many unemployed who sought to make a living through professional boxing during the depression years. He succeeded better than most and his ability as a two-fisted, hard-punching fighter brought him both fame and prosperity. He began his professional career in 1927 and after unsuccessfully challenging Len Harvey (qv) in 1932, he took the British and Empire middleweight title from Harvey the following year. Although he soon relinquished the Empire crown, he made four defences of his British title before moving up to the light-heavyweight division. In March 1936 he lost on points when he challenged John Henry Lewis (USA) for the World light-heavyweight title in New York and later in the year he was also defeated when he took on Jack Petersen for the British heavyweight crown. However, he won the British light-heavyweight title from Eddie Phillips in April 1937, but lost the title to his old rival Len Harvey the following year with a further loss to Harvey in a great fight at the White City in 1939.

Despite these Championship successes, possibly his finest performance came in a non-title bout in New York in December 1935 when he had the American World middleweight champion, Ed 'Babe' Risko, on the floor six times before winning with a first round KO. He retired in 1945, never having been knocked out, but sadly he contracted polio soon afterwards and his last years were spent in a wheelchair.

Career record 1927-45: 148 contests. Won 134 (92 KO), Lost 14.

Willie John McBRIDE

Rugby Union
William James McBride. b. 6 Jun 1940 Toomebridge, Co. Antrim.

During an international career which lasted from 1962 to 1975, 'Willie John' played in a record 17 Tests for the Lions and was capped 63 times (12 as captain) by Ireland. His total of 80 international caps remained a record until bettered by fellow Irishman Mike Gibson (qv) in 1979.

In an era when the robust, physical play of the All Blacks and Springboks dominated, McBride was the only forward from the Home Countries who was their match. In addition to his ability to take on the opposition, he inspired his team-mates to do the same and his outstanding leadership qualities led to his being appointed captain of the 1974 Lions in South Africa. This was his fifth Lions tour and his team stunned the Springboks by winning the Test series 3-0 with one match drawn. After retirement he coached the Irish team and was manager of the 1983 Lions tour to New Zealand.

Robert McCOIG

Badminton
Robert Scrymgeour McCoig. b. 10 Mar 1939 Greenock, Inverclyde.

The greatest Scottish player, he won 39 Scottish titles and a record 67 international caps 1956-76. Although unseeded he was a finalist in the 1968 All-England mixed doubles and at the 1966 Commonwealth Games he was 4th in the singles and won a bronze medal in the mixed doubles with Muriel Ferguson. He was captain and flag bearer of the Scottish team at the 1974 Games. In a lengthy career he played in seven Thomas Cup series, 1957-76, and was awarded the MBE in 1975.

Ally McCOIST

Football
Alistair Murdoch McCoist. b. 24 Sep 1962 Bellshill, North Lanarkshire.

A prolific goal scorer, McCoist's partnership with Mark Hateley has been one of the features of Scottish football in recent years. After spells with St Johnstone 1978-81 and Sunderland 1981-3, he was signed by Rangers in June 1983 where his clinical finishing as a striker quickly paid dividends. He helped Rangers to victories in the Scottish Cup 1992, eight Scottish League Cup wins and eight League titles

between 1984 and 1995 and in 1992 he became the first player to score 200 goals in the Scottish Premier Division. Four times he has scored over 30 goals in a league season, topped by 34 in 1991/2 and 1992/3, in which years he won the Adidas Golden Boot award as Europe's top scorer. He was voted Player of the Year in 1992 by both the Scottish Football Writers and the Scottish Professional Footballers Association. He won 46 caps for Scotland from 1986 to 1993.

Liz McCOLGAN

Athletics
Elizabeth McColgan. née Lynch. b. 24 May 1964 Dundee.

McColgan was world champion at 10,000m in Tokyo in 1991 and at the half-marathon in 1992. A Scottish international who competed for Dundee Hawkhill, she made her first steps to world class while at the University of Alabama, USA, for whom she won the NCAA indoor mile in 1986. In that year she won Scotland's one athletics gold medal at the 1986 Commonwealth Games in Edinburgh with the first of four British records for 10,000m, 31:41.42. In 1987 she was second in the World cross-country and smashed her bests at all events from 800m to 10,000m, at which she was 5th in the World Championships in 31:19.82. Further British records at 10,000m came with 31:06.99 in 1988 and 30:57.07 in 1991.

She married international steeplechaser Peter McColgan (b. 20 Feb 1963) in October 1987. In 1988, after a highly successful campaign on the roads, she took the Olympic silver medal at 10,000m. She set a 10km world road best of 30:38 at Orlando in 1989, just a week after she had taken the World indoor silver at 3000m, having led nearly all the way, and then coming back for sixth at 1500m just 13 minutes later. In 1990 she retained her Commonwealth 10,000m title and was also 3rd at 3000m.

She made an astonishingly fast return after her daughter Eilish was born on 25 Nov 1990 to win a series of important races and then place 3rd in the World cross-country in March 1991. She won her first two marathon races, the fastest ever debut marathon 2:27:32 at New York 1991 and 2:27:38 in Tokyo 1992, but was 3rd in London 1993. In 1992 she ran a world indoor record of 15:03.17 for 5000m and was 5th in the Olympic 10,000m.

Injuries kept her out of major races from April 1993 to October 1994 and on the track until her 4th place for Britain at 10,000m in the 1995 European Cup. She was BBC Sports Personality of the Year for 1991, and was awarded the MBE in the 1992 New Year Honours List.

Won UK 10,000m 1986, 5000m 1988, 3000m 1989, 1991; Scottish 3000m 1985-6. Other best times: 800m 2:05.9 (1987), 1500m 4:01.38 (1987), 1M 4:26.11 (1987), 2000m 5:40.24 (1987), 3000m 8:34.80i (1989), 8:38.23 (1991), 5000m 15:01.08 (1987). Road: 15km 47:43 (1988), Half Marathon 67:11 (1992).

William McCONNELL

Hockey
William David Robert McConnell. b. 19 Apr 1956 Newry, Co. Down.

He shares the record as Ireland's most capped player with Steve Martin (qv). Both played 135 times for their country but as McConnell's 51 appearances for GB was exceeded by Martin (94) the *overall* record goes to Martin.

He won a bronze medal at the 1984 Olympic Games but although still a regular first choice for Ireland in the midfield or as a defender, he failed to make the Olympic team in 1988 and 1992.

Billy McCRACKEN

Football
William McCracken. b. 29 Jan 1883 Belfast. d. 20 Jan 1979 Hull.

As one of great exponents of the original offside trap, McCracken was instrumental in bringing about a change of the law in 1925. Exceptionally fast for a full-back, he won an Irish Cup winners' medal with Distillery in 1903 before moving to Newcastle the following year where he added League Championship medals in

1907 and 1909 and an FA Cup winners' medal in 1910. Although his international career lasted 21 years (1902-23) his frequent disputes with the Irish FA, usually over appearance money, restricted his number of caps to 15. He played his last game for Northern Ireland when manager of Hull City after which he managed Gateshead 1932-3, Millwall 1933-6 and Aldershot 1937-49 before becoming a scout for Watford and for his old club, Newcastle.

David McCREERY

Football
David McCreery. b. 16 Sep 1957 Belfast.

McCreery won 67 caps for Northern Ireland as a midfielder 1976-90. He began his professional career with Manchester United in 1974, coming on as a substitute in the FA Cup finals of 1976 and 1977 and earning a winner's medal in the latter. In 1979 he moved to Queen's Park Rangers, where he spent two seasons followed by a year in America with Tulsa, after which he returned to England, signing for Newcastle United where he spent seven seasons before transferring to Hearts.

More recently he has been player and assistant manager for Hartlepool United 1991-2 and player-coach at Carlisle United from 1992.

Kirsty McDERMOTT – see WADE

Jem MACE

Boxing
James Mace. b. 8 Apr 1831 Beeston, Norfolk. d. 30 Nov 1910 Jarrow, Tyne and Wear.

The last genius of the old school of prize fighting, Mace was the father of modern scientific boxing. He travelled the country as an itinerant fiddler and after many bouts in farmyard barns and other secret locations he was recognised as the British middleweight champion. As a heavyweight he defeated Sam Hurst for the British crown in October 1861 and although he lost the title to Sam King six months later, when King retired immediately after the fight Mace was universally acclaimed as the World champion. After disposing of a challenge from Joe Goss, he had great difficulty in finding anyone willing to take him on and Mace didn't fight again for three years. After a lucrative exhibition tour of Australia, he based himself in America where his defeat of Tom Allen in May 1870 reinforced his claim to the world heavyweight title. He retired the following year at the age of 40.

Held in high esteem on both sides of the Atlantic, he did as much as any man to take pugilism into the modern era of boxing.

Career record (incomplete) 1855-71: 19 contests. Won 12 (12 KO), Drew 2, Lost 3, Stopped by police 2.

Freddie McEVOY

Bobsleigh
Francis Joseph McEvoy. b.12 Feb 1907 St Kilda, Melbourne, Australia. d. 7 Nov 1951 Morocco.

Australian-born, he came to England as a child to attend prep school in Sussex and later Stonyhurst College, Yorkshire. In the years prior to World War II he was Britain's leading bobsledder winning a bronze medal in the four-man event at the 1936 Olympics and gold at the World Championships 1937 and 1938. He was also world champion in the two-man event in 1937.

Despite these successees he was better known for his social life. He never bothered with regular employment and his funds were provided by a succession of super-rich women including the heiresses Barbara Hutton and Doris Duke. He died by drowning while trying to rescue his French wife after a boating accident in high seas off the coast of Morocco.

Ian McGEECHAN

Rugby Union
Ian Robert McGeechan. b. 30 Oct 1946 Leeds.

Although born in England and playing his club rugby for the English club, Headingley, he was an outstanding member of the Scottish back line. Between 1972 and 1979 he was capped 32 times by Scotland, 12 as a fly-half and 20 as a centre, and was equally effective in either position. In 1973 he played at fly-half in all the Five Nations matches and at centre in the same matches in 1975. He toured South Africa (1974) and New Zealand (1977) with the British Lions and played in all four Tests on both tours. All his Test appearances were in the centre except for the third Test against New Zealand when he came on as a replacement for the injured winger J.J.Williams.

On retirement, he was appointed Scotland's assistant coach before taking over as chief coach in 1988. He coached the Lions in Australia in 1989 when they won the series 2-1 and after guiding Scotland to the Grand Slam in 1990, when he was universally recognised as one of the game's greatest coaches, he was awarded the OBE. He again coached the Lions on their 1993 tour of New Zealand and although the series was lost 2-1 he further enhanced his reputation as a brilliant thinker and motivator. He retired from the international scene in 1994 and accepted an appointment with the Northampton club who were struggling to maintain their First Division status in the Courage League.

Walter McGOWAN

Boxing
Walter McGowan. b. 13 Oct 1942 Burnbank, South Lanarkshire.

Taught to box by his father, a former professional fighter, McGowan had a brilliant career as an amateur, losing only two of his 124 fights, and after winning the ABA flyweight title in 1961 he turned professional. In only his 10th fight as a pro he won the British and Empire title by knocking out fellow Scot, Jackie Brown (qv). In June 1966 he had a comfortable points victory over Salvatore Burruni (Italy) to take the WBC world title but in December of that year he lost his crown to Chartchai Chionoi (Thailand) when forced to retire with a cut nose. In a re-match in September 1967 the referee again stopped the fight because of cuts sustained by McGowan.

Soon after winning the world flyweight crown, he took the British and Empire bantamweight title from Alan Rudkin in September 1966, but Rudkin regained the title in May 1968. He was awarded the MBE in 1966 after winning the world title. Career record 1961-9: 40 contests. Won 32 (14 KO), Drew 1, Lost 7.

Danny McGRAIN

Football
Daniel Fergus McGrain. b. 1 May 1950 Glasgow.

A superb full-back, McGrain overcame such handicaps as diabetes and a fractured skull to win 62 Scottish caps (10 as captain) 1972-82. Signing as a professional for Celtic in 1967 he remained loyal to the club throughout his career and was a key member of the team which won the Scottish League Championship and the Scottish Cup five times each and the Scottish League Cup twice.

Paul McGRATH

Football
Paul McGrath. b. 4 Dec 1959 Greenford, Middlesex, London.

Signed from St Patrick's Athletic by Manchester United in 1982, having helped them to win the FA Cup in 1985 he left for Aston Villa in 1989 after a dispute with United manager, Alex Ferguson. With Villa he had a League Cup win in 1994. A fine man-marker or zonal defender, he has built a reputation as one of the top defenders in Europe and has been capped 75 times by Ireland from 1985 to June 1995, scoring 7 goals. He has been handicapped by persistent knee trouble.

Bobby McGREGOR

Swimming
Robert Bilsland McGregor. b. 3 Apr 1944 Falkirk.

The hero of British swimming in the 1960s, he was 2nd at 110y freestyle at the 1962 Commonwealth Games and 2nd again at 100m at the 1964 Olympics, when Don Schollander (USA) passed him in the last five metres and beat him by a tenth of a second. He missed a 100m medal by inches at the 1962 Europeans before recording the fastest split in the relay final to take the British team into 2nd place. At last he won a major gold medal at the 1966 Europeans, despite blatant flyers by two of his opponents. Convinced that there would be a recall, he was left at the start and seemed hopelessly adrift. Sensationally he stormed down the pool and caught the field by the halfway point, holding on to win in 53.7. He also won a silver medal at 4 x 100m freestyle.

He was 4th at 100m in the 1968 Olympics, when his preparations had been affected by his studies for his architecture degree at the University of Strathclyde. He was ASA champion at 110y freestyle 1962-4 and 1966-8 and 220y 1963 and 1966 and won 12 Scottish titles. He set five world records at 110y freestyle to 53.5 in 1966, with four European 100m records in 1963-4 and a final British record of 53.4 in 1967. He was awarded the MBE.

His father **David** (b. 7 Feb 1909) had competed at the 1936 Olympic Games at water polo.

Gregor MacGREGOR

Cricket and Rugby Union
Gregor MacGregor. b. 31 Aug 1869 Merchiston, Edinburgh. d. 20 Aug 1919 Marylebone, London.

MacGregor was a brilliant wicket-keeper for Middlesex and England, and full-back or centre for Scotland, for whom he played in 13 internationals 1890-4. Educated at Uppingham School and Cambridge University, he won Blues for rugby 1889-90 and cricket 1888-91 and made his reputation by standing up to the fierce pace of Sammy Woods. He captained Middlesex at cricket 1899-1907.
8 Tests 1890-3: 96 runs at 12.00, HS 31; 14 catches, 3 stumpings.
First-class 1888-1907: 6381 runs at 18.02, 3 100s HS 141; 411 catches, 148 stumpings.

Yvonne McGREGOR

Cycling
Yvonne McGregor. b. 9 Apr 1961
Bradford, West Yorkshire.

In Manchester on 17 June 1995, McGregor cycled 47.411 kilometres in one hour, thus becoming the first British woman ever to hold this world record. Two weeks later she won her third successive women's national 50 miles time trial championship. Having earlier been a fell runner, who had placed 8th in the world championships, she turned to triathlon and only took up cycling at the age of 30 in 1991.

A youth worker, riding for Swallowdale Cycling Club, she achieved remarkable success in 1993, when she won British National time trial titles at 10, 50 and 100 miles. In 1994, in her first-ever bunch start race, she took the Commonwealth Games gold medal in the 25 km points race in sensational style by lapping every other competitor. By her world record achievement she had won British time trial titles at every distance from 3000m to 100 miles.

Jimmy McGRORY

Football
James Edward McGrory. b. 26 Apr 1904
Glasgow. d. 20 Oct 1982 Glasgow.

McGrory is the most prolific goal scorer in the history of British football. A centreforward with Celtic he scored 550 goals in first-class games which still stands a record: 523 goals were for Celtic in League and Cup games with the remainder coming for Clydebank and in international and representative matches. He scored eight goals v Dunfermline in 1928, a Scottish League record, and averaged more than a goal a game over a 15-year period with more than half the goals coming from his powerful and accurate heading.

He made his debut for Celtic in 1922 and, apart from spending the following season on loan to Clydebank, he stayed with the club until his retirement in 1937. Initially he played on the left wing, but soon established himself at centre-forward. His extraordinary talents helped Celtic win the

Scottish League (1926, 1936) and the Scottish Cup four times (1925, 1931, 1933, 1937), in addition to being losing finalists twice (1926, 1928).

His seven Scottish caps (with six goals) seem poor reward for a player of his phenomenal goal-scoring abilities, but he was a contemporary of the equally talented Hughie Gallacher (qv). On leaving Celtic in 1937 he became manager of Kilmarnock until 1939 when the club closed for the duration. In 1945 he returned to Celtic as manager and when he handed over to Jock Stein (qv) in 1955 he was appointed public relations officer.

Barry McGUIGAN

Boxing
Finbar Patrick McGuigan. b. 28 Feb 1961
Clones, Co, Monaghan.

McGuigan was an Irish hero throughout his career. As an amateur in 1978 at bantamweight he won the Irish title and the gold medal at the Commonwealth Games. Having turned professional he won the British featherweight title in 1983 and in 1985 outpointed Eusebio Pedroza (Pan) to win the world featherweight championship. He was upset in 1986 by Steve Cruz (USA) and retired briefly. He started fighting again but did not mount a serious title challenge. He was voted BBC Sports Personality of the Year 1985.

Career record: 32 Contests: Won 30 (26), Lost 2.

Alister McHARG

Rugby Union
Alister Ferguson McHarg. b. 7 Jun 1944
Irvine, North Ayrshire.

In an international career which began in 1968 he won 44 caps at lock and on his retirement in 1979 he was Scotland's most capped player in that position.

Exceptionally mobile for a second-row, his speed about the field often disconcerted the opposition as he joined in the attacking moves of his backs. He played for West of Scotland and London Scottish.

Jimmy McILROY

Football
James McIlroy. b. 25 Oct 1931 Lambeg,
Co. Antrim.

The complete inside-forward, McIlroy spent 13 years at Burnley after being signed from Glentoran in 1950. He helped Burnley to the League Championship in 1960 and the FA Cup final in 1962 but after playing 437 games (114 goals) for the club a dispute with autocratic chairman, Bob Lord, led to his departure to Stoke City the following season. Unable to command a regular first team place at Stoke, he moved to Oldham Athletic in 1966 and later became manager of the club. He was, by his own admission, not suited to a managerial role and he soon left football to go into business.

First capped by Northern Ireland in 1951, his international career had apparently come to an end in 1963 but while with Stoke he was recalled to the national team in 1965. He won three further caps to bring his total up to 55 (scoring 10 goals) and, at the time, only Danny Blanchflower and Billy Bingham (qqv) had played more times for Northern Ireland.

Bob McINTYRE

Motorcycling
Robert McG McIntyre. b. 7 Nov 1928
Glasgow. d. Aug 1962.

In 1957 the much-respected Glaswegian became the first rider to lap the Isle of Man circuit at over 100 mph. On his 500cc Gilera he first recorded 162.59 km/h *101.03 mph* and then 162.74 km/h *101.12 mph*, finally winning the Senior TT with four laps at over 100. That year he also won the Junior TT race. For much of his career he competed as an independent entrant, and was only a works rider for three seasons, 1954 for AJS, 1957 for Gilera (2nd in the World 500cc and 3rd at 350cc) and 1962 for Honda (2nd in the World 250cc). He set a world 1 hour speed record with 221km/h *141 mph* on a 350cc Gilera at Monza in 1957. He died as a result of injuries sustained when he crashed an experimental five-speed Norton at Oulton Park, Cheshire in August 1962.

Curly MACK (Ireland)

Badminton
Gordon S B Mack. b. 1900 Ireland. d. 1949
Canada.

Mack's partnership with Frank Devlin (qv) at badminton was the greatest of his era. Together they won the All-England doubles six times, 1923, 1926-7, 1929-31. He also won the singles in 1924 and the mixed doubles in 1923. Mack modelled his playing style on Sir George Thomas (qv) with whom he won six of his Irish doubles titles and he also won the singles three times. He was capped by Ireland 21 times, 1919-32, and he also won the men's doubles at the Irish tennis championships in 1929.

A brilliant scholar, he became a schoolmaster, after taking a double first at Trinity College, Dublin, but later took up a more lucrative post as a professional coach in Montreal where he sadly committed suicide at the age of 49.

Kitty McKANE – see GODFREE

Dave MACKAY

Football
David Craig Mackay. b. 14 Nov 1934
Musselburgh, Midlothian.

An indomitable half-back, Mackay's stamina and strong tackling earned him more honours than most other players in history. With Hearts he won a complete set of the major Scottish medals playing on the team which won the League Cup 1955 and 1959, Scottish Cup 1956 and the League Championship 1958. In retrospect his 22 internationals for Scotland 1957-65 (scoring 4 goals) is an amazingly low number, but a broken leg twice held him back. In recognition of the consistent quality of his play he was voted Scottish Footballer of the Year in 1958.

On moving south to Tottenham Hotspur in 1959 he continued to add to his impressive medal collection by helping Spurs to the Cup and League double in 1961, the FA Cup again in 1962 and, after breaking a leg twice in the 1963, he returned as Tottenham's captain to take his third FA Cup winners' medal in 1967. The following year he moved to Derby County and, after leading them to the Second Division title in 1969, he was voted joint Footballer of the Year.

In 1971 he was appointed player-manager at Swindon Town and over the next 20 years he served as manager of Nottingham Forest, Derby County (League champions 1975) and Walsall before spending a number of years as a successful coach in Kuwait and Dubai. On his return to Britain in 1987 he took over at Doncaster Rovers before moving to Birmingham City two years later. He resigned from his post with Birmingham in 1991 and went to Zamelek, Egypt.

Neil McKECHNIE

Swimming
Neil John McKechnie. b. 28 Apr 1939 Wallasey, Merseyside.

When swimming became a popular television sport in Britain in the late 1950s, McKechnie was one of its biggest stars. He was ASA freestyle champion at 110y in 1956-7, 220y 1955-7, 440y 1955-6 and 880y 1956. He competed at the 1956 Olympics, but only won one major championship medal, a bronze at 4 x 100m medley at the 1958 Commonwealth Games. He set British records with 57.8 for 110y and 4:31.6 for 440y in 1956.

Eddie MACKEN (Ireland)

Equestrianism, Show Jumping
Edward Macken. b. 20 Oct 1949 Granara, Co. Longford.

Ireland's top show-jumper, an international 1970-95, Macken had the misfortune to miss major titles narrowly as he was runner-up at the Worlds in 1974 on *Pele* and in 1978 on *Boomerang*. He lost the former to Hartwig Steenken (Ger) in a jump-off and the latter to Gerd Wiltfang (Ger) by just 0.25 point, the smallest ever winning margin. Macken was also runner-up in the European Championship in 1977 on *Kerry Gold*, when he lost the jump-off to Johan Heins (Hol) by just 0.1 sec with four faults apiece, and tied for 3rd in the first World Cup Final in 1979. His four wins in the Hickstead Jumping Derby

equals the record and they were won in successive years, 1976-9 on the great *Boomerang*, who was buried on his death in 1983 at Macken's stud in Kells.

Mary McKENNA (Ireland)

Golf
Mary A McKenna. b. 29 Apr 1949 Dublin.

McKenna played in a record ninth Curtis Cup match in 1986, when for the first time she was on the winning team. Her overall record was 10 wins, 16 losses and 4 halves in her 30 matches from 1970. She was the Irish Ladies' Amateur champion in 1969, 1972, 1974, 1977, 1979, 1981-2 and 1989, and won the British Open Amateur Stroke Play title in 1979.

Duke McKENZIE

Boxing
Duke Roger McKenzie. b. 5 May 1963 Croydon, London.

McKenzie was the first British boxer to win a world title at three different weights. After turning professional in 1982 he beat Danny Flynn for the vacant British flyweight title in 1985 and added the European crown the following year by beating Charlie Magri (qv). After two defences of his European crown, he relinquished both the British and European titles but in October 1988 he won the IBF world title with a victory over reigning champion Rolando Bohol (Phi) and after one successful defence he lost the world crown to Dave McAuley (Ire) in 1989.

McKenzie then moved up to the bantamweight division and after unsuccessfully challenging Thierry Jacob (Fra) for the vacant European title in 1990, he won the WBO world title the following year with a points victory over Gaby Canizales (USA). After two successful defences, he lost his world title in dramatic fashion when substitute Rafael Del Valle, in his first professional fight outside his native Puerto Rico, knocked him out in the first round in May 1992. Later in the year, McKenzie won a world title at a third weight when he took the WBO super-bantamweight crown from Jesse Benavides (USA) but in June

1993 the title passed to Daniel Jimenez (PR) on a majority points decision after a close 12-round contest. In October 1994 he lost to Steve Robinson (UK) in a bid for the WBO world featherweight title and in April 1995 he lost in a bid for the European bantamweight title.

Career record 1982-95: 41 Contests. Won 37, Lost 6.

George McKENZIE

Wrestling
George McKenzie. b. 1890. d. 1957.

McKenzie's remarkable top-class career lasted 25 years, during which time he won nine British Championships from 1909 to 1932, winning both featherweight and lightweight titles in 1922 and 1924, He competed for Britain at five Olympuc Games 1908-28 and was a team official at four further Games 1936-56. At his ninth Games he was awarded the rare honour for an official of carrying the British flag at the Opening Ceremony. He was one of the world's outstanding authorities on the sport, an international referee and British delegate to the International Federation. As secretary of the National and British Amateur Wrestling Association 1935-57, he did much to keep amateur wrestling going in Britain during some difficult years.

Precious McKENZIE

Weightlifting
Precious McKenzie. b. 6 Jun 1936 South Africa. Ex South African, now New Zealand.

The only man to win four gold medals at the Commonwealth Games, McKenzie is also the oldest ever champion. He received his name after surprisingly, but happily, surviving surgery when he was born in South Africa. While very young he lost his father to a crocodile. Although he was his country's best lifter at his weight in 1958, another, white, South African was sent to the Games in Cardiff and indeed won the gold medal.

Precious came to Britain just before the 1966 Games and after special efforts were made to rush through his passport he arrived in Kingston as a member of the English team. He won the gold medal at bantamweight, a feat he repeated in 1970 and at flyweight in 1974. At the latter, held in Christchurch, he was so attracted by New Zealand that he emigrated there and wore NZ colours when he won the Commonwealth bantamweight title in 1978. A three-time Olympian, he was 9th at bantamweight in 1968 and 1972 and 13th at flyweight in 1976. He won eight British titles from 1966.

He also won the world 56kg powerlifting title in 1980.

Mick MACKEY (Ireland)

Hurling
Michael Mackey. b. 12 Jul 1912 Castleconnell, Co. Limerick.

The charismatic captain of the great Limerick team, which reached its peak in winning the all-Ireland title in 1936 and won again in 1940, Mackey became, in 1961, the first player to be elected to the Hurling Hall of Fame. He made his debut for the Limerick senior hurling side in 1930 and played on his first all-Ireland winning side in 1934. He won five National League medals and eight Railway Cup medals and with his club, Ahane, won 20 Limerick championship medals, 15 in hurling and 5 in Gaelic football. He was named at centre-forward on the hurling 'Team of the Century'.

Catherina McKIERNAN (Ireland)

Athletics
Catherina McKiernan.b. 30 Nov 1969 Cornafean, Co. Cavan.

The Irish national senior cross-county champion each year 1990-4, McKiernan was 2nd in the World cross-country championships for four successive years 1992-5. In 1991-2 she won three successive grand prix events in Belgium, France and Mallusk and went on to win the World Cross Country Challenge series. She won this series again in 1993, 1994 and 1995 and at the end of 1994 became the inaugural European women's champion. She has yet to match such success on the track. At 3000m she was eliminated in the heats of the 1991 Worlds and 1992 Olympics and in both 1993 and 1994 she set Irish records for 10,000m. She reached of the major championships finals, but failed to finish in the 1993 Worlds and 1994 Europeans.

In 1993 she recorded a time of 32:14.74 and in 1994 reduced that dramatically to 31:19.11 in winning a European Cup race for Ireland. Further improvement came in 1995, when she started the summer season in magnificent form, following a 5000m best of 14:59.04 with an Irish record for 10,000m of 31:08.41. At 3000m, she was Irish champion each year 1990-3 and has a best time of 8:51.33 (1992).

Other best times: 1500m 4:21.30 (1990), 1M 4:37.74 (1992).

Ken McKINLAY

Speedway
John Robert Vicas McKinlay. b. 7 Jun 1928 Blantyre, South Lanarkshire.

Having first ridden speedway for the British Army in Germany in 1947, McKinlay joined Glasgow in 1948 and retired in 1974, having raced mainly for Glasgow, Leicester, Coventry and West Ham. He scored 5971 points from 703 league matches, made 12 world final appearances and raced in 152 internationals, captaining Scotland, Great Britain, England and British Isles.

Esmé MACKINNON

Alpine Skiing
Esmé Mackinnon. b 2 Dec 1913. Later Mrs Murphy.

In 1930 Mackinnon won the British title for the downhill, slalom and combined at Mürren and the following year, although still only 17 years-old, she won these three events over the same course at the International Downhill Ski-racing meeting which was afterwards recognised as the first Alpine World Championships. She was thus the first British woman ever to win the World title and her feat has subsequently only been matched by Evie Pinching (qv) in 1936.

Christopher MACKINTOSH

Athletics, Bobsleigh and Rugby Union.
Charles Ernest Whistler Christopher Mackintosh. b. 31 Oct 1903 Charville, France. d. 12 Jan 1974 Haddington, East Lothian.

An accomplished all-round sportsman, Mackintosh, after winning the Public Schools tennis doubles in 1921, went up to Oxford where he represented the University at athletics, rugby football and skiing and was an international at each of these sports. At the long jump he won against Cambridge in 1924 and 1925 and was 6th at the 1924 Olympics; his best was 7.14m in 1925. He played one international for Scotland as a winger at rugby in 1924. On leaving Oxford he joined the Alpine travel business of Sir Henry Lunn (qv), and was chairman of the company from 1931 to 1944. In 1938 he was a member of the British team that won the four-man bobsleigh world title.

His daughters Sheena (1948 and 1952) and Vora (1952) were Olympic skiers.

Myrtle MACLAGAN

Cricket
Myrtle Ethel Maclagan. b. 2 Apr 1911 Ambala, India. d. 11 Mar 1993 Farnham, Surrey.

In the first women's Test played between England and Australia at Brisbane in December 1934, Maclagan took 7-10 with her off-spinners for England in skittling Australia out for just 47. She then top-scored with 72 to ensure a 9-wicket victory for England. In the 2nd Test at Sydney in January she scored the first Test century by a woman with 119. In 1937, with 115 at Blackpool, she became the first woman to score a Test century in England.

In her 14 Tests over 17 years she became the first to reach the career figures of 1000 runs and of 50 wickets with 1007 at 41.95 and 60 at 15.58 respectively. She captained England in two Tests in 1951. She was an officer in the ATS during the war and having rejoined the Army in 1951 was awarded the MBE for her services to the

WRAC in 1966. She was a fine all-rounder, also playing for the army at hockey, lacrosse, badminton and tennis.

Archie MacLAREN

Cricket
Archibald Campbell MacLaren. b. 1 Dec 1871 Whalley Range, Manchester. d. 17 Nov 1944 Warfield Park, Bracknell, Berkshire.

After making his name as a handsome batsman at Harrow, MacLaren joined Lancashire in 1890, and scored a century on his debut for them. He was Lancashire captain for 1894-6 and 1899-1907.
In 1895 he made 424 in 470 minutes of majestic batting against Somerset at Taunton; this lasted as the record score in first-class cricket for over 27 years and added 80 to W.G.Grace's previous record. He succeeded W.G. as England captain in 1899 and in all led England in 22 Tests, but was not especially successful, winning 4 to 11 losses, and his authoritarian attitude did not get the most out of his players. At 49 he raised a team that beat the all-conquering Australians at the end of their tour in 1921. He managed the England team to South Africa in 1924/5 and was Lancashire coach in the 1920s.
35 Tests 1894-1909: 1931 runs at 33.87, 5 100s HS 140; 29 catches.
First-class 1890-1921: 22,237 runs at 34.15, 47 100s HS 424; 1 wicket; 453 catches.

Ian McLAUCHLAN

Rugby Union
John 'Ian' McLauchlan. b. 14 Apr 1942 Tarbolton, South Ayrshire.

A small but immensely strong loose-head prop, McLaughlan was universally known as the 'Mighty Mouse'. Capped 43 times by Scotland 1969-79, he took over the captaincy in 1973 and became Scotland's most successful captain, leading his country to 10 wins in 19 matches.
With the Lions in New Zealand (1971) and South Africa (1974) the hosts initially viewed his modest physique with something approaching derision but he gave both the All Blacks and Springboks an object lesson in the technique of front-row play. Playing in all four Tests on both tours, he was only once on the losing side.

William McLEAN

Hockey
William D McLean. b. 6 Mar 1952 Kirkcaldy, Fife.

With 89 international appearances 1972-85 McLean is Scotland's most capped hockey player. He also represented GB 19 times as a forward. Educated at Kirkcaldy HS and Strathclyde University he qualified as an accountant and played for Edinburgh Civil Service and Inverleith and Grange.

Alex McLEISH

Football
Alexander McLeish. b. 21 Jan 1959 Glasgow.

A central defender whose entire League career was spent with Aberdeen, McLeish first signed for the club in 1976 and is still with them 17 seasons later. During his time with Aberdeen they have won the European Cup Winners' Cup 1983, the Scottish Cup four times, the Scottish League title three times and the Scottish League Cup once. He won 77 caps for Scotland between 1980 and 1993.

Hugh McLEOD

Rugby Union
Hugh Ferns McLeod. b. 8 Jun 1932 Hawick, Borders.

A tough prop-forward from Hawick, McLeod made his international debut against France in 1954 and kept his place in the Scottish XV until his retirement in 1962 at the age of 29. Initially a tighthead prop, he later specialised in the loosehead position. His 40 caps came in consecutive matches and he toured twice with the Lions. Although he did not command a place in the Test side in South Africa in 1955, he played in all six Tests against Australia and New Zealand on his second tour in 1959. He was awarded the OBE.

Kenneth MacLEOD

Rugby Union, Cricket and Athletics
Kenneth Grant McLeod. b. 2 Feb 1888
Liverpool. d. 7 Mar 1967 St. James,
Western Cape, South Africa.

A triple Cambridge Blue (rugby, cricket and athletics). McLeod could claim to be Scotland's finest all-round sportsman. While a schoolboy at Fettes he was selected to play rugby against Wales in 1905 but he agreed with his Headmaster that he was too young and the invitation was declined. The match was played just two days after MacLeod's 17th birthday and had the invitation been accepted he would still hold the record as Britain's youngest rugby international.

His debut for Scotland was, however, not long delayed and he won the first of his ten caps against New Zealand while still only 17. A strong running three-quarter, he was awarded his Blue in all four years at Cambridge 1905-08, but after one brother had been seriously injured and another, **Lewis** (1885-1907), who was also capped by Scotland, died following rugby injuries, he gave up the game at his father's request after his final appearance in the University match. His glorious rugby career ended at the age of 20.

As a cricketer, he won his Blue 1908-09 as a lower order bat and fast-medium bowler and then played regularly for Lancashire until 1914 and for the Gentleman v Players in 1909.

He also excelled at athletics, even though he refused to take the sport seriously, and he was unbeaten over 100y while at Cambridge, winning against Oxford in 1906 and 1908 and sharing 1st place in 1907. He was chosen for the 1908 Olympics but did not take part, and he was also the Scottish long jump champion in 1907.

After being gassed serving as a captain in the Gordon Highlanders in World War I he settled in South Africa for health reasons and became a scratch golfer.

First class cricket 1908-13: 3458 runs at 23.84, 6 100s HS 131; 103 wickets at 26.67, BB 6-29; 107 catches.

Frank McLINTOCK

Football
Francis McLintock. b. 28 Dec 1939
Gorbals, Glasgow.

Originally a right-half with Leicester City, McLintock moved to centre-half when he went to Arsenal in 1964. He skippered Arsenal when they won the Cup and League double in 1971, having led them to victory in the Inter-Cities Fairs Cup the previous season. In 1973 he moved to Queen's Park Rangers and on his retirement in 1977 he returned to Leicester City as manager, but the appointment lasted less than a year. He then joined the BBC radio commentary team before taking over as coach at Queen's Park Rangers in 1982 after which he was manager of Brentford from 1984 to 1987 and then assistant manager of Millwall 1988-90.

He was capped nine times by Scotland 1963-71, and was awarded the MBE in 1972.

Ray McLOUGHLIN (Ireland)

Rugby Union
Raymond John McLoughlin. b. 24 Aug 1939 Ballinasloe, Co. Galway.

McLoughlin was a major influence on Irish rugby, not only as a player but also as a planner, tactician and leader. Winning 40 caps for Ireland 1962-75 he was appointed captain in 1965 but, after leading his country to their best season for many years, 1966 was not so successful and he was relieved of the post. This decision took him out of the running as a possible captain of the 1966 Lions but he went on the tour and played in both Tests against Australia and the fourth Test against New Zealand.

His playing abilities as a prop forward were never in doubt but, with hindsight, it can be seen that many of his ideas were ahead of their time and most of his thinking on the game is now widely accepted.

From Gorbally College, he studied chemical engineering at Newcastle University and University College, Dublin, and played for Blackrock College and Gosforth.

His brother **Phelim** won one cap for Ireland as a flanker in 1976.

Jimmy McMULLAN

Football
James McMullan. b. 26 Mar 1895 Denny, Stirling. d. 28 Nov 1964 Sheffield.

The outstanding Scottish half-back of the 1920s, McMullen captained the legendary 'Wembley Wizards' in their 5-1 defeat of England in 1928.

After playing for a number of Scottish clubs he went to Manchester City from Partick Thistle in 1926 and stayed at Maine Road until his retirement in 1933. He was twice on the losing side in the FA Cup final (1926, 1933) and helped Manchester City win promotion to the First Division in 1928. He won 16 Scottish caps between 1920 and 1929 and after his playing days were over he held managerial posts at Oldham Athletic, Aston Villa, Notts County and Sheffield Wednesday before leaving the game in 1942 to take a job in a Sheffield steel works.

Carol McNEILL

Orienteering
Carol McNeill. b. 26 Feb 1944 Crosby, Merseyside.

McNeill won the British women's orienteering title a record six times, 1967, 1969, 1972, 1974-6. She started orienteering while teaching PE in Devizes, Wiltshire and represented Britain from 1968 to 1983, continuing thereafter with much success as a veteran. The best result she obtained at seven World Championships was 7th in 1979. In 1984 she was awarded the MBE and she was coach to the British team in 1984-5. Now teaching in Coniston, she has contributed to books about orienteering and is a keen mountaineer and cross-country skier.

Hugo MacNEILL (Ireland)

Rugby Union
Hugh Patrick MacNeill. b. 16 Sep 1958 Dublin.

After captaining Irish Schools, he won a 'B' international cap before making his full international debut while an undergraduate at Dublin University. He scored tries in his first two internationals and went on to win 37 caps (1981-8) at full-back and was a member of the team which won the Triple Crown in 1982 and 1985. On the 1983 British Lions tour of New Zealand he played in the first two Tests and came on as a replacement in the final Test.

At Oxford University he won a Blue in 1982 and in 1983, when he was captain.

Phil MacPHERSON

Rugby Union
George Philip Stewart MacPherson. b. 14 Dec 1903 Newtonmore, Highland. d. 2 Mar 1981 Thame, Oxfordshire.

One of the greatest Scottish centres, McPherson captained his country in 12 of his 26 international matches. After attending Edinburgh Academy and Fettes he went up to Oxford University and played against Cambridge in 1922-4. A fine all-round athlete, he was the Scottish long jump champion in 1929.

After reaching the rank of Brigadier in World War II he resumed his career as a merchant banker and became a director of many major institutions. He was awarded the CBE for his work.

Colin McRAE

Rallying
Colin McRae. b. 5 Aug 1968 Lanark, South Lanarkshire.

Having led the RAC Rally in three previous years, only to be denied a chance of success by mechanical failure, McRae won the event in 1994 in a Subaru Impreza to become the first British winner of the race since Roger Clark in 1976. He joined Subaru in 1991 and was British Rally champion for them in 1991 and 1992. In the latter year, with co-driver Derek Ringer, he won all six rounds of the championships and also burst into world prominence with a fine 2nd place in the Swedish Rally. He was successively 8th, 5th equal and 4th in the World Championship 1992-4, winning

his first World Championships rally in 1993 in New Zealand, but had been too prone to accidents until 1994 when he again won the New Zealand rally and the Australian rally before his RAC triumph
His father James Worthy **'Jimmy'** (b. 28 Oct 1943) won the British International Open rally five times, 1981-2, 1984, 1987-8, and Colin, who had started racing at motocross as a teenager and who started rallying in 1985, won that title in 1991 and 1992. His brother Alister is also a rally driver.

Paul McSTAY

Football
Paul Michael Lyons McStay. b. 22 Oct 1964 Hamilton, South Lanarkshire.

McStay is one of the few modern British international players who has spent his entire senior career with one club. Signed by Celtic as an attacking midfield player in 1981, he had made 440 League appearances (53 goals) for the club to the end of the 1993/4 season and is currently the Celtic captain. With one of the most devastating long-range shots in the game and also superb passing ability, he was a member of the Celtic team which won the Scottish League Cup in 1983, the Scottish Cup in 1985, 1988-9 and 1995 and the League Championship in 1986 and 1988. For Scotland he has won 71 caps, several as captain, from 1984 to 1994.

Dick McTAGGART

Boxing
Richard McTaggart. b. 15 Oct 1935 Dundee.

The greatest British amateur boxer of modern times, McTaggart came from a family of boxers and as a lightweight he won gold (1956), and bronze (1960) at the Olympics, Commonwealth Games gold (1958) and three ABA titles (1956, 1958, 1960). He won two further ABA titles as a light-welterweight (1963, 1965) and fought at this weight in 1964 to become the only British boxer ever to compete in three Olympic Games. In 1956 he was awarded the Val Barker Trophy as the out-

standing stylist of the Melbourne Olympics. With no great power behind his punches, but considerable ability to say out of trouble, he resisted many offers to turn professional and continued to serve amateur boxing in Scotland after his retirement. He was the coach of the Scottish team at the 1990 Commonwealth Games.

Mike McTIGUE (Ireland)

Boxing
Michael Francis McTigue. b. 26 Nov 1892 Kilmonaugh Parish, Co. Clare. d. 26 Aug 1966 Queen's, New York, USA.

A member of a large Irish family, McTigue emigrated to America in 1908 at the age of 16. Although not a heavy puncher, he was a skilful boxer and after building an impressive record fighting in America he returned to Dublin in March 1923 to win the World light-heavyweight title with a 20 round points victory over Battling Siki (Senegal). After a draw and a 'no decision' result against Young Stribling (USA) he met Paul Berlanbach (USA) in May 1925 when the American experienced little difficulty in taking the world title after inflicting heavy punishment on McTigue. By 1927 the world light-heavyweight title had fallen vacant and McTigue met Tommy Loughran (USA) for the crown but he lost on points and this was his last opportunity to regain the crown he had initially won four years earlier. As his 40th birthday approached his licence was revoked in 1930.
Career record 1909-30: 166 contests. Won 104 (53 KO), Drew 10, Lost 45, No decision 6, declared no contest 1.

George McVEAGH (Ireland)

Hockey, Tennis, Cricket and Squash
Trevor George Brooke McVeagh. b. 14 Sep 1906 Athboy, Co. Meath. d. 5 Jun 1968 Dublin.

McVeagh was considered by some to be Ireland's greatest all-round sportsman. He represented Ireland more than 70 times in four different sports. In one year, 1938, he won international caps for tennis, hockey, squash and cricket. After winning the first of his 24 Irish caps for hockey in 1932, while still at Dublin University, he played in every international match until the outbreak of war. He joined Three Rock Rovers and from the outside-left position captained what was probably Ireland's best ever team to three successive Triple Crown victories, 1937-9.

At tennis, he represented Ireland in 17 Davis Cup matches 1933-8 and twice beat the great Bill Tilden (USA).

At cricket, McVeagh's batting average of 40.88 runs per innings is the second best ever of those playing four or more first-class matches for Ireland. He scored 695 runs in ten matches 1926-34, and scored a century and took 5 catches in the historic Irish victory over the West Indies in 1928. Adding appearances for Dublin University 1925-6, his first-class record was 814 runs at 38.76.

He was Irish national squash champion three times, 1935-7, a first-class billiards player and one of the best game shots in Ireland.

Peter McWILLIAM

Football
Peter McWilliam. b. 21 Sep 1878 Inveravon, Aberdeenshire. d. 1 Oct 1951 Redcar, North Yorkshire.

McWilliam was one of the first international players who went on to become a successful manager. He signed for Newcastle in 1902 where he was quickly recognised as the finest left-half of his era. He played in four FA Cup finals, being on the winning side in 1910, won League Championship honours (1905, 1907, 1909) and he was capped eight times by Scotland 1905-11 before his career was ended by injury in 1911. He was appointed manager of Tottenham Hotspur in 1913 and after the war he was instrumental in developing the great Spurs side of the 1920s before moving to Middlesbrough for a record managerial salary in 1927.

He then went to Arsenal in an advisory capacity in 1934 but in 1938 he returned to Tottenham as manager and remained in the post until his retirement in 1942. Although his achievements as both player and manager are now sometimes overlooked, they were recognised by the Football League when he was awarded their Long Service medal in 1939.

Charlie MAGRI

Boxing
Charles Magri. b. 20 Jul 1956 Tunis, Tunisia.

After a brilliant amateur career which included three successive ABA flyweight titles 1975-7 and a place on the 1976 Olympic team, Magri began his professional career in spectacular fashion. He won his first 23 bouts and took the British flyweight title in 1976 and the European crown in 1979. He made six successful defences of his European title before losing to Duke McKenzie (qv) in 1986 but relinquished his British title in 1981 in order to concentrate on his bid for world honours. He successfully challenged Eleoncio Mercedes (Dominica) for the WBC World title in March 1983. but only six months later he lost his world crown to Frankie Cedeno (Phi) at Wembley. In February 1985 he made an unsuccessful attempt to recover his title when the fight was stopped in the fourth round of his challenge to Sot Chitalada (Thailand). A charming man, he retired to run his sports goods business.
Career record 1977-86: 35 contests. Won 30 (18 KO), Lost 5.

Adrian MAGUIRE (Ireland)

Horse Racing
Adrian Maguire. b. 29 Apr 1971.

Maguire very speedily established himself in the top-flight as a jumps jockey. The champion point-to-point rider in 1990/1 he rode his first winner under National Hunt rules on 12 Mar 1991 (*Omerta* at Cheltenham) and rode the same horse to win the 1991 Irish Grand National, and became the youngest ever winning jockey of that race. Retained by David Nicholson (qv), in 1991/2 he rode 71 winners, the most ever for a conditional jockey, including the Cheltenham Gold Cup on *Cool Ground*.

The following season he rode 124 winners and in 1993/4 he had an epic duel with Richard Dunwoody (qv) for the jockey's championships, leading at one point by 40 but ending with 194 (from a record 915 rides), four short of Dunwoody; he also set a season's money won record at £1,193,917. After his win on *Barton Bank* in the King George in December 1993 he was described by David Nicholson as '...the best I've seen. That's not an accolade, that's the truth'.

Harold MAHONEY (Ireland)

Tennis
Harold Segerson Mahoney. b. 13 Feb 1867 Edinburgh. d. 27 Jun 1905 Caragh Hill, nr Killorglin, Co. Kerry.

Even by the informal standards of his time, Mahoney adopted an exceptionally casual attitude to the game and had a very poor forehand but he was a superb volleyer and still good enough to win the Wimbledon singles in 1896. The following year he lost to Reggie Doherty (qv) in the Challenge Round and he was twice a finalist in the All Comers' event (1893, 1898). He continued to play at Wimbledon until 1904, but he was past his best by the time the Davis Cup competition began and was never a member of the British team.
Although born in Scotland, he was from an old Irish family and won the gold medal for philosophy at Trinity College, Dublin. At the Irish Championships he won the singles 1898 and the mixed doubles 1895-6 and at the 1900 Olympic Games he won silver medals in the singles and mixed doubles and a bronze in the men's doubles. Aged only 38, he was found dead, alongside his wrecked bicycle, at the foot of a hill near his family home.

Devon MALCOLM

Cricket
Devon Eugene Malcolm. b. 22 Feb 1963 Kingston, Jamaica.

Malcolm's potential and fierce pace were recognised when he was selected for England against Australia in 1989 despite a fairly modest record in first-class cricket.

He came to live in England in 1979 and played for Yorkshire Schools in 1981, but made his debut for Derbyshire at the age of 21 in 1984. He took a long time to gain a regular county place, but after 56 first-class wickets in 1988 (his best until he took 69 in 1994) he received his county cap in 1989
In 1990 he took 19 wickets in four Tests in the West Indies, his 6-77 at Kingston helping England to a memorable victory, and he followed that with 15 at 17.93 in three Tests against New Zealand. From 1991, however, he was in and out of the England team, too often bowling erratically and not helped by slow, flat wickets in England. His great moment came when he was recalled to the England team for the final Test against South Africa at The Oval in 1994. After 1-81 in the first innings he produced a devastating burst in the second innings, taking 9-57, the best bowling performance for England since Jim Laker (qv) in 1956.
32 Tests 1989-95: 208 runs at 6.70, HS 29; 111 wickets at 36.27, BB 9-57; 5 catches.
10 One-day Ints 1990-4: 9 runs at 3.00, HS 4; 16 wickets at 25.25, BB 3-40; 1 catches.
First-class 1984-95: 1126 runs at 7.98, HS 51; 562 wickets at 31.57, BB 9-57; 29 catches.

James MALE

Rackets and Real Tennis
James S Male.

Male was world rackets champion after successfully challenging his regular doubles partner, John Prenn (qv) in 1988. He won the British Open singles four times (1987-89, 1991) and the British Amateur singles five times between 1986 and December 1994 and his record in doubles partnering Prenn has been particularly noteworthy. Together they won the World Championship in 1990, the British Open six times (1986-90, 1993) and the British Amateur six times (1988-91, 1993, 1995) after Male had taken the title in 1987 with Rupert Owen-Browne.
He was also the British Amateur real tennis champion winning the singles in 1990 and the doubles in 1987 and 1989-90.

Harry MALLIN

Boxing
Henry William Mallin. b. 1 Jun 1892
Shoreditch, London. d. 8 Nov 1969
Lewisham, London.

Mallin was the greatest amateur boxer ever produced in the UK. He was ABA middleweight champion each year from 1919-23 and never lost a match as an amateur boxer in over 300 bouts. He won the Olympic middleweight title in both 1920 and 1924, becoming the first man to defend an Olympic boxing championship. He worked as a London policeman and in 1936 and 1952 managed the British team at the Olympics. He became a high-ranking officer in the Amateur Boxing Association.

His brother **Fred**erick (1902-87) was also ABA middleweight champion five times, 1928-32.

Wilf MANNION

Football
Wilfred James Mannion. b. 16 May 1918
South Bank, Middlesbrough. / 4 / 4 / 2000

Mannion was a brilliant inside-forward whose ball control and passing skills won him 26 England caps in a short international career 1946-51. But for the lost wartime years (in which he played in four wartime internationals) and a bitter wage dispute with his club in 1948, he would undoubtedly have played many more times for England.

Signing as a professional for Middlesbrough in 1937, he played in four wartime internationals before playing in the first post-war international which marked the beginning of the famous partnership of Carter - Lawton - Mannion as the spearhead of England's attack. He virtually retired in 1954 having scored 99 goals for Middlesbrough in 341 games but he made a few final appearances for Hull City in 1955 (16 matches, 1 goal). He then drifted into non-League football and was associated with a variety of clubs, each of lesser status than the previous one. When he finally gave up football and returned to his native Middlesbrough to look for work he found employment desperately hard to come by: a truly saddening experience for a man who had once been feted as a local hero.

Nigel MANSELL

Motor Racing
Nigel Ernest James Mansell. b. 8 Aug 1953
Upton-upon-Severn, Worcestershire.

Britain's most successful Grand Prix driver of the 1980s, Mansell's tenacity paid off when he became world champion in 1992, two years after declaring his retirement. He had been runner-up in the World Drivers' Championship in 1986, when he was just two points behind Alain Prost (Fra), and again in 1987 and 1991. Rash and aggressive at the outset of his career, he worked hard to achieve his eminence as a fast and determined driver.

He started at kart racing and was in the British junior team, turning to motor racing in the 1970s while also working as an aerospace engineer. He made his Grand Prix debut in 1980, driving for Lotus 1980-4, Williams 1985-8, 1991-2 and Ferrari in 1989-90. His first pole position was in 1984 and his first Formula One win was in the 1985 European Grand Prix at Brands Hatch.

After a short-lived retirement and much speculation he signed for Williams for 1991, reaching his peak with a brilliant year in 1992 when he won the first five Grand Prix races and took the title with 108 points to 56 by the runner-up, his teammate Riccardo Patrese (Ita). Mansell started in pole position a record 14 times in the 16 races, and had a record nine wins. His championship year ended, however, in anger, as he left Formula One after being unable to agree terms with Frank Williams (qv).

He then competed for two years for the Newman-Haas Indy Car team in the USA. He had a triumphant season in 1993, winning his first race, achieving a splendid 3rd in his first ever drive in the Indianapolis 500 and winning the overall IndyCar series with five wins in all. His second year was not quite so successful and he returned to Formula One for four Grand Prix races for Williams in 1994, ending the year by winning the Australian Grand Prix when the rivals for the championship Michael Schumacher (Ger) and Mansell's teammate Damon Hill (qv) collided and left the race. In 1995 he signed for McLaren, but could not fit into the car for the first two Grand Prix races and then had two unsuccessful races before being replaced.

In his career Mansell had 31 GP wins (28 for Williams, 3 Ferrari) and 31 pole positions from 187 starts, totalling 482 points. He was BBC Sports personality of 1986 and 1992, and awarded the OBE 1991.

Terence MANSERGH

Hockey
Terence Walter Mansergh. b. 5 Nov 1900 Hampstead, London. d. 8 Sep 1981 Salisbury, Wiltshire.

Scoring 46 goals for England in only 18 matches 1920-8, his phenomenal strike rate of 2.56 goals per match is by far the best in British international hockey. Full details of the scorers in some of the early international have not been traced but it is known that Mansergh, a brilliant centre-forward, scored 8 goals v France 1922, 7 v Wales 1924, 6 v France 1926 and 1928, and scored a hat trick on at least two other occasions.

From Marlborough he went up to Cambridge where he won his Blue (1920-2) and, while still an undergraduate, made his international debut against Ireland in 1920. On leaving University he played for Bromley and taught at Wellington College before taking up an appointment as headmaster of Hilton College in Natal, South Africa. He died while playing golf.

Andy MAPPLE

Water Skiing
Andrew Mapple. b. 3 Nov 1962.

He had begun water skiing in 1976 and made his international debut in 1981, winning the world slalom title then and again in 1989. He has also had six wins at the US Masters and was British overall champion in 1980 and 1984. He has set three world records for the slalom - all on a 10.25m line, with 3 buoys in 1989, 3.5 buoys in 1991 and 4 buoys in 1994.

In 1987 he married Deena (née Brush, USA) (b. 2 Mar 1960), who was world overall champion in 1987 and 1989 and won her speciality, jumping, in 1981, 1985, 1987, and 1989. In 1988 she set a world record at 47.5m *156 ft*. She also shared the world record for slalom in 1990.

David MARQUES

Rugby Union
Reginald William David Marques. b. 9 Dec 1932 Hertford.

An exceptionally tall lock, Marques won a total of 23 England caps 1956-61, with 22 of them coming in consecutive internationals partnering fellow Harlequin, John Currie (qv), in England's second row. His talents as a superb line-out jumper were often countered by blatantly illegal tactics from overseas opposition but, despite considerable provocation, he remained the calmest of players.

A Cambridge Blue 1954-7, he toured Australia and New Zealand with the British Lions in 1959 playing at No. 8 in two Tests. A natural athlete, he played cricket for Hertfordshire and crewed on the yacht *Sovereign* in the 1966 America's Cup.

Richard MARSH

Horse Racing
Richard John Marsh. b. 31 Dec 1851 Smeeth, Kent. d. 20 May 1933 Great Shelford, Cambridgeshire.

As a jumps jockey he had his first winner in 1866 and rode in eight Grand Nationals before he began training for the Duke of Hamilton at Newmarket in 1876. He was leading trainer in 1897, 1898 and 1900 and had 13 Classics successes from 1883 to 1909. His greatest horses included two full brothers owned by the Prince of Wales (later King Edward VII): *Persimmon*, winner of the Derby and St Leger in 1896, and *Diamond Jubilee*, who took the colt's triple crown in 1900. He also trained for King George V until his retirement in 1924 and was awarded the MVO.

His son **Marcus** Maskell **Marsh** (b. 23

Feb 1904 Stechworth, near Newmarket. d. 12 Dec 1983 Burthorpe, near Newmarket) trained the winners of five Classics, including two who did the Derby and St Leger double: *Windsor Lad* in 1934 and *Tulyar* in 1952, in which year Marsh was leading trainer.

Terry MARSH

Boxing
Terence Marsh. b. 7 Feb 1958 Stepney, London.

ABA welterweight champion in 1980 and 1981 while serving in the Royal Marines, Marsh turned pro having been disappointed to miss selection for the 1980 Olympic Games. He won his first 15 professional fights and after taking the British light-welterweight title from Clinton McKenzie in 1984 he added the European crown the following year. In March 1987 he beat Joe Louis Manley (USA) in 10 rounds to take the IBF World title and four months later, he disposed of the challenge of Akio Kameda (Japan) in six rounds. Shortly afterwards, he gave up boxing due to epilepsy and he retired as the unbeaten world champion and with an unbeaten career record. That condition also caused him to have to abandon his career in the Fire Service.

Following an incident in which his manager, Frank Warren, was shot he was charged with attempted murder but when he was brought to trial at the Old Bailey the prosecution case quickly collapsed.

Career record 1981-7: 27 contests. Won 26, Drew 1.

Bryan MARSHALL (Ireland)

Horse Racing
Bryan A Marshall. b. 29 Feb 1916 Cloughjordan, Co. Tipperary. d. 9 Oct 1991 Reading, Berkshire.

A leading jumps jockey, Marshall rode 508 winners, 1932-54, including the Grand Nationals of 1953 and 1954. His mother Binty was a fine show-jumper and he started riding from the age of three. At 11 he worked in his summer holidays with trainer Atty Persse (qv), and at the age of

12 was apprenticed, riding his first flat race winner in 1929. He spent five years with Hubert Hartigan in Ireland before moving to Penrith, where Noel Murless (qv) was assistant trainer. He then went with Murless when the latter opened his own stable at Hambleton in North Yorkshire. His first winner over fences was in the 1932/3 season. After wartime service, being demobilised as a captain, he was 2nd in 1946/7 and in 1947/8 won the NH jockeys title with 66 winners.

He was not only a natural horseman, but a marvellous judge of pace, and very strong in the finish. He married show-jumper Mary Whitehead in 1953, and trained until 1973, after which he ran a horse transport business.

Peter MARSHALL

Squash
Peter Marshall. b. 12 May 1971.

The double-handed player had a great year in 1994. He started by winning the national title and went on to lose to Jansher Khan (Pakistan) in the finals of the World Open and the Pakistan Open while rising to world No.2 ranking. He also lost to Jansher Khan in the final of the 1995 British Open.

Marshall had won the national Under-12 title, progressing to be Under-19 champion in 1990 and English senior champion in 1992. In the World Open he was a quarter-finalist in 1992 and semi-finalist in 1993. He played on the winning England teams at the European Juniors in 1989 and 1990 and European seniors 1990.

Eamonn MARTIN

Athletics
Eamonn Thomas Martin. b. 9 Oct 1958 Basildon, Essex.

The highlights of Martin's long career have been his marvellous run in Oslo 1988 when he made the fastest ever debut at 10000m with a British record time of 27:23.06, the Commonwealth Games 10,000m title of 1990 and his London Marathon win in 2:10:50 on his debut at the distance in 1993.

Two English Schools titles, junior cross-country in 1973 and intermediate 1500m in 1975, showed his early promise, and he made his international debut at 1500m, at which he was 2nd in the 1983 AAAs. He had operations on both Achilles and missed most of 1985 and 1986 seasons, so his emergence as Britain's top distance runner has been a triumph of perseverance for him and for his coach **Mel Batty** (b. 9 Apr 1940) who set a world record of 47:26.8 for 10 miles in 1964.

A components testing engineer at Ford Motors, Martin won the European Cup 10,000m in 1991, the UK 5000m 1984-5, AAA 5000m 1990-1, 10,000m 1989, 1992, road 10km 1988; and the national cross-country in 1984 and 1992.

Other best times: 1500m 3:40.54 (1983), 1M 3:59.30 (1983), 2000m 5:01.09 (1984), 3000m 7:40.94 (1983), 2M 8:18.98 (1988), 5000m 13:17.84 (1989).

Louis MARTIN

Weightlifting
Louis George Martin. b. 11 Nov 1936 Kingston, Jamaica.

At mid-heavyweight (90kg) Martin was World champion in 1959, 1962-3 and 1965 and Commonwealth champion three times, 1962, 1966 and 1970. He represented England, but when the 1966 Games were held in his hometown of Kingston, Jamaica his weight category was moved to the end, rather than in the usual ascending order of weights, so as to provide a suitable climax. The Olympic title eluded him as he was 3rd in 1960 (hampered by a knee injury) and 2nd in 1964. In 1968 he was in great form, but after his best ever total for press and snatch and knowing exactly what he needed for gold he narrowly failed to complete the weight he needed; three times he lifted the 192.5kg *424 1/4 lb* weight overhead only to fail to hold it. He won a record 12 British titles.

He began as a body-builder, taking up weightlifting as a sport when he emigrated to Britain in 1955. He took part in the 1958 Commonwealth Games (for Jamaica), but did not complete his presses. He won his first British title in 1959 and then caused an amazing upset by matching the total of Arkadiy Vorobyev (USSR) at the World Championships and winning the title on lighter bodyweight. He was awarded the MBE.

World records: 90kg jerk 190.5kg 1965, total 480kg 1962.

Stephen MARTIN

Hockey
Stephen Alexander Martin. b. 13 Apr 1959 Bangor, Co. Down.

With a total of 228 international appearances (135 Ireland; 93 GB), Martin is the most capped player in British hockey.

After winning an Olympic bronze medal in 1984, he won gold in 1988 and made a third Olympic appearance in 1992. A full-back with Belfast YMCA and then Holywood '87, he was awarded the MBE in 1994 for his services to the game. He was coached by Norman Hughes (qv) and works as a sports administrator.

Dan MASKELL

Tennis
Daniel Maskell. b. 11 Apr 1908 Fulham, London. d. 10 Dec 1992.

A ball boy from the age of 15 and then a teaching professional at Queen's Club, Maskell was appointed the first professional coach at the All-England Club in 1929 and, apart from the war years, he remained at Wimbledon until 1955. In 1953 he became the first professional to be honoured with life membership of the All-England Club. He also held various coaching appointments with the Lawn Tennis Association and was attached to the successful British Davis Cup teams of the 1930s. During the war he served with the RAF and was awarded the OBE for his rehabilitation work with wounded airmen.

As a player he won the British Professional singles title 16 times (1928-36, 1938-9, 1946-50) but it was as a TV commentator that he became best known. He did not-miss a day's play at Wimbledon for 68 years and his television commentaries, which began in 1951, continued until he reached the age of 83. With his distinctive voice and extensive knowledge of the game, his broadcasts from the Championships were unrivalled, and in 1982 he was awarded the CBE for services to tennis and broadcasting.

Jack MATTHEWS

Rugby Union
Jack Matthews. b. 21 Jun 1920 Bridgend,

A Welsh junior sprint champion before the war, Mathews's game was marked not only by his exceptional speed but also by his devastating tackling. He played in five Victory internationals before winning his first full cap in 1947 and he scored four tries in 17 matches before his international career ended when he captained Wales in Paris in 1951. On the 1950 Lions tour of New Zealand he played in all four Tests, partnering his Cardiff team-mate, Bleddyn Williams (qv), in the centre in three of the matches. A Cardiff doctor, he was medical officer to the 1980 British Lions in South Africa and the service he gave to Welsh sport, in a medical capacity, was recognised by the award of the OBE in 1981.

Ken MATTHEWS

Walking
Kenneth Joseph Matthews. b. 21 Jun 1934 Birmingham.

The Olympic champion at 20km walk in 1964, while the other British gold medallists received the MBE his feat seemed rather forgotten and it was not until 1978 that the power station electrician also received this honour from the Queen. Matthews had led the 1960 Olympic 20km for 8km, but became dehydrated and had to drop out, but by 1964 he was clearly the world's best competitor, having won the Lugano Cup 20km on the first two occasions that it was contested, 1961 and 1963, and taken the European title in 1962.

An immaculate stylist as well as being very fast, Matthews set unofficial world best times for 5 miles 34:21.2 (1960) and 10 miles 69:40.6 (1964) and British records at all distances from 5 miles to 2 hours. His other best times: track - 2M 13:09.6 (1960), 10,000m 42:35.6 (1960), 7M 48:22.2 (1964), 20,000m 1:28:45.8 (1964), 1 hour 13,927m (1964), 2 hours 25,563m (1964); road 20 km 1:28:15 (1960). Competing for Sutton Coldfield Walking Club he won the RWA 10 miles each year 1959-64 and the 20 miles on his only attempt in 1962, and was AAA champion at 2 miles 1959 and 1961-4 and at 7 miles 1959-61 and 1963-4.

Stanley MATTHEWS

Football
(Sir) Stanley Matthews. b. 1 Feb 1915 Hanley, Stoke-on-Trent. *D 23/2/2000*

Stanley Matthews is one of the legendary names of world soccer. With his dribbling skills and swerve he destroyed the reputations of some of the game's greatest full-backs and was possibly the most popular player in history.

Making his League debut for Stoke City at the age of 17, he became the oldest player ever to appear in the First Division when he played his last League game (his 701st) at 50 years 5 days for Stoke v Fulham in 1965. He was with Stoke until 1947 when he moved to Blackpool, but in 1961 he returned to the Potteries. He twice won Football League Second Division honours with Stoke, first in 1933 and, incredibly, for a second time 30 years later in 1963. With Blackpool, he played in three FA Cup finals (1948, 1951, 1953) but was on the winning side only in 1953 when his superb performance led to the match being known as the 'Matthews Final'.

Although his appearances in the England side were spasmodic during the latter part of his career, he won 54 international caps; after making his debut in 1934 as a 19-year-old he played his last game for England in 1957 at the age of 41. He also played in 29 wartime internationals. He was the first footballer to be awarded the CBE (1957) and the first to be knighted (1965). In 1948 he was the first winner of the Football Writers' Player of the Year award and, after a 15-year interval, he again won the award in 1963. He was also the first winner of the European Footballer of the Year award in 1956.

Following his retirement in 1965 he served

as general manager of Port Vale for three years and later coached in Malta and South Africa.

His son, also **Stanley Matthews**, played Davis Cup tennis for Britain in 1971, and in 1962 won the Wimbledon Boys singles, the last British individual champion at this event.

Stewart MATTHEWS

Trampolining
Stewart Matthews. b. 19 Feb 1962.

The winner of a record five British individual titles 1976-80, Matthews was the world champion in 1980 at both individual and synchronised pairs (with Carl Furrer (qv)).

Peter MAY

Cricket
Peter Barker Howard May. b. 31 Dec 1929 Reading, Berkshire. d. 27 Dec 1994.

May was a strong and elegant batsman, the finest of his generation. His talent blossomed at Charterhouse and continued in his first-class career with Cambridge University (1950-2) and Surrey, whom he captained from 1957 to 1962. He made a lovely century against South Africa on his Test debut at the age of 21 and batted outstandingly for England for most of the 1950s. His highest score of 285* was against the West Indies in the First Test in 1957 when, at a time when England looked in danger of an innings defeat, he put on 411 for the 4th wicket with Colin Cowdrey (qv), still the England Test record partnership.

He succeeded Len Hutton as England captain in 1955 and was highly successful in that role, winning 20 to 10 losses in his 41 matches in charge. However, the strain of captaincy and illness resulted in his retirement at the early age of 31. He first became one of the Test selectors in 1965, and was their chairman 1982-8, President of MCC 1980/1 and awarded the CBE in 1981.

He captained Cambridge at soccer, though not at cricket, and with his brother **John** (1933-88) won the Kinnaird Cup, the amateur championship for Eton Fives each

year 1951-3. He was an insurance broker from 1953 and an underwriting member of Lloyd's from 1962. His daughter Nicola won the European junior three-day equestrian event title in 1979.

66 Tests 1951-61: 4537 runs at 46.76, 13 100s HS 285*; 42 catches.

First-class 1948-63: 27,592 runs at 51.00, 85 100s HS 285*; 282 catches.

Raymond MAYS

Motor Racing
Raymond Mays. b. 1 Aug 1900 Bourne, Lincolnshire.

He started racing while at Cambridge University in 1921 in a Hillman. From then he drove many makes until 1934, when he created E.R.A. (English Racing Automobiles) with Humphrey Cook and designer Peter Berthon, and in these cars he won many important races, notably at Brooklands, including the Campbell Trophy Formula Libre race in 1939. He was hugely successful at hill climbs and won the oldest speed hill climb in Britain, at Shelsley Walsh, Worcestershire 19 times between 1923 and 1950, including achieving the first time under 40 seconds when he averaged 51.14 mph in his E.R.A. in 1935. He won the first Hillclimb Championship of Britain in 1947 in his veteran 2-litre E.R.A.

In 1949 he helped to found B.R.M. (British Racing Machines) with Berthon, and although the cars had many problems for years, eventually he saw the marque win the constructors' championship, with Graham Hill (qv) winning the drivers' championship, in 1962.

Philip MEAD

Cricket
Charles Philip Mead. b. 9 Mar 1887 Battersea, London. d. 26 Mar 1958 Boscombe, Dorset.

It is curious to look back on Mead's career and see that he only won 17 Test caps for England over a 19-year span, yet he scored four centuries and averaged nearly 50 and was for years a most prolific run scorer for Hampshire. A left-handed batsman and occasional slow left-arm bowler, he also proved sure-handed at slip. He went to Australia twice, yet on tours as far apart as 1911/2 and 1928/9. He played, of course, in a great era of English batsmen and, while he lacked the dash and style of some, he was nonetheless a fine technician. In all he scored 1000 runs in a season 27 times, over 2000 nine times and over 3000 twice: 3179 at 69.10 in 1921 and 3027 at 75.67 in 1928.

His idiosyncratic and unchanging routine before every ball - looking round the field, pulling at his cap four times, tapping his bat in the crease four times and shuffling into a crouching stance - was a notable feature of the game of this solemn, but shrewd cricketer. He played minor counties cricket for Suffolk in 1938-9, averaging 76.80 and 71.28 in these seasons. In his youth he had kept goal for Southampton.

17 Tests 1911-28: 1185 runs at 49.37, 4 100s HS 182*; 4 catches.

First-class 1905-36: 55,061 runs at 47.67, 153 100s HS 280*; 277 wickets at 34.70, BB 7-18; 671 catches.

Richard MEADE

Equestrianism, Three-day Event
Richard John Hannay Meade. b. 4 Dec 1938 Chepstow, Monmouthshire.

With three Olympic gold medals at the three-day event, as an individual on *Laurieston* in 1972 and team in 1968 and 1972, Meade is Britain's most successful Olympic equestrian. He made his Olympic debut in 1964 after his victory on *Barberry* at Burghley, and competed again in 1976, when he was 4th.

After being runner-up in the individual event at the World Championships in 1966 on *The Poacher*, he was a member of the winning British team at the 1970 and 1982 Championships and in both those years won at Badminton, on *The Poacher* and *Speculator III* respectively. He was also a member of the winning eventing team at the 1967 European Championships. He was awarded the OBE in 1974.

His parents bred ponies and horses in Chepstow, so he learned to ride at an early age. He is an engineering graduate of Cambridge University and now farms in Wiltshire; he became president of the British Equestrian Federation in 1989.

Stan MELLOR

Horse Racing
Stanley Thomas Edward Mellor. b. 10 Apr 1937 Manchester.

Mellor broke Fred Winter's (qv) record for a jockey of 923 winners under National Hunt rules; his 1000th was on *Ouzo* at Nottingham on 18 Dec 1971, and he ended with a career total of 1049, including 14 abroad, from 1953 to 1972. That record was subsequently beaten by John Francome and Peter Scudamore. Mellor also won three flat races. On his retirement from riding he became a trainer at Lambourn, Berkshire.

He started as an amateur with George Owen at the age of 15, and at 16 turned professional and won on his first pro ride. He was champion jockey in 1959/60 and the following two seasons, with a peak of 118 wins in 1960/1. As a lightweight he was always able to have plenty of rides, and excelled with great timing. As a jockey he had won the Whitbread Gold Cup in 1962, and exceeded this with training successes in this race in 1980 and 1987. He was awarded the MBE in 1972.

Vera MENCHIK

Chess
Vera Francevna Menchik. b. 16 Feb 1906 Moscow, Russia. d. 26 Jun 1944 London.

A pupil of Géza Maróczy, Menchik was the dominant player in women's chess for many years. She was world junior women's champion 1926-7 and won the inaugural women's world championship in 1927, retaining the title throughout her life.

Her family (her father was Czech and her mother English) moved to Hastings in 1921, and she became a British citizen on marrying R.H.Stevenson in 1937. She was killed in an air raid in London in 1944.

Kay MENZIES – see STAMMERS

Joe MERCER

Football
Joseph Mercer. b. 9 Aug 1914 Ellesmere Port, Cheshire. d. 9 Aug 1990 Hoylake, Merseyside.

The son of a professional footballer, Mercer signed for Everton as a 16-year-old in 1932 and helped them to the Football League title in 1939. He played at left-half for England in all their five international matches in 1938/9 but, although he played in 27 wartime internationals, he was not capped again after the war. In 1946 he lost his place in the Everton team and was transferred to Arsenal where, under the shrewd guidance of Tom Whittaker, his career was revived. With Arsenal, he won League Championship honours in 1948 and 1953, and an FA Cup winners' medal in 1950, and he was again an FA Cup finalist in 1952. In 1950 he was voted Footballer of the Year.

Despite his frail physique he was a relentless tackler but his fragile, spindly legs always caused him problems and his playing days ended in April 1954 when he sustained a double fracture.

He went on to enjoy a highly successful career as a manager, holding appointments at Sheffield United, Aston Villa, Manchester City and Coventry. His years at Maine Road were particularly notable, as he led Manchester City to the First Division title 1968, the FA Cup 1969 and to both the League Cup and European Cup-Winners' Cup 1970. He also served as England's caretaker manager between the departure of Sir Alf Ramsey and the appointment of Don Revie (qqv). Held in high regard by his peers and universally popular with spectators, he remained closely connected with the game until he retired as a director of Coventry in 1981. He died on his 76th birthday.

Joe MERCER

Horse Racing
Joseph Mercer. b. 25 Oct 1934 Bradford, West Yorkshire.

Mercer rode 2810 winners in his riding career in Britain, 1950-85. His brother Manny (qv) was also a brilliant jockey. Joe won his first race in 1950 and became champion apprentice in 1952 and 1953. The first of his eight English Classics winners was *Ambiguity* in the 1953 Oaks, but he was perhaps the best jockey never to win the Derby. Undoubtedly the greatest horse that he rode was *Brigadier Gerard* on whom he won 17 races in 1970-2, and he rates as his greatest joy the winning of the Prix Diane on the Queen's *Highclere* in 1974. He rode over 100 winners in a season six times, first with 106 in 1964 and 1965, improving to 115 in 1978 and a peak of 164 in 1979.

He was apprenticed to Major Fred Sneyd 1947-55 and then went to Bob Colling's stable at West Ilsley, which was taken over in 1962 by Dick Hern (qv), with whom he stayed until 1976 when the racing world was amazed to hear that Mercer's services were no longer required. However, he then joined Henry Cecil (qv) and became champion jockey in 1979 at the age of 45. In 1959 he married Anne, the daughter of Harry Carr (qv).

A great sportsman and enormously respected in the racing world, he was a model jockey, renowned for waiting and producing a hard, driving finish. On his retirement from the saddle he became an agent and then racing manager for Maktoum Al Maktoum.

Manny MERCER

Horse Racing
Emmanuel Lionel Mercer. b. 15 Nov 1928 Bradford, West Yorkshire. d. 26 Sep 1959 Ascot, Berkshire.

Brother of Joe (qv), Mercer was a superbly stylish jockey, apprenticed first to James Russell and then to George Colling in 1947. He surpassed 100 winners in a season first in 1953, when he rode the first of his two Classics winners, *Happy Laughter* in the 1000 Guineas, and again each year 1956-9, with a peak of 125 in 1958. In all from 1947 he rode 976 winners until he was killed in a freak accident when *Priddy Fair*, who he was riding to the start at Ascot, whipped round, threw him and kicked him.

Billy MEREDITH

Football
William Henry Meredith. b. 30 Jul 1874
Chirk, nr Wrexham d. 19 Apr 1958
Manchester.

A brilliant outside-right, like Stanley
Matthews (qv) in later years, Meredith
enjoyed a career of remarkable longevity.
He won the first of his 48 Welsh caps in
1895 and made his final international
appearance in March 1920 at the age of 45
years 229 days when Wales beat England
for the first time in their history. His record
of being the oldest player ever to win
international honours still stands. Four
years later, as he approached his 50th
birthday, he was brought into the
Manchester City side for the FA Cup semi-
final although he had made only three
League appearances in the previous two
years. His 670 League appearances
remained a British record until 1963.
After one season with Northwich Victoria
he signed for Manchester City in October
1894, but after being involved in an illegal
payments scandal in 1906 he was forced to
leave the club. He then joined Manchester
United but rejoined City in 1921. He won
an FA Cup winners' medal with both City,
1904, and United, 1909, and twice won
League Championship honours with
United, 1908 and 1911.
Billy Meredith, who always played with a
toothpick in his mouth, was justifiably
known as the 'Prince of Wingers' and his
laconic attitude shielded the fact that he
worked constantly on his dribbling skills
until the end of his career. He was a
founder member of the Players' Union and
after retirement he returned to Manchester
United in 1931 as a coach. He later ran a
hotel in Manchester.

Bryn MEREDITH

Rugby Union
Brinley Victor Meredith. b. 21 Nov 1930
Cwmbrân, Torfaen.

Playing in 34 internationals between 1954,
when he was a student at St Luke's
College, Exeter, and 1962, he is Wales'
most capped hooker. After playing in all

four Tests on the 1955 Lions tour of South
Africa, he toured Australia and New
Zealand in 1959 but skipper Ronnie
Dawson (qv) kept him out of the Test side.
In 1962 Meredith made his third Lions
tour and played in all four Tests against
South Africa. Apart from being an excep-
tionally quick striker in the scrum, his play
in the loose was unusually skilful for a
hooker. He played his club rugby for
Newport.

Leon MEREDITH

Cycling
Lewis Leonard Meredith. b. 2 Jul 1882 St
Pancras, London. d. 27 Jan 1930 Davos,
Switzerland.

The first man to win seven world championships, all in the now-defunct amateur
100km motor-paced event, 1904-05, 1907-
09, 1911 and 1913, Meredith also won
seven British championships, 1902-8. At
the 1908 Olympics he might well have
been favourite to win the individual road
race, but the event was not contested for
one of the few times in Olympic history;
he did win a gold medal at team pursuit. In
1912 he was 4th in the road race at the
Stockholm Olympic Games. He was also
British amateur roller-skating champion in
1911 and 1912. He died of a heart attack
while on his annual winter holiday in
Davos.

Colin MILBURN

Cricket
Colin Milburn. b. 23 Oct 1941
Burnopfield, Co. Durham. d. 28 Feb 1990
Newton Aycliffe, Co. Durham.

Just when Ollie Milburn seemed to have
sealed his place in the England team as
much more than just a formidable hitter
with all the power that his 18 stone frame
could muster, he suffered the loss of his
left eye in a car accident in May 1969.
After a great season with Western
Australia (940 runs at 62.66, including a
thunderous 243 v Queensland) the Notts
player had been summoned to the England
team in Pakistan and in what was to prove
his last Test innings in March 1969 he

scored a splendid 139. He bravely reappeared for Notts in 1973-4, but had to accept that the magic could not be recaptured with one eye. Despite his size he was light on his feat and developed into a magnificent attacking batsman and a useful medium-pace bowler. He had first come to prominence at the age of 17 with a century for the (then) minor county, Durham, against the Indian tourists in 1959 and was soon snapped up by Nottinghamshire, He exceeded 1000 runs in a season each year 1963-8 with a best of 1861 at 48.97 in 1966, when he made his England debut with 316 runs at 52.66 in four Tests against West Indies before being surprisingly droipped for the final match of the series.
9 Tests 1966-9: 654 runs at 46.71; 2 100s HS 139; 7 catches.
First-class 1960-74: 13,262 runs at 33.07, 23 100s HS 243; 99 wickets at 32.0,3 BB 6-59; 224 catches.

Jackie MILBURN

Football
John Edward Thompson Milburn. b. 11 May 1924 Ashington, Northumberland. d. 8 Oct 1988 Ashington.

'Wor Jackie' was a Tyneside legend whose contribution to Newcastle's three post-war FA Cup victories (1951, 1952, 1955) earned him the Freedom of the City. In 1951 he scored in every round of the Cup, including both goals in the final. Initially an inside-forward or winger he later specialised in the centre-forward role where he used his exceptional speed and powerful shot to great effect scoring 177 goals in 353 League matches during his eleven seasons 1946-56 with Newcastle and 10 goals in 13 international matches 1948-55 when he succeeded Tommy Lawton (qv) as England's centre-forward.
After leaving Newcastle in 1957 he was associated, in various capacities, with Linfield, Yiewsley, Reading, Ipswich and Gateshead and he was also a journalist with the *News of the World*. Four of his cousins, George, Jack, Jim and Stanley Milburn, played League football and a fifth, Cissie, was the mother of Bobby and Jack Charlton (qqv).

Anthony MILES

Chess
Anthony John Miles. b. 23 Apr 1955 Edgbaston, Birmingham.

An international master in 1974 when he won the world junior title, Miles became the first officially recognised British Grand Master at chess on 24 Feb 1976. He was British junior champion in 1971, tied for the first UK Grand Prix title in 1974 and won it in 1975, 1982 and 1984 and was British champion in 1982.
Having attained many international victories and been Britain's top player for the best part of a decade, he announced in 1987 that he would represent the USA in future, and in that year was beaten in a play-off for the US title.

Eustace MILES

Rackets and Real Tennis
Eustace Hamilton Miles. b. 22 Sep 1868 Hampstead, London. d. 20 Dec 1948 London.

After briefly attending Eastbourne College, Miles moved to Marlborough where he won his colours at cricket and rugby. On going up to King's College, Cambridge he began to concentrate on rackets and real tennis and soon excelled at both games. At real tennis he won the British Amateur title a then record nine times between 1899 and 1910 and was the US champion in 1900. He was also won the US and Canadian rackets title in 1900 and in the British rackets championship he won the singles in 1902 and was a four-time winner of the doubles.
Eustace Miles carried his sporting versatility into his business life and he was at various times an author, journalist, lecturer, adviser on health and diet and managing director of Eustace Miles Restaurants Ltd.

David MILFORD

Rackets
David Sumner Milford. b. 7 Jun 1905 Headington, Oxford. d. 24 Jun 1984 Marlborough, Wiltshire.

World rackets champion from 1937 to

1947, Milford was the first amateur to hold the title since Sir William Hart-Dyke in 1862. While at Rugby he won the Public Schools Championship in 1923 and 1924 and at Oxford he won Blues for rackets and hockey. In 1930 he won his first amateur singles title at rackets and the first of his 25 international caps for hockey (inside-left or centre-forward). He then concentrated on hockey and did not play again in the Championships until 1935 when he won his second title.

Between 1930 and 1966 he won 18 British amateur rackets titles (7 singles, 11 doubles). After winning the British Open in 1936, he challenged Norbert Seltzer (USA) for the world title. Seltzer won the first leg in New York by a narrow margin (4-3) but Milford was an easy winner (4-0) of the second leg at Queen's and was the overall winner 7-3. He remained world champion until he resigned the title in 1947 but, mainly because of the war, he was never called upon to make a defence.

Robert MILLAR

Cycling
Robert Millar. b. 13 Sep 1958 Glasgow.

Over 15 years of professional riding from 1980, Millar has shown himself not only as one of the world's best climbers, but also as a great team man. In 1995 he was chosen to add experience to a new team, Le Groupement, with the specific task of leading the team in the Giro and hoping to finish the Tour de France for the 12th time. In his first Tour in 1983 he won the long Pyrenées stage to become the first Briton to win a mountain stage in the Tour. He won the same stage the following year and he was King of the Mountains in 1984 and 1985. His 4th place overall in 1984 was the best ever British placing in the Tour.

He won the Vuelta a Catalanya 1985 and Dauphiné Libéré 1990 and also finished 2nd in a major Continental race no less than seven times: Tour de Suisse 1986 and 1990, Vuelta a España 1985-6, Dauphiné Libéré 1989, Vuelta a Catalanya 1993 and Giro d'Italia 1987. He was British amateur road race champion in 1978 and 1979, represented Scotland at the 1978

Commonwealth Games and was 4th in the 1979 World road race. He also won the Kellogg's Tour of Britain in 1989, and in 1995 at last won his first British professional road racing title.

Syd MILLAR

Rugby Union
Sidney Millar. b. 23 May 1934 Ballymena, Co. Antrim.

Millar was a powerfully built tight-head prop who won 37 caps for Ireland 1958-70, although he was dropped by both Ulster and Ireland for three seasons, 1965-7, midway through his international career. He toured Australia and New Zealand (1959) and South Africa (1962, 1968) with the British Lions, playing in a total of nine Tests, including all four in South Africa in 1962 when he switched to loose-head to accommodate the less experienced Kingsley Jones. He later became a leading coach and twice toured South Africa again with the Lions, as assistant manager in 1974 and as manager in 1980.

Sammy MILLER

Motor Cycling
Samuel Hamilton Miller. b. 11 Nov 1933 Belfast.

The greatest trials rider of his time, Miller achieved enormous success after he had been third as a road racer in the world 250cc championship in 1957. He was British trials champion each year 1959-69 and was twice European champion. Many of his greatest successes were on the 500cc Ariel, but in 1964 he switched to Bultaco and maintained his supremacy on a 250cc two-stroke. As a road racer his best placings in Isle of Man TT races were 4th in both 1957 and 1958 at 125cc.

Freddie MILLS

Boxing
Frederick Percival Mills. b. 26 Jun 1919 Parkstone, Dorset. d. 25 Jul 1965 London.

Mills was a popular and courageous light-heavyweight who learned the fight game in the fairground booths. He first captured the public imagination with his all-action style in 1942 when he knocked Len Harvey (qv) out the ring in the second round to take the British and Empire light-heavyweight title and gain recognition in Britain as the world champion. This was the first KO ever inflicted on Harvey. In 1946 Mills lost to the American champion, Gus Lesnevich, but he got the verdict in a return match in 1948 to become the undisputed world champion. A 10th round KO defeat by Joey Maxim (USA) in 1950 ended his reign as world champion and he retired soon afterwards.

In the absence of any worthwhile light-heavyweight opponents, Mills, who possessed a potent punch in his left hook but whose right-hand punching was very crude, was always prepared to take on the heavyweights and challenged twice for the British title losing to Jack London (1944) and Bruce Woodcock (1946). Such was his popularity that he probably earned more than any other British boxer up to that time and he made a number of business investments. He was found with severe gunshot wounds in his car outside his Soho nightclub and died soon afterwards in the Middlesex Hospital. The generally accepted view is that the wounds were self-inflicted, although there are persistent rumours that the cause of death was more sinister.

Career record: 101 Contests. Won 77, Drew 6, Lost 18.

Mick MILLS

Football
Michael Denis Mills. b. 4 Jan 1949
Godalming, Surrey.

Released by Portsmouth when they abandoned their youth policy in 1966, he moved to Ipswich where he captained the club and England with distinction. His 591 League appearances during his 17 years with Ipswich was a club record and he led them to victory in the FA Cup in 1978 and the UEFA Cup in 1981. After many successful years with Ipswich, he moved to Southampton in 1982 and then took over as player-manager of Stoke City in 1985.

A solid, unspectacular full-back, having been a youth and under-23 international, he won 42 England caps between 1972 and 1982 and was awarded the MBE in 1984.

Roger MILLWARD

Rugby League
Roger Millward. b. 16 Sep 1947
Castleford, West Yorkshire.

After establishing a reputation with Castleford as a stand-off of exceptional quality, Millward moved to Hull Kingston Rovers in 1967 where his play contributed to one of the most successful periods in the club's history. In 1967/8 his 38 points topped the League scoring table and was the record number of points scored in a single season by a stand-off. In his years with Hull KR 1966-80 he set a club record with 207 tries and also kicked 597 gals and 10 dropped goals.

First recognised by the GB selectors as an 18-year-old in 1965 as a non-playing substitute against New Zealand, he won his first full cap the following season and went on to win 28 GB caps (plus one as a replacement), 10 as captain, as well as 17 for England (10 as captain). The highlight of his Test career, including three Lions tours to Australia, came in the second match of the series against Australia in 1970 when, with two tries and seven goals, he equalled Lewis Jones' record of scoring 20 points in a single Test match.

A little man at 1.63m and about 65 kg, after he gave up playing, he stayed with Hull Kingston Rovers as a coach from 1977 to 1991, guiding them to victory in every major trophy before taking over as coach at Halifax in 1992. In July 1994 he was appointed coach at the second division club, Ryedale-York, but lack of success led to him being dismissed after only seven months. He was awarded the MBE in 1983 for services to the game.

Iain MILNE

Rugby Union
Iain Gordon Milne. b. 17 Jun 1958
Edinburgh.

A prop with Heriot's FP from 1974 to

1991, except for two years, 1984-6, with Harlequins, he won 44 caps 1979-90 in the Scottish front row although he missed part of the 1981 season and the entire 1987/8 international season through injury. He toured New Zealand with the British Lions in 1983 but didn't play in the Tests. On his return he played in the Scottish front row in all four matches in their 1984 Grand Slam season.

His brother, **Kenneth** Stewart **Milne** (b. 1 Dec 1961 Edinburgh) also plays for Heriot's FP and had won 38 caps from 1989 to the end of the World Cup in 1995 as Scotland's hooker. In 1993 he played in the first Test on the British Lions tour of New Zealand.

Alan MINTER

Boxing
Alan S. Minter. b. 17 Aug 1951 Bromley, London.

Minter was a hard-punching southpaw whose jolting jab earned him the nickname 'Boom Boom'. He won the ABA middleweight title in 1971 and turned professional the following year after winning an Olympic bronze medal at light-middleweight.

Within three years he had taken the British middleweight crown from Kevin Finnegan (qv). He forfeited the title in 1976 for failing to defend his title within the stipulated period, but he beat Finnegan again in 1977 to regain it. During much of this period he was also the European champion. In 1980 he took on three world title fights, in March he became the undisputed world middleweight champion, and the first British boxer to win a world title in the USA since Ted 'Kid' Lewis (qv) in 1915, by beating Vito Antuofermo (Ita) on points in Las Vegas. In the return match in London in June he stopped the Italian in the eighth round and in his third and final World title bout in September, Minter succumbed to Marvin Hagler (USA) in the third round when the referee stopped the fight because of cuts to the defending champion. His eventful reign as world champion had lasted less than six months. In 1981 he made a bid to win back his European title but after a third round KO by Tony Sibson

he retired from the sport.
Career record 1972-81: 49 contests. Won 39 (23 KO), Lost 9, No contest 1.

Derek MINTER

Motorcycling
Derek W. Minter. b. 1932 Kent.

The outstanding short-track racer of his era, 'The Mint' began his racing career at Trials during his National Service in 1951-2. He turned full-time professional in 1958 and reached his peak in the early 1960s. He created numerous lap and race records at most of the British circuits and was particularly outstanding at Brands Hatch. He was British champion at 500cc 1961-4, adding both 250cc and Junior in 1962, in which year he won the Isle of Man lightweight 250cc TT.

A highly skilful rider and an immaculate stylist, he was an outspoken individual and did not like the discipline of being a works rider, so he mostly rode as a freelance, which meant that his talent was seen all too little in World Championship races. He retired at the end of the 1987 season.

Abe MITCHELL

Golf
Abraham Mitchell. b. 19 Jan 1887 East Grinstead, West Sussex. d. 1947.

After being runner-up to John Ball (qv) in The Amateur Championship of 1912, Mitchell turned professional in 1913. He was 4th in The Open in 1914 and again in 1920, but that was after leading the eventual winner, George Duncan (qv), by 13 strokes at the end of the second round. His game collapsed with an 84 in the third round. He was again in the top six in 1925-6 and 1929, but never achieved a top three placing, making him possibly the best player never to have done this.

He won the *News of the World* Match Play title in 1919, 1920 and 1929 and was a force in the Ryder Cup, winning four of his six matches in the ties of 1929, 1931 and 1933. He had been employed as golf professional by Samuel Ryder and captained the British team in a match against the American professionals in 1926 as a result of which Ryder decided to put up a cup for a biennial contest. Mitchell himself had to withdraw from the first match in 1927 through appendicitis.

Elegant of appearance, his short and powerful swing was greatly admired.

Beryl MITCHELL

Rowing
Beryl E. Mitchell. b. 26 Jun 1950 London. Later Mrs Crockford.

A London schoolteacher and a member of the Thames Tradesmen RC, she was Britain's leading oarswoman in the early 1980s. She made her Olympic debut in the coxless pairs in 1976 and was a finalist in the single sculls at the 1980 and 1984 Games, finishing 5th in Moscow and 6th in Los Angeles.

A regular competitor at the world championships in the single sculls, coxless pairs or coxed fours, her best performance was to take the silver medal in the single sculls in 1981 before winning the lightweight double sculls with Lin Clark in 1985. In 1982 she won the first sculling event for women to be held at Henley.

William MITCHELL

Billiards
William Mitchell. b. 13 Oct 1854. d. ?

One of the foremost professionals of his day, Mitchell was the first player to make a four-figure break in public, scoring 1055 in a match against W.J.Peall (qv). Recognised as the unofficial spot stroke champion of the world, his proficiency led to the 'push and spot' stroke being banned in 1898.

Tim MOLONY (Ireland)

Horse Racing
Tim Molony. b. 14 Sep 1919 Co. Limerick. d. 14 Dec 1989 Wymondham, near Melton Mowbray, Leicestershire.

Molony came to England in 1946 and was National Hunt champion jockey five times, each year from 1948/9 to 1951/2 and in 1954/5, with a peak of 95 wins in 1949/50. His first ride in public was in 1936 and he turned professional in 1940.

A bold, brave rider, known as the 'rubber man', he rode 866 winners under NH rules to April 1958, when he retired after breaking a thigh in the only bad fall of his career. Riding *Hatton's Grace* and *Sir Ken* he won four consecutive Champion Hurdles, and he rode *Knock Hard* to win the Cheltenham Gold Cup in 1953. He became a trainer in Leicestershire in 1960. His younger brother **Martin** (b. 1925) showed brilliant skill, and rode the Gold Cup winner *Silver Fame* in 1951 and the winners of the 1944, 1946 and 1950 Irish Grand Nationals, but his career was cut short by a fall in September that year and he retired to own and manage the Rathmore Stud.

Rinty MONAGHAN

Boxing
John Joseph Monaghan. b. 21 Aug 1920 Belfast. d. 3 Mar 1984 Belfast.

Before he had reached the age of 15, Monaghan won his first professional bout on a KO but he did not have his first fight in London for another 12 years when he knocked out Terry Allen (qv) in the first round. An impressive series of performances led to him being matched with Dado Marino (Hawaii) for the vacant NBA World flyweight crown in March 1947 with the Irishman winning on points. In defence of his title he beat former champion, Jackie Paterson, with a seventh round KO and with this victory he also became the British and Empire champion. This was followed by a points victory over Maurice Sandeyron (Fra), which also gave him the European title, and in his third world title defence in September 1949 he was held to a draw by Terry Allen after which he retired, suffering from tuberculosis, as the undefeated champion.

It was his custom to celebrate victory by singing the Irish ballad 'Danny Boy' from the ring and this added further to his popular image.

Career record 1935-49: 66 contests. Won 51, Drew 6, Lost 9.

Terry MONAGHAN

Speed Skating
Terence Austin Monaghan. b. 26 Aug 1933
Mountain Ash, Rhondda Cynon Taff.

His 5th place in the 10,000m in 1960, when he beat the previous world record, is the best ever performance by a British speed skater at the Olympic Games. This was his only Olympic appearance but he competed at six World Championships (1956-60, 1962) where, as at the Olympics, his best performance was 5th place in the 10,000m in 1959.

Colin MONTGOMERIE

Golf
Colin Stuart Montgomerie. b. 23 Jun 1963
Glasgow.

Montomerie was the leader of the European tour in 1993 with £613,682 and in 1994 with £762,719, having been 4th in 1991 and 3rd in 1992. In 1994, having won three European tour events to take his career total to seven, he also tied for 2nd in the US Open and lost to Ernie Els (SAf) in the final of the World Matchplay Championship.
After achieving great success as an amateur, winning the Scottish Strokeplay Championship in 1985 and the Scottish Amateur in 1987, with Walker Cup appearances in both those years, this big, powerful man turned professional in 1988. His first win on the pro tour was the Portuguese Open in 1989 and he was 3rd in the US Open in 1992. He played for Scotland in the Dunhill Cup 1988, 1991-4 and in the Ryder Cup in 1991 and 1993. In 1991 he won one, lost one and halved one, and in 1993 played outstandingly for three wins, a loss and a half.

Robert MONTGOMERIE

Fencing
Robert Cecil Lindsay Montgomerie. b. 15 Feb 1880 South Kensington, London. d. 28 Apr 1939 Westminster, London.

Montgomerie established himself as one of the finest British fencers of his era. After fencing for Oxford for three years (1900-02) in the match against Cambridge, he became the first man to win the AFA épée title fve times (1905, 1907, 1909, 1912 and 1914), and the first to win the foli title four times (1905, 1908-10); his total of nine victories remains a record for the Championships. He competed at both weapons at four Olympic Games, 1908-24, winning a silver medal in the épée team event in 1908 and 1912. A barrister by profession, he served as Hon Secretary of the AFA from 1904 to 1924, when he was appointed a vice-president.

David MOORCROFT

Athletics
David Robert Moorcroft. b. 10 Apr 1953
Coventry, West Midlands.

Already Commonwealth champion at 1500m in 1978 and the European Cup winner at 5000m in 1981, Moorcroft had a wonderful year in 1982, including a magnificent world record, 13:00.41 for 5000m and a European record of 7:32.79 for 3000m. His world record came at the Bislett Games in Oslo, when instead of his usual tactics of relying on his formidable finishing kick, he led from 800m and ran away from the field, taking six seconds off the previous best, set four years earlier by Henry Rono (Kenya), who was to place 4th in this race. Moorcroft went on to win the Commonwealth 5000m, but was past his best when 3rd to Thomas Wessinghage (Ger) at the 1978 Europeans.
A member of Coventry Godiva Harriers, Moorcroft was AAA junior champion indoors and out at 1500m in 1971 and showed his strength and versatility early with 2nd in the National cross-country over 9 miles in 1976. He won the AAA 1500m indoors in 1976 and outdoors in 1978, and the UK 1500m and 5000m in 1980 and 3000m in 1989. He was 3rd at 1500m at the 1978 Europeans and at the Olympic Games was 7th at 1500m in 1976, but was ill at the 1980 Games and in 1984 injury again struck at the wrong time, as he trailed in last in the 5000m final.
Other best times: 800m 1:46.64 (1982), 1000m 2:18.95 (1976), 1500m 3:33.79 (1982), 1M 3:49.34 (1982), 2000m 5:02.86

(1986), 2M 8:16.75 (1982).
Hugely respected and popular in athletics circles, he works in Coventry on youth projects and also on radio and TV for the BBC on athletics. He was awarded the MBE in 1983.

Ann MOORE

Equestrianism, Show Jumping
Ann Elizabeth Moore. b. 20 Aug 1950 Sutton Coldfield, West Midlands.

Riding *Psalm*, Ann Moore was European Ladies' champion in 1971 and 1973. In between she took the Olympic silver in 1972, when she was beaten in the jump-off by Graziano Mancinelli (Italy). On *Psalm* she won the Queen Elizabeth II Cup in 1972 and 1973 (shared with Alison Dawes (qv)). She won team gold medals at the European Juniors of 1965, 1967 and 1968, with an individual bronze on *Kangaroo* in 1965 and gold on *Psalm* in 1968.

Bobby MOORE

Football
Robert Frederick Moore. b. 12 Apr 1941 Barking, London. d. 24 Feb 1993 Putney, London.

Moore was one of England's greatest defenders and captain of the team which won the 1966 World Cup. After making a record 18 appearances for England's Youth team, which he captained, he went on to win a then record 108 caps at senior level 1962-73, playing 90 times as captain. He was voted BBC Sports Personality of the Year 1966.
Starting as an amateur with West Ham United, he signed as a professional in 1958 and made 642 League and Cup appearances for them, which was then a club record, leading them to victories in the FA Cup 1964 and the European Cup Winners' Cup 1965. He then played for Fulham (150 matches) 1974-7 and made a second appearance in the FA Cup final in 1975 when Fulham lost to his old club West Ham. A master tactician and a natural leader, he was an ideal choice as captain of both club and country. He was voted Footballer of the Year in 1964 and was

awarded the OBE in 1967. In the NASL in the USA he played for San Antonio Thunder in 1976 and Seattle Sounders in 1978 and served briefly as player-manager of the Danish club, Herning FC in 1978, before taking up managerial and executive appointments at Oxford City 1979-80 and Southend United 1984-6. He was then sports editor of *Sunday Sport* for three years.
The exemplary off-field image which he developed later led to numerous valuable commercial contracts before his tragically early death from cancer.

Brian MOORE

Rugby Union
Brian Christopher Moore. b. 11 Jan 1962 Birmingham.

With 64 England caps 1987-1995 and five Test appearances for the British Lions, Moore is the world's most capped hooker. On his first tour with the British Lions to Australia in 1989 he played in all three Tests and in New Zealand in 1993 he played in the last two Tests after Kenny Milne had been chosen as hooker for the first match of the series. An aggressive character and a fierce competitor he is an inspirational leader of the England pack.
He played for Nottingham, where he was at University, until 1990 when his work as a lawyer with a financial house took him to London and he joined Harlequins. With his legal skills he is at the forefront of moves for the game to adjust to commercial realities and reward top players while they still retain their amateur status.

Steve MOORE

Water Skiing
Steven Ronald Moore. b. 3 Mar 1963 Sidcup, London.

In 1986 Moore won the inaugural ski racing World Cup, winning all three races and in 1988 he became world champion. He was also Europpean champion 1985-8. He was awarded the MBE in 1989 and is general manager of a Ford dealership.

Adrian MOORHOUSE

Swimming
Adrian David Moorhouse. b. 25 May 1964
Bradford, West Yorkshire.

The winner of many major titles in a long career at breaststroke swimming, Moorhouse's record reads:
Olympic Games: 1984 4th 100m, 1988 1st 200m, 1992 8th 100m; Worlds: 1982 4th 100m, 7th 200m; 1986 disqualified after finishing 1st at 100m, 4th 200m; 1991 2nd 100m; Europeans: 1981 3rd 100m, 1983 1st 200m, 2nd 100m; 1985 1st 100m; 1987 1st 100m, 3rd 200m and silver at 4 x 100m medley; 1989 1st 100m in world record 1:01.49; Commonwealth Games: 1982 1st 100m, 3rd 200m, 2nd 4 x 100m medley; 1986 1st 200m, 2nd 100m and 4 x 100m medley; 1990 1st 100m in world record 1:01.49, 2nd 4 x 100m medley, 4th 200m. He set his third 1:01.49 world record later in 1990. That was also his ninth British record from his first, 1:03.15 in 1982. His best time for 200m was 2:15.78 at the Europeans in 1987.
He made his international debut in 1980 and in 1987 he became the first man to break one minute for 100m breaststroke in a 25m pool, with 59.75. ASA long-course champion 50m 1991, 100m 1981-3, 1985-7, 1989-91; 200m 1981-3, 1985-6. He was awarded the MBE in 1987. A graduate of Bradford Unversity, he was appointed Youth Development Officer for the ASA in 1993.

Cliff MORGAN

Rugby Union
Clifford Isaac Morgan. b. 7 April 1930
Trebanog, Rhondda Cynon Taff.

One of the most talented fly-halves in the history of the game, Morgan was at his best when partnering his Cardiff clubmate Rex Willis (qv). He played a major role when Wales won the Grand Slam in 1952 and the following season he inspired Cardiff and then Wales to victory over the touring All Blacks.
On the 1955 Lions tour of South Africa, a brilliant try in the first Test paved the way for a classic victory and he captained the Lions when they won the third Test. The series ended level at 2-2 and Morgan made an outstanding contribution to the Lions' successes.
Between 1951 and 1958 he won 29 caps for Wales and still holds the record as the most capped Welsh fly-half.
On retirement, he became a successful radio and TV commentator and journalist and was later an inspirational Head of Outside Broadcasts for the BBC, setting by his own example and by his enthusiasm, the highest standards for all who worked for him. He was honoured with the OBE in 1977 and the CVO in 1986.

Janet MORGAN

Squash
Janet Rachael Margaret Morgan. b. 10 Dec 1921 Wandsworth, London. d. 29 Jun 1990 Walton-on-Thames, Surrey. Later Mrs Bisley, then Mrs Shardlow.

Initially a top-class tennis player, Morgan became the best squash player in the world in the 1950s. She learned both games at Surbiton Lawn Tennis Club and as a tennis player she appeared at Wimbledon 14 times and was a non-playing member of the 1946 Wightman Cup squad. She first took up squash in 1946 and within two years was a finalist in the British Open. After losing to Joan Curry (qv) in the final of the British Open in 1948 and 1949, she won the US title in 1949 and then, in 1950, won the first of ten successive British titles. Her greatest year was 1954 when she won the British, Australian and US Opens.
After giving up competitive play in 1960 due to persistent leg and back problems, she became first chairman and then president of the Women's Squash Racquets Association until 1988, and worked tirelessly to promote the sport. She especially encouraged Heather McKay (Aus), who in 1972 surpassed her record number of British Open titles.
Janet also achieved a seven handicap at golf. She married first Joe Bisley, then Ambrose Shardlow, and was awarded the MBE in 1961.

Stewart MORRIS

Yachting
Stewart Harold Morris. b. 25 May 1909
Bromley, London d. 4 Feb 1991 West
Wittering, West Sussex.

Morris was the winner of the prestigious
Prince of Wales Cup for International 14 ft
dinghies a record 12 times: 1932-3, 1935-
6, 1947-8, 1956-7, 1960-2, and 1965.
He was a reserve at the 1936 and 1952
Olympics and the winner of Olympic gold
at Swallow class at the 1948 Games partnering **David Bond** (b. 27 Mar 1922).
He was awarded the OBE in 1945 for
wartime service with the RNVR, after
which he returned to the family hop business. This gave him ample time to
continue his sailing and also to serve on
many committees involved in the administration of the sport.

Tom MORRIS Jnr

Golf
Tom Morris Jnr. b. 20 Apr 1851 St
Andrews, Fife. d. 25 Dec 1875 St
Andrews.

'Young Tom' Morris was probably the
greatest player of the featherie and early
guttie period. His three consecutive wins in
the British Open at Prestwick in 1868-70
retired the championship belt and forced
the cancellation of the 1871 tournament. He
then won in 1872 for a fourth consecutive
time. His 12-stroke margin of victory in 1870
(149 to 161 for Bob Kirk) over 36 holes
has been bettered only by his father's win
by 13 strokes in 1862. Walter Hagen (USA)
in the PGA is the only other golfer to win
a major championship four times consecutively and Morris remains the youngest
ever British Open winner, at 17 years 249
days in 1868. Morris was also 4th in 1867,
joint 3rd in 1873 and 2nd in 1874.
Morris was taught by his father, Old Tom
Morris (qv). They made a formidable pair
and in 1875 were playing a stakes match at
North Berwick when Young Tom received
word that his young bride had died during
childbirth. He never recovered from the
anguish and his death a few months later is
often attributed to 'heartbreak'.

Tom MORRIS Snr

Golf
Tom Morris Snr. b. 17 Jun 1821 St Andrews,
Fife. d. 24 May 1908 St Andrews.

'Old Tom' Morris was the first man to win
the British Open four times, 1861-2, 1864
and 1867, the last making him still the
oldest ever champion, at 46 years 99 days.
He was also runner-up in 1860, 1863 and
1869. He was a leading figure in Scottish
golf for almost 50 years from when he was
apprenticed to Allan Robertson (qv) in
1839 to learn the making of featherie balls.
He was employed at Prestwick from 1851
to 1865, and then returned to St Andrews
to serve as greenkeeper and professional
until his death. He teamed with first
Robertson and then his son, Young Tom, to
make a formidable pair in stakes matches.
At his death he was considered the most
revered man in the game of golf.
His second son **John** Ogilvie Fairlie
Morris (1852-1906) was 3rd in the Open
in 1878.

Stan MORTENSEN

Football
Stanley Harding Mortensen. b. 26 May
1921 South Shields, Tyne & Wear. d. 21
May 1991 Blackpool, Lancashire.

A speedy, high-scoring player, Mortensen
played at inside-right in what was probably England's greatest ever forward line.
He initially signed for Blackpool in 1937
but it was thought that his career was
ended after his bomber plane crashed,
killing two of the crew, during the war.
Fortunately for Blackpool and England he
recovered to become one of the stars of the
game in the immediate postwar years.
In 25 games for England 1947-53 he
scored 23 goals starting with four against
Portugal on his debut and with two more
hat-tricks in his first eight internationals.
After two losing appearances in the FA
Cup final (1948, 1951) he was on the winning side in 1953 when he scored the only
hat trick in a Wembley final. After many
years with Blackpool, he moved to Hull in
1955 and then to Southport where he
closed his career having scored a total of

225 goals in 395 League games. Spells with non-League clubs Bath City and Lancaster City followed before he finally retired in 1962. He returned to the game in 1967 to take over as manager of Blackpool but, after only two years in the job, he was dismissed. This marked the end of his connection with football and he went into the entertainment business in Blackpool.

Angela MORTIMER

Tennis
Florence Angela Margaret Mortimer. b. 21 Apr 1932 Plymouth, Devon. Later Mrs Barrett.

Mortimer was a determined player whose economic use of ground strokes enabled her to enjoy a long career despite her physical frailty. In 1955 she won the French singles and the Wimbledon doubles with Anne Shilcock (qv), but did not win another major title until she took the Australian singles in 1958. Despite this victory she was unseeded at the 1958 Wimbledon for the first time in six years, but reached the final where she lost to Althea Gibson (USA).

Finally in 1961, at her 11th attempt, she beat Christine Truman (qv) in three sets in the only all-British women's singles final since 1914 to become the first British winner of the title since Dorothy Round (qv) in 1937. After being eliminated in the third round of the 1962 singles she did not play at Wimbledon again, but in 1964 she played in her seventh and final Wightman Cup tie.

In April 1967 she married **John Barrett**, who played for Britain in the Davis Cup in 1956 and who is now the leading tennis commentator for BBC television.

Alan MORTON

Football
Alan Lauder Morton. b. 24 Apr 1893 Partick, Glasgow. d. 15 Dec 1971 Glasgow.

Morton was the first Scottish superstar and arguably the greatest of all left-wingers. Although only 1.62m *5 ft 4 in* tall, his speed, dribbling and hanging lobs tormented the finest full-backs of the time.

After signing for Queen's Park in 1913 he remained an amateur for seven seasons, winning his first two Scotland caps before moving to Rangers in 1920. With Morton joining the legendary Alex James and Hughie Gallacher (qqv) in the forward line, Rangers swept all before them winning the League nine times, the Scottish Cup twice (1928, 1930) and they were losing finalists on three other occasions. Morton did not play in the 1932 Cup Final when Rangers again won the trophy. He made his final appearance for Scotland that year and his 31 caps remained a Scottish record until bettered by George Young (qv) in 1952. Possibly his finest international performance came against England in 1928 when the 'Wembley Wizards' beat England 5-1. His Rangers team-mate, Alex Jackson, stunned England with a hat trick of goals, all of them coming from Morton crosses.

A qualified mining engineer, he was unusually well educated for a footballer in that era and, although he played 495 games for Rangers, he was never more than a part-time professional. When he gave up playing in 1933 he was immediately appointed a director of Rangers and remained on the board until one year before his death.

Lucy MORTON

Swimming
Lucy Morton. b. 23 Feb 1898 Blackpool, Lancashire. d. 26 Aug 1980 Blackpool. Later Mrs Heaton.

With the 200m breaststroke in 1924, she became the first British woman to win an individual Olympic swimming title. This came as a surprise as she was the second string to the world record holder Irene Gilbert, who had been ill and placed 5th. She twice set world records for 200y breaststroke, 3:11.4 in 1916 and 3:06.0 in 1920, when there was no breaststroke event at the Olympic Games, and also set a world record for 150y backstroke with 2:17.0 in 1916. She was ASA champion at 150y backstroke and 200y breaststroke in 1920. Married to Henry Heaton in 1927, she taught swimming for many years in Blackpool and was a leading official.

Pat MOSS

Rallying
Patricia Moss. b. 27 Dec 1934. Later Mrs Carlsson.

The most successful woman rally driver, she was the sister of Stirling Moss (qv) and married Erik Carlsson (Sweden), the top male rally driver of his generation. Driving for BMC, she won the European Ladies Championship in 1958 and the Liège-Rome-Liège with Anne Wisdom in an Austin Healey 3000 in 1960. She won the Tulip and German rallies in a Mini Cooper and was 3rd in the Safari rally in 1962. She was European Ladies Touring champion five times. In the RAC Rally she was 2nd in 1961 and 3rd in 1962 and won the Ladies' Prize eight times. She also took the Coupe des Dames eight times in the Monte Carlo Rally between 1959 and 1969 before retiring to train show jumpers.

Stirling MOSS

Motor Racing
Stirling Crauford Moss. b. 17 Sep 1929 West Kensington, London.

Britain's most admired and respected motor-racing driver of his era, Moss was unlucky never to win a world title, but won 16 of his 66 Grand Prix races 1951-61. He was runner-up to Juan-Manuel Fangio (Arg) in the World Drivers' Championship each year from 1955 to 1957 and by just one point to Mike Hawthorn (qv) in 1958; and in all he totalled 186.64 points.

His patriotism meant that he raced uncompetitive British cars up to 1954, when he bought a Maserati and later joined their works team. He was then persuaded to sign for Mercedes in 1955, driving as number two to Fangio. That year he became the first Englishman ever to win the British Grand Prix, a success he repeated in a Vanwall in 1957, after rejoining Maserati in 1956. He also excelled in sports car racing and in 1955 he became the first Englishman to win the Mille Miglia in Italy. Back in British cars he had two highly successful years with Vanwall 1957-8, and was 3rd in the championship with Cooper in 1959 and 1960, and for

Lotus in 1961. In 1962 he was severely injured in a crash at Goodwood, and after a slow recovery realised that he would never regain all his old skills. However, years later he reappeared, racing for fun, retaining all the verve and sparkle which has made him such a revered figure. He was awarded the OBE in 1957 and voted BBC Sports Personality of the Year 1961.

His father Alfred had raced internationally in the 1920s and his mother Eileen had been an expert trials driver in the 1930s. His sister Pat (qv) was a leading rally driver. Stirling started racing at 17 and in 1948 he had ten class wins in sprint and hill-climb events.

Buster MOTTRAM

Tennis
Christopher John Mottram. b. 25 Apr 1955 Wimbledon, London.

As befitted someone whose father and mother were Davis and Wightman Cup players respectively, Mottram showed exceptional talent at an early age. In 1971, at the age of 16, he became the youngest-ever player to win the British Under-21 title and the following year he lost to Björn Borg (Swe) in the boy's final at Wimbledon. As a 20-year-old he was ranked British No. 1 (equal with Mark Cox (qv)) in 1975, the youngest player ever to top the British rankings, and he was again the British No. 1 from 1977-82.

Like his father, Tony (qv), he had a fine Davis Cup record playing in 18 ties between 1975 and 1983 (26/33 singles, 4/6 doubles). With John Lloyd (qv) he played a major part in taking Britain to the final in 1978. In Britain's only final appearance since 1937 he defeated Brian Gottfried (USA) in five sets in the singles after losing the first two sets and having a match point against him in the third.

Tony MOTTRAM

Tennis
Anthony John Mottram. b. 8 Jun 1920 Coventry, West. Midlands.

A promising junior before World War II, Mottram reached the third round in the

Wimbledon singles in 1939. After winning a DFC as a torpedo bomber with RAF Coastal Command, he resumed his tennis career after the war and was nominated by the LTA to play in the 1946 US Championships. Although never winning a major title he was runner-up in the men's doubles at Wimbledon in 1947 and reached the quarter-finals of the singles the following year. At the French Championships he was a semi-finalist in the men's doubles in 1948 and the mixed doubles, 1950-1. He won the British Hard Court singles in 1954 and, partnering Geoffrey Paish (qv), the doubles in 1954 and the British Covered Court doubles 1951-2.

As Britain's leading postwar player, he was a stalwart of the Davis Cup team playing in 19 ties between 1947 and 1955 (25/38 singles, 11/18 doubles). He turned professional in 1955 and was appointed Britain's national coach in 1970.

He married **Joy** Irene **Gannon** (b. Enfield), who was a semi-finalist at Wimbledon 1949-50, won the German singles in 1954 and played in four Wightman Cup ties 1947-52; their son, Buster (qv), became Britain's leading player.

Marion MOULD

Equestrianism, Show Jumping
Marion Janice Mould. b. 6 Jun 1947 Hampshire. née Coakes.

In 1965, at the age of 18, Marion Coakes won the first World ladies' individual title on her Irish-bred pony *Stroller*; she remains the youngest world champion at show jumping. Also that year they won the Queen Elizabeth II Cup, and they went on to win the Hickstead Jumping Derby in 1967 and the individual Olympic silver in 1968. That was the first individual jumping medal ever won by a woman at the Olympics.

Marion's first notable achievements on *Stroller*, owned by her father Ralph, had come at the European Junior Championships, with a team gold in 1962 and silver in 1964. Marion rode *Spring Shandy* when she won a second team gold in 1963. After marriage she took the world individual silver medal in 1970 and was British

champion and won her second Queen Elizabeth II Cup on *Stroller* in 1971. *Stroller* then retired and died on 24 Mar 1986. Marion won the British Ladies' title on *Elizabeth Ann* in 1976.

Her husband **David** Stephen Mould (b. 24 Apr 1940 Ashford, Surrey) was a leading National Hunt jockey, with 606 winners from 1958 to 1975, riding for much of his career for royal trainer Peter Cazalet.

Doug MOUNTJOY

Snooker
Douglas James Mountjoy. b. 8 Jun 1942 Tir-y-Berth Rhymney, Caerphilly.

Having been world amateur champion in 1976 and Welsh amateur champion in 1968 and 1976, Mountjoy started his professional career with great success. In 1977 he won the Benson & Hedges Masters, in 1978 the UK Championship, in 1979 the B & H Irish Masters, and in 1980 the Welsh title. In 1981 he reached the final of the World Championship, where he lost 12-18 to Steve Davis (qv). A fluent potter, he has never won that title, but his further tournament successes include the UK Open 1988, Mercantile Credit Classic 1989, as well as being BBC *Pot Black* champion in 1978 and 1985.

He was also a member of the Welsh team that won the World Cup in 1979 and 1980 and Welsh champion 1979, 1982, 1984, 1987 and 1989. He became a publican in 1984.

Ethel MUCKELT

Figure Skating
Ethel Muckelt. b. 30 May 1885 Moss Side, Manchester. d. 13 Dec 1953 Altrincham, Gt. Manchester.

After taking 4th place in the singles at the 1923 World Championships, Muckelt won a bronze medal at the 1924 Olympics but by the time separate British Championships for women were introduced in 1927 she was rather past her best and never won the British singles title. By way of contrast she won nine successive British pairs titles 1923-31 with John Page (qv).

Internationally, their best performance was

to take the silver medals at the 1924 World Championships. They also placed 4th in 1928 by which time Muckelt was 42 years old. She never married.

Bill MULCAHY (Ireland)

Rugby Union
William Albert Mulcahy. b. 7 Jan 1935 Rathkeale, Co. Limerick.

A strong, reliable lock from Bective Rangers and Bohemians, Mulcahy made his international debut against Australia in 1958 as one of six new caps introduced by the Irish selectors. He retired in 1965 after winning 35 caps and captaining his country 11 times. He partnered Willie John McBride (qv) in the second row in 17 international matches.
He toured with the British Lions to Australia and New Zealand 1959 and South Africa 1962. Hampered by injury he only played in two Tests on his first tour, but in South Africa he was the first choice lock and after playing in his favoured position in the first three Tests he was a surprise choice as a flanker for the final match of the series.

Karl MULLEN (Ireland)

Rugby Union
Karl Daniel Mullen. b. 26 Nov 1926 Courttown Harbour, Co. Wexford.

An outstanding hooker of the immediate post-war era, Mullen won his 25 Irish caps in consecutive matches.
Noted for his brilliant tactical sense and leadership, he first captained Ireland in 1948 at the age of 21 and led them to the Grand Slam that year. In 1949 Ireland won the Triple Crown and Mullen's leadership qualities were recognised when he was chosen to lead the 1950 Lions to Australia and New Zealand. Although only managing one draw in the Test series against New Zealand, the 1950 Lions are still remembered as the most popular team ever to tour New Zealand. On his return, he led Ireland to the International Championship in 1951 and played his last international against Wales in 1952.

Alan MULLERY

Football
Alan Patrick Mullery. b. 23 Nov 1941 Notting Hill, London.

Mullery was an outstanding right-half whose all-round talents won him 35 England caps 1964-71. On a less positive note, in 1968, against Yugoslavia, he became the first England player to sent off in an international.
He began his professional career with Fulham in 1958, moved to Tottenham in 1964 and returned to Fulham in 1972. He was at his peak during his years with Spurs, playing on the winning team in the FA Cup 1967, the Football League Cup 1971 and the Inter-Cities Fairs Cup 1972. During his second spell with Fulham he was a losing FA Cup finalist in 1975. He made 364 appearances for Fulham and 312 for Tottenham
Following his retirement in 1976 he was successively manager of Brighton, Charlton, Crystal Palace, Queen's Park Rangers and Brighton again before he finally left the game in 1987. Voted Football Writers' Footballer of the Year in 1975, he was awarded the MBE in 1976.

Brendan MULLIN (Ireland)

Rugby Union
Brendan John Mullin. b. 30 Oct 1963 Israel.

An Irish international hurdler (best for 110m 14.41 in 1986), Mullin's exceptional speed has been one of his greatest assets but his all-round footballing talents led to a place on the 1989 British Lions tour of Australia where he played in the centre in the first Test.
From Trinity College, Dublin he went to Oxford University (Blue 1986-7) and then joined London Irish. He withdrew from international rugby in 1992 but, having continued to play for Blackrock College, he returned after two years and by the end of the 1995 World Cup he had won 54 Irish caps and scored an Irish record 17 tries. He is a stockbroker.

Noel MURLESS

Horse Racing
(Sir) Charles Francis Noel Murless. b. 24
Mar 1910 Malpas, Cheshire. d. 9 May 1987
Newmarket.

Murless was champion trainer on the flat
in England nine times: 1948, 1957, 1959-
61, 1967-8, 1970 and 1973. He trained the
winners of 19 Classics in England between
1948 and 1973 and two more in Ireland.
He broke the records for highest prize
money three times, being the first trainer to
win more than £100,000 in a year with
£116,898 from 48 winners in 1957, and the
first over £200,000 with £256,899 from 60
winners in 1967.

He was a steeplechase jockey during the
1930s and after assisting the Irish brothers
Frank and Hubert Hartigan, he established
stables first at Hambleton Lodge, Yorkshire,
taking over from Fred Darling (qv) at
Beckhampton in 1947, and then moving to
Warren Place, Newmarket in 1952. His
Derby winners were *Crepello* 1957, *St
Paddy* 1960 and *Royal Palace* 1967, and
his other great horses included *Petite
Etoile*. He was knighted in the 1977 Silver
Jubilee honours.

His brother **Stuart** (1917-94) trained
Nocturnal Spree to win the 1000 Guineas
in 1975 as well as the winners of two Irish
and one French Classic.

Alex MURPHY

Rugby League
Alexander John Murphy. b. 22 Apr 1939 St
Helens, Merseyside

A brilliant scrum half of extraordinary speed,
Murphy played in four winning Challenge
Cup finals for three different teams: St
Helens 1961 and 1966, Leigh 1971 and
Warrington 1974. On the last three occasions he was player-coach but when he
devoted himself exclusively to coaching he
took four teams to the final: Warrington
1975, Wigan 1984 and St Helens 1987,
1989. He won the first of his 27 Great
Britain caps in Australia in 1958, when at
the age of 19 he was the youngest British
player ever to tour there. He played brilliantly, scoring 21 tries in 20 matches, the
majority of which were attributable to his
speed from the base of the scrum. He
played in all three Tests and Great Britain
won the series 2-1. In 1959 he equalled the
GB Test match record by scoring four tries
against France, a record which stood for
32 years until Martin Offiah (qv) scored
five times against France in 1991.

He was also an accomplished stand-off and
played some notable games at senior club
level. One of the most knowledgeable men
in the game, he is now a member of the
TV commentary team.

Jimmy Barry MURPHY (Ireland)

Hurling and Gaelic Football
Jimmy Barry Murphy. b. 22 Aug 1954
Cork.

A great all-rounder he won all-Ireland
medals with Cork for Gaelic football
1973-4 and hurling 1976-8, 1983 and
1986. He was also an outstanding soccer
player and is now deeply involved in greyhound racing.

He won three National League medals, one
in football and two in hurling and is the
holder of seven all-star awards, two in
football and five in hurling.

Noel MURPHY (Ireland)

Rugby Union
Noel Arthur Augustine Murphy. b. 22 Feb
1937 Cork.

One of a legendary family in Irish rugby;
his father, **Noel** Snr (1904-1987) won 11
caps (1930-3) and his son **Kenneth John**
(b. 31 Jul 1966, Cork) made his debut as
Ireland's full-back in 1990.

Noel's 41 caps 1958-69 stood as a record
for an Irish flanker until 1980. Initially an
open-side specialist, he later moved to
blind-side. With the 1959 British Lions he
played in four Tests in Australia and New
Zealand but a serious injury in the 1962
match against England ruled him out of
consideration for a second Lions tour. The
honour was, however, only postponed as
he went to Australia and New Zealand in
1966 when, as in 1959, he played in four
of the six Tests.

He became an Irish selector and after

taking over as Ireland's coach in 1977 was appointed coach for the 1980 Lions tour of South Africa.

John MURRAY

Cricket
John Thomas Murray. b. 1 Apr 1935
North Kensington, London.

An immaculate wicket-keeper, Murray held the record for most dismissals in a first-class career from passing Bert Strudwick's (qv) total in 1975, until his 1527 victims was passed by Bob Taylor (qv). In 1957 he became only the second man ever to achieve the wicket-keeper's double with 1025 runs and 104 dismissals, and he exceeded 1000 runs in a season on six occasions. His batting prowess was best demonstrated with his 112 for England against West Indies at The Oval in 1966, batting at No. 9, and in a dashing century for the Rest of the World in Barbados in 1967, yet earlier in his career much less proficient keepers had often been preferred to him for the Test team as his batting had been considered weak. He was awarded the MBE.
21 Tests 1961-7: 506 runs at 21.00, 1 100 HS 112; 52 catches, 3 stumpings.
First-class 1952-75: 18,872 runs at 23.59, 16 100s HS 142; 6 wickets at 40.50, BB 2-10; 1268 catches, 258 stumpings.

Yvonne MURRAY

Athletics
Yvonne Carol Grace Murray. b. 4 Oct 1964 Musselburgh, Midlothian.

Although she has had some disappointments, such as 8th in the 1992 Olympic 3000m and 9th at the World 3000m, when highly favoured, Murray has amassed a formidable collection of major championships medals. At the Olympics she took the 3000m bronze in 1988 and her first major gold medal was the European Indoor 3000m in 1987, after 3rd in 1984 and 2nd in 1985 at this event. Outdoors at the Europeans, after bronze in 1986, when she improved her 3000m pb by 5.76 sec. in the heat and a further 12.41 in the final, she won in 1990, producing devastating

acceleration with 600m to go, and took the silver medal in 1994. She also won the World Indoor 3000m in 1993. At the Commonwealth Games she was 10th at both 1500m and 3000m in 1982, was 3rd at 3000m and 5th at 1500m on her home track in Edinburgh 1986, 2nd at 3000m and 4th at 1500m in 1990 and finally struck gold with a brilliant win at 10,000m in 1994. This was only her second track race at this distance, but she could undoubtedly have run much faster than the 31:56.97, with which she decisively out-kicked Elana Meyer (SAf). That added to the long list of Scottish records that she has set since 1983.

Having preceded Zola Budd as the UK junior record holder at 3000m, she beat her for the first time in 1986 at 2000m behind Maricica Puica's world record, with a Commonwealth best of 5:29.58, a record she improved to 5:26.93 in 1994. In 1989 she became the first British woman to win a World Cup event (3000m), and she won that event again in 1994.

Her national titles: UK 3000m 1985, 1987, 1993; 5000m 1983; AAA 1500m 1992, 1995; 3000m 1988, 1990-1; Scottish 800m 1987-8, 1500m 1990, 3000m 1982.

She was awarded the MBE in 1991.

Other best times: 800m 2:00.80 (1987), 1000m 2:37.29 (1989), 1500m 4:01.20 (1987), 1M 4:22.64 (1994), 3000m 8:29.02 (1988), 5000m 14:56.94 (1995).

Alfred MYNN

Cricket
Alfred Mynn. b. 19 Jan 1807 Goudhurst, Kent. d. 1 Nov 1861 Southwark, London.

One of the first great champions of cricket, 'The Lion of Kent' was a powerful man, a high scorer in an age of bowling dominance on rough pitches and a fast round-arm bowler despite a shortish run. He played for Kent and was one of the mainstays of the Gentlemen against the Players in the early days of those great matches. His 46 runs and 9 wickets in 1842 and 47 runs and 8 wickets in 1843 restored the fortunes of the Gentlemen. On his death, mourned by all of Kent, he was described by his contemporary as a great player, **Felix** (Nicholas Wanostrocht, 1804-76), as 'one of the noblest specimens of manliness and courage combined with all that was becoming in a man'.

In what may now be regarded as first-class matches, from 1832 to 1859, he took over 1000 wickets at an average of about 10 and scored nearly 5000 runs, with a highest score of 125*.

Tony NASH

Bobsleigh
Anthony James Dillon Nash. b. 18 Mar 1936 Amersham, Buckinghamshire.

Nash was the driver, known for his accuracy, with Robin Dixon (qv) as brakeman of the winning Olympic two-man bobsleigh title in 1964 and of the world title in 1965. They retired after 5th place at the 1968 Olympics.

He was awarded the MBE in 1969. He was the director of a family engineering company and farms in Devon, where he is joint-master of the Tiverton Foxhounds. His daughter Annabel became Britain's top woman lugeist.

Phil NEAL

Football
Philip George Neal. b. 20 Feb 1951 Irchester, Northants.

A remarkably consistent full-back, Neal only missed one League game for Liverpool in ten seasons. After seven seasons with Northampton Town, he moved to Anfield in 1974 and played a key role in one of the greatest ever club teams, which won the League Championship seven times, and the League Cup four times. He was the only player to have appeared in all four of their European Cup wins between 1977 and 1984, also winning the UEFA Cup in 1976, and was captain of the team that lost 1-0 to Juventus in the 1985 European Cup final after the Heysel disaster.

The only major honour that eluded Neal was an FA Cup winners' medal although he came close when Liverpool lost 2-1 to Manchester United in the 1977 final. During his years with Liverpool 1974-85 he played 455 League games, scoring 41

goals, many of them from penalties. His reliable play was rewarded with 50 England caps between 1976 and 1983.

In 1985 he moved to Bolton Wanderers where spent four seasons and was manager of Coventry City from October 1993 to February 1995. He was also an assistant to Graham Taylor for England.

Denis NEALE

Table Tennis
Denis Neale. b. 12 Apr 1944.

Neale's 18 titles in the English Closed Championships, six men's singles, seven men's doubles and five mixed doubles between 1966 and 1977, was a record until passed by Desmond Douglas (qv).

He made 495 England appearances, and was appointed England men's team captain in 1994.

Tony NEARY

Rugby Union
Anthony Neary. b. 25 Nov 1949 Manchester.

Until his record was beaten by Rory Underwood (qv), Neary was England's most capped player. As a flanker with Broughton Park he played for England 43 times, but although he toured with the British Lions to South Africa 1974 and New Zealand 1977, the final match of the series against New Zealand was the only time he was called up for Test duties.

He made his international debut against Wales in 1971 and, after a spell as England's captain in mid-career, he retired after England had won the Grand Slam in 1980.

John NEILL

Hockey
John Whitley Neill. b. 15 May 1934 Surrey

The first player to win 50 caps for Great Britain, Neill first represented GB in 1959, played in three Olympic Games 1960-8, and closed his career in 1968 with a total of 56 GB caps. During the England tour of South Africa in 1958, he came into the team for the second Test and holding his place for the remainder of the series, established himself as a regular member of the team, going on to win 33 England caps 1958-68. A solid and reliable defender, he learned the game at Rugby School and later played for the Army, Southgate and Bowdon. After qualifying as a chartered accountant he became a director of a brewery.

Gwen NELIGAN

Fencing
Gwendoline Frances Elizabeth Neligan. b. 1906 London. d. 10 Apr 1972 Torremolinos, Spain.

As the European Championships held prior to 1936 were subsequently accorded World Championship status, Gwen Neligan, by virtue of her 1933 European victory, became the first British woman to win the world title. Her feat has only been matched among British women fencers by Gillian Sheen (qv) whose 1956 Olympic victory also carried World Championship status.
In 1933 Miss Neligan also won a silver medal in the team event. She came close to defending her individual title in 1934 when she initially tied for the Championship but was relegated to 4th place after a barrage. She did, however, win a second silver medal in the team event.
Her first success came in 1928 when she won the British Junior title and after placing in the British Ladies' Foil championship for three years 1931-3 she won the title for four successive years 1934-7. Her expected challenge for a medal at the 1936 Olympics was thwarted at the last minute when she was forced to withdraw because of appendicitis.

Louise NETTLETON

Archery
Louise Nettleton. b. c.1874. d. 22 Oct 1954 Tunbridge Wells, Kent.

In addition to sharing the World individual title with Mrs Weston Martyr in 1938, Nettleton was on the winning team three times (1935, 1937, 1946) at the World Championships and shares with Nilla de Wharton Burr (qv) the distinction of being the only British archer to have won four gold medals at the Championships. She was the British champion in 1933 and 1939 and in 1946 she won the British long distance championship.
Her husband was also a leading archer in addition to being a noted cyclist, mountaineer and motorist. She shared her husband's love of mountaineering and won fame as the first woman to climb several of the Swiss Alpine peaks, in addition to climbing the Matterhorn seven times. She served as President of the Ladies' Alpine Club from 1920-3.

Bill NEVETT

Horse Racing
William Nevett. b. 26 Mar 1906 Chorley, Lancashire. d. 9 May 1992 Bedale, North Yorkshire.

The 'Cock of the North', the leading northern flat-race jockey for many years, Nevett was runner-up to Gordon Richards (qv) for the jockey's championship four times: 1933 (72 winners), 1936 (108), 1937 (110), 1938 (122) and 1939 (71). He was apprenticed to Dobson Peacock from 1918 and rode the winner of three wartime Derbys, 1941, 1944-5 and one peacetime Classic, the Oaks in 1948 on *Masaka*. After his retirement from riding at the end of the 1956 season, he trained at Epsom for a few seasons.

Queenie NEWALL

Archery
Sybil Fenton Newall. b. 17 Oct 1854 Calderbrook, Gt. Manchester. d. 24 Jun 1929 Cheltenham, Gloucestershire.

In 1908, at the age of 53 years 277 days, Newall took the Olympic archery title and is the oldest woman ever to win an Olympic gold medal in any sport. She first took up archery as a pastime on the family estate in Lancashire and only entered the sport competitively when she joined Cheltenham Archers as a 50-year-old in 1905. Within three years she was the Olympic champion and remains the only British lady to have achieved this honour. She was the British champion in 1911 and

1914 and continued to take part in competitions until the year before her death.

Tom NEWMAN

Billiards
Thomas Newman. né Pratt. b. 23 Mar 1894 Barton-on-Humber, Lincolnshire. d. 5 Oct 1943 Tufnell Park, London.

Winner of a record six world billiards titles under knock-out conditions, Newman learned the game in the saloons owned by his father in Nottingham and later in London. In the early part of his career, he signed a three-year contract with John Roberts Jr (qv) with whom he toured extensively. After winning his first world title in 1921, he was the champion for four of the next five years, losing only to Willie Smith (qv) in the 1923 final. He was again a finalist each year 1928-30 but lost to Joe Davis (qv) on each occasion, although his record of playing in ten successive finals remains unsurpassed. In 1924 he made the first 1000 break in the Championship (1021).

Although he professed to have little interest in the game, he was also an accomplished snooker player and lost to Joe Davis in the 1934 World final.

Alison NICHOLAS

Golf
Alison Margaret Nicholas b. 3 Jun 1962 Gibraltar.

The British Ladies' Open champion of 1987 started playing golf at the age of 17, was Northern girls' champion in 1982 and 1983 and won the 1983 British amateur stroke-play title. She turned professional in 1984 and she was was runner-up in the European Order of Merit each year 1988-90. She has been a stalwart member of the European Solheim Cup teams of 1990, 1992 and 1994 with a record of five wins and four losses. Just 1.52m *5 ft 0 in* tall, but an aggressive player, she has achieved much success with her substantially larger partner Laura Davies (qv). In May 1995 she achieved her first victory on the US tour, when she won the Corning Classic in New York.

Peter NICHOLAS

Football
Peter Nicholas. b. 10 Nov 1959 Newport,.

Renowned for his hard tackling in the midfield, he gave sterling service to variety of clubs. Beginning his professional career with Crystal Palace in 1976 he transferred to Arsenal in 1980, returned to Palace after three seasons at Highbury and then signed for Luton Town, Aberdeen, Chelsea and Watford.

He was capped by Wales while playing for each of these clubs and represented his country 73 times 1979-91; at the end of his international career he was the most capped Welsh player.

Jimmy NICHOLL

Football
James Michael Nicholl. b. 28 Feb 1956 Hamilton, Canada.

After spending his peak years (1974-81) with Manchester United, with a winner's medal in the FA Cup in 1977, Nicholl never really settled after his move to Sunderland in 1981/2. He went to play in Toronto, Canada, rejoined Sunderland then returned to Canada. He came back for one season with Glasgow Rangers, then went to West Bromwich Albion, rejoined Rangers before moving on to Dunfermline Athletic 1989 and Raith Rovers 1990.

He won 73 caps for Northern Ireland between 1976 and 1986.

Gwyn NICHOLLS

Rugby Union
Erith Gwynne Nicholls. b. 15 Jul 1874 Westbury on Severn, Glos. d. 24 Mar 1939 Dinas Powys, Vale of Glamorgan.

Nicholls was the only Welshman on the British tour of Australia in 1899 and the first Welshman to play for a British XV. Playing in the centre in each of the four Tests he scored a try in both the first and second Tests and was the leading points scorer on the tour (12 tries).

A regular captain of Cardiff around the turn of the century, he won 24 Welsh caps 1896-1906, and captained Wales 10 times, including their famous victory over the All Blacks in 1905. One of the greatest early Welsh stars, the Gwyn Nicholls Memorial Gates at Cardiff Arms Park are a lasting tribute to his legendary status.

His brother, **Syd** (1868-1946), was also capped by Wales as was his brother-in-law and business partner, **Bert Winfield** (1878-1919).

Morris NICHOLS

Cricket
Morris Stanley Nichols. b. 6 Oct 1900 Stondon Massey, Essex. d. 26 Jan 1961 Newark, Notts.

One of England's best all-rounders of the 1930s, Nichols performed the double of 1000 runs and 100 wickets in a season in 1929, 1932-3 and each year 1935-9, before his career was ended by the war and the cancellation of the MCC tour to India for which he had been selected. He scored over 1000 runs nine times and took over 100 wickets eleven times, with a best of 171 at 19.92 in 1938. He batted left-handed in the middle order and bowled fast right arm with great stamina for Essex. He was also a soccer goalkeeper for Queen's Park Rangers.

14 Tests 1929-39: 355 runs at 29.58; HS 78*; 41 wickets at 28.09, BB 6-35; 11 catches.

First-class 1924-39: 17,827 runs at 26.56, 20 100s HS 205; 1833 wickets at 21.63, BB 9-32; 325 catches.

Ralph NICHOLS

Badminton
Ralph C.F.Nichols. b. Feb 1911 Oakham, Rutland.

The leading British player in the years preceeding World War II, Nichols won the All-England singles five times (1932, 1934, 1936-8), the doubles three times (1936-8) with his elder brother Leslie and the mixed doubles once (1939). The 36 international caps he won, 1930-51, was at the time an England record. His game was built on subtlety and a solid defence which frustrated many harder-hitting opponents. A Wimbledon tennis player, he married English badminton international Elizabeth O'Beirne.

Frenchy NICHOLSON

Horse Racing
Herbert Charles Denton Nicholson. b. 13 Jan 1913 Rotherham, South Yorkshire.

The son of a professional huntsman, with whom he worked in France, hence his nickname, Nicholson became a most respected trainer, especially noted for the apprentices he brought on, such as Pat Eddery (qv), Tony Murray, Paul Cook and Walter Swinburn (qv).

Nicholson was apprenticed to Stanley Wootton at Epsom and rode *Victor Norman* to victory in the Champion Hurdle in 1936 and *Medoc II* to win the Cheltenham Gold Cup in 1942. He took out a trainer's licence in 1946, although he continued riding for several years.

In 1938 he married Diana Holman, whose father Captain Bill Holman was a top polo player.

Their son **David Nicholson** (b. 19 Mar 1939) was a stylish jumps jockey, who rode 594 winners in his career, including the 1967 Whitbread Gold Cup on *Mill House*. 'The Duke' rode as a professional to 1974, with a best season of 63 winners in 1966/7, before succeeding his father as a trainer. He had 100 winners in 1992/3 and was champion NH trainer on money winnings in 1993/4.

Guy NICKALLS

Rowing
Guy Nickalls. b. 12 Feb 1866 Sutton, London. d. 8 Jul 1935 Leeds.

Nickalls was the winner of a record 23 Henley medals. His son, **Guy Oliver** (b. 4 Apr 1899. d. 26 Apr 1974) also won 10, and had the highest number of wins (7) in the Grand Challenge Cup. Guy Snr also won an Olympic gold medal in 1908 when he rowed with the Leander Club crew in the eights. Guy Jnr won Olympic silver medals at eights in 1920 and 1928. In the Diamond Sculls, Nickalls won six times between 1888 and 1894, failing only in 1892. Between 1890 and 1897 he and his brother, **Vivian** (1870-1947) dominated the Silver Goblets pair oars, winning together in 1894-6. Guy won with Lord Ampthill in 1890-1 and with E.R.Balfour in 1897, while Vivian won with W.A.L.Fletcher in 1892-3. In 1895, their father, Tom, donated the Nickalls Challenge Cup in their honour, to be given to future winners of the pair oars at Henley.

Jenny and John NICKS

Figure Skating
Jennifer Mary Nicks. b. 13 Apr 1932 Brighton. d. 21 Aug 1980 Delta, BC, Canada. Later Mrs Sturrock.

John Allen Wisden Nicks. b. 22 Apr 1929 Brighton.

Great-great niece and nephew of the pioneer cricketer John Wisden (qv), Jenny and her brother John first took up skating when the Brighton Ice Rink opened near their home. They won the British pairs title for six successive years 1947-52, competed in the Olympic Games of 1948 (8th) and 1952 (4th), and at the World Championships they were runners-up in 1950 before taking the title in 1953 to become the first British winners since 1912. Two weeks earlier they were the first-ever British winners of the European title.

After becoming World champions they turned professional and Jenny won the British Open professional singles title (1955-6). Following a mild heart attack while touring in South Africa, she gave up skating and after her marriage she settled in Canada where she taught skating. A sudden second and more serious heart attack resulted in her death at the early age of 48.

After retiring from competition John Nicks became an instructor in America.

Tom NICOLSON

Athletics, Hammer
Thomas Rae Nicolson. b. 3 Oct 1879 Tighnabruich, Argyll and Bute. d. 18 Apr 1951 Glasgow.

Nicolson was the most prolific record-breaker in British hammer throwing history, taking the record in 14 improvements from 40.48m in 1902 to 50.84 in 1908, in which time the diameter of the circle was reduced from 9ft (at which his best was 51.82m in 1911) to its current 7 ft diameter. He was AAA hammer champion six times 1903-05, 1907, 1909 and 1912 and won an extraordinary 21 Scottish titles, including 19 in succession 1902-14 and 1919-24, with those of 1926-7. In all he won 40 Scottish titles, adding 14 for the shot (at which his best was 13.41m in 1903) 1903-05, 1909-14, 1919-23; four at 56lb weight 1921-4 and three at Scots hammer 1921-3. At the Olympic Games hammer he was 4th in 1908 and 6th in 1920. He farmed in Kyles of Bute on the Clyde.

He had a sister and nine brothers. One, **Hugh** (b. 20 Apr 1878) was Scottish shot champion in 1902 and a much younger brother **Andrew** (b. 14 May 1898. d. 1965) succeeded him as Scotland's top shot putter, winning 11 Scottish shot titles between 1924 and 1936 as well as four titles at Scots style hammer and placing 2nd or 3rd 13 times, but never winning.

Paul NIHILL

Walking
Vincent Paul Nihill. b. 5 Sep 1939 Colchester.

The winner of a record 27 UK national walking titles between 1963 and 1975: on the track, Nihill was AAA champion at 2 miles 1965, 3000m 1970-1 and 1975, 7 miles 1965-6 and 1968, 10,000m 1969; and on the roads he won RWA 10 miles 1965, 1968-9, 1972; 20km 1965-6, 1968-9, 1971-2; 20 miles 1963-5, 1968-9, 1971; 50km 1964, 1968, 1971; not only was he the only man to win at all the four road distances, he won them all in one year, 1968.

A member of Surrey Walking Club, he won the silver medal at 50km at his first Olympics in 1964. He won 35 successive walks races from December 1967 to his failure to finish the Olympic 50km in 1968 in the heat and high altitude of Mexico City, but then won a further 51 consecutive races to June 1970, including the European 20km in 1969. He took the European 20km bronze medal in 1971 and was 6th at 20km and 9th at 50km at the 1972 Olympics. In his career 1960-77 he won 355 races.

He set world track bests for 3000m 11:51.2 (1971) and 5000m 20:14.2 (1972),and his numerous other British records included track: 30km 2:28:44.0 (1972), 20 miles 2:40:42.6 (1972), and road: 20km 1:24:50 (1972), 20 miles 2:30:35 (1971), 50km 4:11:31.2 (1964). His track 10,000m best was 42:34.6 (1972).

Susan NOEL

Squash
Susan Diana Barham Noel. b. 8 Jun 1912 London. d. 20 Oct 1991 London. Later Mrs G.F.Powell.

As a player, writer, historian and benefactor, Noel had a considerable influence on the development of women's squash in Britain. She first competed in the British championships in 1922 at the age of nine and in 1932, at the age of 19 years 7 months, she became the youngest ever champion. After retaining the title for the next two years she gave up squash in favour of tennis but she made a comeback in 1939 finishing as runner-up to Margot Lumb (qv). She also won the US title in 1933.

With Mrs G Bryans Wolfe she donated the Wolfe-Noel Challenge Cup in 1933 for competition between Great Britain and the USA, playing in the match three times herself (1933-4, 1939) and in 1949 she was non-playing captain of the British team.

At tennis she was the British Schoolgirls' champion while at Glendower School in 1927-8 and later became a regular at Wimbledon. During the break in her squash career she enjoyed a particularly successful year in 1935 when she won the doubles at Queen's, the South of England and the Welsh Championships and she was also a finalist in the singles at Queen's that year. She represented England at tennis but narrowly failed to make the Wightman Cup team.

Her father **Evan Baillie Noel** (1879-1928)

was the Amateur Rackets champion in 1907 and won an Olympic gold medal in 1908. He served as Secretary of the Queen's Club and was a sporting journalist and the leading historian of court games. Susan also became a journalist and continued the historical research started by her father.

Philip NOEL BAKER – see BAKER

Malcolm NOKES

Athletics, Hammer
Malcolm Cuthbert Nokes. b. 20 May 1897 Edmonton, London. d. 22 Nov 1986 Alton, Hampshire.

Nokes was Britain's top hammer thrower of the inter-war years, after winning a Military Cross in World War I. He was the Olympic bronze medallist in 1924 and 11th in 1928, Empire champion in 1930 and 1934 and AAA champion each year 1923-6. He set British hammer records at 52.42 and 52.76m in 1923 and also set the official English native record for the discus at 38.44 when he won against France in 1927.

A schoolmaster, he played a leading role in the development of the AAA coaching scheme. He won the hammer for Oxford University against Cambridge in 1921 before the event was dropped from the programme, was also a water polo Blue each year 1919-22 and had trials at soccer and rugby.

Wendy NORMAN

Modern Pentathlon
Wendy Norman.

Norman was a member of the British team that won the world team title in 1981 and 1982, and individually placed 3rd in 1981 and won in 1982, and was later 4th in 1984. At the preceding World Cup she was 2nd in 1978 and 1979 and the winner in 1980, and won team gold on each occasion. She won a record seven British titles, 1978-80, 1982 and 1986-8 and was the Sports Writers' Sportswoman of the Year in 1982.

Bob NORSTER

Rugby Union
Robert Leonard Norster. b. 23 Jun 1957
Ebbw Vale, Blaenau Gwent.

A line-out specialist who captained Wales and Cardiff, Norster was first included in the Welsh national squad in 1977 and played v Romania in 1977 but full caps were not awarded for this match. He also played for Wales 'B' 1979-80 and toured North America in 1980 but had to wait until 1982 before winning his first full cap. On his retirement in 1989 he had won 34 caps and shares with Alan Martin the record of being Wales' most capped lock. Only injury prevented him from being the outright holder of the record.

He went on the British Lions tour of New Zealand in 1983 where he played in the first two Tests before a back injury put him out of contention for further honours. On his second Lions tour to Australia in 1989 he played in the first Test but Wade Dooley (qv) was preferred for the two final Tests. On his return home a shoulder injury finally ended his international career but, as a coach and manager of the Welsh team from 1991, he played a major part in the revival of Welsh international fortunes in 1994-5. He is a marketing manager by profession

Betty NUTHALL

Tennis
Betty May Nuthall. b. 23 May 1911
Surbiton, London. d. 8 Nov 1983 New
York, USA. Later Mrs Shoemaker

The daughter of tennis enthusiasts who founded the West Side Club at Ealing, Nuthall won the first of her seven British Junior titles in 1924 (at 13 years 23 days, the youngest ever champion) and was unbeaten at the Championships for three years. Although it was not until 1928 that she started to serve overarm, she had been in 1927 at Forest Hills, at 16 years 80 days, the youngest player ever to represent Great Britain in the Wightman Cup. With a victory over the redoubtable Helen Jacobs (USA) she was the only British singles winner, and two weeks later she reached the final of the singles and women's doubles at the US Championships. She scored her greatest successes at these Championships as in 1930 she became the first overseas player to win the singles, and she also won the women's doubles in 1930-1 and 1933 (with three different partners) and the mixed doubles with George Lott (USA) in 1929 and 1931. She won the French doubles in 1931 with Eileen Whittingstall and the mixed in 1931 and 1932, the latter with Fred Perry (qv).

She surprisingly never progressed beyond the quarter-finals of the singles or the semi-finals of either doubles at Wimbledon, but at the Hard Court Championship won the singles in 1927, five women's doubles and two mixed. She played in her eighth and final Wightman Cup tie in 1939 and made her last appearance at Wimbledon in 1946 when she lost in the fourth round of the singles to Dorothy Bundy (USA). She lived in the USA following her marriage to American Franklin C. Shoemaker.

Judy OAKES

Athletics, Shot and Powerlifting
Judith Miriam Oakes. b. 14 Feb 1958
Lewisham, London.

Oakes is Britain's most prolific national champion at athletics, with 35 senior titles at shot putting: UK (9) 1978, 1982, 1984-9, 1991; WAAA/AAA (13) 1979-80, 1982-8, 1990-1, 1994-5; WAAA/AAA indoors (13) 1977-80, 1982, 1984-8, 1990-1, 1995. Both the latter totals are the record for one event.

She competed for England at five Commonwealth Games, winning medals each time: gold in 1982 and 1994, when she made a come-back after two years out of the sport; silver in 1986, a result she feels very bitter about given that the winner Gael Mulhall (Aus) was later found to be a drugs-taker, and in 1990, and bronze in 1978.

She won a European Indoor bronze medal in 1979 and took advantage of the boycott by many Eastern nations to take a fine 4th place at the 1984 Olympics. She has competed for Britain 70 times, including a record eight times at the European Cup between 1977 and 1995, with a best placing of third in 1991 and 1995. She won three English Schools titles 1974-6, set nine British junior records and seven British senior records between 1978 and her best of 19.36m in 1988. Her discus best is 53.44m in 1988.

Oakes also won world powerlifting titles at 75kg in 1981, 82.5kg in 1982 and 1988, set world records at these weight categories, and also won eight European titles 1983-90. At weightlifting she was European champion in 1989 and 1990 and 3rd in the World Championships in 1989.

Manager of a fitness centre in Wimbledon, she has for long been coached by Mike Winch and competes for Croydon Harriers. She was awarded MBE in 1988.

Alex OBOLENSKY

Rugby Union
(Prince) Alexander Obolensky. b. 17 Feb 1916 St Petersburg, Russia. d. 29 Mar 1940 Norfolk.

Educated at Trent College and Brasenose College, Oxford, Obolensky was one of the greatest wingers ever to play for Oxford but he failed to score in his two appearances in the University match (1935 and 1937). A White Russian Prince, who dropped his title in March 1936, he won all four of his England caps that year and his second try against the visiting All Blacks is still remembered as a classic and invariably referred to as 'Obolensky's try'. In the summer of 1936 he went on the RFU tour of South America and his tally of 17 tries against a Brazilian XV remains a record for representative rugby.

On leaving Oxford, he played for Rosslyn Park and the Barbarians and was the first English international to lose his life in World War II. Serving as a Pilot Officer in the RAF, he was killed in a flying training accident.

Graeme OBREE

Cycling
Douglas Graeme Obree. b. 11 Sep 1965 Ayr.

In 1993 Obree startled the world of cycling by breaking the classic 1 hour record with 51.596km at Hamar in Norway when he was virtually unknown. He went on, however, to win the world pursuit title a month later and to regain his record from Chris Boardman (qv) by recording a distance of 52.713km at Bordeaux on 27 April 1994, with other national records at 10km 11:18.13 and 20km 22:39.03. He had set records at 10km of 11:28.46 and 11:25.813 in the previous five weeks.

Obree's innovations were so drastic that the international governing body, the UCI, changed the rules on bike construction in 1994, disallowing his bike as they considered it to give an unfair advantage with the 'tuck' position for the rider. He was British 4km pursuit champion in 1993-4 and set a national 4km record at 4:20.894 in 1993.

Des O'BRIEN (Ireland)

Rugby Union
Desmond Joseph O'Brien. b. 22 May 1919 Dublin.

A regular member of the Irish back row in the immediate post-war years, O'Brien won 20 caps 1948-52 and played for a variety of clubs including Edinburgh University, London Irish, Cardiff and Old Belvedere. He managed the 1966 Lions tour to New Zealand. A fine all-round sportsman, he played squash for Ireland and worked as sales manager for Guinness and a director of Harp Lager.

Vincent O'BRIEN (Ireland)

Horse Racing
Michael Vincent O'Brien. b. 9 Apr 1917 Churchtown, Co. Cork.

A great Irish trainer for 50 years, O'Brien began his racing career as an amateur jockey and rode his first winner in 1940, before starting training in Co. Cork in 1943. In 1951 he moved to Ballydoyle House, Co. Tipperary, where he established one of the world's great training centres, first achieving immense success as a trainer of jumpers. He won all the major National Hunt races including the Grand Nationals of 1953-5, four Cheltenham Gold Cups and the Champion Hurdle, won three times by *Hatton's Grace*. O'Brien switched to flat racing from 1959, achieving even greater success, training winners of 16 English Classics, including six Epsom Derbys, and 27 Irish Classics; perhaps the greatest of these was the triple crown winner *Nijinsky* in 1970. He also won the Prix de l'Arc de Triomphe three times, with *Ballymoss* 1958 and *Alleged* 1977-8.

In 1966 he began one of the greatest partnerships on the turf, with Lester Piggott (qv) riding many great races for him. Champion trainer in Ireland 13 times, and in Britain on the flat 1966-7 and jumps 1952/3 and 1954/5, he retired after the 1994 season. O'Brien's sons David and Charles followed him as successful trainers.

Leslie O'CALLAGHAN (Ireland)

Croquet
C. Leslie O'Callaghan. b. 1880 Ireland. d. 1944 Ireland

O'Callaghan was the winner of many major honours until in 1922, at the age of 42, he suddenly abandoned croquet, never playing again, and took up golf. He was a three-time winner of both the Open Championship (1910, 1912, 1921) and the Champion Cup (1909-10, 1920) and he won the mixed doubles title five times (1909-10, 1912, 1914, 1921).

The son of a Cork landowner, he spent the winters hunting in Ireland as Master of the Fingal Harriers or with one of the six other packs of which he was a member. His summers were devoted to croquet and later to golf. An unpredictable and flamboyant player, he is said to have had the manner of a stage Irishman.

His brother **Richard** (b. 30 Jun 1879) won the mixed doubles in 1922 and they both died in the same year (1944).

Pat O'CALLAGHAN (Ireland)

Athletics
(Dr) Patrick O'Callaghan. b. 15 Sep 1905 Kanturk, Co. Cork. d. 1 Dec 1991 Clonmel, Co. Tipperary,

O'Callaghan was the Olympic gold medallist at the hammer in 1928 (51.39m) and 1932 (53.92). He set European records at 56.06 in 1931 and 56.94 in 1933 and on 22 Aug 1937 exceeded the world record with 59.56 in the Cork County Championships at Fermoy, but this mark was not recognised by the IAAF as the Irish federation (NACA) was not affiliated to the world body. The IAAF had imposed the boundary rule (i.e. Northern Ireland was part of the UK) in 1935, and the NACA refused to accept the decision. In consequence no Irish team participated in the 1936 Berlin Olympic Games, and perhaps Dr Pat was thus deprived of a third gold medal.

In 1932 O'Callaghan had come through to win with his last throw of the competition (53.92), only able to overtake the 52.27 of Ville Pörhöla (Fin) after he had managed to file down his over long spikes, which were suitable for the grass circles to which he was accustomed, but not the hard surface in use in Los Angeles. In between each of his throws he spent every spare minute working to reduce the spike length Between 1927 and 1936 he won Irish titles: six at hammer 1927-8, 1930-2 and 1935, five at shot 1930-2 and 1934-5, four at 56lb weight 1928 and 1930-2, three at high jump 1930-2, and one at discus 1931.

He started athletics after he had qualified as a doctor at the age of 20, too young to practise in Ireland so he served in the RAF Medical Corps 1926-8. He took up the hammer in 1927 and was Olympic champion a year later.

Mick O'CONNELL (Ireland)

Gaelic Football
Michael O'Connell. b. 4 Jan 1937 Beginish Island, Co. Kery.

A supreme stylist, O'Connell was noted especially for his unmatched and spectacular high fielding ability at midfield and the way he kicked points from a dead ball position. He captained Kerry to the all-Ireland title in 1969 and 1970 and two further medals and also won six National League medals. He had been voted footballer of the year in 1962 and later was elected to the Team of the Century as a midfielder. In 1974 he wrote a best-selling sports book *A Kerry Footballer*.

Christy O'CONNOR (Ireland)

Golf
Christy O'Connor. b. 21 Dec 1924 Dublin.

The greatest Irish golfer ever, known for his smooth and rhythmic swing, O'Connor was probably, between the eras of Henry Cotton and Tony Jacklin (qqv), the best player from the British Isles. He was the dominant player in the early days of the British PGA Tour, with 24 victories. He headed the Order of Merit in 1961 and 1962. and was second five times, 1964-6, 1969-70. He never won the British Open but finished in the top five seven times between 1958 and 1969, with a best of 2nd in 1965.

He started his professional career only in his late 20s, winning his first British title in 1955 at the Swallow-Penfold Tournament. His major wins included the Dunlop Masters in 1956 and 1959, the PGA Match Play in 1957 and the World Seniors in 1976 and 1977. He was Irish Professional champion ten times: 1958, 1960-3, 1965-6, 1971, 1975 and 1978. With Harry Bradshaw (qv) he won the World Cup for Ireland in 1958 and in all played for Ireland in the World Cup 15 times between 1956 and 1975. O'Connor played in a record 10 Ryder Cup matches, consecutively from 1955 to 1973, with a record of 11 wins, 20 losses and 4 halves.

His nephew **Christy O'Connor Jnr** (b. 19 Aug 1948 Galway) followed him as a Ryder Cup player in 1975 and played again in 1989, when the two-iron approach shot that he hit to within tap-in distance at the 18th closed out Fred Couples (USA) and ensured victory for Europe. He had been assistant to his uncle at Royal Dublin and his best tournament wins were the Irish Open 1975 and British Masters 1992. He was 3rd in the Open in 1985 and played six times for Ireland in the World Cup between 1974 and 1992.

Peter O'CONNOR (Ireland)

Athletics
Peter O'Connor. b. 18 Oct 1874 Ashtown, Co. Wicklow. d. 9 Nov 1957 Upton, Newton, Co. Waterford.

O'Connor set five world records for the long jump, the first at 7.51 in 1900 and then four more in 1901, with his last at 7.61 remaining unbeaten for 20 years. It also remained as an Irish record until 1990. In July 1901 he became the first man to jump over 25 ft (7.62m), but his 7.63 mark was ruled out due to a slightly downhill runway. In 1906 he disappointed with Olympic silver at the long jump in Athens, but came back to win gold at the triple jump. At the award ceremony, he caused a stir when he climbed the flagpole to replace the Union Jack with the Irish flag. He then retired to concentrate on his solicitor's practice, but was a judge at the 1932 Olympics in Los Angeles.

He was AAA champion at long jump 1901-06 and high jump 1903-04 and won a total of nine Irish and Gaelic AA titles at high, long and triple jumps.

Dorothy ODAM – see TYLER

George O'DELL

Motorcycling
George O'Dell. b. 13 Nov 1945 Hemel Hempstead, Herts. d. March 1981 Herts.

In 1977 O'Dell became the first British sidecar world champion since 1953. Amazingly he won the title without winning a single Grand Prix race, but, partnered by Kenny Arthur or Cliff Holland, he never finished lower than 4th. In 1975 he achieved the first ever 100 mph lap with a sidecar at Silverstone and in 1977 he achieved the same feat on the Isle of Man. Tragically he took his own life in 1981.

Martin OFFIAH

Rugby League
Martin Nwokocha Offiah. b. 29 Dec 1966 Hackney, London.

Signed by Widnes from the rugby union club Rosslyn Park, Offiah immediately proved to be the most exciting winger to emerge in recent years. In his first four seasons as a League player he was the leading try scorer: 1987/8 (44 tries), 1988/9 (60), 1989/90 (45) and 1990/1 (49) and during the 1993/4 season passed 300 tries in major rugby league (325 tries in 278 games to end 1993/4). In Wigan's Grand Slam year of 1994/5 he scored 53 tries. He set a GB record by scoring five tries against France in 1991. Although he missed the first match for Great Britain against New Zealand in 1993, he returned from injury to score in the second, taking his international record to 26 tries in 33 matches 1988-94, the best strike rate of any GB player in history.

In January 1992 he signed for Wigan for a record transfer of £400,000 and played on their winning Challenge Cup teams each year 1992-5. He won the Lance Todd Trophy as man of the match in the final in both 1992 and 1994, on each occasion scoring two tries. He also helped Widnes to win the Premiership 1988-90 and Wigan in 1992 and 1994-5. A fast, elusive runner, he also has the strength to break through all but the most committed tackles. He won the Man of Steel award as the rugby league personality of the year in 1988.

Kevin O'FLANAGAN (Ireland)

Football and Rugby Union
Kevin Patrick O'Flanagan. b. 10 Jun 1919 Dublin.

An international at both soccer and rugby, he was Ireland's most popular sportsman in the years immediately following World War II. He was also a scratch golfer, the Irish champion at the 100y (1941) and long jump (four times 1938-43) and used his speed to great effect playing on the wing in both sports. Uniquely his brother, **Michael** (b. 29 Sep 1922), was also capped by Ireland at soccer and rugby and they were both members of the association football team which played against England in 1946.

Kevin O'Flanagan began his soccer career with Bohemians in the League of Ireland at the age of 16 and won seven international caps for the Republic before the outbreak of war. In 1945, after graduating from University College, Dublin, he went to Ruislip, London to practise as a doctor, signed as an amateur with Arsenal and won three further caps. He gave up playing

for Arsenal to concentrate on his medical practice but in the 1949/50 season he was persuaded to join Brentford for whom he played eight games. While with Arsenal he also played rugby for London Irish and won his only international cap for rugby against the visiting Australians in 1947. He was medical officer for the Irish Olympic teams in 1960, 1964 and 1968.

On his return to Ireland, he took a keen interest in Olympic affairs and was appointed medical officer to the Irish team at the 1960 Games. He became a member of the Olympic Council of Ireland and in 1976 was elected to the International Olympic Committee, only the third Irishman to be so honoured.

Dan O'KEEFFE (Ireland)

Gaelic Football
Dan O'Keeffe. b. 1907 Fermoy, Co. Cork.

Goalkeeper for Kerry 1931-49, he became the first man to win seven all-Ireland medals, playing for Kerry (Ciarraidhe) when they won in 1931-2, 1937, 1939-41 and 1946 from ten finals in all. He won 15 Munster Senior Football Championship medals and also three Railway Cup medals with Munster in the Interprovincial Championship. He won his only National Football League medal in 1932. He was named as goalkeeper on the Team of the Century.

Chris OLD

Cricket
Christopher Middleton Old. b. 22 Dec 1948 Middlesbrough, North Yorkshire.

Although often bedevilled by injury, Old gave good service to Yorkshire and England as a very controlled right-arm fast-medium bowler and hard-hitting left-handed batsman. He first played for England in two matches against the Rest of the World in 1970 and had his best series with 18 wickets at 13.83 in three Tests against India in 1974. In 1978 at Edgbaston he took four wickets in five balls against Pakistan. His best totals in first-class seasons were 850 runs at 36.95 in 1975 and 74 wickets at 22.62 in 1970. He captained

Yorkshire in 1981 but was dismissed during the following season and replaced by county manager, 50-year-old Ray Illingworth (qv), at this most unhappy time in his county's affairs. He then spent three seasons with Warwickshire 1983-5.

46 Tests 1972-81: 845 runs at 14.82, HS 65; 143 wickets at 28.11, BB 7-50; 22 catches.

32 One-day Ints 1973-81: 338 runs at 18.77, HS 51*; 45 wickets at 22.20, BB 4-8; 8 catches.

First-class 1966-85: 7756 runs at 20.84, 6 100s HS 116; 1070 wickets at 23.48, BB 7-20; 214 catches.

His elder brother **Alan** Gerald Bernard **Old** (b. 23 Sep 1945 Middlesbrough) played minor counties cricket for Durham and one first-class match for Warwickshire, but was best known as fly-half for England in 16 internationals 1972-8. He toured South Africa with the British Lions in 1974 and his 37 points against South Western Districts was a Lions record on any tour.

David O'LEARY (Ireland)

Football
David Anthony O'Leary. b. 2 May 1958 Stoke Newington, London

O'Leary was the bedrock of the defence of Arsenal, for whom he played a record number of games from 1975 to 1993, including 558 in the Football League. He won an FA Cup winner's medal in 1979 and again 14 years later, when he came on as a substitute. He also helped Arsenal to the League title in 1989 and 1991. In 1993 he moved on to Leeds United and in all made 67 international appearances for Ireland 1977-93, having earlier captained their schoolboy and youth teams.

Born in London, he moved with his family to Ireland when he was an infant and there he played for Shelbourne teams from the age of 12 before being signed by Arsenal as a 15-year-old.

Alan OLIVER

Equestrian Events, Show Jumping
Alan Oliver. b. 8 Sep 1932 Newcastle.

Until passed by David Broome (qv),

Oliver held the record for British show jumping titles with five, 1951, 1954, 1959 and 1969-70. He had won the junior national championship in 1947.

Eric OLIVER

Motorcycling
Eric S. Oliver. b. 1911 Crowborough, East Sussex. d. 1981.

Oliver was the first ever world sidecar champion in 1949, with Dennis Jenkinson as passenger, and won again in 1950-1 with Lorenzo Dobelli and in 1953 with Stanley Dibben. When sidecars were reintroduced to the Isle of Man TT in 1954, Oliver won with Les Nutt. Oliver concentrated on sidecar racing after World War II, having raced both solo machines and sidecars before then, making his TT debut as a solo rider in 1937. With supreme skill and determination, in all he won 18 world championship sidecar races in his Norton/Watsonian combination and in 1954 he introduced the kneeler sidecar outfit, soon emulated by most other sidecar competitors.

Frank O'MARA (Ireland)

Athletics
Frank O'Mara. b. 17 Jul 1960 Limerick City.

A fine all-round distance runner, O'Mara achieved his greatest success at the in-between distance of 3000m, at which he was World Indoor champion in 1987 and 1991. Disappointingly he went out in the heats at three Olympics, at 1500m in 1984 and at 5000m in 1988 and 1992, and had a best placing in other major championship of 8th in the 1986 European 1500m. He won Irish titles at 1500m 1983, 1986, 1988 and 1991.

Best times: 800m 1:47.72 (1984), 1500m 3:34.02 (1985), 1M 3:51.06 (1986), 2000m 4:59.00 (1987), 3000m 7:40.41 (1989), 2M 8:17.78 (1988), 5000m 13:13.02 (Irish record, 1987), 10,000m 27:58.01 (1991). He also ran on Ireland's team that set a world best for 4 x 1 mile in 1985.

He obtained a degree in civil engineering and a Masters degree in business administration at the University of Arkansas, where he later studied law. While there he won the 1983 NCAA 1500m.

Jonjo O'NEILL (Ireland)

Horse Racing
John Joseph O'Neill. b. 13 Apr 1952 Castletownroche, Co. Cork.

O'Neill was Champion National Hunt jockey in 1977/8, when he set a record with 149 winners, and in 1979/80 with 115 winners; in his career 1972-86 he rode 885 winners, three times over 100 in a season. Apprenticed for three years to Mick Connolly at the Curragh, where in 1970 he rode his first winner, he then joined the stable of Gordon W.Richards (qv) in 1972. He rode *Dawn Run* to her unique double of Champion Hurdle in 1983 and Gold Cup in 1986, and had previously won those races on *Sea Pigeon* in 1980 and *Alverton* in 1979 respectively.

His natural lightness meant that he had few weight problems. Highly popular, he was the first NH jockey to employ an agent. Soon after he retired he had to begin a tremendously courageous battle against cancer, but overcame that to pursue a successful training career.

Martin O'NEILL

Football
Martin Hugh Michael O'Neill. b. 1 Mar 1952 Kilrea, Co. Derry.

O'Neill was signed from the Irish club, Derry, in 1971 by Nottingham Forest, with whom he stayed for ten seasons winning League, League Cup and European Cup honours. In 1981 he went to Norwich City and then Manchester City before returning to Norwich, after which he moved to Notts County in 1983 and then joined Fulham, where he ended his career in 1985.

A midfield player, he won 64 caps for Northern Ireland 1972-85, scoring 8 goals. From February 1990 he was manager of Wycombe Wanderers, who won the GM Vauxhall Conference in 1992/3 and entered the Football League the following season, moving swiftly up from the Fourth Division to the Second Division, before

returning to Norwich as manager in June 1995.

Peter OOSTERHUIS

Golf
Peter A. Oosterhuis. b. 3 May 1948 London.

Europe's top golfer of the early 1970s, Oosterhuis won the Vardon Trophy for the lowest stroke average on the European tour each year 1971-4. He won the French Open in both 1973 and 1974 and the PGA Championship 1973. In 1973 he led the US Masters by three shots after three rounds, but fell back to finish 3rd. He was 2nd in the Open in 1974 and top British player in 1975 (7th), 1978 (6th) and 1982 (3rd).

After his 1974 successes in Europe Oosterhuis went to play in the USA, but it was not until 1981, with the Canadian Open, that he won a tournament in North America, even so he became only the second British golfer to win on the PGA tour in the modern era.

The British Youth champion in 1966 and Walker Cup player in 1967, Oosterhuis was 2nd in his first ever professional tournament, the Natal Open and 6th in his first in Britain, the Penfold in 1969. A tall man at 1.95m *6 ft 5 in*, his short game was his main strength.

In the Ryder Cup he was highly successful in the singles, taking six and a half points from nine matches – including wins against Arnold Palmer in 1971 and 1973 – in his six ties 1971-81, with an overall playing record of 14 wins, 11 losses and 3 halves.

He was director of golf at the Fosgate Country Club, New Jersey from 1984 and then at the Riviera Golf and Country Club in Los Angeles from 1991.

Lisa OPIE

Squash
Lisa Jane Opie. 15 Aug 1963 Guernsey.

Opie made her international debut in 1981 after victories in the World Junior and the British National Championships where, at the age of 18, she was the youngest ever winner. She went on to further wins in the British National (1983, 1986-7) and the Australian Open (1986-7) and, having been runner-up in 1981, 1983 and 1985-6, in 1991 she became the first Briton for 30 years to win the British Open.

At the World Open she was beaten by Susan Devoy (NZ) in the final in 1985 and 1987, and played on the winning England team title in both those years and in 1990. In 1984 she was fined £1000 for bringing the game into disrepute at the British Open and was banned from the event the following year. She was awarded the MBE in 1995.

Tony O'REILLY (Ireland)

Rugby Union
Anthony Joseph Francis Kevin O'Reilly. b. 7 May 1936 Dublin.

O'Reilly was a strong-running winger, 1.88m *6 ft 2 in* tall, with great crowd appeal. He won 28 caps for Ireland between 1955, when in his first season of senior rugby with Old Belvedere, and 1963. His international career seemed to be over, but, following an injury to the first-choice winger, he was recalled seven years later and made his final appearance against England in 1970. Then he arrived for training in a chaufeur-driven Rolls Royce.

His career span of 16 seasons of international rugby has been matched only by Mike Gibson (qv) among Irish players. Although he scored 15 tries for Ireland in the International Championship, O'Reilly really excelled on tours with the British Lions. He played in every Test in South Africa in 1955 and in Australia and New Zealand in 1959, and his six tries in the 10 Tests remains a Lions scoring record.

Well before he gave up playing, having qualified as a solicitor, he embarked on a highly successful business career to become the 'golden boy' of Irish business, moving on to a world stage. He became president of the Heinz Corporation in the USA in 1979 and is now one of the world's highest paid executives. Additionally, he has substantial investments in a private capacity and is an influential figure in the financial world. He is also a keen racehorse owner.

Wilf O'REILLY

Speed Skating
Wilfred John O'Reilly. b. 22 Aug 1964 Birmingham.

In 1985 O'Reilly not only won his first British title, but won all four short-track events: 500m, 1000m, 1500m and 3000m, and within a year held British records at all distances. He repeated his British championships successes each year to 1988, when he crashed at the World Championships, but came back two weeks later to win both 500m and 1000m races when short-track speed skating was held as a demonstration sport at the Olympic Games. In 1990 he won the 500m and was 2nd overall at the Worlds, improving in 1991 to win the 1000m and take the overall title to become the first ever British champion. He was European champion in 1983, 1986 and 1992, but was 5th at 1000m in the one individual event to be staged when the sport was included for the first time as a medal sport at the Olympics.

He set numerous British records with bests of: 500m 44.07, 1000m 1:31.65 and 3000m 5:13.32 in 1992, and 1500m 2:22.67 in 1993.

Phil ORR (Ireland)

Rugby Union
Philip Andrew Orr. b. 14 Dec 1950 Dublin.

The first of Orr's 49 consecutive matches for Ireland was against France in 1976 and after this sequence was interrupted in 1986 he won nine further caps to bring his total to 58 international appearances, a world record for a prop forward. He toured with the British Lions to New Zealand in 1977, when he played in the first Test. He also toured with the 1980 Lions to South Africa but failed to command a place in the Test team. He retired after the 1987 World Cup. A clothing manufacturer, he went to Trinity College, Dublin and played his club rugby for Old Wesley.

Marcus O'SULLIVAN (Ireland)

Athletics
Marcus O'Sullivan. b. 22 Dec 1961 Cork City.

O'Sullivan inherited fellow-Irishman Eamonn Coghlan's (qv) role as the world's finest indoor miler, like him possessing a scintillating finish. He won the Wanamaker Mile at the Millrose Games in New York five times between 1986 and 1991 and was also 2nd five times to 1995.

In Meadowlands in 1989 he set a world indoor record in the 1500m at 3:35.6 and he won the World Indoor title three times at 1500m: in Indianapolis 1987, Budapest 1989 and Toronto 1993, with 4th place in 1991. He also won the European Indoor silver medal at 1500m in 1985, but at outdoor championships has been less successful, with a best of 6th at the 1986 Europeans, and 8th in 1988, his only final appearance at three Olympics 1984-92. He was Irish champion at 1500m 1984 and 800m 1986, 1989, 1992, and won the AAA 1500m 1985. He has a degree in accountancy from Villanova University.

He ran on Ireland's 4 x 1 mile world best in 1985 and set three Irish 800m records 1984-5 with a best of 1:45.85. Other best times: 1000m 2:19.15 (1987), 1500m 3:34.57 (1992), 1M 3:50.94 indoors (1988), 3:51.64 (1989); 2000m 4:58.08 (1988), 3000m 7:42.53 (1989), 5000m 13:27.32 (1990).

Ronnie O'SULLIVAN

Snooker
Ronald O'Sullivan. b. 5 Dec 1975.

A prodigious young talent, in 1991 at 15 O'Sullivan became the youngest snooker player to score a maximum (147) in competition - in the English Amateur Championship at Aldershot. That year he was also the world junior champion. In November 1993, in winning the UK Open, he beat Stephen Hendry (qv) 10-6 in the final, and superseded Hendry as the youngest ever winner of a ranking event. In 1994 he won the British Open and in 1995 became the youngest ever winner of the Benson & Hedges Masters.

Sonia O'SULLIVAN (Ireland)

Athletics
Sonia O'Sullivan. b. 28 Nov 1969 Cobh, Co. Cork.

In 1991 O'Sullivan became the first Irish woman athlete to break a world track record with the indoor 5000m of 15:17.28. She finished 4th in the 3000m in the 1992 Olympics and was the second Irish woman to appear in an Olympic track final. In 1992 she broke five Irish records from 1500 to 5000m in eleven days and was favourite to win the 3000m in the World Championships in Stuttgart in 1993. Finishing 4th behind three Chinese athletes, she went on to take the silver in the 1500m – thus becoming the first woman representing Ireland to win a medal at any major championship. She won four IAAF Grand Prix events in 1993, finishing 2nd overall in the series and collected $100,000. She had an even better season in 1994 when in successive weeks in July she set the world record for 2000m at 5:25.36 and the European record for 3000m at 8:21.64 before winning the European gold at 3000m. She then won her third successive Grand Prix title, at 5000m, having won at 5000m in 1992 and 3000m in 1993. She now lives in Teddington, England.

She studied accountancy at Villanova University, USA, for whom she won NCAA titles at 3000m in 1990-1 and cross-country 1990. She was World Student Games champion at 1500m and 2nd at 2000m in 1991. Irish titles won: cross-country 1987, 800m 1992, 1500m 1987, 1990; 5000m 1990. Irish records 1990-4: 800m 2:00.69 (1994), 1000m 2:34.66 (1993), five 1500m to 4:01.23 (1992), two 1M to 4:17.25 (1994), three 2000m, six 3000m, three 5000m to 14:45.92 (1993).

Dave OTTLEY

Athletics, Javelin
David Charles Ottley. b. 5 Aug 1955 Thurrock, Essex.

Ottley was ranked as Britain's No.1 javelin thrower ten times between 1976 and 1988 and was in the top ten for 19 successive years 1973-91. His first major championships medal was silver at the 1977 World Student Games and he won the Olympic silver medal on his 29th birthday in 1984. In 1980 he set a British javelin record with 85.52m and 1985 he was ranked 4th in the world and achieved his best throw, 90.70m.

With the new specification javelin he had a best of 80.98m in 1988, and in that year he won his sixth AAA title (also 1977, 1982, 1984-6) which completed 13 successive years in the first three, an all-time record for any event. He again showed his competitive prowess to win the Commonwealth Games title in 1986, after 5th in 1978 and 7th in 1982, and in 1988 he was 11th at his third Olympic Games. He had won English Schools titles as an intermediate in 1971 and senior in 1973 and was UK champion each year 1978-82. Having been at Borough Road College, he became a school teacher and then a youth training scheme supervisor.

Steve OVETT

Athletics
Steven Michael James Ovett. b. 9 Oct 1955 Brighton, East Sussex.

A brilliant middle-distance runner, Ovett led the way for the British domination of these events in the 1970s and 1980s. He competed at three Olympic Games, winning the gold medal at 800m in 1980, when he was also 3rd at 1500m.

He started his championship success at 400m with the English Schools Junior title in 1970 and AAA Youth titles in 1971 and 1972, and emerged internationally in 1973 when he won the European Junior 800m. In 1974 he set a European junior record and took silver against his seniors in the European Championships. He was 5th in the 1976 Olympic 1500m and took a second European 800m silver in 1978 before winning the 1500m title and thereafter concentrating on longer distances, winning 45 successive races at 1500m or 1 mile 1977-80. Indeed he seemed unbeatable at that time, with a devastating win in the 1977 World Cup 1500m in Düsseldorf. However, it was at his original distance of

800m that he took Olympic gold, only to lose to Seb Coe (qv) at 1500m.

Ovett had professed himself uninterested in records, which went regularly to Coe, but in 1980-1 he gave chase and set three world records at 1500m and two at 1 mile. He lost the 1982 season due to a training accident when he impaled his thigh on some church railings, but came back in 1983 to take 4th place in the World 1500m. He was very disappointed with that and determined to do better at the 1984 Olympics, but there he suffered severe bronchial problems and had to trail in last at 800m and pull out of the 1500m final. He won the UK 1500m 1977 and 1981 and AAA 800m 1974-6, 1500m 1979-80. Voted BBC Sports Personality of the Year 1978, he was awarded the MBE in 1982.

He was able to compete outstandingly at a wide range, but the longer distances did not hold the same attraction for him, although at 5000m he won the 1986 Commonwealth title. His final major championship appearance was 10th in the 1987 World 5000m. Now settled in Scotland, he is a regular commentator on athletics for ITV.

Best times: 800m 1:44.09 (1978), 1000m 2:15.91 (1979), 1500m 3:31.36 (1980), 1M 3:48.40 (1981), 2000m 4:57.71 (1982), 3000m 7:41.3 (1977), 2M 8:13.51 (1978, world best), 5000m 13:20.06 (1986).
For season-by-season progress - see Sebastian Coe.

Dickie OWEN

Rugby Union
Richard Morgan Owen. b. 17 Nov 1876 Llandore, Swansea. d. 27 Feb 1932 Swansea. Although always known as Owen, his birth was actually registered as Owens.

A scrum-half with Swansea, Owen's 35 international appearances for Wales between 1901-12 remained a record until beaten by Ken Jones (qv) in 1955. He was first choice for Wales during their first 'Golden Era' and was in the team which won the Triple Crown four times and the Championship on two other occasions. Always an innovative player, it was his unorthodox pass which led to the Welsh try when they beat the 1905 All Blacks 3-0. A steelworker and later a licensee, he took his own life.

Ann PACKER

Athletics
Ann Elizabeth Packer. b. 2 Mar 1942 Moulsford, Oxfordshire. Later Mrs Brightwell.

In 1964 at the Tokyo Olympics, Packer sealed her athletics career with a storybook win at 800m in a world record time of 2:01.1 in her first year at the event. She had been favoured to win the 400m, but although she ran a European record time of 52.20 she had to settle for the silver behind Betty Cuthbert (Aus), while her fiancé Robbie Brightwell (qv) had been disappointed with his 4th place in the men's 400m. They were married after the Games and Ann retired at the age of 22 and was awarded the MBE in 1965.
Ann's athletic success had started with the English Schools 100y title in 1959 and she won WAAA titles at long jump 1960 and 440y 1964. In 1962 she surprised by reaching the final of the European 200m and later that year she was 6th at 80m hurdles and took a silver medal in the sprint relay at the Commonwealth Games. She reached world class when she moved up to 400m in 1963.
Other bests: 100m 11.7w/12.0 (1960), 200m 23.7 (1964), 80mh 11.4 (1960), LJ 5.92m (1960).

Alf PADGHAM

Golf
Alfred Harry Padgham b. 2 Jul 1906 Caterham, Surrey. d. 4 Mar 1966 West Wickham, Greater London.

Padgham won the 1936 Open Championship after 3rd place in 1934 and 2nd in 1935. This was his fourth big professional tournament win in succession, starting with the PGA Match Play title (then the *News of the World* tournament) in September 1935. He had also won that event in 1931, but he lost all six of his matches in his Ryder Cup appearances of 1933, 1935 and 1937. He

was also joint 4th in the Open in 1938. At his best he was a brilliant putter despite an ungainly style, and was known as the smoothest and laziest swinger of a golf club. He was assistant for five years at Warley Woods, Birmingham and professional at Royal Ashdown Forest and then at Sundridge Park, Bromley for 30 years.

Jack PAGE

Figure Skating
John Ferguson Page. b. Apr-Jun 1900 Brooklands, Gt. Manchester. d. 14 Feb 1947 Manchester.

Page was the winner of a record 20 British titles (11 singles 1922-31, 1933; 9 pairs 1923-31). From 1919-27 the only ice rink in Britain was situated in Manchester and the fact that Page lived in the area and was able to practise there gave him a distinct advantage over his rivals from other parts of the country. His partner for each of his pairs victories was fellow-Mancunian, Ethel Muckelt (qv) and, internationally, they won a silver medal at the 1924 World Championships and placed 4th in 1928. Individually, his best placing at the Worlds was 3rd in 1926 and he finished 4th three times, 1924, 1928-9. He partnered Muckelt in the pairs at two Olympic Games finishing 4th in 1924 and 7th in 1928. In the singles he finished 5th in 1924 and 9th in 1928. At the age of 47 he took his own life in his Manchester stockbroking office.

Geoff PAISH

Tennis
Geoffrey Lane Paish. b. 2 Jan 1922 Croydon.

A former schoolboy champion, although his career was interrupted by service in the RAF, immediately after the war, Paish established himself as one of Britain's leading players. At his best in the doubles, he formed an effective partnership with Tony Mottram (qv) and they played together in 16 out of Paish's 17 Davis Cup doubles matches. Between 1947 and 1955 he played in 19 Davis Cup ties (7/23 singles, 10/17 doubles). With Mottram he also won the British Hard Court title in

1955 and the Covered Court doubles in 1951-2. He had two further Covered Court doubles wins with different partners, 1949 and 1956.

The majority of his successes in mixed doubles came with Jean Quertier (later Rinkel-Quertier) as his partner and together they won the British Covered Court title three times, 1949 and 1951-2, and the British Hard Court title twice 1952-3. Paish also won the Covered Court mixed doubles with Anne Shilcock (qv) in 1956. His only notable victories in the singles came in the All-England (Wimbledon) Plate in 1950 and the British Covered Court Championships in 1951.

A civil servant with the Inland Revenue for over 40 years, he was awarded the MBE in 1974 and served the LTA in many capacities, being elected a life vice-president in 1993.

His son, **John** Geoffrey **Paish** (b. 25 Mar 1948 Croydon), also played against France in the Davis Cup in 1972, and in his only Cup appearance he lost both his singles but won his doubles with David Lloyd (qv). The following year, again with Lloyd as his partner, he reached the semi-final of the men's doubles at Wimbledon.

Bob PAISLEY

Football
Robert Paisley. b. 23 Jan 1919 Hetton-le-Hole, Tune and Wear.

An FA Amateur Cup winners' medal with Bishop Auckland in 1939 and a League Championship medal with Liverpool in 1947 were the highlights of Paisley's playing career as a wing-half, but he later made a far greater impact as manager of Liverpool. After giving up playing in 1954, he spent 20 years on the coaching and administrative staff at Anfield before taking over from Bill Shankly (qv) as manager in 1974.

He proved to be the most successful manager in Football League history, leading Liverpool to three victories in the European Cup, one in the UEFA Cup, six League Championship titles and three consecutive wins in the League Cup.

Success in the FA Cup eluded him both as a player and manager although he was voted Manager of the Year a record six times. He was awarded the OBE in 1977 and after he stepped down as manager in 1983 he became a director of Liverpool two years later.

Charles PALMER

Judo
Charles Stuart William Palmer. b. 15 Apr 1930 London.

A pioneer of the sport in Britain, with a 9th dan in 1991 Palmer has achieved the highest grade of any British judo player. He was a British international from 1949 to 1959, studying in Japan 1951-5 and captain of the European Championships team 1958-9. He was president of the International Judo Federation 1965-79 and chairman 1962-85 and president from 1977 of the British Judo Association. He was vice-chairman 1977-83 and chairman 1983-8 of the British Olympic Association (now life vice president), a member of the Sports Council in Britain 1982-93, and secretary general of the General Association of International Sports Federations 1975-84. He was awarded the OBE in 1973.

Pedlar PALMER

Boxing
Thomas Palmer. b. 19 Jan 1876, Canning Town, London. d. 13 Feb 1949, Brighton.

Palmer was an exceptionally skilful bantamweight whose superb ringcraft more than compensated for his lack of a lethal punch. After beating Billy Plimmer in 1895, he claimed the world title but as this was not recognised in America he went to New York in 1900 to take on Terry McGovern who had claimed the title in the USA after the retirement of Jimmy Barry. The Londoner had no opportunity to show his evasive skills as he was overwhelmed by McGovern and knocked out in the first round.

This marked the start of the decline in Palmer's career: he lost his British title later in 1900, failed in his challenge for the vacant world bantamweight crown in 1901 and in 1904 and 1905 both his bids for the

British featherweight title ended in defeat. His career effectively ended in 1907 when he received a five year jail sentence for manslaughter following a fight on a train, although he had eight more rather inconsequential fights after his release. He was a great public favourite, particularly at the National Sporting Club, whose members presented him with gold and diamond belt. Career record 1891-1919: 64 Contests. Won 45 (2 KO), Drew 4, Lost 15.

Willie PARK Snr

Golf
William Park b. 1834 Musselburgh, Midlothian. d. 1903.

Willie Park was the first Open champion in 1860 and won again in 1863, 1866 and 1875, with second places to his great rival Tom Morris Snr (qv) in 1861, 1862 and 1867, and to Andrew Strath in 1865. He was also 3rd in 1868 and 1876, and 4th in 1864.
His brother **Mungo Park** (b. 1839 Musselburgh. d. 1904), for many years greenkeeper and professional at Alnmouth, was Open champion in 1874 and his son Willie Jnr (qv) in 1887 and 1889. The brothers Willie and Mungo were famed for their numerous money matches. A match between Willie and Old Tom Morris in 1882 was brought to an end when spectators interfered with play, but Park claimed the stakes when Morris did not accept his challenge to return to finish the match.

Willie PARK Jnr

Golf
William Park b. 1864 Musselburgh, Lothian. d. 24 May 1925.

Willie Park Jnr followed his father as Open champion, winning in 1887 and 1889 and being runner-up in 1898. He was renowned as a great putter. He played for Scotland v England in 1903-05, 1907 and 1910, and from 1916 worked in the USA as a golf course architect. He also designed several course in Britain, including the Old course at Sunningdale.
His daughter **Doris** (Mrs Aylmer Porter) was an international golfer., playing for

Brin in the first Curtis Cup match against the USA in 1932 and winning the Scottish Ladies' Amateur Championship in 1936.

James PARKE (Ireland)

Tennis and Rugby Union
James Cecil Parke. b. 26 Jul 1881 Clones, Co. Monaghan. d. 27 Feb 1946 Llandudno, Aberconwy and Colwyn.

One of the great all-round sportsmen of his time, Parke was a champion tennis player, a rugby and golf international, a first-class cricketer and sprinter while at Dublin University and a child prodigy at chess, playing competitively from the age of five. He won an Olympic silver medal in the men's doubles in 1908 and at Wimbledon he won the mixed doubles with Ethel Larcombe (qv), 1912 and 1914, and lost four times in the final of the All-Comers' men's doubles, 1911-13, 1920. He won the Irish singles eight times (1904-5, 1908-13), the doubles five times (1903, 1909-12) and the mixed doubles twice (1909, 1912).
His Davis Cup career spanned World War I, during which he was wounded serving as a major with the Leinster Regiment, and he played a vital role in the team which recaptured the trophy for the British Isles in Melbourne in 1912, winning both his singles. While in Australia he also won the singles and doubles at their Championships. Between 1908 and 1920 he played in a total of eight Davis Cup ties (8/15 singles, 0/5 doubles). He was ranked world No. 6 in 1914 and No. 4 in 1920.
As a rugby player he was capped 20 times 1903-07 by Ireland as a centre three-quarter and captained his country on three occasions.

Charlie PARKER

Cricket
Charles Warrington Leonard Parker. b. 14 Oct 1882 Prestbury, Glos. d. 11 Jul 1959 Cranleigh, Surrey.

The total of 3278 wickets taken by this slow-medium left-arm bowler, who spun the ball fiercely, is the third highest of all time in first-class cricket, yet he played only one Test match. His chances were perhaps not helped by the fact that he was surly and strongly opinionated. He made his debut for Gloucestershire in 1903, but it was not until 1920, when he was 37, that he first took 100 wickets in a season; however, he did so every year from then until 1935, with more than 200 in 1922, 1924-6 and 1931. He took six hat-tricks in his first-class career and is one of only seven men to have taken two in the same match (v Middlesex 1924). In 1922 against Yorkshire he hit the stumps with five successive balls, but the second was called "no ball".

On retiring at the age of 52 he was a first-class umpire for two seasons then turned to golf, at which he was a fine player.

1 Test 1921: 3 runs, HS 3*; 2 wickets at 16.00, BB 2-32.

First-class 1903-35: 7951 runs at 10.48, HS 82; 3278 wickets at 19.46, BB 10-79; 248 catches.

Jack PARKER

Speedway
John Parker. b. 9 Oct 1908 Aston Manor, West Midlands. d. 31 Dec 1989 Rugby, Warwickshire.

Parker was a great speedway rider whose career stretched from 1928 to the 1950s. He was runner-up in the British final of the first Star Championship in 1929 and won this title in 1934. In the World Championships he was 4th in 1939, but had to wait until the competition started again in 1949 for his next chance. Then he came 2nd to Tommy Price (qv), after being slowly away in the crucial heat against his great rival. He had a record seven British Match Race wins between 1932 and 1951 and was British Riders' Champion in 1947. He rode in the first England v Australia Test match in 1930 and by the early postwar years had amassed more points in Tests than any other English rider.

Parker joined BSA in 1927, working in their experimental department, later designing and producing their speedway machines. His brother **Norman** (b. 14 Jan 1910 Solihull) was also a speedway international 1936-9.

Jill PARKER - see HAMMERSLEY

Cecil PARKIN

Cricket
Cecil Harry Parkin. b. 18 Feb 1886 Eaglescliffe, Co. Durham. d. 15 Jun 1943 Cheetham Hill, Manchester.

A notable eccentric and comedian, Parkin fell out with authority so that his England career ended after he criticised his captain in a ghosted newspaper article, and his Lancashire career two years later due to disagreement with his county committee. He had great success in league cricket and played one match for Yorkshire in 1906 before it was discovered that, since he had been born 20 yards over the border, he was not eligible to play for them. He first played for Lancashire in 1914 but it was not until 1921 that he was a county regular. He played in all five Tests in Australia in 1920/1 and topped the England bowling averages against Australia in 1921. In the four years 1922-5 he took successively 189 wickets at 17.46, 209 at 16.94, 200 at 13.67 and 152 at 19.30 with his highly varied slow bowling. He became a publican.

10 Tests 1920-4: 160 runs at 12.30, HS 36; 32 wickets at 35.25, BB 5-38; 3 catches.

First-class 1906-26: 2425 runs at 11.77, HS 57; 1048 wickets at 17.58, BB 9-32; 126 catches.

Jonty PARKIN

Rugby League
Jonathan Parkin. b. 5 Nov 1897 Sharlston, West Yorkshire. d. 9 Apr 1972 Wakefield, West Yorkshire.

During a 10-year international career Parkin won 17 Great Britain caps, 11 as captain, and was the first man to make three tours of Australasia (1920, 1924 and 1928, the last two as captain). Although injured for much of the 1928 tour, his qualities of leadership played a major part in Britain's entirely unexpected victory in the Test series against both Australia and New Zealand.

After joining Wakefield Trinity as a boy of 15, he remained with the club for 17 years before asking for a transfer in 1930. As Wakefield were anxious to retain his services they demanded what they thought was an unacceptably high transfer fee for a player nearing the end of his career. Parkin paid the fee out of his own pocket, declared himself a free agent and signed for Hull Kingston Rovers. Wakefield and the League authorities were outraged by this early example of 'player power' and the rules were changed to prohibit players paying their own transfer fees.

An astute and resilient scrum-half, he had a fine tactical brain, but his brilliant leadership was perhaps his finest quality.

Jim PARKS

Cricket
James Michael Parks. b. 21 Oct 1931 Haywards Heath, West Sussex.

Parks made his Test debut in 1954, but although he scored over 2000 runs in 1955 (2314, his best total), 1957 and 1959 he did not appear again until he played the final Test against West Indies in 1960 as a replacement for the ill Peter May (qv). He seized the opportunity to score 43 and 101. During 1958 Sussex had converted him into their wicket-keeper and he was effective enough to do so for England as well, with a fairly regular Test place for the next eight years, although his batting probably suffered.

In 1959 he totalled 93 dismissals in first-class cricket as well as making 2313 runs. He had also been a useful leg-break bowler. He was captain of Sussex for a year and a half 1967-8 and later played for Somerset 1973-6. He made over 1000 runs in 20 seasons, missing only 1968 between 1953 and 1973.

46 Tests 1954-68: 1962 runs at 32.16; 2 100s HS 108*; 1 wicket at 51.00, BB 1-43; 103 catches, 11 stumpings.

First-class 1949-76: 36,673 runs at 34.76, 51 100s HS 205*; 51 wickets at 43.82, BB 3-23; 1088 catches, 93 stumpings.

His father James Horace 'Jim' Parks (b. 12 May 1903 Haywards Heath, West Sussex. d. 21 Nov 1980 Cuckfield, West Sussex) made 21,369 runs at 30.74 and took 852 wickets at 26.74 in his first-class career 1924-47. He achieved a unique double with 3003 runs at 50.89 and 101 wickets at 25.83 with his slow-medium

bowling in 1937, in which year he made his one Test appearance, against New Zealand, opening with Len Hutton on the latter's Test debut.

Jim Snr's brother **Harry** William Parks (1906-84) was an attacking middle-order batsman, who made 21,725 runs at 33.57 in first-class cricket, mostly for Sussex, 1926-50.

Jim's son **Bobby** (b. 15 Jun 1959) kept wicket for Hampshire from 1980 to 1992 and with one match for Kent in 1993 had a career total of 714 dismissals.

John PARROTT

Snooker
John Stephen Parrott. b. 11 May 1964 Liverpool.

Having turned professional in 1983, Parrott soon became established as a highly promising player. He worked his way up the world rankings, was beaten 18-3 by Steve Davis (qv) in the World Championship final in 1989, and reached the peak of his sport by winning the world title in 1991, beating Jimmy White (qv) 18-11 in the final. He went on to win the Dubai Classic in 1991 and 1992 and UK Championship in 1991, before losing in the UK final to White in 1992. In 1988 he was beaten by Steve Davis in the final of the World Match-play, the first tournament with a £100,000 prize for the winner. Other major wins include the European Open 1989 and 1990, the English Professional Championship 1989 and the International Open 1994.

He started playing snooker at the age of 12 and as an amateur won *Junior Pot Black*, on his first appearance on television.

Geoff PARSONS

Athletics, High Jump
Geoffrey Peter Parsons. b. 14 Aug 1964 Margate, Kent.

The tallest ever UK international at 2.03m *6 ft 8 in*, Parsons set a UK age-15 high jump best of 2.06m in 1980 and was the top ranked UK high jumper from the age of 17 in 1982 until 1988. He achieved the unique feat of setting a UK senior record to win an English Schools title in 1983 with 2.25m. He broke through to top international class indoors in 1986, when his European indoor bronze and Commonwealth silver medals were the first by a British high jumpers at senior level in either of these events since Alan Paterson (qv) in 1950. In all he set six British high jump records (and four indoor bests) in 1983-6.

He won a Commonwealth bronze medal in 1990, and some time after being passed at the top of British high jumping by Dalton Grant (qv) and Steve Smith (qv), excelled to win his third Commonwealth medal at his fourth Games (he had been 7th in 1982) in 1994 with 2.31, his first Scottish record for four years and his 14th in all. He was UK champion in 1985-6 and 1988; AAA 1986-8, AAA indoors 1983, 1986, 1988, 1991 and 1995 and Scottish 1985-7, 1989-90 and 1993-4.

Trained as a mining engineer, he now works in marketing for Blue Circle.

Alan PASCOE

Athletics, Hurdling
Alan Peter Pascoe. b. 11 Oct 1947 Portsmouth.

After a most successful athletics career to 1978, headed by his Commonwealth and European gold medals at 400m hurdles in 1974, he has been a highly successful businessman. He formed Alan Pascoe Associates, which took over the marketing of athletics in Britain for the British Board in 1984. His company played a major role in the sport's boom in ensuing years, and he sold his company to Aegis for £9.5 million in 1986, buying it back for £1.5 million in 1992. He is now chairman of The Sponsorship Group.

Coached at Portsmouth by Doug James, whose daughter Della he later married, he was an outstanding junior, winning the English Schools 120y hurdles in 1966. The next year came the first of his 13 AAA titles: indoor 60y/60m hurdles 1967-70 and 1973, outdoor 110m hurdles 1968, 1971-2, 400m hurdles 1973, 1976, 1978; 200m 1971-2. As a hurdler, before moving up to 400m, he won the European Indoor

50m in 1969, and was 3rd in 1969 and 2nd in 1971 in the European 110m, but failed to finish the final of the 1970 Commonwealth Games. He showed fine 400m flat speed with an Olympic relay silver in 1972, and at this event also won European gold in 1974 and Commonwealth silver in 1974. He won the European Cup 400m hurdles in 1973 and 1975, but, having been the world No.1 in 1975, injuries ruined his preparation for the 1976 Olympics although he made the 400m hurdles final. He retired soon after taking the bronze medal at this event at the 1978 Commonwealth Games. He had begun his involvement with the promotion of the sport while at Borough Road College in the early 1970s and became a spokesman for the athletes. He was awarded the MBE in 1975 and was a member of the Sports Council 1974-80.

Best times: 100y 9.7 (1969), 200m 20.92 (1972), 400m 46.8 (1973), hurdles: 50m 6.6i (1969), 60y 7.0i (1969), 60m 7.7i (1972), 110m 13.79 (1972) and 13.7 (1969), 200m 23.0 (1969), 400m 48.59 (1975).

In 1970 he married **Della James** (b. 28 Mar 1949), who was WAAA champion outdoors at 100m 1972 and indoors at 60y 1967, 200m 1969, and who set a British 100m record of 11.36 in the heats of the 1968 Olympics.

Alan PATERSON

Athletics, High Jump
Alan Sinclair Paterson. b. 11 Jun 1928 Glasgow.

With a high jump of 6 ft 5 in *1.95m* in 1946 Paterson became and remains, at 17 years 338 days, the youngest male British athletics record holder. He improved this record to 1.97m and 2.00 that year and to 2.02 at the Rangers' Sports in 1947, having set his first Scottish record at 1.87m a month after his 17th birthday. He is the youngest male medallist at the European Championships with his silver in 1946 and he went on to win in 1950. He was 7th equal at the 1948 Olympics and 2nd equal in the 1950 Empire Games and was ranked best in the world in 1949. It was to be 40 years before Britain had another world class high jumper. A member of Victoria Park AAC and tall at 2.00m, he was Scottish champion 1946 and 1948-51 and AAA champion 1946 and 1949-50.

He emigrated to Canada to pursue his accountancy career, although he returned to compete at the 1952 Olympics.

Rodney PATTISSON

Yachting
Rodney Stuart Pattisson. b. 15 Aug 1943 Campbeltown, Argyll and Bute.

Britain's most successful Olympic yachtsman, Pattisson won medals in the Flying Dutchman class with different partners on each of his three Olympic appearances. He won Olympic gold in 1968 with Iain MacDonald-Smith and 1972 with Chris Davies, and took the silver in 1976 with Julian Brooke-Houghton. During this period, he was unrivalled in the Flying Dutchman class and was world champion 1969-71 and European champion in 1968, 1970, 1972 and 1975.

He went on to win further world titles at Quarter Ton in 1976 and One Ton in 1984. He was awarded the MBE in 1969 for his Olympic successes. After his victory in 1968 he resigned his commission in the Navy and joined a boat-building firm which allowed him more time for training than his naval duties had permitted. In 1983 he was co-skipper of *Victory*, Peter de Savary's entry in the America's Cup.

Peter PATTON

Ice Hockey
(Major) Bethune Minet Patton. b. 5 Mar 1876 London. d. 1939 Tiverton.

Patton was the founding father of ice hockey in Britain. He was educated at Winchester and Wellington Colleges and, at the age of 20, not long after leaving school, he formed an ice hockey club at the Prince's Skating Club and the first properly organized game in Britain was played there in February 1897. The Prince's Club often represented England and Patton was a member of the team which won numerous tournaments on the Continent, including the first indoor international tournament in Berlin 1908 and the first European Championship at Les Avants in 1910. As a player Patton had an unsurpassed record. He took part in most of the early international matches and played on defence until 1923 before taking over as England's goalkeeper for several years. He was a reserve on the 1924 Olympic team and played his last international match against France in 1930 at the age of 54.

He founded the British Ice Hockey Association in 1914 and after it had been disbanded during the war, he was responsible for its revival in 1923. He served as President of the BIHA until 1934 when he became Patron. He was one of the five founders of the International Ice Hockey League and he was also a founder of the International Bobsleigh Association. His other sporting interests also centred on the water (unfrozen): between 1906 and 1920 he won the Royal Canoe Club's Challenge Cup (1 mile) four times when the event was, in effect, the British Championship for Canadian singles. He also won a host of major punting events on the Thames.

René PAUL and family

Fencing
Ronald René Charles Paul. b. 20 Jan 1921 Paddington, London.

The son of the famous fencing master, Professor Leon Paul (1881-1963), René was a distinguished member of the most successful family in the history of British fencing. At four Commonwealth Games 1950-62 he won a total of 10 medals (7 gold, 2 silver, 1 bronze) with his gold medals coming in the individual foil 1950 and 1954, four for foil team 1950-62, and one épée team, 1954. He competed at four Olympic Games 1948-60, and was the AFA foil champion five times (1947, 1949-50, 1956, 1962). He was also AFA runner-up twice in the foil and three times in the épée.

His son Dr **Graham** René Paul (b. 15 May 1947) competed at four Olympic Games 1968-84 and was AFA champion at foil 1966, 1968, 1971 and 1973 and épée 1969 and 1971. He was also runner-up in the foil four times and twice in the épée.

A younger son, **Barry** Christopher Paul (b. 10 May 1948), competed twice in the foil at the Olympic Games 1972-6, and at the 1970 Commonwealth Games he won a gold medal in the foil team event and a silver in the individual foil. He was also the AFA foil champion in 1974-6 and 1979-80 as well as runner-up in 1970-1 and 1977.

René's brother **Raymond** Rudolph Valentine **Paul** (b. 21 Nov 1928) competed at the 1952 and 1956 Olympics where he met his wife, **June** (née **Foulds**), who won bronze (1952) and silver (1956) medals in the 4 x 100m sprint relay.

June is the youngest ever European champion, taking gold with the British sprint relay team in 1950 at 16 years 75 days, just two days after becoming the youngest ever medallist with the bronze at 100m. She set four British records at 100y from 11.0 in 1950 to 10.8 in 1956, two at 100m , 11.9 in 1952 and 11.6 in 1956, and three at 200m at 24.1 in 1956 and 23.7 for half a turn, with 24.1 for 220y when she took the 1958 Commonwealth silver medal. She completed a full set of medals at those Games with gold at relay and bronze at 100y.

Raymond won 1958 Commonwealth gold medals for foil (individual and team) and was the AFA foil champion in 1953, 1955 and 1957-8, as well as runner-up five times for first or second place each year 1951-9. Raymond and June's son, **Steven** (b. 28 Sep 1954) was an Olympic fencer in 1980, 1984 and 1992 and was AFA épée champion in 1980, 1983 and 1993, with three runners-up places. René and Raymond were members of the British team that won world bronze in 1955.

Howard PAYNE

Athletics, Hammer
Andrew Howard Payne. b. 17 Apr 1931 Benoni, Gauteng, South Africa. d. 1 Mar 1992 Sheffield.

Victor Ludorum at school in Johannesburg in 1948, Payne dropped out of athletics until 1954, when he set a Northern Rhodesian discus record. He started hammer throwing in 1955 and represented Rhodesia at the 1958 Commonwealth Games in Cardiff, placing 4th. He returned to Britain in 1959 and settled permanently. By then he had won eight Rhodesian titles: shot and hammer 1956-7. discus 1955-8, and the South African hammer title in 1956.

He made his international debut for Britain in 1960 at the age of 29, first exceeded 200 ft *60.96m* in 1960 and took Mike Ellis's British record with 64.95m in 1968, adding three more records that year to his 68.06 in the Olympic qualifying round (placing 10th in the final). Three more records followed in 1970, in which year he won his third successive Commonwealth title (also 1962 and 1966) on the same day that his wife Rosemary (qv) won the discus. Getting better with age he set his best ever mark with 70.88 in 1974, when he was 2nd at his fifth Commonwealth Games and retired having made a then record 61 international appearances for Britain. His best placing at three European Championships was 8th in 1969.

At the AAA Championships he set a record with 15 placings in the first three at one event, as he won the hammer in 1964, 1969-71 and 1973, was 2nd in 1961-2, 1966-7, 1972 and 1974, and was 3rd 1959-60, 1963 and 1965.

Rosemary PAYNE

Athletics, Discus
Christine Rosemary Payne. b. 19 May 1933 Kelso, Borders. née Charters. Later Mrs Chrimes.

At the 1970 Commonwealth Games in Edinburgh, Rosemary won the discus on the same day that her first husband Howard won the hammer. That was the highlight of a career in which she had competed in 50 internationals for Britain from her late debut at the age of 30 in 1963 to 1974. She competed at three other Commonwealth Games, 10th in 1958, 4th in 1966 and 2nd 1974 (and 7th at shot), and was 12th at the 1972 Olympics.

From ten placings in the first three, and best placed British athlete each year 1964-74, she won the WAAA discus in 1966-7, 1970 and 1962-3 and set 12 British discus records from 48.07m in 1964 to 58.02 in

1972. She was Scottish champion at discus 1964-74, shot 1959, 1965 and 1974. A talented all-rounder, she had a shot best of 14.67m (1974) and achieved world age records for the over 55s at 80m hurdles, high jump, triple jump, shot. discus and hammer in 1988. While at Edinburgh University she was close to a place in the Scottish hockey team.

Eddie PAYNTER

Cricket
Edward Paynter. b. 5 Nov 1901 Oswaldshire, Lancashire.d. 5 Feb 1979 Keighley, West Yorkshire.

A gritty left-handed batsman who took a long time to establish himself in first-class cricket, Paynter came to compile a magnificent Test record, averaging 84.42 for 591 runs in his seven Tests against Australia. He joined the Lancashire staff at the age of 19, but he did not make his first team debut until he was 24 and did not gain a regular place until he was 29. Then, however, in 1931 he not only scored his first century but made his Test debut against New Zealand.
On the 1932/3 tour to Australia, he went into cricket history by rising from his sick bed, where he had spent four days in hospital with tonsilitis, to play a crucial match-winning innings of 83 at Brisbane, ending with a six. After three more Tests on that Tour he was not selected again for a Test until 1937, but in the three immediate prewar seasons he was hugely successful, averaging 101.75 for 407 runs against Australia in 1938, including 216* at Nottingham, and 81.62 for 653 runs against South Africa, including 243 at Durban in 1938/9. He exceeded 1000 runs in a season nine times, including four times over 2000 with a peak of 2904 at 53.77 in 1937.
At the end of World War II he was 45 and decided to play league cricket but he had an amazing final flurry in first-class cricket in England with 154, 73 and 127 (in 85 minutes) in his last three innings at the 1947 Harrogate Festival. He was a brilliant fielder despite having lost the ends of two fingers of his right hand in a brick press as a teenager.

20 Tests 1931-9: 1540 runs at 59.23; 4 100s HS 243; 7 catches.
First-class 1926-45: 20,075 runs at 42.26, 45 100s HS 322; 30 wickets at 45.70, BB 3-13; 160 catches.

W J PEALL

Billiards
William John Peall. b. 31 Dec 1854. d. 6 Jun 1952 Hove, East Sussex.

In 1890 Peall made a world record break at Westminster Aquarium of 3304, including 400 consecutive 'spot' reds. In his career he had eight other breaks over 2000 and won the first English Billiards Championship in 1892.

Stuart PEARCE

Football
Stuart Pearce. b. 24 Apr 1962 Shepherd's Bush, London.

After two seasons with Coventry City, Pearce joined Nottingham Forest in 1985 and established himself as England's regular left-back, winning 59 caps (4 goals) 1987-95. He captained both England and Nottingham Forest, leading the club to victory in the League Cup in 1989 and 1990. A hard-tackling, competitive left-back, he is known for the strength of his free kick although he surprisingly missed a vital penalty which resulted in England's elimination from the 1990 World Cup. He scored 16 goals for Forest in 1990/1, a remarkably high figure for a back.

Frank PEARD (Ireland)

Badminton
Frank Woodley Peard. b. 5 Oct 1919 Ireland.

The dominant Irish player in the immediate postwar years, Peard won 30 international caps and 18 Irish titles including a 'treble' in four consecutive years 1950-3. He later became a leading coach and published a number of papers on the theory of the game. A senior executive with Guinness, he married the former Sue Devlin (see Frank Devlin).

Geoff PECK

Orienteering
Geoffrey Peck. b. 27 Sep 1949 Blackpool, Lancashire.

Peck has been Britain's most successful orienteer. He won the British title five times, 1971, 1973, 1976-7 and 1979, adding the Over-35 title in 1985-6 and Over-40 in 1989. He competed in all World Championships from 1968 to 1981, with a best placing of 11th in 1972, still the highest by a British competitor.
He made the first colour map for the British Championships in 1969 and, as well as continuing his mapping skills, was the senior British squad coach 1980-7. A graduate of Edinburgh University, he was in the RAF from 1972 to 1983, where he flew Jaguars and was a test pilot at Farnborough for his last four years. He then joined British Aerospace as a test pilot, moving on in 1987 to Cathay Pacific, where he is now senior training captain, Boeing 747s.

Cecil PEDLOW (Ireland)

Rugby Union
Alexander Cecil Pedlow. b. 20 Jan 1934 Lurgan, Co. Armagh.

Although a trifle short of pace he had a long international career as a centre and winger. As a 19-year-old, he scored a try on his debut against Wales in 1953 and he closed his career in 1963 having won 30 caps for Ireland. Selected for the 1955 British Lions he was the top scorer on the tour (57 points) and played in two Tests against South Africa. Although handicapped by poor eyesight, he represented Ireland at squash and was a first-class tennis player.

Robert PEEL

Cricket
Robert Peel. b. 12 Feb 1857 Churwell, West Yorkshire. d. 12 Aug 1941 Morley, West Yorkshire.

A top-class slow left-arm bowler, Peel was also a formidable batsman and an excellent cover point fielder. Three times he took 20

wickets or more in a Test series against Australia. His partnership of 292 with Lord Hawke (qv) for Yorkshire v Warwickshire in 1896 is still the English record for the 8th wicket; Peel scored 210* in that match. He took 100 wickets in a season eight times with a high of 180 at 14.97 in 1895 and he did the double in 1896. Sadly his county career came to an abrupt end due to an incident when he took to the field drunk.
22 Tests 1884-96: 427 runs at 14.72, HS 83; 102 wickets at 16.81, BB 7-31; 17 catches.
First-class 1882-99: 12,191 runs at 19.44, 7 100s HS 210*; 1776 wickets at 16.19, BB 9-22; 214 catches.

Jesse PENNINGTON

Football
Jesse Pennington. b. 23 Aug 1883 West Bromwich. d. 5 Sep 1970 Kidderminster.

Pennington formed one of the greatest full-back partnerships in the history of the game. As a beautifully balanced left-back, he played alongside Bob Crompton (qv) in the first 23 of his 25 internationals from 1907. He won two further caps after the war, captaining England in his final international against Scotland in 1920.
Initially on the books of Aston Villa as an amateur, he signed for West Bromwich Albion in 1903 and gave yeoman service to the club until his retirement in 1922, helping them to win promotion from Division II in 1911 and to their first League Championship title in 1920, when he was captain. His 494 League and FA Cup appearances was a club record until beaten by Tony Brown in 1978. After retirement he undertook coaching and scouting and he was made a life member of West Bromwich a few years before his death.

Jonathan PENROSE

Chess
Dr Jonathan Penrose. b. 7 Oct 1933 Colchester, Essex.

The winner of the most British titles at chess, with ten 1958-63 and 1966-9,

Penrose became an International Master in 1961 and International Correspondence Grandmaster in 1969.

His first major title was when he became London champion in 1949. A lecturer in psychology, he limited his chess-playing by deciding to remain an amateur and he cut back further from 1970 by concentrating on the less-confrontational correspondence play at which he became the world's top-rated player and led the British team to victory in the 9th Correspondence Olympiad.

Fred PERRY

Tennis
Frederick John Perry. b. 18 May 1909 Stockport, Gt. Manchester. d. 2 Feb 1995 Melbourne, Australia.

Perry ranks as the outstanding British tennis player and one of the world's greatest players of all time. Since he turned professional in 1936, no British male has won a Grand Slam singles title whereas Perry won eight: three at Wimbledon 1934-6, three US at Forest Hills 1933-4 and 1936, and the 1935 French and 1934 Australian Championships. He was the first player to win all four major singles but as he did not hold the titles concurrently he missed the distinction of being the first winner of the Grand Slam.

Perry also won the Australian and French doubles with Pat Hughes (qv) in 1933 and took four Grand Slam mixed doubles titles with three different partners. His claim to greatness was enhanced by his superb Davis Cup record. In 20 ties 1931-6 he lost only 7 of his 52 matches and just one of his ten singles in the Challenge Rounds, as he helped the British team to win the Cup for four consecutive years 1933-6. In both the 1933 and 1936 finals Perry won the vital fifth rubber to clinch the match 3-2 for Great Britain. He especially cherished his 1933 triumphs when he beat both Jean Borotra and Henri Cochet of France to ensure Britain's first win since 1911.

After winning the 1936 US singles he turned professional and played a series of classic matches with Ellsworth Vines (USA) and Don Budge (USA) until he sus-tained an elbow injury at Madison Square Garden in 1941, after which he never played again seriously. His great strength was his running forehand drive and he had a confident, aggressive attitude to the game.

In the days of the 'gentleman amateur' Perry, son of the Labour Member of Parliament Sam Perry, was unique in that he did not come from a wealthy background. Initially, his main sport was table tennis, at which in 1929 he was the world singles champion. He became an American citizen in 1940 and served with the US Forces during World War II but in his later years he spent more time in England and became a hugely respected commentator on the game for BBC Radio. In 1950 he started the very successful Fred Perry Sportswear business.

To honour the 50th anniversary of his first Wimbledon title a statue of him was erected on the Wimbledon lawns by the All-England club in 1984.

He died while attending the Australian Championships in 1995.

Nora PERRY

Badminton
Nora C. Perry. b. 15 Jun 1954 Essex. née Gardner.

Having won five national under-18 titles and been runner-up at both doubles events at the European Juniors, Nora Gardner made her senior international debut in 1973 and went on to win the All-England mixed doubles six times and the ladies' doubles twice, and to make 90 international appearances for England 1973-85. She also won ten English National doubles titles, five ladies' and five successive mixed doubles with Mike Tredgett (qv). At the European Championships she won the ladies' and mixed doubles in 1978 and 1980, and at the Commonwealth Games she won a mixed doubles silver in 1974 and both doubles and a third gold in the team event in 1978.

At the World Championships she won the ladies' doubles with Jan Webster in 1980 and the mixed with Thomas Kihlström (Swe) in 1983, with silver at mixed doubles 1980 and two doubles bronze medals in 1977. She was awarded the MBE in 1984 and three months after the birth of her daughter, Gemma, that year she won all her matches in the Uber Cup except against the Chinese to whom England lost in the final.

Steve PERRYMAN

Football
Stephen John Perryman. b. 21 Dec 1951 Ealing, London.

An accomplished midfield player, and later a defender, Perryman gave exceptional service to Tottenham Hotspur. Joining the club as an apprentice in 1967 and captain for many years, his 655 League appearances (864 in all matches 1969-86) was a club record, and he helped Spurs to some of their greatest triumphs, notably the FA Cup 1981-2, League Cup 1971 and 1973, UEFA Cup 1984 and the Inter-Cities Fairs Cup 1972. His only senior England cap came late in his career when he played against Iceland in 1982, although he had been a schoolboy and youth international and won a record 17 Under-23 caps.

After 20 years with Tottenham, he signed for Oxford United in 1986 but after less than a year he moved on to Brentford as player-manager. He then managed Watford 1990-3 before returning to Spurs as assistant manager. His loyal service to Tottenham was rewarded with an MBE in 1986.

Atty PERSSE (Ireland/UK)

Horse Racing
Henry Seymour Persse. b. 17 Jun 1869 Galway, Ireland. d. 4 Sep 1960 Windsor, Berkshire.

Persse was a great racehorse trainer, first of jumpers and later on the flat. He trained the winners of four Classics, but his greatest horse was *The Tetrarch*, and he was particularly renowned for his fast two-year-olds. His first Classics winner was in 1912, *Sweeper II* in the 2000 Guineas. He was champion trainer in 1930.

Persse was a boxer while at Oxford University and an amateur steeplechase

jockey before starting training in Ireland in 1902, moving to England in 1906. From 1909 he trained at Stockbridge, Hampshire and then at Kingsdown, Upper Lambourn, Berkshire until his retirement in 1953.

Jim PETERS

Marathon
James Henry Peters. b. 24 Oct 1918 Homerton, London.

A great runner, who set four world best times for the marathon, Peters will always be remembered for his gallant failure in his last race. That was at the 1954 Commonwealth Games in Vancouver, when just after the finish of the epic mile between Roger Bannister (qv) and John Landy (Aus), Peters, who had won the 6 miles bronze medal seven days earlier, entered the stadium some 20 minutes ahead of the marathon field. Severely affected by the 24°C heat and suffering from dehydration, he staggered and reeled many times, before, still 200 yards short of the finish, he collapsed and was rushed to hospital. Later he received a gold medal from the Duke of Edinburgh for his gallant efforts.

As a track runner he won the AAA 6 miles in 1946 and 10 miles in 1947 and was 9th in the 1948 Olympic 10,000m.

Coached by 'Johnny' Johnston, he came back as a marathon runner in 1951 and won the Poly marathon in a British record 2:29:24. A year later in this famous annual race from Windsor to Chiswick he took five minutes off the world best with 2:20:42.2 and went to the Helsinki Olympics as favourite. He led for nearly half the race, but dropped out with cramp as Emil Zátopek (Cs) went on to complete his historic treble. In 1953 Peters ran two more world best times, 2:18:40.2 in the Poly race and 2:18:34.8 at Turku and in 1954 he won his fourth successive Poly in 2:17:39.4, a time that remained the world best for four years. In all he won eight of his eleven marathons.

Best track times: 3M 14:09.8 (1954), 6M 28:57.8 (1954), 10,000m 31:16.0 (1948), 1 hour 11M 986y (1953).

Martin PETERS

Football
Martin Stanford Peters. b. 8 Nov 1943
Plaistow, London.

Peters was a tireless and gifted player whose roving style of play did much to change the pattern of the game. A schoolboy and youth international, he started his professional career in 1960 at West Ham, with whom he won 33 caps and scored England's second goal in the 1966 World Cup final. After his move to Tottenham in 1970 he played for England a further 34 times (for 67 in all 1966-74) and captained the team on several occasions. The circumstances of his departure from West Ham have never been fully revealed but there is no doubt that his free-flowing style was better appreciated at Tottenham, where he fully justified the transfer fee which made him Britain's first £200,000 player.

Although he never won an FA Cup or League winners' medal, he won a European Cup Winners' Cup medal 1965 with West Ham and with Spurs he was in the winning team in the League Cup final in 1971 and 1973 and the UEFA Cup 1972.

In 1975 he moved to Norwich City where he enjoyed five successful seasons, after which he had an unsuccessful year as manager of Sheffield United, resigning when the club was relegated to the Fourth Division. This ended his involvement with the game and he joined his former World Cup colleague, Geoff Hurst (qv), in the insurance broking business, where he is now a sales manager.

Mary PETERS

Athletics
Mary Elizabeth Peters. b. 6 Jul 1939
Halewood, Gt. Manchester.

Peters won the Olympic pentathlon title with a world record 4801 points (4841 on the 1984 tables) on her third attempt in 1972, after placing 4th in 1964 and 9th in 1968. She needed to run a personal best in the last event, the 200m, to win, and did just that, although she had an agonising wait to see if the gap between her and Heide Rosendahl (FRG) – who had won

that race in 22.96 to the 24.08 by Peters – was sufficiently small. It was, and Peters won by 10 points.

She was Commonwealth pentathlon champion for Northern Ireland in 1970 and 1974 and also won the shot in 1970. She won eight pentathlon (1962-6, 1968, 1970, 1973) and two shot (1964, 1970) WAAA titles outdoors, with indoor titles at shot 1964-6, 1970 and 1972 and 60m hurdles 1970, and set British records at 100m hurdles 13.29 (1972), two at shot with bests of 16.31m (1966) and 16.40m indoors (1970), and six at pentathlon.

Voted BBC Sports Personality of the Year 1972, she was awarded the MBE 1973 and the CBE 1990. She went on to be a most successful team manager of UK squads as well as enthusiastic supporter of British sport in a wide range of capacities, including as a member of the Northern Ireland Sports Council 1973-93 and GB Sports Council 1974-7 and 1987-93.

Other bests: 200m 24.08 (1972), high jump 1.82m (1972), long jump 6.04m (1972).

Jack PETERSEN

Boxing
John Charles Petersen. b. 2 Sep 1911
Cardiff. d. 22 Nov 1990 Porthcawl, Vale of Glamorgan.

After winning the ABA light-heavyweight title in 1931, Petersen had a meteoric rise to the top in the professional ranks. In May 1932 he won the British light-heavyweight title, which he relinquished almost immediately, and within two months he was also the British heavyweight champion. Two successful defences earned him a Lonsdale Belt before he lost the title to Len Harvey (qv) in 1933, but the following year he beat Harvey in a return bout to reclaim the British crown and win the Empire title for the first time.

He lost both titles in 1936 when the referee stopped the fight in the third round in favour of the South African, Ben Foord. A third defeat by the German, Walter Neusel, in 1937 added to his growing concern over damage to his eyesight and he wisely retired. A popular fighter, he lacked the physique and strength of the top heavy-weights and never fought for the world title.

After war service in the army he was demobilised in 1945 with the rank of major and then became involved with youth welfare work in Wales. He also remained active in boxing administration and he became the first former profes-sional to serve as President of the British Boxing Board of Control. He was awarded the OBE.

Career record 1931-7: 38 contests. Won 33 (19 KO), Lost 5.

Brian PHELPS

Diving
Brian Eric Phelps. b. 21 Apr 1944
Chelmsford, Essex.

Britain's finest diver, Phelps won an Olympic bronze medal at springboard in 1960, golds for highboard at the European Championships of 1958 and 1962, and gold medals for both events at the Commonwealth Games of 1962 and 1966. At 14, in 1958, he was the youngest ever European champion after taking the high-board silver at the Commonwealth Games.

He was disappointed by 6th place at high-board at the 1964 Olympics and having been unbeaten by a British competitor from 1958 to 1966, he retired after defeat by David Priestley at the 1967 national championships.

He won 14 ASA titles from his first at the age of 13: highboard 1958-62 and 1964-6, 3m springboard 1960-2, plain 1957, 1960-1. In 1965 he married the gymnast **Monica Rutherford** (b. 29 Mar 1944) who had competed at the 1964 Olympic Games and won four British titles.

Brian gave professional diving displays for a few years and with Monica formed a gymnasium and health club business. Brian coached trampolining and at this sport their elder daughter **Erika** was 3rd in the 1980 World championships and won the World Cup event at the age of 13. Both Brian and Monica have worked as televi-sion commentators on their sports.

Richard PHELPS

Modern Pentathlon
Richard Lawson Phelps. b. 19 Apr 1961
Gloucester.

In 1993 Phelps became the first British modern pentathlete to win the men's world title, and in the team event won a world bronze medal in 1985 and silver in 1994. At the Olympic Games he had equalled the best ever placing by a British modern pen-tathlete (Jim Fox in 1972) with 4th in 1984, and four years later he was 6th and won a team bronze medal. He also passed Fox (qv) by winning a record eleven British titles, 1979, 1981-4, 1986, 1988, 1990-1, 1993 and 1995.

He had also won the British junior title in 1979 and 1981-2 and in the World Juniors he was 2nd in 1980 and 3rd in 1982, with a team bronze on each occasion. His talent at fencing brought him 3rd place in the British championship at épee in 1991.

Ted PHELPS

Rowing
Edward Alexander Phelps. b. 17 Jun 1908
Wandsworth, London. d. 1 Nov 1983
Exeter, Devon.

The son of 'Bossy' Phelps, King's Barge-master and Cambridge University coach, Ted Phelps brought further honours to an already famous rowing family. At the age of 20 he took up a coaching appointment in South America but returned home in 1930 to wrest the world championship from Bert Barry in May. He made a suc-cessful defence of his title in a return match with Barry in October and also won the Doggett's Coat and Badge that year. In 1932 he made another successful defence of his title against Major Goodsell in Los Angeles before finally losing his world crown to Bob Pearce (Can) in Toronto in 1934.

His younger brother **Eric** (b. 1912) was the winner of the Doggett race in 1932 and in 1935 went to Germany as private coach to the automobile magnate, George von Opel. Eric was interned in Germany during the war after which he took a coaching appointment in Argentina and on his return home in 1950 he engaged in occasional challenge matches, but the lack of prize money discouraged both Phelps and his challengers and professional sculling matches became a thing of the past.

Mark PHILLIPS

Equestrianism, Three-day Event
Mark Anthony Peter Phillips. b. 22 Sep 1948 Cirencester, Gloucestershire.

Phillips achieved a record four Badminton victories: 1971-2 on *Great Ovation*, 1974 on *Columbus* and 1981 on *Lincoln* before Lucinda Green (qv) surpassed his feat. He also won at Burghley in 1973. A reserve for the 1968 Olympics, he won a team gold in 1972, although *Great Ovation* fell twice in the cross-country and theirs was the discard score. With the British team he won team golds in the 1970 Worlds and 1971 Europeans. In 1988, Phillips again competed at the Olympics in the three-day event. He was forced to withdraw before the cross-country stage because his horse *Cartier* had pulled a muscle, but he earned a silver medal as the fourth member of Britain's second-placed team.
In 1973, Captain Phillips married HRH The Princess Anne (qv), but the marriage was dissolved in 1992. In 1974 he was appointed CVO. He was educated at Marlborough and RMA Sandhurst and now farms at Gatcombe, Gloucestershire. His grandfather Joseph Phillips played first-class cricket for Warwickshire.

Mollie PHILLIPS

Figure Skating
Molly (sic) Doreen Phillips. b. 27 Jul 1907 Clapham, London. d. 15 Dec 1994 London.

A pioneer in many areas of ice skating, Phillips was the first woman ever to carry the flag at an Olympic Opening Ceremony (1932), the first to be elected to the Council of the NSA (1939), the first Briton to act as a judge at the Olympic Games and the first woman referee at a World Championship (1953 ice dance). She competed, without notable success, in the singles at two Olympic Games, three

European and three World Championships but she had a better record as a pairs skater, winning the British title and placing 3rd in the Europeans in 1933 with Rodney Murdoch.
Her achievements were not exclusively sporting. She studied law at Lincoln's Inn and in 1961 she became the first lady High Sheriff of Carmarthenshire where she was well known as a breeder of dairy cattle. In 1978 she was awarded the OBE.

Jean PICKERING

Athletics, Long Jump
Jean Catherine Pickering. b. 4 Jul 1929 Forest Gate, London. née Desforges.

Starting athletics seriously in 1947 she became a highly talented all-rounder, winning the European long jump title in 1954, when she also ran on the 4th placed British sprint relay team and was 6th at 80m hurdles. At the latter event she had been 5th at the 1950 Europeans. She competed at the Empire Games of 1950 and 1954, with bronze medals at 80m hurdles and long jump in 1954. Britain's woman athlete of the year in 1953, when she set British records at long jump (6.10m) and pentathlon (3997 points), she was WAAA champion at 80m hurdles in 1949, 1952-4, long jump and pentathlon 1953-4. She considered her finest performance to be the wind assisted time of 10.9 that she ran in the semi-final of the 80m hurdles at the 1952 Olympics, but she only managed 11.6 for 5th in the final. Her 'legal' best time was 11.1 in 1954. 100y flat best: 10.9w (1952)
She met her husband to be **Ron**ald James **Pickering** (b. 4 May 1930 Hackney, London. d. 13 Feb 1991) at school, Stratford Grammar. Ron became an inspirational National Coach for Wales in 1960 and helped Lynn Davies (qv) to win the 1964 Olympic title and many other successes. Ron moved on to become an athletics commentator for BBC Television, where his enthusiasm and knowledge made him a hugely respected and much-loved figure. In 1986 he was awarded the OBE for his services to athletics, which also included being president of Haringey AC and doing

much work for the development of the sport in the community and for handicapped or disadvantaged sportsmen and women.

Karen PICKERING

Swimming
Karen Denise Pickering. b. 19 Dec 1971 Hove, East Sussex.

In 1993 Pickering became the first British woman swimmer to win a World title with the short-course 200m freestyle in a Commonwealth record 1:56.25 and a bronze at 100m in a UK record 54.39. She also won three bronze medals at the 1993 Europeans, 200m and two relays, with 6th place at 100m. A year later she won Commonwealth golds for 100m and 4 x 100m freestyle, a silver for 4 x 100m medley and a bronze for 200m. She then took her British long-course 100m record down to 55.79 when she was 7th in the World Championships, having set three British records in 1992 from 56.60 to 56.11. In 1990 she had been 4th at 100m and 9th at 50m with relay silver and bronze medals at the Commonwealth Games. Her 200m best is 2:00.33 for 2nd in the B final at the 1992 Olympics.

A British international from 1987, she set a UK record short-course 50m 25.74 (1992). Between 1988 to 1994 she has won 24 national titles including the outdoor ASA 50m 1992-3, 100m 1989-93; 200m 1990, 1992-4, 400m 1992; and short-course 50m 1991-3, 100m 1988, 1991-3; 200m 1991-2, 400m 1990-1 and 800m 1991; thus winnin g all five freestyle titles in December 1991. An outspoken critic of faults in the system of preparation for British swimmers, she was awarded the MBE 1994.

Lester PIGGOTT

Horse Racing
Lester Keith Piggott. b. 5 Nov 1935 Wantage, Oxfordshire.

Piggott has been the greatest jockey of the modern age on the English turf. From his first winner, *The Chase* at Haydock Park on 18 Aug 1948 at the age of 12, to the end of 1994, he rode over 5300 winners worldwide, including 4493 in Britain. There were a record 30 Classics winners between 1954 and 1992: 5 in the 2000 Guineas, 2 the 1000 Guineas, 6 The Oaks, 8 the St Leger, and a record 9 in the Derby, a race with which he is most especially connected in the minds of his admiring public, from *Never Say Die* in 1954 to *Teenoso* in 1983. In 1970 he rode *Nijinsky*, whom he considered the best of the many brilliant horses that he had ridden, to the Triple Crown.

Lester Piggott - Classic Winners		
1954	Derby	Never Say Die
1957	2000G	Crepello
1957	Derby	Crepello
1957	Oaks	Carrozza
1959	Oaks	Petite Etoile
1960	Derby	St Paddy
1960	St Leger	St Paddy
1961	St Leger	Aurelius
1966	Oaks	Valoris
1967	St Leger	Ribocco
1968	2000G	Sir Ivor
1968	Derby	Sir Ivor
1968	St Leger	Ribero
1970	1000G	Humble Duty
1970	2000G	Nijinsky
1970	Derby	Nijinsky
1970	St Leger	Nijinsky
1971	St Leger	Athens Wood
1972	Derby	Roberto
1972	St Leger	Boucher
1975	Oaks	Juliette Marny
1976	Derby	Empery
1977	Derby	The Minstrell
1981	1000G	Fairy Footsteps
1981	Oaks	Blue Wind
1983	Derby	Teenoso
1984	Oaks	Circus Plume
1984	St Leger	Comanche Run
1985	2000G	Shadeed
1992	2000G	Rodrigo de Triano

A child wonder, and twice champion apprentice, Piggott surpassed 100 winners in a season 25 times between 1955 and 1984 and was champion jockey eleven times between 1960 and 1982, with a peak total of 191 winners in 1966, but he sought to find the best rides rather than to maximise his number of wins, particularly after he had startled the racing world by turning freelance. He became undoubtedly the richest British sportsman. He had been first jockey to Sir Noel Murless (qv) 1954-66, in the 1970s rode many major race winners for Vincent O'Brien (qv), and in the early 1980s teamed up with Henry Cecil (qv).

His grandfather Ernest had ridden three Grand National winners, his father Keith trained at Newmarket (champion NH trainer 1963) and his mother Iris was the sister of the famous jockeys Bill (qv) and Fred Rickaby.

A solitary and withdrawn character, due to his partial deafness and speech impediment, Lester brought great strength to bear, driving his horses to many a perfectly judged finish, and he was both a brilliant horseman and a marvellous judge of a horse. In his early days his ruthless will to win cost him a series of suspensions from the Turf for dangerous riding. He had marvellous balance and needed it as he rode exceptionally short.

He retired on 29 Oct 1985 to train at Newmarket with his wife Susan (daughter of the famous trainer Sam Armstrong), and his first winner was sent out from his Eve Lodge stables within a few weeks. In October 1987 he was sentenced to three years imprisonment for a £2.8 million tax fraud, and was released a year later. This cost him the OBE awarded earlier. He obviously missed riding and made a comeback on 15 Oct 1990 at the age of 54, starting to add to his winners the following day and soon showing that he had lost little of his supreme ability, riding the winner of the Breeders' Cup mile in the USA. A record 30th Classics winner came in 1992 with *Rodrigo de Triano* in the 2000 Guineas.

Fuller PILCH

Cricket
Fuller Pilch. b. 17 Mar 1804 Horningtoft, Norfolk. d. 1 May 1870 Canterbury, Kent.

Pilch was the leading batsman in England in the mid-1850s and the founder of a dynasty of Pilches in Norfolk, where the leading sports shop in Norwich still bears the family name. His elder brothers Nathaniel and William played with him for Norfolk, for whom he played from 1820-36 before becoming established in the great Kent team until 1854.

Very tall for his generation at over 6 ft *1.83m* tall, he was a stylish middle-order batsman and a useful slow round-arm bowler, a master of the then-popular single-wicket matches.

First-class 1820-54: 7147 runs at 18.61, 3 100s HS 153*; 142 wickets at c.18.16, BB 7 wkts; 121 catches.

Cherry PILLMAN

Rugby Union
Charles Henry Pillman. b. 8 Jan 1890 Sidcup, Greater London. d. 13 Nov 1955 Bromley-by-Bow, London.

'Cherry' Pillman was the first flanker to develop the tactic of harrying the opposing fly-half with a fast break from the scrum on the opponent's heel. From this innovative move, modern wing-forward play has developed.

First capped against Wales in 1910, in the first international to be played at Twickenham, he played 18 times for England before a broken leg against Scotland in 1914 ended his international career, but after the war, in which he won an MC, he captained Blackheath 1919-20.

Pillman toured South Africa with the British Lions in 1910 where he made a great impression, not only for his fast breaking from the scrum but also for his unorthodox all-round capabilities. Not selected for the first Test, he played at fly-half in the second, making both England tries and converting the second to give the Lions their only Test victory (8-3). In the third and final Test he returned to the pack.

His brother, **Robert** (1893-1916), who was also an England international (1 cap, 1914) and a flanker with Blackheath, lost his life in the war.

Joshua PIM (Ireland)

Tennis
Joshua Pim. b. 20 May 1869 Bray, Co. Wicklow, Ireland. d. 15 Apr 1942 Dublin.

Possibly the best of the early Irish players

he was a Wimbledon singles finalist for four successive years. He met Wilfred Baddeley (qv) in the final in all four years and after losing in 1891 and 1892 he took the title in 1893 and 1894. He also won the doubles in 1890 and 1893 partnering fellow-Irishman Frank Stoker on each occasion. At home he won the Irish singles 1893-5 and the doubles in 1890-1 and 1893-5.

He played little first class tennis after 1895 and was well past his best when he was surprisingly called up for Davis Cup duty in 1902 under unusual circumstances. A doctor by profession, he was nominated as 'Mr X' allegedly to conform with medical ethics, although it is difficult to see what particular ethic would have been breached by the use of his full name, and he sailed for America one week after his team mates, but lost both singles in his only Davis Cup appearance.

Evie PINCHING

Skiing
Evelyn A. Pinching. b. 18 Mar 1915 Norwich, Norfolk.

At the 1936 Olympic Games Evie Pinching took 9th place overall (7th downhill, 11th slalom) and one week later in the World Championships at Innsbruck she won the downhill, finished 2nd in the slalom and took 1st place overall to become, with Esmé Mackinnon (qv), one of only two British skiers to win the world title. She also won the British downhill and combined title in 1935 and was the trainer of the British team at the 1948 Winter Olympics.

Matthew PINSENT

Rowing
Matthew Clive Pinsent. b. 10 Oct 1970 Holt, Norfolk.

After winning a gold medal in the British coxless four at the 1988 World Junior Championships and bronze at coxed fours in the 1989 World Championships, he went up to Oxford University (president 1992-3) and rowed in the winning boat against Cambridge in 1990 and 1991,

although he was in the losing boat in 1993. He then enjoyed many notable successes after teaming up with Steve Redgrave (qv) and after the world bronze in 1990 they were world coxless pairs champions in 1991, 1993 and 1994 and Olympic champions in 1992. They also set a world record time at Lucerne in 1994, and have been unbeaten from 1992 at coxless pairs from 1992 at least until their fourth successive win at Henley in July 1995. In addition to those four Goblets wins, Pinsent has also had Henley wins in the Princess Elizabeth Cup as a schoolboy and fours with the Prince Phillip Cup in 1995. He was awarded the MBE in 1993.

Martin PIPE

Horse Racing
Martin Charles Pipe. b. 29 May 1945 Taunton, Somerset.

Pipe has been champion jumps trainer for a record ten successive seasons 1986-95. In the years from 1988 to 1992 he smashed all records for training horses to win National Hunt races in Britain.

Previously an amateur point-to-point rider, he began training for the 1974/5 season, with his first winner *Hit Parade* at Taunton on 29 May 1975, and obtained a full licence in 1977. His first five years brought only 19 winners, but his number of winners increased each year from 1978/9 to 1989/90; he first trained 50 winners in a season in 1984/5, 106 in 1986/7 and broke Michael Dickinson's season's record of 120 with 129 in 1987/8. He left these figures far behind as in 1988/9 he was responsible for 208 winners. In 1989/90 he again bettered the record, reaching 200 winners on 7 May 1990, 12 days ahead of the previous year, and ending with 224 wins from 639 runs.

A high proportion of his winners were ridden by Peter Scudamore (qv), as he too set brilliant new records. In 1990/1 Pipe added to his records, becoming the first NH trainer to win over £1 million in a season with £1,203,014, and with 230 winners. He was again champion with 224 winners in 1991/2 and 194 in 1992/3. Although his number of winners fell to

127 in 1993/4, this was still the highest in the country, and his first Grand National winner came in 1994 with *Miinehoma*..

Gordon PIRIE

Athletics
Douglas Alastair Gordon Pirie. b. 10 Feb 1931 Leeds. d. 7 Dec 1991 Lymington, Hampshire.

A great distance runner, Pirie helped revolutionise attitudes to hard training. He set five world records: in 1953 at 6 miles and at 4 x 1500m relay, and three in 1956. The first of these was in Bergen on 19 June when he ran 5000m in 13:36.8 (25 secs off his best), beating Vladimir Kuts (USSR) 13:39.6, as both beat the old mark of 13:40.6. Three days later at Trondheim he ran 3000m in 7:55.6, a time which he improved to 7:52.7 in Malmö in September when he beat the great Hungarian trio of Rozsávölgyi, Iharos and Tábori. Later that year at the Olympics he ran an epic race at 10,000m against Kuts, but had to yield and finished eighth; he came back to gain the 5000m silver behind Kuts. At the 1952 Olympics he was 7th at 10,000m and 4th at 5000m, and in 1960 he went out in the heats of the 5000m. In 1958 he was 3rd in the European 5000m and 4th in the Empire Games at both 1 mile and 3 miles. He was AAA champion at 3 miles 1953 and 1961 and at 6 miles 1951-3 and 1960.
He set 24 British records at distances from 2000m to 10,000m, and excelled at cross-country, at which he was English National champion each year 1953-5. He became a professional athlete for a while and coached in Britain and in New Zealand. He also won the first two British titles at orienteering, 1967-8. He was voted BBC Sports Personality of the Year 1955.
Other best times: 1500m 3:42.5 (1961), 1M 3:59.9 (1960), 2000m 5:09.8 (1955), 2M 8:38.8 (1959), 3M 13:16.4 (1961), 6M 28:09.6 (1960), 10,000m 29:15.2 (1960)
He married international sprinter **Shirley Hampton** (b. 5 Sep 1935) in 1956. She won silver at sprint relay and bronze at 220y at the Empire Games and bronze at 200m in a British record 24.4 in the European Championships in 1954, and at 400m set a British record of 55.5 after 4th in the Europeans, with a WAAA title at 440y in a British record 56.4 in 1958.

Jenny PITMAN

Horse Racing
Jennifer Susan Pitman. née Harvey. b. 11 Jun 1946 Hoby, Leicestershire.

A forthright personality, Pitman's first training licence was in 1975 and in 1983 she became the first woman trainer of a Grand National winner, when *Corbière* won. In 1995 she succeeded again, this time with *Royal Athlete*. She also trained *Esha Ness*, who was first across the line in the 1993 Grand National, the race that was abandoned due to the chaotic and faulty start.
Jenny was formerly married (from 1965) to **Richard** Thomas **Pitman** (b. 1943), who was first jockey to Fred Winter's stable from 1972 to 1975, whose successes included *Lanzarote* in the 1974 Champion Hurdle, and later a journalist and TV commentator.
Their son **Mark** Andrew **Pitman** (b. 1 Aug 1968) rode *Garrison Savannah*, trained by his mother, to victory in the 1991 Cheltenham Gold Cup and is now assistant trainer to his mother. Jenny had also trained *Burrough Hill Lad* to win the Gold Cup in 1984. Both Richard and Mark had narrow misses in the Grand National, Richard riding the gallant *Crisp* whose huge lead was to no avail when *Red Rum*, to whom he was conceding 23 lb, swept past in the long finishing straight for his first win in the race in 1973. Mark's best season as a jockey was 1989/90 when he rode 57 winners.

David PLATT

Football
David Andrew Platt. b. 10 Jun 1966 Chadderton, Gt. Manchester.

An attacking midfield player, one of Platt's greatest assets is his ability to time his runs into the box to perfection and he has been England's leading goalscorer in recent years. He was appointed England captain by Terry Venables (qv), when the latter took over the team management in March 1994.

Platt joined Manchester United as an apprentice in 1984, but was released after a year, joining Crewe Alexandra on a free transfer. He scored 53 goals in 134 League appearances for Crewe before being signed by Graham Taylor for Aston Villa for £200,000. He made his England debut in 1989 and a year later was voted PFA Footballer of the Year award after scoring three goals to help England to the World Cup semi-finals. To June 1995 he has scored 26 goals in 54 internationals for England.

His series of brilliant performances as a midfield player in the World Cup led to him joining the Italian club, Bari, for a British record fee of £5.5 million in 1991, having scored 50 goals in 121 League games for Aston Villa. His 12 goals in 28 *Serie A* games for Bari were followed by another huge transfer fee, as Juventus paid £6.5 million for him. He first captained England in 1993, when he was transferred again, this time for £5.2 million to Sampdoria. His transfer fee total reached record proportions when he moved to Arsenal in July 1995 in a £4.75 million deal.

Susan PLATT

Athletics, Javelin
Susan Mary Platt. b. 4 Oct 1940 Mill Hill, London.

Platt so nearly took the javelin silver medal at the 1960 Olympics. The best throw of her life sailed out over 54m in the third round, but she was so excited that although she had completed her throw well before the scratch line, she walked out over it, so that the throw had to be ruled a foul. She had to settle for 7th at 51.00m and rue what might have been.

She won eight WAAA titles, 1959-62 and 1966-9 and set seven British records, from 49.04m in 1959 to 55.60m in 1968. Her top competitive achievement came with Commonwealth gold in 1962, and she was also 4th in 1958 and 6th in 1966. Her other Olympic placings were 9th in 1964 and 15th in 1968. She was a member of

London Olympiads and Spartan Ladies AC.

Marjorie POLLARD

Hockey and Cricket
Marjorie B. Pollard. b. 3 Aug 1899 Rugby, d. 21 Mar 1982 Bampton, Oxfordshire.

Pollard was a major pioneer of women's sport. She was a founder member of the Women's Cricket Association in 1926, a high-scoring international hockey player, and also played tennis and golf to county standard. Her international hockey career was divided into two parts, 1921-8 and 1931-7, and she won a total of 41 caps. Details of the scorers in some of the earlier matches have not been reliably recorded, but it is known that she scored more than 115 goals in international matches. Amongst her scoring feats were 13 of England's 20 goals against Wales in 1926, and the following season, 6 out of 8 against Ireland, 5 of 11 against South Africa and 4 of 11 against Wales.

After some outstanding performances as a Peterborough schoolgirl, she joined the town club and later founded the North Northants HC. As a journalist she wrote for several national newspapers, and edited the magazines *Hockey Field* 1946-70 and *Women's Cricket* for 20 years. She also became the first woman radio commentator on cricket when she commentated on the women's Tests in 1937. She served as vice-president of the All-England Women's Hockey Association and in 1965 was awarded the OBE for services to sport.

Hugh PORTER

Cycling
Hugh William Porter. b. 27 Jan 1940 Wolverhampton.

Porter was the finest ever British pursuit cyclist, at least until Chris Boardman (qv) came on the scene; in addition to his four world professional titles, 1968, 1970, 1972-3, he was 2nd in 1967 and 1969, and 3rd in 1971. As an amateur he won a bronze medal at the 1963 world championships in the pursuit, but had difficulty at the 1964 Olympics, losing in the quarter-finals at Tokyo, before winning the 1966 Commonwealth gold. He competed on the road as well, including the 1968 Tour de France (he did not finish), but with less success. Porter married British swimming gold medallist Anita Lonsbrough (qv) on 1 Jun 1965. He was awarded the MBE.

John PORTER

Horse Racing
John Porter. b. 2 Mar 1838 Rugeley, Staffs. d. 21 Feb 1922 Newbury, Berkshire.

Between 1868 and 1900, Porter trained the winners of over 1000 races, including 23 English Classics, with a record-equalling seven Derbys. In all, in 43 seasons, he trained the winners of 1063 races. He was apprenticed to John Barham Day (qv) in 1852, and rode occasionally. He became a trainer in 1863 for Sir Joseph Hawley, first at Cannons Heath and then at Kingsclere, Berkshire, which he bought on his patron's death in 1875. His best horses included the triple crown winners *Ormonde, La Flèche, Common* and *Flying Fox*. After his retirement from training in 1905 he managed Newbury racecourse.

Jon POTTER

Hockey
Jonathan Nicholas Mark Potter. b. 19 Nov 1963 Paddington, London.

Great Britain's most capped player, Potter was also the first to win 100 caps.
Inspirational in midfeld or defence, he made his debut for Britain against Pakistan in 1983, and passed Richard Leman's record 228 internationals for Britain and England in December 1994, He then retired from international hockey, having played in 106 matches for England and 128 for Britain. After winning a bronze medal at the 1984 Olympics, he won silver at the 1986 World Cup and 1987 European Cup and an Olympic gold medal in 1988. Before making his third Olympic appearance at Barcelona, he won a bronze medal in the 1991 European Cup.
After graduating from Southampton University he played for Hounslow and is a marketing manager.

Martin POTTER

Surfing
Martin Potter. b. 28 Oct 1965 Blyth, Northumberland.

In 1989 Potter became the first Briton to win a world surfing championship, having won six events on the world pro tour. Born in Britain, his family had moved to Durban, South Africa in 1970, so that he was brought up in an ideal surfing location. He turned professional in 1980 with immediate success to become at 16 the youngest competitor in the world championships. He had his first tour win in 1983.

Ronald POULTON

Rugby Union
Ronald William Poulton. b. 12 Sep 1889 Oxford. d. 5 May 1915 Ploegsteert Wood, Belgium. Later Poulton-Palmer.

Poulton was the outstanding player in English rugby immediately prior to World War I. An elusive runner on the wing or in the centre and a deadly finisher, he scored a record five tries in the 1909 Oxford v Cambridge match and four tries for England against France in 1914, which was then a record for an international. In all, he scored eight tries for England in 17 internationals and 24 points for Oxford in three University matches 1909-11. He also won a hockey Blue at inside-forward in these three years.
On inheriting a fortune from his uncle, he changed his name to Poulton-Palmer in 1913 and on leaving Oxford he joined the family biscuit firm of Huntley and Palmer. A handsome, popular officer, he was killed by a sniper's bullet while serving with the Berkshire Regiment.

Paddy PRENDERGAST (Ireland)

Horse Racing
Patrick Joseph Prendergast. b. 5 Aug 1909 Co. Kildare. d. 20 Jun 1980 Kildare.

A great Irish trainer, Prendergast's Meadow Court stables were at Maddenstown near the Curragh. After an unsuccessful career as a jumps jockey, he worked in Australia and for the Epsom trainer Harry Hedges before being granted his trainer's licence in Ireland in 1941. He trained 17 Irish Classics winners and four in England (between 1960 and 1964), where he was leading trainer 1963-5.

His sons Kevin (b. 5 Jul 1932 Australia) and Paddy Jnr (b. 19 Mar 1935 Co. Kildare) both became trainers, **Kevin** training the winners of five Irish Classics between 1972 and 1981 and *Nebbiolo* to win the 2000 Guineas in England in 1977.

John PRENN

Rackets
John Allen Nicholas Prenn. b. 30 Aug 1953 London.

After winning the 1971 Public Schools rackets championship for Harrow with Mark Thatcher as his partner, Prenn went on to become the World singles champion. A successful challenge to William Surtees (qv) in 1981 gave him the World title for the first time and after exchanging the crown with Willie Boone (qv) in 1984 and 1986 he finally lost the World title in 1988 when the honour passed to his doubles partner John Male (qv).

Together Prenn and Male won the World doubles Championship (1990), six British Open titles (1986-90, 1993) and six British Amateur titles (1988-91, 1993, 1995) after Prenn had taken the title in 1985 with Charles Hue-Williams.

As a singles player he won the British Amateur five times (1979-80, 1982-3, 1991), the British Open six times (1977, 1980-3, 1985), the Canadian Amateur eight times (1979, 1981-6, 1992) and the US Open three times (1980, 1982, 1985). He also won the British mixed doubles title at real tennis in 1995.

Alan PRESCOTT

Rugby League
George Alan Prescott. b. 17 Jun 1927 Widnes, Cheshire.

After starting his career as a winger, Prescott later moved into the pack and in 1956 became the first forward ever to captain Great Britain. He signed for Halifax in 1946 as a winger but moved to loose for-ward when his weight increased, and after he transferred to St Helens in 1948/9 he developed into an outstanding prop for-ward. As was to be expected from a former winger, he showed unusual speed for a for-ward and scored an exceptional try when St Helens won the 1956 Challenge Cup final.

In an international career which started in 1951 he won 28 caps, 17 as captain, and led the British team to victory in the 1958 Test series in Australia, playing for 76 minutes of the second test with a broken arm. Steel plates were put in his forearm, but his career ended soon after that; he stayed on as a coach at St Helens.

Berwyn PRICE

Athletics, Hurdling
Berwyn Price. b. 15 Aug 1951 Tredegar, Blaenau Gwent.

Britain's No.1 high hurdler for much of the 1970s, Price's greatest triumph came when he won the Commonwealth 110m hurdles title in 1978, after being a semi-finalist in 1970 and silver medallist in 1974. He was AAA junior champion in 1969, European Junior champion in 1970, and World University Games champion in 1973 in 13.69, a British record on automatic timing. At 60m hurdles he achieved his best European Championships result with a silver in 1976 in a British auto-timed record of 7.80. At 110m hurdles he won AAA titles each year 1973-8, UK 1977-8 and Welsh 1971, 1977-9 and 1981-2, and set hand-timed British records at 13.5 in 1973 and 1976. He was also AAA indoor champion at 60m hurdles 1971, 1975-6 and 1978.

He represented Britain in 50 international matches 1971-82, a record for a Welshman, and was a member of Cardiff AAC for most of his career, but later of Swansea Harriers, when he was Head of Sport and Recreation in the city.

Graham PRICE

Rugby Union
Graham Price. b. 24 Nov 1951 Moascar, Egypt.

Price is the most capped Welsh prop, with 39 of his 41 caps 1975-83 coming in consecutive matches. He packed down at tight-head with Charlie Faulkner and Bobby Windsor in the formidable Pontypool front row which played together in 19 internationals. Three British Lions tours took him to New Zealand (1977, 1983) and South Africa (1980); he played in every Test on each tour and his total of 12 Test appearances for the Lions is a record for a front-row and has only been bettered by lock Willie John McBride (17) and scrum-half Dickie Jeeps (13).

Leo PRICE

Hockey and Rugby Union
Herbert Leo Price. b. 21 Jun 1899 Sutton, Surrey. d. 18 Jul 1943 Manchester.

At Oxford, Price won Blues for rugby, hockey and water polo and also played cricket for the University. He was chosen to play hockey and rugby for England on the same day (18 Mar 1922). He chose rugby but as he had played hockey against Ireland the previous weekend, he had the unique distinction of representing England at different sports on successive Saturdays. At rugby, he won four England caps (1922-3) as a flanker and in the 1923 match against Wales he scored one of the fastest ever international tries when he caught the ball from the kick-off and scored before any Welsh player had touched the ball.
He won 12 England caps at hockey in 1921-4 before his sporting career was ended by injury playing rugby for London v All Blacks in December 1924.
Educated at Bishop's Stortford College, he taught at Uppingham and Christ's Hospital before returning to his old school as Headmaster in 1932.

Ryan PRICE

Horse Racing
(Captain) Henry Ryan Price. b. 16 Aug 1912 Hindhead, Surrey. d. 16 Aug 1986 Findon, West Sussex.

Price was the leading NH trainer in 1954/5, 1958/9, 1961/2, 1965/6 and 1966/7. Having been a point-to-point rider, he took out a trainer's licence in 1937, and, after war service as a commando, saddled his first winner at Plumpton in 1946. He trained in West Sussex at Wisborough Green and Lavant before moving to Findon in 1951.
His horses won the Champion Hurdle three times, the Grand National (*Kilmore* 1962), and Cheltenham Gold Cup (*What A Myth* 1969). In the 1960s he began to train more horses for the flat, and in 1970 handed over his jumpers to Josh Gifford (qv) so as to concentrate on the flat, winning the Oaks in 1972 and St Leger in 1975 before retiring in 1982.

Tommy PRICE

Speedway
Thomas Price. b. 11 Jun 1911 Cambridge.

In 1949, on the resumption of that event for the first time since 1938, Price became the first Englishman to be world speedway champion. He had, however, won the British Championship in 1946, when that event took the place of the World Championship.
He captained Wembley and rode for them from 1936 to 1955. Having ridden for England at the age of 44, the oldest ever to do so, he emigrated to Australia, where he lives in Perth.

Lucinda PRIOR-PALMER – see Green

Jeff PROBYN

Rugby Union
Jeffrey Alan Probyn. b. 27 Apr 1956 London.

England's most capped prop until Jason Leonard (qv) passed his record of 37 caps in 1995, Probyn made his international debut against France in 1988 and, playing at tighthead prop scored three tries for England before his retirement in 1993. Starting with Old Albanians from 1971, he played for Streatham & Croydon 1977-80, Richmond 1980-4 and for Wasps from 1984, as well as briefly for Askeans towards the end of his career.

John PULLIN

Rugby Union
John Vivian Pullin. b. 1 Nov 1941 Aust,
Gloucestershire

With 42 international appearances 1966-76, Pullin was England's most capped player until overtaken by Tony Neary (qv). Seven Tests for the British Lions brought his international total to 49 and he then shared the record as the world's most capped hooker with Ken Kennedy (Ire, qv).

An inspirational captain, he led England on 13 occasions including wins over South Africa, New Zealand and Australia. Only the win over Australia was on home territory and the Bristol hooker was the first man to lead his team to victory over the three Dominion countries. With the British Lions he toured South Africa in 1968 and New Zealand 1971, playing in seven Tests and missing only the first Test on the South African tour.

John PULMAN

Snooker
John Pulman. b. 12 Dec 1923 Teignmouth, Devon.

Pulman turned professional after winning the English Amateur snooker title in 1946 and steadily progressed until he reached the World Matchplay championship semi-final in 1954. He was beaten by Fred Davis (qv) in the final in 1955 and 1956 but won in 1957, when the event was held for the last time.

When the World Championship was revived in 1964 Pulman was challenged by Fred Davis for the title and won 19-16. He retained the title against six successive challenges in 1964-8, but was beaten by John Spencer (qv) in the first round in 1969 when the Championship was contested for the first time since 1951 as a knock-out tournament. In 1970 he was beaten by Ray Reardon (qv) in the final. His standard declined thereafter, but he reached the world semi-final in 1978. Since the 1970s he has commentated regularly on the game for television.

Alexander PURVES

Rugby Union
Alexander Buckholm Campbell Laidlaw Purves. b. Aug 1886, d. 20 Sep 1945 London.

A winger for London Scottish, the Army and Scotland, Purves is noted for scoring a try in six consecutive internationals. After scoring against England and South Africa in 1906, he added tries against Wales, Ireland and England in 1907 and began the 1908 season with a try against Wales. First capped against Wales in 1906 he marked his tenth and final appearance for Scotland with a dropped goal against England in 1910.

His brother, **William** (1888-1964) also won six caps as a lock 1912-3.

Malcolm PYRAH

Equestrianism, Show Jumping
Malcolm John Pyrah. b. 26 Aug 1941 Nottingham.

Pyrah was a member of the British team which successively won gold, bronze and silver medals at the World show jumping Championships of 1978, 1982 and 1986, with the individual silver on *Towerlands Anglezarke* in 1982. With this horse he won the King George V Gold Cup in 1985 and 1987 and the European silver medal in 1981. In the European team event he won gold in 1979 and 1985 and silver in 1983. He also competed at the 1988 Olympic Games.

Carole QUINTON

Athletics, Hurdling
Carol(e) Louise Quinton. b. 11 Jul 1936 Birmingham. Later Mrs Barr, then Mrs Kibble-White.

A member of Birchfield Harriers, Quinton won her first Midland title in 1954 and reached the Olympic semi-finals in 1956. In 1958 she took the silver medal at the Commonwealth Games in a wind-assisted time of 10.77, her fastest ever, just 0.05 sec. behind the winner, Norma Thrower (Aus) and then set her first British record with 10.9 in the semi-final of the European

Championships, where she was 4th in the final; she also earned a silver medal at sprint relay. She equalled that British record time of 10.9 four times, including twice at the 1960 Olympics in Rome, where she took the silver medal behind Irina Press (USSR). She was WAAA champion in 1958 and 1960 and retired after her marriage to water polo coach David Barr in 1961.

Other best times: 100y 10.8 (1959), 100m 11.9 (1960), 200m 25.2 (1959).

Peter RADFORD

Athletics
Peter Frank Radford. b. 20 Sep 1939 Walsall.

Having overcome a serious kidney illness as a child, which long confined him to a wheelchair, Radford became Britain's fastest man as a teenager and in 1960 won the Olympic bronze medal at 100m. He started running at the age of 12, and burst through at the age of 18 in 1958, when he was 4th at 100y, a semi-finalist at 220y and won a sprint relay gold medal at the Commonwealth Games, with a bronze at 100m and silver at the relay at the Europeans.

A member of Birchfield Harriers, he set the following British records: four each at 100y, 9.6 twice in 1958 and 9.4 in 1959 and 1960, 100m, all 10.3 1958-60, with an auto-timed 10.31 in 1958, and 220y, where after three 21.0s 1958-60 he ran a world record 20.5 at the Staffordshire Championships in 1960. He had also run a 200m record of 20.8 in 1958, which like the 100m 10.3 was also a world junior record, and a 300y best of 29.9 in 1960, with a world indoor best for 50m of 5.5 in 1958.

He was not such a force after 1960, although he won a second Commonwealth relay gold in 1962 and helped the British team to equal the world record of 40.0 for 4 x 110y in 1963. In 1962 he was a semi-finalist at both sprints in both Commonwealth and Europeans and he was a quarter-finalist at both 100m and 200m at the 1964 Olympics. He was AAA champion at 100y 1959-60.

Having been founder professor of the chair of PE and sports science at Glasgow University, he became chairman of the British Athletics Federation in 1993 and executive chairman in 1994.

Paul RADMILOVIC

Swimming and Water Polo
Paulo Radmilovic. b. 5 Mar 1886 Cardiff. d. 29 Sep 1968 Weston-super-Mare, Somerset.

The winner of Olympic gold medals for water polo with the British team at successive Games, 1908, 1912 and 1920, and also for 4 x 200m freestyle swimming in 1908, Radmilovic also competed at the Games of 1924 and 1928.

He had a Yugoslav father and an Irish mother, and eventually competed in international swimming and water polo for almost 30 years. He won nine ASA championships at an amazing range of distances and an enormous time span: 100y in 61.0 in 1909, 440y 1925, 880y 1926, 1 mile each year 1925-7 and the long-distance swim of five miles in the River Thames in 1907, 1925 and 1926.

His first Welsh title was at 100y in 1901 and his last at 440y in 1929 at the age of 41 in a championship record that stood for nine years. In 1967 he was the first Briton inducted into the International Swimming Hall of Fame.

Ronan RAFFERTY (Ireland)

Golf
Ronan Patrick Rafferty. b. 13 Jan 1964 Newry, Co. Down.

The leader of the Order of Merit in 1989, when he scored his first three wins on the European tour, Rafferty has not since matched that success. In the 1989 Ryder Cup he lost twice but won his singles against Mark Calcavecchia (USA). In 1990 he won two more tournaments and was 5th in the Order of Merit, but dropped to 35th in 1991.

As an amateur he played for Ireland at boy, youth and full international level in 1979; at 15 years 9 months he is the youngest ever Irish international. He was British Boys' champion in 1979 and became the youngest Irish champion in 1980, when he also tied for the English Amateur stroke-play title. At 17 in 1981 he became the youngest ever Walker Cup player before turning pro.

His first professional win came with the Venezuelan Open of 1982. He made his Dunhill Cup debut for Ireland in 1986, but it was not until that great year of 1989 that he lived up to the reputation earned as a boy prodigy.

He has played seven times for Ireland in the World Cup 1983-93 and his career earnings on the European tour 1981-94 amount to £2,255,558.

Alf RAMSEY

Football
(Sir) Alfred Ernest Ramsey. b. 22 Jan 1920 Dagenham, London. ⅔) 30/4/99

Although he was England's regular choice at right-back for four seasons, Ramsey is best remembered for his shrewd managerial skills. Beginning his professional career with Southampton, he made his first-team debut in 1946 and won his first England cap shortly before moving to Tottenham in May 1949, helping them to win the Football League Second Division in 1950 and First Division in 1951. He went on to win 32 caps 1948-53, including a run of 29 consecutive appearances, scoring three goals, including in each of his last two internationals.

He retired from playing in 1955 and that year he was appointed manager of Ipswich Town, There, after he had taken them to the Third Division title in 1956/7, he repeated the rare feat he had accomplished at Tottenham as a player by taking them to the Second Division and First titles in successive years, 1961-2.

In May 1963 he was appointed England's manager and became the most successful ever, winning the World Cup in 1966; of 123 matches in charge to May 1974, 78 were won, 32 drawn and only 13 lost. He was knighted in January 1967 for his role in England's World Cup success. In 1977 he had a brief spell as manager of Birmingham City.

Mary RAND

Athletics
Mary Denise Rand. b. 10 Feb 1940 Wells, Somerset. née Bignal. Later Mrs Toomey, then Mrs Reese.

A brilliantly talented all-rounder, Rand made up for the disappointment of placing 9th in the long jump at the 1960 Olympics when favourite for the title by winning in great style in 1964, when she set three British and Olympic records culminating in a world record 6.76m. That year she also won the silver medal at pentathlon with a British record 5035 points and bronze in the sprint relay; she was 4th at 80m hurdles in 1960.

She set the first of her six British records at pentathlon at the age of 18 when 7th with 4466 points in the European Championships in 1958, and that year she won the Commonwealth long jump silver medal. She set 11 British records at the long jump from 6.19 in 1959, and also set British records at 100y 10.6 (1964) and 80m hurdles 10.8 (1963). Four months after the birth of her daughter Alison she won European long jump and sprint relay bronze medals in 1962, and she won the Commonwealth long jump in 1966. She was WAAA champion at 80m hurdles 1959, 100m hurdles 1966, high jump 1958, long jump 1959, 1961, 1963-5; pentathlon 1959-60. She was awarded the MBE in 1965 and voted BBC Sports Personality of the Year 1964.

Mary Rand's British Long Jump Records		
Metres	*Venue*	*Date*
6.19	White City	1 Aug 1959
6.23	Chiswick	14 May 1960
6.27	Chiswick	14 May 1960
6.33	Rome	31 Aug 1960
6.35	Hurlingham	13 Jul 1963
6.44	White City	5 Aug 1963
6.53	White City	4 Jul 1964
6.58	White City	4 Jul 1964
6.59	Tokyo	14 Oct 1964
6.63	Tokyo	14 Oct 1964
6.76	Tokyo	14 Oct 1964
This beat the world record set at 6.70 by Tatyana Shchelkanova (USSR) in 1964. As Mary Bignal in 1959 and 1960.		

She married in 1960 rower Sidney Rand (who competed for Britain at the 1956 and 1960 Olympics), in 1969 Bill Toomey (USA, the 1968 Olympic champion and world record holder for the decathlon) and later John Reese.

Other bests: 100m 11.7 (1963), 200m 23.9 and 23.6w (1967), high jump 1.72m (1964).

Derek RANDALL

Cricket
Derek William Randall. b. 24 Feb 1951 Retford, Nottinghamshire.

A great character, always on the move and taking to himself (or anybody who would listen) Randall gave great pleasure to England and Nottinghamshire supporters with his brilliant cover fielding and enterprising batting.

Always willing to serve, his Test career was not helped by movement up and down the order, but he had some notable innings, most especially his superb 174 in the Centenary Test at Melbourne in 1977, in his fifth Test. Indeed, he showed his best form in Australia as his best series were with 385 runs there in 1978/9 and 365 runs in 1982/3.

His fitness enabled him to perform with distinction for his county into his 40s. He scored over 1000 runs in a season 11 times with a best of 2151 at 53.77 in 1985.

47 Tests 1972-84: 2479 runs at 33.37, 7 100s HS 174; 31 catches.

49 One-day Ints 1976-84: 1067 runs at 26.67, HS 88; 1 wicket; 25 catches.

First-class 1972-93: 28,456 runs at 38.14, 52 100s HS 237; 13 wickets at 31.76, BB 3-15; 361 catches.

Ted RAY

Golf
Edward Rivers Ray. b. 28 Mar 1877 Gorey, Jersey. d.26 Aug 1943 Watford, Herts.

Ray was the Open champion of 1912 after seven previous top ten finishes, of which the best was his 3rd place in 1908. In 1913 he was runner-up and tied for the US Open with Harry Vardon (qv) and Francis Ouimet (USA) and he was also 3rd in

1920 and joint runner-up in the Open in 1925 with Archie Compston, just one shot off the winning score of Jim Barnes (USA).

He was beaten in the final of the *News of the World* Match Play Championship three times, 1903, 1911 and 1912, losing twice to James Braid (qv) and once to Vardon. After World War I he won the 1920 US Open by one shot from Vardon and played in the first Ryder Cup match in 1927, losing both his matches.

A large and lumbering figure, noted for his long driving and usually seen with a pipe in his mouth, he was professional at Ganton and then at Oxhey, Hertfordshire from 1912 to 1941.

Thomas RAY

Athletics, Pole Vault
Thomas Ray. b. 5 Feb 1862 Staveley-in-Cartmel, Cumbria. d. 26 Aug 1904 Ulverstone, Cumbria.

Pole vaulting was a strong tradition in the Lake District a century ago, and Ray, who developed the technique of 'climbing' the pole - a style now banned - by slipping his hands up the stiff hickory shaft with three spikes on the end when it became vertical, was the best of its practitioners there.

He won a record seven AAA titles, 1881-2 and 1884-8 and remains the youngest men's world record holder in athletics from his first record at 11 ft 2 3/4 in *3.42m* in 1879 with a further nine records to 11 ft 8 in *3.55m* in 1888. He also won the championships of USA and Canada in 1887, but his beer drinking became a problem and his weight rose from 12 stone *76 kg* in 1881 to 14 st 11 lb *94kg* in 1887.

He retired in 1891 and trained five-time AAA champion **Richard Dickinson** (b. 1867) who improved the world record to 3.58m in 1891 – the last world record from the age of the poleclimbers.

Phil READ

Motorcycling
Philip William Read. b. 1 Jan 1939 Luton, Bedfordshire.

Read was eight times world motorcycling

champion, at 250cc in 1964-5, 1968 and 1971; at 125cc in 1968, all riding for Yamaha; at 500cc for MV in 1973-4 and at Formula One for Honda in 1977. In his career between 1961 and 1975 he achieved 52 Grand Prix victories: 10 at 125cc, 27 at 250cc, 4 at 350cc and 11 at 500cc, 39 for Yamaha, 11 MV Augusta and 2 Norton. He won eight Isle of Man TT races 1961-77.

He bought his first bike, a 250cc side-valve Matchless, at the age of 13, started racing in 1956 when he was an apprentice engineer, and had his first win at Castle Combe in 1957. His first major wins were on Nortons before being selected by Geoff Duke (qv) to ride for Gilera in 1963; after that unsuccessful year he started his hugely successful Yamaha era.

A most determined competitor, his feud with Bill Ivy (qv) brought him some noto-riety in 1968, and he enjoyed fierce rivalry with Giacomo Agostini (Ita) when they were team-mates in 1973. He was awarded the MBE in 1979.

Ray REARDON

Snooker
Raymond Reardon. b. 8 Oct 1932 Tredegar, Blaenau Gwent.

Reardon was the top snooker player of the 1970s, winning the world title at his second attempt in 1970, each year 1973-6 and in 1978, the latter making him, at 45 years 6 months, the oldest ever champion. He was ranked as world No.1 from the introduction of rankings in 1976 until 1980 and again in 1982. Other major wins: Benson & Hedges Masters 1976, British Open 1982. He was also the BBC TV *Pot Black* champion in 1969 and 1979 and helped Wales to win the World Cup in 1979 and 1980.

His first important success was at 17 when he won the first of six successive Welsh Amateur titles, 1950-5. He left his colliery job in Wales to become a policeman when his family moved to Stoke-on-Trent. It was not until 1964 that he won the English Amateur title and he turned pro in 1967. He was awarded the MBE in 1985.

Steve REDGRAVE

Rowing
Steven Geoffrey Redgrave. b. 23 Mar 1962 Amersham, Buckinghamshire.

Redgrave was Olympic gold medallist in 1984 at the coxed fours and in 1988 at the coxless pairs with **Andrew Holmes** (b. 15 Oct 1959), with whom he also took the bronze at coxed pairs. He equalled the all-time record with a third Olympic gold in 1992, at the coxless pairs with Matthew Pinsent (qv).

He was runner-up in the World Junior double sculls in 1980 and started his world championships career with 6th places at quad sculls in 1981 and 1982. Since then he has been world champion at coxless pairs with Holmes in 1987 and with Pinsent in 1991, 1993 and 1994, and at coxed pairs in 1986. At coxless pairs he was also 2nd in 1989 (with Simon Berrisford) and 3rd in 1990 (with Pinsent) and at coxed pairs 2nd in 1987 (with Holmes). In 1986 he became the first rower ever to win three gold medals at the Commonwealth Games, at single sculls and with Holmes at coxless and coxed pairs.

At Henley he has recorded 15 wins to 1995, including the Diamond Sculls in 1983 and 1985, and a record seven win in the Silver Goblets and Nickalls' Cup (cox-less pairs). In 1995 Pinsent and Redgrave became the first coxless pair to break seven minutes in this race, and by this time were unbeaten anywhere as a pair for three years. Redgrave also had five consecutive successes at the Wingfield Sculls from 1985 to 1989 and was awarded the MBE in 1986. In 1989 he took up bobsledding and was a member of the crew which won the British 4-man championship that year.

Tom REECE

Billiards
Thomas Reece. b. 12 Aug 1873 Oldham, Gt. Manchester. d. 16 Oct 1953 Lancing, West Sussex.

Although he failed in his lifetime ambition to win the world billiards title, Reece's break of 499,135 assures him of a place in the history of the game. This phenomenal score was made in London in the summer of 1907 against Tom Chapman and took almost five weeks to compile. Even then it was 'unfinished' but it was not officially recognised as the press and public were not continually present. The break was based on 249,552 'cradle' or 'anchor' cannons, involving repeated use of the same shot. After a rule restricting the number of ball-to-ball cannons to 25 was introduced, Reece devised the 'pendulum' cannon which led to further inflated scores. It soon became apparent that the game would suffer if unlimited scoring, entirely by specialist means, was permitted and in 1932 the important Baulk line rule was introduced.

He reached the final of the World Championship six times, 1912-14, 1921 and 1924-5, but lost to Melbourne Inman (qv) in his first three finals and to Tom Newman (qv) in the next three.

Dai REES

Golf
David James Rees. b. 31 Mar 1913 Barry, Vale of Glamorgan. d. 15 Nov 1983 London.

Rees is surpassed only by Ian Woosnam (qv) as the greatest ever Welsh golfer. In his 35-year career Rees had 20 British PGA tour victories, but never the one he most wanted, the British Open, in which he was joint 2nd in 1953 and 1954 and runner-up just one shot behind Arnold Palmer in 1961. He was also joint 3rd in 1950. In 1946 he had gone into the final round tying for the lead with Sam Snead (USA) only to collapse with an 80.

He won the Dunlop Masters in 1950 and 1962 and the *News of the World* Match Play in 1936, 1938 and 1949-50. He often showed his best in that tournament, and was runner-up twice in his 50s, in 1967 and 1969. Rees made nine Ryder Cup appearances as a player between 1937 and 1961, winning 7, losing 10 and halving 1 of his 18 matches, and captained the British PGA team that won the Cup for the first time for 24 years in 1957, in which year he was voted BBC Sports Personality of the Year. He was also selected for the

match in 1939 which was cancelled due to the outbreak of War, and was non-playing captain in 1967. He was a smallish man, but was known as a long hitter, especially for his size. In his early days in particular he was a brilliant putter.

His father was the professional at Aberdare GC and Rees was assistant there 1929-34, before taking up appointments at Surbiton and Hindhead, going on to South Herts, where he taught until his retirement. His first important win was the Assistants Championship in 1935. He was awarded the CBE.

Dick REES

Horse Racing
Frederick Brychan Rees. b. 30 Nov 1894 Tenby, Pembrokeshire. d. 14 Aug 1951 Lewes, East Sussex.

The son of a Pembrokeshire vet, he was a complete horseman and five times champion NH jockey, in 1920-1, 1923-4, 1927. Employing tactical mastery and with the ability to produce his mounts with driving finishes, he was the first great jumping jockey in Britain. After riding as an amateur for two years, he turned professional in 1921 and won the Grand National that year on *Shaun Spadah*. His elder brother **Bilby** won the following year on *Music Hall*, and his nephew **Bill** rode *Pas Seul* to win the 1960 Cheltenham Gold Cup.

As with so many jockeys, weight troubles curtailed his career.

Leighton REES

Darts
Leighton Rees. b. 17 Jan 1940 Ynysybwl, Pontypridd, Rhondda Cynon Taff.

One of the early stars in the days when darts became hugely popular on British television, he won the first World professional championship, held in 1978, two months after he had clinched the 1977 World Cup for Wales and won the individual title. He worked as a storeman until turning professional after losing in the final of the 1976 *News of the World* tournament. He played for Avon for many years and Glamorgan from 1980.

Athletics, Long Jump
Susan Diane Reeve. b. 17 Sep 1951
Birmingham. née Scott, later Mrs
Herrington.

Sue Scott was a brilliantly talented all-rounder as a junior, and as Sue Reeve she became Britain's top long jumper. She joined Birchfield Harriers at the age of 11 and at 14 in 1966 won the WAAA junior and English schools intermediate long jump. In 1967 she made her senior international debut as well as winning the WAAA intermediate titles at long jump and pentathlon and in 1968 was 10th in the pentathlon at the Olympic Games. In 1969 she was 2nd in the European Indoor long jump and 7th in the European pentathlon. A week before the 1970 Commonwealth Games she suffered an ankle injury, but competed to place 5th at pentathlon and 6th at 80m hurdles. The ankle, however, suffered further damage and she eventually had an operation on it in 1972. By then married to coach Kevin Reeve, she fought back to fitness and was a world-class long jumper in the late 1970s.

In 1978 she won the Commonwealth title, and was 3rd indoors and 6th outdoors at the Europeans. She placed 9th at the 1976 Olympics and had to resist severe government pressure on her as a civil servant to compete and place 10th at the 1980 Games, which Prime Minister Thatcher wanted Britain to boycott.

She was later married to discus thrower Gary Herrington.

At long jump she was WAAA champion outdoors 1976-7 and 1980 and indoor 1969, 1976-8, and UK champion 1978-9. Best performances: 100m 12.0 (1980), 200m 24.3 (1968), 100m hurdles 13.7 (1970), high jump 1.65m (1969), long jump 6.69m (1979), 6.84w (1977); shot 13.17m (1978).

Athletics
John Paul Lyndon Regis. b. 13 Oct 1966
Lewisham, London.

The powerfully built sprinter won the European Junior bronze at 100m and gold at sprint relay in 1985, and achieved his first senior gold medals in 1989, with individual 200m wins at the World Indoors and European Cup, after silver at the European Indoors.

At the World Championships he very nearly won the 200m in 1987, as he led at 195m, but had to settle for 2nd in 20.18, the first of his four UK records. He added two relay medals, bronze at 4 x 100m and gold at 4 x 400m, in 1991 after going out in the 200m semi-finals. Then in 1993 he won silver medals at 200m, in a British record time of 19.94, and on the 4 x 100m team. He has often expressed his dislike of the 400m, but has shown great ability in relays, most notably with his 43.93 third leg to ensure Britain's gold at the 1990 Europeans, when he won four medals, the most ever by a man at one Championships, adding gold at 200m, silver at 4 x 100m and bronze at 100m.

At the Olympics he won a sprint relay silver in 1988 and was 6th at 200m (after a British record 20.09 in his semi-final) with a 4 x 400m bronze in 1992. In 1994 he improved his 200m record to 19.87 at the high altitude Italian resort of Sestriere. He then had to miss the Europeans through Achilles injury, but came back for Commonwealth silver at 200m to match his 1990 medal, when he had also won a sprint relay gold. His other major wins: European Cup 200m 1993; UK 100m 1988 and 200m 1985 (tie), 1986, 1991 and 1993; AAA 200m 1986-7, 1990, 1992 and 1995. He was awarded the MBE in 1994.

Other best times: 60m indoors 6.71 (1991), 100m 10.15 (1993), 10.07w (1990), 300m 31.67 (1992, European best), 400m 45.48 (1993), 200m hurdles 22.79 (1991).

His cousin **Cyrille Regis** (b. 9 Feb 1958 Maripiaoula, French Guyana) played five times for England at football 1982-8 as a centre-forward, having been PFA Young Footballer of the Year in 1979 while with West Bromwich Albion. From there he moved to Coventry City in 1984, Aston Villa in 1991 and Wolverhampton Wanderers in 1993.

Lawrie REILLY

Football
Lawrence Reilly. b. 28 Oct 1928 Edinburgh.

Reilly was a high-scoring centre-forward whose habit of claiming match winning goals in the closing minutes earned him the nickname 'Last-Minute Reilly'. For Scotland, he played at outside-left and at centre-forward scoring 22 goals in 38 matches between 1948 and 1957 and he was at the time the most capped Hibernian player.

He signed for Hibs in 1945 and his exceptional scoring abilities helped them to the Scottish League title in 1951 and 1952. Seventy-nine of his 185 League goals came in just three seasons 1951-3, and he topped the scoring list in the Scottish League in each of these years. A knee injury in 1958 ended his playing career and he became a licensee in the Edinburgh area.

Sharon RENDLE

Judo
Sharon Susan Rendle. b. 18 Jun 1966 Hull.

When women's judo was held as a demonstration sport at the 1988 Olympics, Rendle won the 52 kg category. She was world champion in the years either side of that victory in 1987 and 1989, bronze medallist in 1986 and silver medallist in 1991. She also won the 52 kg title in 1990 on the only occasion that judo was included on the Commonwealth Games programme. She was European champion 1990, Japanese Open champion in 1987 and 1988 and British champion at 52kg 1984-9 and 1992. When judo became a medal sport at the Olympics in 1992 she took a bronze medal. She took a European bronze on 1995. She was awarded the MBE in 1993.

William RENSHAW

Tennis
William Charles Renshaw. b. 3 Jan 1861 Leamington, Warwickshire. d. 12 Aug 1904 Swanage, Dorset.

Renshaw was the winner of a record seven singles titles at Wimbledon (1881-6, 1889) and five doubles with his twin **Ernest** (1884-6, 1888-9). In 1880 and 1881 they also won the Oxford doubles which was recognised as the premier event prior to the introduction of the official All-England doubles championship at Wimbledon in 1884.

In ten singles appearances at Wimbledon, William Renshaw lost only three matches. His defeat by O.E.Woodhouse in the 3rd round on his debut in 1880 was followed by six successive Championships and in 1887 he did not defend his title. He lost to Irishman Willoby Hamilton in the quarter-final although family honour was restored as Ernest Renshaw won the title in 1888. William was again champion in 1889 and on his last appearance in 1890 he lost again to Hamilton.

The Renshaws are generally recognised as the founders of modern tennis and credited with turning a game into a sport. The twins, who came from a wealthy family and were both educated at Cheltenham, had tremendous crowd appeal and after their retirement, attendances at Wimbledon dropped significantly. Although not the inventor of the overhead serve and smash, William developed their technique and was the first to employ them consistently and effectively. Marginally the older of the twins, William had the better championship record but both were well ahead of their contemporaries.

Jim RENWICK

Rugby Union
James Menzies Renwick. b. 12 Feb 1952 Hawick, Borders.

Starting with a try on his international debut against France in 1972, Renwick went on to win 52 Scottish caps, scoring 67 points, including 8 tries. Heheld the record of being Scotland's most capped player and when he retired in 1983 he was the world's most capped centre. He toured South Africa with the British Lions in 1980 and played in one Test.

Don REVIE

Football
Donald George Revie. b. 10 Jul 1927
Middlesbrough, North Yorkshire. d. 26
May 1989 Edinburgh.

Despite an outstanding record as a player Revie will be remembered as a successful and innovative manager. In a playing career which lasted from 1944 to 1963, he played for Leicester, Hull, Manchester City, Leeds and Sunderland. He spent his best years with Manchester City where he won six England caps 1954-6, the 1955 Player of the Year award and an FA Cup winners' medal in 1956, after being on the losing side in the 1955 final. He was a key figure in Manchester City's revolutionary 'Revie plan' in which he played as deep-lying centre-forward. The plan, based on one used by the great Hungarian team of the time, was the first really significant tactical innovation seen in Britain since before the war.

In 1961 he was appointed as player-manager at Leeds, and although he gave up playing after two seasons he remained as manager until 1974. He transformed Leeds' fortunes and under his guidance, after several near misses, the club won the League Cup in 1968, FA Cup 1972, Football League 1969 and 1974 and the UEFA Cup 1968 and 1971.

Taking over as manager of England in 1974 he held the post for three years, but was unable to recapture his highly successful club atmosphere at national level and took up a lucrative offer to be coach to the United Arab Emirates team. He was awarded the OBE in 1970.

Ronald RHODES

Canoeing
Ronald Rhodes. b. 31 Oct 1937. d. 12 Jan 1962 Twickenham, London.

Rhodes was 5th in the kayak singles at 1000m in the 1960 Olympic Games, for the best ever performance by a British competitor at this sport. He was British Open champion at K1 500m in 1958, at K1 and K2 1000m in 1959 and 1961, and at K1 nd K2 10,000m in 1960.

He was killed in a motorcycle crash near Twickenham Bridge.

Wilfred RHODES

Cricket
Wilfred Rhodes. b. 29 Oct 1876
Kirkheaton, West Yorkshire. d. 8 Jul 1973
Bransome Park, near Poole, Dorset.

Rhodes was the greatest wicket-taker of all-time in first-class cricket, and an all-rounder whose runs total is exceeded by only 15 batsmen. Throughout his exceptionally long career, in which he made a record number of 1107 first-class appearances, he was a masterly slow left-arm bowler, and his sound batting progressed so that from an England No. 10 or 11 in his first series in 1899 he developed to be able to open the innings in the period 1909-21, mostly with Jack Hobbs (qv), with whom he made 8 century opening partnerships. He is one of only three cricketers to have batted in every position in the order in Tests.

His 16 doubles of 1000 runs and 100 wickets in a season is the all-time record, as is his 23 seasons of 100 or more wickets. He captured 154 wickets at 14.60 in his first season of 1898, and went on to his peak seasons with 261 wickets at 13.81 in 1900 and 251 at 15.12 in 1901. He averaged under 20 runs per wicket in each season from then until 1930, apart from 1904 and 1911-13, when for a while he concentrated on his batting. He scored over 1000 runs in each of the 20 seasons in England between 1903 and 1926, with a peak of 2261 runs in 1911.

At Kingston, Jamaica in 1930 he became, at 52 years 165 days, the oldest ever Test player and his span as a Test cricketer of 31 years 315 days is easily the record. He later coached at Harrow School.

58 Tests 1899-1930: 2325 runs at 30.19, 2 100s HS 179; 127 wickets at 26.96, BB 8-68; 60 catches.

First-class 1898-1930: 39,802 runs at 30.83, 58 100s HS 267*; 4187 wickets at 16.71, BB 9-24; 764 catches.

ACS figures: 39,969 runs at 30.58; 4204 wickets at 16.72; 765 catches.

Dean RICHARDS

Rugby Union
Dean Richards. b. 11 Jul 1963 Nuneaton, Warwickshire.

After playing in France for a season, Richards moved to Leicester in 1982 where he joined the local police force and began to establish a reputation with their rugby club. He scored two tries against Ireland on his England debut in 1986 and his considerable body strength and shrewd positional sense soon made him one of the world's most respected back-row players.
He toured twice with the British Lions, playing in all three Tests against Australia in 1989 and against New Zealand in 1993. His international career was interrupted by shoulder injuries and he was no longer an automatic choice as the England selectors had an abundance of talented back row players to choose from. However, he returned as a regular, and tower of strength, for the 1995 Five Nations campaign and by the end of the season he was the world's most capped No. 8 taking his number of England caps to 46 by the end of the World Cup,with another 6 for the British Lions.
In 1994/5 he also captained Leicester to win the Courage league title, which they had previously won in 1987/8.

Gordon RICHARDS

Horse Racing
Sir Gordon Richards. b. 5 May 1904 Oakengates, Shropshire. d. 10 Nov 1986 Kintbury, Berkshire.

Richards bestrode the Turf in Britain, where he rode a record 4870 winners (over 2000 more than the previous record) and was champion jockey a record 26 times. In his final year he rode his one Epsom Derby winner, *Pinza*, just a few days after it had been announced that he was to be the first professional jockey to be knighted. The first of his 14 Classics winners (5 St Leger, 3 1000 Guineas and 2000 Guineas, 2 Oaks, 1 Derby) had been *Singapore* in the 1930 St Leger, and his greatest success came in winning the fillies Triple Crown on *Sun Chariot* in 1942.

At the age of 15 he answered an advertisement for stable-lads and joined the trainer Martin Hartigan. He had his first ride in public in October 1920 and his first winner was *Gay Lord* at Leicester on 31 Mar 1921. Champion with 118 winners in 1925, he contracted tuberculosis in 1926 but returned as champion with 164 winners the following year, and from then until 1953 he was champion every year except 1930, when Freddie Fox (qv) beat him by one, and 1941 when he broke a leg. He surpassed Fred Archer's season's record with 259 winners in 1933, when on 3-5 October he rode a world record 12 successive winners. He improved the season's record to 269 in 1947, with 12 years in all at 200 or more. After an accident in 1954 he retired from riding, and trained from 1955 to 1970, when he became a racing manager. He was first jockey to Tommy Hogg 1925-31, Fred Darling (qv) 1932-47, and then for Noel Murless (qv).
A strong and determined, if unorthodox, jockey, riding on a long rein, he displayed perfect balance and said that his success came from his will to win. Unlike some of his rivals he had little difficulty in making his riding weight of less than 8 stone. He was a model sportsman, adored by the racing public and respected by his colleagues.

Gordon W. RICHARDS

Horse Racing
Gordon (Waugh) Richards. b. 7 Sep 1930 Bath.

Having been a jockey, when he was apprenticed with Jack Waugh and then Ivor Antony before moving north and switching to National Hunt, he trains at the Greystoke stables in Cumbria, having taken out his first licence in 1964. His big race winners have included the Grand National with *Lucius* in 1978 and *Hello Dandy* in 1984. He added Waugh to his name, after his trainer, during World War II as the Jockey Club required a middle name to distinguish him from the famous jockey.

Gordon Richards - season by season

Year	Wins	Mounts	Best other jockey	
1920	0	1	Steve Donoghue	143*
1921	5	47	Steve Donoghue	141*
1922	5	72	Steve Donoghue	102*
1923	49	324	Steve Donoghue	89*
			Charlie Elliott	89*
1924	61	517	Charlie Elliott	106*
1925	118*	730	Charlie Elliott	86
1926	5	53	Tommy Weston	95*
1927	164*	771	Tommy Weston	78
1928	148*	863	Harry Wragg	89
1929	135*	777	Freddy Fox	116
1930	128	832	Freddy Fox	129*
1931	145*	899	Harry Wragg	110
1932	190*	945	Harry Wragg	102
1933	259*	975	Bill Nevett	73
1934	212*	965	Freddy Fox	132
1935	210*	942	Harry Wragg	102
1936	177*	1000	Bill Nevett	108
1937	214*	987	Bill Nevett	110
1938	206*	971	Eph Smith	114
1939	155*	726	Bill Nevett	71
1940	68*	344	Harry Wragg	38
1941	22	84	Harry Wragg	71*
1942	67*	311	Eph Smith	52
1943	65*	281	Tommy Carey	44
1944	88*	333	Bill Nevett	37
1945	104*	406	Eph Smith	67
1946	212*	725		
1947	269*	835	Doug Smith	173
1948	224*	808	Edgar Britt	145
1949	261*	779	Doug Smith	137
1950	201*	868	Doug Smith	151
1951	227*	835	Doug Smith	117
1952	231*	806	Doug Smith	97
1953	191*	728	Doug Smith	112
1954	54	275	Doug Smith	129*

* Champion jockey

Tom RICHARDS

Marathon
John Thomas Henry Richards. b. 15 Mar 1910 Upper Cwmbrân, Torfaen. d. 19 Jan 1985 London.

The Olympic marathon silver medallist in 1948, when he came strongly through the field in the latter stages of the race to finish just 16 seconds behind Delfo Cabrera (Arg). He won the Poly marathon in 1945 and 1946, and after 4th at the 1950 Empire Games marathon achieved great success when a veteran, with his first Welsh cross-country title at the age of 41 in 1951 and Welsh marathon titles in 1950, 1952-3 and 1955-6, with a Welsh marathon best of 2:30:40 in 1952. He had started in athletics as a walker and won the Welsh junior title in 1932 and at cross-country ran ten times for Wales in the International Championship 1934-53.

Peter RICHARDSON

Cricket
Peter Edward Richardson. b. 4 Jul 1931 Hereford.

England found the answer to an opening batsman problem with Richardson, who scored 81 and 73 on his Test debut against Australia in 1956 and remained an England regular for the rest of the 1950s. After four series he had scored 1386 runs at 46.20, but after a modest tour to Australia and New Zealand he lost his place in the side. That loss of form came at the end of his career with Worcestershire, whom he captained in 1956-8. His best year until then had been 1953 when he scored 2294 runs. He then played for Kent 1959-65, and returned to form with over 2000 runs in 1961 and 1962 and was recalled for nine Tests in 1961-3.

He was a patient accumulator of runs with nudges and deflections, although strong arms made him capable of hitting hard; he was also a fine fielder at cover point as well as a renowned practical joker. In December 1956 against South Africa at Johannesburg he took 488 minutes to reach his century, then the slowest ever in Tests.

34 Tests 1956-63: 2061 runs at 37.47, 5 100s HS 126; 3 wickets at 16.00, BB 2-10; 6 catches.

First Class 1949-65: 26,055 runs at 34.60, 44 100s HS 185; 11 wickets at 45.36, BB 2-10; 220 catches.

His brother **Dick** (b. 3 Nov 1934) also played for Worcestershire (career record 16,303 runs at 27.40 with 16 centuries) and played once for England in 1957, when the brothers became the first to play for England since the Hearnes in 1892.

T.D. RICHARDSON

Figure Skating
Thomas Dow Richardson. b. 16 Jan 1887
York. d. 7 Jan 1971 London.

Richardso was the foremost British authority on ice skating. A fine all-round sportsman, he won a boxing Blue at Cambridge (featherweight, 1906) and, although he did not have the usual physique of an oarsman, he stroked Thames RC in the Grand Challenge Cup at Henley. In 1923 he was runner-up with his wife (née Mildred Allingham) for the British pairs skating title and they competed at the 1924 Olympic Games. As a competitor, judge, author and journalist he made an immense contribution to British skating and his book *Modern Figure Skating* (1930) provided an unprecedented analysis of technique. In 1958 he overcame many difficulties to found the first Commonwealth Winter Games.

His forceful personality was better understood at home than it was abroad and he was often at odds with the ISU. He was awarded the OBE in 1955.

Tom RICHARDSON

Cricket
Thomas Richardson. b. 11 Aug 1870
Byfleet, Surrey. d. 2 Jul 1912 St Jean
d'Arvey, France.

A splendidly built fast bowler, at his prime in the 1890s Richardson was the world's finest bowler. He made his debut in 1892 and the following year took 174 wickets at 15.40, figures that he improved in 1894 to 196 at 10.33, and in 1895 to 290 at 14.38. That total was the season's record until Tich Freeman took 304 wickets in 1928. Richardson again took over 200 wickets with 246 in 1886 and 273 in 1897, but thereafter although he exceeded 100 wickets in five more seasons, his form began to decline, and eventually increasing weight cost him his county place.

He reached 1000 wickets in first-class cricket in just 174 matches, easily the all-time record. He took five wickets in each of his first six Test innings in England 1893-6.

14 Tests 1893-8: 177 runs at 11.06, HS 25*; 88 wickets at 25.22, BB 8-94; 5 catches.
First-class 1892-1905: 3424 runs at 9.65, HS 69; 2104 wickets at 18.43, BB 10-45; 125 catches.

Ken RICHMOND

Wrestling
Kenneth Alan Richmond. b. 10 Jul 1926
Kensington, London.

Best known as the man who struck the gong in the introduction to films made by the J.Arthur Rank organisation (succeeding 'Bombadier' Billy Wells (qv) in that rôle), Richmond was also Britain's most successful wrestler with a freestyle bronze medal at the second of his four Olympics in 1952 and gold at heavyweight at the 1954 Commonwealth Games, following bronze in 1950.

He began wrestling after returning from an Antarctic whaling expedition in 1945. He also represented Britain at judo in the 1955 European Championships. He became a Jehovah's Witness circuit minister.

Bill RICKABY

Horse Racing
William Anthony Rickaby. b. 15 Jul 1917
Norwich, Norfolk.

A most popular flat race jockey, Rickaby rode his first winner in 1931. His best years came after the war, in which he had risen to the rank of major, with a best total of 83 winners in 1953. He was first jockey to Jack Jarvis (qv) from 1949 to 1956. In 1961 he won the 1000 Guineas and Oaks on *Sweet Solera* and he had a third Classics success with the 2000 Guineas in 1962. He retired after the 1968 season and became assistant stipendiary steward at the Royal Hong Kong Jockey Club, but he was very seriously injured in a car crash in February 1970 and had to return to Newmarket.

His father **Frederick** Lester **Rickaby** (1894-1918) rode five Classics winners and Bill's sister Iris was the mother of Lester Piggott (qv).

Jon RIDGEON

Athletics, Hurdling
Jonathan Peter Ridgeon. b. 14 Feb 1967
Bury St Edmunds, Suffolk.

A brilliantly talented hurdler, Ridgeon's career was ruined by Achilles tendon injuries. He alternated with Colin Jackson (qv) as Britain's top young athlete. In 1985 he beat Jackson to win the European Junior 110m hurdles in a record time of 13.46, was 2nd to Jackson in the World Juniors in 1986, when he was also 5th at the Commonwealth Games, but had a brilliant season in 1987 when he was voted UK Athlete of the Year. He showed smoother hurdling, as well as his accustomed aggression, to set UK records of 13.38 in semi-final and 13.29 in the final of the World Student Games, won the AAA title, and he equalled his UK record to gain the World silver medal. He was 5th in the Olympic final despite a virus infection in 1988, but missed the 1989 outdoor and 1990 seasons when he had operations on both Achilles tendons.

He switched to 400m hurdling with immediate success in 1992, improving from 51.30 on his debut in July to 48.73 in September and was 2nd at the World Cup. Further injury problems brought his career to a premature close.

At 60m hurdles indoors he won silver medals at the 1985 Worlds and 1988 Europeans and had a best time of 7.56 in 1988. He had a record five wins for Cambridge University v Oxford in 1987 and is now working in television on athletics as well as in sports sponsorship. His mother, then Mary Allum, won the 1954 English Schools junior girls 70y hurdles.

Fred RIMELL

Horse Racing
Thomas Frederick Rimell. b. 24 Jun 1913 Newmarket, Suffolk. d. 12 Jul 1981 Upton upon Severn, Worcestershire.

Leading National Hunt trainer in 1950/1, 1960/1, 1968/9, 1969/70, 1975/6, Rimell was the first to win over £1 million in prize money. First apprenticed to his father, Tom, at Kinnersley, Worcestershire, he switched from flat racing, at which he rode his first winner at the age of 12, to the jumps in 1932 and was champion NH jockey four times between 1938/9 and 1945/6. A natural horseman, he brought both power and balance to his steeplechase riding.

He took a trainer's licence in 1945 and, after injury, retired from riding in 1947. His horses won the Grand National four times, the Cheltenham Gold Cup twice and Champion Hurdle twice. After his death, his wife **Mercy** (née Cockburn) carried on training at Kinnersley until her retirement in 1989.

Christy RING (Ireland)

Hurling
Christy Ring. b. 20 Oct 1920 Cloyne, Co. Cork.

Remembered as perhaps the most spectacular performer in the history of hurling, Ring was the second player to be elected to the Hall of Fame in 1971. He was the first man to win eight all-Ireland hurling titles, 1941-4, 1946 and 1952-4 from ten finals with Cork, captaining their team in 1946 and 1953-4. He also won four National League medals with Cork, but among his greatest records is that he played with Munster in a record 22 Railway Cup inter-provincial finals 1942-63 and was on the winning side 18 times. He was voted Hurler of the Year in 1959. In Cork he won a record 11 county senior championship hurling medals with Glen Rovers between 1941 and 1967. He was named as right-half forward on the Team of the Century.

Antony RINGER

Shooting
Thomas Antony Ringer. b. 5 Sep 1966 Norwich.

In 1992 Ringer not only won the individual world long range shooting championship, but also won the Fulton Trophy as top scorer in the team competition. In the latter he achieved a record score of 449.26 out of 450 at 800, 900 and 1000 yards on 20 inch bulls-eyes at all ranges, with no telescopic sights. Three years later, in 1995, he retained both titles. With wins in major competitions all round the world, he has become established in the very highest class. He was a Norfolk Under-21 hockey player before concentrating on shooting, at which he made his GB debut in 1988. He won the Queen's Prize at Bisley in 1992 and at the Commonwealth Games won a pairs silver medal with Glyn Barnett.

Andy RIPLEY

Rugby Union
Andrew George Ripley. b. 1 Dec 1947 Liverpool.

As befits a man who showed his all-round ability by winning the all-sport British Superstars TV competition in 1980, Ripley was a fine basketball player and a useful 400m hurdler for Polytechnic Harriers (best time 53.69). He was an athletic No. 8 for Rosslyn Park and England. He won 24 caps for England 1972-6 and also went on the Lions tour to South Africa in 1974., but did not play in any of the Tests.
He maintained his fitness well, playing top level rugby for many years, so that he was unlucky not to have a longer England career.
He is a graduate of the University of East Anglia and became a chartered accountant.

Frank RISELEY

Tennis
Frank Lorymer Riseley. b. 6 Jul 1877 Clifton, Bristol. d. 6 Feb 1959 Torquay, Devon.

With his West Country partner, Sydney Smith (qv), Riseley formed a doubles pairing which was second only to the legendary Doherty brothers (qv). Riseley and Smith reached the Challenge Round at Wimbledon for five successive years where they met the Dohertys on each occasion, taking the title in 1902 and 1906 and losing to the famous brothers, 1903-05.
With a particularly effective serve and smash Riseley was also a fine singles player, reaching the Wimbledon Challenge Round three times, 1903-4 and 1906, losing to Laurie Doherty on each occasion.

He also won all three titles at the 1906 Irish Championships.
In the 1904 Davis Cup Challenge Round against Belgium he won both his singles and he later captained the Davis Cup team (1922, 1924-5). In 1922, at the age of 44, and 18 years after his last appearance, he was called on to play against Italy and by winning his doubles he maintained his unbeaten Cup record. Two years later he won the doubles with John Wheatley at the first British Hard Court Championships.

Bev RISMAN

Rugby Union and Rugby League
Augustus Beverley Walter Risman. b. 23 Nov 1937 Salford, Gt. Manchester.

The son of league legend Gus Risman (qv), he had a brilliant rugby union career before turning professional. While at Loughborough College and Manchester University he won eight England caps at fly-half or centre and on the 1959 Lions tour of Australia and New Zealand he played at fly-half in four Tests, only missing the other two due to injury.
On switching codes, he started wth Leigh and then won a Challenge Cup winners' medal with Leeds. He won five GB caps at full-back in 1968 and kicked seven goals against New Zealand in his final Test appearance, emulating his father by captaining Britian in the World Cup series. He retired in 1970 after taking an MA degree from Leeds University and became a schoolmaster, briefly serving as team manager of London Crusaders in 1988.

Gus RISMAN

Rugby League
Augustus John Risman. b. 21 Mar 1911 Barry, Vale of Glamorgan. d. 17 Oct 1994 Cumbria.

Equally talented as a centre or full back, Risman's career spanned 27 seasons and included tours of Australia in 1932, 1936 and, as captain, in 1946. He won 17 caps between 1932 and 1946, the longest international career of any Great Britain rugby league player, and was captain nine times.

He signed for Salford shortly before his 18th birthday in 1929 and led them to victory in the 1938 Challenge Cup. He remained with the club until 1946 when he moved to Workington Town as player-manager.

After winning the Championship in 1951, Workington won the 1952 Challenge Cup, so after a 14-year interval the 41 year-old had his second Cup winner's medal and the distinction of being the oldest player ever to appear in a Cup Final. His career ended at Batley in 1954 by which time he had amassed 4050 points, including 1677 goals and 232 tries in 873 matches, the third highest ever points total. He was, however, as great a creator of tries as a scorer. He also captained Wales in five wartime rugby union internationals.

His son **Bev** (qv) was also a double international and his younger son **John** won three international caps at rugby league for Wales in 1978-9.

Margaret RITCHIE

Athletics, Discus
Margaret Elizabeth Ritchie. b. 6 Jul 1952 Kirkcaldy, Fife.

Ritchie, who competed for Edinburgh Southern Harriers, set ten UK, including five Commonwealth, discus records from 58.36m in 1977 to 67.48 in 1981; she also set six UK, and one Commonwealth (unratified), shot records from 16.40m in 1978 to 18.99 in 1983.

Her best distances came in the USA, where she studied at the University of Arizona and now coaches, winning NCAA shot and discus titles in 1982. She competed at three Commonwealth Games, placing 6th in 1974 and 4th in 1978 at the discus before winning the title in 1982. At the Olympics she was 9th in 1980 and 5th in her final season of 1984. She was UK discus champion 1977-80; and WAAA 1975, 1977 and 1981, with Scottish titles at shot 1978-9 and 1982 and discus 1972, 1975-9 and 1982.

She made 39 international appearances for Britain from 1973 to 1984.

Herbie ROBERTS

Football
Herbert Roberts. b. 19 Feb 1905 Oswestry, Shropshire. d. 19 Jun 1944.

Known as 'Policeman' Roberts because of his wholly defensive play at centre-half, he adopted this role to counter the new off-side law on instructions from his manager Herbert Chapman (qv). Although unattractive to the spectators, this tactic proved effective and Roberts made a major contribution to Arsenal's four League Championships, 1931 and 1933-5, and their FA Cup victory in 1936. Chapman's tactical innovation was not adopted by England and Roberts was capped just once, against Scotland in 1931. He retired due to injury in the 1937/8 season and died from erysipelas while on active service with the Royal Fusiliers.

John ROBERTS

Billiards
W. John Roberts Jnr. b. Aug 1847 Ardwick, Manchester. d. Dec 1919.

The first great billiards player, Roberts made a record seven successful defences of the world title he first won in 1870. Initially raised in Lancashire, he moved to London in 1866 when his father took a saloon at Leicester Square. At the first World Billiards Championship in February 1870, William Cook beat John Roberts Snr, but within weeks John Roberts Jnr avenged his father's defeat by taking the title from Cook, an odds-on favourite. In the early days, the championship was decided by challenge matches and Roberts played in 11 of these, winning eight and losing three. After beating Joseph Bennett in June 1885 he declined to make any further defences, mainly owing to a dispute over the rules, but he remained supreme for at least another decade.

During his peak years the title sometimes passed to lesser players, as Roberts preferred to tour the world rather than play in the Championships. He visited Australia three times and went twice to New Zealand and America and once to South Africa, but 11 times to India for supervision of the billiard-table factory he owned in Calcutta, and due to his appointment as court billiards player to the Maharajah of Jaipur. This involved an annual visit of one month to the Palace and carried a salary of £500 a year.

An arrogant, self-assured and wealthy man, he finally retired from competitive play in 1906 when problems with his eyesight worsened, but he was one of the greatest sporting heroes of his time and a great entertainer.

Philippa ROBERTS

Water Skiing
(Dr) Philippa Mary Elizabeth Roberts. b. 11 Apr 1960 Manchester.

Roberts has won 44 senior national titles from her first at slalom in 1974 to 1995, including a record 12 overall British water-skiing titles, 1977, 1982, 1985-92 and 1994-5. She set a personal best jump at 41.7m in winning the 1994 British title.

At European championships she was junior champion 1974-8 and won the overall gold in 1986 and 1990 with silver in 1993 and individual titles at jump 1985 and slalom 1991.

Other gold medals include the European Masters jump 1990, slalom 1991-2, overall 1992; World Games slalom 1989, 1993. She was awarded the MBE in 1993.

Allan ROBERTSON

Golf
Allan Robertson. b. 1815 St Andrews, Fife. d. Sep 1859.

The greatest player of the pre-tournament and featherie era, Robertson died two years before the first real championship, the British Open, was started. The tournament was actually begun to settle the argument of who was the best player in the world, an argument which had a pat answer while Robertson was alive - it was Robertson. It was said he never lost an individual stakes match. He never faced the other great player of that era, Old Tom Morris (qv), in an individual match, though it is recorded that they were unbeaten as a team. They later had a parting

of the ways when Morris began making gutta percha balls, which Robertson saw as a threat to his trade of making featheries. Robertson's fame is also based on his great feat of once going round St Andrews in 147 strokes for 36 holes.

Belle ROBERTSON

Golf
Isabella Robertson. b. 11 Apr 1936 Southend, Argyll and Bute. née McCorkindale.

Robertson was the British Ladies' Open Amateur champion of 1981, when at 45 she became the oldest ever champion. She had been runner-up in 1959, 1965 and 1970 and was the British amateur stroke-play champion of 1971, 1972 and 1985. She made the last of seven Curtis Cup appearances from 1960 in 1986, to become at 50, the oldest ever player in the event; her record was 5 wins, 12 losses and 7 halves.

She was Scottish Ladies' champion in 1965-6, 1971-2, 1978 and 1980, was named as Scottish Sportswoman of the Year four times, and was awarded the MBE in 1973.

Keith ROBERTSON

Rugby Union
Keith William Robertson. b. 5 Dec 1954 Hawick, Borders.

Capped 20 times as a centre and 24 times on the wing Robertson's international career with Scotland spanned 11 seasons 1978-89. He scored eight international tries and was a member of Scotland's 1984 Grand Slam team and also played in the inaugural World Cup in 1987. He was 34 when he won his last cap; few backs have continued to play internationally at that age.

Walter ROBINS

Cricket
Robert Walter Vivian Robins. b. 3 Jun 1906 Stafford. d. 12 Dec 1968 Marylebone, London.

An energetic cricketer, Robins captained Middlesex from 1935-8 and in 1946, 1947, when they won the County Championship, and 1950, as permitted by his business interests. He was a Test selector in 1946-8 and again, as chairman, 1962-4 and managed England on the 1959/60 tour to West Indies.

Although at times erratic he spun his leg breaks and googlies fiercely and was a fast-scoring batsman. He achieved the double with 1134 runs and 162 wickets in 1929, in which year he made his Test debut, and on three more occasions exceeded 1000 runs in a season. He captained England against New Zealand in 1937. Much his best Test bowling was his 6-32 against the West Indies at Lord's in 1933. He won his Blue at Cambridge each year 1926-8. At soccer he played inside-left for Cambridge, Corinthians and Nottingham Forest.

19 Tests 1929-37: 612 runs at 26.60, 1 100 HS 108; 64 wickets at 27.46, BB 6-32; 12 catches.

First-class 1926-51: 13,884 runs at 26.39, 11 100s HS 140; 969 wickets at 23.30, BB 8-69; 221 catches.

Brian ROBINSON

Cycling
Brian Robinson. b. 3 Nov 1930 Mirfield, West Yorkshire.

British hill climb champion in 1952, Robinson competed in the Olympic road race that year and later became the first Briton to compete sucessfully in the classic road races on the Continent. He became a full-time professional in 1954 and in his first race won a stage of the Tour of Europe. In 1955, although lacking team support, he became the first Briton to finish the Tour de France and in 1959 the first to win a stage when he took the 20th by a massive 20 minutes, then the largest winning margin in a postwar race. In all he rode in the Tour seven times 1955-61; his best placing was 14th in 1956 and he failed to finish only twice. His most notable victory on the Continent came in the mountainous Dauphine Libéré in 1961.

Eleanor ROBINSON – see ADAMS

Jem ROBINSON

Horse Racing
James Robinson. b. 1793 Newmarket. d. 15 Jan 1973 Newmarket.

Robinson's total of 24 Classics winners, between 1817 and 1848, is still the third highest ever for a jockey, including a record 9 in the 2000 Guineas and the former record of 6 Derbys. He was apprenticed to Robert Robson (qv), and learned much from champion jockey Frank Buckle (qv). A ruthless rider, his career ended with a bad fall in 1852, which left him with a permanent limp. Renowned during his career for high living in London out of season, his extravagance left him destitute in his later years.

Val ROBINSON

Hockey
Valerie Robinson. née Walsh,

Robinson played for England from 1963 to1984, captain in 1972, and won a record 149 caps, scoring 38 goals. She also scored 8 goals in 21 appearances for Britain 1978-81 and was awarded the OBE. She won the televised women's Superstars competition in 1978.

Bobby ROBSON

Football
Robert William Robson. b. 18 Feb 1933 Langley Park, Co. Durham.

Having played 20 times for England as an inside-forward 1957-62, later becoming a right-half, he managed the England football team 1982-90. In his Football League career he scored 133 goals in 584 games for Fulham 1950-6 and 1962-7, and West Bromwich Albion 1956-62. In 1968 he played for the Vancouver Whitecaps, before managing Fulham, November 1968 to January 1969, and Ipswich Town 1969-82. After his career as England manager, which culminated in incessant hounding by the tabloid press, he managed the Dutch team PSV Eindhoven, winning two successive Dutch championhips, and then Sporting Lisbon and Porto in Portugal. Sporting Lisbon sacked him in mid season when they were top of the Portuguese league, but his Porto then beat them in the Cup Final in 1994 and went on to win the league in 1994/5. He was awarded the CBE in 1991.

Bryan ROBSON

Football
Bryan Robson. b. 11 Jan 1957 Chester-le-Street, Co. Durham.

After being on the books of West Bromwich Albion as a schoolboy and an apprentice, he signed professional forms in 1974. In 1981 he moved to Manchester United for the then record British fee of £1.5 million and while with United he became the first captain to lead a team to three victories in the FA Cup (1983, 1985, 1990). Although he missed many games, he helped United to their first League title in 26 years in 1992/3 and was again a member of the squad of their double winning team in 1993/4. Then, after 39 goals in 197 League appearances for Hartlepool and 74 in 345 for Manchester United, he moved to become player-manager of Middlesbrough.

After a fine performance in the 1982 World Cup he was forced out of the next two competitions (1986, 1990) because of injury. He was troubled by many injuries throughout his career but he still won 90 caps (with 26 goals) 1980-91, and took over the captaincy of England and Manchester United from Ray Wilkins (qv) in 1982. He is recognised as one of the most complete midfield players ever to represent England. He was awarded the OBE in 1990.

His younger brother Gary (b. 6 Jul 1965) has played for West Bromwich Albion.

Robert ROBSON

Horse Racing
Robert Robson b. 1765. d. 2 Apr 1838 Newmarket.

Robson set a record, later surpassed by John Scott (qv), by training the winners of 34 English Classicss between 1793 and 1827, including records for the Oaks (12), 1000 Guineas (9) and Derby (7), many for

the 3rd and 4th Dukes of Grafton. He was known as 'The Emperor of Trainers'. He started as private trainer at Lewes, East Sussex to Sir Ferdinand Poole in 1793, when he achieved his first Classics success, the Derby with *Waxy*, and then moved to Newmarket.

Stephen ROCHE (Ireland)

Cycling
Stephen Roche. b. 20 Nov 1959 Dublin.

Roche had a year in 1987 that has been matched by only one rider ever - the great Eddy Merckx. He won both the Tour de France and Giro d'Italia and also won the rainbow jersey as world road champion and the Super Prestige Pernod Trophy for the cyclist of the year. His Tour de France win was the stuff of high drama. In 2nd place entering the Alps, with Pedro Delgado (Spa) close in 3rd, Roche fell off the pace as Delgado attacked up the Villard de Lans, took over the race, and was the leader on the road, as he opened up a huge margin. But Roche countered and closed to within four seconds at the finish. It was an almost superhuman effort which earned him the yellow jersey but also put him in hospital overnight. However, he recovered enough to race the next day and keep the yellow jersey into Paris.

Roche's career was hampered by knee problems both before 1987 and in the ensuing years.

Starting his career with the Orwell Wheelers in Dublin, Roche was 45th in the Olympic road race in 1980 and turned pro in 1981, winning the Paris-Nice and the Tour of Corsica in his first season. He was 3rd in the world pro road race in 1983 and in the Tour de France in 1985. Other major wins included the Criterium International in 1985 and 1991. In his last season as a pro, 1993, he was 13th in the Tour de France.

Budge ROGERS

Rugby Union
Derek Prior Rogers. b. 20 Jun 1939 Bedford.

Rogers played in 34 internationals between 1961 and 1969, by when he was England's most acpped player, He captained England seven times, and also the British Lions in two Tests in South Africa in 1962.

His foraging, fast-breaking play from the open side of the scrum is said to have been one of the influences that led to a change in the laws which restricted the activities of roving wing-forwards. He remained loyal to the Bedford club throughout his career and, after retiring, served England as a coach and a selector. He was awarded the OBE for his services to the game.

Iris ROGERS

Badminton
Iris Lilian Rogers b. 23 Feb 1930. née Cooley.

Rogers was a back-court player whose partnership with June Timperley brought them three All-England doubles titles, 1953, 1955 and 1959. She also won the All-England mixed doubles in 1954. Her 52 caps for England (1952-69) was then a record for a lady international from any country.

At the 1966 Commonwealth Games she won a silver medal with Angela Bairstow for women's doubles.

John ROGERS

Rugby League
John Henry Rogers. b. c.1893, d. 26 Jul 1958.

Rogers was a small, tough Welshman, who first saw a Rugby League game when he played in a trial match in 1913, after which he was immediately signed by Huddersfield.

He toured Australia in 1914 and 1920 but had the misfortune to fracture his leg in New Zealand on the second tour. He made a complete recovery and played in all three Tests when the Australians visited Britain in 1921/2. After playing in a total of seven Test matches, he was transferred to Wakefield Trinity in 1925.

David ROLLO

Rugby Union
David Miller Durie Rollo. b. 7 Jul 1934.

A tough tight-head prop, Rollo had few equals in this combative position. He only took up rugby as an 18-year-old having been captain of soccer at school, but with 40 caps 1959-68 he equalled Hugh McLeod's (qv) record as the most capped Scottish player of all time. He toured South Africa with the British Isles in 1965 but failed to win a Test place as the Lions fielded an unchanged front-row of Syd Millar (qv), Bryn Meredith (qv) and Kingsley Jones throughout the series.

A Fife farmer, he was the first player to be capped from the Howe of Fife club.

Chloe RONALDSON

Roller skating
Chloe Ronaldson. b. 30 Nov 1939 Epping, Essex.

Having started roller skating at the age of 12, Ronaldson won a record 54 British speed skating titles, 40 individual and 14 ladies' team, from 1958 to 1985. She represented Britain for 20 years, excelling particularly as a sprinter, and in her second world championships in 1962 she won a silver medal, adding a team gold in 1967. In 1969 she set six British records, some of which remain unsurpassed, and in 1970 won the World Cup 500m. She became chairman of the Roller Speed Committee of the NSA and has been British team manager for many years. She now works as a supervisor for Securicor Omega Express.

Herbert ROPER BARRETT – see Barrett

Dorothy ROUND

Tennis
Dorothy Edith Round. b. 13 Jul 1909 Dudley. d. 12 Nov 1982 Kidderminster, Worcestershire. Later Mrs Little.

Round was the outstanding British player of the 1930s. After being runner-up to Helen Wills Moody (USA) at Wimbledon in 1933 she beat Helen Jacobs in the final the following year, when with Fred Perry (qv) winning the men's title they completed the first British 'double' in the Wimbledon singles since 1909. In 1935 she became the first overseas player to win the Australian women's title, but although the top seed, she was eliminated in the quarter-finals at Wimbledon in both 1935 and 1936, before regaining her title in 1937. After marrying Dr Douglas Little later in 1937 she did not defend her title in 1938 and made her last Wimbledon appearance in 1939 when she was eliminated in the fourth round.

She won the Wimbledon mixed doubles with the Japanese Davis Cup captain, Ryuki Miki, in 1934 and with Fred Perry in 1935 and 1936.

She had a surprisingly poor Wightman Cup record, winning only 4 of her 11 singles and losing both doubles. An unspectacular player, her strength was her forehand drive which she supplemented with a shrewd drop-shot. A dedicated Sunday School teacher, she refused to play on Sundays, which on one occasion posed difficulties for the authorities at the French Championships.

Stanley ROUS

Football
(Sir) Stanley Ford Rous. b. 25 Apr 1895 Mutford, Lowestoft, Suffolk. d. 18 Jul 1986 Westminster, London.

One of the most influential figures in the history of football, Rous trained as a teacher at St Luke's College, Exeter, where he was captain of soccer and tennis. After war service he accepted his rather modest playing abilities and took up refereeing, taking charge of 34 international matches throughout Europe from 1920 to 1934, when he left his teaching job to become secretary of the Football Association. He remained in that job until 1961 when he was appointed president of FIFA, a position he held until his retirement in 1974. He was one of the founders of the Central Council for Physical Recreation (CCPR) and a member of many sporting bodies, all of whom benefited immensely from his forward thinking and planning talents. He was awarded the CBE in 1943 and knighted in 1949.

Arthur ROWE

Athletics, Shot
Arthur Rowe. b. 17 Aug 1937 Barnsley, South Yorkshire.

Commonwealth and European shot champion in 1958, Rowe was England's first truly world-class thrower. He set 15 British records, from 16.94m in 1958 to 19.56 in 1961; five of these were also European records, and he was AAA champion each year 1957-61.

Sadly he ended his amateur athletics career on the edge of greatness at the age of 25 when he signed to play professional rugby league for Oldham. Little came of that, but he enjoyed much success for many years on the Scottish Highland Games circuit as a thrower, being proclaimed world caber-tossing champion in 1970. A member of Doncaster Plant Works AC, he had been a blacksmith.

Diana ROWE

Table Tennis
Diana Rowe. b. 14 Apr 1933 Marylebone, London. Later Mrs Schöler.

The left-handed Diana and her right-handed identical twin, Rosalind, formed a brilliant partnership. Together they won the world doubles in 1951 and 1954 and were runners-up three times, in 1952-3 and 1955. They also won six consecutive English Open doubles 1950-5, after which the partnership broke up following Rosalind's marriage.

Diana, who was also runner-up with Johnny Leach for the world mixed doubles title in 1952 and for the women's doubles in 1957 with Ann Haydon and 1963 with Mary Shannon, continued tournament play and won six more English women's doubles titles with three different partners. She also won the singles for the first time in 1962 and won the mixed doubles four times.

She won European team titles in 1958 and 1964 and women's doubles titles with Shannon in 1962 and 1964, and was again a finalist in 1970. She married the West

German champion Eberhard Schöler in 1966 and reached the quarter-finals of the world mixed doubles with him in 1971.

Rosalind ROWE

Table Tennis
Rosalind Rowe. b. 14 Apr 1933
Marylebone, London. Later Mrs Cornett.

An orthodox player who shared in the early successes of her twin sister, Diana (qv), Rosalind was the English singles champion in 1953 and 1955 and retired from championship play following her marriage in October 1955 to Jack Cornett, a ship's doctor whom she had met two years earlier when the twins travelled by sea to play in New Zealand.

She also won the English Open mixed doubles with Viktor Barna in 1953.

Arthur ROWLEY and Jack

Football
George Arthur Rowley. b. 21 Apr 1926
Wolverhampton.

John Frederick Rowley. b. 7 Oct 1920
Wolverhampton.

The Rowley brothers gave exceptional service to their respective clubs and were both noted for their goal scoring abilities, particularly with their left feet.

The elder brother, **Jack,** had the more distinguished career. After being on Wolverhampton's books, he played for Bournemouth before signing for Manchester United in 1937. He played in the team which won the FA Cup in 1948 and the League Championship in 1952. In only six matches for England 1948-9 he played in every position in the forward line except outside-right and scored four of his six goals in one match, against Northern Ireland in 1949.

He had also played in a wartime international for England in 1944. After finally leaving Manchester United, having scored 208 goals in 422 games for them, he played 1955-7 for Plymouth Argyle, continuing as manager for three years. His subsequent managerial appointments at

Oldham Athletic, Wrexham and Bradford were interrupted by a spell as coach with Ajax (Amsterdam). He returned to Oldham as manager in 1968 but finally retired after little more than a year.

Unlike his brother, **Arthur** Rowley never won a full international cap but he played for England 'B' and for the Football League. After spells with West Bromwich Albion and Fulham he moved to Leicester City in 1950 and spent eight seasons there before moving to Shrewsbury Town where he ended his playing career in 1964. He made a total of 619 League appearances for his four clubs and his aggregate of 434 goals still stands as a Football League record. He also scored 32 goals in the FA Cup and one for England 'B'. He scored 20 Football League goals or more in a record 13 seasons to 1962/3.

Ian RUSH

Football
Ian James Rush. b. 20 Oct 1961 St Asaph, Denbighshire.

One of the most dangerous strikers of recent years, Rush was one of six brothers; the others all played for Flint Town in the Clwyd League. After winning Welsh international honours at Schoolboy, Youth and Under-21 level, he made his debut in a full international at the age of 18 in May 1980 and later that month he was transferred for £300,000 to Liverpool from Chester City. To April 1995 he has scored 28 goals in 70 internationals.

He was a vital member of the superb Liverpool teams which won the European Cup 1984, FA Cup 1986, 1989 and 1992, Football League Cup 1981-4 and 1995, and the League Championship 1982-4, 1986 and 1990. Rush missed Liverpool's League Championship success of 1988 as he spent that season with Juventus in Italy, but he soon returned and in 601 appearances for Liverpool to 3 December 1994 he scored 330 goals. By March 1995 he had scored 41 goals in the FA Cup, 3 for Chester City and 38 for Liverpool, the second equal highest total ever and his total of five Football League Cup winner's medals is a record.

He won both the Football Writers' and PFA Footballer of the Year award in 1984, having been PFA Young Footballer of the Year in 1983.

Jack RUSSELL

Cricket
Robert Charles 'Jack' Russell. b. 15 Aug 1963 Stroud, Gloucestershire

After some years of being regarded as a contender for the title of England's best wicket-keeper, Jack Russell made his Test debut at the age of 25 against Sri Lanka and came within six runs of scoring a maiden first-class century. That was followed by a great year in 1989, when he played in all six Tests against Australia, and remarkably, for a man to whom others had been preferred due to their better batting, scored 314 runs at 39.25 in the series, including that maiden century, 128* at Old Trafford. His keeping was such that he was regarded as the best in the world. Alec Stewart (qv), a capable keeper, not as good as Russell but a world-class batsman, was preferred in 1993 and although Russell came back in 1994 against the West Indies his keeping was not as immaculate as usual, and Steve Rhodes took over in the England team

Russell joined his father in playing for Stroud CC before taking eight dismissals on his first-class debut for Gloucestershire at the age of 17. A year later, in 1982, he played for Young England.

He was appointed Gloucestershire captain for 1995. He is a very talented artist, with exhibitions of his work attracting much interest.

36 Tests 1988-94: 1255 runs at 26.70, 1 100, HS 128*; 90 catches, 8 stumpings.

26 One-day Ints 1987-91: 261 runs at 20.07, HS 50; 26 catches, 5 stumpings.

First-class 1981-94: 9469 runs at 28.01, 4 100s, HS 128*; 1 wicket; 701 catches, 94 stumpings.

Mary RUSSELL-VICK

Hockey
Mary Russell-Vick. b. July 1922. née de Putron.

Russell-Vick scored more than 70 goals in 30 England appearances 1947-53, only failing to score in one match. She scored four goals on her debut against Wales in 1947 and six in a 13-1 win over the same opponents in 1949. She was a member of the team that played in the first women's hockey international held at Wembley, scoring three goals against Ireland in 1951. In her final year as an international, 1953, she scored 33 goals in 12 internationals. On the England tour to the USA in 1947 the team's record was: goals against 5, goals for 208, of which Russell-Vick scored 79.

John RUTHERFORD

Rugby Union
John Young Rutherford. b. 4 Oct 1955 Selkirk, Borders.

Retiring in 1987 after 42 international appearances, Rutherford was Scotland's most capped fly-half. He partnered scrum-half Roy Laidlaw (qv) In 35 of these matches, which was a world record for an international half-back pairing. Once Rutherford had made his debut against Wales in 1979, he was never dropped by Scotland, although he missed several matches due to injury

On the British Lions tour of New Zealand in 1983 he was second choice to Ollie Campbell (qv) for the fly-half position but played at centre in the third Test and scored one of the Lions' two tries. He scored 12 dropped goals in internationals.

Ian ST JOHN

Football
Ian St John. b. 7 Jun 1938 Motherwell.

Tiny as the sum might appear now, the £35,000 that Liverpool paid Motherwell for Ian St John in 1961 was then the club record, but certainly represented a bargain. Having scored 79 goals in 113 league games for Motherwell, St John maintained a high striking rate in his early years for Liverpool, with 18, 19, and 21 league goals in his first three seasons, but he moved back from his centre-forward role to control the midfield.

An indispensable member of Bill Shankly's team until 1971, he helped Liverpool to win the Second Division in 1963 and the League in 1964 and 1966, with his great header late in extra time of the 1965 FA Cup Final took the Cup to Anfield for the first time. He played in 21 internationals for Scotland 1959-64, scoring 9 goals.

In 1970 he reached the finals of a BBC TV competition to find an extra commentator for the World Cup finals in Mexico and he has gone on to be a leading football pundit on ITV, particularly well known for the long-running Saint and Greavsie show with Jimmy Greaves (qv).

Roy SALVADORI

Motor Racing
Roy Francesco Salvadori. b. 12 May 1922 Dovercourt, Essex.

Salvadori won the Le Mans 24-hour race, the climax of a successful era driving Aston Martin sports cars, with Carroll Shelby (USA) in 1959, and was 3rd at Le Mans with Jim Clark (qv) in 1960.

Having started racing in 1946, a Londoner, born of Italian parents, he was very popular on British tracks in the 1950s and a fine all-round driver. In 47 Formula One Grand Prix starts 1952-62 he scored 19 points; his best year being 1958 when he was 4th in the drivers' world championship. Driving for Cooper he had his best ever results with 2nd in the German and 3rd in the British Grand Prix. He retired from racing in 1965 and managed the Cooper team in 1966-7 before moving to live in Monaco.

Tessa SANDERSON

Athletics
Theresa Ione Sanderson. b. 14 Mar 1956 St Elizabeth, Jamaica.

The Olympic javelin champion in 1984, Sanderson is the only British athlete to compete at five Olympic Games from her 10th place in 1976 to 4th in 1992. Other highlights of a 20-year international career include three Commonwealth titles, 1978, 1986 and 1990 and, after five top-three placings, a win in her sixth European Cup

in 1991, with a win in the 1992 World Cup in her last competition. She was 4th in the World Championships in 1983 and 1987 and won the European silver in 1978. She won the UK title in 1977 and 1978 and nine WAAA titles, 1975-7, 1979-80, 1985, 1989-90, 1992.

She started her senior international career at the Commonwealth Games (5th) and Europeans (13th) in 1974, and set the first of her ten UK records at the javelin with 56.14m in 1976, taking the record to 73.58 in 1983. The last five were also Commonwealth records, as were her heptathlon scores of 5857 and 6125 points in 1981. In all she made 57 international appearances for Britain 1974-92. She had a great rivalry with Fatima Whitbread (qv), and although Whitbread was superior in the period 1984-7, overall Sanderson had a 27-18 advantage in clashes between them 1977-88. She was awarded the MBE in 1985, and became a TV presenter with Sky News.

Cecil SANDFORD

Motorcycling
Cecil C Sandford. b. 1928 Gloucestershire.

Sandford was the first British rider to win world titles at 125cc, which he did in the inaugural season of that championship in 1952, also gaining MV its first world title, and at 250cc, riding for Mondial in 1957. In each of those years he won the lightweight TT races on the Isle of Man. He was also 2nd in the World Championship at 125cc in 1953 and 3rd at 250cc in 1955. When Mondial pulled out of road racing after the 1957 victories he retired to concentrate on his father-in-law's motor business in Shipston-on-Stour.

He had begun his racing career on grass tracks in 1947, progressing to road racing after a couple of years.

Andrew SANDHAM

Cricket
Andrew Sandham. b. 6 Jul 1890 Streatham, London. d. 20 Apr 1982 Westminster, London.

Sandham was a top-class opening bats-man, forging a great partnership with Jack Hobbs (qv), with whom he shared 66 cen-tury partnerships, mostly for Surrey. But with Herbert Sutcliffe (qv) partnering Hobbs for England, Sandham did not get many Test opportunities. However he scored the first Test treble century, 325 v West Indies at Kingston in 1930. This was in his last Test match and he also scored a century in his last match for Surrey, against Sussex at Hove in 1937.

A small man, he was a fine hooker and cutter, and was also a splendid outfielder. He scored over 1000 runs in 18 successive seasons 1920-37, with eight years over 2000 (1921, 1924-5 and 1927-31) and bests of 2565 at 51.30 in 1929 and 2532 at 58.88 in 1928. He also scored over 1000 runs on two overseas tours.

He coached at The Oval 1946-58 and was Surrey scorer for a further 12 years.

14 Tests 1921-30: 878 runs at 38.17, 2 100s HS 325; 4 catches.

First-class 1911-37: 41,284 runs at 44.83, 107 100s HS 325; 18 wickets at 31.11, BB 3-27; 158 catches.

Mike SANGSTER

Tennis
Michael John Sangster. b. 11 Sep 1940 Torquay, Devon. d. 30 Apr 1985 Torquay.

Noted for his big serve, Sangster was the leading British player of the 1960s, reach-ing the closing stages at all the 'majors'. He was a semi-finalist in the singles at Wimbledon and the US championships in 1961, when he also reached the Australian quarter-finals. He was also a semi-finalist at the French Open in 1963 and again reached the Australian quarter-finals in 1964. He won the British Covered Court singles in 1964 and doubles with Bobby Wilson (qv) in 1960. His best perfor-mances in the doubles came in 1964 when he finished as runner-up in the men's at the US Championships and the mixed at the Australian.

Between 1960 and 1968 he played a British record 65 Davis Cup rubbers (26 ties) (29/48 singles, 14/17 doubles).

Kenny SANSOM

Football
Kenneth Graham Sansom. b. 26 Sep 1958 Camberwell, London.

A left-back with Crystal Palace and Arsenal, Sansom won 86 England caps between 1979 and 1988. He signed as a professional for Palace in 1975, making his Football League debut at 16, and after helping them win promotion to the First Division in 1979 he moved to Arsenal the following year and won a winners' medal in the League Cup in 1987. After nine sea-sons with Arsenal he went to Newcastle United in 1988 and then played for Queen's Park Rangers, Coventry City, Everton and Brentford. He was noted for his exceptionally long throw in and good passing ability.

Dean SAUNDERS

Football
Dean Nicholas Saunders. b. 21 Jun 1964 Swansea.

A powerful striker, Saunders has scored 16 goals in 48 internationals for Wales from 1986 to April 1995. Having joined Swansea City as an apprentice, he has been much travelled, playing successively for Swansea, Cardiff (on loan), Brighton, Oxford, Derby County, Liverpool and Aston Villa. He gained an FA Cup winner's medal with Liverpool in 1992 and helped Villa to win the Coca Cola Cup in 1994. In July 1995 he signed for the Turkish club, Galatasaray.

His father **Roy** (b. 4 Sep 1930) played for Liverpool and Swansea City 1952-63.

Ron SAUNDERS

Football
Ronald Saunders. b. 6 Nov 1932 Birkenhead, Merseyside.

Before joining Portsmouth in 1958, Saunders played for Everton, non-league Tonbridge and Gillingham. After a number of successful years with the Hampshire club he closed his playing career with Watford and Charlton Athletic. A solidly built centre-forward, he scored 130 goals in 234 appearances for Portsmouth but never added a full England cap to those he won at Youth level.

On leaving Charlton in 1966 he became a successful manager, firstly with Yeovil Town and Oxford United, before taking over at Norwich City 1969-73, leading them into the First Division for the first time in their history in 1972. He was at Manchester City 1973-4 and then had a successful eight years at Aston Villa 1974-82, consolidating his managerial reputation by taking them back into the First Division, winning the League Cup in 1975 and 1977 and the League Championship for the first time in 71 years in 1981.

He then completed a tour of the big Birmingham clubs, by managing Birmingham City 1982-6 and West Bromwich Albion 1986-7.

Vivien SAUNDERS

Golf
Vivien Inez Saunders. b. 24 Nov 1946 Sutton, Surrey.

Saunders was the British Ladies' Open champion of 1977 and runner-up in the British Ladies' Amateur in 1966. She played in the Curtis Cup in 1968 and turned professional soon afterwards, becoming the first European to qualify for the LPGA tour in the USA in 1969. She helped to found the WPGA and was its Chairman 1978/9. As coach and journalist she wrote instructional books on golf. She graduated in psychology from Bedford College, University of London and qualified as a solicitor in 1981.

David SAVAGE

Hockey
David Austin Savage. b. 15 Dec 1940 St Asaph, Denbighshire.

A goalkeeper with Oxton HC, Savage won a record 100 international caps for Wales 1962-81. He also played 20 times for Great Britain 1966-72, including the 1972 Olympic Games. Educated at Holywell GS and the University College of North Wales he is now a schoolteacher.

Sammy SAVILLE

Hockey
Stanley Herbert Saville. b. 21 Nov 1889 Tottenham, London. 22 Feb 1966 Eastbourne, East Sussex.

With 37 caps at inside-right between 1913 and 1930, Saville held the record as England's most capped player until 1958, a remarkable achievement as he played in an era when opportunities for international honours were far less frequent than they were in the postwar years.

He captained England from 1926-30 and scored 34 international goals. Educated at Marlborough and Trinity College, Cambridge he won his Blue at both hockey and cricket for four years 1911-14. At cricket he played 50 first class-matches for Middlesex 1910-28 as a middle order batsman scoring 2784 runs at an average of 21.75 with a highest score of 141*.

He served as President of the Hockey Association from 1951-66 and was awarded the OBE for his services to the game.

Garry SCHOFIELD

Rugby League
Garry Edward Schofield. b. 1 Jul 1965 Leeds.

An outstanding junior with Hunslet Parkside, Schofield captained the Great Britain amateur youth team to New Zealand in 1983 and signed for Hull that year. In his first season as a professional he topped the League scoring list with 38 tries, and at the age of 18 years 10 months in 1984 he was selected to go to Australia to become the youngest-ever member of a Great Britain touring party. His brilliant play in the centre brought him a host of scoring records and his four tries against the formidable New Zealanders in 1985 remains one of his finest performances.

Financial difficulties at Hull caused the club to sell many of their leading players in 1987/8 and Schofield commanded the then record transfer fee of £155,000 when he moved to Leeds after scoring 107 tries in 117 appearances for Hull. He won the Man of Steel award as the rugby league personality of the year in 1991. In 1994 he was awarded the OBE and in November he equalled Mick Sullivan's record of 46 caps for Great Britain; only Sullivan (qv) has bettered his total of 31 international tries. He was an inspiring captain of the Great Britain team.

Ken SCOTLAND

Rugby Union
Kenneth James Forbes Scotland. b. 29 Aug 1936 Edinburgh.

As an attacking full-back Scotland was years ahead of his time and his running out of defence brought a new dimension to the game. His talents were such that he was also capped by Scotland as a fly-half, played in a Test for the 1959 British Lions as a centre and also appeared at scrum-half for the Lions in two provincial matches. To these astonishing abilities as running back, he added a talent as a line, drop and place kicker, all which made him the outstanding Sevens player of his time.

With the 1959 Lions in Australia and New Zealand he played in five of the six Tests and the discerning New Zealanders voted him one of the five Players of the Year.

His first cap for Scotland came as a result of some fine performances for the army while he was a National Serviceman and he celebrated his international debut in 1957 with a penalty and a dropped goal against France in Paris to score all Scotland's points in their 6-0 victory. After the army, he went up to Cambridge University (Blue 1958-60) and then had a spell with Leicester before returning to Edinburgh and Heriot's FP.

He closed his international career in 1965 having equalled the Scottish record of winning 25 caps in that position. Additionally he won two caps as a fly-half. He also played cricket for Scotland.

Elisha SCOTT

Football
Elisha Scott. b. 24 Aug 1894 Belfast. d. 16 May 1959 Belfast.

Scott was possibly the greatest goalkeeper of his era. After making his debut for Liverpool in 1913 he went on to make 430 appearances for the club, which stood as a record for almost a quarter of a century. His reflex saves were a significant factor in Liverpool winning the League Championship in 1921 and 1922. At a time when Northern Ireland only played the other Home Countries he won 31 caps between 1920 and 1936 and on his last international appearance he was approaching his 42nd birthday. In 1934 he left Liverpool to become player-manger of Belfast Celtic. He retired as a player in 1936 but remained as manager until 1949, even though the club had by then dropped out of League football. Exceptionally lithe and agile, he had superb judgement and many of his contemporaries, including the great 'Dixie' Dean (qv), rated him the finest goalkeeper they ever played against.

His brother **William Scott**, goalkeeper for Everton, preceded him with a record 25 caps for Ireland (then united), 1903-13.

John SCOTT

Horse Racing
John Scott. b. 30 Nov 1794 Chippenham, near Newmarket. d. 4 Oct 1871 Malton, North Yorkshire.

Scott trained the winners of a record 40 English Classics between 1827 and 1863 at his Whitewall stable in Malton. His total was made up of 16 winners of the St Leger, eight of the Oaks, seven 2000 Guineas, five Derby and four 1000 Guineas. His most notable horses were *Touchstone* and *West Australian*, which in 1853 became the first Triple Crown winner. His brother Bill (qv), was his stable jockey for his first 18 years at Whitewall.

Peter SCOTT

Yachting and Gliding
(Sir) Peter Markham Scott. b. 14 Sep 1909 London. d. 29 Aug 1989 Bristol.

The son of the famous Antarctic explorer, Sir Robert Falcon Scott (1868-1912), Peter Scott excelled in many fields and was eventually best known as an ornithologist and for his watercolour paintings. As one of Britain's leading single-handed dinghy sailors, he won an Olympic bronze medal in the Monotype class in 1936 and was the winner of the Prince of Wales Cup in 1937-8 and 1946. He was a member of the international jury for yachting at three Olympic Games 1956-64. Taking up gliding, he won the British championship in 1963 and was chairman of the British Gliding Association 1968-70.

As a young man he won several pairs competitions as a figure skater, but felt that training for the highest honours as a solo skater would be too time-consuming. During the war he won the DSC and bar serving with the Royal Navy. He founded the World Wildlife Fund and was its chairman 1961-82. After being awarded the CBE in 1953 he was knighted in 1973 and in 1987 was appointed a Companion of Honour.

Susan SCOTT – see REEVE

Will SCOTT

Horse Racing
William Scott. b. 1797 Chippenham, nr Newmarket. d. 26 Sep 1848 Malton, North Yorkshire.

Will Scott was stable jockey for his first 18 years of the tenure of his brother John (qv) at Whitewall. He rode 19 Classics winners 1821-46, including a record nine of the St Leger (six for John), four of the Derby, and three each of the 2000 Guineas and Oaks. He died prematurely due to heavy drinking, and indeed in 1846 lost the chance of riding his own horse *Sir Tatton Sykes* to triple crown success; they had won the 2000 Guineas and St Leger but were beaten by a neck in the Derby, when Scott was palpably drunk. He was a strong, reckless and aggressive rider.

Peggy SCRIVEN

Tennis
Margaret Croft Scriven. b. 17 Aug 1912 Leeds. Later Mrs F H Vivian.

Scriven was an unorthodox left-hander who won the British Junior singles in 1929 without ever having had a tennis lesson. A four-time singles quarter-finalist at Wimbledon (1931, 1933-4, 1937) she had greater success at the French Championships where she was the winner in 1933 and 1934 before taking the doubles title in 1935.

Her punishing forehand and patient style were well suited to harder surfaces and at the British Covered Court Championships she won the singles (1932, 1935, 1937-8), the doubles (1933) and the mixed doubles (1934-5). She also won the singles in 1938 and mixed doubles 1935 at the Hard Court Championships and, after taking the singles titles at both Championships in 1938, she was ranked as the British No. 1 that year.

She played in three Wightman Cup ties 1933-8 but lost all six of her singles matches.

Peter SCUDAMORE

Horse Racing
Peter Michael Scudamore. b. 13 Jun 1958 Hoaruntby, Herefordshire.

Scudamore was the most successful jockey in National Hunt history, having ridden a total of 1678 winners from 7521 mounts, from his first in 1979 at Devon and Exeter to his retirement after winning on his last ride, at Ascot on 7 Apr 1993 to become assistant trainer to Nigel Twiston-Davies. In the 1988/9 season he rode 221 winners (from 663 rides) compared to the previous record of 149.

Peter Scudamore - career record				
Season	Wins	Mounts	Best other jockey	
1978/9	9	81	John Francome	95
1979/80	34	193	Jonjo O'Neill	115
1980/1	91	570	John Francome	105
1981/2	120	623	John Francome	120
1982/3	93	694	John Francome	106
1983/4	98	644	John Francome	131
1984/5	50	508	John Francome	101
1985/6	91	537	Simon Sherwood	77
1986/7	124	578	Mark Dwyer	81
1987/8	132	558	Chris Grant	80
1988/9	221	663	Mark Dwyer	92
1989/90	170	523	Richard Dunwoody	102
1990/1	141	423	Richard Dunwoody	127
1991/2	175	510	Richard Dunwoody	137
1992/3	129	416	Richard Dunwoody	173

Having shared the jockey's championship title in 1981/2 with his first century (120 winners), he was champion for seven successive seasons from 1985/6 to 1991/2. On 18 Nov 1989 he passed John Francome's (qv) career record 1138 winners. His most important winners have been in the Champion Hurdle: *Celtic Shot* in 1988 and *Granville Again* in 1993.

He rode for David Nicholson (qv), to whom he had been assistant trainer, before he turned professional at 21, and for Fred Winter (qv) before beginning his record-breaking partnership with Martin Pipe (qv). He was awarded the MBE in 1990. He had first ridden on the flat in 1975, with his first winner on 31 Aug 1978 at Devon and Exeter.

His father **Michael** John Scudamore (b. 17 Jul 1932) rode a total of 496 winners under NH rules 1952-69, including *Oxo* to win the 1959 Grand National.

Dick SEAMAN

Motor Racing
Richard John Beattie-Seaman. b. 4 Feb 1913 Aldingbourne, West Sussex. d. 25 Jun 1939 Liège, Belgium.

Having started racing as an amateur in 1931, Seaman was the most successful British driver in Continental races in the 1930s. His first major win was after leaving Cambridge University at Berne in 1934 with an MG Magnette. He won there again, and at Pescara and Brno in an E.R.A. in 1935 and had several more wins in 1936 in a 1926 Delage.

Such achievements led to his signing by Mercedes-Benz in 1937, and for them he won the 1938 German Grand Prix. He was killed in a fire resulting from his car's crash after skidding into a tree while leading the Belgian GP at Spa.

Greg and Johnny SEARLE

Rowing
Gregory Mark Pascoe Searle. b. 20 Mar 1972 Ashford, Kent.

Jonathan William Courtis Searle. b. 8 May 1969 Walton, Surrey.

The greatest successes achieved by the brothers Searle have come when they were rowing together. They won the coxed pairs at the 1992 Olympics and at the 1993 world championships with Garyy Herbert as cox on both occasions.

Johnny, the elder brother, was the first to make a name in rowing circles when he won a silver medal (1986) and a gold (1987) in the junior coxless fours at the world championships. As a senior, he won a bronze in the eights at the world championships in 1989 and 1991. He was President of Oxford University BC and rowed in the winning Oxford boat, 1988-90, and was also in the Leander crew which won the Grand at Henley in 1991.

Greg was a world junior gold medallist in 1989 and 1990 in the coxless fours and after graduating to the senior ranks he joined his brother in the eights boats which were 4th in 1990 and took the bronze medals at the 1991 world championships. Both brothers and their cox, **Garry Herbert** (b. 3 Oct 1969), were awarded the MBE after their 1992 Olympic victory. In 1994 the brothers earned world bronze medals with the British coxless fours.

Paul SEATON

Water Skiing
Paul Seaton. b. 3 Jul 1951.

Having won a (then) record four British overall titles, 1971-3 and 1975, Seaton incurred a serious injury at the 1975 World Championships which brought a premature end to his competitive career. He set several British records, including the European jump record of 53.80m in 1975. He then concentrated on coaching and now operates a water-ski school at Thorpe Park, Surrey.

Jimmy SEED

Football
James Marshall Seed. b. 25 Mar 1895 Blackhill, Co. Durham. d. 16 Jul 1966 Bromley, London.

After being gassed in World War I, Seed's football future seemed to be in jeopardy but after playing non-league football with

Mid-Rhondda in South Wales he went on to a successful career as an inside-forward with Tottenham Hotspur, Sheffield Wednesday and England.

Signed by Tottenham in 1919, he won an FA Cup winners' medal in 1921 and was capped five times by England 1921-5, before moving to Sheffield Wednesday in 1927. He captained Wednesday to two successive League titles, 1929-30, before he retired early in 1931. After two years as manager of Clapton Orient he took over at Charlton where he established a reputation as an exceptionally shrewd manager. He took them from the Third to the First Division in two years and, in their first season in the First Division, they only missed taking the 1936/7 League title by four points.

After the war, with Seed still at the helm, Charlton were losing finalists in the FA Cup in 1946 before taking the trophy the following year with a 1-0 victory over Burnley after extra time. In 1956, after some 25 years, Jimmy Seed finally parted company with Charlton and was associated with Bristol City as a consultant and then with Millwall as manager until 1959; he was appointed a director of the club the following year.

Henry SEGRAVE

Motor Racing
(Sir) Henry O'Neal Dehane Segrave. b. 22 Sep 1896 Baltimore, USA. d. 13 Jun 1930 Lake Windermere.

Segrave was the first man to hold the world land and water speed records simultaneously. He was the first man to exceed 200 mph on land to set the world land speed record at Daytona, USA, with 327.96 km/h *203.79 mph* in a Sunbeam in 1927, improving to 372.47 km/h *231.445 mph* in the 23-litre Irving Napier *Golden Arrow* in 1929. In that year he also won the International Championship for racing boats. He was killed attempting to improve the world water speed record, which he had just set at 98.76 mph, when his *Miss England II* hit an underwater obstruction.

Born of an Irish father and American mother, Segrave was a wartime pilot and aviation attaché in the USA. He had a successful motor racing career from 1917 until retiring in 1927 to concentrate on speed records, with a record of 31 wins in 49 races, which included the 1923 French and 1924 San Sebastián Grands Prix in Sunbeams. He had joined the Sunbeam Talbot-Darracq works team in 1921. He was knighted in 1929 for services to British prestige.

Edgar SELIGMAN

Fencing
Edgar Isaac Seligman. b. 14 Apr 1867. d. 27 Sep 1958 London.

The pioneer of modern British fencing, Seligman gave unrivalled service to the sport as a competitor, coach, judge and administrator. He was the AFA champion with the foil (1906-7) épée (1904, 1906) and sabre (1923-4) and only Bill Hoskyns (qv) has matched his feat of winning the British title with all three weapons.

At the Olympic Games he was a silver medallist in the épée team event at three successive Games (1906-12) and on his fifth and final Olympic appearance in 1924 at the age of 57 he came close to winning a medal. In the individual foil he reached the final pool but was forced to withdraw through injury after winning his first fight and the gold medal went to Roger Ducret (Fra) whom Seligman had beaten earlier in the competition.

A member of a well-known family of City financiers, he was educated in London and Belgium where, as a schoolboy, he won the 100m swimming championship of Brussels.

Derek SHACKLETON

Cricket
Derek Shackleton. b. 12 Aug 1924 Todmorden, West Yorkshire.

A marvellously accurate medium-fast bowler, for year after year Shackleton was outstandingly successful for Hampshire, exceeding 100 wickets for a record 20 successive years from 1949 to 1968, with a peak of 172 in 1962. He averaged under 20 runs per wicket in 15 of his 22 seasons and under 22 in all but the first three. He could surely have been successful in Tests, but had few opportunities in a great era of England pacemen, most of them with the extra speed perhaps more appropriate at this level. After three Tests in 1950-1 he had to wait until four Tests against West Indies in 1963, when he took 15 wickets, before he was asked again.

His batting declined, but in his second season of 1949 he missed the double by only 86 runs: 914 runs and 100 wickets, and on his Test debut against West Indies in 1950 he top scored with 42 in England's first innings. After retiring in 1969 he coached, played for Dorset in the Minor Counties 1971-4, and was a first-class umpire in 1979-81. His son Julian played for Gloucestershire 1971-8.

7 Tests 1950-63: 113 runs at 18.83, HS 42; 18 wickets at 42.66, BB 4-72; 1 catch.
First-class 1948-69: 9574 runs at 14.61, HS 87*; 2857 wickets at 18.65, BB 9-30; 221 catches.

Len SHACKLETON

Football
Leonard Francis Shackleton. b. 3 May 1922 Bradford, West Yorkshire. 28/11/2000

One of the most talented inside-forwards in the history of English football, Shackleton had uncanny ball control skills and his entertaining style led to him being known as the 'Clown Prince of Soccer'. Capped three times by England as a schoolboy in 1936, he joined the Arsenal ground staff but was not signed on a permanent basis as he was considered too frail, and his senior career really began as a part-time professional with Bradford Park Avenue during the war.

After scoring more than 160 goals during the restricted wartime seasons, he played a few League games for the club in 1946 but quickly moved to Newcastle United where he scored six goals on his debut for his new club in their 13-0 win against Newport County and helped them to win promotion to the First Division and reach the FA Cup semi-final. After two seasons with Newcastle he was transferred for a record £20,000 to Sunderland, where he

remained until injury ended his career 10 years later. Despite his extravagant talents he seldom found favour with the England selectors, winning only five caps between 1948 and 1954, after playing in the 'Victory' international against Scotland in 1946.

The fact that he made no secret of his contempt for officialdom certainly didn't help his case, but it was also felt that the intricacies of his play even confused his team-mates at times. His autobiography *Clown Prince of Soccer* contained a chapter entitled 'The Average Director's Knowledge of Football', which consisted of a blank page. On retirement, he became a journalist, was also a qualifed boxing referee, and served briefly as a director of Fulham in 1976.

Bill SHANKLY

Football
William Shankly. b. 2 Sep 1913 Glenbuck, South Lanarkshire. d. 28 Sep 1981 Liverpool.

Shankly was the driving force behind the emergence of Liverpool Football Club as a great team. He had been a fine player for Carlisle United before transferring to Preston North End in 1933. With them he won an FA Cup winners' medal in 1938, and played five times for Scotland 1938-9 as well as seven wartime internationals. He was known as 'Willie' Shankly when he captained Scotand in 1941.

In 1949 he returned to Carlisle as manager, moving on to Grimsby 1951, Workington 1953 and Huddersfield 1955, before joining Liverpool in December 1959. There he developed a strong youth policy and teams that would become the powerhouse of English football. They won the Second Division in 1962 and began their drive to the top with the the First Division title in 1964. Under Shankly Liverpool won the Football League again in 1966 and 1973, the UEFA Cup in 1973, and the FA Cup in 1965 and 1974, after which he retired. Under his chosen successor Bob Paisley, Liverpool went on to even more titles and honours.

Shankly, awarded the OBE in 1974, was

one of five brothers who played professional football; one of them, Bob, managed Dundee when they won the Scottish Championship in 1962.

Janet SHARDLOW – see MORGAN

Richard SHARP

Rugby Union
Richard Adrian William Sharp. b. 9 Sep 1938 Mysore, India.

Born into a rugby-playing family, Sharp developed into a brilliant attacking fly-half for Redruth, Wasps, Oxford University (Blue 1959-61) and Bristol. First brought into the England team against Wales in 1960, after Bev Risman (qv) was injured, he went on to win 13 caps 1960-3, and after a premature retirement won one more international and captained England for the fifth time, when England lost 23-11 to the visiting Australians in 1967. On the 1962 British Lions tour of South Africa he suffered a fractured cheek bone in an early provincial match but recovered sufficiently to play in the two final Tests. His marvellous try against Scotland at Twickenham in 1963 brought England victory 10-8 and the International Championship. Initially a schoolmaster, he has worked for English China Clays from 1968 and also as a journalist, and was awarded the OBE in 1986.

Graham SHARPE

Figure Skating
Henry Graham Sharpe. b. 19 Dec 1917 London. d. 2 Jan 1995 Poole, Dorset.

The first Briton to win the men's world figure skating title, Sharpe took up skating when his father opened the Westover Rink in Bournemouth in 1930 and made his Championship debut there when he placed 2nd to Jack Page's 11th and final British title. Sharpe was never beaten again in a British singles event and the following year he won the first of his eight British titles, 1934-8 (twice in 1937) and 1946-7. In 1934 he was 6th in the World Championships and 4th in the Europeans and he took the silver medals in both championships each year 1936-8; he was

also 5th at the 1936 Olympics. He then enjoyed his finest year when he took the European and World title in 1939.

During the war, he saw action at Dunkirk and in Africa and was wounded in the Italian campaign. After demobilisation he won his final British title in 1947 and placed 7th at the Olympics and 6th at the World Championships in 1948.

On the death of his father later in the year he took over as managing director of the family-owned ice rink until a take-over forced his retirement in 1964. He then spent some years as an instructor in America where a near-fatal accident in a swimming pool in 1974 prevented him from working again. With his debonair style and geometric accuracy he was one of Britain's greatest skaters and would undoubtedly have been a contender for top Olympic honours had the Games of 1940 and 1944 not been cancelled.

Alfred SHAW

Cricket
Alfred Shaw. b. 29 Aug 1842 Burton Joyce, Notts. d. 16 Jan 1907 Gedling, Notts.

The bowler of the first ball in Test cricket (3-51 and 5-38 in the first ever Test), Shaw was England's finest bowler of his era, and a useful batsman as well. At medium or slow-medium pace he employed flight and artistry and was relentlessly accurate. His fluent, easy action enabled him to bowl for long spells and he has the lowest career average for any bowler taking over 1000 wickets. In three seasons, 1875, 1879 and 1880 he averaged less than ten runs per wicket for over 100 wickets.

He was involved in six tours to Australia, captaining the England team that toured there in 1881/2, and later acting as manager. He played for Nottinghamshire for over 30 years, captaining them in 1883-6, when they were the unofficial county champions each year. A strong personality, he fought hard to improve conditions for professional cricketers. He was a first-class umpire from 1898 to 1905.

7 Tests 1876-82 (captain in 4): 111 runs at 10.09, HS 40; 12 wickets at 23.75, BB 5-38; 4 catches.

First-class 1864-97: 6585 runs at 12.83, HS 88; 2027 wickets at 20.12, BB 10-73; 368 catches.

Norma SHAW

Bowls
Norma Shaw. b. 8 Jun 1937 Wakefield.

The World singles champion in 1981, Shaw won team gold in 1981 and 1988, and was also a bronze medallist at pairs in 1981 and 1985, silver medallist at triples and bronze at fours in 1988, with further bronze medals at singles and triples in 1993. At the Commonwealth Games she won a pairs bronze in 1978 and she won seven English women's titles to 1989. She was awarded the MBE.

Alan SHEARER

Football
Alan Shearer. b. 13 Aug 1970 Newcastle-upon-Tyne.

Shearer was the Professional Footballers' Association Player of the Year in 1995, near the end of his second successive season of scoring more than 30 goals in the Premier League, a feat that only Jimmy Greaves (qv) could match since World War II. This, with a growing reputation as one of Britain's few world-class players, came just two years after a demanding knee operation.

On his debut for Southampton he became, at 17 years 240 days, the youngest ever to score a hat-trick in the First Division, but had only 23 goals in 118 League appearances for them and had made three England appearances when Blackburn Rovers paid a British record fee of £3.2 million for him in July 1992.

He has since played a major part in his team's surge to the top of British football, with 81 League goals for Blackburn, including 34 in their Premier League success in 1994/5. He made seven appearances for England Under-17 and scored 13 goals in 11 games for England Under-21, followed by 5 goals in 16 England appearances from 1992 to June 1995; he scored on his debut at each international level.

John Joe SHEEHY (Ireland)

Gaelic Football
John Joe Sheehy. b. 1898 Tralee, Co. Kerry.

Sheehy is regarded as one of the most influential players in the history of Gaelic football. He won four all-Ireland football medals and played with Munster in the Interprovincial Championship in both hurling and Gaelic football, having the distinction of captaining Munster to their first win in 1927. He was the first player elected to the Gaelic Football Hall of Fame in 1963.

Three of his sons, Paudie, Niall and Seán Ogh, also won all-Ireland senior football medals, with Seán (b. 24 May 1939) following in his footsteps by captaining Kerry to victory in 1962.

Gillian SHEEN

Fencing
Gillian Mary Sheen. b. 21 Aug 1928 Willesden, London. Later Mrs Donaldson.

Sheen is the only British fencer to win an Olympic gold medal, achieving this when she was a surprise winner at Melbourne in 1956. In her two other Olympic appearances (1952, 1960) she was eliminated in the early stages of the competition. She won a record ten British titles (1949, 1951-8, 1960) and other successes included gold medals at the 1951 World University Games and the 1958 Commonwealth Games.

She gave up competitive fencing in 1963 and settled in New York where she joined her husband in a dental practice.

Barry SHEENE

Motor Cycling
Barry Stephen Frank Sheene. b. 11 Sep 1950 Holborn, London.

A charismatic motorcycling champion, Sheene overcame serious injuries to attain success and great popular esteem. He was world champion at 500cc for Suzuki in 1976 and 1977, and still holds the record for the fastest ever average speed for a world championship race, 217.37 km/h *135.07 mph* with a lap record at 220.721

km/h *137.150 mph* at Spa-Francorchamps, Belgium in 1977. His first Grand Prix wins were for Suzuki in 1971, one at 50cc and three at 125cc. Then he won 19 at 500cc between 1975 and 1981, the last for Yamaha, all the others for Suzuki.

His father Frank Sheene was a notable rider and his brother-in-law Paul Smart raced in Britain and the USA in the 1960s and 1970s. Barry made his racing debut in 1968, won the British 125cc title in 1970 and was just beaten by Angel Nieto (Spain) to the world 125cc title in 1971. He was awarded the MBE in 1978 and retired in 1984.

From 1987 he has lived in Queensland, Australia where he is a TV commentator.

Norman SHEIL

Cycling
Norman Shiel.

Sheil was the world amateur pursuit champion in 1955 and 1958, having earlier won a bronze medal in 1954. He was also a double gold medallist at the Commonwealth Games, winning the individual pursuit in 1954 and 1958. He started in the Tour de France in 1960 but didn't finish the race. At home he won the British pursuit title three times (1954-5, 1959), the 10 miles title in 1957 and was also the 25 miles time trial champion that year.

He held the British track records at 5, 10 and 25 miles and on retirement he was appointed as national coach.

David SHEPPARD

Cricket
David Stuart Sheppard. b. 6 Mar 1929 Reigate, Surrey. *5/3/2005*

Bishop of Liverpool from 1975, Sheppard is the only ordained minister to have played Test cricket. He was a most determined opening batsman, who made his first-class debut for Sussex while still at school at Sherborne. He scored a record 3545 in his three years at Cambridge University 1950-2, including a season's record of 1281 runs including seven centuries in his final year when he was captain. He made his Test debut in 1950

and his maiden Test century against India in 1952, when he topped the first-class averages with 2262 runs at 64.62. He also exceeded 2000 runs in 1951 and 1953 when he captained Sussex.

Thereafter, however, his studies for holy orders and ordination in 1955 restricted his cricket. Nonetheless he captained England in Len Hutton's (qv) absence in two matches against Pakistan in 1954 and was recalled to the England team in 1956, scoring 113 against Australia. His appearances became less frequent and he did not play at all in 1961, but he came back in 1962, made a hundred for the Gentlemen at Lord's, played in the last two Tests and, taking a sabbatical from his work as warden of the Mayflower Family Centre, went on the 1962/3 tour to Australia, where he scored a century in the 2nd Test and preached almost as much as he batted. That was the end of his cricketing career. He was a suffragan bishop of Woolwich 1969-75 before translating to Liverpool.

22 Tests 1950-64: 1172 runs at 37.80, 3 100s HS 119; 12 catches.

First-class 1947-64: 15,838 runs at 43.51, HS 239*; 2 wickets at 44.00, BB 1-5; 195 catches.

Eileen SHERIDAN

Cycling
Eileen Sheridan. b. 18 Oct 1923.

Sheridan was the greatest British woman cyclist until the arrival of Beryl Burton (qv). A road racing specialist, she was the British champion at 25 miles in 1945 and at 50 and 100 miles in 1950. She rode for Coventry CC. Her many long-lasting place-to-place women's records included London to Bath and back 10:41:22 in 1952, London to York 9:05:20 in 1953, London to Edinburgh (380 miles *610 km* in 20:11:35 in 1954, and Land's End to John O'Groats (1414 km) in 2 days 11 hour 7 min in 1954, a record that lasted for 36 years. She went on to complete 1000 miles *1609 km* in 3 days 1 hour and her other straight out distance records included 50 miles in 1:55:00 in 1954 and 100 miles in 4:16:01 in 1952.

John SHERWOOD

Athletics, Hurdling
John Sherwood. b. 4 Jun 1945 Selby,
North Yorkshire.

When David Hemery (qv) swept to victory in the 1968 Olympic final in Mexico City at 400m hurdles in a world record time of 48.12, TV commentator David Coleman uttered the instinctive phrase 'Who cares who's third?', but we did for it was another British athlete, John Sherwood. His time of 49.03 compared to the British records of 49.37 that both he and Hemery had run in their semi-finals and his pre-Games best of 50.2. He had won silver medals at the 1967 World Student Games at hurdles and 4 x 400m relay, and in 1968, while a schoolteacher he married long jumper Sheila Parkin. Both won Commonwealth Games gold medals in 1970, John at 400m hurdles (with a relay bronze) and Sheila at long jump. John also took the European hurdles silver medal in 1969.

A fine all-round athlete, ideally built at 1.87m tall and weighing 83kg, Sherwood made his international debut for Britain while a student at Loughborough in 1964, when he was an Olympic relay reserve, competed internationally until his third Commonwealth Games in 1974 and went on for his club, Sheffield, with much success for several more years. He was AAA hurdles champion in 1966 and 1967 (both in British record times), 1969 and 1971 and his best 400m on the flat was 46.8 in 1969, although he often ran much quicker in relays.

His younger brother, **Steve Sherwood** (b. 10 Dec 1953 Selby), played as a goalkeeper in the Football League from 1971 to 1992 principally for Chelsea, Brentford, Watford and Grimsby Town. He played in the 1988 FA Cup final for Watford.

Sheila SHERWOOD

Athletics, Long Jump
Sheila Hilary Sherwood. b. 22 Oct 1945
Sheffield. née Parkin.

Having been an international long jumper from the age of 16, the Sheffield schoolteacher reached her peak in taking the Commonwealth gold medal in 1970 with her personal best jump (and third equal on the world all-time list) of 6.73m. All six of her jumps were superior to the best of silver medallist, Ann Wilson (6.50), and she achieved her ambition of jumping 22 feet *6.71m* three times. Her husband John (qv) had earlier won gold for 400m hurdles. At previous Commonwealth Games she was 5th in 1962 and 2nd in 1966 and went on to 7th in 1974. At the three Olympic Games 1964-72 she was respectively 13th, 2nd and 9th, and the best of her four European Championships was 4th in 1971. She was WAAA champion in 1968-9 and 1971-2 and indoors in 1962-3 and 1965. Her best sprint times, in 1964, were 10.8 for 100y and 11.8 for 100m.

Anne SHILCOCK

Tennis
Jacqueline Anne Shilcock. b. 13 Jun 1932
Hartfield, East Sussex. Later Mrs J K
Spann.

Shilcock was an aggressive serve-volleyer who reached her peak in 1955 when she won the Wimbledon doubles with Angela Mortimer (qv), all three events at the British Covered Court Championships and the mixed doubles at the Hard Court championships. She also won the Covered Court singles in 1958, the doubles, 1953, 1956 and 1958, the mixed doubles 1956, and the Hard Court doubles in 1958.

She played in four Wightman Cup ties between 1953 and 1958 but lost all five of her matches (2 singles, 3 doubles).

Peter SHILTON

Football
Peter Leslie Shilton. b. 18 Sep 1949
Leicester.

As goalkeeper for England 125 times between 1970 and 1990, Shilton holds the British record for international caps.

After making his debut for Leicester City as a 16-year-old he later played for Stoke City 1974-7, Nottingham Forest 1977-82, Southampton 1982-7, Derby County 1987-92 and Plymouth Argyle as player-manager from 1992 until he resigned following financial problems in 1994, and one game for Bolton Wanderers in 1995. His major honours came when he was with Forest, helping them win the European Cup 1979 and 1980, the League title 1978 and the League Cup 1979.

A complete master of all the goalkeeping skills, he made a total of 1380 senior UK appearances, including a record 996 League appearances with his seven clubs 1966-95. For his contribution to the game he was awarded the MBE in 1986 and OBE 1990.

Nigel SHORT

Chess
Nigel David Short. b. 1 Jun 1965 Leigh, Gt. Manchester.

Having been a boy prodigy, Short progressed to become Britain's highest ever rated chess player, with a peak of 2685 points on the Elo system at the end of 1991, when he was 4th in the world. In 1979 at the age of 14 he tied for the British title only to lose the tie-break. He was an International Master in 1980 when he was runner-up to Gary Kasparov (USSR) for the world junior title, and a Grand Master in 1984.

He was British champion in 1984 and 1987, and after a string of international successes in 1988 he and Jon Speelman (qv) became the first British players to qualify for the quarter-finals of the World Championship candidates tournament. Speelman beat him there, but in 1992-3 Short went further. First he beat former world champion Anatoliy Karpov (Rus) and then Jan Timman (Hol) to win the right to challenge Gary Kasparov for the world title. Short and Kasparov determined to contest the title outside the control of the world governing body, FIDE, and set up a Professional Chess Association. While FIDE recognised a series between Karpov and Timman for the world title, Kasparov and Short battled it out with the former winning 12.5 to 7.5.

He won silver medals with the English team at the Chess Olympiads in 1984, 1986 and 1988, and bronze in 1990 and 1994.

Sue SHOTTON

Trampolining
Susan Carol Shotton. b. 11 Aug 1965. Later Mrs Challis.

In 1984 Shotton won three gold medals at the World Championships, individual, synchronised pairs with Kirsty McDonald and team. She has also been 3rd in the individual event in 1982, 1990 and 1992. At the European Championships she shared the individual title with Andrea Holmes (qv) in 1983 and won again in 1993. She has been British individual champion overall a record nine times, 1980-2, 1984-5, 1987 (shared), 1990 and 1992-3, and won the World Cup singles in 1981, 1983 and 1986.

Stanley SHOVELLER

Hockey
Stanley Howard Shoveller. b. 2 Sep 1881 Kingston Hill, London. d. 24 Feb 1959 Broadstone, Dorset.

Shoveller was the first man in Olympic history to win two gold medals for hockey and England's highest scoring player. After Kingston Grammar School, he joined Hampstead and represented Surrey and the South before making his international debut in 1902. He went on to win 35 caps for England at centre-forward and accumulated a record total of 79 goals, scoring in all but ten of his international matches.

He captained England from 1909 until his retirement in 1921 when he became a leading administrator. During World War I he won an MC serving as a captain in the Rifle Brigade.

Arthur SHREWSBURY

Cricket
Arthur Shrewsbury. b. 11 Apr 1856 New Lenton, Notts. d. 19 May 1903 Gedling, Notts.

W.G.Grace's famous tribute was 'Give me Arthur', when asked which of his contemporaries he rated the highest. For much of his career Shrewsbury was the finest professional batsman in the country, a master of the turning ball, and he was the first player to reach 1000 runs in Test cricket, reaching that milestone in the last of his three centuries against Australia in 1893.

With James Lillywhite and Alfred Shaw (qqv) he helped to organise four tours to Australia in the 1880s, and he captained two of them, winning five of the seven Tests played on those.

In an age of much lower scoring than at any time since, he consistently scored at a higher level than anybody but Grace, and made 10 double hundreds. He shot himself less than a year after his final first-class match, unable to cope with life after cricket.

23 Tests 1881-93: 1277 runs at 35.47, 3 100s HS 164; 29 catches.

First-class 1875-1902: 26,505 runs at 36.65, 59 100s HS 267; 376 catches.

Alf SHRUBB

Athletics
Alfred Shrubb. b. 12 Dec 1879 Slinfold, Horsham, West Sussex. d. 23 Apr 1964 Boumanville, Ontario, Canada.

The world's greatest distance runner at the turn of the century, Shrubb set world records from 2 miles to 1 hour, many of which lasted for a very long time. His greatest run was at Glasgow on 5 Nov 1904, when his world records included those for 6 miles 29:59.4, 10,000m 31:02.4, 10 miles 50:40.6 and 1 hour 18,742m. That last time remained a British record for 48 years 296 days. Earlier in 1904 he had set records at 2 (9:09.6), 3 (14:17.2), 4 (19:23.4) and 5 (24:33.4) miles.

He won the first two International cross-country races 1903-4, but did not compete at the 1904 Olympics as Britain did not send a team. At the end of that year the AAA declared him to be a professional and he ran in professional marathons in the USA in 1909. After the war he became Oxford University's first professional coach (1920-6), before emigrating to Canada.

He won the English National cross-country each year 1901-4 and was AAA champion at 1 mile 1903-4 and 4 miles 1901-4.

Max SIMMERS

Rugby Union
William Maxwell Simmers. b. 7 Aug 1904 Glasgow. d. 14 Nov 1972 Helensburgh, Argyll and Bute.

A determined and reliable winger with Glasgow Academicals, Simmers won 28 caps 1926-32, scoring six tries for Scotland. He married Wightman Cup player, Gwen Sterry, the daughter of five-time Wimbledon singles champion, Charloote Cooper (qv). Their son, **Brian** (b. 26 Feb 1940), was capped by Scotland seven times 1965-71, and served as President of the Scottish RU 1956-7.

Cyril SIMPSON

Rackets
Sir John Cyril Finucane Simpson. b.10 Feb 1899. d.21 Dec 1981 Wylam, Northumberland.

From Rugby School, Simpson went up to Oxford, where he won his singles against Cambridge for three successive years 1920-2. A hard-hitting left-hander, he then went on to win the Open singles twice, 1929-30, the Amateur singles three times, 1926-8, and the Amateur doubles six times between 1922 and 1937, three with Roddy Williams and three with Cosmo Crawley.

Jimmy SIMPSON

Motorcycling
James H Simpson.

Simpson set three successive speed milestones in Isle of Man TT races and eight lap records. He recorded the first lap in excess of 60 mph in 1924 on an AJS, the first over 70 mph in 1926 on an AJS and the first over 80 mph in 1931 on a Norton, though on none of these occasions did he win the race. He did, however, produce a consistent record: in the Senior TT he was 2nd in 1933 and 1934, 3rd in 1930 and 1932; and in the Junior he was 2nd in 1926 and 1934, 3rd in 1925 and 1927. His one win came at Lightweight on a Rudge in 1934.

In 1930 he became the world's fastest road racer with a lap of 84.63 mph *136.19 km/h* in the Ulster Grand Prix riding a works

Norton. The Jimmy Simpson Trophy for the fastest speed around the TT course was inaugurated in 1948.

Judy SIMPSON

Athletics
Judy Earline Veronica Simpson. b. 14 Nov 1960 Kingston, Jamaica. née Livermore.

A very talented all-rounder, Simpson had her greatest season in 1986, when she excelled in Stuttgart with five personal bests in the seven events to take the bronze medal at the Europeans with a score of 6623 points, her fourth Commonwealth record since 1981. She also improved from silver in 1982 to gold in the Commonwealth heptathlon.

She was 7th at the 1982 Europeans and was WAAA champion in 1982 and 1983. At the Olympics she was 13th in the pentathlon in 1980 and 5th at heptathlon in 1984, and she won World Student Games bronze medals in 1983 and 1985. Bursitis in her knee caused her to miss the 1987 World Championships, and she withdrew after two events in Seoul 1988, but she returned to take the Commonwealth bronze in 1990. She also ranked regularly in the British top ten at high jump (best 2nd 1983), long jump (best 6th 1986) and shot (best 6th 1984 and 1988) and was a former UK champion at taekwan-do. She is now a public relations officer for the Duke of Edinburgh's Award scheme, and a television personality, acting as *Nightshade* in ITV's *Gladiators*.

Best performances: 100m 12.13 (1990), 200m 24.75 (1983), 400m 53.76 (1981), 800m 2:11.49 (1982), 60m hurdles 8.21i (1985), 100m hurdles 13.05 (1986), high jump 1.92m (1983), long jump 6.40m (1984), 6.56mw (1986), shot 15.23m (1988), javelin 40.92m (1986).

Her husband Robin Simpson competed as a pole vaulter for Birchfield Harriers, with a best of 4.60m.

Reg SIMPSON

Cricket
Reginald Thomas Simpson. b. 27 Feb 1920 Sherwood Rise, Nottingham.

A stylish opening batsman, outstanding against fast bowling and a brilliant fielder, Simpson had to contend with Cyril Washbrook (qv) for a place on the England team in the late 1940s and early 1950s when Len Hutton (qv) was the number one choice. His finest moment came with his 156* in the 5th Test against Australia in 1950/1 which helped England to their first win over Australia since 1938.

He made his first-class debut in India in 1944/5 while serving with the RAF, but was 26 when he made his county debut in 1946. He then scored over 1000 runs in England each year from 1947 to 1960 except for 1957, including five times over 2000, with 2525 at 63.12 in 1949, 2576 at 62.82 in 1950 and 2505 at 45.54 in 1953. He captained Nottinghamshire from 1951 to 1960.

27 Tests 1948-55: 1401 runs at 33.35, 4 100s HS 156*; 2 wickets at 11.00, BB 2-4; 5 catches.

First-class 1944-63: 30,546 runs at 38.32, 64 100s HS 259; 59 wickets at 37.74, BB 3-22; 189 catches.

Tommy SIMPSON

Cycling
Thomas Simpson. b. 30 Nov 1937 Co. Durham. d. 13 Jul 1967 Mont Ventoux, France.

Tommy Simpson was the first truly great British road professional, and he remains the greatest. He turned professional in 1960 after an amateur career which included an Olympic bronze medal in the 1956 team pursuit and a silver in the individual pursuit at the 1958 Commonwealth Games. He lacked only the ability to climb strongly, which made him more of a factor in one-day classics than in the major tours. With the Tour of Flanders in 1961 he became the first British rider to win a classic for 65 years and added wins: Bordeaux-Paris 1963, Milan-San Remo 1964, Paris-Nice 1967.

In 1962 he became the first Briton to wear the *maillot jaune* at the Tour de France, though he held it only for a day and ended the race 6th overall, still the best ever by a British rider to that date. His greatest year was 1965 when he won the Tour of Lombardy and the world professional road race and was voted BBC Sports Personality of the Year. Those wins occurred after a disastrous fall in the Tour de France when doctors feared they might need to amputate his arm.

In 1967, Simpson was ascending Mont Ventoux in the Tour de France when he collapsed and fell from his bike. He could not be revived and died that day. He was later found to have been quite heavily drugged with stimulants and his death was directly responsible for many of the anti-drug regulations put in place by international sporting organisations.

Janet SIXSMITH

Hockey
Janet Teresa Sixsmith. b. 5 Sep 1967 Sutton Coldfield. Now Mrs Beeton.

After playing for England at Under-18 and Under-21 levels, Sixsmith made her international debut as a senior in 1987 and won a silver medal at the European Championships that year before winning gold in 1991. She represented Britain at the 1988 Olympic Games and again in 1992 when she won a bronze medal.

A talented winger, she plays for the First Personnel club in Sutton Coldfield and was voted Hockey Writers 'Player of the Year' in 1992. In June 1995 he played her 100th international for England, in which she has scored 23 goals, and she has also played 82 times for Great Britain, scoring 34 goals.

Nick SKELTON

Equestrian events
Nicholas David Skelton. b. 30 Dec 1957 Coventry, West Midlands.

Skelton was a member of the British silver-medal winning team at the European Junior Championships in 1974 at the age of 16. He made his senior international debut in 1978 and became a regular member of the British show jumping team. Individually on *Apollo* he won a World bronze in 1986 and European bronze in 1987 and in the team event at the World

Championships he took silver in 1986 and bronze in 1982 and 1990, and at the Europeans gold in 1985 and 1987 and silver in 1993. He also competed at the Olympic Games of 1988 and 1992. Riding *St James* he was British champion in 1981 and won the King George V Gold Cup in 1984. He won a second King George on *Limited Edition* in 1993 and also won the Hickstead Jumping Derby three times, 1987-9. In 1995 he had his greatest triumph, winning the World Cup on *Everest Dollar Girl*.

Reg SKRIMSHIRE

Rugby Union
Reginald Truscott Skrimshire. b. 30 Jan 1878 Crickhowell, Powys. d. 20 Sep 1963 Worthing, West Sussex.

Skrimshire won all three of his Welsh caps in 1899 and four years later, although no longer a current international, he was the only Welshman to be selected for the 1903 British Lions tour of South Africa. On tour, he had the remarkable record of playing in all 22 matches and was the Lions leading points (59) and try (10) scorer.

A centre with Newport, his exceptional speed often distanced him from his support and this - perhaps unfairly - led to him being labelled an individualist; this was a quality that did not appeal to the Welsh selectors.

Bill SLATER

Football
William John Slater. b. 29 Apr 1927 Clitheroe, Lancashire.

Slater was one of the last amateurs to play at the highest level. Originally an inside-left and later a half-back, he played with Blackpool, Brentford and Wolverhampton Wanderers, before signing as a professional with Wolves in 1954 at the age of 27. He was still an amateur with Blackpool when he played in the 1951 FA Cup final and, as a professional, he was in the Wolves team which won the Cup in 1960. That year he was voted the Football Writers' Footballer of the Year. He also won three League championship medals

---

with Wolves 1954 and 1958-9. He won 12 full England caps between 1954 and 1960, including the 1958 World Cup, to add to his 21 amateur caps, which included playing at the 1952 Olympic Games.

A graduate of Carnegie College, Leeds he held a number of senior appointments in sports administration and education.

Fergus SLATTERY (Ireland)

Rugby Union
John Fergus Slattery. b. 12 Feb 1949 Dún Laoghaire, Co. Dublin.

With 61 international appearances between 1970 and 1984, Slattery was Ireland's most capped flanker. On the Lions tour of New Zealand in 1971 he was unable to command a place in the Test side but on his second Lions tour in 1974 he played in all four Tests against South Africa. He made his international debut against the touring Springboks in 1970 and played in 28 consecutive matches before he lost his place through injury. After returning to the side he made a further 33 consecutive appearances for Ireland.

Kendra SLAWINSKI

Netball
Kendra Slawinski. b. 11 Nov 1962 North Yorkshire.

Slawinski is England's most capped netball player, with 118 apearances for England 1982-95, as goal defence, goal keeper or wing defence. Now teaching in Luton, where she plays for Vauxhall Golds and is player-coach for Bedfordshire, she has been an exceptional leader of the England team at Under-18, Under-21 and senior level. She led the England team at her 4th World Championships in 1995, having previously played in 1983, 1987 and 1991. Her charismatic personality and dedicated work have done much to raise the profile of netball.

Mike SLEMEN

Rugby Union
Michael Anthony Charles Slemen. b. 11 May 1951 Liverpool.

With 31 international appearances between 1976 and 1984, Slemen was England's most capped winger until his record was beaten by Rory Underwood (qv) in 1989.

A composed, elusive runner he scored eight tries for England and was the top try scorer for the British Lions in South Africa in 1980 even though he had to return home for personal reasons after playing in the first Test. A Liverpool schoolmaster, he played for the local club throughout his career and is now a member of the England coaching team.

Kathy SMALLWOOD – see COOK

Charlie SMIRKE

Horse Racing
Charles James William Smirke. b. 23 Sep 1906 Lambeth, London. d. 20 Dec 1993 Leatherhead, Surrey.

Smirke rode 11 Classics winners in England from Derby winners *Windsor Lad* in 1934 to *Hard Ridden* in 1958. Six of these, including *Mahmoud* in 1936 and *Tulyar* in 1952, were owned by the Aga Khan for whom he rode for 30 years.

He was apprenticed to Stanley Wootton from 1920 and rode his first winner in 1922. His most wins in a year was 78 in 1924 until he passed that in 1948 with 98. An cocky and aggressive Cockney, he lost his licence to ride in 1928 due to a miscarriage of justice by the Stewards of the Jockey Club and did not regain it until 1933. An undoubted talent, he had disagreements with several of the trainers for whom he rode and was not especially popular with his fellow jockeys.

Anne SMITH

Athletics
Anne Rosemary Smith. b. 31 Aug 1941 Amersham, Bucks. d. 9 Nov 1993 London.

After a British mile record of 4:44.2 in 1966, Smith set two world records for the 1 mile in 1967, 4:39.2 and 4:37.0, the latter a race in which she also set a world record for 1500m of 4:17.3, the first record for the distance to be officially accepted by the IAAF. Unfortunately the 1500m was not a major championship event when she was at her peak, and she was 8th at 800m at the 1964 Olympics, having set a British record of 2:04.8 in her semi-final. She improved that best to 2:03.4 in 1968 and had a 440y best of 56.0 (1967). She was WAAA champion at 880y each year 1964-7, with a British 880y record of 2:04.2 in 1966, in which year she also won a Commonwealth Games bronze.

A PE teacher, she was coached by Gordon Pirie (qv).

Arthur SMITH

Rugby Union
Arthur Robert Smith. b. 23 Jan 1933 Castle Douglas, Dumfries & Galloway. d. 3 Feb 1975 Edinburgh.

After playing in only three matches for Scotland, Smith was chosen for the 1955 Lions tour of South Africa but he broke his hand in the first match and did not play again until the end of the tour. In 1962 he again toured South Africa with the Lions, this time as captain, and in the three Tests he played the Lions won twice and drew once. Between 1955 and 1962 he was capped 33 times (15 as captain) on the wing and scored 12 tries with his fast elusive running, being especially known for his change of pace. A brilliant scholar, he also was the Scottish long jump champion in 1953, with a best of 7.03m, before going to Cambridge University where he won his rugby Blue for four years.

After his early death at the age of 42 he will be best remembered for his outstanding qualities as a captain.

Charles SMITH

Water polo
Charles Sidney Smith. b. 26 Jan 1879 Worlsey Mesnes, Pemberton, Gt. Manchester. d.6 Apr 1951 Southport, Merseyside.

Smith was England's goalkeeper for 25 years 1902-26 and a member of the winning team at the 1908, 1912 and 1920 Olympic Games; at the last he was, at 41 years 270 days, the oldest water polo player ever to win an Olympic gold medal.

He made a fourth Olympic appearance in 1924 at 45. Initially a member of Salford SC, he later joined Southport SC and he was the flag carrier for the British team at the 1912 Olympic opening ceremony.

Doug SMITH

Horse Racing
Douglas Smith. b. 21 Nov 1917 Shottesbrooke, Maidenhead, Berkshire. d. 11 Apr 1989 Suffolk.

Doug Smith was champion jockey in Britain in 1954-6, 1958-9, in all he rode 3111 winners, 1931-67, with a highest season's total of 173 in 1947, when runner-up to Gordon Richards (qv), as he also was each year 1949-53.

The son of a Berkshire farmer, he won prizes in the show ring before starting his career as an apprentice jockey, with his brother Eph (qv), to Major Fred Sneyd. His first ride was at Salisbury in 1931, and his first winner in the same race a year later. His first Classics success was on the King's *Hypericum* in the 1946 1000 Guineas, when retained by Cecil Boyd-Rochfort (qv). He won the 2000 Guineas on *Pall Mall* in 1958 and the 1000 Guineas on *Petite Etoile* in 1959.

He excelled on stayers, notably the great *Alycidon*, and won the Cesarewitch five times. He trained in Newmarket 1968-79, winning the Oaks with *Sleeping Partner* 1969, and then became a bloodstock agent before committing suicide at his home.

Eph SMITH

Horse Racing
Eric Ephraim Smith. b. 4 May 1915 Shottesbrooke, Maidenhead, Berkshire. d. 12 Aug 1972 Newmarket.

Although not quite reaching the eminence of his younger brother Doug (qv), Eph Smith rode 2313 flat race winners from 1930 to 1965, including three Classics, the 2000 Guineas and Derby on *Blue Peter* in 1939, and the St Leger on *Premonition* 1953.

He was champion apprentice each year 1933-5 and second in the jockey's championship in 1938, 3rd in 1939 and in the war years successively 3rd, 2nd, 2nd, 3rd, 4th and 2nd 1940-5, missing military service due to deafness. From 1949-63 he rode for leading owner Jim Joel.

In 1972 his body was found in a brook near Newmarket.

G.O. SMITH

Football
Gilbert Oswald Smith. b. 25 Nov 1872 Croydon. d. 6 Dec 1943 Lymington, Hampshire.

The greatest centre-forward of his day, Smith was educated at Charterhouse and Oxford University and was the quintessential amateur in the Corinthian mould. He won the first of his 20 England caps (1893-1901) while still at Oxford and was a member of the Old Carthusian team which won the FA Amateur Cup in 1897. In 1899 he scored an English international record five goals against Ireland.

He was also a fine cricketer, winning his Blue at Oxford, for whom he scored a century against Cambridge in 1896, and playing for Hertfordshire and Surrey.

For many years he was joint Headmaster of Ludgrove Preparatory School with another England soccer international, William Oakley. Although lacking speed and a robust physique, he possessed a lethal shot and was a consummate tactician.

Harvey SMITH

Equestrianism, Show Jumping
Robert Harvey Smith. b. 29 Dec 1938 Bingley, West Yorkshire.

A Yorkshire farmer, Smith recorded his first major show jumping win in 1958 with *Farmer's Boy*. He went on to win the King George V Gold Cup in 1970 on *Mattie Brown* and set records for seven wins in the John Player Trophy (1962, 1965-7, 1972-3, 1978) and four in the British Jumping Derby (1970-1, 1974, 1981). He was also British champion in 1960, 1963 and 1975.

Smith took part in both the 1968 and 1972 Olympics but failed to win a medal. He earned a World bronze medal in 1970,

European silver in 1967 and 1971, and bronze in 1963.

His worldwide fame is due as much to his fighting spirit and his no-holds-barred approach to his sport as to his prowess as a rider. He also wrote several popular books about equestrian sport and now trains National Hunt horses.

His son **Robert** Walter **Smith** (b. 12 Jun 1961) became the youngest ever winner of the King George V Gold Cup at 18 in 1979 and won again in 1988, and was British champion in 1987. He also won a European Junior team gold, with individual bronze in 1977.

Ian SMITH

Rugby Union
Ian Scott Smith. b. 31 Oct 1903 Melbourne, Australia. d. 18 Sep 1972 Edinburgh.

Although educated at a soccer school (Winchester), Smith became the leading international try scorer after he concentrated on rugby at Oxford. After winning his Blue in 1923, he went on to win 32 caps on the wing for Scotland between 1924 and 1933 and set a host of scoring records. On his international debut against Wales in 1924 he scored three tries and the following season he scored four tries against both Wales and France. In all, he scored a record 24 tries for Scotland, but on the Lions tour of South Africa in 1924 he failed to cross the line in the two Tests he played. He captained Scotland in his last season (1933) when they won all three matches, their first Triple Crown for eight years.

He qualified as a chartered accountant and later as a solicitor at the age of 48.

Jeff SMITH

Moto-cross
Jeffrey Vincent Smith. b. 14 Oct 1934 Colne, Lancashire.

Smith was world 500cc moto-cross champion in 1964-5, 2nd in 1967 and 3rd in 1963 and 1966 with a 2nd at 250cc in 1962. He also rode on eight winning British teams in the Moto Cross des Nations, 1956-7,

1959-60, 1963-5 and 1967. A qualified engineer, he had started scrambling at 20 and won a record nine A-CU Stars scrambling titles at 500cc (1955-6, 1960-5 and 1967), having won the trials titles in 1953 and 1954, riding for BSA virtually throughout his career.

He was awarded the MBE in 1970, the first motorcycle sportsman outside road racing to be so honoured, and emigrated to Canada in 1972 to pursue his engineering career. There he joined the Can-Am Company as a development rider.

Joyce SMITH

Marathon
Joyce Esther Smith. b. 26 Oct 1937 Stoke Newington, London. née Byatt.

Having been a reserve for the English cross-country team in 1956, Smith made her international debut for Britain at 800m in 1960, She suffered, however, for much of her career from the lack of long-distance events for women, but was hugely successful in her 40s at marathon running. In 1979 she set the first of six British marathons records when she won the WAAA title in 2:41:37. She improved this to 2:36:27 that year and to 2:33:32 and 2:30:47 in 1980 before becoming the first British woman to better two and a half hours when she won the first London marathon in 1981 in 2:29:57, a win she repeated the following year in 2:29:43. In 1983 she was 9th at the World Championships and in 1984 11th at the Olympics.

The much shorter distance of 1500m was first run at the Olympics in 1972 and Smith set British records in her heat (4:11.27) and semi-final (4:09.37). The 3000m was first added to the international programme in 1974 at the Europeans and Smith took the bronze medal, having set six British records for the distance from 9:52.2 in 1970 to 8:55.53 in 1974. She won WAAA titles at 1 mile 1965, 3000m 1971 and 1976, indoor mile 1966.

Smith first achieved world-class performances as a cross-country runner, winning the English National title in 1959 and 1960 and again in 1973 after four 2nd places.

Reaching her peak in her mid-30s, after her daughter was old enough to go to playschool, Smith was successively 3rd, 1st, 2nd and 7th in the International Cross-country 1971-4. She was awarded the MBE in 1984.

Other best times: 800m 2:08.8 (1972), Mile 4:45.6 (1971), 10,000m 34:26.4 (1980).

Mike SMITH

Cricket
Michael John Knight Smith. b. 30 Jun 1933 Westcotes, Leicestershire.

Smith was a free-scoring batsman in county cricket for Leicestershire 1951-5 and then for Warwickshire, whom he captained from 1957-67. He had won a Blue at Oxford University 1954-6, scoring a century in the University match each year, including 201* in 1954. He scored 1000 runs in a season 19 times, with six over 2000 and a peak of 3245 at 57.94 in 1959. At Test level he did not quite establish himself as a batsman, although he was a highly respected captain of England for 25 matches 1963-6, especially successful as a tourist. He was awarded the OBE.

Despite wearing spectacles, he was also a brilliant short-leg fielder and was the last man to double as an international for England at cricket and rugby, at which he won one cap as a fly-half in 1956.

He played for Leicester and formed a notable half-back combination at Oxford with David **Onllwyn Brace** (b. 16 Nov 1932 Gowerton), who won nine caps for Wales at scrum-half and who became head of sport for BBC Wales.

50 Tests 1958-72: 2278 runs at 31.63, 3 100s HS 121; 1 wicket; 53 catches.
First-class 1951-76: 39,832 runs at 41.84, 69 100s HS 204; 5 wickets; 593 catches.

Robin SMITH

Cricket
Robin Arnold Smith. b. 13 Sep 1963 Durban, South Africa.

Smith was marked out as a potentially great batsman from an early age. A brilliant all-round athlete (South African

Under-17 shot champion in 1980), rugby player and cricketer at school, he followed his elder brother **Chris** (b. 15 Oct 1958) in leaving South Africa to play for Hampshire and qualify for England. Chris played in eight Tests 1983-6, but Robin has established himself as one of the world's best batsmen and an England regular from his debut in 1987 until he was dropped in 1994.

Against Australia in 1989, while the side was disintegrating around him, he scored 553 runs at 61.44. He hits a cricket ball with ferocious power, particularly strong in square driving and cutting. That power was shown to best effect in his marvellous 167* in a one-day international against Australia in 1993, but he has shown vulnerability to top-class spin bowling.

He returned to the England team in 1995, initially, and unsuccessfully as an opening batsman, but returning to the middle order to excel in England's epic win over the West Indies in the second Test and to be the one player able to cope with the West Indian pace men in the next Test.

He played for Natal 1980-5 and for Hampshire from 1982.

53 Tests 1987-94: 3677 runs at 44.30, 9 100s HS 175; 35 catches.

64 One-day Ints 1988-94: 2218 runs at 40.32; 4 100s HS 167*; 22 catches.

First-class 1980-94: 17,813 runs at 44.31, 45 100s HS 209*; 12 wickets at 57.75, BB 2-11; 174 catches.

Steve SMITH

Athletics, High Jump
Stephenson James Smith. b. 29 Mar 1973 Liverpool.

Smith set his first senior British record as a teenager in 1992, when having won the AAA title with a British junior record of 2.31m, he went to the World Juniors in Seoul and in a magnificent battle with the Australian Tim Forsyth not only won the title but improved his record to 2.33, 2.35 and 2.37, the latter matching the World junior record in an astonishing display of high talent and coolness under pressure. He had earlier been most disappointed to have been 12th at the Olympics at 2.24,

when the title was won at 2.34. Smith cleared 2.37 again twice in 1993 to win World Championships bronze medals both indoors and out, and in 1994 he improved his Commonwealth record to 2.38 indoors. Despite losing much time through injury he still won European and Commonwealth silver medals outdoors in 1994.

Relatively small for a high jumper at 1.86m, he had first come to notice when he won the English Schools junior title in 1987. He won the 1991 European Junior title, was AAA champion in 1992 and 1995, and won at the European Cup in 1995. He is also a capable long jumper with bests of 7.51 (1992) and 7.65w (1993).

Sydney SMITH

Tennis
Sydney Howard Smith. b. 3 Feb 1872 Stroud, Glos. d. 27 Mar 1947 Stroud.

Although handicapped by playing in a leg iron, Smith was one of the greatest players of his time and was noted for his ferocious forehand drive. With fellow West countryman, Frank Riseley (qv), he won the Wimbledon doubles in 1902 and 1906 beating the renowned Doherty brothers (qv) on both occasions. In the singles he reached the Challenge Round at Wimbledon in 1900 and was a finalist in the All-Comers' in 1899 and 1905. He had a remarkable record at the Welsh Championships. winning the singles nine times in ten years 1897-1906.

He played on the winning Davis Cup team in 1905 and 1906 and, winning both singles in the Challenge Round each year, he had an unbeaten Cup record.

He was also first winner of the All-England men's singles at badminton in 1900.

Willie SMITH

Billiards
William Smith. b. 25 Jan 1886 Darlington, Co. Durham. d. 2 Jun 1982 Leeds.

Smith was the winner of the world billiards title in 1920 and 1923, on the only two occasions he played in the championships. Although the latter was his last major win, he remained a force in the game during the dominant years of Inman, Davis and Lindrum. The son of a sporting journalist, he was declared a professional at the age of 15 for accepting a modest amount of travel expenses after playing in a Middlesbrough club. He made a sensational London debut in 1912 with a break of 736 to beat the renowned Tom Newman (qv) and his score of 2743 against Newman in 1928 is often considered to be the finest break ever made, as it did not include any repetitive cannons and was compiled solely by all-round play. He toured Australia in 1929 for a series of matches against Walter Lindrum and was instrumental in persuading the Australian to come to England after the death of his young wife.

Smith was also an outstanding snooker player, losing to Joe Davis (qv) in the final of the World Championship in 1934 and 1936. Never a relaxed character, he became increasingly morose and awkward as the years passed and was constantly at loggerheads with the governing bodies, retaining a cynical view of their capabilities until his death at the age of 96.

Steve SMITH ECCLES

Horse Racing
Stephen Smith Eccles. b. 9 Jun 1955 Pinxton, Derbyshire.

Apprenticed for six years to Harry Thomson Jones, Smith Eccles became a jumps jockey after just one ride on the flat, joining Nicky Henderson's stable.

A cool, balanced and controlled rider, his first winner was in 1975 and he rode *See You Then* to victory in the Champion Hurdle for three successive years 1985-7. In 1990 he became the eighth jumps jockey to ride over 700 winners in his career, and his total reached 861 by 1995.

Karen SMITHIES

Cricket
Karen Smithies. b. 20 Mar 1969 Ashby de la Zouch, Leics. née Hickin.

A member of Newark and Sherwood CC, Smithies made her England debut in one-day internationals in 1986 and Tests in

1987. She bats left-handed and is a right-arm seam bowler. In 1993 she captained the England team that won the Women's World Cup and her miserly bowling played a major part in the team success as she took 15 wickets in the tournament at 7.93, conceding just 1.54 runs per over. She was awarded the OBE in 1994.
5 Tests 1987-92: 127 runs at 25.40, HS 64; 5 wickets at 45.00, BB 3-63; 4 catches.
32 One-day Ints 1986-93: 262 runs at 15.41; HS 41; 30 wickets at 15.00, BB 3-6; 11 catches.

Pat SMYTHE

Equestrianism, Show Jumping
Patricia Rosemary Smythe. b. 22 Nov 1928 East Sheen, Greater London. Later Mrs Koechlin-Smythe.

From her international debut at the age of 17 in 1949, Smythe built up a great reputation and became Britain's best-known show-jumper of the 1950s and early 1960s, in which period she won 13 Nations Cups. In 1957 she won the first European Ladies' Championship, riding her great horses *Flanagan* and *Prince Hal*. With *Flanagan* (and also *Scorchin* in 1961 and 1963) she was 2nd in 1959 and won again in 1961, 1962 and 1963.

When women were first admitted to Olympic show jumping events in 1956 she took a team bronze, and in 1960 she was equal 11th in the individual event, on both occasions riding *Flanagan*. She was national champion eight times, 1952-3, 1955, 1957-9 and 1961-2, and in 1954 set a European high jump record of 2.22m on *Prince Hal*.

She was awarded the OBE in 1954 and married the Swiss rider Sam Koechlin in 1963. She was president of the BSJA 1983-6.

Chris SNODE

Diving
Christopher Snode. b. 22 Mar 1959 Sutton, London.

Having competed as a 17-year-old at the 1976 Olympics, Snode went to the University of Florida at Gainesville, where he progressed to top world class. He was Commonwealth diving champion at both highboard and springboard in both 1978 and 1982 and in the 1979 World Cup he beat three-time world champion Phil Boggs (USA) into 2nd place at springboard and was also 4th at highboard. He was ill at the 1980 Olympics, but still placed 6th at the springboard, improving by only one place at his third Games in 1984, when he was also 7th at highboard. At the Europeans his best was 3rd at springboard in 1983.

ASA junior champion at highboard 1974-5, 3m springboard 1973-5 and senior champion at 1m springboard 1975-6, 3m springboard 1975-6 and 1978, highboard 1979 and 1983.

John SNOW

Cricket
John Augustine Snow. b. 13 Oct 1941 Peopleton, Worcestershire.

Snow was England's best fast bowler in a period when he was often the only top-class paceman in the team. He played for Sussex from 1961 to 1977, and took over 100 wickets in a season in 1965, in which year he made his England debut, and in 1966, but in later years tended to reserve his best for the big occasions. His best Test series were against Australia in 1970/1 when he played a major part in enabling England to win the Ashes with 31 wickets at 22.83, and in the West Indies in 1968, 27 wickets at 18.66.

He had a smooth, high action, generating genuine pace despite his relatively slim build. He could also be a useful tail-end batsman, notably when he made 59* and put on 128 for the last wicket with Ken Higgs against West Indies at The Oval in 1966. He made his highest score of 73 against India at Lord's in 1971, but was excluded from the next Test for running into Sunil Gavaskar. In 1980 he made a brief comeback to play one-day games for Warwickshire and helped them to win the Sunday League title.

His autobiography was appropriately titled *Cricket Rebel*.

49 Tests 1965-76: 772 runs at 13.54, HS 73; 202 wickets at 26.66, BB 7-40; 16 catches.
9 One-day Ints 1971-5: 9 runs at 4.50, HS 9*; 14 wickets at 16.57, BB 4-11; 1 catch.
First-class 1961-77: 4832 runs at 14.17, HS 73*; 1174 wickets at 22.72, BB 8-87; 125 catches.

Julian SNOW

Real Tennis
Julian Piercy Snow. b. 16 Jun 1964 Hereford.

A brilliant junior while at Radley, Snow won various age group titles before winning eight British Amateur singles titles (1987-9, 1991-5) and four doubles titles (1987, 1991-3). He also won the British Open singles in 1992-4.

A much travelled player, he enjoyed a particularly successful year in 1992 winning the British and US Amateur and the British, French and Australian Open singles.

Betty SNOWBALL

Cricket
Elizabeth Alexandra Snowball. b. 9 Jul 1908 Burnley, Lancashire. d. 13 Dec 1988 Colwall, Worcestershire.

As a wicket-keeper Betty Snowball was likened to Bert Oldfield (Aus) by the Australian press. She claimed 21 victims (13 catches, 8 stumpings) in her ten Tests, including four stumpings in an innings for England against Australia at Sydney in 1935. She was also a prolific opening bat, making the highest score by an England Test player of 189 in 222 minutes, including 22 boundaries, against New Zealand at Christchurch in 1935. In that match she contributed heavily to a record 2nd-wicket partnership of 235 with Molly Hide (qv). Her Test batting record was 613 runs at 40.86.

Snowball was coached by Learie Constantine at Nelson CC in Lancashire, and was the England vice-captain from 1934 to 1948. She was a teacher for many years and also represented Scotland at both lacrosse and squash.

David SOLE

Rugby Union
David Michael Barclay Sole. b. 8 May 1962
Aylesbury, Bucks.

By leading Scotland in 1990 to only the third Grand Slam in their history in his first season of captaincy, David Sole joined the immortals of Scottish rugby. A regular as a prop forward since 1986, he took over the captaincy from Finlay Calder (qv).

He played for Exeter University, Bath, with whom he won a John Player Cup winners' medal in 1987, and Edinburgh Academicals.

He announced his retirement after the 1992 game against Wales but was persuaded to lead Scotland on their 1992 tour of Australia, where Sole had earlier played in all three Tests for the 1989 Lions. Having won 44 caps and captained Scotland a record 25 times, he finally retired after that tour. He was awarded the OBE in 1993.

John SOLOMON

Croquet
John William Solomon. b. 22 Nov 1931
Wandsworth, London.

Solomon was the most successful and possibly the greatest croquet player of all-time. He made his tournament debut in 1948 while a schoolboy at Charterhouse and went on to win 31 major British events. Between 1951 and 1972 he won the Open championship, the men's championship and the men's doubles ten times each and the mixed doubles once. He also won the President's Cup on nine occasions, 1955, 1957-9, 1962-4, 1968 and 1971, and was a four-time winner of the Champion of Champions tournament. After first representing England in New Zealand in 1950, at the age of 19, he went on to play in a record 25 Test matches over five tours and captained England in Australia in 1969.

Some traditionalists held the view that his play was rather too adventurous, but his unsurpassed record provides undeniable proof of his abilities.

Tommy SOPWITH

Yachting
(Sir) Thomas Octave Murdoch Sopwith. b. 18 Jan 1888 London. d. 27 Jan 1989 Romsey, Hampshire.

A leading aircraft pioneer, he founded the Sopwith Aviation Company in 1912 and from 1935 to 1963 was president of the Hawker Siddeley Group. At yachting, in 1934 he made his first challenge for the America's Cup. Just before leaving England, his crew struck for higher wages, so his yacht *Endeavour* was manned by a crew including 13 amateurs from the Royal Corinthian YC in the races against Harold Vanderbilt's *Rainbow* in the USA. *Endeavour* proved faster and won the first two races but the Americans came back to win the next four and retain the trophy. Sopwith challenged again in 1937 but his *Endeavour II* was easily beaten 4-0 by *Ranger*.

He had also been the goalkeeper on the winning British team at the first European Championships in ice hockey in 1910. At powerboat racing he drove his *Maple Leaf IV* to victory in the Harmsworth Trophy in 1912 and 1913. He was awarded the CBE in 1918 and was knighted in 1953.

His son, Thomas Edward Brodie '**Tommy**' **Sopwith** (b. 15 Nov 1932 London), who married Gina Hathorn (qv), won the Cowes-Torquay powerboat race three times, 1961, 1968 and 1970.

Graeme SOUNESS

Football
Graeme James Souness. b. 6 May 1953
Edinburgh.

A masterly midfield player whose precision passing was a feature of his game, Souness was thought by many to adopt an unnecessarily aggressive attitude. Initially an apprentice with Tottenham Hotspur, he was transferred to Middlesbrough in 1972 for £30,000 without ever playing a League game for Spurs, and helped them win promotion to the First Division in 1974. In 1978 he moved to Liverpool and became a key player in the brilliant team which won the European Cup (1978, 1981, 1984), the

Football League (1979-80, 1982-4) and the Football League Cup (1981-4). In June 1984 he signed for Sampdoria in Italy, but returned home in 1986 to become player-manager of Rangers, whom he took to the Scottish League Championship in 1987, 1989 and 1990. In 1991 he took over as manager of Liverpool and won the FA Cup in 1992 after undergoing heart surgery, but by their own high standards the club did not yet far so well under his stewardship. In 1995 he moved on to manage the Turkish club, Galatasaray.

After winning Scottish International honours at schoolboy, youth and Under-23 level, he went on to win 54 senior caps between 1975 and 1986.

Neville SOUTHALL

Football
Neville Southall. b. 16 Sep 1958
Llandudno, Aberconwy and Colwyn.

After some brilliant performances in goal for a variety of Welsh non-League clubs, Southall signed for Bury in 1979 but after two seasons he moved to Everton where his agility and lightning reflexes played a major part in the club's successes of the 1980s. With Southall in goal, Everton won the League Championship in 1986 and 1987, the FA Cup 1984 and the European Cup Winners' Cup 1985. First capped in 1981 and maintaining a very high level of fitness, he went to play a record 80 times (to May 1995) for Wales, and kept magnificently to win a second FA Cup winner's medal for Everton in 1995. He was voted the Football Writers' Player of the Year in 1985.

Jon SPEELMAN

Chess
Jonathan Simon Speelman. b. 1956.

British champion in 1978, 1985 and 1986 and International Grand Master in 1980, Speelman shared the distinction with Nigel Short (qv) of being the first British players to qualify for the quarter-finals of the World Championship candidates tournament. Speelman beat Short easily to become Britain's first semi-finalist, at

which stage he lost narrowly to Jan Timman (Hol). He played for England at each Chess Olympiad 1980-90, winning silver medals in 1984, 1986 and 1988 and bronze in 1990. A leading analyst, he has written several books on the game.

John SPENCER

Snooker
John Spencer. b. 18 Sep 1935 Radcliffe, Gt. Manchester.

Having played snooker as a boy, Spencer did not play from the age of 18 to 28. Then he succeeded in winning a series of money matches, and was persuaded to enter the 1964 English Amateur Championship. He lost in the final, as he did in 1965, but he won in 1966, when he was also runner-up in the World Amateur. In 1969 he entered the World Professional Championship, played that year for the first time since 1951 on a knock-out basis, and he won.
A period of great success followed, with *Pot Black* wins in 1970-1 and 1976, and the World title again in 1971 and 1977. It was, however, a major shock when he was beaten in the 1972 final by Alex Higgins (qv). His last major success was when he was a member of the England World Cup winning team in 1981. In 1979 he recorded, at the Holsten Lager International at Slough, the first maximum break of 147 ever scored in a major tournament.
He became chairman of the World Professional Billiards and Snooker Association in 1990.

Terry SPINKS

Boxing
Terence George Spinks. b. 28 Feb 1938
West Ham, London.

An apprentice jockey, Spinks gained his early boxing experience in stable lads' competitions and in his first year of senior competition he won the 1956 ABA flyweight title. Later in the year he won an Olympic gold medal before turning professional early in 1957. In September 1960 he won the British featherweight title, defeating Bobby Neill in seven rounds, but after one successful defence against Neill he lost the title to Howard Winstone (qv) in May 1961.

Career record 1957-62: 49 contests. Won 41, Drew 1, Lost 7.

Reg SPOONER

Cricket
Reginald Herbert Spooner. b. 21 Oct 1880 Litherland, Merseyside. d. 2 Oct 1961 Lincoln.

Renowned as one of the most stylish players of the great era of the amateur, with a fiercely majestic off-drive, Spooner opened the innings for Lancashire for nearly 20 years apart from three years military service in the Boer War. Also a graceful cover point, he exceeded 1000 runs in a season six times, with a best of 2312 runs at 51.37 in 1911.

He was offered the England captaincy for the tour to Australia in 1920/1, but had to drop out through injury.

At rugby football he played for Liverpool as a centre three-quarter and played once for England, against Wales in 1903, and he also played county soccer. He became land agent to Lord Londesborough.

10 Tests 1905-12: 481 runs at 32.06, 1 100 HS 119; 4 catches.

First-class 1899-1923: 13,681 runs at 36.28, 31 100s HS 247; 6 wickets at 97.00, BB 1-5; 142 catches.

Sarah SPRINGMAN

Triathlon
(Dr) Sarah Marcella Springman. b. 26 Dec 1956 London.

Springman was the first British triathlete to win a European title, winning at the Ironman distances in 1985 and 1986 and at short distance in 1988. She was British triathlon champion a record eleven times and became a vice-president of the International Triathlon Union in 1992. While a student at Cambridge University, where she now lectures in soil mechanics, she was a squash Blue and also British Universities cycling champion. She has been a member of the GB Sports Council from 1993.

Jeff SQUIRE

Rugby Union
Jeffrey Squire. b. 23 Sep 1951 Pontywaun, Caerphilly.

Winner of 29 caps in the Welsh back row 1977-83, Squire is one of the few men to have played in a Test on three separate British Lions tours. In 1977 he flew out to New Zealand as a replacement for the injured Roger Uttley (qv) and played in the 4th Test. In South Africa in 1980 he played in all four Tests and back in New Zealand in 1983 he played in the 1st Test before a shoulder injury ruled him out of the remainder of the tour.

Initially with Newport, he moved to Pontypool in 1978 and took over as captain the following year. He also captained Wales in six matches and later served as a Welsh selector. He is now a director of a sportswear company.

Tommy STACK (Ireland)

Horse Racing
Thomas Brendan Stack. b. 15 Nov 1945 Co. Kerry.

Starting his career with Bobby Renton, Stack proved to be a natural rider and within three months had ridden his first winner. He rode *Red Rum* to his third Grand National victory in 1977, but Stack's career ended when he broke his pelvis falling when riding *Red Rum* in his last race a year later. By then he had ridden 606 winners under National Hunt rules, and was champion jockey with 97 winners in 1976/7.

He bred horses and became the manager of the Longfield Stud, Cashel, Co. Tipperary before turning to training in the late 1980s. He sent out *Las Meninas* to win the 1000 Guineas in 1994, his first runner in an English Classic.

Kay STAMMERS

Tennis
Katherine Esther Stammers. b. 3 Apr 1914 St Albans, Herts. Later Mrs M.Menzies then Mrs T.W.Bullitt.

A charming and attractive left-hander,

Stammers was Britain's most popular lady player and delighted her supporters by reaching the Wimbledon singles final in 1939. She was also a semi-finalist in the singles at the US Championships (1935-6, 1939) but had a better record as a doubles player winning at Wimbledon in 1935 and 1936 with Freda James and at the 1935 French Championships with Peggy Scriven (qv).

She continued her career after the war, reaching the quarter-finals of the singles and the semi-finals of the doubles at Wimbledon in both 1946 and 1947. Her Wightman Cup career also spanned the war and between 1935 and 1948 she played in eight matches (4/14 singles, 1/5 doubles) after which she was non-playing captain, 1959-60.

Although a major singles title eluded her, she claimed some notable victories, particularly over the leading Americans. She beat the near-invincible Helen Wills-Moody (USA) 6-0, 6-4 at Beckenham in 1935, she defeated Helen Jacobs (USA) in the Wightman Cup in 1935 and 1936 and again in the Wimbledon quarter-finals in 1939, and she beat Alice Marble (USA) in the 1938 Wightman Cup. She also had an excellent record at the British Hard Court Championships winning the singles (1935-6, 1939) and the doubles (1936, 1946, 1948). After the death of her first husband, Michael Menzies, she married Thomas Bullitt in Philadelphia in 1975.

Larry STANLEY (Ireland)

Gaelic Football
Larry Stanley. b. 1896 Co. Kildare. d.?

Stanley won all-Ireland football medals with both Kildare and Dublin in his playing career, which lasted from 1916 to 1932, and in 1970 was elected to the Hall of Fame.

He was Irish high jump champion in 1924 and 1925 and won the English AAA title in 1924, in which year he recorded his best jump of 6 ft 3 in *1.907m* and carried the flag for Ireland, before placing 10th at high jump at the Olympic Games.

David STARBROOK

Judo
David Colin Starbrook. b. 9 Aug 1945 Croydon.

Starbrook won a record nine British titles, middleweight 1969-70, light-heavyweight 1971-5 and the Open division 1970-1. A strong and determined competitor, he won the world bronze medal at middleweight in 1971 and, moving up to light-heavyweight, the Olympic silver in 1972 when he was beaten in the final by Shoto Chochoshvili (USSR), against whom he had been awarded a split decision in the preliminary rounds. In 1973 he won the European silver and World bronze. He returned to the Olympics to win a bronze medal in 1976. He was awarded the MBE.

Ian STARK

Equestrianism, Three-day Event
Ian David Stark. b. 22 Feb 1954 Galashiels, Borders.

In 1991 Stark won double gold at the European Championships for three-day event, as his team gold followed those of 1985, 1987 and 1989, and his individual win on *Glenburnie* followed silver medals in 1985 and 1987. At the Olympic Games he won team silver medals in 1984 and 1988, with 9th individually in 1984 on *Oxford Blue* and 2nd in 1988 on *Sir Wattie*. He also rode *Sir Wattie* to victory at Badminton in 1986 and 1988.

He was awarded the MBE in 1989 and farms in the Borders.

Greville STARKEY

Horse Racing
Greville Michael William Starkey. b. 21 Dec 1939 Lichfield, Staffordshire.

Starkey rode his first winner at Pontefract in 1956, when he was apprenticed to Harry Thomson Jones, and retired in 1989. He was first jockey to John Oxley 1961-9 and Henry Cecil (qv) 1970-4, before a spell as a freelance and then teamed up with Guy Harwood. He rode *Homeward Bound* to win The Oaks in 1964 and *Star Appeal* to win the Prix de l'Arc de Triomphe in 1975, but had few other major successes until a marvellous year in 1978, when he had 10 Group One winners, including the English and Irish Derby and Oaks double with *Shirley Heights* and *Fair Salinia*. In all he won five English Classics.

He was champion apprentice in 1957 and his highest number of winners in a season was 107 in 1978. He also reached exactly 100 in 1978 and 103 in 1982-3. He is now an assistant trainer and owns a stud farm in Newmarket.

Brian STATHAM

Cricket
John Brian Statham. b. 17 Jun 1930 Gorton, Manchester. *10/6/2000*

Statham was a wonderfully accurate fast bowler for England in the 1950s, forming famous partnerships with Frank Tyson and with Fred Trueman (qqv). He had a beautifully rhythmic action and his effectiveness was marked not only by his own fine figures, but also by the enormous help that his relentless accuracy gave to his partners. After just one part-season in which he had taken 37 wickets for Lancashire, he was a replacement on the England tour of Australasia in 1950/1, making his Test debut against New Zealand. His best Test series figures were 27 wickets at 18.18 against South Africa in 1960, and he exceeded 100 wickets in 13 English seasons, all at an average of 21.63 or better, with a low of 12.29 for his 134 wickets in 1958.

In 1963 he passed the record for most wickets in Tests, set at 236 by Alec Bedser (qv), but Statham, in turn, was passed two months later by Trueman.

Nicknamed 'George', this highly popular and much respected cricketer was also a brilliant fielder and captained Lancashire in 1965-7. He was awarded the CBE in 1966.

70 Tests 1951-65: 675 runs at 11.44, HS 38; 252 wickets at 24.84, BB 7-39; 28 catches.

First-class 1950-68: 5424 runs at 10.80, HS 62; 2260 wickets at 16.36, BB 8-34; 230 catches.

Allan STEEL

Cricket
Allan Gibson Steel. b. 24 Sep 1858 Liverpool. d. 15 Jun 1914 Hyde Park, London.

Steel topped the first-class averages, taking 164 wickets at 9.43 with his right-arm bowling of varied pace, spinning the ball both ways, in his first full season, 1878. This was the first of the four years that he was in the Cambridge University team and he also gained Blues for rugby and racquets. He had made his debut for Lancashire the previous year and went on to captain England in four Tests against Australia, including three in 1886, which were all won. Also an aggressive middle-order batsman, he was regarded as second only to W.G.Grace (qv) as an all-rounder, although his work as a barrister - he became a KC and Recorder of Oldham - reduced his ability to play regular cricket.

He was MCC president in 1902 and had three brothers who played for Lancashire.

13 Tests 1880-8: 600 runs at 35.29, 2 100s HS 148; 29 wickets at 20.86, BB 3-27; 5 catches.

First-class 1877-95: 7000 runs at 29.41, 8 100s HS 171; 788 wickets at 14.80, BB 9-63; 137 catches.

Billy STEEL

Football
William Steel. b. 1 May 1923 Denny, Falkirk. d. 13 May 1982 San Francisco, USA.

Blessed with exceptional pace and devastating shooting power with his left foot, Steel had a meteoric rise to fame.

Although he signed as a professional with Greenock Morton in 1941, the start of his League career was delayed by the war but on his international debut, in the first post-war match between England and Scotland in 1947, he gave such a brilliant performance at inside-left that he was selected for Great Britain v The Rest of Europe the following month. Another impressive showing resulted in him being signed by Derby County in the summer for £15,000 which was the first time a five figure fee had been paid by an English club to a Scottish club. His days at Derby were not happy ones and, after several well-publicised disputes with the management, he returned to Scotland, joining Dundee in 1950 for a Scottish record fee of £23,000, helping them to win the League Cup twice, 1952-3, and to reach the Scottish FA Cup final in 1952. Between 1947 and 1953 he won 30 Scottish caps but after being dropped from Dundee's first team he left, without warning, for America where he played in the unofficial leagues. When he eventually gave up playing he worked in advertising in Los Angeles.

Dorothy STEEL

Croquet
Dorothy Dyne Steel. b. 21 Apr 1884 Woodsetts, South Yorkshire. d. 22 Jan 1965 Biddenham, Bedfordshire.

Steel was the greatest woman croquet player of all-time and the equal of any of her male contemporaries. The daughter of a Yorkshire clergyman, she learned the game on the vicarage lawn, and with her effective but unexciting style she won 4 Open Championships (1923, 1933, 1935-6), 15 women's Championships (8 of them in succession), 5 women's doubles and 7 mixed doubles for a total of 31 titles. She also won the President's Cup six times and rated her last victory in 1937 as the best of her many fine performances.
She played for England in 1925, 1928 and 1939 but refused to go on the 1927 tour of Australia following a dispute over expenses. After the war, when her hands were crippled by arthritis, she was forced to give up playing but continued to make her presence felt in the game as a notable team manager. DD, as she was always known, spent much of her life at Biddenham, Bedford where she played croquet for the local club and was a keen rider to hounds.

David STEELE

Cricket
David Stanley Steele. b. 29 Sep 1941 Bradeley, Staffordshire.

While Steele had an all-too-short Test career he became a national hero, and BBC Sports Personality of the Year in 1975 when he stepped into the beleaguered England team to combat the pace of the Australians Dennis Lillee and Jeff Thomson. He was 33 and looked older, with his prematurely grey hair, and had until then been thought of as an ordinary county standard batsman. His dogged determination and courage were just what was wanted and he scored 365 runs at 60.83 in his three Tests that summer, his six scores all between 39 and 92. He scored a century in the first of his five Tests against the West Indies the next summer, but doubts about his ability against spin bowling meant that he was not selected for the tour of India that followed – and he was never again called upon for England.
He scored over 1000 runs in a season ten times with bests of 1756 at 48.77 in 1975 and 1618 at 52.19 in 1972. He did not bowl much in the mid 1970s but was also an accurate slow left-armer and excelled in that vein towards the end of his career, which, after playing Minor Counties cricket for Staffordshire, was with Northants 1963-78 and 1983-4 and Derbyshire 1979-81.
8 Tests 1975-6: 673 runs at 42.06, 1 100 HS 106; 2 wickets at 19.50, BB 1-1; 7 catches.
1 One-day Int 1976: 8 runs at 8.00, HS 8.
First-class 1963-84: 22,346 runs at 32.47, 20 100s HS 140*; 623 wickets at 24.89, BB 8-29; 546 catches.
His brother **John** (b. 23 Jul 1946) played as a right-hand batsman and slow left-arm bowler for Leicestershire 1970-85 and Glamorgan 1986, with a career record of 15.054 runs at 28.95 with 21 100s, and 584 wickets at 27.04, and 412 catches.

Mavis STEELE

Bowls
Mavis Mary Steele. b. 9 Sep 1928 Kenton, London.

Steele was a world champion bowler and leading administrator of the game. At the World Championships she won six medals: gold in the fours and team event in 1981, three silver (singles and pairs 1973, triples 1981) and one bronze at fours 1985. She won the Commonwealth games bronze medal at triples in 1982 and was runner-up in the World indoor singles in 1989.

She won a total of 11 English titles, including the singles outdoors in 1961-2 and 1969 and indoors in 1989, and represented England internationally for 33 successive years. During the latter part of her career she became involved in the administration of the game and served as assistant secretary of the English Women's Bowling Association and as president of the English Women's Indoor Bowling Association in 1989-90. In 1983 she was awarded the MBE for her services to the game.

Jock STEIN

Football
John Stein. b. 6 Oct 1922 Hamilton, South Lanarkshire. d. 10 Sep 1985 Ninian Park, Cardiff.

Stein was the most successful of all Scottish football managers and one of the greatest in the history of the game. His playing career took him to Albion Rovers and Llanelli before he joined Celtic in 1951 to help with the coaching of the junior teams. He made such a favourable impression that he became captain of the first team, leading them to the Scottish League and Cup double in 1954.

His playing career was ended by injury in 1955 and after managerial appointments at Dunfermline and Hibernian he returned to Parkhead in 1965 as manager of Celtic. In his first season Celtic won the Scottish Cup, the first of many successes. In 1967 Celtic became the first British club to win the European Cup and under his guidance they went on to win the League Championship ten times, the Scottish Cup eight times and the League Cup six times between 1966 and 1977. Following some internal disagreements at Celtic he left to take over as manager of Leeds in 1978 but after just 44 days he returned to Scotland to become manager of the national team. He was awarded the CBE in 1970 and died of a heart attack at the end of Scotland's match against Wales in Cardiff in 1985. The 1-1 draw ensured that Scotland qualified for the 1986 World Cup finals.

Although Jock Stein never lived to see his team play in Mexico he will always be remembered as a kindly. dignified and gracious monument to the some of the best years of Scottish football.

Rees STEPHENS

Rugby Union
John Rees Glyn Stephens. b. 16 Apr 1922 Neath, Neath and Port Talbot.

The start of Stephens's international career was delayed by the war, and after playing in four Victory Internationals, he made his full international debut against England in 1947. He was not a regular in the Welsh XV until the latter part of his career but when he retired from international rugby in 1957 he had won 32 caps at lock or no. 8 and at the time he was the most-capped Welsh forward.

With the 1950 British Lions an injured shoulder contributed to his failure to win a Test place against New Zealand but he played in the second-row in both Tests against Australia.

On his return, he commanded a regular international place and finally retired after 11 seasons of international rugby. One of the stars in a golden age of Welsh rugby, he captained both Neath and Wales.

His father, **Glynn** (1891-1965), also won four caps and they are the only father and son to have captained Wales. Both were stalwarts of the Neath club.

Arthur STEPHENSON

Horse Racing
William Arthur Stephenson. b. 7 Apr 1920 Leasingthorne, Co. Durham. d. 3 Dec 1992 Middlesbrough.

Although Stephenson came from a notable training family, he made a late start to his career as a trainer, farming at Bishop Auckland until he took a licence in 1959. Then he speedily became established. In 1969/70 he became the first man to train more than 100 winners in a National Hunt season in Britain. While he did not exceed that season's total of 114, he went on to top the 100 mark seven times in all, each year to 1974 and again in 1975/6 and

1976/7 and was champion trainer ten times. In all he won a record 2644 races over jumps, plus 344 on the flat, in Britain 1946-92.

His cousin **Willie** (b. 9 Oct 1911) rode from 1925 to 1945 and trained the three-time Champion Hurdle winner *Sir Ken*, the 1951 Derby winner *Arctic Prince*, and the 1959 Grand National winner *Oxo*.

George STEPHENSON (Ireland)

Rugby Union
George Vaughan Stephenson. b. 22 Dec 1901. d. 6 Aug 1970 Lambeth, London.

Stephenson was one of the greatest Irish players; with 42 caps 1920-30 he was the world's most capped player until Jackie Kyle (qv) beat his record in 1956, and his 14 international tries remained an Irish record until beaten by Brendan Mullin (qv).

A forceful, hard-running centre he made his international debut as an 18 year-old against England in 1920 and only missed two internationals, both due to injury, over the next 10 seasons. He captained Ireland in his last 13 matches. Much of his rugby was played in England while he was a medical student at the London Hospital.

His brother, **Henry** (1900-58), also won 14 Irish caps as a winger, 1922-8.

Charlotte STERRY – see COOPER

Gary STEVENS

Football
Michael Gary Stevens. b. 27 Mar 1963 Barrow-in-Furness, Cumbria.

After serving as an apprentice at Everton, Stevens signed as a professional for the club in 1981 and played at right-back on the team which won the FA Cup in 1984, the European Cup Winners' Cup 1985 and the League Championship 1985 and 1987. In 1988 he was transferred for a fee of £1 million to Rangers where he gained winners' medals in the Scottish Cup 1992 and the Scottish League Cup 1989, 1991 and 1994, plus the League title each year to 1995.

His exceptional speed and his long throw were his greatest assets, as he earned 46 England caps between 1985 and 1992.

Ray STEVENS

Badminton
Raymond Philip Stevens. b. 23 Jun 1951 Walthamstow, London.

Stevens was England's leading player of the 1970s and an all-out attacker. A European Junior doubles champion in 1969, he formed an outstanding partnership with Mike Tredgett (qv) when he entered the senior ranks. Together they won the European title in 1976 and 1978, were gold medallists at the 1978 Commonwealth Games and won seven English National titles, 1983 and six successive 1976-81. They were finalists at the All-England Championships in 1972 and 1980, but lost to an Indonesian pairing in both years.

Stevens also won the English National singles five times (1973, 1977, 1979-81), was European singles runner-up in 1982 and won 111 caps for England from 1970 until cartilage trouble ended his playing career in 1982. He later became the national coach for Wales.

His nephew is Darren Hall (qv).

H.W. STEVENSON

Billiards
Henry William Stevenson. b. 15 Jul 1874 Hull. d. 11 Jun 1964 Isleworth, London.

Universally known by his initials 'H.W.', Stevenson was the dominant figure in world billiards after the retirement of John Roberts, Jnr (qv). Beginning as a marker in his native Hull, he made a name for himself in South Africa where he lived for a number of years before playing his first professional game in England. After finishing as runner-up to Charles Dawson in the 1900 World Championship, he beat Dawson for the title in 1901. Over the next decade the title changed hands frequently and Stevenson claimed the Championship four more times. He was still a contender in 1919 and 1920 when approaching 50.

Many professionals of the time went on tour to boost their earnings, but Stevenson travelled more than most. In 1921, accompanied by Claude Faulkiner, he embarked on a tour which lasted almost two years and took him to South and East Africa, India, Burma, China, Japan, New Zealand and Australia.

Alec STEWART

Cricket
Alec James Stewart. b. 8 Apr 1963 Merton, London.

A classy right-handed batsman, Stewart has established a regular place in the England team, although his batting has proved much more successful when he has not also been asked to handle the wicket-keeping duties. His all-round abilities have presented the selectors with a problem, in that although he is a high capable keeper and his role as much allows England to play another batsman, it does seem to be asking too much of anyone to have to concentrate on both opening the batting and keeping wicket at Test level.

Usually batting at No. 4 for Surrey, whom he has captained from 1992, he has proved a most effective opener for England, always prepared to attack the bowling. His best Test series to date has been in the West Indies in 1994, when he opened and scored 477 runs at 53.00, his centuries in each innings at Bridgetown, Barbados inspiring England's epic victory and being a first for any Englishman against West Indies. He has been vice-captain to both Graham Gooch and Mike Atherton (qqv), and led England in two Tests in 1993.

He has scored over 1000 runs in a season eight times with a peak of 1637 in 1989. That year he also tied the world record with eleven catches in a match, for Surrey v Leicestershire. In 1994 he set a NatWest Trophy record with seven catches in an innings for Surrey against Glamorgan.

45 Tests 1990-5: 3055 runs at 40.19, 7 100s HS 190; 55 catches, 4 stumpings.
64 One-day Ints 1989-95: 1665 runs at 30.27, 1 100 HS 103; 50 catches, 4 stumpings.
First-class 1981-95: 15,815 runs at 39.63, 31 100s HS 206*; 3 wickets at 125.00, BB 1-7; 345 catches, 13 stumpings.

His father **Michael** James Stewart (b. 16 Sep 1932 Herne Hill, London) played as an opening batsman for England and Surrey, whom he captained from 1963 to 1972, leading them to their last County Championship success in 1971. He scored over 1000 runs in a season 15 times, with a peak of 2045 at 44.45 in 1962 and in 1957 held 77 catches, just one short of Wally Hammond's record and including a world first-class record seven in one innings against Northants. He was Surrey manager from 1979 and became England team manager; being awarded the MBE in 1993. At football he was an amateur international and played for Charlton Athletic 1956-8.
8 Tests 1962-45: 385 runs at 35.00, HS 87; 6 catches.
First-class 1954-72: 26,492 runs at 32.90, 49 100s HS 227*; 1 wicket; 634 catches.

Ian STEWART

Athletics
Ian Stewart. b. 15 Jan 1949 Handsworth, Birmingham.

Stewart was a determined competitor who compiled a fine racing record. Coached by Geoff Warr at Birchfield Harriers from the age of 15, he worked very hard and his first successes came at cross-country, the Midland youths title in 1966 and the Midland and National junior titles in 1968. In the summer that year he set five European Junior records from 3000 to 5000m. In his first year as a senior in 1969 he won the European indoor 3000m and outdoor 5000m. Then in 1970 he won the Commonwealth Games 5000m in a European record of 13:22.8. This was one of the great races of all time, as Stewart battled with fellow-Scot Ian McCafferty down the finishing straight, leaving the all-time greats Kip Keino (Ken) and Ron Clarke (Aus) behind them.

He missed most of the 1971 season through injury, but was back in 1972, when he was 3rd in the International cross-country and took the Olympic bronze at 5000m. Disappointed with 5th at 5000m and 6th at 10,000m at the 1974 Commonwealth Games, he turned to cycling for a while, but came back in superb style in 1975, when he won his second European Indoor 3000m title and just a week later won the World cross-country title. In 1976 he was 7th in the Olympic 5000m. He won AAA titles at 5000m in 1969 and indoor 3000m in 1972-3 and 1975, and the UK 10,000m in 1977 after setting a world best time for 10 miles on the roads of 45:13. In 1978 he ran in the England National cross-country for the first time as a senior and came 2nd.

He was awarded the MBE in 1979, and after coaching and working to promote distance running, he succeeded Andy Norman as promotions officer for the BAF in 1994. Other British records: 1500m 3:39.12 (1969), 2000m 5:02.98 (1975), 2M 8:22.0 (1972). Other best times: 1M 3:57.3 (1969), 3000m 7:46.83 (1976), 10,000m 27:43.03 (1977).

His brother **Peter** (b. 8 Aug 1947) won the European Indoor 3000m in 1971 and set British records at 2 miles, 8:26.8 in 1970, and at 1500m 3:38.22 and 1 mile 3:55.3 in 1972. Unfortunately after winning the 1972 AAA 1500m he had to withdraw from the Olympic team through injury. He was 4th in the 1970 Commonwealth 1500m and won the AAA indoor 3000m in 1971. His other best times: 800m 1:50.8 (1971), 5000m 13:57.4 (1972).

His sister Mary (qv) set British records and won European Indoor and Commonwealth titles.

Jackie STEWART

Motor Racing
John Young Stewart. b. 11 Jun 1939 Dumbarton, Dumbarton and Clydebank.

Stewart was Britain's most successful driver, world champion in 1969, 1971 and 1973, and runner-up in 1968 and 1972. In his Formula One career from 1965 to 1973 he set a record, since surpassed by Alain Prost (Fra), of 27 Grand Prix wins and 360 points (from 99 races), driving for BRM 1965-7, Matra 1968-9, March 1970 and Tyrrell 1971-3.

His father was a Jaguar dealer and his elder brother Jimmy had raced in the 1950s. At trap shooting Jackie won a

series of major events, including the British Championships in 1959-60, but was bitterly disappointed to fail at the trials for the 1960 Olympic Games.

He first raced in 1960 and his ability was soon apparent, as he was the most successful British driver in club races in 1963 and won 11 Formula Three races for Cooper-BMC in 1964. Signed by BRM for Formula One in 1965 he was an immediate success, with a point in his first race, a win in the Italian GP at Monza and 3rd place overall. He campaigned hard to sell the sport, pushing it into a modern big business enterprise, and he became by far the sport's biggest money-earner.

After he retired at the top of his profession, he continued his jet-set life, promoting the sport and campaigning vigorously for improved driver safety standards. BBC Sports Personality of the Year 1973 and *Daily Express* Sportsman of the Year 1971 and 1973, he was awarded the OBE in 1972.

Mary STEWART

Athletics
Mary Stewart. b. 25 Feb 1956 Birmingham. Later Mrs Cotton.

Mary emulated the athletics success of her elder brothers, Peter and Ian Stewart (qv). At 1500m she won the European Indoors in 1977 and the Commonwealth title in 1978 and she set British records for 1000m 2:39.42 (1974) and 1 mile 4:36.1 (1977) and a world indoor 1500m record of 4:08.1 in 1977. She improved her best mile time to 4:34.3 indoors and 4:35.17 outdoors in 1979 and her other best times were: 800m 2:03.11 (1977), 1500m 4:06.0 (1978), 3000m 9:05.4 (1984).

She set a world best time for a 14-year-old at 1500m in 1970 and won the National cross-country title for intermediates in 1971 and 1972, capturing the senior title in 1978. Competing for Scotland at the 1974 Commonwealth Games, she was 4th at 1500m, but switched allegiance to England for her 1978 triumph. After that she had the misfortune to fall in her heat of the European 1500m. She was a semi-finalist at the 1976 Olympics. She retired in 1980 at the age of 24, but came back to win the Midland 1500m in 1984, although she did not compete at international level. By then she had married David Cotton, who competed for Britain in the 1978 Europeans at 50km walk.

Jeannette STEWART-WOOD

Water Skiing
Jeannette Stewart-Wood. b. 1946. Later Mrs Williamson.

Stewart-Wood was the first British water-skier to win a world title, which she achieved at jumping and overall in 1967. A student at London University, she had been runner-up at this event in 1965. She began water-skiing at the age of ten, won the European junior title at jumping in 1961, and in 1963 she became, at 17, the youngest British overall champion, a title she won again in 1966-7, when she won all four titles. She then retired briefly, but came back to win the European jumping title in 1968. She had earlier taken European titles at jumps in 1964 and 1966-7, slalom 1966-7 and overall 1967.

With jumping her speciality, she became the first European to exceed 100 ft *30.48m* in 1965, and her jump of 32.39m at Ruislip in 1967 exceeded the then world record by 9cm, although the rules stated that to be recognised a new record had to beat the old by at least 20cm.

Nobby STILES

Football
Norbert Peter Stiles. b. 18 May 1942 Salford, Gt. Manchester.

Stiles was an unlikely-looking hero of England's World Cup successes in 1966, with his false teeth and glasses off the pitch, the combative litlle man fully justfied Alf Ramsey's (qv) faith in him. He had been a schoolboy international and first played for Manchester United as an inside-forward, but had settled at right-half as United won League Championship honours in 1965 and 1967 and the European Cup in 1968. He made 28 appearances for England 1965-70, and in 1971 was transferred to Second Division Middlesbrough.

Andrew STODDART

Cricket and Rugby Union
Andrew Ernest Stoddart. b. 11 Mar 1863 South Shields, Tyne and Wear. d. 4 Apr 1915 London.

Stoddart was the first man to captain England to wins at both rugby and cricket. He made his first-class cricket debut for Middlesex and gained the first of his ten caps for England as a wing three-quarter at rugby (four as captain, including uniquely on his first appearance) in 1885. He took England cricket teams to Australia in 1894/5 and 1897/8, having toured there earlier in 1887/8 and 1891/2. His best season in England was in 1893, when he scored 2072 runs at 42.28 in first-class matches.

A stockbroker, he made 221 in his last first-class innings in cricket, for Middlesex against Hampshire in 1900, and scored prolifically for Hampstead in club cricket, including the then record of 485 against the Stoics in one afternoon in 1886. He was a stylish right-handed opening batsman and medium-paced bowler. At rugby he captained the first Barbarians side in 1890/1. He took his own life in 1915 after declining health and financial problems.

16 Tests 1888-98: 996 runs at 35.57, 2 100s HS 173; 2 wickets at 47.00, BB 1-10; 6 catches.

First-class 1885-1900: 16,738 runs at 32.12, 26 100s HS 221; 278 wickets at 23.63, BB 7-67; 257 catches.

Adrian STOOP

Rugby Union
Adrian Dura Stoop. b. 27 Mar 1883 London. d. 27 Nov 1957 Hartley Witney, Hants.

The most famous of all Harlequin players, Stoop joined the club on leaving Oxford University (Blue 1902-04) and served as club captain 1906-14, secretary 1920-38 and president 1920-49; the 'Quins Adrian Stoop Memorial Ground at Twickenham is named in his honour. For England he won 12 caps at fly-half and two at scrum-half and his brother, **Frederick** (1888-1972), played with Adrian in three of his four international appearances.

Apart from his dedication to the Harlequins with his great leadership and development of three-quarter play, Adrian Stoop served the sport in a wider field: he was an England selector 1927-31, president of the RFU 1932-3 and also a first-class referee. A qualified barrister, he was awarded the Military Cross in 1919.

Billy STOTT

Horse Racing
William Stott. d. 1933.

Stott was champion National Hunt jockey for five successive years from 1927/8 to 1931/2, with 88, 76, 77, 81 and 77 winners respectively. He completed the spring double at Cheltenham in 1933 for trainer Basil Briscoe by riding *Insurance* to win the Champion Hurdle and then *Golden Miller* to the second of his five Cheltenham Gold Cup wins in 1933, but he was replaced as *Golden Miller*'s jockey for the Grand National by Ted Leader. Soon afterwards he was forced to give up riding because of heart trouble and he died following a car crash later in the year.

Michael STOUTE

Horse Racing
Michael Ronald Stoute. b. 22 Oct 1945
Barbados.

Son of the Chief of Police in Barbados, Stoute came to Britain and worked for Pat Rohan at Malton 1965-8, Douglas Smith 1968-70 and Harry Thomson Jones 1970-2, before gaining his trainer's licence in 1972.

He first trained over 100 winners in a year in 1980 and was champion trainer in 1981 and again in 1986, 1989 and 1994. His progressive record has been: 101 winners in 1980, 103 in 1982, 120 in 1985. In 1986 he set a record for worldwide earnings by a British trainer of £2,778,405 and in 1989 he set a record in Britain of £2,000,330.

His first Classics winner was *Fair Salinia* in the 1978 Oaks and his first English and Irish Derby winner the ill-fated *Shergar* in 1981. In 1995 he sent out his 10th winner of an Irish Classic.

John H. STRACEY

Boxing
John Henry Stracey. b. 22 Sep 1950
Bethnal Green, London.

After winning the British (1973) and European (1974) welterweight titles, Stracey challenged the legendary José Napoles (Cuba) for the WBC World title in December 1975 in Mexico City. Stracey was floored in the first round but came back in sensational fashion to take the title with a sixth round stoppage. His first successful title defence, against Hedgemon Lewis (USA) in March 1976, also ended inside the distance when the referee called a halt in the 10th round. His third and final World title fight came just three months later and although Stracey felt that he needed a rest, his manager Terry Lawless and promoter Mickey Duff eventually persuaded him to put his title on the line against Carlos Palomino (Mexico) at Wembley. Stracey's misgivings proved well-founded and the Mexican's devastating body attack gave him the title in the 12th round. His last big fight was a 10th round defeat by Dave 'Boy' Green in 1977.

As an amateur he fought at lightweight at the 1968 Olympics and won the ABA light welterweight title in 1969.

Career record 1969-78: 51 contests. Won 45 (37 KO), Drew 1, Lost 5.

Gordon STRACHAN

Football
Gordon David Strachan. b. 9 Feb 1957
Edinburgh.

In an exceptionally long career the slight, red-haired Strachan won the highest honours in Scottish and English football. A tireless midfield player, he made his League debut with Dundee in 1975 and on moving to Aberdeen in 1977 he helped them win the European Cup Winners' Cup (1983), the Scottish Cup (1982, 1983, 1984) and the Scottish League (1980, 1984). In the summer of 1984 he was transferred to Manchester United where he won an FA Cup winners' medal in his first season. From Manchester United he went to Leeds in 1988, quickly becoming captain and helping them win promotion to Division I in 1990 and the League Championship in 1992. His international career ended in 1992 after he had won 50 Scottish caps since his debut in 1980, and he was awarded the OBE in 1993. He announced his retirement in 1995, and was appointed assistant manager at Coventry City.

Shirley STRONG

Athletics, Hurdling
Shirley Elaine Strong. b. 18 Nov 1958 Northwich, Cheshire.

Strong was Commonwealth champion in 1982 with silver medals at the 1978 Commonwealth Games and 1984 Olympics at the 100m hurdles.

A glamorous blonde, coached by Joe Harris at Stretford throughout her career, she set five British records from 13.06 in 1980 to 12.82 in 1983, with a wind-assisted best of 12.78 when 5th at the 1983 World Championships. She won a record six successive WAAA titles 1979-84 and was also UK champion in 1979-80 and 1983.

Herbert STRUDWICK

Cricket
Herbert Strudwick. b. 28 Jan 1880 Mitcham, London. d. 14 Feb 1970 Shoreham, West Sussex.

England's best wicket-keeper of his era, Strudwick set a record number of first-class career dismissals (since passed by John Murray and Bob Taylor (qqv)) from his Surrey debut in 1902. His 91 dismissals in his first full season was at the time a record. Better batsmen were often preferred to him in the Test team and he was aged 41 before he kept in a Test in England. He was quiet and unobtrusive but very quick on his feet. He became Surrey's scorer for many years.
28 Tests 1910-26: 230 runs at 7.93, HS 24; 60 catches, 12 stumpings.
First-class 1902-27: 6445 runs at 10.89, HS 93; 1 wicket; 1242 catches, 255 stumpings.

Nik STUART

Gymnastics
Wray Stuart. b. 20 Jul 1927.

Britain's top gymnast and unbeaten as national champion between 1956 and 1963, Stuart was a pioneer of the sport in Britain. In 1957 he became the first British holder of the FIG pin.
Serving in the army, he took up the sport relatively late but retained his supreme fitness. Leaving the army he became a professional coach in 1963 and was awarded the MBE for his services to the sport. He became National Staff Coach.

Colin STURGESS

Cycling
Colin Andrew Sturgess. b. 15 Dec 1968 Wakefield.

Educated at Marian College, Johannesburg, South Africa and Loughborough University, as an amateur Sturgess won national junior titles at 3km pursuit 1985-6, and senior 4km 1987, 5km 1989-91 and competed at the 1986 Commonwealth and 1988 Olympic Games. He was then world professional pursuit champion in 1989, and 3rd in 1991 and won British professional titles at 5km pursuit 1990-1 and road 1990.

William STURGESS

Walking
William James Sturgess. b. 2 Apr 1871 Dublin. d. 27 Jun 1945 West Ealing, London.

Sturgess was the winner of the AAA walk titles at 4 miles each year 1895 to 1900 and at both 2 and 7 miles in 1902. He also won a Danish title in 1897.
Best times: 1M 6:33.6 (1896), 2M 13:24.2 (1897), 7M 51:27.0 (1895), 1 hour 8M 274y (1895).

Jim SULLIVAN

Rugby League
James Sullivan. b. 2 Dec 1903 Cardiff. d. 14 Sep 1977 Wigan.

Sulivan was the most prodigious goal

kicker of all time. Between 1921 and 1946 he kicked 2867 goals and scored 6192 points in a record 928 club, representative and international matches, including records for one club, Wigan, with totals of 2317, 4883 and 774 respectively.

He became full-back in Cardiff's rugby union XV at 16 and had the distinction of being, at the age of 17 years 26 days, the youngest player ever to represent the Barbarians, at Newport in December 1920. Six months later he signed for Wigan to begin his epic league career. He made a record 60 international appearances, 25 of which were for Great Britain and the remainder for Wales and Other Nationalities and toured Australia in 1924, 1928 and as captain in 1932. In 1936 he became the only player ever to be selected for a fourth tour but declined the invitation. His 160 goals and 329 points is a record at international level.

He played in five successive Test match victories during his three visits to Australia and kicked 246 goals on the tours. It was the consistency of his goal kicking that made him unique among full backs, and he kicked more than 100 goals in every season from his debut in 1921/2 to 1938/9. His best year was 1933/4 with the then record total of 194 goals (and 406 points). In 1925 he kicked a record 22 goals in a Cup game, against Flimby and Fothergill. On his retirement he stayed on at Wigan as coach and later coached at St Helens, where he transformed the side into an outstanding one in the 1950s.

Mick SULLIVAN

Rugby League
Michael Sullivan. b. 12 Jan 1934.

Mick Sullivan, who was not related to the legendary Jim Sullivan, is Britain's most capped player with 46 caps for Great Britain 1954-63 and a further 5 for England; he also scored a record 45 international tries. On the 1958 tour of Australia he scored a record 38 tries and he set a further record by making 36 consecutive international appearances, thereby emphasising his clear superiority over his contemporaries.

He won three amateur caps for England and turned professional in 1952, from when he played for Huddersfield, Wigan and St Helens during his peak years and later for York, Dewsbury and the Australian club Junee.

At international level his speed, swerve, sidestep and devastating tackling made him the most formidable winger of his era. Although his speed gradually diminished, his other talents remained and served him well when he played at loose forward after his international career ended. He scored 342 tries in first-class games in England 1952-66.

John SURTEES

Motor Cycling and Motor Racing
John Surtees. b. 11 Feb 1934 Tatsfield, Surrey.

Surtees is the only man to have become world champion on both two wheels and four. In his motorcycling career for MV Agusta 1956-60 he won 38 Grand Prix races, 22 at 500cc and 15 at 350cc, including the unprecedented feat of winning all of the 25 world championship events he contested in 1958 and 1959, being world champion at 350cc and 500cc in both those years and in 1960. He was voted BBC Sports Personality of the Year in 1959.

His father Jack had a motorcycle business in Croydon and John acted as his passenger, racing sidecars on grass tracks before becoming an engineering apprentice with Vincent, on whose machines he achieved his earliest successes. He made his solo debut in 1951, and in 1955, racing for Norton, beat the great Geoff Duke in 68 out of 76 races. He began his brilliant career with MV in 1956 when he won the Senior TT and the world championship at 500cc. On the Isle of Man he won further Senior TT races in 1958-60 and Junior in 1958-9.

Surtees, introspective, but determined and with plenty of skill, based on mechanical ability, was awarded the MBE in 1959 for his services to motorcycle racing. He started motor racing in 1960, when he made his Formula One debut in a Lotus and was 2nd in the British Grand Prix. Driving for Ferrari, he was world champion in 1964 and runner-up in 1966, but halfway through that season left Ferrari for Cooper. In 1967-8 he ran the Honda team and placed 4th in the 1967 world championship. In 1969 he moved to BRM and in 1970 he built his own Formula One car, but ended his own racing career in 1972, with a record of six wins and 180 points from 111 Grand Prix races. He also won the first Can-Am Challenge in 1966.

William SURTEES (UK/USA)

Rackets
William James Conyers Surtees. b. 29 June 1947 Windsor, Berkshire.

Surtees was world rackets champion 1972-3 and again from 1975-81, and an eight-time winner of the US Amateur singles, 1971-2, 1974-9. After winning the Public Schools rackets championship for Rugby in 1965 he attended Balliol College, Oxford before settling in America where he now works in real estate in Florida.

When winning his second US Amateur title in 1972 he beat Howard Angus (qv) for the world title which had fallen vacant following the retirement of Geoffrey Atkins (qv). Angus reversed the decision when he challenged in 1973 but Surtees reclaimed the title in 1975 and remained the champion until 1981.

Herbert SUTCLIFFE

Cricket
Herbert Sutcliffe. b. 24 Nov 1894 Summer Bridge, Harrogate, North Yorkshire. d. 22 Jan 1978 Crosshills, nr Keighley, West Yorkshire.

Immaculate of appearance, Sutcliffe was a hugely reliable and prolific opening batsman, who formed memorable opening partnerships with Jack Hobbs (qv) for England and with Percy Holmes (qv) for Yorkshire.

He played for Yorkshire 2nd XI in 1914 and his first-team career fitted exactly into the period between the wars, the first, in which he had been commissioned as a 2nd Lieutenant, delaying his debut in first-class cricket until he was 24. He was then an immediate success, scoring 1839 runs in 1919, a record aggregate for a debut season and over 1000 runs each season up to World War II, including over 2000 runs each year 1922-35 and in 1937, with three years over 3000: 3002 at 76.97 in 1928, 3006 at 96.96 in 1931 and 3336 at 74.13 in 1932. In that last year he made his highest score, 313, for Yorkshire v Essex at Leyton, putting on a world record 555 runs for the first wicket with Holmes.

He made a sensational start in Test cricket, as his first three series were: 303 runs at 75.75 v South Africa 1924, 734 at 81.55 with 4 100s v Australia 1924/5, and 472 at 78.66 v Australia 1926. He maintained brilliant form at Test level for a decade and has the best record of any England batsman against Australia, his 2751 runs being made at an average of 66.85. He became a successful businessman and was a Test selector 1959-61. His son **Billy** (b. 10 Oct 1926) captained Yorkshire 1956-7.

54 Tests 1924-35: 4555 runs at 60.73, 16 100s HS 194; 23 catches.

First-class 1919-45: 50, 138 runs at 51.95, 149 100s HS 313; 14 wickets at 40.21, BB 3-15; 466 catches.

Charlie SWAN (Ireland)

Horse Racing
Charles Franan Thomas Swan. b. 21 Jan 1968 Cloughjordan, Co. Down.

Having ridden his first winner on the flat in 1983, when apprenticed to Kevin Prendergast, Swan turned to jumping with Dessie Hughes. He became Irish champion jumps jockey for five successive years from 1989/90 to 1993/4, with 104 winners in 1992/3 and 123 in 1994. He won the Ritz Trophy as top jockey at the Cheltenham National Hunt Festival in both 1993 and 1994 and rode rode *Ebony Jane* to win the Irish Grand National in 1993.

His father Captain Donald Swan was a trainer.

Frank SWIFT

Football
Frank Victor Swift. b. 24 Dec 1913 Blackpool, Lancashire. d. 6 Feb 1958 Munich, Germany.

Swift was a spectacular goalkeeper who was immensely popular with the fans. After signing professional forms for Manchester City in 1932, he made his first-team debut in 1933 and proved so successful that he did not miss a match for the next five years, making 192 consecutive League appearances.

He was goalkeeper in the City team which won the FA Cup in 1934 and the Football League in 1937. After that Cup final the 20-year-old Swift collapsed from nervous exhaustion.

Despite these prewar successes, he did not win international honours until a wartime match in 1943. He played in 14 'wartime' internationals for England to 1946, and then won the first of his 19 full England caps in 1946 at the age of 32. In 1948 he became the first goalkeeper to captain England.

After his retirement he became a licensee and soccer journalist and lost his life in the Munich air disaster while working for the *Sunday Empire News*. His brother Fred kept goal for Bolton Wanderers.

Walter SWINBURN (Ireland)

Horse Racing
Walter Robert John Swinburn. b. 7 Aug 1961 Oxford.

Hailed as a boy wonder when he won his first Derby on *Shergar* in 1981, by June 1995 Swinburn had ridden eight English and nine Irish Classics winners. His father Wally was a top Irish jockey when Walter began his apprenticeship with 'Frenchie' Nicholson (qv) in 1977 and had his first winner at Kempton Park the following year. In 1983 he was retained as first jockey by Michael Stoute (qv) and in that year rode *All Along* to victory in the Prix de l'Arc de Triomphe, as well as three major races in North America, culminating in the Washington International.

In 1984 he rode 99 winners in Britain and achieved his first century with 111 in 1990. In his career in Britain to the end of 1994 he has ridden 1258 winners.

In 1995 he won his third Epsom Derby driving *Lammtarra* to an astonishing finishing burst to break the 62-year-old race record time.

Edgar SYERS

Ice Skating
Edgar Morris Wood Syers. b. 18 Mar 1863 Brighton, East Sussex. d. 16 Feb 1946 Maidenhead, Berkshire.

As the first Englishman to master the International style of skating, Syers had an immeasurable influence on the development of the sport in Britain. It was mainly due to his insistence that British Championships were introduced for the English style in 1902 and for the International style the following year. Syers never won either of these titles although with his wife, Madge (qv), he won the World pairs championship in 1902 and 1904 and at the 1908 Olympics they took the bronze medals. At the age of 45 yrs 225 days, he is the oldest winner of an Olympic medal for figure skating. He was an NSA badge holder for speed, ice and roller skating.

After the death of his first wife and skating partner in 1917, he married 24-year-old Eva Critchel in 1921. He was a founder member of the Ski Club of Great Britain in 1903 and, apart from sending a message to the Club on their 30th Anniversary, he apparently maintained no sporting contacts following his second marriage.

Madge SYERS

Ice Skating
Florence Madeline Syers. née Cave. b. Oct-Dec 1881. d. 9 Sep 1917 Weybridge, Surrey.

Syers was the most influential figure in the development of women's skating and also a notable swimmer, golfer and shot. As there was, at the time, no specific rule prohibiting women, she entered the 1902 World Championships at skating and caused a sensation by finishing 2nd to the great Ulrich Salchow (Swe). The authorities immediately barred women from the Championships and in 1906 introduced a separate World Championship for Ladies. She easily won the title in 1906 and 1907 and the gold medal at the 1908 Olympics by a huge margin. She also won the British title in 1903 and 1904, beating the leading male skaters on both occasions. She owed much to her husband, Edgar Syers (married 1900), who encouraged her to give up the restrictive 'English' and adopt the free-flowing 'International' style. Together they won the bronze medal in the pairs at the 1908 Olympics. She died of complications after giving birth to a short-lived daughter.

Graham SYKES

Swimming
Graham Sykes. b. 20 Jul 1937 Coventry, West Midlands.

Sykes equalled the record of Jack Besford and John Brockway (qqv) by winning seven ASA backstroke titles, 110y 1956-60 and 220y 1961-2. He was Commonwealth champion at 110y in 1962, and at the medley relay won a bronze in 1958 and silver in 1962. He was 6th at 100m back-stroke at the Olympic Games of 1956 and also competed in 1960.

Pat TAAFFE (Ireland)

Horse Racing
Patrick Taaffe. b. 12 Mar 1930 Rathcoole, Dublin. d. 7 Jul 1992 Dublin.

A superb horseman, even though he was very tall for a jockey, Taaffe rode the winner of the Grand National twice (*Quare Times* 1955 and *Gay Trip* 1970), the Irish Grand National a record six times and the Cheltenham Gold Cup four times, including thrice on the supreme champion *Arkle*. After riding as an amateur from 1945 (with his first winner in 1947) he turned professional in 1950, when he became first jockey to Tom Dreaper (qv). Turning to training after his retirement in 1970, he trained *Captain Christy* to the Cheltenham double, Champion Hurdle in 1972 and Gold Cup in 1974.

He was the second son of **Tom Taaffe**, who trained *Mr What* to win the 1958 Grand National. His own son Thomas James 'Tom' (b. 15 Jun 1963) was a leading jumps jockey, riding the winner of the Irish Grand National in 1987, with a season's best of 59 winners in 1991/2, and becoming a trainer from 1994,

Derek TALBOT

Badminton
Derek Talbot. b. 23 Mar 1947.

Capped 83 times by England 1969-81, Talbot formed a brilliant mixed doubles partnership with Gillian Gilks (qv). Together they won the European title 1972, 1974, 1976; All-England 1973, 1976-7; Commonwealth Games 1974, and the English National 1972 and 1974-6.

At the Commonwealth Games Talbot also won gold medals in the team event 1978 and in the mixed doubles (with Margaret Boxall) in 1970 and men's doubles (with Elliot Stuart) in 1974, and at men's singles took silver in 1978 and bronze in 1974. Apart from his four mixed doubles titles at the English Nationals, he won the singles four times and the men's doubles three times.

Bill TANCRED

Athletics, Discus
(Dr) William Raymond Tancred b. 6 Aug 1942 Quetta, India (now Pakistan).

Tancred improved the British discus record 18 times from 57.76m in 1969 to 64.94 in 1974, although that was not recognised and his 64.32 later that year was the ratified mark. He was AAA discus champion seven times, 1966-70 and 1972-3, being placed in the first three each year 1964-75. At the shot he was AAA indoor champion in 1969 and 1976 and had a best of 19.43m (1974).

His best international performances came at the Commonwealth Games, where he won discus bronze in 1970 and silver in 1974; he was also 4th at shot in 1974. He made 53 international appearances for Britain 1964-76. Having been an Army PT instructor, he went to Loughborough University, becoming a university lecturer and then director of physical education and recreation at the University of Sheffield 1980-93. He was awarded the MBE in 1992. His brother **Peter** (b. 20 Oct 1949) was AAA discus champion in 1977-8 and UK champion 1977, 1980 and 1983, and 6th in the Commonwealth Games in 1978 and 1982, with a best of 62.36m (1980).

Haydn TANNER

Rugby Union
Haydn Tanner. b. 9 Jan 1917 Gowerton, Swansea.

As an 18-year-old schoolboy Tanner played scrum-half in the Swansea team which defeated the 1935 All Blacks 11-3. As a result of his impressive display he was immediately brought into the Welsh XV and again played a significant part in a second defeat (13-12) of the touring New Zealanders. He won 13 caps with Swansea before the war and a further 12 after the war when he played for Cardiff.

His international career lasted 14 seasons, 1935-49, and matches the longest of any Welsh international. In addition to his 25 Welsh caps, he played in one Test on the Lions tour of South Africa in 1938. A penetrating runner in attack and solid in defence, his greatest attribute was his ability to serve his fly-half in the most adverse playing conditions.

Nel TARLETON

Boxing
Nelson Tarleton. b. 14 Jan 1906 Liverpool. d. 12 Jan 1956 Crosby, Merseyside.

Tarleton was a British featherweight champion noted for his outstanding defensive skills and his long reach. Although he was exceptionally tall, he carried a powerful enough punch to win 40 of his fights by a KO. During an unusually lengthy career he took part in eleven British title bouts, winning the crown on three separate occasions (1931, 1934, 1940). His last title fight was in 1945 when, at the age of 39, he beat Al Phillips over 15 rounds to win his second Lonsdale Belt. He retired two years later as the undefeated champion.

He twice (1934, 1935) fought Freddie Miller (USA) for the world featherweight title before his home-town crowd in Liverpool but lost narrowly on points on both occasions. All this despite having only one lung due to tuberculosis as an infant.

Career record 1926-45: 144 contests. Won 116 (40 KO), Drew 8, Lost 20.

Maurice TATE

Cricket
Maurice William Tate. b. 30 May 1895 Brighton, East Sussex. d. 18 May 1956 Wadhurst, East Sussex.

Originally a slow-medium bowler, like his father **Fred** (1867-1943) who played once for England in 1902 and took 1331 first-class wickets at 21.55 in his career, Tate became the best medium-fast bowler of his era and the back-bone of the England attack in the late 1920s.

A genial and powerful man with large hands and feet, 'Chubby' to his friends, he swung the ball late and both ways, generating considerable pace off the pitch from a short run. He was a genuine all-rounder, achieving 1000 runs and 200 wickets in a season each year 1923-5; three of six times that this feat has ever been achieved. He had eight doubles of 1000/100 in England and one in India and Ceylon in 1926/7. There his 116 wickets at 13.78 remains the most ever in a first-class season outside England.

Having made his debut for Sussex in 1912 it was not until 1922 that he broke through to top class, taking 100 wickets in a season for the first time (119 at 17.42) and improving to 219 at 13.97 in 1923, although he made his 1000 runs each year 1919-29, with a peak of 1713 at 36.44 in 1927. He took a wicket with his first ball in Test cricket, and his most successful series were his first two: 27 wickets at 15.70 against South Africa in 1924, and 38 wickets at 23.18 in Australia in 1924/5, then a record for an Ashes series. After leaving Sussex he coached at Tonbridge School and then was a publican at Wadhurst.

39 Tests 1924-35: 1198 runs at 25.48, 1 100 HS 100*, 155 wickets at 26.16, BB 6-42; 11 catches.
First-class 1912-37: 21,717 runs at 25.04, 23 100s HS 203; 2784 wickets at 18.16; BB 9-71; 284 catches.

Alec TAYLOR

Horse Racing
Alexander Taylor. b. 15 Mar 1862 Fyfield, Wiltshire. d. 28 Jan 1943 Thorpe, nr Chertsey, Surrey.

Taylor was champion trainer in Britain 13 times, 1907, 1909-10, 1914, 1917-23, 1925-6. He was the first to pass £50,000 in a season in 1910, when his total was £52,929 from 47 races.

Known as 'The Wizard of Manton', he trained over 1100 winners in all. His 21 English Classics successes between 1905 and 1927 included eight of the Oaks, and the colts' Triple Crown winners *Gay Crusader* 1917 and *Gainsborough* 1918. He retired after the 1927 season and died a very wealthy man. He took over the Manton stables in 1902 from his father, **Alec Taylor** (1821-94), whose horses had won 12 Classics 1851-87; his brother Tom was also a leading trainer.

Bob TAYLOR

Cricket
Robert William Taylor. b. 17 Jul 1941 Stoke-on-Trent.

Apart from one Test in 1971, Taylor had to wait a long time for his chance at international level, for while his excellence as a wicket-keeper was well known, he had to act as reserve for the great Allan Knott (qv), who was five years younger than him. Knott, however, went to play in World Series cricket, and at the age of 36 Taylor was at last in the England team. For the next six years he showed himself the best 'keeper in the world. Against India at Bombay in February 1980 he equalled the world Test record with seven dismissals in the first innings and with three more in the second set a world Test record of ten dismissals (all caught).

He ended his career with a record number of dismissals in first-class cricket. He was also a most useful batsman, who sadly just missed a Test hundred when he made his then highest-ever score of 97 for England v Australia at Adelaide in 1979. He made his maiden first-class century at the age of 39 in 1981 having played a record 744 innings before this achievement. He captained Derbyshire in 1975-6 and was awarded the MBE in 1981.

57 Tests 1971-84: 1156 runs at 16.28, HS 97; 167 catches, 7 stumpings.

27 One-day Ints 1973-84: 130 runs at 13.00, HS 26*; 26 catches, 6 stumpings.

First-class 1960-88: 12,065 runs at 16.92, 1 100 HS 100; 1 wicket; 1473 catches, 176 stumpings.

Dennis TAYLOR

Snooker
Dennis James Taylor. b. 19 Jan 1949 Coalisland, Co. Tyrone.

The hugely popular Taylor won one of snooker's greatest ever matches when he defeated Steve Davis (qv) in the final of the World Professional Championship in 1985. His 18-17 victory came on the black in the last frame in the early hours of the morning, watched by 18.5 million people, by some definitions the largest viewership ever for a sporting event on UK television. Taylor had won the British junior billiards title in 1968 and after representing England on a residential qualification in 1971 he turned professional. He reached the World Championship semi-final in 1975 and 1977 and lost in the final to Terry Griffiths (qv) in 1979. He won the Irish Professional Championship in 1982 and 1985-7, the Rothmans Grand Prix in 1984 and the Benson & Hedges Masters in 1987. He was also a member of the Irish team that won the World Cup three times 1985-7.

Henry TAYLOR

Swimming
Henry Taylor. b. 17 Mar 1885 Oldham. d. 28 Feb 1951 Chadderton, Manchester.

Taylor's eight Olympic medals is a record for a British sportsman at any sport. In 1906, when the swimming events were held in the sea off Athens, he won the 1 mile freestyle, was 2nd at 400m and 3rd at 4 x 250m freestyle relay, and in 1908 he won the 400m and 1500m in world record times of 5:36.8 and 22:48.4 respectively, with a third gold at 4 x 200m relay. He added further medals with silver in 1912 and bronze in 1920 at 4 x 200m.

An orphan, raised by his brother, he worked in Lancashire cotton mills and trained as best he could in canals and streams as well as 'dirty water' (cheap) days at the local baths. He won 15 ASA titles: 440y 1906-07, 500y 1906-08, 1911; 880y and 1 mile 1906-07, 1911; long distance 1909, 1912, 1920. In 1920, at the age of 35, he also played water polo for England. His time of 11:25.4 for 880y in 1906 was the first world record officially accepted at the distance and was unbeaten until 1920.

Ian TAYLOR

Hockey
Ian Charles Boucher Taylor. b. 24 Sep 1954 Bromsgrove, Worcs.

Taylor, who was regarded as the world's best goalkeeper for several years, became the most capped player in this position for England (91 outdoor, 4 indoor) and GB (80). He started out with Slough, but for the majority of his international career, which lasted more than a decade (1977-88), he played for East Grinstead. A medallist at all the major competitions: Olympic gold 1988 and bronze 1984; World Cup silver 1986 and European Cup silver 1987 and bronze 1978.
He was given the honour of carrying the British flag at the Olympic Opening Ceremony at Seoul in 1988.

J.H. TAYLOR

Golf
John Henry Taylor. b. 19 Mar 1871 Northam, Devon. d. 10 Feb 1963 Northam.

Taylor, with Harry Vardon and James Braid (qqv), comprised the 'Great Triumvirate' of golf at the turn of the century. He won the British Open five times, 1894-5, 1900, 1909 and 1913, and was also 2nd six times: 1896, 1904 (=), 1905(=), 1906, 1907 and 1914, and 3rd in 1901. He was in the top six a record 18 times. He also won the PGA in 1904 and 1908, the French Open in 1908-9 and the German Open in 1912, and was 2nd in the 1900 US Open. He represented England nine times against Scotland and frequently partnered Vardon or Braid in stakes matches.
He had started as a caddie on the Westward Ho golf course, and soon became a professional, first at Burnham, then successively at Winchester, Wimbledon and Royal Mid-Surrey. He helped to found the Professional Golfers Association, was a golf course architect and wrote on the sport for many years for a Sunday newspaper.

John TAYLOR

Rugby Union
John Taylor. b. 21 Jul 1945 Watford, Herts.

Although he was no match for the majority of his opponents in physical terms, Taylor usually outplayed far larger forwards with his speed and devastating tackling. He won 26 Welsh caps 1967-73 as a flanker but, apart from internationals and representative matches, he played little rugby in Wales.
Educated at Watford Grammar School and Loughborough Colleges, he later played for and captained London Welsh. He toured South Africa with the 1968 British Lions but injury restricted his appearances to just five games. He then declined, on principle, to play against the Springboks when they visited Britain the following year. In 1971 he enjoyed a highly successful Lions tour to New Zealand, playing at open-side in all four Tests.
He played a major role in the successful Welsh team which won the Grand Slam in 1971 having previously won (or shared) the International Championship three times 1969-71. On retirement, he gave up his position as a schoolmaster and has developed a highly successful career as a journalist and ITV commentator on gymnastics and rugby.

Megan TAYLOR

Figure Skating
Megan Devenish Taylor. b. 25 Oct 1921 Rochdale, Gt. Manchester. d. 23 Jul 1993 Jamaica. Later Mrs R.R.Mandeville-Ellis.

Trained by her father, who was an accomplished speed skater, Taylor won the British title at her first attempt in 1932 and took the title again in 1933 and 1934 with her great rival Cecilia Colledge (qv) placing 2nd in all three years. Taylor went to the 1932 Winter Olympics as an 11-year-old and only her team-mate, Colledge, who was born one month later, has ever competed at the Winter Games at a younger age.

At the 1932 Olympics and at the World Championships in Montreal later in the month, Taylor was the best placed of the British competitors finishing 7th on both occasions. In 1933, she placed 4th at the World Championships and improved to take the silver medal in 1934, 1936 and 1937. After missing the 1935 World Championships and the 1936 Olympics through injury, she finally won gold at the World Championship in Stockholm in 1938 with defending champion, Colledge, finishing 2nd.

Taylor successfully defended her world title in Prague in 1939 to share with Madge Syers (qv) the distinction of being the only British lady figure skater to win two World singles titles. She turned professional shortly after the outbreak of the war.

Phil TAYLOR

Darts
Phillip Taylor.

Taylor became world professional champion in 1990 and 1992, and runner-up in 1994, and winner of the WDC world title in 1994/5. His other major wins have included the World Masters in 1990.

Roger TAYLOR

Tennis
Roger Taylor. b. 14 Oct 1941 Sheffield.

A rugged, big-serving left-hander, Taylor is one of only two British players to have reached the semi-finals of the Wimbledon singles since the war. The first was Mike Sangster (qv) who reached the last four in 1961, but Taylor was a semi-finalist three times (1967, 1970, 1973). He claimed many notable scalps at Wimbledon, most notably that of the defending champion Rod Laver (Aus) in the 4th Round in 1970. In 1973 Taylor was one of the few players who defied the ATP ban on the tournament. He reached the closing stages of both singles and doubles at the major

championships on numerous occasions but his only victories came in the US doubles in 1971 and 1972.

Between 1964 and 1976 he played in 18 Davis Cup ties (26/36 singles, 3/5 doubles). He is now the owner of a tennis ranch in Spain.

Mike TEAGUE

Rugby Union
Michael Clive Teague. b. 8 Oct 1950 Gloucester.

A hard-driving flanker, Teague played for England at Under-23 and 'B' levels before winning full international honours. He made his England debut in 1985 but did not win a regular place in the team until 1989 and that year went on the British Lions tour of Australia when, after missing the first Test through injury, his sterling play in the two remaining Tests led to him being voted Player of the Series. He went on a second Lions tour in 1993 when he again played in two Tests. Injury caused him to miss England's first two games in 1990, but he returned to play at no. 8, in place of the injured Dean Richards, for the remaining three internationals of the season.

After many years with Gloucester, he moved to Moseley and was with the Midlands club when he won his 27th and final England cap in 1993, but he soon returned to Gloucester where he continues to turn in some outstanding performances.

Jim TELFER

Rugby Union
James William Telfer. b. 17 Mar 1940 Pathhead,Midlothian.

A schoolmaster who played for Melrose, Telfer gave outstanding service to Scottish and British rugby. Primarily a no. 8, he was at one time Scotland's most capped player in that position, winning 22 caps in the middle of the back-row and a further three as a flanker. During his international career 1964-70 he captained Scotland 12 times.

As a player, he toured twice with the British Lions, going to Australia and New

Zealand in 1966 and South Africa in 1968 and playing a total of 8 Tests (5 at no. 8, 3 as flanker). After retiring in 1970, he became Scotland's leading coach and was appointed the coach for the 1983 British Lions in New Zealand. Having been impressed by the standard of the All Blacks, he instilled some of the better qualities of the New Zealanders into the Scottish team and guided them to their first Grand Slam for 59 years in 1984.

Simon TERRY

Archery
Simon Duncan Terry. b. 27 Mar 1974 Stirling.

With a bronze medal at the 1992 Olympics, Terry became the first Briton to win an Olympic medal in an individual archery event since Willie Dod (qv) in 1908. He also won a second bronze medal in Barcelona in the team event. He competes for Lincoln Archery Club.

Delme THOMAS

Rugby Union
William Delme Thomas. b. 12 Sep 1942 Bancyfelin, Carmarthenshire.

Thomas was chosen for the 1966 British Lions tour of New Zealand before he had been capped by Wales. His performances at lock were so impressive in provincial matches that he was promoted to the Test team ahead of tour captain, Mike Campbell-Lamerton (qv). He rose to the challenge magnificently and although the selectors were reluctant to leave the captain out of the side for another Test they were equally reluctant do without Thomas's services. A compromise was reached and Thomas played at prop in the 3rd Test, but injury prevented him from being considered for the final Test.

On his return home he won the first of his 25 Welsh caps 1966-74, and having established himself in the Welsh second-row he was a member of the 1971 Grand Slam team. He toured twice more with the Lions, playing as a prop in two Tests (one as a replacement) in South Africa in 1968 and, as a lock, in three Tests (one as a

replacement) in New Zealand in 1971. Loyal to Llanelli throughout his senior career, he captained the club to victory over the 1972 All Blacks and was awarded the BEM for this memorable achievement.

George THOMAS

Badminton
(Sir) George Alan Thomas Bt. b. 14 Jun 1881 Constantinople (now Istanbul), Turkey. d. 23 Jul 1972 London.

Between 1903 and 1928 Thomas won 21 All-England badminton titles, still the record. He was singles champion each year 1920 to 1923, won the men's doubles nine times with three different partners and the mixed doubles eight times with five partners. A magnificent stylist, he played in every England international match from 1903 to 1929.

In 1934 he was elected president of the newly formed International Badminton Federation, and remained in that office for 21 years. In 1940 he donated the Thomas Cup for the men's world team championship, although it was not until 1949 that it was first contested.

He was British champion at chess in 1923 and 1934 and represented England at lawn tennis, at which he reached the Wimbledon doubles semi-finals in 1907 and 1912. He also played hockey for Hampshire.

Neil THOMAS

Gymnastics
Neil Roderick Thomas. b. 6 Apr 1968 Chirk, Devon.

Thomas became the first British gymnast to win a world championship medal when he took silver at floor exercises in 1993, a feat he repeated in 1994, when he was 16th in the all-around. At the 1992 Olympics he was 8th equal in the floor exercises, but missed competing in the final on countback. He won his speciality floor exercises at the Commonwealth Games, as well as a team silver in 1990, and in 1994 took the all-around title as well as the floor gold.

A British junior international from 1986 and senior from 1988, he became the first gymnast to win each individual event at the British Championships in 1992. He had won his first British senior titles at floor exercises and high bar in 1987. He was awarded the MBE in 1995.

Parry THOMAS

Motor Sports
John Godfrey Parry Thomas. b. 1885 Wrexham. d. 3 Mar 1927 Pendine Sands, Carmarthenshire.

Parry Thomas set world land speed records at 169.30 mph *272.46 km/h* and 171.02 mph *275.23 km/h* at Pendine Sands in 1926. A year later, however, he was killed in his aero-engined Higham Special *Babs* when attempting to improve the record. It was believed that he was killed when a driving chain broke loose after the collapse of a rear wheel. Before modification this car had been, at 27-litres, the largest-engined car ever to race at Brooklands and he bought it for £175 from Count Zborowski in 1926. The car was buried in the sands, but was dug up in 1969.

Thomas trained as an electrical engineer, set up his own business in 1907 developing electrical transmissions, and became chief engineer for Leyland in 1917. He lived near Brooklands, where he won many races and set world 1 hour records at average speeds of 109.09 mph *175.56 km/h* and 110.64 mph *178.06 km/h* in 1925.

Daley THOMPSON

Athletics
Francis Morgan Thompson. b. 30 Jul 1958 Notting Hill, London.

Thompson was the world's greatest decathlete, so often displaying unparalleled competitive ability. He was Olympic champion in 1980 and 1984, World in 1983, European in 1982 and 1986 and Commonwealth in 1978, 1982 and 1986, and he set four world records (8648 in 1980, 8730 and 8774 in 1982, 8847 in his Olympic triumph at Los Angeles 1984).

He contested his first decathlon in 1975 and a year later took part in the Olympics, learning much while placing 18th. He progressed fast, with three world junior records 1976-7 and the first of ten UK and Commonwealth records in 1976. He won 19 decathlons in all, including 12 in succession from his European silver in 1978 to his 9th in the World Championships in 1987, when he had his preparations marred by a groin injury. He came back to place 4th at the 1988 Olympics, but after an operation to remove a bone growth in his left knee in September 1989 and further injuries, he was unable to achieve his goal of a fifth Olympics in 1992 and announced his retirement. Curiously he never contested a decathlon in England!

He was a top class performer at a wide range of events, winning sprint relay medals in 1986 with Commonwealth silver and European bronze, and taking national titles at the long jump, AAA in 1977 and UK in 1979. He was awarded the MBE and voted BBC Sports Personality of the Year in 1982. Individual event bests: 100m 10.26 (1986), 200m 20.88 (1979), 400m 46.86 (1982), 1500m 4:20.3 (1976), 110mh 14.04 (1986), 400mh 52.14 (1986), high jump 2.14mi (1982), 2.11 (1980); pole vault 5.25m (1986), long jump 8.01m (1984), 8.11w (1978); shot 16.10m (1984), discus 49.10m (1986), javelin 65.38m (1980).

Don THOMPSON

Walking
Donald James Thompson. b. 20 Jan 1953 Hillingdon, London.

The 'Mighty Mouse' was Britain's hero of the 1960 Olympic Games, where he won the 50km walk by 17 seconds from John Ljunggren (Swe). The story of how he prepared for the heat and humidity of Rome by spending many hours sweating in his bathroom heated to 100°F *38°C* was an inspiration for the nation. With this triumph the diminutive (1.68m tall) man made up for his disappointment in having to drop out of the 1956 Olympic 50km, the first time he had ever failed to complete a race.

Thompson had started in athletics at 880y and javelin, taking up walking only in 1951 due to an Achilles tendon injury. He was immediately successful and in 1954 won his first Middlesex title. Always highly proficient at the longest distances,

Daley Thompson's Decathlon Career

All competitions rescored on the 1984 IAAF Decathlon Tables

Date	Venue	Competition	Score	Place	Records
28-29 Jun 1976	Cwmbrân	Welsh Open		1st	6523	
30-31 Aug 1975	Cwmbrân	AAA Juniors		1st	6845	
4-5 Oct 1975	Cwmbrân	UK v France		2nd	6941	UKJR
22-23 May 1976	Cwmbrân	AAA Championships		1st	7517	UKJR
26-27 Jun 1976	Copenhagen	UK v 3 nations		10th	6649	
	(no height in pole vault)				
29-30 Jul 1976	Montreal	Olympic Games		18th	7330	
4-5 Sep 1976	Talence			4th	7748	UKR, UKJR
21-22 May 1977	Götzis			3rd	7865	UKR, UKJR
25-26 Jun 1977	Madrid	UK v 3 nations		1st	8056	UKR, WJR
30-31 Jul 1977	Sittard	European Cup semi		1st	8082	UKR, WJR
19-20 Aug 1977	Donetsk	European Juniors		1st	7568	
27-28 May 1978	Götzis			2nd	8226	UKR
7-8 Aug 1978	Edmonton	Commonwealth Games		1st	8470w	
30-31 Aug 1978	Prague	European Champs		2nd	8258	UKR
28-29 Jul 1979	Flein			dnf	(6954)	
	(no height in polevault, did not run 1500m)				
17-18 May 1980	Götzis			1st	8648	WR
25-26 Jul 1980	Moscow	Olympic Games		1st	8522	
13-14 Jun 1981	Saskatoon	UK v Canada		1st	7797	
22-23 May 1982	Götzis			1st	8730	
7-8 Sep 1982	Athens	European Champs		1st	8774	WR
4-5 Oct 1982	Brisbane	Commonwealth Games		1st	8424	
7-8 Jun 1983	Etobicoke			1st	8529w	
12-13 Aug 1983	Helsinki	World Champs		1st	8714	
23-24 May 1984	Los Angeles			dnf	(7938)	
	(did not run 1500m)				
8-9 Aug 1984	Los Angeles	Olympic Games		1st	8846	WR
17-18 May 1986	Arles	UK v FRA, CAN		1st	8667	
27-28 Jul 1986	Edinburgh	Commonwealth Games		1st	8663	
27-28 Aug 1986	Stuttgart	European Champs		1st	8811	
3-4 Sep 1987	Rome	World Champs		9th	8124	
28-29Sep 1988	Seoul	Olympic Games		4th	8306	
15-16 Sep 1989	Talence			dnf	(4085)	
	(contested first day only)				
4-5 May 1991	Irvine			dnf	(6938)	
	(did not run 1500m)				
1-2 Jun 1991	Alhama	UK v Spain		dnf		
	(only contested seven events through injury)				
28-29 Sep 1991	Emmitsburg			dnf	(6743)	
	(did not run 1500m)				

Records: WR = world record, WJR = world junior record, UKR = British record, UKJR = British junior record. dnf = did not finish, w = at least one event with wind assistance over the 4 m/s permitted for decathlon records.

he was 2nd that year in the London-to-Brighton walk, a race he was to win a record eight times, successively 1955-62, setting a record time for the 86km course of 7 hours 35 mins 12 secs in 1957. He also won a record eight national titles at 50km walk: 1956-62 and 1966 and won the RWA 20 miles in 1961. At the European Championships he was 5th in 1958, 3rd in 1962 and 9th in 1966 at 50 km, and he was 4th in the 1966 Commonwealth 20 miles. At his third Olympics he was 10th in the

1964 50km. His first British records came at 25 miles and 4 hours in 1955 and he improved the best time for 50km five times from 4:24:39 in 1956 to 4:09:15 in 1961. His best time at 20 km was 1:34:45 (1961), with track bests in 1960: 20M 2:41:43.8, 25M 3:36:37.4, 30M 4:08:11.6, 50km 4:17:29.8.

Maintaining his fitness he became Britain's oldest full international when he competed in the 200km walk at Bazencourt, France at 58 years 89 days in 1991. He was awarded the MBE in 1970.

Ian THOMPSON

Marathon
Ian Reginald Thompson. b. 16 Oct 1949 Birkenhead, Merseyside.

Regarded as just an ordinary club athlete, Thompson suddenly broke through to world class as a marathon runner on 27 Oct 1973. That day he ran the AAA marathon championship just to make up the numbers for his club, Luton United. It was his first race beyond 10 miles, but he won in 2:12:40, the fastest ever debut at the distance. Thus he qualified for the Commonwealth Games three months later - and he won again, this time in 2: 09:12, the fastest ever run in a championship race and a British record. Further victories followed in 1974 in Athens and at the European Championships and he was the best marathon runner in the world.

In 1976 he suffered cramp and finished only 7th in the trials for the Olympics, for which he was not selected to the consternation of some. Although for many years among Britain's best, he never regained his 1974 eminence and contested only one more major championship. His best times each year between 1977 and 1982 were in the 2:12 to 2:15 range. He won the AAA title in 1980 to gain Olympic selection but dropped out at the Games. By profession he was a sales manager. Other best times: 1500m 3:51.0 (1969), 5000m 14:05.4 (1971), 10,000m 29:33.0 (1979).

His wife Margaret was an early pioneer of marathon running for women in Britain and ran a British best time of 3:07:47 in 1975.

Joe THOMPSON

Rugby League
Joseph Thompson. b. 22 Dec 1902 Harnbrook, Glos.

Signed by Leeds in 1923 from Rugby Union club Cross Keys, Thompson's many years of outstanding service to the Yorkshire club were rewarded by his election as a life member. A versatile forward, he was capped by GB in three positions - prop, second row and loose forward - and is the only forward to have played in three Ashes-winning series in Australia, 1924, 1928, 1932. In all he won 12 caps for GB 1924-32.

He kicked 921 goals at home 1923-33, but the presence of Jim Sullivan (qv) in the Lions party on all three visits to Australia meant that Thompson was never called up as a kicker in the Tests.

John THOMPSON

Rackets
John Ross Thompson. b. 10 May 1918 Berkhamsted, Herts.

After attending Tonbridge School, Thompson went up to Cambridge where he represented the University at rackets and squash in 1938 and won a cricket Blue in 1938-9. After war service with the Royal Artillery, he became a master at Marlborough where David Milford (qv) was also on the staff. With the advantage of being able to practice together, they became the most successful rackets pairing in history. Together they won a record ten British Amateur doubles titles (1948, 1950-2, 1954-9) and Thompson won an eleventh title in 1966 with a different partner. Other successes included victories in the US and Canadian Amateur in 1953. Thompson also won the British Amateur singles five times (1954-5, 1957-9) and was British Open champion in 1959.

His success at rackets naturally restricted his cricketing career, but he found time to play 44 matches for Warwickshire between 1938 and 1954 with a first-class career record of 3455 runs at an average of 31.12; he scored six centuries with a highest score of 161. He also played cricket for Wiltshire 1955-63.

Phil THOMPSON

Football
Philip Bernard Thompson. b. 21 Jan 1954 Kensington, Liverpool.

Thompson was a hard-tackling central defender with a deceptively frail appearance. Joining Liverpool as an apprentice from local schoolboy ranks, he signed as a professional in 1971 and stayed with the club throughout virtually the whole of his career. In the twilight of his career he spent little more than a year with Sheffield United before returning to Anfield to join the coaching staff.

He was a member of the great Liverpool team which won the European Cup twice, the UEFA Cup once, the League Championship seven times, the FA Cup once and the League Cup twice. In all, he made 340 appearances for the club and was capped 42 times by England (1 goal) 1976-82.

Andy THOMSON

Bowls
Andrew Edward Thomson. b. 26 Nov 1955 St Andrews.

Thomson won the Buckhaven club championship at the age of 16 and a year later the Fife Under-30 title. After taking the Scottish junior title in 1978 and making his international debut a year later for Scotland he moved to Kent in England, for whom he competed thereafter. In 1981 he was EBA singles champion and won the EIBA triples, followed by the EIBA fours in 1983-4 with the Cyphers team.

He struck up a formidable pairing with Gary Smith for Blackheath and Greenwich. Together they won the EIBA pairs in 1986 and 1991, EBA pairs in 1992, the British Isles pairs indoors in 1987 and 1992 and outdoors in 1993, and the world indoor pairs in 1993. With the EIBA singles in 1989-91 he became the first player ever to have won all four national indoor titles. In 1995 Thomson won the world indoor singles title. At the Commonwealth Games he was 6th in the singles 1986, and 5th in 1990 and 3rd 1994 in the pairs.

Paul THORBURN

Rugby Union
Paul Huw Thorburn. b. 24 Nov 1962 Rheindalen, Germany.

A prodigious goal kicker, Thorburn's 304 points in 37 international matches 1985-91 was a Welsh record until beaten by Neil Jenkins (qv). He achieved this total with 69 penalties, 43 conversions and 2 tries. Among his subsidiary records he holds the Welsh record for the most points in an International Championship season (52 pts 1986) and the most points in an international match (21 pts v Barbarians 1990). He also set the record for the most penalties (16) in a Five Nations season (1986) but lost this record to Simon Hodgkinson (England) in 1991.

For Wales against Scotland on 1 Feb 1986 he achieved the longest penatlty kick in international rugby, when he succeeded from 64.22m, just over 70 yards.

Not surprisingly, he also holds numerous scoring records for his club, Neath, for whom he continues to play after announcing his retirement from the international game in 1991. In 1989 he was appointed captain of Wales but following the extraordinary gestures he made towards the press box after Wales had surprisingly beaten England at Cardiff Arms Park he fell out of favour with the authorities. He was passed over for the 1989 Lions tour of Australia and was not invited to captain Wales in the Five Nations the following season.

Graham THORNER

Horse Racing
Graham Edward Thorner. b. 27 Jan 1949 Coxley, Somerset.

Champion jumps jockey in 1970/1 with 74 winners, Thorner increased his total to 75 in 1971/2, 14 short of the winning total, but including his greatest success, the Grand National on *Well To Do*, He joined Tim Forster's stable on leaving school, and continued to ride for him. His first winner was at Newton Abbot in 1966 and in all rode 650 winners before starting training in 1981.

Dave THORPE

Moto-cross
David Thorpe.

Thorpe was three times world champion at 500cc moto-cross, in 1985-6 and 1989, and also 3rd in 1984 and 1988, all riding for Honda. He had been British junior schoolboy champion in 1967 and 1969-70 and senior champion in 1976 and 1977. In his first year of adult racing he won the AMCA 250cc and superclass (55) championships and the following year won the British Under-18 title sanctioned by the ACU.

Lenox TINDALL

Athletics
(Rev.) Henry Charles Lenox Tindall. b. 4 Feb 1863 Margate, Kent. d. 10 Jun 1940 Peasmarsh, East Sussex.

Tindall was AAA champion at 440y in 1888 and in 1889 won both 440y and 880y in championships records. The former was a world record at 48 $^1/2$ and this lasted as a championships best for 48 years. His 880y time later the same afternoon was 1:56$^2/5$.
He won his Blue at Cambridge each year 1883-6, winning at 100y and 440y in the 1886 Inter-Varsity match, and although he did not play at Cambridge, played county cricket for Kent 1893-5. He was also an originator of Rye Golf Club.

Bob TISDALL (Ireland)

Athletics, Hurdling
Robert Morton Newburgh Tisdall. b. 16 May 1907 Ceylon (now Sri Lanka).

With film-star good looks and hugely popular, Tisdall had only run in six previous races over the distance when he won the Olympic gold medal at 400m hurdles in 1932 in a world record time of 51.7. However, conforming with the rules at that time, Tisdall's record was not officially recognised because he had hit a hurdle. The American, Glen Hardin, in 2nd place, was given the new record of 51.9 secs. Tisdall was also 8th in the decathlon at these Games.
From an Anglo-Irish family, born in Ceylon and raised in Nenagh, Co. Tipperary, Tisdall had won the public schools 440y while at Shrewsbury and established a reputation as a fine all-rounder while at Cambridge University, winning a record four events, 440y, 120y hurdles, long jump and shot, in the annual match against Oxford in 1931. The Irish authorities accepted his desire to run at a new event and he qualified by setting an Irish record at 54.2 for 440y hurdles. He improved marvellously to 52.8 for 400m in his semi-final and then that 51.7 in the Olympic final.
He left England in 1934 to teach in South Africa, and helped form the South African Irish Regiment in World War II, which he finished as a major. He later lived in Kenya, Rhodesia, Tanzania and Ireland before settling in Queensland, Australia.

Fred TITMUS

Cricket
Frederick John Titmus. b. 24 Nov 1932 Kentish Town, London.

From his debut for Middlesex at the age of 16, Titmus's career spanned five decades, and since his retirement he has stayed in close touch with the game, serving as a Test selector in several seasons. He took 100 wickets in a season 16 times between 1953 and 1971, with a peak of 191 at 16.31 in 1955. That year he made his England Test debut, although he did not play again for seven years. As an effective lower middle-order batsman he completed the double with over 1000 runs in 1955-7, 1959-62 and 1967. He is one of only five players to have made over 20,000 runs and taken over 2500 wickets in first-class cricket. His best batting season was 1961 when he scored 1703 runs at 37.02.
With consistent control of line and length, he was for long England's top off-spinner, and a Test regular for much of the sixties until he lost four toes to the propeller blade of a boat while swimming in the sea on England's tour to the West Indies in 1968. He recovered in time for his fourth season as captain of Middlesex and returned to the England team for four Tests in Australia in 1974/5. His most successful Test series

was against India in 1963/4, when he took 27 wickets at 27.66 and scored 143 runs at 35.75, and with the bat he made 258 runs at 64.50 against Australia in 1965/6. He retired after the 1976 season to become coach at Surrey, playing once for them in 1978, but left in 1979 and played again for Middlesex in a few matches 1979-82.
53 Tests 1955-75: 1449 runs at 22.29, HS 84*; 153 wickets at 32.22, BB 7-79; 35 catches.
2 One-day Ints 1975: 11 runs at 11.00, HS 11; 3 wickets at 17.66, BB 3-53; 1 catch.
First-class 1949-82: 21,588 runs at 23.11, 6 100s HS 137*; 2830 wickets at 22.37, BB 9-52; 473 catches.

Colin TODD

Football
Colin Todd. b. 12 Dec 1948 Chester-le-Street, Co. Durham.

A highly reliable defender, very fast and strong in the tackle, Todd made his League debut for Sunderland in 1966 and won the first of his 27 England caps, 1972-7, after moving to Derby County in 1971. In his first season with Derby he helped them to the League Championship in 1972 and again in 1975 when he was voted Player of the Year by his fellow professionals.
After 293 League games for Derby, he went to Everton in 1978 and then continued his career with Birmingham City, Nottingham Forest, Oxford United, Vancouver Whitecaps (Canada) and Luton Town.
When his travels finally ended, he took up a coaching appointment at Middlesbrough in 1986, manager 1990-1, before becoming assistant manager at Bolton Wanderers in 1992.

Alan TOMES

Rugby Union
Alan James Tomes. b. 6 Nov 1961 Hawick, Borders.

With 48 international appearances 1976-87, Tomes is Scotland's most capped lock. He started playing in England with Gateshead Fell and moved to the Hawick club in 1973. His powerful scrummaging earned him a place on the 1980 British Lions tour of South Africa but he failed to win a Test place. In 1984 he played in all four internationals in Scotland's Grand Slam season.

Freddie TOMLINS

Figure Skating
Frederick William Edwin Tomlins. b. 5 Aug 1919 Lambeth. d. 20 Jan 1943 in action.

Tomlins showed a rare versatility by being a top-ranking figure skater in both singles and pairs and a record-breaking speed skater. After placing 3rd in the pairs (with Joy Ricketts) at the 1934 British championships he made his international debut in the singles in 1936 but finished well down the field at both the Olympic Games and the Europeans. He then improved to finish 5th twice (1937-8) at the World Championships before taking the silver medal in 1939. Tomlins was unfortunate to be a contemporary of Graham Sharpe (qv), who not only beat him for the 1939 World title but also deprived him of many British titles. Even while competing as a figure skater at the highest level he set British speed skating records at 880y and 1 mile in 1937 and, as the event is no longer held, he still holds the British record for 220y.
On the outbreak of war he was commissioned into the RAF and after training in Canada he was killed in an action against a German submarine while flying with Coastal Command. His name is perpetuated by the Freddie Tomlins speed skating trophy donated by his father in his son's memory.

Daniel TOPOLSKI

Rowing
Daniel Topolski. b. 4 Jun 1945 London.

Son of the artist Feliks Topolski, he became the most successful coach in Boat Race history, guiding Oxford to victory for ten successive years, 1976-85 as well as in 1975-4 and 1987 in his tenure of office 1973-87. He has been a leading competitor for more than 30 years, an Oxford Blue 1967-8 and winning a world silver medal at lightweight coxless fours in 1975 and gold at lightweight eights in 1977. He was national coach at major championships 1979-84 and has been a writer on travel and sport, and a journalist, returning to Oxford as coaching director in 1994.

Sam TORRANCE

Golf
Samuel Robert Torrance. b. 24 Aug 1953 Largs, North Ayrshire.

Torrance turned professional in 1970 after winning the Scottish Boys' title. A Ryder Cup regular, his greatest moment came with his putt in 1985 to beat Andy North (USA), which ensured that the trophy was won for Europe. In seven Cups from 1981-93 he won 4, lost 13, and halved 5 of his 22 matches. He has also played in 7 Dunhill Cups for Scotland from 1985 and 10 World Cups from 1976. Although yet to win a major he has 20 European tour wins from the Zambian Open of 1975 to his second Italian Open and Irish Open in 1995. His highest positions on the European Order of Merit have been 2nd in 1984 and 3rd in 1976 and 1982.
His putting has been a problem for him, but has been helped from 1988 by his use of a putter with an elongated shaft. He is coached by his father Bob.
European tour earnings 1971-94: £2,520,973.

Jayne TORVILL

Figure Skating
Jayne Torvill. b. 7 Oct 1957 Nottingham. Later Mrs Christensen.

Partnering Christopher Dean (qv), Torvill won four world titles and the 1984 Olympic gold medal, when their interpretation of Ravel's *Bolero*, was one of the most memorable and dramatic performances in the history of any sport. Having won a British junior and senior title with Michael Hutchinson, she joined Dean and they won the first of a record six successive British Championships in 1978. *See Dean's entry for details.*
In September 1990 Torvill married Phil Christensen, a technician with the Phil Collins show. Along with other professionals, Olympic eligibility was returned to Torvill and Dean in 1993 and they made a triumphant return to competition in 1994, even though the Olympic title eluded them. She was awarded the MBE in 1981.

Diane TOWLER

Figure Skating
Gay Diane Margaret Towler. b. 16 Dec 1946 London.

Towler was a four-time World, European and British ice dance champion with Bernard Ford (qv for details).

Dave TRAVIS

Athletics, Javelin
David Howard Travis. b. 9 Sep 1945 Twickenham, London.

The Commonwealth javelin champion of 1970 and silver medallist of 1974, and World University Games champion of 1967, Travis made his international debut for Britain at the decathlon in 1965. A teacher, who competed for Surrey AC, he won the AAA javelin title in 1965, 1968, 1970-4 and was placed in the first three each year 1965-75 and in 1977. He competed in 46 internationals for Britain 1965-78, including the Olympic Games of 1968 and 1972 and counted his greatest win as that over Olympic champion Janis Lusis (USSR) in the European Cup semi-final in 1970.
He set British javelin records at 82.22m and 83.44 in 1970 and also set a British record at the decathlon with 6791 points (6653 on the current tables) in 1965, later improving his best to 6921 points in 1968.

John TREACY (Ireland)

Marathon
John Treacy. b. 4 Jun 1957 Villierstown, Co. Waterford

Treacy was twice winner of the World Cross Country Championships, in Glasgow 1978 and Limerick 1979, having been 3rd in the juniors in 1974 and 1975; later he was 5th in 1985. He set Irish records on the track at distances from 3000m to 1 hour, with bests of 3000m 7:45.22 (1980), 5000m 13:16.81 (1984), 10,000m 27:55.80 (1989),

1 hour 19,625m and 20,000m 61:10.1 (1987). At 5000m he was the European Junior silver medallist in 1975 and was 4th in the 1978 Europeans and 7th at the 1980 Olympics. His greatest success came, however, at the marathon, at which he took the silver medal behind Carlos Lopes (Por) in a time of 2:09:56 in 1984, when he was also 9th at 10,000m.

With Olympic appearances also in 1980, 1988 and 1992 he emulated yachtsman David Wilkins as a four-time Olympian for Ireland. He was 6th in the 1986 European 10,000m. His fastest marathon was 2:09:15 in 1988 when 3rd in Boston, where he was 3rd again in 1989; he was also 3rd in the New York Marathon in 1988 and 2nd in the Tokyo Marathon in 1990. His major marathon wins came at Los Angeles 1992 and Dublin 1993. He was Irish champion at 5000m 1978, 1980-1, 1983-4; 10,000m 1978, 1985, 1987 and also won the AAA 10,000m in 1979.

He gained an MBA from Providence University, USA and is the first sportsman to be given the Freedom of the City of Waterford.

Mike TREDGETT

Badminton
Michael G Tredgett. b. 5 Apr 1949 Cheltenham.

Tredgett has been considered by many to be England's finest doubles player and winner of a then record 137 caps 1970-84, adding one more in 1987. At the All-England Championships he won the mixed doubles three times with Nora Perry (1978, 1980-1) and at the English National he won 16 doubles titles (ten men's 1973, 1976-81, 1983-5; six mixed 1977-81, 1983). He was also a doubles gold medallist at the European Championships (men's 1976, 1978 and 1984, mixed 1978 and 1980) and the Commonwealth Games (men's and mixed 1978, with a third gold at team event). With Nora Perry (qv) he lost in the final of the World mixed doubles in 1980.

The majority of his men's doubles successes were with Ray Stevens (qv) but when injury brought Stevens' career to an end he formed a fruitful partnership with Martin Dew. He was awarded the MBE for his services to the game.

Roger TREDGOLD

Fencing
Roger Francis Tredgold. b. 23 Oct 1911 Guildford, Surrey. d. 24 Dec 1975 Old Heathfield, East Sussex.

Tredgold won a record six AFA sabre titles (1937, 1939, 1947-9, 1955) and was a finalist each year that the championship was held between 1934 and 1963. He was also runner-up in the AFA foil in 1947. He competed in three Olympic Games (1936, 1948 and 1952). A graduate of Cambridge University, he was a doctor and editor of *The Sword* when this magazine was first published in 1948.

Billy TREW

Rugby Union
William James Trew. b. 1878 Swansea. d. 20 Aug 1926 Swansea.

Trew was one of the brightest stars of Welsh rugby in the pre-World War I era. A versatile back, he won 14 caps as a centre, 9 in his preferred position as a fly-half and 6 as a winger, and contributed to three Grand Slams, five Triple Crowns and six Championship wins. In 29 games for Wales 1900-13 he was on the losing side only four times and scored 11 international tries.

He captained Swansea when they beat Australia in 1908 and South Africa 1912 and he led Wales 14 times. Initially a boilermaker and later a publican, he was part of a dedicated rugby family: his son-in-law, **Thomas Day** (1907-80), was capped by Wales, his son captained Swansea and two brothers also played for the club.

Helen TROKE

Badminton
Helen Suzanne Troke. b. 7 Nov 1964 Southampton.

A brilliant junior, Troke won English National titles at all levels, including the senior singles in 1986, and was the European Junior singles champion in 1981 and 1983, making her senior international debut in 1981. In the senior ranks she was the Commonwealth Games singles gold medallist in 1982 (at 17 years 335 days the youngest ever at the sport) and 1986, and 3rd in 1990, and the European champion in 1984 and 1986. She also won a Commonwealth women's doubles bronze in 1986 and three team gold medals.

A member of the British team when badminton was introduced into the Olympics in 1992, she had the misfortune to meet the world champion in her opening match. She made 115 appearances for England 1980-92 and was awarded the MBE in 1987.

Fred TRUEMAN

Cricket
Frederick Sewards Trueman. b. 6 Feb 1931 Scotch Springs, Stainton, South Yorkshire.

A great fast bowler, Trueman devastated the Indians on his Test debut in 1952, when he took three wicket and Alec Bedser (qv) one to reduce India to 0-4 at the start of their second innings. He took 29 wickets at 13.31 in the four Tests of that series and went on to become the first man to take over 300 wickets in Test cricket.

He was all that a fast bowler needed to be, aggressive and strong with a perfect action. As his career progressed and he lost a little of his extreme pace, his skill, late outswinger and control of line and length meant that he retained his wicket-taking ability. He took over 20 wickets in six successive Test series 1959-63 followed by 14 wickets in two Tests against New Zealand 1962/3 and 34 at 17.47 against West Indies in 1963.

He was a hard-hitting and effective tail-end batsman and a brilliant fielder, either at short-leg or in the deep, where he was a fine thrower. Early in his career 'Fiery' Fred's forthright views and behaviour brought him some trouble with selectors, but he matured into a most astute cricketer and a fine captain when he deputised for Yorkshire. After playing for his native county 1949-68 he played in Sunday League games for Derbyshire in 1972.

A great personality, he has become a regular radio and TV commentator on cricket and a notable speaker. He was awarded the OBE in 1989.

67 Tests 1952-65: 981 runs at 13.81, HS 39*; 307 wickets at 21.57, BB 8-31; 64 catches.

First-class 1949-68: 9231 runs at 15.56, 3 100s HS 104; 2304 wickets at 18.29, BB 8-28; 439 catches.

Christine TRUMAN

Tennis
Christine Clara Truman. b. 16 Feb 1941 Loughton, Essex. Later Mrs G.T.Janes.

A free hitting player, particularly on the forehand, Truman's attractive playing style and exemplary court manners made her a great favourite with the crowd.

A Wimbledon singles semi-finalist at the age of 16 in 1957 she was, understandably, tipped as a future champion but it was not to be although she again reached the semifinals in 1960 and 1965. In 1961 she met Angela Mortimer (qv) in the first all-British final since 1914 but she twisted an ankle, when apparently holding a winning lead, and lost in three sets.

In 1959 she won the French and Italian singles and in 1960 took the Australian doubles partnering Maria Bueno (Bra). Possibly her best performance came in the 1958 Wightman Cup when she beat Althea Gibson (USA) and helped Britain to their first victory since the war. She played in 11 Cup ties between 1957 and 1971 (7/18 singles, 5/9 doubles).

Her sister, Frances Ellen 'Nell' (b. 12 Dec 1945, Loughton, Essex, later Mrs C Robinson) took part in five Wightman Cup matches 1965-72, playing only in the doubles and winning two of her five matches. The sisters formed an effective partnership winning the British Hard Court doubles in 1968. Their brother, Humphrey was also a top-class tournament player.

After retirement she became well-known as a BBC radio and television commentator at the major championships.

Andrew TUCKER

Shooting
Andrew St George Tucker. b. 17 Jul 1937 Edinburgh.

Tucker is the only person to have both principal events at Bisley at both fullbore and smallbore rifle shooting. At smallbore he won the Earl Roberts Trophy in 1975 and the Grand Aggregate in 1964 and 1975. At fullbore he won the Queen's Prize in 1979 and 1987 and the Grand Aggregate in 1986.
He made his debut for Britain at smallbore in 1962 and was still shooting for Britain in 1994 at fullbore, having reprseented England and Britain for smallbore and fullbore on more occasions than any other shooter. At the 1990 Commonwealth Games he took pairs gold and individul silver at fullbore rifle. At smallbore rifle long range he won the English title in 1975 and 1977 and the GB title 1975.

Sam TUCKER

Rugby Union
John Samuel Tucker. b. 1 Jun 1895 Bristol. d. 4 Jan 1973 Bristol.

Although wounded in the Battle of the Somme, Tucker recovered to command a regular place in the Gloucester team and made his England debut against Wales in 1922. After a disappointing performance, he missed the next eleven games but was recalled for the match against New Zealand in 1925 after which he held his place as England's regular hooker, winning 27 caps up to his retirement. He captained England in his last three internationals in 1930-1.
In the days before private flying was commonplace, he made news in 1930 by flying from Bristol to Cardiff in response to a last-minute request to replace the injured Henry Rew. He arrived at Cardiff Arms Park minutes before the international against Wales kicked off. A rugged, tough forward his occupation as a solicitor's clerk somehow seemed rather inappropriate.

Raymond TUCKEY

Tennis
Charles Raymond Davys Tuckey. b. 15 Jun 1910 Godalming, Surrey.

Tuckey was the most successful member of a talented tennis playing family. A Cambridge Blue and a regular army officer with the Royal Engineers he won the Wimbledon men's doubles with his Davis Cup partner, Pat Hughes (qv) in 1936. Tuckey played in three Davis Cup finals, being on the winning team in 1935-6 and on the losing side in 1937. He lost two of his three Davis Cup doubles matches.
Tuckey and Hughes first came together in 1935, both had a powerful serve and their attacking play brought them some notable victories. In the 1935 London Grass Court Championships at Queen's they disposed of former Wimbledon and US champions, Wilmer Allison and John van Ryan before beating two more formidable Americans, Gene Mako and Don Budge, in the final. They beat Allison and van Ryan again in the Davis Cup Challenge round in 1935 and in 1936, in addition to winning at Wimbledon, they took the British Hard Court title. The previous year Tuckey had won the Hard Court mixed doubles with Peggy Scriven (qv).
His mother, the former **Agnes** Katharine Raymond **Daniell** (b. 8 Jul 1877 Marylebone. d. 13 May 1972 Winchester) won the All England women's doubles at Buxton in 1909 and in 1913 was the winner of the inaugural mixed doubles championship at Wimbledon. In 1927, at the age of 50, she won the women's doubles with M.Chamberlain at the British Hard Court Championships but her remarkable career did not end there, as in 1931 and 1932, by now in her mid-50s, she played with her son in the mixed doubles at Wimbledon. Not surprisingly, the mother-son pairing made little progress in either year but they established a unique record for the Championships.
His sister, **Kathleen** Lilian Agnes **Tuckey** (later Mrs J.A.C.Maule (b. 24 Dec 1921 Godalming, Surrey) played in three Wightman Cup matches, 1949-51, losing all four of her matches (1 singles, 3 doubles).

Bruce TULLOH

Athletics
Michael Bruce Swinton Tulloh. b. 29 Sep 1935 Datchet, Berkshire.

Renowned for running barefoot in many of his major races, Tulloh's greatest moment came with his victory in the European 5000m in 1962. Although he had won the Hong Kong 5000m title in 1955 while on national service, he broke through very rapidly in 1959 to win the AAA 3 miles and make his international debut while a student at Southampton University and member of Portsmouth AC. In 1960 he set a British record at 3 miles of 13:17.2, a time he improved to 13:12.0 in 1961, but he did not qualify from the heats at the Olympic Games. In 1962 he ran his best ever mile (3:59.3) and a British record 8:34.0 for 2 miles in New Zealand in January before his European triumph, and 4th at 3 miles and 9th at 1 mile at the Commonwealth Games.
In 1966 he ran a British record 27:23.78 for 2nd place in the AAA 6 miles and was 6th in the Europeans in his best time for 10,000m of 28:50.4. He was also AAA 3 miles champion in 1962 and 1963. Other best times: 1500m 3:46.7 (1963), 5000m 13:49.4 (1964). In 1969 he ran across the USA, 2876 miles in 65 days.
An agricultural scientist, he has remained a top-class veteran runner and coach, notably of Richard Nerurkar, World Cup marathon winner in 1993.

Dick TURPIN

Boxing
Richard Turpin. b. 26 Nov 1920 Leamington Spa, Warwicks. d. 7 Jul 1990 Leamington Spa.

The elder brother of Randolph (qv), Turpin began his professional career in 1937 but despite an excellent record he was denied the opportunity of a championship challenge because of the colour bar which precluded black boxers from fighting for a British title. On his return from three years service in the RAF, his obvious abilities made it impossible for the British authorities to maintain their prejudiced stance and

in May 1948 he took the Empire middleweight crown from Bos Murphy (NZ) with a first round KO. The following month he defeated Vince Hawkins for the British title and defended both titles against Albert Finch in June 1949, but later in the year he lost his Empire title when he was knocked out in the first round by Dave Sands (Aus). In March 1950 he lost his British title to Albert Finch and after losing his next two fights he retired. Although not as talented as his brother he was nevertheless a fine boxer and had it not been for the colour bar and war service he would have been a title contender much earlier in his career.
Career record 1937-50: 103 contests. Won 76, Drew 6, Lost 20, No decision 1.

Randolph TURPIN

Boxing
Randolph Adolphus Turpin. b. 7 Jun 1928 Leamington Spa, Warwicks. d. 17 May 1966 Leamington Spa.

One of five sons of an English woman and a seaman from British Guiana, Turpin was ultimately the most successful of the three brothers who became professional boxers. After winning the ABA welterweight (1945) and middleweight (1946) titles he turned professional at the age of 18 and was soon hailed as 'the most exciting fighter raised in Britain for a generation' with a reputation as a knockout puncher.
He won his first British title in 1950 with a fifth round KO of Albert Finch, who had taken the middleweight crown from his elder brother, Dick (qv), earlier in the year. In February 1951 he won the European title in just 48 seconds by knocking out Luc van Dam (Hol) and in July 1951 he gave one of the finest performances ever seen from a British boxer when he outpointed the seemingly invincible American, Sugar Ray Robinson, who had lost only one of his previous 133 fights, to take the world middleweight title. Such was the excitement and interest aroused by this bout that a return match was held just 64 days later. Robinson regained his title when the referee stopped the fight after 10 rounds and Turpin, after taking heavy punishment, was

never quite the same fighter again. After Robinson retired, Turpin was recognised as the world champion outside the USA, whereas the Americans acknowledged Carl 'Bobo' Olsen (USA) as the champion. The two met in New York in October 1953 and following Olsen's win on points he became the undisputed champion.

Turpin was also a champion in the light-heavyweight division. He first won the British and Empire titles in 1952 from a weight-weakened Don Cockell (qv), relinquished and then regained both titles on two separate occasions and was still the title holder when he retired in 1958. Like many before him, Turpin had little money left when he gave up boxing, professional wrestling and work in a Midlands scrapyard did little to alleviate the situation and in 1962 he was declared bankrupt. Saddened by what life held for him he shot himself at the age of 37.

Career record 1946-58: 75 contests. Won 66 (45 KO), Drew 1, Lost 8.

Ernest TYLDESLEY

Cricket
George Ernest Tyldesley. b. 5 Feb 1889 Roe Green, Worsley, Gt. Manchester. d. 5 May 1962 Rhos-on-Sea, Aberconwy and Colwyn.

With a Test batting average of 55, it seems amazing that Tyldesley, by 15 years the younger brother of the great J.T. (qv), played in only 14 Tests for England, but then such was the strength in depth of English batting in those days. In his only Test at Lord's, seven years after his debut, he made 122 against the West Indies in 1928. He made seven double centuries for Lancashire and scored over 1000 runs in 18 successive seasons 1913-14 and 1919-34, with six years over 2000, headed by 3024 at 79.57 in 1928 and 2826 at 64.22 in 1926, which included a record ten successive fifties, eight of them 100s. Even in his last regular season, at the age of 45 in 1934, he scored 2457 runs at 57.83. He became the first professional cricketer to serve on the Lancashire committee.

14 Tests 1921-9: 990 runs at 55.00, 3 100s HS 122; 2 catches.

First-class 1909-36: 38,874 runs at 45.46, 102 100s HS 256*; 6 wickets at 57.66, BB 3-33; 293 catches.

Johnny TYLDESLEY

Cricket
John Thomas Tyldesley. b. 22 Nov 1873 Roe Green, Worsley, Gt. Manchester. d. 27 Nov 1930 Monton, Manchester.

Tyldesley was a stylish and quick-footed right-hand batsman and brilliant fielder for Lancashire and England. He exceeded 1000 runs in a season each year 1897-1914 and in 1919, over 2000 five times and had a peak of 3041 at 55.29 in 1901. His 97 and 62 out of 103 for England on a terrible wicket at Melbourne in 1904 were regarded as his best in Tests. After his retirement he became the Lancashire coach.

His younger brother **Ernest** (qv) followed him into the Lancashire team. Ernest scored more runs and at a better average, but regarded J.T., who had to play on poorer wickets, as the better player.

31 Tests 1899-1909: 1661 runs at 30.75, 4 100s HS 138; 16 catches.

First-class 1895-1923: 37,897 runs at 40.66, 86 100s HS 295*; 3 wickets; 355 catches.

Dorothy TYLER

Athletics, High Jump
Dorothy Jennifer Beatrice Tyler. b. 14 Mar 1920 Stockwell, London. née Odam.

As Dorothy Odam in 1936 and Dorothy Tyler at the 1948 Olympics she cleared the same height as the high jump winner, respectively (1.60m and 1.68m), only to take 2nd place under the rules then in operation for settling ties. Under later rules she would have been champion.

She was also 2nd in the 1950 Europeans and 1954 Commonwealth Games, but won the Commonwealth title in 1938 and 1950. She first jumped over 5ft in 1935 at 15 and was still clearing that height 31 years later, and her 20-year span of competing at Olympic Games is a British women's record for any sport, as she went on to 7th equal in 1952 and 12th equal in 1956. She is the youngest ever British record holder in athletics with her 1.65 high jump in 1936 at 16 years 39 days. This tied the world record, but was not ratified, but her 1.66m in 1939 was, until it was superseded by an earlier, 1938, performance by Dora Ratjen (Ger). However, Ratjen was then shown to have been a man and Tyler's mark was put back in its rightful place in the record books.

Tyler set further British records at 1.66 and 1.68 at the 1948 Olympics. She was WAAA high jump champion eight times outdoors, 1936-9, 1948-9, 1952 and 1956, placing in the first three 14 times over 22 years, and four times indoors 1936-9; and also won the long jump and pentathlon in 1951, the latter in a British record 3953 points (1954 tables). She became a leading coach.

Other bests: 80m hurdles 11.8 (1950), long jump 5.73m (1951), 5.75w (1956).

Frank TYSON

Cricket
Frank Holmes Tyson. b. 6 Jun 1930 Farnworth, Gt. Manchester.

Tyson had a short but dramatic career. Selected for the 1954/5 England tour of Australia after just one full season in county cricket for Northamptonshire, his very fast bowling, in combination with Brian Statham (qv). did much to win the series for England as he took 28 wickets at 20.82. Australia had won the first Test b y an innings, but Tyson took ten wickets in the second at Sydney, including his best Test performance of 7-27 in the second innings, to turn the course of the series.

Now known as 'Typhoon', he added 11 wickets at 8.18 against New Zealand and 14 at 18.42 in 1955 against South Africa, but thereafter injuries, perhaps exacerbated by his ungainly action, limited his appearances and effectiveness. A graduate of Durham University, he emigrated to Australia where he became first a schoolteacher in Melbourne and subsequently a coach, journalist and TV commentator.

17 Tests 1954-9: 230 runs at 10.95, HS 37*; 76 wickets at 18.56, BB 7-27; 4 catches.

First-class 1952-60: 4103 runs at 17.09, HS 82; 767 wickets at 20.89, BB 8-60; 85 catches.

Betty UBER

Badminton
Elizabeth Uber. née Corbin. b. 2 Jun 1906 Epsom, Surrey. d. 30 Apr 1983. Poole, Dorset.

One of the finest badminton players, especially at doubles, in her very long career Uber set an English record with 37 international appearances from 1926 to 1951, winning every match until 1948. In 1956 she donated the Uber Cup to the International Badminton Federation, and that has since been regularly contested as the women's world team championship.

She was the British junior champion at lawn tennis, and at the All-England Badminton Championships she won eight mixed doubles titles in nine years, first from 1930 to 1932 with her husband **Bertie**, then 1933-6 with Donald Hume and in 1938 with Bill White. She was women's singles champion in 1935 and won the women's doubles with Marianne Horsley in 1931, Diane Doveton 1937-8 and Queenie Allen 1949.

George ULYETT

Cricket
George Ulyett. b. 21 Oct 1851 Pitsmoor, Sheffield. d. 18 Jun 1898 Pitsmoor

Regarded as the best Yorkshire batsman of the 19th century and also a top-class fast round-arm bowler, Ulyett played in the first ever Test match and in 25 of the first 33 ever played. His best series was when he opened against Australia in 1881/2, scoring 438 runs at 54.75 and taking 8 wickets at 22.50.

A powerful striker of the ball, he exceeded 1000 runs in a season ten times and his attitude earned him the nickname 'Happy Jack'. He died of pneumonia contracted while watching Yorkshire play Kent at Sheffield.

25 Tests 1876-90: 949 runs at 24.33, 1 100 HS 149; 50 wickets at 20.40, BB 7-36; 18 catches.

First-class 1873-93: 20,823 runs at 23.44, 18 100s HS 199*; 653 wickets at 20.14, BB 7-30; 367 catches.

Derek UNDERWOOD

Cricket
Derek Leslie Underwood. b. 8 Jun 1945 Bromley, London.

With his medium pace left-arm spin bowling Underwood fully lived up to his nickname of 'Deadly', for so he was on any sort of wicket that gave him some assistance. In an age when pace bowling dominated, he could and should have played more often for England, for he was from time to time left out of the team. Despite that, he took nearly 300 wickets in Tests. He also lost the chance to play Test cricket when he played World Series Cricket in 1978-9 and when he went on a rebel tour to South Africa in 1982. In his best Test series he took 24 wickets at 9.16 in three Tests against New Zealand in 1969 and 29 wickets at 17.55 in five against India in 1976/7.

He first played for Kent at 17 and in that first season showed impressive maturity to take 101 wickets at 21.12. That was the first of ten 100-wicket hauls, despite the fact that most of his career was played at a time when the number of first-class games was reduced and that target very rarely achieved. His 157 at 13.80 in 1966 is the last instance of a bowler taking over 150 wickets in a season. At his peak from 1966 to 1984 he averaged less than 20 runs per wicket in 12 seasons in England. He was awarded the MBE in 1981.

86 Tests 1966-82: 937 runs at 11.56, HS 45*; 297 wickets at 25.83, BB 8-51; 44 catches.
26 One-day Ints 1973-82: 53 runs at 5.88, HS 17; 32 wickets at 22.93, BB 4-44; 6 catches.
First-class 1963-87: 5165 runs at 10.19, 1 100 HS 111; 2465 wickets at 20.28, BB 9-28; 261 catches.

Rory UNDERWOOD

Rugby Union
Rory Underwood. b. 19 Jun 1963 Middlesbrough.

A measure of his brilliance and consistency is that Underwood is both England's most capped player and their leading try scorer. He was the first English player to win 50 caps, and in 79 matches to the end of the 1995 World Cup has scored 46 tries, including a record five against Fiji in 1989. First capped in 1984, he played in the World Cup in New Zealand in 1987. He also toured with the British Lions to Australia in 1989 and to New Zealand 1993 (three Tests on each tour, with a try on the second), but his duties as an RAF officer (fighter pilot) prevented him from joining a number of other touring teams.

Primarily a left-winger, he could play with equal facility on the opposite wing. He announced his retirement after helping England to their second successive Grand Slam in 1992 but reversed the decision early the following season and again made himself available for international selection. Too often starved of the ball in his early internationals for England, his try-scoring try has improved markedly in recent years, even if many supporters still wish that England would employ a yet more expansive game.

He started his senior career with Middlesbrough and made his county debut for Durham in 1981. From 1983 he has played for Leicester, helping them to the club championship in 1988 and 1995 and the Pilkington Cup in 1993.

His brother **Tony** (b. 17 Feb 1969 Ipoh, Malaysia), an investment banker who also plays for Leicester, played with him for England in 1992-5, scoring 10 tries in 20 internationals, and also went on the Lions tour to New Zealand 1993. He won Blues at Cambridge University for both rugby (1990-2) and athletics, as a sprinter.

Roger UTTLEY

Rugby Union
Roger Miles Uttley. b. 11 Sep 1949 Blackpool, Lancashire.

Capped from the Gosforth club 23 times by England 1973-80, Uttley later became a successful coach with England and the British Lions. Tall, strong, robust and an excellent ball player, he won eleven caps as a lock, seven as a no. 8 and finally five as a flanker. When the 1974 British Lions comprehensively won the series in South Africa he played as flanker in all four Tests and made a major contribution to their success with his superb loose forward play. He was also selected for the 1977 Lions tour of New Zealand but was prevented by injury from accepting.

Unfortunately his career was plagued by injury but, after missing the 1976 international season because of back troubles, he returned to captain England in 1977 and he closed his international playing career as a member of the 1980 Grand Slam team.

The highlights of his coaching career were as assistant to Ian McGeechan (qv) with the successful 1989 Lions in Australia and as coach to England's 1991 Grand Slam team. He is the only man to have both played in and coached an England Grand Slam team. He retired as England's coach after the 1991 World Cup and was awarded the OBE that year. Now a master at Harrow, he continues to coach at school and club level.

Dave VALENTINE

Rugby League
David Donald Valentine. b. 12 Sep 1926 Hawick, Borders. d. 14 Aug 1976 Leeds.

After winning two rugby union caps for Scotland in 1947, Valentine signed professional forms for Huddersfield and won 15 GB caps 1948-54 at rugby league. Experience gained as a flanker for Hawick in the tough school of Borders rugby stood him in good stead in his new environment and he was a member of the Huddersfield team which won the Challenge Cup in 1953.

He toured Australia and New Zealand with the 1954 Lions and crowned his international career by captaining the victorious Great Britain team in the 1954 World Cup. Rated as complete outsiders before the tournament, the British team responded magnificently to Valentine's inspiring leadership and he was chaired from the field in Paris after GB beat France 16-12 in the play-off. After he retired he stayed on at Huddersfield as a coach.

Jesse VALENTINE

Golf
Jessica Valentine. b. 18 Mar 1915 Perth. née Anderson.

Valentine was the British Ladies' Open Amateur champion of 1937, 1955 and 1958 (then the oldest ever winner at 43) and runner-up in 1950. Her record in seven Curtis Cups 1936-58 (then a record number of appearances) was two wins and nine losses. In her first Cup she holed a fine putt on the last green to win her single and halve the entire contest.

She had won the British Girls title in 1933, the New Zealand Ladies in 1935, and the French in 1936 and was Scottish ladies champion in 1938-9, 1951, 1953 and 1955-6. 'Wee Jessie', noted as a very controlled player, was a Scottish international from 1934 to 1958, before turning professional in 1959, in which year she was awarded the MBE, the first woman so honoured for golf.

Harry VARDON

Golf
Harry Vardon. b. 9 May 1870 Grouville, Jersey. d. 20 Mar 1937 Totteridge, London.

Vardon was the greatest player of the guttie era and considered the greatest ever until the advent of Bobby Jones (USA). He won six British Opens, 1896, 1898-9, 1903, 1911 and 1914, still a record, and was 2nd four times, 1900, 1901, 1902 (=) and 1912, 3rd in 1906 and 1913 (=) and in the top six 16 times in all. He also won the US Open in 1900, lost the play-off in 1913 and was equal 2nd in 1920. He had a serious illness in 1901, after which it was said he never completely recovered his old dominance, but he won the 1911 German Open and 1912 British PGA. The overlapping grip, which he popularised, is still often termed the 'Vardon grip'. A calm and likeable man, he was known primarily for his upright, graceful swing and his tremendous talent as a fairway wood player.

His younger brother **Tom** finished 2nd to him, six strokes behind, in the 1903 Open Championship.

Harry VASSALL

Rugby Union
Henry Vassall. b. 22 Oct 1860 Tadcaster, North Yorkshire. d. 5 Jan 1926 Repton, Derbyshire.

Although winning only five England caps 1881-3, Vassall was rated the greatest player of the Victorian era. He scored three tries on his international debut and captained England twice. Converting his Oxford University team to a revolutionary passing game, he led the University to an unbeaten record of 70 matches. A strongly built forward, his plan of the forwards linking with the backs proved particularly effective and was adopted by England with considerable success. His influence on the development of the game is unmatched by any other individual.

A schoolmaster by profession, he served as Treasurer of the RFU 1884-94, and his nephew, **Henry Holland 'Jumbo'** (1887-1949) won one cap for England in 1908 and played in the centre during Oxford's second 'Golden Era' 1907-12.

Terry VENABLES

Football
Terence Frederick Venables. b. 6 Jan 1943 Dagenham, London.

After much deliberation Venables was appointed England coach in January 1994. His appointment had been delayed, possibly because of allegations concerning his business affairs, notably during his period as manager and later chief executive of Tottenham Hotspur from 1987 until 1993 when he was sacked by chairman Alan Sugar.

A born leader, Venables was the first player to win international honours for England at five different levels: schoolboy, youth, amateur, Under-23 and full, as he won two senior caps in 1964. He joined Chelsea as an apprentice in 1958, turning pro in 1960. Initially an assured right-half, later moving into the midfield, he scored 31 goals in 237 senior appearances for Chelsea before being transferred for £80,000 in 1966 to Tottenham Hotspur, for whom he scored 19 goals in 115 games, and for £70,000 fees to Queen's Park Rangers in 1969 and to Crystal Palace in 1974. He won winners' medals for the League Cup in 1965 and for the FA Cup in 1967. He was appointed manager of Crystal Palace in 1976, moving to QPR in 1980. From 1984-7 he managed Barcelona, who won the Spanish League in 1985 and were beaten in the European Cup final of 1986. He managed the Spurs team that won the FA Cup in 1991.

Apart from playing and managing he has also been a players' agent, a TV scriptwriter and novelist and proprietor of the club, Scribes West.

Hedley VERITY

Cricket
Hedley Verity. b. 18 May 1905 Headingley, Leeds. d. 31 Jul 1943 Caserta, Italy.

Verity was the world's best slow medium left-arm spinner of the 1930s and the most famous cricketing casualty of World War II, when he died of his wounds in an Italian prisoner-of-war camp as a captain in the Green Howards.

With Wilfred Rhodes (qv) in the Yorkshire team, he had to wait until he was 25 for his debut, but then followed in his county's great tradition of bowlers of his type and was an immediate success, as in his first season of 1930 his 64 wickets averaged just 12.42. His impressive record continued as he took at least 150 wickets in each season for the rest of the decade - his worst seasonal average was 17.63 - to have the best career average figures of any major bowler of the 20th century. He took over 200 wickets each year 1935-7 and was close to the double when he scored 855 runs to go with his 216 wickets in 1936. In 1932 for Yorkshire v Nottinghamshire at Leeds he took 10-10 in 19.4 overs, the most economical ten-wicket haul ever and the only one to include a hat-trick. In 1934 for England against Australia at Lord's he took 7-61 and 8-43, these 15 wickets being the most to fall to a bowler on one day of Test cricket.

Tall and unhurried in his bowling, he was also a useful batsman, who was pressed into service to open the innings for

England in one Test against South Africa in 1937.

40 Tests 1931-9: 669 runs at 20.90, HS 66*; 144 wickets at 24.37, BB 8-43; 30 catches.

First-class 1930-9: 5605 runs at 18.08, 1 100 HS 101; 1956 wickets at 14.90, BB 10-10; 269 catches.

Stan VICKERS

Walking
Stanley Frank Vickers. b. 18 Jun 1932 Lewisham, London.

Vickers was European champion at 20km walk in 1958, and at the Olympics at this event was 5th in 1956 (in a British record time of 1:32:35) and 3rd in 1960. He was succeeded as Britain's number one by Ken Matthews (qv), and the two had some great contests, not least the AAA 2 miles championship of 1960, a race in which both men broke the British record that Vickers had equalled two weeks earlier, but which had stood at 13:11.4 to George Larner (qv) since 1904. Vickers won in 13:02.4 with Matthews 2nd in 13:09.6.

Vickers was regarded by walking experts as one of the most stylish of the great walkers. His other best times: track: 5M 35:24.2 (1960), 10,000m 43:43.6 (1960), 7M 50:09.0 (1958), 10M 1:14:31.4 (1957), 1 hour 13,517m (1958), road 20km 1:31:43 (1960). He won the RWA 10 miles in 1957-8 and the 20 miles in 1960, and was AAA champion at 2M 1957-8 and 1960 and at 7M 1957-8.

Bill VOCE

Cricket
William Voce. b. 8 Aug 1909 Annesley Woodhouse, Notts. d. 6 Jun 1984 Nottingham.

The name of Voce will ever be linked with that of his Nottinghamshire colleague Harold Larwood (qv) for their fearsome 'bodyline' bowling on the 1932/3 tour to Australia, but unlike his partner he returned to Australia for two further tours, 1936/7 and 1946/7, and on the former returned his best figures with 26 wickets at 21.53 in the series. After the controversy,

however, he played only three Tests in England and never against Australia. Having joined Nottinghamshire as a left-arm spinner, this burly ex-miner became a magnificent fast bowler, and took over 100 wickets in a season six times in the 1930s; his 120 wickets at 17.02 in 1929 helping Notts to their first Championship since 1907. He was also a capable attacking batsman and a magnificent fielder, with a very strong throw from the boundary. He was Notts coach from his retirement from regular county cricket in 1947 until 1952.

27 Tests 1929-47: 308 runs at 13.39, HS 66; 98 wickets at 27.88, BB 7-70; 15 catches.

First Class 1927-52: 7590 runs at 19.21, 4 100s HS 129; 1558 wickets at 23.08, BB 8-30; 286 catches.

Gordon WADDELL

Rugby Union
Gordon Herbert Waddell. b. 12 Apr 1937 Glasgow.

Son of Herbert (qv), The Waddells were the only Scots to play at fly-half in a Test for the British Lions until Craig Chalmers (qv) won his place on the 1989 tour.

After a series of brilliant performances with the unbeaten Fettes team, he won his first cap the year after leaving school. On going up to Cambridge University he won his Blue 1958-61 and an excellent game at fly-half in the 1958 'Varsity match, together with some impressive performances for Scotland, earned him a place with the 1959 Lions. Because of examinations, he missed the Australian leg of the tour and, although the Lions called on three different fly-halves for the four Tests in New Zealand, Waddell failed to win a Test place.

On his second Lions tour, to South Africa in 1962, his solid physique was an invaluable asset against the robust Springboks and he played in the first two Tests in place of the injured Richard Sharp (qv). Having won 18 caps 1957-62 for Scotland and being appointed captain at the age of 21, he ended his first-class rugby career after the Lions tour and spent two years at Stanford University in America pursuing business studies. He then settled in South Africa where he rose to become a senior executive with the influential Oppenheimer Group and a member of the South African Parliament.

Herbert WADDELL

Rugby Union
Herbert Waddell. b. 19 Sep 1902 Scotland. d. 5 Jan 1988 Scotland.

Like his son, Gordon (qv), Waddell was capped at fly-half by Scotland and the British Lions. For Scotland he won 15 caps 1924-30 and with the Lions he played in three Tests in South Africa in 1924. After the tour he helped Scotland to the Grand Slam in 1925 and the Championship in the two succeeding years. He excelled as a tactical kicker and with the drop goal. He became a leading administrator and served as President of the Scottish RU 1963-4.

Sheila WADDINGTON

Equestrianidsm, Three-day event
Sheila Waddington. b. 12 Mar 1936 Sutton Coldfield, West Midlands. née Wilcox.

The first great woman three-day eventer, Sheila Wilcox was for three successive years the winner of the Badminton Horse Trials, on *High and Mighty* in 1957-8 and on *Airs and Graces* in 1959, and she also won at Burghley on *Fair and Square* in 1968. Women were not allowed to compete at the Olympic events until 1964 so she was asked to put her *High and Mighty* at the disposal of the selectors for someone else to ride at the 1956 Olympics, but the horse went lame and did not take part. Back together again Sheila won the European title, the most important event open to her, on him in 1957.
Her brother **John** (b. 16 Feb 1937) won 16 England caps for rugby union at full-back. He also won a boxing Blue at Oxford in 1960.

Chris WADDLE

Football
Christopher Roland Waddle. b. 14 Dec 1960 Hepworth, nr. Gateshead, Tyne and Wear.

Waddle signed for Newcastle United in 1980 and although he made his England debut in 1985 didn't fully develop into a world-class forward until he went to Tottenham Hotspur later that year. In 1989 he moved to Marseille for a then British record fee of £4.25 million and in 1992 he returned to England when Sheffield Wednesday paid the French club £1 million.
A winger or central striker known for his tricky running and balance on the ball he was voted the Football Writers' Player of the Year in 1993 when he was one the stars of the Sheffield Wednesday team which lost to Arsenal in the final of both the FA Cup and the League Cup.
He scored 6 goals in his 62 England appearances 1985-92, but after brilliant play in the 1990 World Cup he was discarded by England manager Graham Taylor apart from a couple of appearances as a substitute and an isolated recall in 1992.

Kirsty WADE

Athletics
Kirsty Margaret Wade. b. 6 Aug 1962 Girvan, South Ayrshire. née McDermott.

Having won the Commonwealth 800m for Wales in 1982 and married Tony Wade in March 1986, she became, in Edinburgh 1986, the first woman to win both 800m and 1500m at the Commonwealth Games. She reached top world class in 1985 when she set UK and Commonwealth records at 800m (1:57.42), 1000m (2:33.70) and 1 mile (4:19.41) and in all set 12 Welsh records from 1981 to 1987, adding bests at 1500m 4:00.73 and 3000m 8:47.7 in 1987. At 1500m she was 6th at 1500m in both 1987 and 1991 World Championships and 7th in the 1986 Europeans, with a win in the 1987 European Cup. She had long shown her promise as at 800m she won the WAAA girls title in 1976 and intermediates 1978 with the English Schools in 1980. She won ten successive Welsh 800m titles 1979-88, with the 400m 1981-2 and 1987 and 1500m 1987.

Virginia WADE

Tennis
Sarah Virginia Wade. b. 10 Jul 1945
Bournemouth, Dorset.

Wade's victory in the 1977 Wimbledon singles was received with acclaim by the spectators: this was Wimbledon's Centenary year and success by a home player was particularly welcome and at the end of the year she was voted BBC Sports Personality of the Year. Approaching her 32nd birthday this was Wade's 16th challenge for the title and although she had been a world-class player for many years, previous Grand Slam singles honours had been restricted to the 1968 US and 1972 Australian titles. She gained her only major clay-court success in 1971 when she took the Italian title.

At women's doubles she won the US, French and Australian Championships in 1973 and the US title again in 1975; all with Margaret Court (Aus), but they did not play together at the 1973 Wimbledon and missed the opportunity of a Grand Slam of doubles titles that year.

Although born in Hampshire, Wade was raised in South Africa where her father was Archdeacon of Durban. She returned to England when she was 15 and then took a science degree at Sussex University. Although she later settled in New York, Wade remained a loyal member of British teams and played in more Federation Cup rubbers (100) and more ties (57) than any player of any country, winning 36 of 56 singles and 30 of 44 doubles. She also played in a record 20 Wightman Cup ties. Apart from her prowess as a player she did much for the game and in 1983 became the first woman to be elected to the Wimbledon Championships Committee. No woman has exceeded the 25 Wimbledon Championships at which she played.

Harold WAGSTAFF

Rugby League
Harold Wagstaff. b. 19 May 1891
Huddersfield, West Yorkshire. d. 19 Jul
1939 Huddersfield.

A teenage prodigy who was universally recognised as the 'Prince of Centres', Wagstaff first played for Huddersfield at the age of 15 years 175 days, represented Yorkshire aged 17-141 and was only 17-228 when he became the youngest-ever international for England. In order to convince sceptics among the Huddersfield supporters who doubted his age, a facsimile of his birth certificate was printed in the official match programme.

He led Great Britain to Australia in 1914 and 1920 and established himself in the legends of the game as captain of the winning team in the famous 'Rorke's Drift Test' in 1914 when Great Britain won 14-6 despite being reduced to 10 men after 50 minutes play. He won every honour in the game, but World War I curtailed his international career and he played in only 12 matches for Great Britain.

After retirement he coached at Halifax and Broughton Rangers, and at the time of his death was the licensee of a hotel in Huddersfield and a committee member of his former club.

Wavell WAKEFIELD

Rugby Union
William Wavell Wakefield. b. 10 Mar 1898
Beckenham, London. d. 12 Aug 1983
Kendal, Cumbria.

Both as a player and an administrator, Wakefield made an immeasurable contribution to the sport. A wing forward for Leicester, Harlequins, RAF, Cambridge University and England, he pointed the way to the advantages of mobile forward play and he introduced the concept of the back row working together as a team. His 31 caps (1920-7) remained an England record until beaten by 'Budge' Rogers (qv) in 1969; he captained England 13 times and led them to three Grand Slams.

He entered Parliament as a Conservative in 1935, served as president of the Rugby Football Union in 1950-1 and was a member of the International Board from 1954-61. He was also sometime president of tne national organistaions for b oth skiing and water-skiing. He was knighted during the war and in 1963 became the first Baron Wakefield of Kendal.

Billy WALKER

Football
William Henry Walker. b. 29 Oct 1897 Wednesbury, West Midlands. d. 28 Nov 1964 Sheffield.

Originally a centre-forward, Walker later switched to inside-left and played for England in both positions. During his 19-year career with Aston Villa, which began in 1919, he won an FA Cup winners' medal as captain in his first full season of 1920 and again played in the final in 1924. Between 1920 and 1927 he was capped 17 times by England (scoring nine goals) and after an interval of nearly six years he won his 18th and final cap when he was recalled as captain against the Austrian 'Wunderteam' in December 1932, a game England won 4-3.

After more than 500 appearances for Aston Villa (with 213 goals in 480 League games) he retired in 1933 to become manager of Sheffield Wednesday, guiding them to victory in the 1935 FA Cup final. After a brief spell at Chelmsford City, he took over at Nottingham Forest in 1939 and 20 years later he had his second FA Cup success as a manager when Forest beat Luton in the 1959 final. He retired owing to ill health the following year and was appointed to the club committee, a position he retained up until his death.

Shaun WALLACE

Cycling
Shaun Patrick Wallace. b. 20 Nov 1961 Christchurch, Dorset.

Wallace won Commonwealth silver medals for the pursuit 12 years apart – in 1982 and 1994. In between he broke the world record for kilometre from a flying start with 59.505 in 1985, a time he improved to 58.995 in 1986, when he also set a British 500m record of 29.55. He was twice runner-up in the world professional pursuit championship (1991-2), with 4th place in 1993.

He had first set a British record with 31.157 for a flying start 500m in 1980. He went to the University of Nottingham, and lived in the USA in the mid-1980s.

Fulke WALWYN

Horse Racing
Fulke Thomas Tyndall Walwyn. b. 8 Nov 1910 Wrexham. d. 18 Feb 1991 Upper Lambourn, Berkshire.

A fine trainer under National Hunt Rules, Walwyn saddled a total of 2188 winners in a 50-year career 1939-90. His horses won all the major races, one Grand National (*Team Spirit* in 1964), four Cheltenham Gold Cups, two Champion Hurdles and seven times the Whitbread and Hennessy Gold Cups. Perhaps the best horses he trained were *Mandarin* and *Mill House*. He was a master of getting his horses right for the big occasion.

The son of an army officer, a career he followed after school until 1935, he started riding as a youngster. The peak of his amateur career, 1929-36, was his win on *Reynoldstown* in the 1936 Grand National. He then turned professional, but switched to training at Lambourn in 1939, after serious injuries from falls. He was leading trainer in 1946/7, in which year he started training for Dorothy Paget, and again in 1947/8, 1948/9, 1957/8 and 1963/4. In 1973 he took over from Peter Cazalet as trainer of the Queen Mother's horses. He was awarded the CVO.

Peter WALWYN

Horse Racing
Peter Tyndall Walwyn. b. 1 Jul 1933 Hastings, East Sussex.

Walwyn had a few rides under NH rules, but was an assistant trainer from the age of 20, and took out his own licence in 1961 to start training at Lambourn. He was champion trainer in 1974 and in 1975, when his horses earned a record £382,527, led by *Grundy*, the winner of the Derby, King George VI and Queen Elizabeth Stakes and the Irish 2000 Guineas. In that year he became the first trainer since Dobson Peacock in 1932 to send out more than 100 winners in a season. After 121 winners that year he again passed the century in 1976 and 1977, when he was 2nd and 3rd respectively in the table. His first Classics winner had been *Humble Duty* in the 1000

Guineas in 1970 and he won the Oaks with *Polygamy* in 1974.

He is a first cousin to National Hunt trainer Fulke Walwyn (qv).

David WARBURG

Real Tennis
David John Warburg. b. 22 Aug 1923 Kensington, London. d. 10 Nov 1987 Hampton Court, London.

From Rugby School, Warburg served in the war, after which he continued his education at Cambridge where he represented the University at real tennis, lawn tennis and squash rackets. He went on to become an outstanding real tennis player and between 1951 and 1969 he was a finalist in the British Amateur singles 14 times, winning the title in 1959, 1961 and 1965. Although his father founded the publishing house, Secker & Warburg, he chose not to join the family business and he became a schoolmaster. He died while playing real tennis at Hampton Court.

Angela WARD – see BONALLACK

Ernest WARD

Rugby League
Ernest Ward. b. 30 Jul 1920 Dewsbury, West Yorkshire. d. 9 Jul 1987.

Although his father was Dewsbury's coach at the time, Ward signed for Bradford Northern on his 16th birthday. His career was interrupted by war service, but he developed into Britain's finest centre in the immediate post-World War II era. His speed and eye for an opening and his accomplished goal kicking gave him a career total of 862 goals and 151 tries.

He went on tour to Australia and New Zealand in 1946 and 1950 and captained the Lions on the second tour. In all he won 20 Test caps, 9 as captain, and captained Bradford Northern in three successive Challenge Cup finals 1947-9, leading them to victory in 1947 and 1949 and winning the Lance Todd Trophy in 1949.

After many years at Bradford he spent two seasons as player-coach at Castleford but in his later years most of his time was devoted to organisations concerned with the welfare of former rugby league players.

Pat WARD

Tennis
Patricia Evelyn Ward. b. 27 Feb 1929 London. d. 22 Jun 1985 Brighton, East Sussex. Later Mrs R Hales.

After winning the British Junior doubles in 1946, Ward developed into one of Britain's leading players in the 1950s. Although at her best in the doubles she also produced some fine singles performances, winning the Italian title and reaching the US finals in 1955, the Wimbledon semi-finals in 1956 and the finals of the British Hard Court Championships in 1957.

She reached her peak as a doubles player in 1955 when, with Shirley Bloomer (qv) as her partner, she was runner-up at Wimbledon and the French Championships and took the British Hard Court title and the Covered Court title with Anne Shilcock (qv). She also won the Hard Court doubles in 1958-9 and the Covered Court doubles in 1956 and 1958-9, the Italian doubles 1954 and German doubles 1957.

Between 1951 and 1958, she played in five Wightman Cup ties but lost all five of her doubles matches.

Tony WARD

Rugby Union
Anthony Joseph Patrick Ward. b. 8 Oct 1954 Dublin.

Ward was a high-scoring and record breaking fly-half. In his only Test appearance for the British Isles (v South Africa 1980) he set a Lions scoring record with 18 points (5 penalties, 1 dropped goal) in the match. He won 19 Irish caps 1978-87, scoring 113 points, including 38 points in his debut season of 1978, which was then a record for the Five Nations Championship.

The more orthodox Ollie Campbell (qv) was often preferred by the Irish selectors but Ward proved himself a match winner on more than one occasion. In 1978 he kicked two drop goals and converted one try when Munster inflicted on the All Blacks their first ever defeat (12-0) on Irish soil.

Janet WARDELL-YERBURGH

Fencing
Janet Clouston Wardell-Yerburgh. b. 15 Feb 1940 Gomshall, Guildford, Surrey. née Bewley-Cathie.

Wardell-Yerburgh was the leading British lady fencer after the retirement of Gillian Sheen (qv); resolute and strong but not as quick on her feet as Sheen had been. She won gold medals in the individual and team foil at both the 1966 and 1970 Commonwealth Games and was the AFA champion six times between 1965 and 1972. She took part in three Olympic Games (1964, 1968, 1972) the last two being after her marriage to rower **Hugh Wardell-Yerburgh** (1938-70) who was killed in a car crash. He won an Olympic silver medal in the coxless fours in 1964.

Johnny WARDLE

Cricket
John Henry Wardle. b. 8 Jan 1923 Ardsley, South Yorkshire. d. 23 Jul 1985 Hatfield, Doncaster, S outhYorkshire.

A colourful character, Wardle maintained the great tradition of Yorkshire slow left-arm bowlers, and had considerable success for England, even though he had to contend with Tony Lock (qv), whom the selectors usually preferred on English wickets, for a place in the team. His most successful Test series were 20 wickets at 8.80 against Pakistan in 1954 and 26 at 13.80 in South Africa 1956/7. A year later his first-class career ended dramatically. He had been selected for the England tour to Australia 1958/9 but Yorkshire, for whom he had been a regular since 1947, announced that his county engagement was not to be renewed.
He had taken over 100 wickets in a season each year 1948-57, with a peak of 195 at 16.14 in 1955, but he could hardly be said to have lost form with 91 wickets at 15.39 in 1958. Wardle reacted virulently and lent his name to scathing newspaper articles about the Yorkshire cricket scene. Yorkshire dismissed him immediately and his Tour invitation was withdrawn. Sadly, at the age of 35, his first-class career was over, although he played in a match in India in 1968. He also played Minor Counties cricket for Cambridgeshire 1963-9. As a batsman he was a renowned hitter and often an effective lower order player.
28 Tests 1947-57: 653 runs at 19.78, HS 66; 102 wickets at 20.39, BB 7-36; 12 catches.
First-class 1946-68: 7333 runs at 16.08, HS 79; 1846 wickets at 18.97, BB 9-25; 256 catches.

Jack WARDROP

Swimming
John Caldwell Wardrop. b. 26 May 1932.

In 1954, with 4:41.7 for 440y medley at the US Indoor Championships, Jack Wardrop became the first British man to break a swimming world record for 40 years. He was competing there for Yale University, and went on to set four more world records: with 2:03.9 and 2:03.4 for 220y freestyle (the latter also a record at 200m) and 4:36.9 for 440y medley in 1955. Before going to America he held British records at all distances from 100y to 1 mile and he was the first Briton to swim 100m in less than a minute. He competed at each Olympic Games 1948-56, with a best placing of 5th at 400m in 1952, and won 11 ASA titles, all five freestyle titles from 100y to 1 mile in 1952, and the 220y 1950 and 1954, 440y 1950-1, and 880y 1949-50; and 21 Scottish titles between 1947 and 1952.
His twin Robert '**Bert**' also swam at the 1952 Olympics (6th 100m backstroke) and 1954 Commonwealth Games. Both he and Jack won bronze medals on Scotland's medley relay team at the latter, when Jack was silver medallist at 440y freestyle. Bert was ASA 100y backstroke champion in 1952 and Scottish backstroke champion 1947-52.

Pelham WARNER

Cricket
(Sir) Pelham Francis Warner. b. 2 Oct 1873 Port of Spain, Trinidad. d. 30 Jan 1963 West Lavington, West Sussex.

A stylish batsman, 'Plum' Warner dedicated much of his life to cricket. He was a Test selector on various occasions between 1905 and 1938 and managed the England team to Australia in 1932/3. His services to the game were recognised by a knighthood in 1937. He was for nearly 60 years on the MCC committee and president in 1950/1. The Warner Stand at Lord's was named in his honour in 1958. He played for Oxford University 1894-6 and for Middlesex, whom he captained from 1908 to 1920. He scored a century in his first Test, against South Africa in 1899, captained England 10 times, leading them on the Ashes winning tour to Australia in 1903/04 and in South Africa 1905/06. He founded the *Cricketer* magazine in 1921 and wrote or edited many books on cricket.

His elder brother **Aucher** (1859-1944) captained the West Indies in 1900 and succeeded his father as Solicitor-General and Attorney-General of Trinidad.

15 Tests 1899-1912: 622 runs at 23.92, 1 100 HS 132*; 3 catches.

First-class 1894-1929: 29,028 runs at 36.28, 60 100s HS 244; 15 wickets at 42.40, BB 2-26; 183 catches.

Derek WARWICK

Motor Racing
Derek Warwick. b. 27 Aug 1954
Alresford, Hampshire.

Warwick won the Le Mans 24-hour race in 1992 for Peugeot with Mark Blundell and Yannick Dalmas (Fra) and shared the world sports car title that year with Dalmas, having been runner-up for the title in 1986 and 1991.

From stock car and Formula Ford racing (European champion 1976), he moved into F3 in 1977 and in 1978 won the Vandervell series and was 2nd in the BP series. He moved up to F2 in 1979 and was runner-up in the 1980 European championship, won by his Toleman teammate Brian Henton. Toleman then went into Formula One and Warwick drove for them for three years, ending with his best results, four successive places between 4th and 6th in 1983. In 1984 he switched to Renault and was leading comfortably on his debut for them in Rio, when he had engine failure. He was

destined never to win a Grand Prix, his best being 2nd twice in 1984, when he was 7th in the World Championship. To 1993 he started 147 races, accumulating 71 points.

His brother **Paul** (b. 20 Jan 1969) was British F3000 champion posthumously in 1991, having been killed in an accident at Oulton Park on 21 July,

Cyril WASHBROOK

Cricket
Cyril Washbrook. b. 6 Dec 1914 Barrow, Clitheroe, Lancashire. *D 30/4/99*

After playing one Test against New Zealand in 1937, Washbrook lost an important part of his career to World War II, but for the first five postwar years he was Len Hutton's regular opening partner for England. A most resolute player of fast bowling and a brilliant cover-point, his best seasons were those of 1946 and 1947 when he scored 2400 runs at 68.57 and 2662 at 68.25 respectively in first-class cricket. In all he hit over 1000 runs in a season 20 times, three of them overseas.

After more than five years out of Test cricket, Washbrook, by then a selector, was recalled against Australia in 1956 at the age of 41, and proved any doubters wrong with an innings of 98, coming in at no. 5 with his side then 17-3. He captained Lancashire 1954-9 and, after being team manager and committee member, became the county president in 1989. His benefit of £14,000 in 1948 remained the record until 1971. He was awarded the CBE in 1991.

37 Tests 1937-56: 2569 runs at 42.81, 6 100s HS 195; 1 wicket; 12 catches.

First-class 1933-64: 34,101 runs at 42.67, 76 100s HS 251*; 7 wickets at 44.14, BB 2-8; 212 catches.

Split WATERMAN

Speedway
Squire Francis Waterman. b. 27 Jul 1921
New Malden, London.

Having turned to speedway from sand racing in 1947, Waterman came closest to the world speedway title in 1951 when runner-up to Jack Young (Aus) and again in 1953 when runner-up to Freddie Williams (qv). He took the Golden Helmet Match Race championship in 1951 and 1952. His skill and cavalier personality made him a great favourite with speedway crowds. He captained England captain and rode in five World finals, scoring 48 points.

David WATKINS

Rugby Union/League
David Watkins. b. 5 Mar 1942 Blaina, Blaenau Gwent.

After winning 21 caps for Wales 1963-7 and playing for Newport at rugby union, Watkins signed professional forms for Salford in 1967. An entertaining stand-off and superlative goal-kicker, his 221 goals in 47 matches in 1972/3 remains the record for the most goals kicked in one season; this was in the midst of his record sequence of scoring for Salford in 92 consecutive matches. Despite these talents, he only won two caps (plus four as substitute) for Great Britain.

He left Salford in 1979 and spent two seasons with Swinton before becoming managing director of the Cardiff Blue Dragons, but the attempt to revive rugby league in Wales was short lived. In his first-class rugby league career 1967-83 he scored 3117 points, including 1342 goals. He was awarded the MBE in 1986.

John WATSON (Ireland)

Polo
John Watson. b.? d. 12 Nov 1908 Ireland.

Watson was the world's leading polo player of the 1880s and early 1890s and the first man to demonstrate the full effectiveness of backhand strokes. When a captain in the 13th Hussars in India he was called on by his commander-in-chief to revise the rules of polo. He captained England to victory in the first two Westchester Cups against the USA, in 1886 and 1900, and led the world's top private team, the Freebooters. He was Master and huntsman of the Meath Foxhounds 1891-1908.

John WATSON

Motor Racing
John Watson. b. 4 May 1946 Belfast.

The Northern Irishman had a long career in Formula One, at which his record was five wins and 169 points from 152 starts 1973-85. He had started racing in 1963 and persistence brought its reward as over the next ten years he fought his way up to Formula One. There his first win came at the Austrian GP in 1976, when he was 6th in the drivers' world championship for Penske. He matched that position and had two wins in 1981 for McLaren, for whom he drove from 1979, replacing James Hunt (qv). He then had his best year in 1982, winning the US and Belgian GPs, and placing 2nd in the championship, five points behind Keke Rosberg (Fin). He was 6th again in 1983, but was dropped by McLaren in favour of Alain Prost and thereafter concentrated on sports car and endurance racing. He had his best year in the World Sports Car Championship in 1987, when he won three times and was 2nd equal overall.

He became director of the performance driving school at Silverstone and a TV commentator for Eurosport. He was awarded the MBE.

Maud WATSON

Tennis
Maud Edith Eleanor Watson. b. 9 Oct 1864 Harrow, London. d. 5 Jun 1946 Charmouth, Dorset.

Watson was the first Wimbledon Ladies' singles champion. At the age of 19 she won the inaugural title in 1884 beating her elder sister, Lilian, in the final. She retained her title in 1885 with a straight sets victory over Blanche Bingley (qv) but Bingley beat Watson in the Challenge Round the following year and this marked the end of Maud Watson's Wimbledon career. She also won the singles (1884-5) and the doubles (1885) at the Irish Championships and she was the Welsh singles champion in 1887. She was awarded the MBE for her nursing work in World War I.

Willie WATSON

Cricket and Football
Willie Watson. b. 7 Mar 1920 Bolton-on-Dearne, South Yorkshire.

The fair-haired Yorkshireman's epic stand of 163 in 5 ³/₄ hours with Trevor Bailey (qv) in the Lord's Test in 1953 ensured that that game was saved for England and the scene set for Ashes victory (15 years after England's last series win against Australia) in the 5th Test of that summer.

Watson had played all five Tests against South Africa in 1951 and made 109 in 346 minutes in this innings, his debut against Australia. He scored another Test century in the West Indies in 1954, but thereafter he did not gain a regular England place, as he was in and out of the side until 1959. In that year he had his best first-class season with 2212 runs at 55.30, one of 14 seasons in which he scored over 1000 runs. A stylish left-hander and fine outfielder, he moved from Yorkshire to be captain of Leicestershire 1958-61 and he was a Test selector 1962-4.

A tenacious left-half for Huddersfield Town (for whom his father had played as a professional footballer), Sunderland and Halifax Town, he made four international appearances for England at football in 1949-50

23 Tests 1951-9: 879 runs at 25.85, 2 100s HS 116; 8 catches.

First-class 1939-64: 25,670 runs at 39.86, 55 100s HS 257; 295 catches.

Jim WATT

Boxing
James Watt. b. 18 Jul 1948 Glasgow.

After winning the ABA title, Watt turned professional in 1968. He only had 14 fights in his first four years as a pro, but he won ten inside the distance, three on points and his only defeat came as the result of a cut eye. He first challenged for the British lightweight title in February 1972 when he lost to Willie Reilly in the 10th round. Reilly then forfeited the title and three months later Watt became the champion after stopping Tony Riley in 12 rounds. The following year he lost to Ken Buchanan

(qv) who then relinquished the title and in the absence of Buchanan, Watt regained the title in 1977 and then relinquished it himself in 1978.

In April 1979 he challenged Alfredo Pitalua (Colombia) for the vacant WBC world lightweight title, and with the referee stopping the contest in the Scotsman's favour in the 12th round, he became the world champion. Watt made four successful defences of his title - winning three of the fights inside the distance - before losing on points to Alexis Arguello (Nicaragua) in June 1981.

Having reigned as world champion for more than two years he then retired and is now an accomplished ITV summariser.

Career record 1968-81: 46 contests. Won 38 (28 KO), Lost 8.

Jack WATTS

Horse Racing
John Watts. b. 1861 Stockbridge, Hampshire. d. 29 Jul 1902 Sandown Park, Esher, Surrey.

Watts was the most successful jockey in the Classics in the last two decades of the 19th century, as he rode four winners each of the Derby, Oaks and 1000 Guineas, five of the St Leger and two of the 2000 Guineas for 19 winners between 1883 and 1897.

Apprenticed to Tom Cannon (qv), he rode his first winner in 1876 and he retired to train at Newmarket in 1900. His health had, however, been undermined by fasting and he died two years later.

Successive generations of Watts have succeeded him as a trainer, each winning a Classic:

His son **John** Evelyn (1887-1959), who trained the Derby winner in 1927 and 1000 Guineas winner in 1944, his grandson John Frederick '**Jack**' (b. 30 May 1911 Newmarket, d. 7 Feb 1988 Newmarket), who trained Indiana, the 1964 St Leger winner, and great-grandson John William '**Bill**' (b. 16 Mar 1942), who moved to Richmond, North Yorkshire, trained *Waterloo* to win the 1000 Guineas in 1972.

Jonathan WEBB

Rugby Union
Jonathan Mark Webb. b. 24 Aug 1963 London.

Webb was England's leading scorer until his total of 296 points was overtaken by Rob Andrew (qv) against Scotland in 1995. Initially with Northern (Newcastle) he joined Bristol when studying medicine at Bristol University and made his first appearance as England's full-back when he came on for the concussed Marcus Rose in the 1987 World Cup match against Australia. He retained his place until Simon Hodgkinson was preferred for the 1990 season after which Webb returned to the side. He had by now moved from Bristol to Bath and he held his place in the England team until the end of the 1993 season when he retired to concentrate on his duties as a surgeon.

His 67 points in the International Championship (4 matches) in the 1991/2 season remains a record for the competition.

Matthew WEBB

Swimming
(Captain) Matthew Webb. b. 19 Jan 1848 Irongate, nr Dawley, Shropshire. d. 24 Jul 1883 Niagara Falls, Canada.

Webb earned his place in history by being the first person to swim the English Channel. On 24-25 Aug 1875 he took 21 hr 45 min to cross from Dover to Calais, swimming an estimated 61 km *38 miles* to make the 33 km *21 mile* crossing. No other swimmer matched this feat until 1911 and his time was not beaten until 1934.

He had learned to swim at the age of eight and at the time of his crossing was a captain in the Merchant Navy, standing 1.73m *5ft 8in* and weighing 92 kg *14 ½ stone*. The previous year he had been awarded the Stanhope Gold Medal for the bravest deed of 1874, having jumped overboard in heavy seas in a vain attempt to save one of his crew. He drowned in 1883 in attempting to swim the rapids above the Niagara Falls.

Steve WEBSTER

Motorcycling
Steve Webster. b. 7 Jan 1960 York.

With Tony Hewitt as passenger, Webster was sidecar world champion each year 1987-9 for Yamaha. With **Gavin Simmons** (b. 2 Sep 1960 York) he won again in 1991 for LCR Krauser and was runner-up each year 1992-4. Third places in 1986 and 1990 meant nine successive years in the top three.

His father Mick had been a sidecar champion and Steve started racing in 1979, gaining his first title with the British Clubman's sidecar championship in 1982. A year later, at Silverstone, he won his first Grand Prix race and he was British champion in 1985 and 1986. He was awarded the MBE in 1990.

Harry WEETMAN

Golf
Harold Weetman. b. 25 Oct 1920 Oswestry, Shropshire. d. 19 Jul 1972 Warlingham, Surrey.

Weetman was a fine match player, as shown by his record in the PGA Match Play Championship, which he won in 1951 and 1958 and lost in the final in 1955, 1959 and 1960. His other main successes included the Dunlop Masters 1952 and 1958, Irish Open 1953 and German Open 1957, but his best British Open placing was only joint 5th in 1955.

He represented England in the World Cup four times and played in each of the seven Ryder Cups 1951-63, with a playing record of just two wins, eleven losses and two halves. One of those wins, was, however, considered by him to be his greatest triumph, when after being four down with six to play he beat Sam Snead (USA) one up in 1953. He was also non-playing captain in 1965.

A powerful man, he was a very aggressive and entertaining player, but it was felt that he could have done even better had he been able to play safe when needed; he was also a sure putter. Professional at Hartsbourne, then at Selsdon Park, he was killed in a car accident.

Dermot WELD (Ireland)

Horse racing
Dermot Charles Kenneth Weld. b. 29 Feb 1948 Tandridge, Surrey.

Weld was champion amateur jockey in Ireland in 1969, 1971 and 1972 and in the latter year took out his first trainer's license. He had earlier been an assistant trainer to his father Charlie Weld in Ireland and to Tommy Smith in Australia. He has now become well established as Ireland's premier trainer from his base at the Curragh. His winners have included *Blue Wind* of the Oaks in both England and Ireland in 1981 and five further Irish Classics as well as the 1988 Irish Grand National. In 1991 he trained 120 winners on the flat and 30 over jumps. With the Irish St Leger now open to older horses, his *Vintage Crop* won the race in 1993 and 1994, and between these races, in November 1993, was ridden, as usual by Michael Kinnane (qv), to the first ever victory in the Melbourne Cup in Australia by a horse trained in Europe.

Frank WELDON

Equestrianism. Three-day Event
Francis William Charles Weldon. b. 2 Aug 1913 Bombay, India. d. 21 Sep 1993

After war service with the Royal Artillery in which he was awarded the MC and later the MBE for helping a fellow escapee from Colditz, Lt Col. Frank Weldon became the first British rider to win an individual Olympic equestrian medal. This came in 1956, five years after he had taken up eventing, with a bronze for the three-day event, as well as a team gold, riding his own horse, the bay gelding *Kilbarry*. On this horse, who was killed in a fall in 1957, he had won at Badminton in 1955 and 1956 and took the European title in 1955 after placing 2nd in 1953 and 1954; winning team gold on each occasion. Weldon was again 2nd in 1959.

He also rode *Kilbarry* in the Queen's Coronation procession when he commanded the King's Troop of the Royal Horse Artillery. Having left the Army, at his second Olympics, in 1960, Weldon was

25th individually and the British team finished 4th. He had also been a point-to-point rider, winning races from 1934 to 1959. After retiring from competition, he was director of the Badminton Horse Trials from 1966 to 1988 and equestrian correspondent of the *Sunday Telegraph* for many years.

Allan WELLS

Athletics
Allan Wipper Wells. b. 3 May 1952 Edinburgh.

Wells became Olympic champion at 100m in 1980, when at the age of 28 he was then the oldest ever champion at the event. Due to the US boycott he was denied the opportunity of showing that he could have beaten the top Americans in Moscow, but he did so after the Games and when he won the IAAF Golden Sprints and the World Cup 100m (2nd at 200m) in 1981.
Although in his first season of athletics in 1970 he won the Scottish junior triple jump title, he only took up sprinting seriously six years later at the age of 24, having trained as a marine engineer.
He won a record six medals at the Commonwealth Games, gold at 200m and sprint relay in 1978, and gold at both 100m and 200m (when he tied with Mike McFarlane) in 1982; he was 2nd at 100m in 1978 and earned a bronze medal on Scotland's relay team in 1982. He was 4th at both 100m and 200m at the 1983 Worlds. He would have loved to have sealed his career with success in his home town at the Commonwealth Games of 1986, but was unable to get fit enough in time, although he returned to place 5th at both 100m and 200m in the European Championships a month later.
At the European Cup he won the 100m in 1981 and the 200m in 1979 and 1983. He was Scottish champion at 100m 1977-80 and 1983, and at 200m 1979-80, and set two British records at 100m and five at 200m from 1978 to his bests of 10.11 and 20.21 in 1980. He also had wind-assisted bests of 10.02 for 100m (1982) and 20.11 for 200m (1980). Other bests: 60m indoors 6.68 (1978), long jump 7.32m (1972).

He was coached by his wife **Margot** (nee Wilkie), who sprinted for Scotland at the 1978 Commonwealth Games.

Bombardier Billy WELLS

Boxing
William Thomas Wells. b. 31 Aug 1889 Mile End, London. d. 11 Jun 1967 Ealing, London.

One of the great unfulfilled talents of the British ring, Wells had the physique, skill and punching power to become a contender for the world heavyweight title, but he lacked the killer instinct and his defence was sometimes suspect, particularly against top ranked opponents who carried a powerful punch. The combination of these talents and deficiencies resulted in an interesting career record with 57 of his 59 professional fights ending in a KO and he was never beaten on points.

While serving in the army, he won the All-India championship and on his return he took the British heavyweight title from Iron Hague in 1911. Superbly fit, he was a good enough athlete to compete in the Powderhall professional sprint in 1912 where, although he entered under the pseudonym of 'T. James London', he was soon recognised by the crowd. He then went to America where he won two and lost two fights with all four bouts ending in a KO. On his return home he was knocked out twice by the 19-year-old Georges Carpentier (Fra) in 1913, but on the domestic scene he experienced little trouble. He won the first heavyweight Lonsdale Belt and made a record 14 successful defences of his British title before losing to Joe Beckett in 1919.

He retired in 1925 and with his good looks and urbane manner he remained a popular figure with the British sporting public. He became a 6 handicap golfer and was well-known to the film-going public as the striker of the gong in the introduction to all J.Arthur Rank productions.

Career record 1908-25: 59 contests. Won 48 (40 KO), Lost 11.

Freddie WELSH

Boxing
né Frederick Hall Thomas. b. 5 Mar 1886 Pontypridd, Rhondda Cynon Taff. d. 29 Jul 1929 New York, USA.

Welsh was world lightweight champion 1914-17 and one of the finest boxers in the history of the division. Although not a heavy puncher, he was a master of in-fighting and his defensive skills have seldom been matched. He first won the British lightweight title in 1909, but then lost to Matt Wells in 1911 and, after beating Wells in a return match in 1912, he remained the champion until he relinquished the title in 1919 on his return to America. He won the world title at Olympia in 1914 after a desperately close fight with the reigning champion, Willie Ritchie (USA).

This was the last time that Welsh fought in Britain but he successfully defended his title twice in America in 1916, beating Ad Wolgast (USA) and Charlie White (GB). After winning the world title, the majority of his fights in America were 'no decision' bouts which protected his title unless he was defeated inside the distance. In 1917 Benny Leonard (USA) succeeded in doing this and took the title with a ninth round KO in New York. This was the only time in his career that Welsh was knocked out and, although he didn't officially retire until 1922, he undertook few fights after this defeat.

He was the first outright winner of a Lonsdale Belt and had the remarkable record of losing only four of his 168 contests. Having invested all his money in a health farm which failed, he died penniless at the early age of 43.

Career record 1905-22: 168 contests. Won 76 (32 KO), Drew 7, Lost 4, No decision 81.

Arthur WENTWORTH GORE – see GORE

Mike WESTON

Rugby Union
Michael Philip Weston. b. 21 Aug 1938 Durham.

Playing in 29 internationals between 1960

and 1968, Weston once held the record as England's most capped three-quarter and was a brilliant tactical player at either fly-half or centre. He toured with the Lions to South Africa in 1962, when he played in all four Tests, and to Australasia in 1966 when after playing in both Tests against Australia he suffered from injury and loss of form and failed to make the team for the matches against New Zealand. Between these two Lions tours, he captained England on a short tour of Australia and New Zealand in 1963.

Born and educated in Durham, he remained loyal to Durham City for most of his career and he also played Minor Counties cricket for the county. After retirement, he served as an England selector for many years and was chairman of the selection panel in 1985-6.

His son **Philip** captained the England Under-19 team at cricket and now plays for Worcestershire.

Tommy WESTON

Horse Racing
Thomas Weston. b. 4 Feb 1902 Dewsbury, West Yorkshire. d. 22 Jan 1981 Ely, Cambridgeshire.

Weston was champion jockey in 1926 with 95 winners and runner-up to Gordon Richards (qv) in 1927, with a peak total of winners of 101 in 3rd place in 1930. He rode his first winner in 1918 and from 1924 to 1934 was first jockey for the 17th Earl of Derby, whose *Hyperion* he rode to win the Derby and St Leger in 1933. In all, this fine horseman rode 11 Classics winners 1924-46; he retired in 1950.

Alison WESTWOOD – see DAWES

Jean WESTWOOD

Ice Dance
Jean T Westwood. b. 1 Nov 1931 Manchester.

After winning the unofficial World title in 1951, Westwood won four consecutive official World titles 1952-5 with Lawrence Demmy (qv) as her partner and they were also European champions 1954-5. Her partnership with Lawrence Demmy ended when he retired to concentrate on his business interests and she then became an ice dance teacher in America where she still lives. She never married.

Joyce WETHERED

Golf
Joyce Wethered (Lady Heathcoat-Amory). b. 17 Nov 1901 Malden, London.

Wethered is usually considered, with the Americans Mickey Wright and Babe Zaharias, as one of the greatest female golfers ever. Bobby Jones once commented that he had never seen a better player – male or female. Tall and strong, she had a fine swing that produced long and accurate driving and firm iron play.

She played in the British Ladies' Amateur only six times, winning four (1922, 1924-5, 1929), losing once in the final to Cecilia Leitch in 1921, and being a semi-finalist on the other occasion. She retired from individual competition after 1925 but came back in 1929 to play this championship at St Andrews, where in the final she defeated the great American champion, Glenn Collett. She was English Ladies' Amateur champion each year 1920-4, but after 1925 she limited her competitive play to such events as the Worplesdon Mixed Foursomes, which she won eight times with seven different partners. She did, however, play in the Curtis Cup in 1932 and toured the USA as a professional in 1935.

Her brother **Roger** Henry **Wethered** (b. 3 Jan 1899 Malden, London. d. 12 Mar 1983 Wimbledon) was British Amateur champion in 1923 and tied for the British Open in 1921, before losing the play-off to Jock Hutchison (USA). No British amateur has come so close to winning the Open since. He also played in five Walker Cups between 1922 and 1934, with a record of five wins, three losses and one half, and was captain of the R & A in 1946.

Her husband Sir John Heathcoat-Amory (1894-1972) played cricket for Oxford University and Dorset.

Peter WHEELER

Rugby Union
Peter John Wheeler. b. 26 Nov 1948
London.

Wheeler was a consistent and talented hooker who won 42 caps for England 1975-84, a total then only exceeded by Tony Neary and John Pullin (qqv), who Wheeler replaced as England's hooker.

Selected as understudy to Bobby Windsor for the 1977 Lions tour of New Zealand, he took over from the Welshman for the last three Tests. After being a member of the England team which won their first Grand Slam for 23 years in 1980, he was selected for his second Lions tour that year, and in South Africa the Lions fielded an unchanged front row for all four Tests with Wheeler as hooker in each match.

His outspoken nature almost certainly precluded his appointment as England's regular captain and he was passed over three times before being given the captaincy in 1983; spurred by his dynamic leadership England claimed their first win over New Zealand at Twickenham since 1935.

Technically skilled in the set pieces and tireless in the loose his attributes did much to make Leicester the outstanding club in English rugby and he led them to three successive victories in the John Player Cup 1979-81.

John WHITAKER

Show Jumping
John Edwin Whitaker. b. 5 Aug 1955
Huddersfield, West Yorkshire.

Riding *Milton* John Whitaker has achieved one of the most successful partnerships in show jumping history, taking European team gold and individual silver in 1987, team and individual gold in 1989, and winning the World Cup in 1990 and 1991, with 2nd place in 1993.

On *Ryan's Son* he won his first national title in 1976, and was most unlucky to miss selection for the Olympic Games that year. They also missed the 1980 Games due to the team's boycott, taking team and individual silver at the alternative Games, but won team silver at the 1984 Olympics as well as bronze at the 1982 Worlds and team and individual European silver medals in 1983. He has won the King George V Gold Cup twice - on *Ryan's Son* in 1986 and on *Milton* in 1990, and further national titles in 1992 and 1994. On *Hopscotch* he won European team gold and individual bronze in 1985 and World team silver in 1986. He brought his European medal collection to ten with team silvers in 1991 and 1993. A very controlled and steady rider, he was awarded the MBE in 1991. He married Claire Barr, whose father owned *Ryan's Son*.

Michael WHITAKER

Show Jumping
Michael Whitaker. b. 17 Mar 1960
Huddersfield, West Yorkshire.

A more pushing rider than John (qv), Michael shared his brother's three European team gold medals (1985, 1987, 1989) and Olympic (1984), World (1986) and two European (1991, 1993) team silver medals, and was the individual silver medallist at the 1989 European Championships on *Monsanta* and bronze medallist on *Midnight Madness* in 1993. In 1984 he won the British title on *Amanda* and had the individual Olympic gold in his sight, only for *Amanda* to stop suddenly in the final round.

The brothers learned to ride at their family's farm in West Yorkshire. Michael won a team bronze in 1976 and gold in 1978 at the European Junior Championships, making his senior international debut in 1982. He has won the King George V Gold Cup four times, 1982, 1989, 1992 and 1994, Hickstead Jumping Derby four times 1980, 1991-3 and took his second British title in 1990.

His wife **Véronique** (b. 15 Jan 1959 Ville, Belgium, née Daems-Vestapane) won a European Junior team gold for Belgium in 1975 and silver medals individually in 1976 and 1977. She made her British debut in 1982, won the Queen Elizabeth II Cup in 1984 and was British show jumping champion in 1991 and ladies' champion in 1993.

Fatima WHITBREAD

Athletics
Fatima Whitbread. b. 3 Mar 1961 Stoke Newington, London. Born of Cypriot parents, former name Vedad.

Fatima Whitbread set a world javelin record of 77.44m at 9.18 am in qualifying for the 1986 European Championships and went on to win that event and the 1987 World title. At Commonwealth Games she placed successively 6th in 1978, 3rd in 1982 and 2nd in 1986, when having won all ten competitions that year she was overtaken in Edinburgh by Tessa Sanderson's fifth round throw, to Fatima's intense dismay.

At the Olympics, after failing to qualify for the final in 1980, she took bronze in 1984 and silver in 1988. In 1979 she won the European Junior title and set three British junior records to 58.20m. She also won the European Cup in 1983, and was WAAA champion five times (1981-4, 1986-7) and UK champion seven times (1981-5, 1987-8).

Between 1978 and 1988 she was ranked UK no.1 six times and 2nd five times behind her great rival Tessa Sanderson (qv), who beat her on the first 17 times that they met, but against whom the full record is: Sanderson 27, Whitbread 18.

Whitbread's career was ended by a series of injuries to her back and shoulder in 1992, although a comeback has remained possible. She was awarded the MBE and voted BBC Sports Personality of the Year in 1987.

She was adopted by Margaret Whitbread, UK javelin coach and international (best of 45.18m in 1959).

Reg WHITCOMBE

Golf
Reginald Arthur Whitcombe. b. 10 Apr 1898 Burnham, Somerset. d. 11 Jan 1957 Godalming, Surrey.

Although thought by some to be the least gifted of the Whitcombe brothers, the youngest, Reg, was the one to win the Open, which he did in 1938. In his only Ryder Cup appearance he lost to Johnny Revolta in a singles match in 1935. He won the 1936 Irish Open.

His elder brother **Charles** Albert (b. 21 Sep 1895 Burnham, Somerset. d. 1981) was a fine natural golfer, although an unreliable putter, who played in six Ryder Cups 1927-37, captaining the team three times, with a record of three wins, two losses and four halves. He twice beat Henry Cotton in the final of the PGA Match Play Championship (1928 and 1930) and was 3rd in the Open in 1935. He was also the first winner of the Vardon Trophy in 1937.

In 1935 the third brother **Ernest** Robert (b. 11 Oct 1890 Axbridge, Somerset. d. 14 Jul 1971 Bury St Edmunds, Suffolk) also played in the Ryder Cup on three occasions, 1929, 1931 and 1935 (one win, four losses, one half), so that in 1935 all three brothers participated, a unique family achievement. In 1924 Ernest was 2nd in the Open, beaten by one shot by Walter Hagen (USA) and won the PGA title.

Belle WHITE

Diving
Isabella Mary 'Belle' White. b. 1 Sep 1894 London. d. 7 Jul 1972 St Austell, Cornwall.

White became Britain's first Olympic diving medallist with the bronze medal in 1912, and was also Britain's first European champion 15 years later at the first championships in 1927.

Between these successes she was 4th in 1920 and 6th in 1924 at the Olympic Games and she was to compete at a fourth Games in 1928. The first ASA championship for women's diving was not held until 1924, but White won each year from then until 1929. She had, however, won the Ladies Plain Diving Bath championship organised by the Amateur Diving Association (which became a part of the ASA) nine times from their first championship in 1916.

She was an official and administrator for the rest of her life, and the Belle White Memorial Trophy is now presented each year to Britain's most successful club in women's competitions.

Jack WHITE

Cricket
John Cornish White. b. 19 Feb 1891
Holford, Somerset. d. 2 May 1961 Combe-
Florey, Somerset.

'Farmer' White relied on flight and changes of pace rather than great spin for his economical slow left-arm bowling. Playing for Somerset for 28 years (captain 1927-31), he achieved his greatest success for England when he was vice-captain in Australia in 1928/9. His 25 wickets for a miserly 760 runs from 406.4 overs was vital for England's 4-1 series victory and at Adelaide in the 4th Test his figures were 5-130 and 8-126. Although by then a grey-haired veteran of 37 he had previously played in only two Tests, but he played in another eight to 1931, captaining England four times in all and was also a selector in 1929-30. Showing great stamina, he took over 100 wickets in each English season 1919 to 1932, with a peak of 168 at 15.76 in 1929, and did the double in 1929 and 1930.

15 Tests 1921-31: 239 runs at 18.38, HS 29; 49 wickets at 32.26, BB 8-126; 6 catches.

First-class 1909-37: 12,202 runs at 18.40, 6 100s HS 192; 2356 wickets at 18.57, BB 10-76; 426 catches.

Jimmy WHITE

Snooker
James Warren White. b. 2 May 1962
Tooting, London.

White is the finest snooker player never to win the world title, although he has been a top-ranked player for more than a decade, since winning the English Amateur title at 16 and in 1979 becoming, at 18 years 191 days, the youngest ever amateur world champion. In the World Professional Championship he was beaten in the final in 1984 and for five consecutive years 1990-4, losing only in the final frame in 1994, when he was beaten for the third successive year by Stephen Hendry (qv). In 1992 he scored a maximum 147 break in the first round. White made his first century break at 13 and won the British boys (Under-16) title

in 1977. Since then his outstanding natural talent has brought the left-hander rich reward. His major titles include: British Open 1987 and 1992; UK Open 1992, Benson & Hedges Masters 1984, European Open 1992, World Matchplay 1989-90 and World Masters 1991.

Wilf WHITE

Equestrianism, Show Jumping
Wilfred Harry White. b. 30 Mar 1904
Nantwich, Cheshire.

On *Nizefella* White scored his first major win in 1949 and earned two Olympic medals - team gold in 1952 and bronze in 1956. They were 5th and equal 4th respectively in the individual competition, losing a medal in the jump-off in Helsinki, when five men tied on eight faults.

A Cheshire farmer, White was awarded the OBE for his services to the sport in 1958 and was a member of the executive committee of the British Show Jumping Association.

Johnny WHITELEY

Rugby League
John Whiteley. b. 20 Nov 1930.

Whiteley was an outstanding loose forward, who won 15 GB caps 1957-62 and toured Australia and New Zealand in 1958. He made his debut for Hull in 1950 and remained loyal to the club throughout his career. After he gave up playing, he became a successful coach and was put in charge of the GB team to meet the Australians in 1982. Great Britain were outplayed in all three Tests, with the Australians running up a total of 99 points. These heavy defeats can be attributed to the brilliance of the Australians and inadequacies of the British team, rather than to any failing on the part of the coach, Johnny Whiteley.

Arthur WHITFORD

Gymnastics
Arthur John Whitford. b. 2 Jul 1908
Swansea.

Britain's leading gymnast between the wars, Whitford won the British individual title a record ten times, 1928-36 and 1939, and was a member of four winning teams with Swansea YMCA. He also won the Irish, Welsh and Scottish individual titles and is the only man to have been champion of all four home countries, A member of the 1928 Olympic team, he was later the only British competitor at the 1931 World Championships in Paris.

He was coach to the 1948 and 1952 Olympic teams, and his son **John** (b. 1924) competed at the 1952 Games,

Harold WHITLOCK

Walking
Hector Harold Whitlock. b. 16 Dec 1903 Hendon, London. d. 27 Dec 1985 Wicklewood, Norfolk.

After 2nd place in 1931, Harold Whitlock won his first national title at 50km in 1933. He won this event again each year 1935-9, recording his best ever time of 4:30:38 in 1936 and also won the national 20 miles title in 1939. He reached his peak success by winning gold medals at 50km at both the 1936 Olympics and 1938 Europeans. The winner of the race each year 1934-7, he was the first man to break 8 hours for the annual London to Brighton walk, and his time of 7:53:50 in 1935 remained the record until broken by Don Thompson (qv) in 1956. He also set British records at 20km walk, 1:36:02 in 1938, and at 40 and 50 miles, 6:07:07 and 7:44:47.2 in 1935.

His brother **Rex** (b. 8 Sep 1910. d. 26 Jun 1982) won the London to Brighton race four times, 1947-8 and 1950-1, was national champion at 20 miles and at 50km in 1948, but did not finish the Olympic Games 50km. Four years later he was 4th in the Olympic 50km, and elder brother Harold placed 11th, becoming, at 48 years 218 days, the oldest international athlete for Britain.

A motor mechanic by profession, Whitlock worked on several record attempts at Brooklands in the 1930s. After his active days he was a leading coach and judge, a member of the International Walking Commission, and was awarded the MBE in 1966.

Harry WHITTLE

Athletics, Hurdling
Harry Whittle. b. 2 May 1922 Bolton, Gt. Manchester. d. 11 May 1990 Bolton.

Whittle became the fourth athlete to win seven successive AAA titles, achieving this at 440y hurdles 1947-53. He was also AAA champion at 220y hurdles in 1953, long jump 1947 and 1949 and decathlon 1950. At the Olympics in 1948 he was 7th at long jump and in 1952 he was 5th at 400m hurdles. In 1950 he was European bronze medallist at 400m hurdles and at the Empire Games was 5th at both 440y hurdles and long jump. He set four British records at 440y hurdles from 53.7 in 1949 to 52.7 in 1953 and three at decathlon to 5938 (current tables) in 1950. Other bests: 220y hurdles 24.2w (1953), 24.6 half turn (1950), long jump 7.25m (1947).

Simon WIGG

Speedway
Simon Antony Wigg. b. 15 Oct 1960 Aylesbury.

Wigg has won a record five world long-track speedway titles, 1985, 1989-90 and 1993-4. After his fourth win he was initially accused of having excess caffeine at a drugs test, but there were found to be errors in the testing procedures and he retained his title. In his first ever world speedway championship final appearance in 1984 he placed equal 6th. He won the British final in 1988 and the British and Commonwealth finals in 1989 before placing 2nd in the World Championship itself. He rode for Oxford and Coventry. With Kelvin Tatum he was 2nd in the world pairs in 1987. At grass-track racing he was British champion five times, 1981-3, 1985 and 1989. He came back from being close to paralysis following an accident in Italy in 1990.

Jimmy WILDE

Boxing
William James Wilde. b. 12 May 1892 Pontygwarth, Rhondda Cynon Taff. d. 10 Mar 1969 Cardiff.

Considered the first flyweight champion of the world and one of the greatest ever, Wilde was a very unorthodox boxer with tremendous hitting power for his size. This earned him several nicknames, such as 'The Mighty Atom', 'The Tylorstown Terror', and 'The Ghost With a Hammer in His Hand'.

Wilde won the British flyweight title in 1916 by stopping Joe Symonds, and a few months later he defeated Johnny Rosner and claimed the world title, confirming that with a win over Young Zulu Kid later in the year. He retired after he was defeated in 1921, when he attempted to wrest the bantamweight championship from Pete Herman (USA). He came out of retirement in 1923 but was knocked out in a title bout against Pancho Villa (Phi). He later became a boxing journalist.

Career record: 140 contests. Won 132 (101), Lost 6, Drawn 2.

Sheila WILCOX – see WADDINGTON

David WILKIE

Swimming
David Andrew Wilkie. b. 8 Mar 1954
Colombo, Sri Lanka.

In 1976 Wilkie became the first British male swimmer for 68 years to win an Olympic title, when he set a world record of 2:15.11 in the 200m breaststroke. At this event he had been a silver medallist in 1972, after which he went on a scholarship to the University of Miami in Florida, and he also took the 100m silver in 1976.

His family returned to Scotland from Sri Lanka in 1965. Tall and broad-shouldered, he won three world titles, 100m in 1975 and 200m in both 1973 (in his first world record, 2:19.28) and 1975, setting European records at both events (1:04.26 and 2:18.23) in 1975. He also won world bronze medals at 200m medley in 1973 and at medley relay in 1975.

Wilkie's first major championships medal was a Commonwealth bronze at 200m breaststroke (also 5th at 100m) in 1970. Four years later he won gold medals at both 200m breaststroke and at 200m IM, with a silver at 100m breaststroke.

In all he set 17 British individual event

records, five at 100m breaststroke from 1:06.20 in 1972 to 1:03.43 in 1976; seven at 200m breaststroke from 2:32.50 in 1970 to 2:15.11 in 1976; and five at 200m IM to 2:06.25 in 1976. ASA champion at breaststroke 100m 1973-4, 200m 1972-4; 200m IM 1974. NCAA breaststroke champion 100y 1974, 200y 1973 and 1976. He was awarded the MBE in 1974.

Ray WILKINS

Football
Raymond Colin Wilkins. b. 14 Sep 1956
Hillingdon, London.

Wilkins was a talented central midfield player whose accuracy and range of passing earned him many honours, including 84 caps for England 1976-86. From an apprentice at Chelsea he signed as a full professional in 1973 and when still only 18 when he was appointed club captain in 1975. He left Chelsea in 1979 and then played for Manchester United 1979-84, winning an FA Cup winners' medal in 1983, AC Milan (Italy) 1984-7, Paris St Germain (France), and Glasgow Rangers 1987-9 before playing for Queen's Park Rangers 1989-94. He played briefly for Crystal Palace in 1994 before returning to QPR as manager later that year. He was awarded the MBE in 1993.

His father **George** played professional football for Brentford, Bradford and Nottingham Forest and his brothers Dean, Graham and Steve were also with Football League clubs.

Cyril WILKINSON

Hockey and Cricket
Cyril Theodore Anstruther Wilkinson. b. 4 Oct 1884 Durham. d. 16 Dec 1970 Honiton, Devon.

A Surrey cricketer from 1909, Wilkinson captained them to the County Championship in 1914. In his final season as a county cricketer (1920) he won the first of his four England caps at hockey at the age of 35 and he was a member of the winning team at the Olympic Games that year. He was later a leading administrator, serving as an international umpire, as a member of the

International Rules Board for 27 years and as a vice-president of the Hockey Association. In 1954 he was awarded the CBE.

He was the Registrar of Probate and Divorce 1936-59, and on his retirement to Devon he continued to play club cricket for many years taking all 10 wickets for Sidmouth in a club match in 1953 at the age of 69. His father, **Anthony** (1835-1905), played first-class cricket for Middlesex and Yorkshire.

First-class cricket: 1773 runs at 25.32, 3 100s HS 135; 23 wickets at 31.47, BB 6-43; 25 catches.

Diana WILKINSON

Swimming
Diana Elizabeth Wilkinson. b. 17 Mar 1944 Stockport. Later Mrs Bishop.

At the age of 13 in 1957 Wilkinson made her senior international debut, became the first British woman to swim 100 yards freestyle in less than a minute, with 57.3, won the ASA 110y freestyle title in another British record time of 65.7 and also set a record for 220y freestyle at 2:28.0. All that earned her the *Daily Express* Sportswoman of the Year award. The next year she set British records at 220y, 2:25.2, and 440y, 5:13.1, and swam the last, freestyle, leg for the England team that won the medley relay title in a world record time at the Commonwealth Games. She won further medals at these Games, silver at medley relay 1962 and bronze at 4 x 100m freestyle in 1958, 1962 and 1966.

At the Europeans she won her only major championships medal at an individual event with the silver at 100m freestyle in 1962, when the first three shared the same time of 63.3, and also won silvers at 4 x100m freestyle and bronzes at medley relay in both 1958 and 1962. She set a European 110y/100m record with 62.4 in 1962, took part in the Olympic Games of 1960 and 1964, and went on to win further ASA titles at 110y 1961-4 and 220y 1961-2. By then a PE teacher, she retired in 1967, and later became a development officer for her hometown of Stockport.

Her brother **Chris** was ASA champion at 220y breaststroke in 1961-2.

George WILKINSON

Water polo
George Wilkinson. b. 3 Mar 1879 Gorton, Manchester. d. 7 Aug 1946 Hyde, Gt. Manchester.

A prolific goalscorer with a variety of scoring shots, Wilkinson is generally recognised as the world's first great water polo player. When little more than a novice he was included in the Manchester Osborne club team which won the 1900 Olympic title and then won gold medals in 1908 and 1912, captaining the British team in Stockholm. He was also a reserve for the 1920 and 1924 Olympic teams.

He won 24 caps for England 1900-22 at water polo and he was an excellent swimmer, often placing well at ASA Championships, although never winning a title. He became a publican and was landlord of the Wheatsheaf Hotel in Hyde for many years.

Sheila WILLCOX – see WADDINGTON

Bleddyn WILLIAMS

Rugby Union
Bleddyn Llewellyn Williams. b. 22 Feb 1923 Taff's Well, Rhondda Cynon Taff.

After playing in three Services and seven Victory internationals, Williams made his full international debut for Wales as a fly-half against England in 1947. In all of his further 21 internationals he played in the centre. To his powerful midfield play he added perfectly timed passes to his wing, and these attributes made him a valuable member of the 1950 Lions party in Australasia, when he played in five Tests and only injury prevented him from appearing in the sixth. He captained the Lions in three Tests and although he only captained Wales five times they won each match.

He was a master of all the skills of the game and in the 1947/8 season scored 41 tries in 31 matches for Cardiff, who were unbeaten that year. In 1953 he led Cardiff to a memorable victory over the touring All Blacks. One of the legends of Welsh rugby, he later became a respected writer on the game.

Denzel WILLIAMS

Rugby Union
Denzel Williams. b. 17 Oct 1938 Trefil,
Blaenau Gwent

A prop-forward with Ebbw Vale, part of
his immense strength came from his
employment as a steelworker, but Williams
also possessed the rugby skills which kept
him in the Welsh front-row for nine seasons
1963-71. He retired in 1971, having won
36 caps, and was then the most capped
Welsh forward of all time.
On the 1966 Lions tour of Australia and
New Zealand he played in five of the six
Tests, missing only the third match against
the All Blacks.

Frank WILLIAMS

Motor Racing
Francis Owen Williams. b. 16 Apr 1942.

Having launched his team under his name
in 1975, Williams has had such success
since then that by the end of 1994 he had
achieved 77 Grand Prix wins, winning the
constructors' championship seven times, in
1980-1 with Ford engines, 1986-7 with
Honda engines and 1992-4 with Renault.
He broke his neck in a car crash in France
in March 1986, but despite being a quadri-
plegic has continued to run his team with
enormous enthusiasm and determination.
He came into the sport as a driver, but
described himself as erratis. After two
years buying and selling racing cars, he
moved into management in 1969. He was
awarded the CBE in 1987.

Freddie WILLIAMS

Speedway
Freddie Williams. b. 12 Mar 1926 Port
Talbot, Neath and Port Talbot.

Williams was a Welshman who, with victories in 1950 and 1953, became the first
British rider to win two world championships. At the time of his 1950 win he
was still using a provisional licence on the
road, later passing his motorcycle test.
Williams, who rode for Wembley, was also
runner-up for the world title in 1952 and
his brothers Eric and Ian also rode in the

world championship finals.

J.J. WILLIAMS

Rugby Union
John James Williams. b. 1 Apr 1948
Nantyffyllon, Bridgend.

As a sprinter (100m 10.4w/10.5), Williams
represented Wales at the 1970 Commonwealth Games in Edinburgh and his speed
was to prove an invaluable asset on the
rugby field. Playing on the wing, he scored
12 tries for Wales in 30 consecutive
matches 1973-9, and he had the distinction
of scoring against all seven International
Board countries.
Twice a British Lion, he played in four
Tests against South Africa 1974 and three
against New Zealand 1977. Against the
Springboks, he scored two tries in both the
second and third Tests to set a new Lions
record of four tries in a Test series. On his
second tour, he scored the winning try
against New Zealand in the second Test
before an injury in the third Test ended his
participation in the tour. After qualifying
as a schoolmaster, he played for Bridgend
before moving to Llanelli and after his
employers had baulked at his visiting
South Africa with the Lions, he gave up
teaching to begin a business career.

J.P.R. WILLIAMS

Rugby Union
John Peter Rhys Williams. b. 2 Mar 1949
Cardiff.

Always known as 'J.P.R', Williams was
initially an outstanding tennis player and
won the Wimbledon Junior singles in
1966, but he became the most capped
Welsh rugby player. After deciding to concentrate on rugby, he was first chosen for
Wales in 1969 and went on to play 55 times
for his country and 8 times for the Lions at
full back. Unusually, he also played in one
international as a flanker on the 1978 Welsh
tour of Australia.
The ferocity of his tackling commanded
immense respect from his opponents and
apart from his resolute defence he was a
brilliant counter-attacking runner. During
the years he spent in London as a medical

student he played for London Welsh, but after he had qualified as an orthopaedic surgeon he was welcomed back to Bridgend where he finished his playing career.

'J.P.R.' had been a member of the team which won the Triple Crown six times and captained Wales in the 1978/9 season after which he retired from international rugby, although he returned to play one last game against Scotland in 1981. One of the greatest full-backs of all time, he was certainly rated as the best in the world in that position on his two Lions tours of South Africa (1971 and 1974). He was awarded the MBE in 1977 for his outstanding contribution to the game.

Rex WILLIAMS

Billiards
Rex Williams. b. 20 July 1933 Stourbridge, Worcestershire.

British junior (Under-16) champion at snooker and billiards in 1948-9, Williams excelled at both games in the senior ranks. After winning the English Amateur snooker title in 1951, he was largely responsible for the revival of the World Professional Championships in 1964 and twice challenged John Pulman (qv) for the title, but lost on both occasions, 1964-5. He then concentrated on billiards and won the 1968 World Championship when the event was revived after an interval of 17 years. After four successful defences he lost to Fred Davis (qv) in 1980 but was again the world champion in 1982 and 1983. He decided not to defend his title in 1984 and reverted to snooker and the development of his business interests. Similarly he had won the UK professional title in 1979 when the championships were staged for the first time since 1951 and he won again in 1981.

He was a regular member of the early TV commentary teams and his involvement in the leisure industry included the ownership of a successful pool and snooker table manufacturing business.

Rhys WILLIAMS

Rugby Union
Rhys Haydn Williams. b. 14 Jul 1930 Cwmllinfell, W Glamorgan. d. 27 Jan 1993 Whitchurch, Cardiff.

A line-out specialist, Williams was rated as the best in world by both team-mates and opponents. The big Llanelli lock won 23 caps for Wales 1954-60, but produced his best performances while on tour with the British Lions. In South Africa 1955 and Australia and New Zealand 1959 he played in every Test on both tours and his ten consecutive Test appearances for the Lions equalled the record of Tony O'Reilly (qv). On his return, he captained a Welsh side, including seven Lions, which surprisingly lost to an inexperienced England team at Twickenham. This proved to be his last international; he was one of several players to be dropped and he retired at the end of the season.

After the University College of Cardiff he became an education officer in the RAF, then a production superintendent for the Steel Company of Wales and finally assistant director of education for mid-Glamorgan. He maintained his interest in the game and later became chairman of the Welsh selectors.

Norman WILLIAMSON (Ireland)

Horse racing
Norman Williamson. b. 16 Jan 1969.

Williamson hit the headlines in March 1995 at the Cheltenham Festival when, for trainer Kim Bailey, he rode *Alderbrook* to win the Champion Hurdle and *Master Oats* to win the Gold Cup. With no Festival winners previously, 'Stormin Norman' rode two more winners at the meeting. He rode his first winner at Clonmel in 1987 and his first major win was on *Multum in Parvo* in the 1990 Mackeson Gold Cup.

Bob WILLIS

Cricket
Robert George Dylan Willis. b. 30 May 1949 Sunderland, Tyne and Wear. He added his third name as a teenager in honour of Bob Dylan.

Bob Willis peaked for Test matches, leading the England attack with his often devastating fast bowling. His best return, 8-43 at Headingley in 1981, gave England an unlikely victory over Australia by 18 runs. He played for Surrey 1969-71, making his Test debut in Australia in 1970/1 while still an uncapped county player. He then moved to Warwickshire, whom he captained for his last five years in the game 1980-4, also captaining England in 18 matches 1982-4. Very tall at 1.98m *6 ft 6 in*, he was an awkward-looking but most effective bowler, who established himself as a Test regular from the mid-1970s, and he passed Fred Trueman's record of most wickets for England in his 84th Test (Trueman had played fewer at 67) against New Zealand in January 1984. Since his retirement he has worked with the England management and as a TV commentator. He was awarded the MBE in 1982.

90 Tests 1970-84: 840 runs at 11.50, HS 28*; 325 wickets at 25.20, BB 8-43; 39 catches.
64 One-day Ints 1973-84: 83 runs at 10.37, HS 24; 80 wickets at 24.60, BB 4-45; 22 catches.
First-class 1969-84: 2690 runs at 14.30, HS 72; 899 wickets at 24.99, BB 8-32; 134 catches.

Rex WILLIS

Rugby Union
William Rex Willis. b. 25 Oct 1924 Ystrad, Rhondda Cynon Taff.

In 1949 Willis took over from the great Haydn Tanner (qv) as Cardiff's scrum-half and then immediately followed Tanner into the Welsh team. He played in every match for the Welsh 1950 Grand Slam team and was then selected as the No. 1 scrum-half for the British Lions tour of Australasia. Initially, in the face of strong challenges from Gus Black and Gordon Rimmer, he had difficulty in justifying his position, but he finally earned his place for the last Test against New Zealand and he then played in both Tests against Australia. Having captained both Cardiff and Wales he was approached to lead the 1955 Lions to South Africa but he declined for personal reasons and retired that year having won 21 Welsh caps.

Philip WILLS

Gliding
Philip Aubrey Wills. b. 26 May 1907 Kensington, London. d. 16 Jan 1978 London.

Wills became Britain's first world champion at gliding when he won the Open category in 1952, and he was also 2nd in 1954. Having learnt to fly in 1928, he began gliding in a Zögling in 1933 and chaired the general meeting of the British Gliding Association in 1934 which restructured the governing body so as to develop advanced gliding in the clubs. He set a British distance record of 104 miles in 1936 (a record he improved to 232.6 miles *374.33 km* in 1949), competed in the first seven World Championships from 1937 to 1958, and led British gliding to prominence in the sport. He was involved with the BGA council for over 30 years and its chairman for 19 years. Director of operations of the ATA in the War, he was awarded the CBE in 1945. He was general manager (technical) of British European Airways 1946-8.

His son **Justin** set a British distance record with 828km in 1986, and was 2nd in the 1989 World Championships in the 15-metre class.

Bobby WILSON

Tennis
Robert Keith Wilson. b. 22 Nov 1935 Hendon, London.

After winning the Wimbledon Boy's title in 1952, Wilson developed into Britain's leading player. A quarter-finalist in the Wimbledon singles in 1958 he was only the second British player since the war to reach this stage (after Tony Mottram (qv)). He again reached the last eight in 1961 and 1963 but never progressed further. In 1964 he lost in the first round but went on to win the Plate. He formed an excellent doubles partnership with Mike Davies (qv) and after winning the British Hard Court title in 1958 they were Wimbledon finalists in 1960. Wilson was particularly successful at the British Covered Court Championships winning the singles (1962-3, 1965) and the doubles (1954, 1958, 1960, 1962, 1964-5). With 34 Davis Cup appearances between 1955 and 1968 (16/29 singles, 25/33 doubles), he set a new record for ties played by a British player, and he played on the British teams which won the European men's team championship each year 1964-7, captain in the last three years.

Enid WILSON

Golf
Enid Wilson. b. 15 Mar 1910 Stonebroom nr Alfreton, Derbyshire.

Having become British girls champion in 1925, Wilson went on to win the English Ladies' Amateur title in 1928 and 1930, winning her finals by the commanding scores of 9 & 8 and 12 & 11, and the Ladies' British Open Amateur Championship each year 1931-3. She was a semi-finalist in the US Ladies' in 1931 and 1933 before being declared a 'non-amateur' in 1934.
She played in the first Curtis Cup of 1932, winning her singles but losing in the foursomes, but retired early to become a leading writer on the game, including as golf correspondent of *The Daily Telegraph*.

Gerry WILSON

Horse Racing
Gerald Wilson. b. 12 Oct 1903 Wing, Buckinghamshire. d. 29 Dec 1968 Wantage, Oxfordshire.

Wilson was champion National Hunt jockey a record seven times, each year 1932/3 to 1937/8 and in 1940/1. He rode *Golden Miller* to win both Cheltenham Gold Cup and Grand National in 1934. In 1935 he completed the Cheltenham double, on *Golden Miller* again and in the Champion Hurdle on *Lion Courage*. As a trainer he won the latter race with *Brains Trust* in 1945, and later was the landlord of a pub near Newbury.
His brother **Anthony** was also a leading jumps jockey.

Jocky WILSON

Darts
John Thomas Wilson. b. 22 Mar 1950 Kirkcaldy, Fife.

At 1.62m and 102kg Wilson has been probably one of the least athletic people in this book, but this fine and popular darts player was World Champion in 1982 and 1989. He did not start playing darts until he was in his 20s, but progressed to become one of Scotland's best players and to win his first major event with the British Matchplay in 1980. He retained that title in 1981, when he won the first of a record four British Professional Championships (winning again in 1983, 1986, 1988), and a year later he had his finest year, winning the British Open as well as the World title. He also won the World Pairs with Ritchie Gardner in 1988.

Ray WILSON

Football
Ramon Wilson. b. 17 Dec 1934 Shirebrook, Derbyshire.

Wilson was one of the greatest left-backs of all time. Although not making his international debut until he was 25 and playing for Second Division Huddersfield, he went on to win 63 caps for England 1960-6, including the 1962 and 1966 World Cups.
He was first signed by Huddersfield Town as a left-winger in 1952 but was quickly converted to a full-back by manager Bill Shankly (qv). He moved to Everton in 1964 and had his golden year in 1966, first by helping Everton to win the FA Cup and then to return to Wembley for England's World Cup triumph. He suffered a badly twisted knee in 1968 and thereafter lost his pace. In 1969-70 he played for Oldham Athletic and closed his career in football with Bradford City as player, coach and caretaker manager before joining the family undertaking business.
A devastating tackler and superb distributor of the ball, he fully earned the esteem in which he was held.

Howard WINSTONE

Boxing
Howard Winstone. b. 15 Apr 1939
Merthyr Tydfil. 30/9/2000

Winstone was an outstanding amateur who won the ABA bantamweight title and a gold medal at the Commonwealth Games in 1958. On turning professional the following year he fought as a featherweight and his unbeaten record in his first 34 contests included a victory over Terry Spinks (qv) in 1961 which gave him the British featherweight title. He made six successful defences before retiring undefeated in 1969.

He also held the European title from 1963-7 but lost three times to the Mexican, Vicente Salvidar, when challenging for the World title. After Salvidar's retirement, Winstone, who was nearing the end of his career, was matched with Mitsunori Seki (Jap) for the vacant WBC World crown in January 1968 and with the referee stopping the contest in his favour in the ninth round the Welshman became the World champion. Later in the year he met Jose Legra (Cuba) and lost his title when a cut eye caused the fight to be stopped in the fifth round. Winstone then retired from boxing and was awarded the MBE.

Career record 1959-68: 67 contests. Won 61 (27 KO), Lost 6.

Fred WINTER

Horse Racing
Frederick Thomas Winter. b. 20 Sep 1926 Andover, Hampshire.

Acclaimed by his contemporaries as the greatest ever rider under National Hunt Rules, Winter set a new record with a total of 923 winners (929 from 4298 races including overseas) until his retirement in 1964, when he became a highly successful trainer.

The son of a jockey/trainer, also Fred (1894-1965) who rode the winner of the Oaks in 1911, he rode at show jumping and then on the flat, with his first winner in 1939 at the age of 13 at Salisbury. After war service as a lieutenant in the Parachute regiment, he had his first jumps success in

1947. His partnership with Ryan Price (qv) began in 1949, and in 1951/2 he rode 81 winners for 2nd place. The following year he became champion jockey with a new record of 121 wins, and the first century since 1924. He was champion jockey again in the three years from 1955/6.

He twice rode the winner of the Grand National, *Sundew* in 1957 and *Kilmore* in 1962, and trained the winner in his first two years: *Jay Trump* in 1965 and *Anglo* in 1966. His Gold Cup winners were two as a jockey, *Saffron Tartan* in 1961 and *Mandarin* in 1962, and *Midnight Court* in 1978 as a trainer; and in the Champion Hurdle he had three wins as a jockey and four as a trainer. Leading trainer eight times, 1970/1 to 1974/5, 1976/7, 1977/8 and 1984/5, he retired in 1989 when he sold his Uplands stable to his assistant Charlie Brooks. He was awarded the CBE in 1963.

Peter WINTERBOTTOM

Rugby Union
Peter James Winterbottom. b. 31 May 1960 Horsforth, Leeds.

Winterbottom became England's most capped forward. A hard-driving flanker, he won 58 caps for England from making his international debut against Australia in 1982 to the declared end of his International Championships career in 1993. Among English players, only Rory Underwood (qv) had won more caps to that time.

Initially with Headingley, he moved to Harlequins at the start of the 1989/90 season and led them to victory in the 1991 Pilkington Cup final. He played club rugby in Canada, South Africa and New Zealand (for Hawkes Bay in 1982/3) and returned to New Zealand with the 1983 and 1993 Lions, playing in all seven Tests on these two tours. He is a Eurobond broker.

John WISDEN

Cricket
John Wisden. b. 5 Sep 1826 Brighton, East Sussex. d. 5 Apr 1884 Westminster, London.

Wisden was the founder of *Wisden*

Cricketers' Almanack, first issued in 1864 and also the founder of the cricket equipment firm of John Wisden & Co. Known as the 'Little Wonder' as he was just 1.63m *5 ft 4 in* tall, he was an outstanding bowler for Sussex with fast off-breaks and also a useful batsman, and in the pre-Test match era played for the All-England and United England XIs. At Lord's on 15 Jul 1850 for the North v South he became the first and only bowler to take all ten wickets, all bowled, in a first-class innings. In all cricket he averaged 225 wickets per season from 1848 to 1859, with a peak of 455 in 1851. In 1859 he toured North America with the first-ever English cricket team to tour overseas. He died in his London office in Cranbourn Street.

First-class 1845-63: 4140 runs at 14.12, 2 100s HS 148; 1109 wickets; 169 catches, 1 stumping.

Willie WOOD

Bowls
William Walker Wood. b. 26 Apr 1938 Haddington, East Lothian.

Wood was highly successful over nearly 30 years as an international bowler. At the Commonwealth Games he won gold at singles 1982 and fours 1990, silver at pairs 1978 and bronze at singles 1974, and he was world champion at team 1984 and fours and team 1992. His other World Championship medals: silver fours 1980, singles 1984, singles and triples 1988; bronze triples 1992.

Indoors he was a member of the winning fours team in 1992. He was awarded the MBE in 1992.

Bruce WOODCOCK

Boxing
Bruce Woodcock. b. 18 Jan 1921 Doncaster.

Woodcock was the leading British heavyweight in the years immediately following World War II. He won the ABA light-heavyweight championship in 1939 and turned professional in 1942. After winning his first 19 fights he knocked out Jack London in 1945 to take the British and Empire heavyweight title, and the following year he won the European title. Despite his successes at home, including over the light-heavyweight champion Freddie Mills (qv), he was usually troubled by the top American fighters. At Harringay on 15 April 1947, he took a beating from Joe Baksi before retiring with a fractured jaw after seven rounds, and when he fought Lee Savold for the British and European version of the world heavyweight championship in 1950 he was forced to retire in the fourth round with a badly cut eye. Later in 1950 he lost his British and Empire titles to Jack Gardner when he retired after eleven hard-hitting rounds. Woodcock wisely gave up boxing after this fight and, in retrospect, his chances of becoming a truly world-class heavyweight were ended by the severe punishment he took from Baksi. He was voted British Sportsman of the Year in 1947.

Career record 1942-50: 39 contests. Won 35 (32 KO), Lost 4.

Tony WOODCOCK

Football
Anthony Stewart Woodcock. b. 6 Dec 1955 Nottingham.

Woodcock was a Nottingham Forest apprentice who graduated to the first team, where his stunning acceleration gave added penetration to the forward line in the team which won the European Cup in 1979, the League Cup in 1978 and 1979 and the League Championship in 1978, in which year he was voted the PFA Young Footballer of the Year. After his successful years with Forest he moved to FC Köln in 1979 for a German record fee of £650,000, he came home to join Arsenal in 1982 but returned to Cologne in 1986. During his two spells in Germany he made 131 Bundesliga appearances.

He retained his place in the England team while with Forest, Cologne and Arsenal and scored 16 goals in 42 internationals between 1978 and 1986. In 1994 he signed as trainer of VfB Leipzig.

Sydney WOODERSON

Athletics
Sydney Charles Wooderson. b. 30 Aug
1914 Camberwell, London.

Denied by World War II of some of his
best years, Wooderson won European titles
before and after, the 1500m in 1938 and
5000m in 1946. In the latter he posted the
second fastest ever time with 14:08.6. Two
years later he sealed his career with the
1948 English National cross-country title.
The small (1.68m), bespectacled Wooderson
looked anything but a world-beater but he
had both speed and strength, with world
records at 800m/880y 1:48.4/1:49.2 in
1938 and 1 mile 4:06.4 in 1937. He was
AAA champion at the mile each year from
1935 to 1939 and at 3 miles in 1946, when
he set a British record of 13:53.2.
An untimely cracked ankle cost him the
chance of Olympic success in 1936,
although he beat Jack Lovelock (NZ) in
four of six mile races in 1934-6. Lovelock,
however, had beaten him to win the 1934
Empire Games title. In 1939 Wooderson
ran a world best 2:59.5 for ³/₄ mile and
after the War set his third British mile
record with 4:04.2 (with his best 1500m of
3:48.4 en route) behind Arne Andersson
(Swe) in 1945.

W.B. WOODGATE

Rowing
Walter Bradford Woodgate. b. 20 Sep
1840. d. 1 Nov 1920 Southampton.

Woodgate was one of the most talented of
the early English oarsman. Between 1861
and 1868 he won 11 times at Henley in six
different events and in 1862 he won three
events and dead-heated in the final of the
Diamonds, losing the re-row. He was the
amateur sculling champion three times and
was in the winning Oxford crew in the
Boat Race in 1862 and 1863.
Educated at Radley and Brasenose
College, Oxford, he was responsible for a
remarkable development in British rowing.
At Henley in 1868 he instructed the
Brasenose cox to jump overboard at the
start of the Stewards' Cup, then a coxed
event. Brasenose duly won the race but

were disqualified. In 1867 a special cup for
coxless fours was introduced at Henley; in
1873 the Stewards' Cup, and eventually
other four-oared races, became coxless
events and it was not until 1963 that
coxed-four rowing was reintroduced at
Henley.

Chris WOODS

Football
Christopher Charles Eric Woods. b. 14
Nov 1959 Swineshead, nr Boston, Lincs.

Woods, who became Britain's highest
priced goalkeeper, set a British first-class
record (since surpassed by Tim Flowers)
of playing in 13 consecutive matches without conceding a goal in the 1986/7 season.
He signed first as a professional with
Nottingham Forest in 1976 and won a
League Cup winners' medals in 1978,
when he deputised for the cup-tied Peter
Shilton (qv), but was sold to Queen's Park
Rangers in 1979 for £250,000, then a
record for a player yet to make his League
debut.
From QPR he went to Norwich two years
later, where he won a second League Cup
winners' medal in 1985, and then to
Rangers in 1986 for a British record fee
for a goalkeeper of £600,000. In his first
season he set a British record by going
1196 minutes without conceding a goal, 26
Nov 1986 to 31 Jan 1987 and he helped
Rangers win the Scottish League Cup
(1987-9, 1991) and the League Championship (1987, 1989-90). From Rangers he
went to Sheffield Wednesday in 1991 and
he was capped 43 times by England
between 1985 and 1993.

Stanley WOODS (Ireland)

Motor Cycling
Stanley Woods. b. 1903 Dublin. d. Aug
1993 Downpatrick, Co. Down.

Woods was the outstanding motorcycling
champion of the 1920s and 1930s, the
great hero of an era regarded by many as a
golden age of the sport in Britain. He set a
record with ten TT victories on the Isle of
Man, a record eventually surpassed by
Mike Hailwood (qv). His first win was the

Junior TT on a Cotton in 1923; on Nortons he won the Junior TT in 1932-3 and Senior 1926, 1932-3; both Lightweight 250cc and Senior on a Moto Guzzi in 1935; and the Junior on a Velocette in 1938-9. During these years he set numerous lap speed records and also excelled at speedway, hill climbs, scrambling and long-distance events.

He started his racing career as a Cotton works rider, having simply written to them asking for a ride. He was a successful businessman as a toffee manufacturer in his native Dublin.

Clive WOODWARD

Rugby Union
Clive Ronald Woodward. b. 6 Jan 1956 Ely, Cambs.

Stylish and elusive, Woodward was one of the finest centres of modern times. He made his England debut as a replacement against Ireland in 1980 following an injury to Tony Bond and held his place for the rest of the Grand Slam season. After a brilliant first international season he was chosen for the 1980 British Lions tour of South Africa where he played in the second and third Tests. He toured again with the Lions in 1983 but failed to make the Test side in New Zealand and in 1984 he won his 21st and final England cap.

After Loughborough College, he played for Harlequins and Leicester and also for Manley in Sydney when he lived in Australia.

Vivian WOODWARD

Football
Vivian John Woodward. b. 3 Jun 1879 Kennington, Londony. d. 31 Jan 1954 Ealing, London.

A brilliant amateur centre-forward, Woodward stood above the professionals of his time and is rated among the greatest ever. He won two Olympic gold medals (1908, 1912) and scored 58 goals in 44 appearances in amateur internationals for England. He won 23 full international caps 1903-11, scoring 29 goals, which remained a record until 1958 when both Tom Finney

(qv) and Nat Lofthouse (qv) brought their international tally up to 30. Woodward twice scored four goals and twice three in England internationals, and he scored six in an amateur international against Holland in 1909.

After playing for various Essex clubs he joined Tottenham Hotspur in 1902 when they were still members of the Southern League and, when they were elected to the Second Division of the Football League in 1908, he scored their first-ever goal in League football. With 19 goals in 27 matches he was Tottenham's top scorer for the season and played a key role in their immediate promotion to the First Division. He moved to Chelsea in 1909 and stayed at Stamford Bridge until 1916 when he was forced to give up the game after being wounded in action serving as an officer with the Middlesex Regiment.

He served as a director of both Tottenham and Chelsea and, having previously been an architect, he took up farming after World War I.

Wilf WOOLLER

Rugby Union
Wilfred Wooller. b. 20 Nov 1912 Rhos-on-Sea, Aberconwy and Colwyn.

A naturally gifted all-round sportsman, Wooller won Blues for rugby 1933-5 and cricket 1935-6 while at Cambridge, played squash for Wales and soccer as centre-forward for Cardiff City in 1939.

One of seven new caps, he made his international debut against England in 1933 when Wales claimed their first-ever win at Twickenham. He also played a full part in another memorable victory when Wales beat the 1935 All Blacks. As a centre or wing, Wooller won 18 caps - the last three as captain - up until the outbreak of war. The privations suffered in a Japanese prison camp left him unable to resume his rugby career but fortunately his cricketing days were not over. A hard-hitting batsman and medium-fast right-arm bowler, he first played for Glamorgan in 1938 and after the war he was a hugely influential captain of the county from 1947 to 1960, winning the Championship in

1948. He scored over 1000 runs in a season five times and took 100 wickets in a season twice, completing the 'double' in 1949, but declined an invitation to tour South Africa with the MCC in 1948/9 due to business commitments. He then served as Glamorgan secretary until 1977 and was a Test selector from 1955-1961. He was also a respected rugby journalist and a cricket commentator on Welsh television.
First-class 1935-62: 13,593 runs at 22.57, 5 100s HS 128; 958 wickets at 26.96, BB 8-45; 413 catches.

Frank WOOLLEY

Cricket
Frank Edward Woolley. b. 27 May 1887 Tonbridge, Kent. d. 18 Oct 1978 Halifax, Nova Scotia, Canada.

Woolley was a peerless left-hander, whose beautiful and exciting batting has long been cited as the model for all aspiring cricketers. His career runs figure has been exceeded only by Sir Jack Hobbs (qv). A big man, he was a great all-rounder, a graceful slow left-arm bowler and a brilliant slip fielder, with a career total of catches well in excess of any other player in the history of the game.
From his Test debut in 1909, he played in 52 successive Tests for England until 1926, a record until matched by Peter May (qv), although his figures were not, on paper, as impressive as might be expected. He considered his innings of 95 and 93 (out of 187 and 283) in the Second Test against Australia in 1921 as the finest he ever played. His total of 28 seasons with 1000 runs matches the record held by W.G. Grace (qv), and he had 13 years over 2000 with a peak of 3352 at 60.94 in 1928. Despite that, he was not selected for the England tour of Australia in 1928/9.
In eight of those years scoring over 1000 runs he also took 100 wickets, and had a record four years (1914, 1921-3) at over 2000 runs and 100 wickets.
64 Tests 1909-34: 3283 runs at 36.07, 5 100s HS 154; 83 wickets at 33.91, BB 7-76; 64 catches.
First-class 1906-38: 58,969 runs at 40.75, 145 100s HS 305*; 2068 wickets at 19.85, BB 8-22; 1018 catches.
His elder brother **Claude** (1886-1962) was a right-handed opening batsman and slow-medium bowler for Northants 1911-31, making 15,395 runs at 24.67 and taking 352 wickets at 33.10 in his first-class career.

Ian WOOSNAM

Golf
Ian Harold Woosnam. b. 2 Mar 1958 Oswestry, Shropshire.

Woosnam is the greatest Welsh golfer ever, reaching the status of world No.1 in 1991 shortly before winning his first major - the US Masters. Just 1.64m *5 ft 4 1/2ni* tall, Woosnam is a powerful hitter who turned pro in 1976, although he did not qualify for the European tour until 1978.
In 1982 he had his first tour victory in the Swiss Open and leapt from 104th in the European Order of Merit in 1981 to 8th. Since then he has been a top ten regular, being ranked first in a marvellous year in 1987, when he had five wins, including the World Matchplay and set a money record of £439,075. Adding overseas earnings, with three more wins including the first Sun City challenge, he set a world record with £1,062,662, and also in that year partnered David Llewellyn to Wales' first World Cup win. After being runner-up in 1989 he again won the World Matchplay in 1990, when top ranked on the European tour with a new record of £574,166. His total European tour earnings 1978-94 are £3,805,781 with 28 wins and he also has two US PGA tour wins.
He first played for Wales in the World Cup in 1980 and was the top individual in both 1987 and 1991. He played in each Ryder Cup 1983-93, and had great success playing with Paul Way in 1985 and Nick Faldo (qv) in 1987. In 1991 he disappointed, but he won all four pairs matches in 1993 as well as halving his singles, taking his overall playing record to 12 wins, 10 losses and 4 halves in 26 matches. He was awarded the MBE in 1992.

Max WOOSNAM

Tennis and Football
Maxwell Woosnam. b. 6 Sep 1892
Liverpool. d. 14 Jul 1965 Westminster,
London.

Woosnam was the outstanding all-round sportsman of his generation - an Olympic gold medallist, a Wimbledon champion, a soccer international and a Cambridge Blue at four different sports. At tennis he won the men's doubles with Oswald Turnbull and won a silver medal in the mixed at the 1920 Olympics, and won the men's doubles with Randolph Lycett (qv) at Wimbledon in 1921. His best performance in the Wimbledon singles was to reach the quarter-finals in 1923. He played in six Davis Cup ties, 1921-4 (0/2 singles, 3/6 doubles).

At football he played for the Corinthians and Chelsea while still an undergraduate and after the war he made 89 first-team appearances for Manchester City 1919-25 and won two amateur international caps, before captaining the full England team against Wales in 1922. In addition to representing Cambridge at these two sports he also won his Blue for golf and real tennis, but he narrowly failed to win a fifth Blue for cricket, at which he had made 144 and 33* for the Public Schools against the MCC at Lord's in 1911. In 1912 he played in every game before the match against Oxford but he lost his place at the last minute and only went to Lord's as 12th man. Educated at Winchester and Trinity College, Cambridge, he joined the staff of ICI in 1919 and remained with the company until his retirement in 1954.

His nephew **Phil Woosnam** (b, 22 Dec 1932) played 17 internationals for Wales at soccer 1959-63, scoring 4 goals, while with Leyton Orient, West Ham and Aston Villa.

Harry WRAGG

Horse Racing
Harry Wragg. b. 10 Jun 1902 Hallam,
Sheffield, South Yorkshire. d. 20 Oct 1985
Newmarket.

A fine tactician, nicknamed the 'Head Waiter', Wragg was champion jockey in England in 1941 when Gordon Richards (qv) was injured, having been runner-up to that great man five times between 1928 and 1940. In all he rode 1762 winners in Britain and Ireland, with five years over 100 and a season's peak of 110 in 1931. He rode 13 Classics winners, his first being *Felstead* in the 1928 Derby. Apprenticed to Bob Colling, he rode from 1921 to 1946.

He trained at Abington Place, Newmarket, sending out winners of six English and nine Irish Classics, perhaps the best of whom was *Darius*, winner of the 1954 2000 Guineas. He handed over to his son **Geoffrey** (b. 9 Jan 1930 Newmarket), who saddled the Derby winner *Teenoso* in his first season of 1983.

Billy WRIGHT

Football
William Ambrose Wright. b. 6 Feb 1924
Ironbridge, Shropshire. d. 3 Sep 1994
Barnet.

A hero to a generation of football enthusiasts, Wright was the first British player to win 100 caps and such was his demeanour that he was never even cautioned on the field. A versatile player in any of the half-back positions, he won a total of 105 England caps 1946-59: 51 at right-half, 46 at centre-half in consecutive matches from 1954 and 8 at left-half. He had also played in four 'wartime' internationals for England in 1946.

A superb motivator, he captained England in a record 90 games. Although short for a central defender, at 1.75m tall, he was very effective in the air, as well as speedy and incisive in tackling.

Joining the ground staff of Wolverhampton Wanderers as a boy, he turned professional in 1941 and remained with the club throughout his career, becoming their captain in 1947 after just one full season in league football. He made 490 League appearances in 13 seasons, helping Wolves win the FA Cup in 1949 and the Football League in 1954, 1958 and 1959. He was voted Footballer of the Year in 1952.

Following his retirement in 1959 he was

awarded the CBE for his services to sport, and went on to manage the England Youth and Under-23 teams before taking over as manager of Arsenal in 1962. He was, however, unable to repeat his successes on the field as a manager there and his contract was terminated in June 1966.

He was head of sport for ATV, the former Midlands television company, 1966-81 and then Controller of Sport at Central Television from 1985 until his retirement at the age of 65. A year later, in 1990, he became a director of Wolverhampton Wanderers. He was elected an Honorary Life Member of the FA.

Doug WRIGHT

Cricket
Douglas Vivian Parson Wright. b. 21 Aug 1914 Sidcup, London.

Although Wright's wickets were extremely costly at Test level, the figures belie his worth, for Wright, with his pacy and fiercely spun leg breaks and googlies was always capable of doing something special. In 1945 he took five wickets in each innings for England in their great match against the Dominions. The Kent player took a world record seven hat-tricks in first-class cricket, and took over 100 wickets in a season ten times between 1937 and 1955, with a best of 177 at 21.12 in 1947. He was Kent captain 1954-6 and later coached at Charterhouse School.
34 Tests 1938-51: 289 runs at 11.11, HS 45; 108 wickets at 39.11, BB 7-105; 10 catches.
First-class 1932-57: 5903 runs at 12.34, HS 84*; 2056 wickets at 23.98, BB 9-47; 182 catches.

Ian WRIGHT

Football
Ian Wright. b. 3 Nov 1963 Woolwich, London.

Wright has been a top-scoring striker for Arsenal, with 100 goals for them from his £2.5 million transfer from Crystal Palace in September 1991, to May 1995. He had played for Palace since his signing from Greenwich Borough in 1985.

In 1994/5 he achieved the unique feat of scoring for Arsenal in every match, nine goals in all, of their campaign to retain the European Cup Winners' Cup leading up to the final, where they lost 2-1 to Zaragoza. Wright had missed the previous year's final through suspension. Domestic honours came with the double of FA Cup and League Cup in 1993.

Mark WRIGHT

Football
Mark Wright. b. 1 Aug 1963 Dorchester-on-Thames, Oxon.

After only 10 League appearances for Oxford United, Wright moved to Southampton in 1982 after he which he went to Derby County in 1987 before moving in 1991 to Liverpool, whom he captained to win the FA Cup in 1992. A skilled central defender and particularly strong in the air, his total of 43 England caps, 1984-92, would have been greater but for the fact that he missed the 1986 World Cup because of a broken leg. He was highly praised for his performances as sweeper in the 1990 World Cup.

Bob WYATT

Cricket
Robert Elliott Storey Wyatt. b. 2 May 1901 Milford, Surrey. d. 20 Apr 1995 Cornwall.

A tough and resourceful cricketer, Wyatt became an indispensable member of the England team, which he captained in 16 Tests 1930-5. From 1930 to 1937 he captained Warwickshire, before resigning after a disagreement with their committee. After the war he played for Worcestershire, as joint captain in 1949 and captain in 1950. He maintained splendid form and made his last first-class appearance for the Free Foresters at the age of 56.
A sound and most consistent batsman he hit over 1000 runs in 17 seasons in England between 1926 and 1948 plus once overseas and went on to pass 2000 runs five times, with a best of 2630 at 53.66 in 1929. He was also a good outfield and a medium-paced outswing and off-break

bowler, with a season's best of 92 wickets in 1926. He was a Test selector 1949-53, chairman in 1950.

40 Tests 1927-37: 1839 runs at 31.70, 2 100s HS 149; 18 wickets at 35.66, BB 3-4; 16 catches.

First-class 1923-51: 39,405 runs at 40.04, HS 232; 901 wickets at 32.84, BB 7-43; 413 catches, 1 stumping.

Norman YARDLEY

Cricket
Norman Walter Dransfield Yardley. b. 19 Mar 1915 Barnsley, South Yorkshire. d. 3 Oct 1989 Lodge Moor, Sheffield.

A natural games player and fine all-round cricketer, Yardley, having missed his peak years due to the war, succeeded Walter Hammond (qv) as England captain in 1947. Having been five years in the St Peter's York school team, he made scores of 90 and 101 for Cambridge in the Varsity matches of 1936 and 1937. He also won hockey and squash Blues and was North of England squash champion for six years in succession.

He was an attractive middle-order batsman for Yorkshire, whom he captained from 1948 to 1955, and in first-class matches scored over 1000 runs in a season eight times, with much his best year in 1947, 1906 runs at 44.32. Although only an occasional bowler for Yorkshire, his medium pace came in useful for England. Having taken 10 wickets in the 1946/7 series against Australia, he surprisingly headed the England averages against them with 9 at 22.66 in 1948. Apart from his business in the wine trade, he was a Test selector 1951-4 (chairman 1951-2) and wrote and broadcast on the game.

20 Tests 1938-50: 812 runs at 25.37, HS 99; 21 wickets at 33.66, BB 3-67; 14 catches.

First-class 1935-55: 18,173 runs at 31.17, 27 100s HS 183*; 279 wickets at 30.48, BB 6-29; 328 catches, 1 stumping.

Sean YATES

Cycling
Sean Yates. b. 18 May 1969 Forest Row, East Sussex.

Yates was a member of the GB team which became the first to record a sub 4:20 time for 4km at the Olympics in 1980, only to finish out of the medals. Having been 2nd in 1979, he was national pursuit champion in 1980, before turning pro. He was national pursuit champion in 1982 and 1983 and national road race champion in 1992, ten years after being 2nd. He also won the Grand Prix Eddy Merckx in 1989. A climax to his career came in 1994 when he wore the *Maillot Jaune* of race leader in the Tour de France, following his compatriot Chris Boardman (qv) for a remarkable display of early British success. Much respected by his fellow riders, they allowed him to lead them through his home village in Sussex when the Tour passed through on their first visit to England a day or two later. He had to pull out of his final Tour de France in 1995, having finished nine in his career.

George YOUNG

Football
George Lewis Young. b. 27 Oct 1922 Grangemouth, Falkirk.

At centre-half or right-back Young dominated the defence for club and country in the seasons immediately following World War II. He joined Rangers in 1941, and played for Scotland in two wartime internationals in 1943. After the war he won a record 53 caps in full internationals 1946-57, captained Scotland a record 48 times and set a record for the number of consecutive matches played for Scotland. Although these records have now been surpassed, he had the finest record of any Scottish international up to his time.

George Young remained loyal to Rangers throughout his playing career and helped them to win six Scottish League Championships, the Scottish Cup four times and the Scottish League Cup twice. In 1949 they won the treble for the first time in their history. Following his retirement in May 1957, he concentrated on his business interests which included a newspaper column and hotel management, but from 1959 to 1962 he was manager of Third Lanark.

A man of imposing physique with a devastating tackle and an immensely powerful kick, he is sometimes only remembered for physical aspects of his game but he was also a fine tactician with excellent ball skills.

AWARDS

BBC Sports Personality of the Year

First awarded in 1954, winners of this prestigious annual award, voted for by television viewers, for British sports men and women have been:

1954 Chris Chataway (athletics)
1955 Gordon Pirie (athletics)
1956 Jim Laker (cricket)
1957 Dai Rees (golf)
1958 Ian Black (swimming)
1959 John Surtees (motorcycling)
1960 David Broome (show jumping)
1961 Stirling Moss (motor racing)
1962 Anita Lonsbrough (swimming)
1963 Dorothy Hyman (athletics)
1964 Mary Rand (athletics)
1965 Tommy Simpson (cycling)
1966 Bobby Moore (football)
1967 Henry Cooper (boxing)
1968 David Hemery (athletics)
1969 Ann Jones (tennis)
1970 Henry Cooper (boxing)
1971 Princess Anne (three-day event)
1972 Mary Peters (athletics)
1973 Jackie Stewart (motor racing)
1974 Brendan Foster (athletics)
1975 David Steele (cricket)
1976 John Curry (ice skating)
1977 Virginia Wade (tennis)
1978 Steve Ovett (athletics)
1979 Sebastian Coe (athletics)
1980 Robin Cousins (ice skating)
1981 Ian Botham (cricket)
1982 Daley Thompson (athletics)
1983 Steve Cram (athletics)
1984 Jayne Torvill & Christopher Dean (ice skating)
1985 Barry McGuigan (boxing)
1986 Nigel Mansell (motor racing)
1987 Fatima Whitbread (athletics)
1988 Steve Davis (snooker)
1989 Nick Faldo (golf)
1990 Paul Gascoigne (football)
1991 Liz McColgan (athletics)
1992 Nigel Mansell (motor racing)
1993 Linford Christie (athletics)
1994 Damon Hill (motor racing)

Sports Writers Sportsman of the Year

Voted annually from 1951 by the Sports Writers' Association, which was formed in 1948.
A sportswoman award was introduced in 1959.

1951 Randolph Turpin (boxing)
1952 Len Hutton (cricket)
1953 Gordon Pirie (athletics)
1954 Roger Bannister (athletics)
1955 John Disley (athletics)
1956 Chris Brasher (athletics)
1957 Derek Ibbotson (athletics)
1958 Ian Black (swimming)
1959 John Surtees (motorcycling)
1960 Don Thompson (walking)
1961 Terry Downes (boxing)

1962 Brian Kilby (marathon)
1963 Jim Clark (motor racing)
1964 Lynn Davies (athletics)
1965 Tommy Simpson (cycling)
1966 England World Cup XI (football)
1967 Mike Hailwood (motor cycling)
1968 David Hemery (athletics)
1969 Tony Jacklin (golf)
1970 Tony Jacklin (golf)
1971 Ken Buchanan (boxing)
1972 Richard Meade (three-day event)
1973 Jackie Stewart (motor racing)
1974 John Conteh (boxing)
1975 David Wilkie (swimming)
1976 James Hunt (motor racing)
1977 Barry Sheene (motorcycling)
1978 Daley Thompson (athletics)
1979 Sebastian Coe (athletics)
1980 Sebastian Coe (athletics)
1981 Sebastian Coe (athletics)
1982 Daley Thompson (athletics)
1983 Steve Cram (athletics)
1984 Sebastian Coe (athletics)
1985 Steve Cram (athletics)
1986 Lloyd Honeyghan (boxing)
1987 Nick Faldo (golf)
1988 Sandy Lyle (golf)
1989 Nick Faldo (golf)
1990 Nick Faldo (golf)
1991 Kriss Akabusi (athletics)
1992 Linford Christie (athletics)
1993 Linford Christie (athletics)
1994 Colin Jackson (athletics)

Sports Writers Sportswomen of the Year

Voted annually by the British sports writers.

1959 Mary Bignal (athletics)
1960 Anita Lonsbrough (swimming)
1961 Angela Mortimer (tennis)
1962 Anita Lonsbrough (swimming)
1963 Dorothy Hyman (athletics)
1964 Mary Rand (née Rand) (athletics)
1965 Marion Coakes (show jumping)
1966 Linda Ludgrove (swimming)
1967 Beryl Burton (cycling)
1968 Lillian Board (athletics)
1969 Ann Jones (tennis)
1970 Mary Gordon-Watson (three-day event)
1971 Princess Anne (three-day event)
1972 Mary Peters (athletics)
1973 Ann Moore (show jumping)
1974 Gillian Gilks (badminton)
1975 Lucinda Prior-Palmer (three-day event)
1976 Gillian Gilks (badminton)
1977 Virginia Wade (tennis)
1978 Sharron Davies (swimming)
1979 Caroline Bradley (show jumping)
1980 Sharron Davies (swimming)
1981 Jayne Torvill (ice skating)
1982 Wendy Norman (modern pentathlon)
1983 Jo Durie (tennis)
1984 Tessa Sanderson (athletics)

1985	Virginia Holgate (three-day event)
1986	Fatima Whitbread (athletics)
1987	Fatima Whitbread (athletics)
1988	Liz McColgan (athletics)
1989	Yvonne Murray (athletics)
1990	Tracy Edwards (yachting)
1991	Liz McColgan (athletics)
1992	Sally Gunnell (athletics)
1993	Sally Gunnell (athletics)
1994	Sally Gunnell (athletics)

Daily Express Sportsman of the Year

The Daily Express Sports Awards were first given in 1946 - initially for the British Sportsman of the Year. A Sportswoman of the Year award was introduced in 1952.

1946	Bruce Woodcock (boxing)
1947	Denis Compton (cricket)
1948	Denis Compton (cricket)
1949	Reg Harris (cycling)
1950	Reg Harris (cycling)
1951	Geoff Duke (motorcycling)
1952	Len Hutton (cricket)
1953	Gordon Pirie (athletics)
1954	Roger Bannister (athletics)
1955	Gordon Pirie (athletics)
1956	Chris Brasher (athletics)
1957	Derek Ibbotson (athletics)
1958	Ian Black (swimming)
1959	John Surtees (motorcycling)
1960	Don Thompson (walking)
1961	Johnny Haynes (football)
1962	Brian Phelps (diving)
1963	Jim Clark (motor racing)
1964	Robbie Brightwell (athletics)
1965	Tommy Simpson (cycling)
1966	Bobby Moore (football)
1967	Harvey Smith (show jumping)
1968	Lester Piggott (horse racing)
1969	Tony Jacklin (golf)
1970	Henry Cooper (boxing)
1971	Jackie Stewart (motor racing)
1972	Gordon Banks (football)
1973	Jackie Stewart (motor racing)
1974	Willie John McBride (rugby union)
1975	David Steele (cricket)
1976	James Hunt (motor racing)
1977	Geoff Boycott (cricket)
1978	Steve Ovett (athletics)
1979	Sebastian Coe (athletics)
1980	Sebastian Coe (athletics)
1981-9	*no awards*
1990	Paul Gascoigne (football)
1991	Graham Gooch (cricket)
1992	Nigel Mansell (motor racing)
1993	Damon Hill (motor racing)
1994	Linford Christie (athletics)

Daily Express Sportswoman of the Year

1952	Jeanette Altwegg (ice skating)
1953	Pat Smythe (show jumping)
1954	Pat Smythe (show jumping)
1955	Pat Smythe (show jumping)
1956	Judy Grinham (swimming)
1957	Diane Wilkinson (swimming)
1958	Judy Grinham (swimming)
1959	Mary Bignal (athletics)
1960	Anita Lonsbrough (swimming)
1961	Angela Mortimer (tennis)
1962	Anita Lonsbrough (swimming)
1963	Dorothy Hyman (athletics)
1964	Mary Rand (née Rand) (athletics)
1965	Marion Coakes (show jumping)
1966	Ann Jones (tennis)
1967	Beryl Burton (cycling)
1968	Marion Coakes (show jumping)
1969	Ann Jones (tennis)
1970	Lillian Board (athletics)
1971	Princess Anne (three-day event)
1972	Mary Peters (athletics)
1973	Ann Moore (show jumping)
1974	Virginia Wade (tennis)
1975	Virginia Wade (tennis))
1976	Debbie Johnsey (three-day event)
1977	Virginia Wade (tennis)
1978	Sharron Davies (swimming)
1979	Caroline Bradley (show jumping)
1980	Linsey Macdonald (athletics)
1981-9	*no awards*
1990	Tracy Edwards (yachting)
1991	Liz McColgan (athletics)
1992	Sally Gunnell (athletics)
1993	Sally Gunnell (athletics)
1994	Sally Gunnell (athletics)

British Athletics Writers' Association Athletes of the Year

Year	Male	Female
1963	Maurice Herriott	Dorothy Hyman
1964	Lynn Davies	Mary Rand
1965	Maurice Herriott	Anne Smith
1966	Lynn Davies	Pam Piercy
1967	Lynn Davies	Lillian Board
1968	David Hemery	Sheila Sherwood
1969	Ian Stewart	Lillian Board
1970	Ian Stewart	Rosemary Stirling
1971	David Bedford	Barbara Inkpen
1972	David Hemery	Mary Peters
1973	Brendan Foster	Verona Bernard
1974	Ian Thompson	Joyce Smith
1975	Alan Pascoe	Andrea Lynch
1976	Brendan Foster	Sonia Lannaman
1977	Steve Ovett	Tessa Sanderson
1978	Daley Thompson	Tessa Sanderson
1979	Sebastian Coe	Christine Benning
1980	Steve Ovett	Kathy Smallwood
1981	Sebastian Coe	Kathy Smallwood
1982	Daley Thompson	Kathy Smallwood
1983	Steve Cram	Fatima Whitbread
1984	Sebastian Coe	Tessa Sanderson
1985	Steve Cram	Zola Budd
1986	Roger Black	Fatima Whitbread
1987	Jon Ridgeon	Fatima Whitbread
1988	Linford Christie	Liz McColgan
1989	Steve Backley	Yvonne Murray
1990	Steve Backley	Yvonne Murray
1991	Kriss Akabusi	Liz McColgan
1992	Linford Christie	Sally Gunnell
1993	Colin Jackson	Sally Gunnell
1994	Colin Jackson	Sally Gunnell

Football Writers' Player of the Year

The Football Writers' Association was founded in 1947 and since 1947/8 its members have voted for their Player of the Year.

1948 Stanley Matthews (Blackpool)
1949 Johnny Carey (Manchester United)
1950 Joe Mercer (Arsenal)
1951 Harry Johnston (Blackpool)
1952 Billy Wright (Wolverhampton Wanderers)
1953 Nat Lofthouse (Bolton Wanderers)
1954 Tom Finney (Preston North End)
1955 Don Revie (Manchester City)
1956 Bert Trautmann (Ger, Manchester City)
1957 Tom Finney (Preston North End)
1958 Danny Blanchflower (Tottenham Hotspur)
1959 Syd Owen (Luton Town)
1960 Bill Slater (Wolverhampton Wanderers)
1961 Danny Blanchflower (Tottenham Hotspur)
1962 Jimmy Adamson (Burnley)
1963 Stanley Matthews (Stoke City)
1964 Bobby Moore (West Ham United)
1965 Bobby Collins (Leeds United)
1966 Bobby Charlton (Manchester United)
1967 Jackie Charlton (Leeds United)
1968 George Best (Manchester United)
1969 Tony Book (Manchester City) & Dave Mackay (Derby County)
1970 Billy Bremner (Leeds United)
1971 Frank McLintock (Arsenal)
1972 Gordon Banks (Stoke City)
1973 Pat Jennings (Tottenham Hotspur)
1974 Ian Callaghan (Liverpool)
1975 Alan Mullery (Fulham)
1976 Kevin Keegan (Liverpool)
1977 Emlyn Hughes (Liverpool)
1978 Kenny Burns (Nottingham Forest)
1979 Kenny Dalglish (Liverpool)
1980 Terry McDermott (Liverpool)
1981 Frans Thijssen (Hol, Ipswich Town)
1982 Steve Perryman (Tottenham Hotspur)
1983 Kenny Dalglish (Liverpool)
1984 Ian Rush (Liverpool)
1985 Neville Southall (Everton)
1986 Gary Lineker (Everton)
1987 Clive Allen (Tottenham Hotspur)
1988 John Barnes (Liverpool)
1989 Steve Nicol (Liverpool)
1990 John Barnes (Liverpool)
1991 Gordon Strachan (Leeds United)
1992 Gary Lineker (Tottenham Hotspur)
1993 Chris Waddle (Sheffield Wednesday)
1994 Alan Shearer (Blackburn Rovers)
1995 Jürgen Klinsmann (Ger, Tottenham Hotspur)

Professional Footballers' Association Player of the Year

At the end of each season the professional players in the Football League and FA Premier League, vote for their Player of the Year, a trophy much cherished by its winners. The first such award was made in 1974. A Young Player award is also presented annually, as well as a Merit Award.

Player of the Year

1974 Norman Hunter (Leeds United)
1975 Colin Todd (Derby County)
1976 Pat Jennings (Tottenham Hotspur)
1977 Andy Gray (Aston Villa)
1978 Peter Shilton (Nottingham Forest)
1979 Liam Brady (Arsenal)
1980 Terry McDermott (Liverpool)
1981 John Wark (Ipswich Town)
1982 Kevin Keegan (Southampton)
1983 Kenny Dalglish (Liverpool)
1984 Ian Rush (Liverpool)
1985 Peter Reid (Everton)
1986 Gary Lineker (Everton)
1987 Clive Allen (Tottenham Hotspur)
1988 John Barnes (Liverpool)
1989 Mark Hughes (Manchester United)
1990 David Platt (Aston Villa)
1991 Mark Hughes (Manchester United)
1992 Gary Pallister (Manchester United)
1993 Paul McGrath (Aston Villa)
1994 Eric Cantona (Fra, Manchester United)
1995 Alan Shearer (Blackburn Rovers)

Young Player of the Year

1974 Kevin Beattie (Ipswich Town)
1975 Mervyn Day (West Ham United)
1976 Peter Barnes (Manchester City)
1977 Andy Gray (Aston Villa)
1978 Tony Woodcock (Nottingham Forest)
1979 Cyrille Regis (West Bromwich Albion)
1980 Glenn Hoddle (Tottenham Hotspur)
1981 Gary Shaw (Aston Villa)
1982 Steve Moran (Southampton)
1983 Ian Rush (Liverpool)
1984 Paul Walsh (Luton Town)
1985 Mark Hughes (Manchester United)
1986 Tony Cottee (West Ham United)
1987 Tony Adams (Arsenal)
1988 Paul Gascoigne (Newcastle United)
1989 Paul Merson (Arsenal)
1990 Matthew Le Tissier (Southampton)
1991 Lee Sharpe (Manchester United)
1992 Ryan Giggs (Manchester United)
1993 Ryan Giggs (Manchester United)
1994 Andy Cole (Newcastle United)
1995 Robbie Fowler (Liverpool)

Merit Award

1974 Bobby Charlton & Cliff Lloyd
1975 Denis Law
1976 George Eastham
1977 Jack Taylor
1978 Bill Shankly
1979 Tom Finney
1980 Sir Matt Busby
1981 John Trollope
1982 Joe Mercer
1983 Bob Paisley
1984 Bill Nicholson
1985 Ron Greenwood
1986 Alf Ramsey, Harold Shepherdson & the 1966 England World Cup winning squad
1987 Sir Stanley Matthews
1988 Billy Bonds
1989 Nat Lofthouse
1990 Peter Shilton
1991 Tommy Hutchison
1992 Brian Clough

1993   The 1968 Manchester United team
1994   Billy Bingham

Scottish Footballer Player of the Year

Awarded annually by the Scottish PFA.

1965   Billy McNeill (Celtic)
1966   John Greig (Rangers)
1967   Ronnie Simpson (Celtic)
1968   Gordon Wallace (Raith Rovers)
1969   Bobby Murdoch (Celtic)
1970   Pat Stanton (Hibernian)
1971   Martin Buchan (Aberdeen)
1972   Dave Smith (Rangers)
1973   George Connelly (Celtic)
1974   Scotland World Cup squad
1975   Sandy Jardine (Rangers)
1976   John Greig (Rangers)
1977   Danny McGrain (Celtic)
1978   Derek Johnstone (Rangers)
1979   Andy Ritchie (Morton)
1980   Gordon Strachan (Aberdeen)
1981   Alan Rough (Partick Thistle)
1982   Paul Sturrock (Dundee United)
1983   Charlie Nicholas (Celtic)
1984   Willie Miller (Aberdeen)
1985   Hamish McAlpine (Dundee United)
1986   Sandy Jardine (Hearts)
1987   Brian McClair (Celtic)
1988   Paul McStay (Celtic)
1989   Richard Gough (Rangers)
1990   Alex McLeish (Aberdeen)
1991   Maurice Malpas (Dundee United)
1992   Ally McCoist (Rangers)
1993   Andy Goram (Rangers)
1994   Mark Hateley (Rangers)
1995   Brian Laudrup (Den, Rangers)

Rugby League - Man of Steel

The RFL personality judged to have made the greatest impact on the season. Sponsored by Trumans Steel 1977-83, Greenall Whitley 1984-9, Stones Bitter from 1990.

1977   David Ward (Leeds)
1978   George Nicholls (St Helens)
1979   Doug Laughton (Widnes)
1980   George Fairbairn (Wigan)
1981   Ken Kelly (Warrington)
1982   Mick Morgan (Carlisle)
1983   Allan Agar (Featherstone Rovers)
1984   Joe Lydon (Widnes)
1985   Ellery Hamley (Bradford Northern)
1986   Gavin Miller (Hull KR)
1987   Ellery Hamley (Wigan)
1988   Martin Offiah (Widmes)
1989   Ellery Hamley (Wigan)
1990   Shaun Edwards (Wigan)
1991   Garry Schofield (Leeds)
1992   Dean Bell (Wigan)
1993   Andy Platt (Wigan)
1994   Jonathan Davies (Warrington)
1995   Denis Betts (Wigan)

Rugby Union - Rugby World Player of the Year

Voted annually by readers of *Rugby World* magazine. The award is now sponsored by Whitbread Flowers.

1970   Ken Goodall
1971-2   Barry John
1973   David Duckham
1974   Mike Gibson
1975   Mervyn Davies
1976   Gareth Edwards
1977   Phil Bennett
1978   Gareth Edwards
1979   Tony Ward
1980   Bill Beaumont
1981   Huw Davies
1982   Ollie Campbell
1983   Terry Holmes
1984   David Leslie
1985   Ciaran Fitzgerald
1986   Jonathan Davies
1987   John Rutherford
1988   Jonathan Davies
1989   Andy Robinson
1990   Brian Moore
1991   Dean Richards
1992   Will Carling
1993   Ieuan Evans
1994   Ben Clarke
1995   Gavin Hastings

THE GREATEST OF THEM ALL

The selection of sports men and sports women for this book inevitably involves subjective assessment, although we are sure all the main candidates as all-time greats are included. As an embellishement to this book, the publishers have invited us to select our Top Ten British sporting greats. That involves comparing people from one sport with another and of course there can be no definitive answers, but purely for fun, and to invite comparisons with readers' lists, we have had a go. More precisely two gos, as we have produced separate lists for men and women. The names in these lists are concentrated on the major sports and indeed this seems appropriate as these are the sports in which there is the stiffest competition and the greatest national interest. We did the exercise independently, and it is interesting to see that we agreed on six men and only four women.

So here are our lists - in alphabetical order.

Peter Matthews

Men	Women
Bobby Charlton	Beryl Burton
Sebastian Coe	Laura Davies
Gareth Edwards	Lottie Dod
W G Grace	Sally Gunnell
David Hemery	Ann Jones
Jack Hobbs	Anita Lonsbrough
Stanley Matthews	Mary Peters
Fred Perry	Marjorie Pollard
Lester Piggott	Mary Rand
Gordon Richards	Joyce Wethered

Ian Buchanan

Men	Women
Sebastian Coe	Jeanette Altweg
Nick Faldo	Beryl Burton
W G Grace	Lottie Dod
Reg Harris	Gillian Gilks
Jack Hobbs	Alice Legh
Nigel Mansell	Virginia Leng
Stanley Matthews	Janet Morgan
Fred Perry	Mary Rand
Lester Piggott	Gillian Sheen
Rory Underwood	Joyce Wethered

And who is the greatest of all them?

We all have our favourites, but our choice is the man who was a colossus to his generation, a man whose 40-year career spanned the age when sports became developed for the masses and who was, for them, the champion, perhaps the best known figure on the land - William Gilbert Grace.

INDEX: WHO'S WHO BY SPORT

Rugby League

Eric Ashton
John Atkinson
William Batten
Billy Benyon
Dennis Betts
Tommy Bishop
Billy Boston
Stanley Brogden
Jim Brough
Douglas Clark
Lee Crooks
Jonathan Davies (*also* Rugby
   Union)
Colin Dixon
Des Drummond
Shaun Edwards
Joseph Egan
Alf Ellaby
Keith Elwell
George Fairbairn
Joe Ferguson
Neil Fox
Frank Gallagher
Kenneth Gee
Albert Goldthorpe
Andrew Goodway
Andy Gregory
Ellery Hanley
Alan Hardisty
Tommy Harris
Gerry Helme
Martin Hodgson
Keith Jarrett (*also* Rugby Union)
Lewis Jones
Vince Karalius
Joe Lydon
Roger Millward
Alex Murphy
Martin Offiah
Jonty Parkin
Alan Prescott
Bev Risman (*also* Rugby Union)
Gus Risman
John H Rogers
Garry Schofield
Jim Sullivan
Mick Sullivan
Joe Thompson
Dave Valentine
Harold Wagstaff
Ernest Ward
David Watkins
Johnny Whiteley

Rugby Union

Carl Aarvold

Paul Ackford
Rob Andrew
Gary Armstrong
Billy Bancroft
Johnny Bannerman
Stuart Barnes
George Beamish
Bill Beaumont
Dewi Bebb
Darkie Bedell-Sivright
Phil Bennett
Gordon Brown
Norman Bruce
Jeff Butterfield
Finlay Calder
Jim Calder
Ollie Campbell
Mike Campbell-Lamerton
Will Carling
Sandy Carmichael
Craig Chalmers
Maurice Colclough
Fran Cotton
Ronnie Cove-Smith
John Currie
Gerald Davies
Mervyn Davies
Phil Davies
Terry Davies
W.J.A. Davies
Eugene Davy
John Dawes
Ronnie Dawson
Colin Deans
Wade Dooley
David Duckham
Willie Duggan
Gareth Edwards
Douglas Elliot
Eric Evans
Ieuan Evans
Jimmy Farrell
Kevin O'Flanagan (*also*
   Football)
Mike Gibson
Arthur Gould
Jeremy Guscott
John Hall
'Dusty' Hare
Gavin Hastings
Scott Hastings
Noel Henderson
David Hewitt
Bob Hiller
Cyril Holmes
Terry Holmes
Monkey Hornby (*also* Cricket)

Andy Irvine
Peter Jackson
Carwyn James
Dickie Jeeps
John Jeffrey
Albert Jenkins
Neil Jenkins
Vivian Jenkins
Barry John
Cliff Jones
Ivor Jones
Jack Jones
Ken Jones
Robert Jones
Ronnie Kavanagh
Moss Keane
John Kendall-Carpenter
Ken Kennedy
Cecil Kershaw
Michael Kiernan
Tom Kiernan
Jackie Kyle
Roy Laidlaw
Donal Lenihan
Jason Leonard
Willie Llewellyn
Cyril Lowe
Gregor MacGregor (*also*
   Cricket)
Willie John McBride
Ian McGeechan
Alistair McHarg
William Maclagan
Ian McLauchlan
Hugh McLeod
Kenneth MacLeod
Ray McLoughlin
Hugo MacNeill
Phil Macpherson
David Marques
Jack Matthews
Bryn Meredith
Syd Millar
Iain Milne
Brian Moore
Cliff Morgan
Bill Mulcahy
Karl Mullen
Brendan Mullin
Noel Murphy
Tony Neary
Gwyn Nicholls
Bob Norster
Des O'Brien
Tony O'Reilly
Alex Obolensky
Phil Orr

Dickie Owen
Cecil Pedlow
Cherry Pillman
Robert Poulton
Graham Price
Terry Price
Jeff Probyn
John Pullin
Alexander Purves
Jim Renwick
Dean Richards
Andy Ripley
Keith Robertson
Budge Rogers
David Rollo
John Rutherford
Ken Scotland
Richard Sharp
Max Simmers
Reg Skrimshaw
Fergus Slattery
Mike Slemen
Arthur Smith
Ian Smith
David Sole
Jeff Squire
Rees Stephens
George Stephenson
Andrew Stoddart (*also* Cricket)
Adrian Stoop
Haydn Tanner
John Taylor
Mike Teague
Jim Telfer
Delme Thomas
Paul Thorburn
Alan Tomes
William Trew
Sam Tucker
Rory Underwood
Roger Uttley
Henry Vassall
Gordon Waddell
Herbert Waddell
Wavell Wakefield
Tony Ward
Jonathan Webb
Mike Weston
Peter Wheeler
Bleddyn Williams
Denzil Williams
J J Williams
John P.R. Williams
Rhys Williams
Rex Willis
Peter Winterbottom
Clive Woodward

Wilf Wooller
Running - see Athletics

Shooting
Alister Allan
Bob Braithwaite
Malcolm Cooper
Arthur Fulton
Antony Ringer
Andrew Tucker
Shot - see Athletics
Show Jumping - see Equestrian

Skiing
Davina Galica
Gina Hathorn
Arnold Lunn
Peter Lunn
Esmé Mackinnon
Evie Pinching

Snooker
Fred Davis
Joe Davis
Steve Davis
Walter Donaldson
Allison Fisher
Terry Griffiths
Stephen Hendry
Alex Higgins
Joe Johnson
Doug Mountjoy
Ronnie O'Sullivan
John Parrott
John Pulman
Ray Reardon
John Spencer
Dennis Taylor
Jimmy White
Soccer – see Football

Speedway
Nigel Boocock
Peter Collins
Peter Craven
Tom Farndon
Gary Havelock
Bill Kitchen
Eric Langton
Michael Lee
Ken McKinlay
Jack Parker
Tommy Price
Split Waterman
Simon Wigg
Freddie Williams

Squash
Jonah Barrington

Norman Borrett (*also* Rugby Union)
Don Butcher
Joyce Cave
Nancy Cave
Victor Cazalet
Joan Curry
Jack Giles
Tommy Jameson
Martine Le Moignan
Margot Lumb
Peter Marshall
Janet Morgan
Susan Noel
Lisa Opie

Surfing
Martin Potter

Swimming
Andrew Astbury
Jack Besford
Ian Black
Brian Brinkley
John Brockway
Joyce Cooper
June Croft
Sharron Davies
Rob Derbyshire
Margaret Edwards
Mark Foster
Nick Gillingham
Duncan Goodhew
Elenor Gordon
Judy Grinham
Jack Hale
Sarah Hardcastle
Phyllis Harding
Martin Harris
Jack Hatfield
Philip Hubble
Andrew Jameson
John Jarvis
Margaret Kelly - Hohmann
Liz Long
Anita Lonsbrough
Linda Ludgrove
Bobby McGregor
Neil McKechnie
Adrian Moorhouse
Lucy Morton
Karen Pickering
Graham Sykes
Henry Taylor
Jack Wardrop
Matthew Webb
David Wilkie
Diana Wilkinson

RELATIVES

Brief entries on the following, who were or are notable sports men and women in their own right, may be found under the name of their relative - brother, sister, father, mother, husband, wife etc. - of the same surname, unless otherwise indicated.

Sidney Abrahams	Athletics
Daniel Ahearn	Athletics (Triple Jump)
Len Allchurch	Football
Peter Allday	Athletics (Hammer)
John Arnull	Horse Racing
Samuel Arnull	Horse Racing
John Badcock	Rowing - see Joyce Cooper
Toby Balding	Horse Racing
Ian Balding	Horse Racing
Jack Bancroft	Rugby Union
Eric Batten	Rugby League
Julius Beresford	Rowing
Jackie Blanchflower	Football
Sally Bonallack	Golf
Peter Brown	Rugby Union
Ralph Kilner Brown	Athletics - see Godfrey Brown
Denise Burton	Cycling
Joseph Cannon	Horse Racing
Mel Charles	Football
Sylvia Cheeseman	Athletics – see John Disley
Samuel Chifney Jnr	Horse Racing
William Chifney	Horse Racing
Nigel Clough	Football
Harry Collier	Motorcycling
Leslie Compton	Football/Cricket
Garry Cook	Athletics
Christopher Cowdrey	Cricket
George Dawson	Horse Racing
Judy & Sue Devlin (USA)	Badminton
Jim Dreaper	Horse Racing
Ted Edgar	Equestrian
Kevin Finnegan	Boxing
Harold Gilligan	Cricket
Billy Gunn	Cricket
Edith 'Eddie' Halstead	Athletics
Garry Herbert	Rowing – see Greg and Johnny Searle
Howard Hipwood	Polo
Richard Hutton	Cricket
Madeline Ibbotson	Athletics
Bob Jack	Football
Clement Jackson	Athletics
Della James	Athletics – see Alan Pascoe
Gay Kelleway	Horse Racing
William Lillywhite	Cricket
Wendy Line	Bowls
David Lloyd	Tennis
Jenny Loriston-Clarke	Equestrian – see Jane Bullen
Sharon McPeake	Athletics (High Jump) – see Tim Hutchings
Jimmy McRae	Rallying
Marcus Marsh	Horse Racing
Kenny Milne	Rugby Union
Martin Molony	Horse Racing
Michael 'Mouse' Morris	Horse Racing – see Lord Killanin
David Mould	Horse Racing
Stuart Murless	Horse Racing
David Nicholson	Horse Racing
Vivian Nickalls	Rowing
Evan Baillie Noel	Rackets
Christy O'Connor Jr	Golf
Alan Old	Rugby Union
John Paish	Tennis
Mungo Park	Golf
Jim Parks Sr	Cricket
Barry Paul	Fencing
Graham Paul	Fencing
Raymond Paul	Fencing
Steven Paul	Fencing
June Paul	Athletics
Ron Pickering	Athletics
Mark Pitman	Horse Racing
Richard Pitman	Horse Racing
Kevin Prendergast	Horse Racing
Derek Redmond	Athletics – see Sharron Davies
Cyrille Regis	Football
Clive Rowlands	Rugby Union – see Robert Jones
Monica Rutherford	Gymnastics - see Brian Phelps
William Scott	Football
Robert Smith	Equestrian
Tommy Sopwith	Powerboating
Willie Stephenson	Horse Racing
Mickey Stewart	Cricket
Peter Stewart	Athletics
Peter Tancred	Athletics
Fred Tate	Cricket
Harry Thrift	Rugby Union – see Maeve Kyle
Kathleen Tuckey	Tennis
Tony Underwood	Rugby Union
Jumbo Vassall	Rugby Union
Bert Wardrop	Swimming
Roger Wethered	Golf
Véronique Whitaker	Equestrian

OTHERS

Onllwyn Brace	Rugby Union – see Mike Smith

473

THE GUINNESS ENCYCLOPEDIA OF INTERNATIONAL SPORTS RECORDS & RESULTS, 4TH EDITION

by Peter Matthews

Containing all the very latest records and results, this book is the most comprehensive guide to the statistics of some 100 international sports.

With comprehensive coverage of the leading international events and championships, major national competitions in the UK, USA and Australia along with results from the most recent Super Bowls, FA Cup Finals, Boxing Championships, Tennis Finals and Motor Sport Championships, this is a must for all sporting fans.

New features for this spectacular 1994/5 sporting year include the Winter Olympics, Soccer World Cup, Commonwealth Games, European Athletics Championships and the Rugby World Cup.

ISBN: 0-85112-686-3   Price: £15.95 net

THE GUINNESS
INTERNATIONAL WHO'S WHO
OF SPORT

by Peter Matthews, Ian Buchanan and Bill Mallon

All the great names in the history of international sport can be found in this definitive compendium of sporting personalities. Presented in A-to-Z format, this book contains over 2,500 concise biographies from more than 100 different sports.

ISBN: 0-85112-980-3   Price: £14.99 net

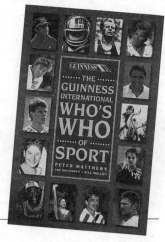

THE GUINNESS BOOK OF
SPORTING BLUNDERS

by Cris Freddi

A ghoulishly entertaining collection of true sporting nightmares. Cris Freddi's ready with not only hilariously recounts the blunder, but also the drastic consequences. A collection of 'foot in mouth' entries leave you wondering how people can say such bizarre things – usually live to millions!

ISBN: 0-85112-770-3   Price: £9.99 net

THE ALL TIME GREATS OF
BRITISH AND
IRISH SPORT

by Peter Matthews and
Ian Buchanan

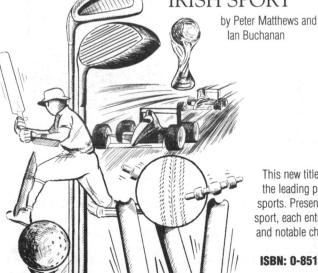

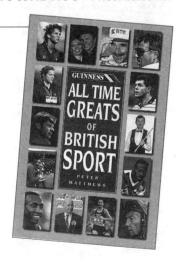

This new title is packed with over 2,000 biographies of the leading personalities from up to 100 different sports. Presented in A-to-Z format, and arranged by sport, each entry lists personal details, a career résumé and notable characteristics of style.

ISBN: 0-85112-678-2   Price: £12.99 net

THE GUINNESS FOOTBALL ENCYCLOPEDIA, 3RD EDITION

by Graham Hart

This encyclopedia offers detailed coverage of all the major tournaments at domestic, European and world level including an extended section on the 1996 European Championships. Containing over 100 profiles of the game's greatest players, features on all the English and Scottish League clubs and other topical issues, such as crowd safety and stadium development, this encyclopedia offers both an informative history of soccer and a useful panorama of the game.

ISBN: 0-85112-664-2   Price: 14.99 net

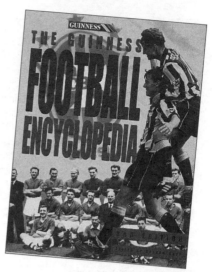

THE GUINNESS SOCCER WHO'S WHO

by Jack Rollin

This ultimate reference on every player active in the Premier League, Football League and Scottish Premier Division is the fan's favourite pocket annual. Personal and career details are listed as a season-by-season record giving any Fantasy Football League Manager the chance to pick the 'Dream Team'.

ISBN: 0-85112-672-3   Price: £7.99 net

THE GUINNESS RECORD OF WORLD SOCCER, 2ND EDITION

by Guy Oliver

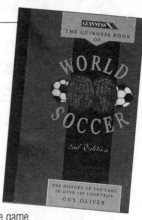

Almost 1,000 pages of world soccer information in a single volume! The history of the game in each and every country is presented in quite breathtaking detail. Also included are result histories of the World Cup, European Championship, European club competitions, Africa Nations Cup, South America's Copa Libertadores and Copa America.

ISBN: 0-85112-654-5   Price: £19.95 net

THE GUINNESS CRICKET ENCYCLOPEDIA

by Alan Rustad

Covering all the test-playing countries, including profiles of over 100 great Test players past and present, all the first-class counties in England together with all the major domestic competitions including the County Championship, Sunday League, Benson & Hedges Cup and the NatWest Trophy. Village Cricket, the Universities' and the women's games are also included. Features on other general topics offer a useful history and panorama of the game.

ISBN: 0-85112-650-2   Price: £17.95 net

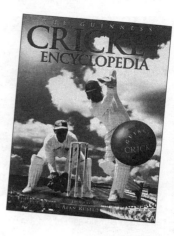

THE DAILY TELEGRAPH CHRONICLE OF CRICKET

by Norman Barrett

Compiled from The Daily Telegraph newspaper, these articles and despatches from each of the last 100 years give the essential flavour of the nation's favourite summer game. These reports relive the great moments of cricketing history through the pens of E W Swanton, Michael Melford and Christopher Martin Jenkins.

ISBN: 0-85112-746-0   Price: £17.95 net

THE JOHNNIE WALKER ENCYCLOPEDIA OF GOLF

by Bob Ferrier and Graham Hart

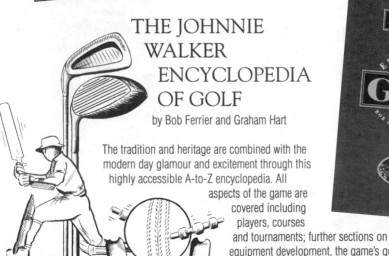

The tradition and heritage are combined with the modern day glamour and excitement through this highly accessible A-to-Z encyclopedia. All aspects of the game are covered including players, courses and tournaments; further sections on equipment development, the game's governing bodies and the handicapping system explained, make this book a uniquely comprehensive and authoritative guide to the sport.

ISBN: 0-85112-747-9   Price: £19.95 net

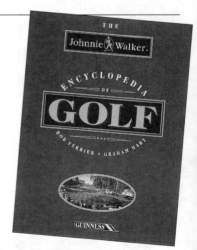

SENIOR GOLFER
by Les Jones and Tony Moore

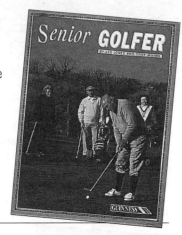

The first instructional book of its kind to address the needs of the more mature player. This book is suitable for both beginners and high-handicappers and contains invaluable tips on how best to adapt their game.

ISBN: 0-85112-731-2   Price: £12.99 net

YOUNG GOLFER
by Peter Smith and Beverley Lewis

As so many younger players take up the sport at an increasingly early age, this book not only offers the essentials of the game but also how best to overcome the limitations of physical size and strength - the major obstacles to improving their performance.

ISBN: 0-85112-533-6   Price: £9.99 net

THE GUINNESS GUIDE TO GOLF EQUIPMENT
by David Graham

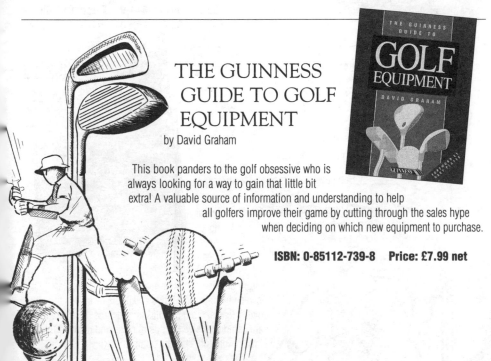

This book panders to the golf obsessive who is always looking for a way to gain that little bit extra! A valuable source of information and understanding to help all golfers improve their game by cutting through the sales hype when deciding on which new equipment to purchase.

ISBN: 0-85112-739-8   Price: £7.99 net

THE DAILY TELEGRAPH
CHRONICLE OF HORSE RACING
by Norman Barrett

Compiled from The Daily Telegraph newspaper, these articles and despatches from each of the last 100 years give the essential flavour of racing, on the flat and over the jumps. These reports relive the great moments of racing history with correspondents such as Lord Oaksey and Tony Stafford.

ISBN: 0-85112-649-9   Price: £17.95 net

THE GUINNESS BOOK OF
FLAT RACING
by Gerry Cranham and Chris Poole

Written as an introduction to the multi-million pound world of the 'sport of kings', this book is illustrated throughout with specially commissioned colour photographs for which Gerry Cranham is famed. The book introduces famous jockeys, trainers and race horses both past and present and offers detailed explanations on racing development and how the sport is administered.

ISBN: 0-85112-344-9   Price: £19.95 net

THE GUINNESS GUIDE
TO INTERNATIONAL
MOTOR RACING
by Peter Higham

From Formula One to Indy Car, World Sportscar to European Formula 3000 the history of these and other major championships are presented in quite exhaustive detail: the races, results, drivers, teams, circuits, rules and records. Also included are comprehensive listings of races and results from major 'one-off' championships.

ISBN: 0-85112-642-1   Price: £19.95 net